Preface

This book deals with more than jus[t] ... [marketing]
communications perspective whic[h] ... [direct]
response communications, below-t[he-line]

Students of advertising may regard it as a textbook, the advertising community
as a handy guide, while I believe marketers (advertisers) will benefit greatly from
reading this book. The reason is that it was written by those in the industry who
are experts in their particular fields – people with years of experience who were
prepared to share their perspectives with us rather than quoting from other
textbooks.

The objective of this book is to give a South African perspective that outlines
the real-life excitement and experiences of the marketing communications world.
As one of my ex-partners used to say: 'Advertising is the most fun you can have
with your clothes on'.

We want the students of marketing communications courses to sense the
excitement and fun of this unique world, to get to grips with the nature, scope
and techniques involved in the topics discussed. We want the advertising frater-
nity to perhaps get back to basic perspectives and the young stars in the industry to become even more knowledgeable and as professional as the contributors
to this book. We want advertisers to realise that we are not merely a crowd of
weird people mumbling a language seasoned with ever-changing buzzwords
that few people understand – we are, in fact, an extension of your company,
we are practical and sometimes illogical, but always creative. We don't spend
your money, we invest it to give you the highest return on your investment.

The book was planned to include an introductory part dealing with the history, nature and scope of advertising, advertising's role in society, advertising
control (including the Code of Advertising Practice) and the role of advertising
in marketing. In order to build up to the important aspect of the management
of an advertising campaign, perspectives on the South African consumer (demographics, psychographics and geographics) are given, followed by perspectives on the role of the advertising agency.

Media planning and the various media available are extensively covered to
present arguments for (and sometimes against) using a particular medium. This
part of the book also includes a comprehensive case study on media planning
and a guide to the media opportunities in the black market.

Creating the advertising involves perspectives on overseas and local creative
philosophies and 'how to' strategies. Checklists for use by creative teams are
presented. Marketers will be able to provide more useful information to their advertising, direct response and promotions agencies by making use of these checklists.

A comprehensive guide to researching the advertising message and media
is provided to enable researchers and students to plan and conduct such surveys.

A number of unique perspectives in the field of marketing communications
management are included, covering aspects such as industrial advertising, black
market, direct response, below-the-line, retail advertising, advertising of services
and the promotion of prescription pharmaceuticals.

A must for students, practitioners and marketers is the final chapter, a comprehensive glossary of advertising, media, research and direct response terms.

I trust that this book will stimulate creative thought and play a role in the development of more efficient and successful advertising in South Africa.

**Marketing Communications Management
A South African Perspective**

Marketing Communications Management
A South African Perspective

Ludi Koekemoer

In collaboration with
David Buirski
Christina Burlock
Simon Copland
Clive Corder
D'Arcy Masius Benton & Bowles
Elana de Swardt
Janice Dickson
Erik du Plessis
John Edmunds
Jock Falkson
Mike Falkson
Coen Gous
Gordon Hooper
Reuel J Khoza
George Klein
Jocelyn Kuper
Laurance Kuper
Marius Leibold
Dick Reed
Grahame Tomes
Gerrie Uys
Annemarie van der Walt
Brian van der Westhuizen
Marinda van Niekerk
Joost van Nispen
Dirk van Rooyen
Chris van Veijeren
Len van Zyl
Retha Vermeulen
Christiane von Ulmenstein

Butterworths
Durban

Butterworths
Professional Publishers (Pty) Ltd
Reg No 87/03997/07

©1987

Reprinted 1988, 1989

ISBN: 0 409 10730 1

Durban
8 Walter Place, Waterval Park, Mayville
Durban 4091

Johannesburg
108 Elizabeth Avenue
Benmore 2010

Pretoria
Third Floor, Hatfield Forum, 1077 Arcadia Street, Hatfield
Pretoria 0083

Cape Town
3 Gardens Business Village, Hope Street
Cape Town 8001

Edited by Megan Hills
Design and typography by Jeremy Woodhouse
Cover design by Thelma Albasini, a student of Graphic Design at the University of Pretoria
Typesetting and reproduction by Positone Pinetown
Printed and bound by Interpak Natal
The imprint Butterworths is used under licence

Acknowledgements

This book was made possible by a number of great advertising people and academics, dedicated men and women who worked under severe time pressures but who were prepared to share their wealth of knowledge and practical experience with me. I would like to thank these men and women.

I would also like to thank the various companies and their advertising agencies who gave me permission to use their visual material as examples or to emphasise a particular point.

To my friend and colleague, Dirk van Rooyen, I would like to express my sincere thanks for your support and hard work in bringing this book to completion. You were more than a contributor.

To my wife, Annette, my lovely daughters, Minette, Carlé and Lize-Marié, my thanks for your loving support. If I hadn't tackled this project, you might have seen more of me.

Finally, I thank God for blessing this venture.

LUDI KOEKEMOER
Pretoria
July 1987

Contents

Preface

Acknowledgements

Contributing authors

1 The history, nature and role of advertising
Introduction to advertising *3*
The nature and process of advertising *16*
The role of advertising in marketing *23*

2 Advertising in the South African society
The role of advertising in society *37*
Advertising control in South Africa *48*

3 The South African consumer
Geo-segmentation *79*
Black values, lifestyles and psychographics *85*
The status of the black consumer *91*
Appendix: Demographics *99*

4 The role of the advertising agency
The role of the advertising agency *107*
The hot agency and how to handle it *114*

5 Management of the advertising campaign
The importance of a good advertising brief *121*
Establishing advertising objectives *132*
The total involvement philosophy and methodology in
  planning a campaign *136*

6 Media planning
Media planning *145*
Television in South Africa *162*
The power of radio *182*
Cinema *198*
Outdoor advertising: the neglected hero *210*
Direct advertising: media planning depends on identification *218*
Media planning case study: Sparkle *228*
Appendix: Media opportunities for the black market *247*

7 Creating the advertising
Creative approaches and styles *261*
Creating effective advertising *269*

8 Advertising research

Will the consumer be able to decode your advertising
  message correctly? *295*
The pre-testing of advertisements *310*
Measuring advertising effectiveness *320*
Multivariate analyses: understanding data *328*
Advertising research: the media *334*
Marketing research into industrial advertising and media *344*

9 Industrial advertising

Advertising industrial goods, specifically capital equipment *355*
Communicating effectively with industrial buyers *369*

10 Advertising to Blacks

Advertising to Blacks in print media *379*
Communicating with the black market on television *391*

11 Retail advertising

Retail advertising *399*

12 Advertising services

Advertising the products and services of
  non-profit organisations *411*

13 Direct response advertising

Direct response advertising *429*

14 Telemarketing

Telemarketing: the medium of the 80s *439*

15 Below-the-line advertising

Below-the-line activities *453*

16 Promoting prescription pharmaceuticals

Promoting prescription pharmaceuticals *463*

17 Glossary of advertising terminology

Glossary of advertising terminology *477*

Index *499*

Contributing authors

David Buirski

is Group Managing Director of Young & Rubicam Retail units – by far South Africa's biggest retail agency. He always wanted to go into advertising on the creative side and after finishing at art school started out as a junior artist with Lindsay Smithers in Cape Town. He was promoted to Creative Director and then to Account Service. The gaining of the Pick 'n Pay account began, in his own words, 'a fantastic association with Pick 'n Pay and Raymond Ackerman – a truly masterful communicator'.

David was recently nominated Argus Businessman of the Week.

Christina Burlock

qualified as a graphic designer at the East London School of Art. She gained a grounding in advertising through working for Lintas, Barker McCormac and Lindsay Smithers. Her experience below-the-line began in retailing and she was a member of the team that founded Game Discount World, her responsibility being store layout, display and advertising. In 1972 she joined Paton Tupper Associates, Durban and in 1975 she opened the Johannesburg office. She is Managing Director of Paton Tupper and a past President of the Institute of Sales Promotion.

Simon Copland

was founder and Director of Outdoor Research International Ltd, Research Manager of London and Provincial Poster Group and Chief Executive of the Poster Audit Bureau. His outdoor experience extended to South Africa, where he was Marketing Services Manager of Advertising Displays (Pty) Ltd until the end of 1986. He is currently New Business Development Manager of Maister Outdoor Marketing (Pty) Ltd.

Clive Corder

is Chairman and Managing Director of Market Research Africa (Pty) Ltd, Managing Director of Lopex International SA (Pty) Ltd and Chairman of Delcas (Pty) Ltd, a computer subsidiary. He is a Director of Lopex Public Limited Company.

After graduating from Cambridge with a degree in Economics and Psychology he joined Lintas Advertising in London. He managed MRA Rhodesia from 1961 to 1963 and since then has worked with MRA in South Africa. He has been involved in over 1 500 research surveys, published a number of articles and addressed numerous conferences and seminars and is registered as a research psychologist with the South African Medical and Dental Council.

Clive is a past Chairman of the South African Marketing Research Association (SAMRA) and of the Association of Marketing Research Organisation (AMRO).

Elana de Swardt

joined Datsun Nissan as Market Research Analyst after graduating from the University of Pretoria with a BCom Marketing degree. In 1978 she joined D'Arcy MacManus and Masius as Trainee Media Planner and then moved to Lindsay Smithers – FCB where she was Senior Media Planner and then Media Manager. During this time she was responsible for implementing what is now the best-known computerised media administration system. In 1984 she joined Preller Sharpe Rice as Media Manager and in 1986 she moved to Young & Rubicam as Media Manager and Centralised Buying Supervisor.

Janice Dickson

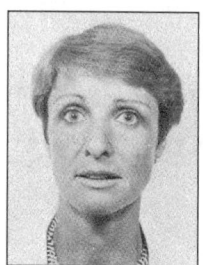

obtained a BA degree in Psychology and Industrial Sociology from the University of the Witwatersrand. She joined Market Research Africa in 1974 and since then has gained extensive experience in the field of ad hoc research, with particular involvement in the Human Resources and SocioMonitor surveys.

Erik du Plessis

is the recipient of two BCom Honours degrees (Stellenbosch and UNISA) and the Post-Graduate Diploma in Market Research and Advertising (SA).

He was Information Manager at SFW for seven years and then became Media and Research Director of BBDO, where he developed a number of advertising research techniques with BBDO New York researchers. He served as Chairman of a BBDO International Marketing Services Board Committee and has been a speaker at several conferences on Marketing and Marketing Research.

Erik is currently Managing Director of Impact Information.

John Edmunds

career began in a retail pharmacy. He worked his way up in the pharmacy industry on both the production and marketing sides and as a medical representative and detailman. In 1972 he obtained the Diploma in Pharmacy and in Production Engineering and joined GD Searle as Marketing Manager. He was awarded the Diploma in Advanced Management by the SA Institute of Management in 1976 and in 1978 was appointed Managing Director of GD Searle South Africa. John was the driving force behind GD Searle's growth programme and the highly successful launch of Canderel Sweeteners.

In 1982 he was awarded an MBA by the University of Columbia Pacific, from which he received a PhD in 1983. Since June 1987 John has been Managing Director of Knoll LTd in the UK. He is a member of a number of societies, councils and institutes.

Jock Falkson

is one of the pioneers of direct mail advertising in South Africa. Starting out with only one automatic typewriter he built his company, Effective Letters, into a leading direct marketing agency which celebrated its 27th anniversary in 1986. He founded Effective Telemarketing (Pty) Ltd – the first professional company of its kind – in 1979 and Prestige Bulk Mailing (Pty) Ltd – the first bulk mail processing plant – in Bophuthatswana in 1986.

Jock has won awards for his creativity, including Europe's 1984 Best-of-the-Year Award for a fundraising campaign, and has served as a judge for the US Direct Marketing Association's annual awards presentation. He is the innovator of many of the new developments, promotional techniques and formats used in direct advertising, some of which have been patented. In 1972 he founded the SA Direct Marketing Association and served as its first Chairman. His personal forte is direct mail copywriting and, not surprisingly, he is a prolific writer of articles, speeches and newsletters.

Mike Falkson

has been Managing Director of Effective Telemarketing for the past six years. He is Founder and Chairman of the South African Telemarketing Association and has helped to pioneer the telemarketing industry in South Africa.

Mike has studied telemarketing services in Britain and Germany and has attended various symposia and conferences in the United States and Europe to keep abreast of the state of the art and future developments. He has written profusely on the subject of telemarketing and his articles have been published in many trade publications. He consults and lectures and keeps up a lively contact with telemarketing executives in New York and other US cities, as well as in London, Frankfurt, Amsterdam and Zurich.

Coen Gous

holds a BCom (Marketing) and an MBA from the University of Pretoria. He has held various positions in the fields of Marketing, Marketing Research, Advertising and Media Planning and is currently Marketing Manager: Media and Research at the SABC.

Gordon Hooper

studied to be a Civil Engineer and started out working for SATS and then for a firm of Civil Engineering Contractors, for whom he designed and implemented computerised planning, budgeting and control systems.

He completed an MBA degree part-time and began his marketing career at Metricomp Programmes, a technical software house, as Marketing and Sales Manager. In 1985 he joined DMB & B, was promoted to Planning Manager in which capacity he concentrated his efforts on understanding consumers' minds, and is currently Account Planning and Research Manager of Freedman & Rossi/BBDO.

Reuel Khoza

holds a BA Honours in Psychology from the University of the North and obtained an MA in Marketing from the University of Lancaster (UK). He has lectured at the University of the North and held marketing positions with Lever Brothers and Shell South Africa. In 1981 he formed Co-ordinated Marketing, a Black marketing and management company, of which he is Managing Director. Reuel is also on the Board of Directors of Stannic, Stancor and Information Systems Management (formerly IBM).

George Klein

holds an MSc from the University of Stellenbosch and an MBA from the University of Cape Town. He is Managing Director of George Klein and Associates (Pty) Ltd and a member fo the Institute of Marketing Management and the South African Marketing Research Association.

George has lectured in Marketing Research to the Institute of Marketing Management, Wits Business School, Damelin Management School and the now defunct National Development and Management Foundation. He is the author of several articles on Marketing Research.

Ludi Koekemoer

is Professor and Head of Marketing Management Education at the University of Pretoria. During the course of 12 years in advertising he worked for Van Zijl & Schultz, Lund & Tredoux and De Villiers Schönfeldt and was a Partner and Deputy Managing Director of Mortimer Tiley until February 1986.

Ludi acts as a marketing consultant to various companies and has published numerous articles on marketing, advertising and the Black market. His book *Print Media Advertising, Some Basic Principles* has been prescribed at a number of South African universities and his PhD thesis investigated the principles of communicating effectively with Blacks through press advertisements.

Jocelyn Kuper

received a BSc Honours from the University of the Witwatersrand and UNISA. She has worked as an executive in the Psychometrics Division of the National Institute for Personnel Research (NIPR), for Action Research, and acted as consultant to various research companies.

In 1980 she joined *The Star* as Research Manager and in 1985 she was appointed Managing Director of Marketing and Media Research (MMR), a wholly owned subsidiary of the Argus Group.

Jocelyn founded the Retail Data Library (RDL) in 1980 and it has grown to be the leading retail survey in South Africa, with more than 17 000 interviews conducted for the last survey. She was recently appointed Deputy Managing Director of the Newspaper Marketing Bureau, adding to her busy schedule as MD of MMR.

Laurance Kuper

holds a BA in Psychology and Sociology. He gained thorough experience in every agency department with several major South African advertising agencies and has had a taste of the media world. Laurance is Managing Director of Kuper Hands, an agency he established 13 years ago, Executive Director of the AAA and convenor of the Creative Directors Forum, an official body of the Association of Advertising Agencies.

Marius Leibold

is head of the Unit for Marketing Studies at the University of Stellenbosch, from which university he received his DCom. He is very active in research, has published many articles and books on aspects of marketing and is a business consultant to many Western Province companies. He specialises in marketing research and the development of corporate and marketing strategies.

Dick Reed

was Media Director of J Walter Thompson Company for many years. He holds the Diploma of the International Advertising Association and was Chairman of the Media Association of South Africa and the Audit Bureau of Circulations of South Africa. Dick is probably the most experienced Media Director in South Africa and is currently Managing Director of The Media Shop.

Grahame Tomes

spent a number of years in the newspaper business in the United Kingdom and South Africa before moving into advertising. He first joined an advertising agency in 1974 and has held a number of senior positions in the BBDO stable in Australia and South Africa. Grahame is currently Group Managing Director of Freedman & Rossi/BBDO.

Gerrie Uys

worked in the Department of Health and Justice as Prosecutor of the Industrial Court of the Transvaal and the OFS until 1951. He joined the Federation of Master Printers as Assistant Secretary and was appointed General Manager of the South African Press Union in 1958. He acted as Secretary of the ABC, the Circulation Bureau of South Africa, until 1982, when he retired, but was called out of retirement by the Advertising Standards Authority to act as Secretary of the ASA, which he did until the end of 1985 when he retired for a second time.

Annemarie van der Walt

is Head of Marketing in the Department of Business Economics at UNISA. She is Co-Director of a marketing consultancy firm and a member of a research unit. In the latter capacity she is involved in several research projects commissioned by a large non-profit organisation in South Africa. Annemarie is co-author of two books, *The task of marketing management* (1983) and *Introduction to management science* (1986).

Brian van der Westhuizen

is a senior consultant with a specialist consulting company owned by Wesbank and is responsible for training, consulting and research for client companies.

He holds a BCom (UNISA), an MBA (Wits Graduate School of Business) and a Diploma in Banking (Institute of Bankers in South Africa) and recently completed his PhD thesis, entitled 'The impact of the local content programme on commercial vehicle marketing in South Africa'.

Brian has served as Vice-Chairman of the Education Committee of the Institute of Marketing Management since 1981 and has been guest lecturer at Wits Graduate School of Business, the University of Pretoria and the University of Natal. He has won a number of special marketing awards, has published locally and abroad and has a number of South African, British and American professional affiliations.

Marinda van Niekerk

graduated from RAU with a BA Communication in 1980. She spent five-and-a-half years in the marketing department at the SABC and has recently joined Reeva Products as a distributor.

Joost van Nispen

holds an MSc from Harvard and Massachusetts Institute of Technology and is a leading expert in all aspects of direct response advertising. He came to South Africa from Holland in 1982 to start up the local office of Ogilvy & Mather Direct in Johannesburg as Managing Director. Ogilvy & Mather Direct is now the largest direct response agency in South Africa. Joost transferred to Ogilvy & Mather Direct Frankfurt as Managing Director in April 1986.

Dirk van Rooyen

holds a BCom Honours degree, MBA and DBA from the University of Pretoria.

He worked for the Land and Agricultural Bank of South Africa and the Bantu Investment Corporation before joining the University of Pretoria as lecturer in 1972. In 1984 he was made professor. His academic interests are mainly Financial Management, Purchasing and Materials Management and Marketing Management, with special emphasis on Advertising, and in each of these areas he has co-authored or contributed to academic textbooks. He has also published several articles locally and abroad.

Dirk is Director of a number of companies, including Bates Wells Pretoria, and a consultant to private practice.

Chris van Veijeren

received a BSc Eng, an MBA and a DBA from the University of Pretoria and ITP from Harvard Business School and has attended courses at Harvard, Columbia and the University of Geneva, Switzerland. He is Professor of Business and Marketing Strategy at the School of Business Leadership, UNISA, and is Associate Director of the School. He is an active consultant to business, has published many articles and books and has addressed conferences locally and abroad.

Len van Zyl

worked as a management trainee at Unilever after completing his BCom degree at Rhodes. He moved into the Marketing Department and after training in sales distribution and market research was appointed Product Manager.

Len worked for J Walter Thompson (Cape Town) and Van Zijl & Robinson (Cape Town and Johannesburg) before joining Lindsay Smithers (Johannesburg) as Account Supervisor in 1968. He was made Manager of the Johannesburg office in 1970 and in 1972 was appointed Group Managing Director. He is also Vice-President of FCB International.

From 1977 to 1979 he served three terms as President of the Association of Accredited Practitioners in Advertising (AAPA) and he has served continuously on the Executive Council of this body up to the present. Len is also a Director of the Advertising Standards Authority of South Africa.

Retha Vermeulen

holds a BA Communication Honours degree from the University of Potchefstroom. She has eight years' experience in the fields of Public Relations, Publishing, Sales and Marketing and is currently Senior Marketing Executive at the SABC.

Christiane von Ulmenstein

received both the BCom and the BCom Honours degrees *cum laude* from the University of Stellenbosch before completing the Public Relations Institute of South Africa Diploma Course in Public Relations in 1979. In 1986 she was awarded an MBA by Wits Graduate School of Business and she is currently a member of a number of professional associations.

Christiane worked for J Walter Thompson as Research Manager before joining Young & Rubicam Transvaal in 1983 as Research and Planning Manager. In 1986 she was appointed Account Director.

1

The history, nature and role of advertising

Introduction to advertising *3*

The nature and process of advertising *16*

The role of advertising in marketing *23*

Introduction to advertising
Dirk van Rooyen

Introduction	3
A historical review of advertising	3
Summary	15
References	15

☐ Introduction

Advertising is certainly not a modern phenomenon. As a matter of fact, since the earliest times that trading took place and ideas were presented to the community, advertising in one form or another has played an important role in life. Sampson (1930:33), for example, maintains that advertising has been used since time immemorial.

Advertising means different things to different people. The adjectives which have been used to describe advertising vary widely, for example: 'Ubiquitous . . . brash . . . pervasive . . . materialistic . . . intrusive . . . dynamic . . . alluring . . . annoying . . . pesky . . . indispensable . . . fascinating' (Wright et al 1982:8). An interesting remark about advertising which appeared in *Advertising Age*, 15 November 1963, reads: '. . . advertising is much like electricity – we know a great deal about it and its uses, but we are not very successful in defining it or delimiting it' (quoted by Ray 1982:5).

Today an individual is continually exposed to advertising. In fact, each individual's lifestyle is affected to a large extent by advertising, be this directly or indirectly. One can hardly imagine a community in which there is no advertising – how else can the consumer be informed about new products, special offers, sales, flats to rent and the many other products or services available to him? As the mass communication media expanded and became more sophisticated, the community's involvement in communication increased.

In order to place advertising in perspective, it is necessary to examine the historical development of advertising briefly, first world-wide and then in South Africa.

☐ A historical review of advertising

The earliest forms of advertising

For obvious reasons it is difficult to say with absolute certainty when and where the first advertisement was used. However, there is evidence of advertising on the walls of ancient Babylonian buildings dating back to around 3000 BC. Such wall signs often commemorated the name of the King who commissioned the erection of the building and were also used to identify the nature of the business activity or craft practised there. In addition, Babylonian clay tablets inscribed with the names of, inter alia, an ointment dealer and a shoemaker have been found.

One of the oldest written advertisements is preserved in a British museum. Inscribed on papyrus, it originated from the Egyptian state of Thebes. This three thousand-year-old advertisement consists of a notice offering a reward of half a gold coin for news of the whereabouts of a runaway slave. A whole gold coin was offered for his return to the shop of Hapu, the Weaver (Presbey 1929:5-9).

Before the invention of movable type printing in the 15th century, three specific forms of advertising were used, namely signs, town criers and trademarks. *Signs* were introduced as a result of increasing competition and were used to identify certain places such as shops, etc. At the excavations at Pompeii several examples of signs with explanatory illustrations were found. One depicted a mule at a mill to identify a bakery, while another depicted a goat to advertise a dairy. There was even one of a teacher whipping a little boy to identify a teacher's classroom. Furthermore, signs consisting of notices of theatrical performances, sports gatherings, gladiator contests and houses to let and invitations to tourists to visit certain taverns were found (Presbey 1929:5-9).

It is interesting to note that the size of these signs and wall paintings increased to such an extent that in England in 1614 legislation prohibiting signs from extending more than eight feet from a building was passed. Another law stipulated that signs should be high enough to give clearance to an armoured man on horseback! (Kleppner 1983:4).

Town criers were hired by the ancient Greeks and Romans (3000 BC) to circulate through the streets and announce important events such as forthcoming slave and cattle sales. In Egypt and other countries town criers were used to announce the arrival of ships and their cargoes. By approximately 1100 BC several French tavern owners were making use of town criers to inform the public of the good wines they served. The criers had to blow on a horn, gather together a number of people and offer them samples of the wines. Town criers were hired by local craftsmen to advertise their products, and hawkers and tradesmen also made use of their services. Some countries began to realise the need to protect the profession and formed town criers' guilds, so that any aspirant town crier had to obtain legal permission (charters from the government) to perform. For example, in the year 1141 12 criers in the Province of Berry in France obtained a charter from Louis VII granting them exclusive privileges to exercise their occupation. (See also Presbey in Sandage et al 1975:17 and Hermes 1949:63.)

Evidence of *trademarks* has been found in ancient Greek civilisation. The purpose of trademarks was to differentiate products from one another and to give proof of a certain quality. Trademarks were often placed on goods such as pottery and furniture. A guild system that offered legal protection to manufacturers of certain products who used the guild's trademark emerged during the 14th century. The use of trademarks made it possible to limit, if necessary, supplies by any one member and to penalise a member if his goods did not comply with the required standards.

The foregoing brief review of the earliest forms of advertising should serve to show that advertising existed in ancient times, albeit on a limited scale. Significant advances in the field of advertising took place from the 15th century onwards with the invention of the printing press, and these will now be discussed.

Advertising since the invention of the printing press

One of the most important events contributing to the development of advertising was the invention of the printing press in 1438 by the German, Johann Gutenberg. New advertising media, including printed posters, handbills and newspapers, were made possible. Of course, this changed the whole world's methods of communication.

The first printed advertisement appeared in England in 1472 in the form of a pamphlet or poster, and was printed by William Caxton. Through this advertisement Caxton informed the public about a prayer book he had written, namely *The Salisburi Pye*, which contained the rules for the guidance of the clergy at Easter. The pamphlet was tacked onto church doors and informed interested people that the book was for sale at Westminster Abbey. Handbills and other printed announcements for various purposes then followed, for example the introduction of a shop together with a short description, advertisements of slaves, announcements about runaway slaves and advertisements placed by people wanting servants or servants seeking positions. (See also Sandage et al 1975:16.)

Although printed newspapers were still a thing of the future, printing had made a definite impression and would soon spread to many other countries. Kleppner states: 'The first ad in any language to be printed on a disseminated sheet appeared in a German news pamphlet about 1525 – and what do you think this ad was for? A book extolling the virtues of a mysterious drug!' (Kleppner et al 1983:4). Meanwhile, handwritten announcements for public posting were done by scribes. They were called *Siquis*, meaning 'If anybody' – followed by the intention, such as desires, knows of, etc.

Advertising advanced significantly with the advent of the first newspapers during the 17th century. The first English newspaper, *The Weekly News of London*, was published in 1622. According to advertising historian Henry Sampson, the first bona fide newspaper advertisement appeared in 1650 on the back of a London newspaper called *Several proceedings in Parliament*. This ad offered a reward for the return of 12 stolen horses. Products with which we are still familiar today were advertised in England, for example coffee ads appeared in 1652, chocolate ads in 1657, and tea ads in 1658. Advertisements in the earliest newspapers were, however, more informative in nature. They were what we would describe today as classified notices and announcements.

The first newspaper to appear in the United States of America was *The Boston Newsletter*. The first edition appeared on 14 April 1704, and it is interesting to note that in this edition reference was made to the usefulness of the newspaper as an advertising medium. The edition of 1 to 8 May 1704 contained three classified advertisements under the heading 'Advertisements'. (See Cohen 1972:51.) Shortly afterwards the first 'Advertising Specialist', Benjamin Franklin, made extensive use of advertising to promote his own ideas and enterprises. Franklin made advertisements more readable by using large headlines and surrounding them with considerable white space. He also used appropriate illustrations to emphasise the benefits of the products.

The number of newspapers published increased steadily. According to Presbey (1929:75), in 1850 there were more than 500 in existence in England and some 2 300 in the United States of America. Although a few magazines were published during the middle of the 18th century, it was not until the last three decades of the 19th century that this medium advanced significantly.

During the 19th century important technological innovations had a stimulating effect on the printing industry and, likewise, on advertising. These included the invention of the rotary printing press in 1849, the manufacturing of paper from wood-pulp in 1866 and improved lithographic methods. Furthermore, the level of literacy increased substantially during this time, resulting in a large reading public and a much better understanding of advertising messages.

A historical review of advertising should inevitably refer to the origin of advertising agencies. While some agencies existed in England as early as 1800, Volney Palmer is generally accepted as being the father of advertising agencies in the United States (Holland 1973:107-111). From 1842 onwards Palmer acted as the agent for most newspapers by contracting large volumes of space at discount rates and then selling this space to advertisers. He usually received a commission of 25% and rendered services such as media selection and preparing copy for his clients. Although initially known as a 'newspaper agent' (space seller), he adopted the concept 'advertising agency' in 1849 for his business.

The Industrial Revolution gained momentum from about the middle of the 19th century and was characterised by mass production on a large scale. This had a tremendous influence on advertising. The need for communication with an unknown market increased, the infrastructure – and particularly the means of transport – expanded enormously, and the level of education increased substantially. The Industrial Revolution also brought about additional media. For example, Marconi invented the radio and the first radio message was broadcast in 1895. However, it was not until the 1920s that the radio was used on a large scale as a communication medium. Television was invented in 1939, introducing a new world of communication opportunities to advertisers.

The development of advertising in South Africa

As a result of its strong ties with the United Kingdom and Western Europe, developments were also introduced in South Africa. The printing industry thus also evolved during the early history of South Africa. Johann Christian Ritter, a German immigrant, started the first printing works in South Africa shortly after his arrival at the Cape in 1780. Even before the end of the 18th century he was printing calendars, handbills and advertising pamphlets.

In 1800, following representations to the Dutch East India Company, a printing press was installed at Cape Town. On 16 August 1800 the first weekly newspaper, *The Cape Town Gazette and African Advertiser*, appeared. It was printed by Walker and Robertson and was the only newspaper published for 24 years. Other newspapers began to appear from 1824 onwards (Rosenthal 1963:38), namely:

☐ *The South African Commercial Advertiser* (7 January 1824)
☐ *De Zuid-Afrikaan* (9 April 1830)
☐ *The Grahamstown Journal* (30 October 1831)
☐ *De Ware Afrikaan* (13 September 1838)
☐ *Kaapsche Grensblad* (18 July 1844)
☐ *Eastern Province Herald* (31 December 1845)
☐ *Friend of the Free State* (10 June 1850)

The advantages of newspaper as an advertising medium were well recognised, the first advertisements taking the form of notices and announcements. The layout and format were much like that of the *Government Gazette* today.

Probably the first newspaper to release circulation figures was the *Afrikaanse Patriot*, which informed its readers in 1893 that the average circulation was 1 625 copies. DF du Toit and Co, who also published *The Paarl*, guaranteed a joint circulation of not less than 3 000 per month for these two newspapers (Rosenthal 1963:49).

Apart from newspapers, outdoor signs and posters played an important role in early South African advertising. Posters, for example, were placed in prominent positions to advertise events such as boat arrivals, auctions and lost goods. (See also Potgieter 1963:20.) There is much evidence that outdoor signs were commonly used to identify various businesses as early as the beginning of the 19th century.

In his comprehensive analysis of the nature of advertising media up to 1910, Potgieter (1963:33) found that the following were used: Press advertising, outdoor signs, word of mouth advertising and exhibitions.

Today more than 700 regular newspapers, periodicals and journals are published annually in South Africa. The advertising industry has grown significantly since 1910 and various factors have contributed to this state of affairs, the following being the most important:

The increased value of manufactured goods

The value of manufactured goods increased dramatically. Similarly, the *Gross National Product* (GNP) increased from approximately R300 million in 1911 to nearly R120 billion in 1985. The need for and role of advertising should thus be quite evident − businesses had to make increasing use of advertising in order to gain the favour of the consumer, especially with regard to luxury products.

Growth in the nature and extent of methods of communication

More than 900 newspapers and magazines are published on a regular basis. Similarly, *radio* communication has grown substantially since the first broadcast on 29 December 1923 by the South African Railways. Broadcasting was taken over in 1927 by the Schlesinger group's subsidiary *The African Broadcasting Company*. Financial problems led to an in-depth investigation in 1936 into all matters relating to broadcasting. The result of this investigation was acceptance of Act No 22 of 1936, according to which all broadcasting was placed exclusively under the jurisdiction of the *South African Broadcasting Corporation* (SABC). Of special significance, from an advertising point of view, was the introduction of a bilingual commercial service, Springbok Radio, on 1 May 1950. On 25 December 1961 the first FM broadcast took place and a few years later the various regional services, namely Radio Highveld (1 September 1964), Radio Good Hope (1 July 1965), and Radio Port Natal (1 May 1967) started operating.

During 1985, the SABC's 22 stations broadcast for just over 107 000 hours in total. The potential available advertising time was 15 707 hours (due to economic conditions all the time was not taken up). However, 1 884 840 advertisements were broadcast during 1985 (information supplied by the SABC).

Another communication medium which would later become a significant vehicle for advertising was *cinema*. The pioneers in this field were Edgar Hyman and Karel Hertz. Their first show was presented on 9 May 1896 in the Palace of Varieties in Johannesburg. Since its inception the cinema has attracted great interest from the public. Financial difficulties caused the fragmented cinema industry to be taken over by the Schlesinger group, which was then placed under the control of its subsidiary, the *African Theatres Trust*. During 1927 a company called *Kinemas South Africa Limited* entered the cinema arena, thus breaking the monopoly that existed. The group expanded quite rapidly, gaining control of 44 theatres in 1928. This number more than doubled in the following year to 106 theatres. At present there are about 330 cinemas for Whites, 118 for Non-Whites, and 96 drive-ins in South Africa. The yearly attendance figure for cinemas is in excess of 60 million people, whilst spending is in the region of R107 million per annum.

Advertising films for cinemas had already been prepared as early as 1938 by William Boxer's company, Alexander Films. However, as a result of Alexander Films' progress, African Theatres also started producing advertising films from 1940 onwards. Today cinema advertising is channelled mainly through Cinemark (Pty) Ltd.

A relatively recent communication medium of great significance to advertising in South Africa is *television*. Test broadcasts started on 5 May 1975, and the service officially opened on 5 January 1978. The first commercial advertisements were broadcast on 1 January 1976. The dramatic growth of television is evident from the number of licences issued. At the end of 1975, for example, just over 214 000 licences were issued, and this figure more than doubled to 509 000 in the following year (1976). Latest figures show that more than 1 877 000 licences are issued annually. Approximately 770 000 licences are issued to Whites, whilst corresponding figures for Coloureds are 225 000, for Asians 113 000 and for Blacks 770 000. During 1985 the four television stations broadcast nearly 6 000 hours, which included 528 hours of advertising. The total number of advertisements shown during 1985 was in excess of 63 000. (Information supplied by the SABC.)

Television has gained a substantial portion of the total advertising revenue since the introduction of commercial advertising in South Africa. This has been further expanded by the introduction of TV2, TV3 (which is aimed specifically at the black population) and TV4. Television's impact as part of the total advertising expenditure can be seen clearly in table 1.4.

It should be evident that the growth in the field of communication offers exciting opportunities to advertisers.

The development of the infrastructure

Either directly or indirectly, the development of the infrastructure contributed to the advancement of the advertising industry in South Africa. If one takes into consideration that the first *railway line* from Durban to the Point, built in 1860, was only three kilometres long, and that 50 years later (1910) it had increased to 11 000 kilometres, this advancement speaks for itself. At present there are more than 23 000 kilometres of railway line (route kilometres) in South Africa. Similarly, the amount and length of *roads* being built have increased at a significant rate. As against 120 000 kilometres of roads completed up to 1935, the latest total distance (1985) is in excess of 184 000 kilometres. *Electricity* supplies were initially privately generated, but the Electricity Supply Commission (ESCOM) began to supply most of the country's electricity needs from 1925. Gross electricity generated and net purchases outside South Africa increased from 1 277 million kWh during 1920 to over 141 000 million kWh during 1985 (information supplied by the Central Statistical Service).

The population growth

This is another obvious factor contributing to the development of advertising in South Africa. More and more people with different needs have had to be exposed to advertising.

The phenomenon of the increasing urbanisation of the South African population is of particular importance from an advertising point of view. The following percentages show clearly the urbanisation trend for the various population groups:

	1904	1980
Whites	53,6	88,7
Coloureds	49,0	77,4
Asians	36,5	91,3
Blacks	10,4	38,0

From a marketing point of view, urbanisation brought about new lifestyles with particular needs. Indeed, it created many marketing opportunities because advertising had to inform, remind and persuade prospective customers to buy particular products.

Increased education and literacy

This has placed greater demands on those responsible for advertising. Improved education has resulted in a more *critical* audience and in order to influence the consumer advertising has to be more convincing, imaginative and exciting. However, the advertising industry was also stimulated by a large number of graduates who entered the field of advertising and applied their theoretical knowledge and skills.

The inception of advertising agencies

As business enterprises accepted the merits of advertising in their marketing programmes to a greater extent, the opportunity was created for experts to handle

R·H·GRIFFIN
PUBLICITY PROMOTIONS

IDEAS UNLIMITED

OVER
35 YEARS
SUCCESSFUL
ADVERTISING

PRESS

LAYOUTS

CATALOGUES

BIOSCOPE
SLIDES

POSTERS

PROMOTIONAL
SCHEMES

FOR
RESULTS

ADVERTISING CONSULTANT

253, MUCKLENEUK STREET
NEW MUCKLENEUK
PRETORIA

Telephone • 78-5593

AS BREAD IS TO LIFE — SO ADVERTISING IS TO BUSINESS

Courtesy: RH Griffin. One of the earlier advertising consultants

advertising more scientifically. The development of advertising agencies was initially strongly influenced by overseas agencies which established branch offices in South Africa. Only a few agencies were established prior to 1910, but the majority have been in existence since the Second World War (1945). At present there are nearly 100 advertising agencies operating in South Africa, half of these being relatively large agencies with various branches operating in different centres and being members of the AAA (Accredited Advertising Agencies). Although advertising agencies were initially concerned mainly with media selection and creating advertisements, today they provide a wide range of marketing advisory services such as package design, marketing research, and others.

The brief review above shows that many factors contributed to the development of advertising in South Africa. However, it is worthwhile to pay some attention to advertising expenditure, not only in South Africa but also elsewhere.

Advertising expenditure in South Africa and elsewhere

In comparison with the free world's total advertising expenditure of nearly 134 billion dollars (US) during 1983, South Africa's total expenditure was relatively low, that is just over one billion dollars (US). Although advertising expenditure has increased steadily in South Africa during the past years, its share of the total has decreased as a result of the depreciation of the Rand, especially during 1985.

More than half of the total expenditure (56%) during 1983 came from the United States of America. Only 14 countries accounted for 91% of the total world advertising expenditure. The top 14 are listed in table 1.1.

Table 1.1
Top 1983 ad
expenditures

Country	Expenditure (in millions of US dollars)
United States	$75 850,0
Japan	$11 670,5
United Kingdom	$ 5 980,2
West Germany	$ 5 522,6
Canada	$ 4 338,4
France	$ 4 035,3
Italy	$ 3 082,3
Brazil	$ 2 462,4
Australia	$ 2 263,6
Netherlands	$ 1 934,3
Spain	$ 1 495,8
Switzerland	$ 1 415,1
South Africa	$ 1 070,0
Sweden	$ 1 068,8

Source: Figures obtained from Market Research Africa. *Research in Action,* (79), April 1986.

The per capita advertising expenditure averaged $47,30 in 1983, with 11 countries spending more than $100. The figures in table 1.2 show countries exceeding $100 per capita:

Table 1.2
Per capita adver-
tising expenditure
in excess of $100,
1983

Country	Per capita advertising expenditure, 1983
United States	$323,18
Switzerland	224,62
Norway	189,57
Finland	188,71
Bermuda	179,00
Canada	172,84
Australia	146,99
Denmark	137,59
Netherlands	134,32
Sweden	128,77
United Kingdom	107,56
South Africa	34,06*

*Including black states

Source: Market Research Africa. *Research in Action*, (79), April 1986.

Another yardstick often used to measure advertising expenditure is a calculation of the percentage of advertising in relation to the GNP. The United States
was the only country that spent more than 2% in 1983. The figures in table 1.3
reflect the advertising expenditures as a percentage of GNP.

Table 1.3
Advertising
expenditure as
% of GNP

Country	Top advertising expenditures as % of GNP, 1983
United States	2,40
Puerto Rico	1,79
Bermuda	1,79
Finland	1,68
Canada	1,48
Dominican Republic	1,38
Israel	1,37
Switzerland	1,30
Australia	1,29
Norway	1,28
South Africa	1,26
Taiwan	1,25
Netherlands	1,19
Bahamas	1,10
United Kingdom	1,09
New Zealand	1,08
Denmark	1,08
Jamaica	1,05
Egypt	1,02

Source: Market Research Africa. *Research in Action*, (79), April 1986.

The lowest percentage of advertising expenditure in proportion to GNP appeared
in the less developed countries of Africa and Asia and the oil rich countries of
the Middle East.

Within a South African context, table 1.4 shows the dramatic increase in total advertising expenditure since 1978, when television advertising was first introduced. It is interesting to note that whilst television's share of the total was only 11,48% during the first year (1978), it increased substantially to 22,47% in 1985.

Table 1.4   Estimated total advertising expenditure in South Africa, 1978-1985

Media category	1978	1980	1982	1983	1984	1985
	Rm	Rm	Rm	Rm	Rm	Rm
Press – branded						
Newspapers (daily, weekend, country)	97 896	139 586	228 007	261 390	281 479	284 656
Magazines and black publications	38 956	58 126	107 810	116 909	115 840	118 925
Trade and technical	14 173	24 173	43 541	52 045	62 857	58 644
Production costs	18 425	28 845	45 523	53 793	59 823	59 700
PRESS 'BRANDED'	169 450	250 730	424 881	484 137	519 999	521 925
Press – other						
Financial and mining						
Hotels and restaurants						
Property and auctions	39 661	69 975	93 918	105 480	115 500	94 297
Selling – classifieds						
Theatre and entertainment						
Recruitment advertising		39 899	42 154	41 500	40 850	22 633
TOTAL PRESS	209 111	360 604	518 799	589 617	635 499	616 222
Radio						
Time	33 662	39 334	69 755	76 315	72 033	75 921
Production	3 861	3 540	5 789	5 724	5 042	5 314
TOTAL	37 523	42 874	75 544	82 039	77 075	81 235
Outdoor						
Space	13 321	16 962	22 030	25 087	25 267	25 685
Production	2 397	2 640	3 304	4 265	4 295	4 366
TOTAL	15 718	19 602	25 334	29 352	29 562	30 051
Cinema						
Screening	4 287	6 306	10 765	12 504	12 156	12 885
Production	2 016	2 228	2 025	2 171	2 361	2 576
TOTAL	6 303	8 534	12 790	14 675	14 517	15 461
Television						
Time (SABC only)	38 927	70 080	124 576	170 713	209 192	229 560
Production	4 800	12 800	35 530	42 400	48 100	68 372
TOTAL	43 727	82 880	160 106	213 113	257 292	297 932
Direct mail						
Total estimate only	24 592	29 448	55 896	74 500	88 600	96 881
Exhibition and shows*						
Total estimate only	4 732	6 133	10 349*	12 212	13 738	15 380
Window displays and point of sale*						
Total estimate only	12 735	15 378	22 280*	24 950	27 400	42 900

Table 1.4 Estimated total advertising expenditure in South Africa, 1978-1985 (*continued*)

Media category	1978	1980	1982	1983	1984	1985
	Rm	Rm	Rm	Rm	Rm	Rm
Public relations* Total estimate only	5 204	8 160	19 820*	23 388	26 311	26 604
Miscellaneous* (General, Yellow Pages sports spon- sorship, Yellow Pages (separated '80)	21 097	6 220 37 000	15 890* 61 500	19 714 69 000	23 640 79 000	21 276 82 000
GRAND TOTAL	380 742	616 833	978 308	1 152 560	1 272 834	1 325 932
PERCENTAGE CHANGE	+17,0%	+62,0%	+58,6%	+17,8%	+11,1%	+3,7%

Note: Figures for media 'Press - branded' to 'Television' are based on factual analyses, but media 'Direct mail' to 'Mis-cellaneous' can best be described as 'qualified guestestimates'. Under 'Miscellaneous' extra items were added in 1982.
    * Based on special surveys.
    1984 production costs were based on a special agency survey.

Source: Market Research Africa. *Summary of Estimated Advertising Expenditure in South Africa,* Johannesburg, and *Management,* 'Advertising Survey 1985'.

Table 1.5 shows the *media* expenditure for some 32 product groups.

Table 1.5 Media expenditure for main product groups - South Africa and South West Africa (R'000), 1983-1985

Product groups		Total expenditure		
		1983	1984	1985
01	Agricultural and garden products	6 146	6 196	6 362
02	Alcoholic beverages	30 528	36 537	40 512
03	Beauty preparations	19 416	19 093	17 317
04	Biscuits and confectionery	11 308	11 634	12 611
05	Breakfast cereals	5 199	5 281	5 460
06	Canned foods	2 567	2 699	2 044
07	Chain store and retailers	129 706	141 738	155 772
08	Colleges and universities	5 293	6 167	6 748
09	Dental products	7 206	7 250	6 427
10	Engineering and industrial	36 827	40 854	34 418
11	Financial institutions	47 896	57 198	65 531
12	Food products	38 953	43 735	45 279
13	Frozen food products	3 774	5 731	7 367
14	Household appliances	13 217	12 013	8 479
15	Household equipment	10 728	11 376	9 996
16	Household stores and services	33 690	37 047	32 022
17	Medicinal	24 400	25 456	26 101
18	Men's clothing	3 623	2 501	2 054
19	Musical equipment	17 387	16 528	10 196
20	Motor vehicle industry	81 054	90 369	98 474
21	Office equipment	14 794	18 112	17 732
22	Petroleum products	9 143	9 407	13 827
23	Photographic	3 573	2 922	1 924
24	Reading matter and stationery	9 146	10 274	9 588

Table 1.5 Media expenditure for main product groups - South Africa and South West Africa (R'000), 1983-1985 (*continued*)

	Product groups	Total expenditure		
		1983	1984	1985
25	Shoes	3 508	4 147	3 055
26	Sports equipment	1 543	1 631	1 570
27	Non-alcoholic beverages	26 305	28 255	29 056
28	Tobacco and associated products	37 766	37 412	41 442
29	Toiletries and personal care	21 114	23 875	22 626
30	Travel and tourism	20 667	25 790	32 433
31	Tyres and tubes	4 429	4 784	5 828
32	Women's and children's clothing	4 495	4 910	3 506
33	Miscellaneous	29 550	33 804	30 506
	Grand total	714 950	784 826	806 263

Note: All figures to the nearest R1 000, but excluding GST.
             'Media' includes press, radio, cinema, outdoor and television.

Source: MRA. *Adindex*, Johannesburg.

From the table it can be deduced that the following product groups spend in excess of R40 million:

Industry	R million
Chain store and retailers	155,8
Motor vehicle industry	98,5
Financial institutions	65,5
Food products	45,3
Tobacco and associated products	41,4
Alcoholic beverages	40,5

During 1985 46 big spenders spent more than R3 million on advertising. These spenders' combined advertising expenditure totalled R300 million or 37% of all media advertising expenditure in 1985. Table 1.6 reflects expenditure by the big spenders.

Table 1.6
The big advertising spenders in South Africa - over R3 million, 1985*

	R'000		R'000
OK Bazaars	18 237	Coca-Cola	5 530
Pick 'n Pay	15 040	Dion	5 408
Lever Brothers	14 478	Van den Berg & Jurgens	5 267
Toyota	14 204	American Cigarette Co	5 257
SA Breweries	12 818	Rothmans of Pall Mall	5 141
Nissan	9 455	Edgars	4 840
Oude Meester	9 440	Mercedes Benz	4 260
Amcar	9 075	Ster Kinekor	4 178
Checkers	8 960	Cadbury Schweppes	4 083
Ford	8 689	SAPM	4 070
United Tobacco	8 590	SAR	3 906
SFW	7 971	United Building Society	3 776
Volkswagen	7 949	Spar	3 772
General Motors	6 870	Beckett TW	3 729
Standard Bank	6 780	Clicks	3 540
Elida Gibbs	6 528	Gilbeys	3 507

Table 1.6
The big advertising spenders in South Africa - over R3 million, 1985* (*continued*)

	R'000		R'000
Colgate Palmolive	6 373	Winston Tobacco Corp	3 503
Food & Nutritional Products	6 286	Riggio Tobacco Co	3 443
Meat Board	6 090	Tedelex	3 438
Reckitt & Coleman	6 085	Game	3 221
Beecham	6 028	Barlow Appliance & TV Co	3 168
SA Airways	5 759	Wilson Rowntree	3 055
Barclays	5 714	Volkskas	3 010

The combined advertising expenditure of these 46 big spenders totalled R300m or 37% of *all* advertising expenditure in 1985.

* Total of all-media advertising expenditure, that is print, radio, television, cinema and outdoor.
Source: MRA. *Adindex,* Johannesburg.

Adindex of MRA offers much more useful and comprehensive information. The intention here, however, is to present a broad overall picture without too much detail.

☐ Summary

Advertising is certainly not a modern invention. Certain forms of advertising were used before 3000 BC by the early Greeks, Romans and Phoenicians. Advertising was stimulated by technological advances and new opportunities to convey messages were created. The invention of the printing press by Gutenberg opened a new door to advertising. Similarly, the Industrial Revolution created new advertising opportunities with the advancement of methods of communication.

Various factors contributed to the development of advertising, the most important of these being mass production for an unknown market; the population growth together with changing needs, expanded transportation and infrastructure; and increased literacy and specialist advertising by advertising practitioners. Advertising executives had to cope with the challenging demands of their clients within a highly competitive market environment and the vast amounts spent on advertising obviously require the very best agencies.

☐ References

Cohen, D. 1972. *Advertising*. New York: John Wiley & Sons.
Hermes, HJA. 1949. *De Bedrijfseconomische betekenis van de reclame*. Leiden: Dissertation.
Holland, OR. 1973. 'The story of Volney Palmer, the nation's first agency man'. *Advertising Age*, 23 April: 107-111.
Kleppner, O, et al. 1983. *Advertising Procedure*. 8th ed. Englewood Cliffs, New Jersey: Prentice-Hall.
Mandell, MI. 1984. *Advertising*. 4th ed. Englewood Cliffs, New Jersey: Prentice-Hall.
Potgieter, LJ. 1963. ''n Ontleding van 'n paar ekonomiese aspekte van reklame in Suid-Afrika' (unpublished DCom dissertation). PU for CHE.
Presbey, F. 1929. *The History and Development of Advertising*. Garden City, New York: Doubleday & Co.
Ray, ML. 1982. *Advertising and Communication Management*. Englewood Cliffs, New Jersey: Prentice-Hall.
Rosenthal, E. 1963. *Manne en Maatskappye*. Cape Town: Human & Rousseau.
Sampson, H. 1930. *A history of advertising from the earliest times*. London: Chatto & Windus.
Sandage, CH & Fryburger, V. 1975. *Advertising theory and practice*. 9th ed. Homewood, Illinois: Richard D Irwin.
Wright, JS, Winter, WL & Ziegler, SK. 1982. *Advertising*. 5th ed. New York: McGraw-Hill.

The nature and process of advertising

Ludi Koekemoer

Advertising defined	16
The process of advertising communication	18
Specific characteristics of advertising communication	19
How effective advertising works	21
References	22

☐ Advertising defined

For the purpose of this book, advertising will be considered from the point of view of the 'sender' of the advertising message. The sender could be a manufacturer, wholesaler or retailer or an advertising agency acting on behalf of the manufacturer, wholesaler or retailer. To the sender, that is the advertiser, advertising is a means of informing existing and potential customers about his product and its special features and benefits and a means of persuading them to buy his product or to buy it more often.

Furthermore, advertising will be viewed primarily in terms of what it is designed to accomplish, that is its objectives. When the advertiser attempts to put into words any description of his product or service, he is engaging in a fundamental task of advertising, that is the communication of news, opinions or ideas to other people (Wright et al 1971:5).

Many definitions of advertising approach it from the viewpoint of the functions it performs or its marketing role in stimulating the movement of goods and services from producer to consumer or user.

The South African Market Research Association (SAMRA 1974:1) defines advertising as 'All forms of paid, non-personal promotion by an identified sponsor'. From the above definition it is clear that four aspects of a definition of advertising are important. These aspects are considered separately below and help to distinguish advertising from other activities with which it is often confused, such as publicity, personal selling and propaganda (Wright et al 1971:5 & 6).

Paid form

The phrase 'paid form' distinguishes advertising from publicity. When a favourable comment about a company, product or service appears in the press media to provide information to the readers, no payment is made by the benefited organisation. Advertising, however, is an openly sponsored message disseminated through one or more media because the advertiser has, for example, purchased space in the printed media to place his advertisement.

Non-personal presentation

When a personal face-to-face presentation of a product or service is made, the process is called personal selling. Advertising is a process or a series of activities necessary to prepare the message and get it to the intended market in a non-personal way through various media such as newspapers, magazines or radio.

Ideas, goods and services

Advertising is concerned with ideas such as how, when and where to use a product, tangible goods such as consumer products, and intangible services offered by, for example, banks, insurance companies and travel agents.

Identified sponsor

Advertising discloses or identifies in some way or other the source of the opinions and ideas it represents. The source could be a business firm, non-profit organisation, or individual. Propaganda, however, attempts to present opinions and ideas with the objective of influencing consumer attitudes and actions while the propagandist remains anonymous.

The above definitions do not, however, include two basic elements of advertising:

The target group that the advertising message is to reach

Advertisements are not aimed at the total population of a particular country. Each advertisement has a certain target group of people it is intended to reach. An advertisement for a washing powder may be aimed primarily at married housewives with children, because they constitute the largest segment of the market for washing powders. A whisky advertisement may be directed at higher income males. The visual or oral messages are therefore addressed to *selected target groups* and owing to the different characteristics and media behaviour of the various target groups, different advertising approaches and media will be used by advertisers for advertising different products.

The objective of the advertisement

The specific objective of advertisements varies from one advertisement to another. One advertisement may announce a special offer, while another may remind consumers of the special features or benefits of the particular product or service. Regardless of this specific purpose, every advertisement conveys information or an impression to change or reinforce the selected target group's attitude towards the product or service advertised. The ultimate aim is to persuade them to buy the product, use the service, or to be favourably inclined towards the product. Some definitions of advertising emphasise persuasion in advertising. Kirkpatrick (1964:33), for example, states that advertising devoid of persuasion is ineffective and if an advertisement fails to influence anyone, either immediately or in the future, money has been wasted. Persuasion is found in every aspect of advertising. An advertisement should persuade the target audience to pay attention to it, to read the message, to become interested in the message, to believe the special features or benefits communicated and to buy the product or service.

Taking into account these two elements of advertising, the author therefore suggests the following functional definition of advertising:

> *Advertising is any paid form of non-personal presentation of ideas, goods and services by an identified sponsor, addressed to selected target groups with the objective of informing, influencing and persuading them to buy or to be favourably inclined toward these ideas, goods or services.*

☐ The process of advertising communication

Advertising is a communication process whereby verbal and non-verbal symbols are transmitted through a channel to a receiver. The objective is to communicate an idea, change or reinforce an attitude, or provide important information about a particular product or service.

A simple communication process consists essentially of a transmitter at one end and a receiver of the message at the other end. Advertising communication is a more complex communication process. It is concerned with *who* says *what* to *whom* through *which channel* with *what effect* (Lasswell in Dunn 1969:59 & 60).

The *who* is the communication source, the *what* is the message itself (the advertisement), the *whom* is the audience the communicator hopes to reach, the *which* is the medium used (for example, the newspaper) and the *what* (effect) may be the number of readers who saw the message, the amount of copy read, how the message changed the readers' attitudes or the extent to which it impelled them to buy the product or service advertised.

The process of communication includes three elements, a *source*, a *message* and a *destination* (or receiver) for the message. In personal or direct communication, the source is an individual. In mass communication, however, the source is not in direct contact with the receiver, and the receiver is part of a group. Mass communication therefore requires a fourth element – a *medium* (such as a newspaper) to deliver the message simultaneously to many persons (Wright et al 1971:100). In order to communicate an encoded message to many consumers, the sender (advertiser) should be able to put the basic appeals into relatively few meaningful words. The advertiser is limited by the amount of space he can afford, and consequently either a small illustration and a few bold sentences or a larger illustration and more sentences in smaller type are used to explain the rewards and product features.

The receiver of the message should be able to comprehend the message exactly as was intended by the sender. Comprehension of a message is mediated by personal experiences and it is the sender's task to express the message in terms of the reader's experience.

The process of expressing the message in terms of the reader's experience is shown in figure 1.1. This indicates that the sender, with his experience and knowledge of the product or service, encodes a particular message which is transmitted to the receiver by means of a signal (newspaper or magazine). The receiver or decoder, with his experience and knowledge of the advertised product or service, is then confronted with the task of decoding the sender's message.

Figure 1.1
The encoding and decoding process

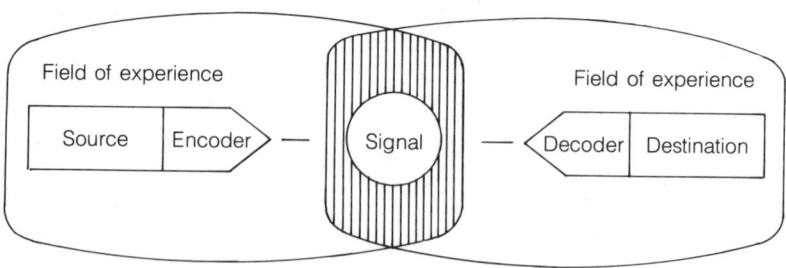

Source: Schramm (in Dunn 1969:59)

Figure 1.2 shows that advertising research measures the received meaning (that is, feedback) of the advertiser's message. In this case advertising research can assess whether the receiver perceived the message in the manner that was intended by the sender.

Figure 1.2
Mass
communication
system

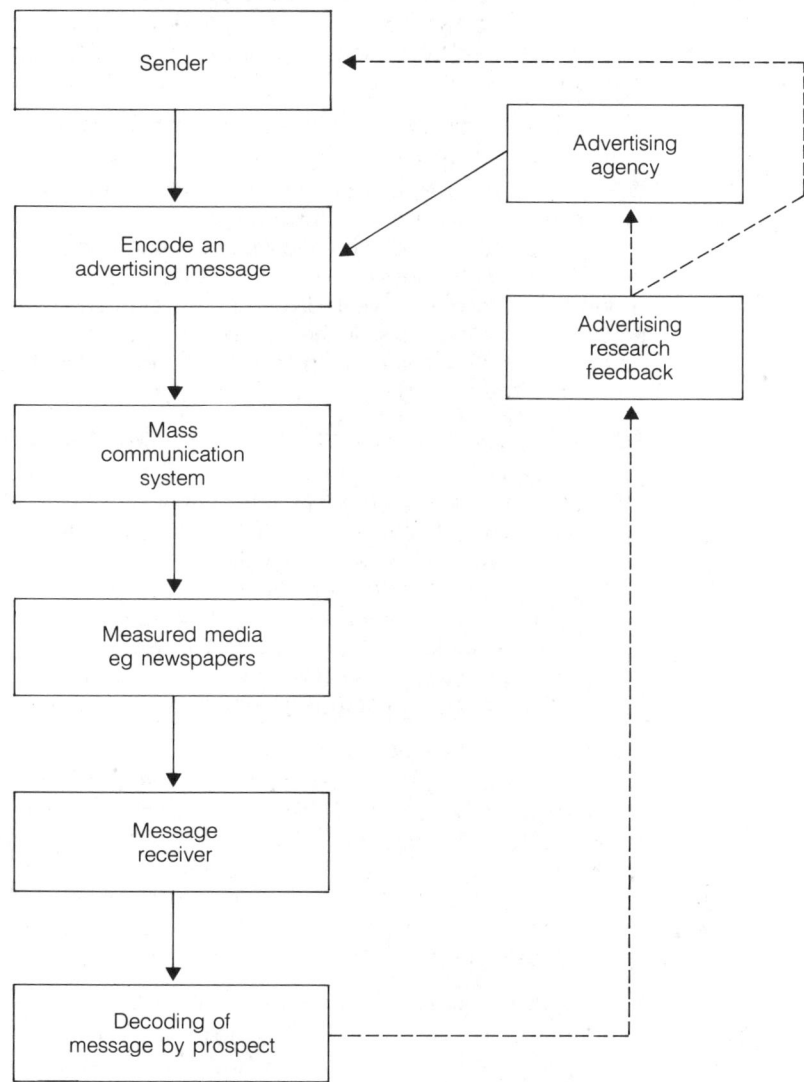

☐ Specific characteristics of advertising communication

Having identified the mass communication system, one must take a closer look at the specific characteristics of advertising communication:

Advertising communication is mainly one-way

Advertising messages move primarily one-way because the reader has no opportunity to comment on the advertising message read, to ask questions or to inform the advertiser whether he is receiving or understanding the message.

The one-way nature of advertising communication puts a special burden on the advertiser to ensure that his message will be seen, read and comprehended, that it will be found interesting and that it will motivate his target market (depending on the purpose of the specific advertisement).

Advertising communication talks to groups of consumers

In personal selling the salesman talks to one person, or perhaps to two, and he can change his approach and tactics to suit the specific situation or type of person(s) he is addressing. Advertising is non-personal communication and has to address thousands of men and women, each with a unique personality make-up, with the same message (Dunn 1956:32). Consumers have different backgrounds and religions, live in different parts of the country, have attained different educational levels and, in the case of Blacks especially, have different cultures. Somehow the advertiser has to make each one feel that he is being addressed personally.

Advertising communication depends heavily on symbols

Advertising uses both symbolic words and pictures to convey ideas in order to help the reader to identify an advertisement quickly and easily. Havakawa (in Dunn 1956:36) puts it as follows: 'Advertising attempts to make the objects of experience symbolic of something beyond itself. Readers of advertising are invited to look upon themselves as smart housewives and hostesses, as men of distinction, as responsible and prudent fathers, as well-regulated families'. People use symbols to classify not only themselves, but also their fellow beings. To be effective, symbols used in advertising should fit the product and the reader. The readers should be able to refer the symbols to their own experience.

Advertising is 'low-cost' mass communication

Advertising is that means of communication which enables advertisers to deliver a message to a large number of potential customers at the lowest possible cost (Crawford 1960:6). The cost of an advertisement is relatively high when it reaches only one or a small group of potential customers. By delivering frequent and economical messages, the advertiser is able to speak to thousands of consumers in a matter of a few days or even a few hours. This reduces the cost per consumer substantially.

In advertising communication selectivity is experienced

Readers in South Africa are, for example, currently exposed to a large number of daily and weekend newspapers and magazines. Each publication contains a large number of different advertisements covering a wide range of products and services.

Readers cannot possibly read all the advertising material to which they are exposed and every reader must inevitably practise selection. Readers will choose to read an advertisement if they think they might gain something from reading it or if the advertisement offers a promise of some reward.

Advertising communication is important information

Consumer advertising communication deals primarily with a specific product (that is, a brand) or service. Information about the brand or service is important to the consumer to enable him to make sound decisions, but it is also important to the advertiser because through it he can inform consumers about his product's qualities and create a specific desired brand image. The information to be put in a specific advertisement is within the control of the advertiser, who should provide consumers with relevant information about the product.

Relevant information is information which will encourage the consumer to see the product as satisfying an existing or latent need or desire. Irrelevant information is information which does not apply directly to the product or service and should therefore be avoided.

Advertising is persuasive communication

Persuasion is the ultimate aim of the advertising message. Persuasion should not be viewed only in terms of persuading a potential consumer to buy a product or a current consumer to buy it more often. It should also be viewed in relation to its task of creating favourable brand images and convincing consumers that the advertised brand is generally more desirable than alternative brands. This will be achieved if the advertisement can convince the consumer that the brand is better than others on the strategically important benefits.

Advertising is commercial communication

To the advertiser, advertising is an expense that must be justified. Effective advertising at the lowest possible cost-per-message may stimulate demand for the product and help assure the advertiser of a long business life with profitable sales. Advertising should make a contribution to the advertiser's net profit by increasing demand for the product. Higher demand may result in lower production and marketing costs which could result in higher profits.

☐ How effective advertising works

Over the years different theories about how effective advertising communication works have been developed. Early theories implied basically that an important task of effective advertising was to implant factual, logical messages in the minds of consumers, that is to provide information.

An advertisement was assumed to provide the consumer with logical and rational propositions which should be seen, read, believed and acted upon. It was believed that information about the product would help the consumer to buy more intelligently and an advertisement should conform to the generally accepted standards of good taste (McClure & Fulton 1964:21).

The modern theories indicate that providing information in an advertisement means considerably more than merely stating rational claims. To discover whether an advertisement has successfully achieved its objective requires a more sophisticated approach to the way in which advertising works. Considering all the recent theories, the following factors are essential in the communication and persuasion process:

Attract the target reader's attention and create initial interest

An effective advertisement will immediately and repeatedly attract the maximum number of target readers' attention to make them aware of the particular product advertised and impel the target reader to want to read the message contained in the advertisement by creating initial interest in the message.

Communicate relevant understandable information about the product and maintain interest in the information

An effective advertisement will communicate information relevant to the product, with the following qualifications:

☐ By 'relevant' is meant the information must encourage the target reader to perceive the product as offering an important advantage and satisfying an existing need or desire. It could also establish a new need or increase the salience of a latent need or desire and encourage the target reader to think of the product as satisfying it.

☐ By 'understandable information' is meant that an effective advertisement will communicate signals that are understood in exactly the same way by both the sender (advertiser) and the receiver. These signals include verbal and non-verbal items, suggestions, innuendo and direct statement.

☐ The advertisement must hold the target reader's attention to the information at least until the main message is perceived and understood. Ideally, it should maintain interest in the information until all the relevant information is perceived.

Induce adoption of the relevant information into the target reader's systems of emotions, beliefs, images and attitudes about the product

The relevant information must be perceived by the target reader as being directed at him, as the answer to one of his needs or desires. It must influence emotions, images and attitudes about the product among current users and non-users of the product, that is all the target readers.

Persuade the target reader to buy the product, to buy it more often or to be favourably inclined towards the message

An effective advertisement will increase the reader's interest in buying the product or service or improve its status among his purchase priorities. It will also, either directly or indirectly, persuade the target reader that the product or service will benefit him and induce him to buy the product or service or buy it more often.

Persuasion may be achieved by effectively doing what is outlined under the above, by appealing rationally or emotionally to the target reader and by asking for action.

☐ References

Crawford, GW. 1960. *Advertising Communications for Management.* New York: Allyn & Bacon.

Dunn, SW. 1956. *Advertising Copy and Communication.* New York: McGraw-Hill.

Dunn, SW. 1969. *Advertising, Its role in modern marketing.* 2nd ed. Hinsdale, Illinois: Holt, Rinehart & Winston.

Kirkpatrick, CA. 1964. *Advertising, Mass Communication in Marketing.* 2nd ed. Boston, New Jersey: Houghton Mifflin.

McClure, LW & Fulton, PC. 1964. *Advertising in the Printed Media.* London: The Macmillan Company.

SAMRA. 1974. *List of Market Research Terms and Definitions.* Johannesburg: SAMRA.

Wright, JS, Warner, DS & Winter, WL. 1971. *Advertising.* 3rd ed. New York: McGraw-Hill.

The role of advertising in marketing
Brian van der Westhuizen

Advertising's place in marketing communications
and the promotion mix 23

Specific tasks of advertising 24

Supporting the sales force 28

Pull-through effect 29

Integrating advertising strategy with total
marketing strategy 30

Problems peculiar to the South African market 32

Concluding remark 33

References 33

☐ Advertising's place in marketing communications and the promotion mix

Marketing communication

Fundamentally all marketing communication is concerned with the needs and wants of people, both as individuals and in groups. Successful marketers understand people or, more technically, consumer behaviour. Knowing what makes his customers 'tick' and formulating a product/service offer to satisfy their needs, wants, hopes, aspirations, dreams and desires is the hallmark of the successful marketer. The means by which this is achieved is *effective marketing communication*. It must be remembered that communication is a two-way process. The effective marketer must 'listen' to his customers as well as 'speak' to them.

Communication is achieved in a variety of ways and few forms of communication succeed on their own. An effective marketing communications strategy must encompass the whole *promotion mix*. Advertising is a key element in the promotion mix and is certainly the most visible. It is also by far the most glamorous, but at the same time most controversial aspect of marketing. However, advertising must work in total harmony with the other elements of the promotion mix. Effective marketing communication takes place when there is effective integration of all four elements of the promotion mix in a marketing communications strategy. This means establishing objectives for each of the four elements of the promotion mix and ensuring that they are all aimed at achieving the goal of the organisation, which should be customer satisfaction.

**The
promotion mix**

The four elements of the promotion mix are the following:

☐ **Advertising** – which is defined as 'any form of non-personal presentation and promotion of ideas, goods or services by an identified sponsor'

☐ **Sales promotion** – which is defined as 'short-term incentives to encourage purchase or sale of a product or service'

☐ **Publicity** – which is defined as 'non-personal stimulation of demand for a product, service or business unit by planting commercially significant news about it in a published medium or obtaining favourable presentation of it upon radio, television or stage that is not paid for by the sponsor'

☐ **Personal selling** – which is defined as 'oral presentation in a conversation with one or more prospective purchasers for the purpose of making sales' (Kotler 1984:603).

Few people would deny that advertising is indeed the most visible of the promotion mix elements. But it cannot work successfully in total isolation from the other three elements. What is needed is an effective *balance* of the four elements.

Not much research has been carried out (both here in South Africa and overseas) to determine how firms establish their promotion mix. A recent research study carried out in South Africa produced some very interesting results. The most significant finding of the study was that in the firms surveyed in South Africa, personal selling dominated the promotion mix. The firms surveyed were in the fast-moving consumer goods, consumer durables, services, capital goods and industrial goods sectors. Advertising played a very significant *supporting* role in the promotion mix. A summary of the findings of this study is given in table 1.7.

**Table 1.7
Schedule of
percentage
expenditure on
the elements of
the promotion mix**

Sector	Total	Personal selling	Sales promotion	Publicity	Advertising
Fast-moving consumer goods	100	35,97	30,65	1,62	31,76
Consumer durables	100	44,36	14,96	4,02	36,66
Services	100	64,52	16,15	3,54	15,79
Capital goods	100	68,96	16,59	5,69	8,76
Industrial goods	100	83,95	4,04	2,74	9,27

Source: Unpublished MBA Research Report, University of the Witwatersrand, Graduate School of Business Administration, 1984, by BIC van der Westhuizen.

Taking these results as our departure point, we will examine the role of advertising in marketing in South Africa.

☐ Specific tasks of advertising

An interesting way of examining the specific tasks of advertising is to relate them to the various stages of the product life cycle as well as to consumer behaviour in the relevant stages.

Awareness building

Generally speaking, it is easy to understand that awareness building is one of the specific tasks of advertising when a new product or service is introduced. It is the act of taking potential customers or consumers from a state of blissful ignorance to interested awareness. Advertising is focused on getting attention, and should therefore be creative, bold and aggressive. The relevant consumer behaviour characteristic at this stage is that of extensive problem solving, which means that the consumers are being faced with new concepts, ideas and/or products and therefore have to resolve problems which arise in their own minds. There are many forms of awareness building advertisements, the most common of which is the straight announcement of a new product or service. Note, however, that once the initial announcement has been made, advertising still has the task of creating further awareness, since it is highly likely that in the initial stages of the advertising campaign not all prospective consumers or customers will be reached. This is due to factors such as selective perception and the readiness of the particular consumers or customers for that particular product or service.

Comprehension building

Once again this type of advertising is used predominantly in the *introduction* stage of the product life cycle in an attempt to educate the consumers or customers and to build their comprehension of what it is that the product or service can do for them. It is logically most effective while the relevant consumer behaviour pattern is one of extensive problem solving, since in this situation consumers are obviously looking for as much relevant information as possible to build up their understanding of the product or service. Typically, advertisements of this type are very informative, giving much technical detail of products and services and explaining, perhaps in fairly substantial detail, how the product or service works. Often these advertisements are tied in with offers of further information such as explanatory booklets or manuals and customers are invited to respond to ask for further information.

Dissemination of knowledge

Closely allied to the previous section (ie comprehension building), the dissemination of knowledge task of advertising is, in a general sense, that of 'spreading the gospel'. In other words, this is a type of missionary work in which the main purpose of advertising is to persuade people to try something new. An example is, say, microwave ovens: many consumers might be nervous of this new product and the manufacturers could persuade people that it is worth trying by putting out extensive knowledge on the product. This type of advertising is used predominantly in the *introduction* stage of the product life cycle and again in the extensive problem solving phase of consumer behaviour. It stands to reason that knowledge will break down any fears or concerns that consumers may have about trying something new. This type of advertising is sometimes referred to as pioneer advertising which, at its simplest, informs people about a product – what it is, what it does, how it can be used and where it can be purchased.

Some other, slightly more subtle aspects of the dissemination of knowledge are suggesting new uses for a product, informing the market of a price change and explaining how the product has been adapted to additional functions.

Overcoming misconceptions

Often consumers have misconceptions about products or services which prevent them from purchasing these items. Unfortunately, manufacturers may not know of these secret fears, concerns or misconceptions and are therefore mystified when their marketing efforts are not successful. Research is the answer for establishing what it is that is inhibiting consumers from purchasing such products and once their misconceptions have been established, advertising is a very powerful medium for overcoming them. Advertising can articulate a secretly held fear or concern and then proceed to eliminate this misconception. It stands to reason that such advertising calls for high quality, creative and credible advertising from a source which is perceived to be reliable. Advertising to overcome misconceptions can be used during any of the first three phases of the product life cycle, that is the *introduction, growth* and *maturity* stages. It is highly unlikely that it will be required during the decline phase of the product life cycle.

Generating interest

Once awareness of a product or service has been created, the next and very vital task of advertising is to generate interest on the part of the consumer. This is done in a number of fairly obvious ways. The secret is to appeal to one or more of the consumer's basic needs. These range from the basic physiological needs (such as the need for food) through the well-known hierarchy of needs (developed by Maslow) including the need for safety and security, social needs, ego needs and, finally, self-actualisation needs. There is no disputing the fact that advertising plays an extremely important role in generating consumer interest. Understandably, this type of advertising is used predominantly during the *introduction* and early *growth* stages of the product life cycle and it is self-evident that it is, in fact, very necessary.

Developing preference

Once a basic interest in the product has been established and the consumers have been informed where to purchase it, a fairly obvious development takes place. This is that competitors enter the market and the consumer is faced with a different type of problem. He now has to choose between different brands or manufacturers. His consumer behaviour pattern is described as limited problem solving, which is basically choosing between alternatives offered to him. In this regard the very important function of building brand preference for a particular manufacturer's product is the challenge facing advertising. Encouraging consumers to switch to a particular brand or to remain with it if they have already purchased it is the basic task of advertising in this phase of the product life cycle.

It is probably true to say that, having developed a preference, a manufacturer never stops having to maintain that consumer preference for his product. Hence his advertising will always in some way or another reflect the brand attributes which differentiate his product from his competitors' and which he seeks to use to convince the consumer to stay with his brand.

Reminding

When a product reaches the *maturity* stage of the product life cycle and consumers are no longer attracted by its novelty, they nevertheless have to be reminded about its existence. Advertising plays a significant role in this respect and does a number of very specific things. First, it reminds consumers about the product and their perhaps successful use of it over a long period of time. It also reminds consumers where the product is available. It seeks to maintain what is known as 'top-of-mind' awareness of the product so that the moment the consumer requires a product of that particular category, the manufacturer's particular brand will pop into focus as a result of the continuous advertising to which he (the consumer) has been exposed over a long period of time.

In this phase of the product life cycle consumer behaviour is often referred to as routinised response behaviour. This implies that the consumer makes a purchasing decision as a matter of routine, and therefore needs constant reminding of what to select. Advertising is the most powerful element of the promotion mix with which this can be done.

Generating leads

This is the so-called direct response task of advertising in marketing. It simply means that an advertisement will generate a direct inquiry from a customer which the firm can follow up and, hopefully, convert to a sale. Of course, it is used predominantly during the *introduction* and *growth* stages of the product life cycle, although many firms successfully use this type of advertising throughout the product life cycle. It stands to reason that the type of product involved will be an important factor here, since it is self-evident that a low unit price product would not use this type of advertising. On the other hand, a very sophisticated high unit price product which would justify an individual follow-up would certainly use this type of advertising.

Legitimation of firms and products

Marketers should never underestimate the power of the printed word! If consumers see a product advertised regularly and in a consistent way, there is no doubt that the legitimacy of the firm and its products is established in their minds. This is particularly relevant during the *growth* stage of the product life cycle. Legitimation of the firm and its product is a particularly useful task of advertising for sales people. They are frequently supplied with pulls of their company's advertising which they hand to prospective customers to establish the status of their company as a potential supplier.

Product positioning

This is a most important task of advertising. It is most commonly used during the *growth* stage of the product life cycle, when consumers are starting to see competitive products advertised and are therefore seeking to establish some position for a particular product in their own minds. The easiest way to get into a person's mind is, of course, to get in first! But if it cannot be first, then the firm concerned must find a way to position itself against the competitive product that got there first. Perhaps the most successful positioning strategy in advertising is the now famous one implemented by Avis, which came up with the slogan 'We try harder'. This implies that someone was better than them, but they were in fact worth trying as a potential supplier of hired cars since they would try harder to satisfy their customers. It is now a matter of historical record that this strategy proved to be eminently successful for Avis. There is no doubt whatsoever that advertising plays a highly significant role in product positioning. Judicious marketers attempt to differentiate their product quite subtly in their advertising message so that consumers automatically position their product in a spot different to that of competing products.

Image building

Once again this task of advertising is particularly relevant during the *growth* stage of the product life cycle. Closely allied to product positioning above, image building simply means that the marketer attempts to build a unique image for his product as compared with competitive products. Advertising is well known for its ability to create a particular image. An important factor to be taken into consideration when image building is that there should be consistency of the advertising message over a long period. If consumers perceive that the advertiser is changing his basic message fairly regularly, they will be confused as to what image he is trying to convey for the particular product or service. Hence image building as part of the advertising strategy has to be carefully designed and is something that should not be undertaken without a long-term commitment if it is to achieve success.

Reassuring purchasers

The task of advertising in reassuring purchasers of the firm's product or service is a very important one. It is used in virtually all stages of the product life cycle, although obviously it has major application during the *introduction* and *growth* stages. The phenomenon referred to when a customer has a potential concern about his or her purchase is *cognitive dissonance*. This simply means that after purchasing a product a consumer may have fears that he has done the wrong thing and be concerned about the wisdom of his decision. It is, for example, a well-known fact that the most avid readers of motor car advertisements are people who have just purchased that particular make of car! They read the advertisement simply to reassure themselves that they have indeed made a wise purchasing decision. There are many subtle ways of reassuring purchasers that they have done just that, that is made a wise purchasing decision. One of the subtle ways that has been employed is to include a small note with the product, congratulating the purchaser for making a wise choice. The manufacturers of a particular brand of shirt include in the packaging a note complimenting the purchaser on his choice and reassuring him that he has bought a top quality garment that will give him maximum satisfaction.

☐ Supporting the sales force

This task of advertising is particularly relevant in the marketing of industrial and capital goods. Various research studies have been conducted to establish the effectiveness of advertising in supporting the sales force, one of the better known ones being that by Morrill (1970:4), who studied the influence of industrial product advertising on the effectiveness of sales representatives. His conclusion was that the cost of selling was 10 to 30% lower to customer groups exposed to the company's advertising compared with unexposed customer groups. It was suggested that advertising did change opinions and attitudes and that this led to improvements in both share of customers and share of market, which provided empirical support for the hierarchy of effects model.

Perhaps one of the best-known advertisements which itself was an advertisement for advertising (McGraw-Hill ad) was developed by McGraw-Hill Publishing Company many years ago. The advertisement depicted a stern-looking buyer facing the reader and the caption read as follows: 'I don't know who you are. I don't know your company. I don't know your company's product. I don't know what your company stands for. I don't know your company's customers. I don't know your company's record. I don't know your company's reputation. Now – what was it you wanted to sell me?' This advertisement has frequently been used to promote industrial and capital goods advertising and seeks to convince manufacturers of these products that the sale actually starts before a salesperson calls. There is no doubt whatsoever that advertising does support the sales force, and other studies have indicated that products that are regularly advertised are also able to command higher prices in the market-place. This would obviously be of major benefit to the sales force.

It goes without saying that the way in which advertising supports the sales force has also to do with many of the things outlined above under the specific tasks of advertising, for example creating awareness, generating interest, building brand image and preference, reminding, generating leads, product positioning

"I don't know who you are.

I don't know your company.

I don't know your company's product.

I don't know what your company stands for.

I don't know your company's customers.

I don't know your company's record.

I don't know your company's reputation.

Now—what was it you wanted to sell me?"

MORAL: Sales start **before** your salesman calls—with business publication advertising.

McGRAW-HILL MAGAZINES
BUSINESS • PROFESSIONAL • TECHNICAL

and reassuring purchasers. All of these tasks undoubtedly support the sales force, and a sales force that goes into the field without the benefit of adequate advertising back-up starts at a distinct disadvantage.

☐ Pull-through effect

The pull-through effect of advertising is simply the way of describing the demand created on retail outlets for a particular product by advertising. The theory is that the advertising will be so persuasive that consumers will be motivated to go to outlets and demand the product. This means that the product is in effect being *pulled through* the distribution channel by means of the advertising effect. For many types of consumer products this is a very valid task of advertising. It is self-evident that mass produced and mass distributed consumer products are typically advertised on this basis and consumer demand is generated by heavy advertising. However, it should be noted that this pull-through effect can take place only if the product is correctly promoted to the retail outlets, usually by means of a combination of direct personal selling as well as effective sales promotion and merchandising and display in the retail outlet.

☐ Integrating advertising strategy with total marketing strategy

As was stated earlier on, advertising is not a stand-alone element of the promotion mix or the marketing strategy for that matter. It has to be integrated with the other elements of the promotion mix and the promotion mix in turn has to be integrated with the other elements of the marketing mix.

However, in order to give some clearer focus as to practical ways in which this can be done, the following should be borne in mind:

Keep your objectives reasonable
Over-ambition is a common pitfall of many strategies. Do not try to talk to everyone, to sell a product for all occasions or to ask people to change their habits. Changing deeply ingrained habits may be the hardest job for your advertising or marketing strategy. Therefore, in order to keep your objectives reasonable they should be achievable. Perhaps the objective should be built up over some time so that at the initial stage your objective would be to persuade people to change their brand before changing total buying habits.

Make your strategy easy to use
In order that people in the company should be able to understand and, more importantly, put into operation your marketing strategy, it should be short, sharp and leave no room for misunderstanding. If your total marketing strategy can be communicated on one page, so much the better.

Be single-minded
Great ideas are usually simple ideas. If your advertising strategy and your marketing strategy is clear and single-minded, it follows that the creative people will be able to reach the consumer that much more easily. Understandably, everything about one's product is important to you, the manufacturer. To consumers, however, some product characteristics are more important than others. Try to establish what it is about your product that is most important to customers and convey that point with single-mindedness to your target market.

State a business objective
Much advertising fails because the advertiser does not actually tell the consumer what to do after hearing the message. If you tell the consumer that you want him to try your product he might well be persuaded to do just that. But if your advertising leaves the customer confused as to what it is that you want him to

do, then understandably he will remain confused and hence will not respond to your advertising.

Decide where your business is going to come from

Probably one of the most often overlooked factors in a marketing and/or advertising strategy is that marketers fail to aim at a specific target market. Unless you have a unique new product that brings totally new consumers into the market, your business will generally come from someone else's business. Strategies should therefore clearly recognise this problem and should not be naïve in the way they address existing users of competitor's products.

Understand your target market

Following on logically from the above, it is obvious that in order to communicate with your target market you should first of all understand it. Most strategies spend too much time on product attributes and too little time on the consumer. Go beyond the obvious demographic factors such as age and income. Spend some time getting to know the AIO factors of psychographic consumer behaviour (attitudes, interests and opinions). Try to write a very simple profile of your typical consumer. This exercise will help you to see your potential customer as an individual and not as a statistic.

Make a meaningful promise to the consumer

If your advertising is to do its job the promise it makes to the consumer must be meaningful and strong. A me-too type product or promise will not be of interest to any consumer. Therefore you have to look for a differential advantage in your product in order to make such a promise to your consumer.

Support your promise

Logically, having made a promise you would look very foolish if you were unable to support that promise. You must do something to make it convincing.

Set yourself apart

Earlier on reference was made to product positioning and there is no question but that setting yourself apart from your competitors is an absolutely vital aspect of your marketing strategy. Look for an empty or unserved niche in the market and try to position your product where it will be seen to be different from competitive products.

Give your product a distinctive personality

Following on from product positioning, one should attempt to build product personality. Admittedly this is very hard to do and many products never ever achieve a brand image of their own. Product personality goes beyond the product itself and in fact reflects the philosphy of the company marketing the product, which undoubtedly sets it apart from competitors. Every advertisement you place should contribute to the long-term image building of your brand.

Advertise what is important, not what is obvious

Research has indicated that many advertisements waste a great deal of money by talking about product benefits that are obvious to the consumer. To some extent this is an insult to the consumer's intelligence. The right strategy, of course, is to point out important benefits that are not so obvious and which perhaps differentiate your product from competitors.

Think ahead

Obviously, being first with anything is best. If you are first with a particular product or service it will sometimes take your competitors a long time to catch up with you, and this pre-emptive strategy is very successful. However, do not underestimate your competition. Just because you have been first once does not mean that your competitors will not attempt to leapfrog you and beat you to the draw next time! Therefore keep thinking ahead if you want to stay ahead.

Keep your strategy up to date

The world is constantly changing, and with it your market and your consumers. Although your basic strategy, that is the key benefits and personalities of your product or service, should never change or, if they do, only for the better, and, with the real understanding of the implications of such a change, you should keep your strategy as up to date as possible as new information becomes available. Hone and refine the strategy rather than changing it for change's sake.

Do not change your strategy without good reason

As mentioned above, do not change for change's sake. Sometimes diminishing sales are the result of poor execution of a good strategy and not merely of a bad strategy. New competition may enter the market, in which case it is obvious that you will have to change your strategy. Whatever you do, take a very hard look at all aspects of your business before you think about changing your strategy. Then test what it is that you have changed so that you can make a meaningful comparison between the old and the new.

Put the strategy in writing

It is very easy to have a rush of blood to the head, develop a new advertising campaign and then forget some vital elements of strategy development. Therefore, a simple discipline is to put your strategy in writing and refer to it frequently. Make sure that this written strategy is distributed throughout the organisation to all parties who will have anything to do with implementing it. The first question that should always be asked about any potential advertisement is: 'Does it fit with our basic marketing strategy?'.

Have a better product

It has been said that better marketing starts with a better product. There is no doubt that the best marketing strategy and the best advertising in terms of creativity will never sell a bad product. Therefore, if your product is not up to scratch have the guts to admit this and go back to the drawing board in order to correct the fault. Very frequently a bad product is not necessarily technically bad, but is bad because of some small design or quality flaws. Very frequently these can be corrected quite easily, but the tragedy is that many companies are loathe to admit that they have made a mistake and hence try to get sales of a potentially bad product off the ground with massive expenditure on advertising. When sales are not forthcoming the advertising and not the poor product is blamed. This is a tragedy that no top management should ever allow to happen in its company.

☐ Problems peculiar to the South African market

There are, of course, some obvious problems which are peculiar to the South African market and which indeed affect the role of advertising in marketing. These are language, culture, size of the market (ie its limitation), geographical dispersion of the market and the available advertising media. Naturally, the astute marketer will take all of these factors into consideration when devising his marketing communications strategy.

However, there are some less obvious problems which affect marketing in South Africa and probably the most significant of these is the difficulty of operating in a first and third world market simultaneously. This means to say that there is an automatic dilution of marketing communications effectiveness by virtue of the fact that if a message is targeted at the first world segment of the market, it will at the same time be exposed to the so-called third world segment of the market. This could easily mean that the message is entirely wasted on that segment of the market. The converse will also apply, and a very simplistic message beamed at the third world segment of the market may even have a negative effect on the first world segment of the market. Just how a marketer overcomes this particular problem is an immense challenge in a market such as South Africa. Because of the diversity of our population, its geographic dispersion and the overlapping of the various advertising media, it seems that there is no simple solution to this problem and that there will always be a wastage factor in this regard.

Another factor that should be taken into consideration is the growing effects of the globalisation of marketing. This means that many advertising messages are beamed directly from overseas sources to South Africa and these sometimes have a confusing effect on the local market. There is obviously not much that local marketers can do to counteract this, except to ensure that their own advertising is in no way contradictory to such overseas advertising which may find its way into this market or into certain of the South African media. It is self-evident that if there were any contradicions this could be disastrous for the product or brand.

☐ Concluding remark

As can be seen from the above, the function of advertising is to present, promote and sell ideas, products and services. It is not an independent force on its own, but an integral part of the marketing effort and its effectiveness depends not only on its own quality, but on its relationship with other elements in the promotion mix and in the marketing mix as a whole.

☐ References

Kotler, P. 1984. *Marketing Management.* London: Prentice-Hall.
Morrill, JE. 1970. 'Industrial Advertising Pays Off'. *Harvard Business Review*, 48.

2

Advertising in the South African society

The role of advertising in society *37*
Advertising control in South Africa *48*

The role of advertising in society

Dirk van Rooyen

Introduction	37
Economic arguments against advertising	37
Societal factors and advertising	41
The merits of advertising for society	46
Conclusion	46
References	47

☐ Introduction

No other aspect of business invites more controversy than advertising. It is certainly the most visible and obvious vehicle of communication today, and every one of the world's citizens is exposed to it, in some form, to a greater or lesser extent every day. It generates social and economic forces which are keenly felt by business, the overall economy and, of course, the general public. The extent of this impact is evident from both the sums of money being spent on advertising and the accumulated evidence of the services (and disservices) performed by advertising. There is wide divergence of opinion concerning the role of advertising and the influence it has. Its protagonists and defenders weigh up equally, with advertising being broadly considered with regard to its social and economic merits. This contribution attempts to evaluate advertising from an economic point of view, as well as from the point of view of its social impact.

☐ Economic arguments against advertising

Classical economists, in particular Adam Smith, give advertising no recognition in their discussions on ideal economic systems. In fact, under perfect competition conditions there is no need for advertising. One of the assumptions of a perfectly competitive market is a condition of complete information and of course an undifferentiated, homogeneous product. Who would need to advertise under these conditions? On the other hand, however, where do such phenomena exist? Perfectly competitive conditions exist more in the minds of economists than in real life.

Neo-classicists such as Marshall and Pigou distinguish between advertising which has *information value* and advertising which has *competitive implications*. Advertising which is valuable for its informative function is approved of, while the latter is regarded as being economically wasteful. And it is, of course, this latter form of advertising that has borne the brunt of some economists' attention.

Some common points of criticism are the following:

☐ Advertising causes misallocation of productive resources in that consumers are manipulated in such a way that they are unable to exercise their preferences rationally.

☐ Advertising does not contribute to economic utility in any way.

☐ Advertising gives rise to monopolies.

☐ Advertising causes costs to increase and this in turn causes increased consumer prices.

Advertising and competition

As has been mentioned, some economists, while recognising the information function of advertising, have been critical of its competitive implications. Boulding (1955:672), for example, argues: 'There is a case for a certain amount of advertising, such as purely informative advertising, which is descriptive of the qualities and prices of commodities. This is a form of consumer education which is necessary if consumers are to make intelligent choices; in fact, it makes competition more nearly perfect . . . Most advertising, unfortunately, is denoted to an attempt to build up the minds of the consumer's irrational preferences for certain brands of goods'. And Scitovsky (1958:401-402) says: 'To the extent that it [advertising] provides information about the existence of available alternatives, advertising always renders the market more perfect. If advertising is mainly suggestive and confined to emotional appeal, however, it is likely to impede rational comparison and choice, thus rendering the market less perfect'. Similar judgement has been passed on advertising by such eminent modern economists as Nicolas Kaldor and Paul Samuelson.

The obvious problem that springs to mind when this criticism is evaluated, however, is: How can the information aspect be separated from the competitive aspect in any given advertisement? The very fact that an advertisement carries information creates at the same time a 'recall' effect concerning a product which will or can lead to sales.

It should also be remembered that advertising can only affect an already subconscious need. Advertising a new bacon in Israel, or a new deep-freeze at the North Pole will hardly have an effect. Advertising cannot create the demand for a product – a want-satisfying product must exist. It is also not the only element in a marketing mix which may have a causative effect on sales. That advertising saves the consumer a considerable amount of search time in his pursual of want satisfaction goes without saying.

Examples of perfectly competitive markets are harder to find than needles in haystacks. Today most markets are what economists call *monopolistically competitive*. A monopolistically competitive market is one in which a relatively small number of producers, all seeking economies of scale, offer their products to a relatively large number of buyers, these products not being identical in the true sense of the word. Price is therefore not the only instrument of competition. The product is differentiated from essentially similar competitive products by design, colour, packaging or any other means in an attempt to stimulate sales. The essential role of advertising is to point out these product differences and to convince consumers to buy the particular product.

And so it would seem that economists' criticism in the context of today's world does not hold water in the real sense. This is underlined by the fact that so many other variables determine the success or failure of, in essence the demand for, a firm's product. Neil Borden's classic essay, written in 1942, still holds today. He said: 'Advertising can and does increase the demand for many individual companies, but the extent to which it does so, varies widely and depends upon the circumstances under which the enterprises operate' (Borden 1942:433).

In a free market system producers compete for the consumer's favourable attention. The consumer is free to choose what he wants to buy, just as producers are free to choose whether to compete in the system or withdraw from it. And let us not forget Stuart Britt's observation: 'Doing business without advertising is like winking at a girl in the dark. You may know what you're doing but nobody else does' (Smit 1980).

Advertising and the creation of economic utility

The concept *utility* has been used by economists to explain the value contribution of an economic activity. Thus production contributes form utility, transport creates place utility, storage creates time utility and ownership possession utility. At first glance it would seem that advertising does not fit in, and as such it has been regarded as wasteful by certain economists – put simply it has no value for consumers because it creates no utility.

However, it can be argued that advertising creates a psychological utility for consumers. Psychological product differentiation by means of advertising can be of value to the consumer, as in the case of expensive motor cars or exotic wines. There has never been and probably never will be the rational consumer so beloved by economists. Consumers are certainly not led purely by economic considerations in their buying decisions, but also by motivational factors such as recognition, prestige, status and acceptance. A fictitious 'value' attributed and accepted by the consumer cannot be regarded as non-existent in every sense of the word. It has happened that two essentially identical products marketed under different brands and advertising themes have taken on different values for consumers, and this certainly does not imply irrationality on the part of the consumer. As Mayer (1958:315) has it: 'Outside standards of judgement cannot be applied to assess the reality of private gratifications'.

If advertising is to be successful it must carry the message of product uniqueness – a particular reason why the product should be used. In this way advertising often initiates product differentiation so that this particular product attribute may be emphasised. Many products have improved with time due to the inclusion of this 'Unique Selling Proposition' message, and it can therefore be argued that advertising has been indirectly responsible for the creation of form utility. Advertising research has also brought to light certain consumer preferences which, after having been incorporated into products, have been to the consumer's advantage – once again contributing indirectly to the creation of form utility.

Because it enables the availability of a formed product at the right place and time, it has been successfully argued that marketing creates time, place and possession utility for the consumer. In reality the role of advertising here is important in that it informs the consumer of the where and when of product availability. This information enables consumers to make more economical decisions – certainly more so than decisions made without information.

Advertising and monopolies

Because larger companies are able to spend vast amounts on advertising, it is the contention of some critics of advertising that it discourages competition and leads to monopoly at worst or oligopoly at best. Even in South Africa, the beer and wine markets are held up to be good examples of this. It is reasoned that advertising makes it considerably difficult for new firms to enter the market and for smaller firms to stay there. Furthermore, larger companies are in a better position to negotiate more advantageous advertising tariffs. And the result of this, say the critics, is greater economic concentration, higher prices and, of course, higher profits for the few.

Advertising has been criticised for its so-called tendency to manipulate demand in the wrong direction, especially as a result of its exploitation of product differentiation. It seems ironic that on one hand advertising should be held responsible for promoting monopolies and on the other be responsible for unnecessary product differentiation.

Advertising is being overly flattered – it is not the only factor which stimulates sales. The success of 'big' firms is in most cases due to excellent products, a fine distribution network, good people, sufficient capital and efficient management, and certainly not entirely due to advertising – how much easier if it were!

Advertising is also *available to all firms*. A relatively small company can also appear 'big' in an advertisement – as big as any large company. As Sandage and Fryburger have put it: 'The opportunity to advertise gives the small firm a chance to get started. If he has a good product or service fairly priced, he can advertise and build a market. He obviously cannot match the giant firms on a national scale, but he might be able to outspend them in his local market area. As his business grows he can use advertising to enter new markets and expand his own competitive capabilities' (Sandage & Fryburger 1975:41). In advertising, as in most things, the watchword is quality and not quantity – small advertisers can become giant killers merely through the quality of their advertising.

Authoritative studies on the relationship between advertising and monopoly formation seem to support the contention that advertising does not intensify monopolistic conditions. Backman (1967:157) found that while in most cases a causative relationship existed between advertising and sales and profits, there was no concrete proof of advertising contributing to monopolistic conditions. In a later study, Pearce, Cunningham and Miller (1971:326) also drew the conclusion that there is no evidence whatsoever that advertising promotes monopoly and that there is no relationship between intensity of advertising and monopolistic market position.

Advertising and consumer prices

Probably the most common criticism of advertising today is that it is a major cause of higher consumer prices. 'If they did not spend so much on silly advertising, we would not have to pay these outrageous prices' is a gripe heard daily. Of course, it is accepted from the outset that the consumer *does* pay for advertising – the manufacturer recoups the cost in his selling price. Whether he (or in most cases she) pays *more* because of this is open to debate. It would seem to depend on the effect of advertising on:

☐ production costs
☐ selling costs
☐ the value of a product as perceived by the management of the manufacturing firm.

If it is accepted that advertising does stimulate sales, then it can certainly be postulated that advertising contributes to lower manufacturing costs by making possible larger production capacities, which in turn lead to greater economies of scale. This implies lower cost (fixed) per unit, which could be passed on to the consumer in the form of lower prices.

A look at the total marketing costs of any firm will show that advertising usually represents a very small percentage of the total. The lion's share − in many cases in excess of 80% − is normally taken up by distribution. The use of representatives entails a cost per contact conservatively estimated at around a thousand times more than advertising. And if anyone has found a cheaper way of informing prospective consumers about a new product than advertising, we certainly have not heard about it! This does not, of course, imply that the effectiveness of advertising can be compared with that of personal selling.

The prices consumers pay for products should always be evaluated against the background of management's chosen price policy − compare, for example, penetration or skim-the-cream policies. Manufacturing and marketing costs are often not used as bases for price determination − long-term profitability objectives are more often the deciding factor. Furthermore, products are evaluated by management in terms of quality, guarantee, availability, image, exclusiveness, economy, convenience and many other product attributes. In most cases products are aimed at a certain market segment, and so pricing often becomes a question of asking what the market will bear. Development costs for many new products are astronomical, and these costs must be recovered. Further development, however, becomes more economical and very often leads to lower prices − developments in the fields of data processing and microchip technology are perfect examples.

The phenomenal investment in new product development over the past decades could hardly have taken place without advertising informing consumers of their existence − and this certainly implies that economic growth rates would have been considerably lower. Thus advertising has contributed to the expansion of markets and in this way has created higher living standards by enabling the swift dissemination of information. Advertising should and does ensure that where one product is not satisfactory, enough information on alternatives is available to ensure market freedom.

What then, in summary, are the merits of advertising in a free market economy? Advertising certainly stimulates demand, but at the same time stimulates competition and new product development. For most products stimulation of demand also results in the creation of employment opportunities, and resultant economic growth. Consumers obtain added value benefits in the form of information, and possibly lower prices as a result of longer production runs. Finally, advertising is in most cases the only, and certainly the most economical, way of communicating with existing and potential customers. One of the characteristics of market freedom is adequate availability of information − with an optimal condition of consumers being fully aware of the available alternatives in order to make their own decisions.

☐ Societal factors and advertising

In addition to being criticised from an economic perspective, advertising is also being criticised from a societal point of view. Some common criticisms are:

☐ Advertising is false and misleading.
☐ Advertising manipulates people to buy products or services they cannot afford or do not need.
☐ Advertising controls the mass communication media.
☐ Advertising is detrimental to moral values.

TRUTH
IN
ADVERTISING

!

THATS THE MOTTO
OF OUR ADVERTISING
DEPARTMENT

AND

THE TRUTH
OF THE VALUES OFFERED
DURING THIS

ADVERTISING
SALE

MUST BE SEEN
TO BE BELIEVED

Truth In Advertising designed in 1932 by RH Griffin

Let us now examine the criticisms mentioned above briefly.

Is advertising false and misleading?

The criticism that advertising is false and misleading and often contains misinterpretation and distortion should be evaluated against the following background. First, it must be accepted that the *consumer himself* will identify such advertisements, with detrimental results for the business of the advertiser concerned. Therefore, it may be contended that an advertiser cannot afford to place misleading advertisements and thus endanger his existence and image.

Second, the consumer is protected by *legislation* concerning false and misleading advertisements. Amongst others, the Trade Practices Act, 1976 (Act 76 of 1976) as amended by Act 78 of 1978 and the 1980 Act provides for the control of certain advertisements. Section 9(*a*) explicitly states that '... no person shall publish or display any advertisement which is false or misleading in material respects or cause such advertisement to be published or displayed'. Formal control over advertising is also exercised directly or indirectly by a number of other laws, ordinances and regulations of local authorities.

Third, in South Africa there are a number of voluntary control measures which are applied by various institutions involved with advertising. The South African Broadcasting Corporation (SABC), for example, exercises control over the advertisements which are broadcast. The Newspaper Press Union (NPU) supervises advertising in terms of the code of practice formulated by the Association of Advertising Agencies (AAA), which was drawn up with the co-operation and agreement of the South African Society of Marketers. As regards advertising practices, certain major objectives of the AAA need to be mentioned, namely:

☐ to continually improve the standard of advertising in South Africa
☐ to discourage dishonest and undesirable practices in advertising and related fields of activity
☐ to specify commonly accepted practice in the industry so that both advertisers and agents are aware of their respective rights and obligations.

The AAA recognises the power and influence of advertising on consumers and is a vigorous campaigner for responsibility and self-regulation. It is involved in all the significant disciplinary mechanisms of the industry and was a prime mover and foundation member of the Advertising Standards Authorities (ASA), the senior regulatory body in South Africa.

The principles of the ASA are dealt with by Gerrie Uys in his contribution entitled 'Advertising control in South Africa'. Suffice it to say that this association advertises on a regular basis in the various media, inviting the public to report any transgressions of its code and stipulations. Where necessary, action is taken against advertisers who are found guilty.

During 1985, for example, 1 711 complaints, of which some 60% related to misleading advertising, were received by the ASA. In 83% of these cases the ASA paid attention to the particular complaint. However, only half of these cases needed further investigation. In the other cases the ASA found the complaints to be unfounded and that the advertisements concerned were indeed acceptable. The majority of complaints were received from the competitors of a specific product and the nature of complaints related mainly to misleading advertising. Obviously, competitors are more critical of transgressions of the ASA's code and stipulations.

In order to evaluate the number of complaints objectively, they should be judged against the background of the total number of advertisements which appeared during the course of a year. If this norm is applied it may be stated that the percentage of complaints is indeed insignificant.

Apart from the abovementioned institutions and associations, there are a number of other bodies exercising control (directly or indirectly) on advertising. To mention just a few there are the Newspaper Press Union, the South African Media Council, the Federation of Master Printers, the Typographical Union and the Audit Bureau of Circulation.

To summarise, South Africa is fortunate in having the legislative and self-regulating measures applied by the various media and institutions. They are of the best in the world to combat false and misleading advertising. A great deal depends upon the *perception* of the receiver of advertising and these perceptions may differ from person to person. This makes a real description of false or misleading advertising very difficult indeed. Besides, undesirable trade practices surely take place in fields other than advertising.

Does advertising manipulate people?

Critics of advertising very often attack advertising on the grounds that it manipulates consumers in a public and unfair way to buy things that they do not need or even cannot afford. A very explicit condemnation is made by Vance Packard in his book *The Hidden Persuaders*, in which he states:

> Large scale efforts are being made, often with impressive success, to channel or move habits, our purchasing decisions, and our thought process by the use of insights gleaned from psychiatry and social sciences. Typically these efforts take place beneath our level of awareness; that the appeals which move us, are often, in a sense, hidden. (Packard 1957:3).

Most critics pretend that the uninformed, ignorant and even irrational customer is exposed to the mercy of the advertiser and is being manipulated by psychological techniques. If the above criticism were true, one would expect consumers to react against their own conviction when exposed to advertising. One would expect, for example, that consumers' attitudes towards a certain brand would remain unchanged and that they would not switch to other brands. This, we know, is not reconcilable with reality.

Advertising must influence the attitude of the individual first of all, and thereafter his behaviour. When attitudes are changed, a change in behaviour follows. Achenbaum, for example, states that '... even changed attitudes do not have a one-to-one relationship with behaviour; other market elements are involved', and further:

> Interestingly enough, contrary to what many believe, the transmission of information through advertising is not correlated with either attitudes or behaviour. Thus, it becomes quite apparent that consumers know what they want, and if you offer and communicate it to them in a persuasive manner, they will react upon it (in Aaker 1975:392).

One should also accept persuasion as a fact of life. It is found in our everyday existence – teachers, preachers, boyfriends (girlfriends), borrowers, charity organisations, political parties and many others are in one way or another busy with persuasion. Is it fair to single out advertising alone?

A prerequisite for successful advertising is a need-satisfying product. Some views are psychologically motivated, that is subjective and psychological motives lead to the buying of certain goods or services. A trip abroad may have significant psychological satisfaction for a certain person. Whether this person could have spent these funds on something else more rationally is of no concern to him, even if he cannot afford it. It is for this very reason that the needs of consumers differ, that different market segments exist and that consumers do not react in the same way to advertisements. An advertising message is received favourably only by someone with an unsatisfied need.

It is clear that the myth of the defenceless consumer should be duly qualified. The consumer is not passive, but *selective* in reacting to advertising. If the consumer buys things for 'non-economic' reasons this does not imply that his motives are unjustified or irrational. Most needs are learned and form part of our modern standard of living. People are free in a free society to choose from available products. If a person buys something that later seems to be unnecessary, this may be regarded as poor judgement and not a reflection on advertising.

Does advertising control the mass communication media?

The largest portion of the various mass media's income (in the order of two thirds) is derived from advertising. Therefore it is contended that the mass media are in fact controlled and manipulated by advertising. It is difficult to accept this criticism, especially in view of the fact that media are controlled by their own autonomous boards of directors or corporate bodies.

The advertising income of the mass media is really advantageous to the consumer. If there was no advertising, he would pay two to five times more for the various media.

The consumer thus saves substantially as a result of advertising. Besides, if no advertising income existed the price would have to be increased or the state would have to subsidise the media. If the state had to subsidise the media it would be likely to demand more control over the media's affairs, and this would bring into question the freedom and independence of the mass media.

Does advertising lower the community's moral values?

Some critics pretend that the permissive influence of advertising is offensive to the moral values of the community. Suggestive illustrations, liquor advertisements, cigarettes, violence or emphasis on sex are some of the common grounds for this criticism.

However, the question arises: Is advertising the *only factor* contributing to moral decline, or are other factors such as the editorial content of magazines, movies and books also to be blamed? Moral standards (including bad taste) are certainly very controversial and highly subjective. They may differ from person to person. What is acceptable to one person may be offensive to another. The continuous controversies in which the Board on Publications is involved are surely evidence of this.

It is interesting to note that research has shown that many of the so-called permissive advertisements are by no means effective. The consumer, for example, may recall the model in the advertisement, but not the product, which is obviously not the objective of the advertisement. As stated earlier, the various institutions concerned with advertising in South Africa accept in their codes the principle of advertisements being of acceptable norms, in *good taste*, of a certain *moral* standard and adhering to the principle of *decency*. These concepts are, however, difficult to define.

On the other hand, advertising has done a lot to improve cultural values and the educational content for the betterment of the community should also be acknowledged. Advertising may have no impact if an advertisement is rejected by the consumer. In fact, it may have exactly the opposite effect: The consumer may also reject the product being advertised. This is by no means the objective of advertising. Ultimately, the person exposed to advertising has the right to veto/ignore advertising of questionable moral content.

A recent Consumer Pulse study carried out by Markinor Research Group (Markinor, *People and Marketing*, May 1986) shows that the overwhelming majority of South Africans – black and white – approve of advertising. They claim that advertising is informative, entertaining and helps keep down prices.

☐ The merits of advertising for society

In the above overview, criticism of advertising from an economic and societal point of view has been examined. In presenting it the intention was to place this criticism in perspective. However, in order to summarise the merits of advertising within an economic and societal context, the following points can be listed:

☐ Advertising provides the consumer with *information value*, enabling him to make more economical decisions. The consumer receives information on new merchandise, special prices and where these are available. The industrial user receives information on new materials, new equipment and technological innovations.

☐ Advertising reduces *marketing costs* by means of less expensive pre-selling and thus reduces or even eliminates the cost of personal selling.

☐ Advertising encourages *competition* and contributes to product development. It stimulates mass production and consumption. This leads to economic growth, investment, job creation and personal income.

☐ Advertising adds *value* to products by providing time, place and possession utility to the consumer.

☐ Advertising promotes the *standard of living* of the community by making consumers aware of products which will improve their standard of living. In this way it stimulates people to work harder (be more productive) to possess such products.

☐ Advertising can help to *stabilise the economic tendency* through manipulation of the extremes of the business cycle, for example stimulating demand in weak economic conditions or even trying to prolong periods of high economic activity.

☐ Advertising can help to solve *social problems* by informing and educating the general public regarding matters such as family planning, bush fires, road safety, pollution, and many others.

☐ Advertising enables the *mass media* to remain *independent* through the income derived from it. In this way advertising indirectly promotes the freedom of speech as well as a democratic community.

☐ Conclusion

It must be accepted that advertising is an essential instrument in the marketing mix of businesses and other institutions. There is ample evidence of businesses which failed to appreciate the importance of advertising and cut back on advertising, with detrimental results. Many studies have shown that advertisers who reduced advertising expenditure during times of recession or depression subsequently could not regain the market share they enjoyed before.

☐ References

Aaker, DA. 1975. *Advertising Management, practical perspectives.* Englewood Cliffs, New Jersey: Prentice-Hall.

Backman, J. 1967. *Advertising and Competition.* New York: University Press.

Borden, NH. 1942. *The Economic Effects of Advertising.* Homewood, Illinois: Richard D Irwin.

Boulding, KE. 1955. *Economic Analysis.* 3rd ed. New York: Harper & Row.

Mayer, M. 1958. *Advertising and values added.* New York: Harper & Row.

Packard, V. 1957. *The Hidden Persuaders.* New York: David McKay.

Pearce, M, Cunningham, SM & Miller, A. 1971. *Appraising the economic and social effects of advertising.* Cambridge: Marketing Science Institute.

Sandage, LH & Fryburger, V. 1975. *Advertising theory and practice.* 9th ed. Homewood, Illinois: Richard D Irwin.

Scitovsky, T. 1958. *Welfare and Competition.* Chicago: Richard D Irwin.

Smit, HH. 1980. *The Marketing Mix*, January.

Advertising control in South Africa
Gerrie Uys

The reason for an Advertising Standards Authority
and its Code 48

Structure of the ASA 49

Sanctions 50

Code of advertising practice 50

Conclusion 53

Appendix: Code of Advertising Practice 54

☐ The reason for an Advertising Standards Authority and its Code

In order to defend freedom of speech and expression and to enhance the credibility of advertising, it is desirable that the advertising industry should, on its own initiative, impose restraints on advertising through co-operation and agreement among those concerned with advertising and not through legal restrictions or Government intervention.

With the object of promoting and encouraging the highest standards in advertising in all media, in 1969 the Advertising Standards Authority of South Africa (ASA) was established as an independent body, set up and paid for by the advertising industry, to ensure that a system of self-regulation is implemented in the public interest. All of the main organisations within the advertising industry, including the media, are members of the Authority and have subscribed to its Code of Advertising Practice. This Code provides that all advertisements should be legal, decent, honest and truthful and prepared with a sense of responsibility to the consumer. Advertisements must also conform to the principles of fair competition in business and should not bring advertising into disrepute or reduce confidence in advertising as a service to industry and to the public. These are the basic principles from which all of the detailed provisions of the Code stem.

The code adopted by the ASA is based on the British Code of Advertising Practice and the International Code of Advertising Practice prepared by the International Chamber of Commerce, which is accepted internationally as a basis for domestic systems of self-regulation. In the ASA Code the basic principles of the International Code are related to the circumstances peculiar to advertising in South Africa.

The main purpose of the Code is twofold. For those in advertising it lays down criteria for professional conduct, and to the public it gives a clear indication of the self-imposed limitations accepted by those using or working in advertising. Its rules form the basis for arbitration where there is a conflict of interests within the business, or between advertisers and the general public.

The provisions of the Code are mostly general, but special rules covered by appendices to the Code apply to particular audiences such as children and young people, and to certain categories of products and services.

The question is often asked: With legislation protecting the consumer from dishonest and fraudulent trading practices, is there any need for a code of advertising practice? The answer is an emphatic *yes* for three reasons.

First, legal controls are not adapted to distinguishing between advertisements which live up to the best professional standards and those which do not. This is the concern of advertising people themselves, and this is why they have voluntarily adopted a code of conduct to maintain the standards of fair dealing and honest trading in advertising that the community is entitled to expect. They believe that professional regulations, voluntarily applied, can ensure the elimination of dubious practices more speedily and with less cost than Government legislation, and are also more readily adaptable to changing economic and social conditions.

The second reason for a self-regulating code is that all concerned agree to observe it in the broad spirit as well as to the letter, and not to circumvent it by dubious ingenuity. All accept a straightforward obligation to the public and to one another. This obligation involves advertisers in making promises that are honest and intelligible, offering performance that matches promises, and in using fair methods of selling. Advertisers also recognise that continued observance of the Code does much to advance the standing of advertising as an essential element in the marketing of goods and services and thus to promote goodwill and understanding between them and the consumer.

Third, a code of practice can maintain standards in an area of communication that defies legal definition – that of good manners and taste. Advertisers are expected at all times to be scrupulous in their respect for individual privacy and personal susceptibilities.

Whilst the Code is obviously there to protect the interests of advertisers and also of the media, its main concern is the consumer. The application of the Code protects the consumer against advertisements which may be dishonest and not truthful, or even indecent. Research has shown that although people are quite interested in advertisements, to the majority advertising is not an important subject – it is not one which is uppermost in their minds and does not worry them. They do not see it as being in urgent need of reform. Consumers appreciate and value the role advertising plays in their decision making and would not like advertising to disappear from the media.

Consumers – shoppers, real people – know what advertisements are. They expect them to be partial, to put the product's best face forward. But, increasingly, they are helping the ASA to trace and stop the tiny minority of advertisements which do not meet the standards of the ASA Code – which are not legal, decent, honest and truthful.

☐ Structure of the ASA

At each annual general meeting of the constituent member organisations of the ASA, an Executive Committee is elected. In turn, this Committee elects a Copy

Committee and an Appeal Committee. The main function of the Executive Committee is to carry on the ordinary business of the Authority. As its name indicates, the Copy Committee adjudicates the acceptability of advertising copy and considers complaints against advertisements. Any person who feels aggrieved by a decision of the Copy Committee has a right to appeal against such a decision to the Appeal Committee.

The members of the Executive, Copy and Appeal Committees are all persons elected from within the industry. The Constitution of the ASA provides, however, that the Chairman must be an independent person, in no way concerned with advertising and preferably a retired member of the judiciary.

The Executive Committee meets approximately once a quarter, whilst the Copy Committee holds monthly meetings at which complaints which could not be resolved administratively are considered and disposed of. The Appeal Committee meets as and when appeals are lodged against the decisions of the Copy Committee.

☐ Sanctions

Being a body set up voluntarily by the advertising industry and not having statutory backing, which it does not want, the sanctions which the ASA can apply are principally the withholding of advertising space or time from advertisers and the withdrawal of trading privileges from advertising agencies. These sanctions are applied by the ASA through its media members. To these sanctions has been added the sanction of adverse publicity. This is wielded by the ASA, which has the right to publish details of the outcome of investigations it has undertaken, naming those who have offended against the Code.

☐ Code of Advertising Practice

Unlike the codes of similar organisations in other countries in the western world, the South African Code of Advertising Practice covers all advertising, whatever the medium. The ASA is very much aware of the fact that certain groups in the population are especially vulnerable and that they need special protection which can be afforded by the Code of Advertising Practice.

The ASA Code is supplemented by individual codes which are enforced by the various member organisations. All such codes conform to the general principles laid down by the ASA and differ only in detail where the individual needs of the medium are to be met.

No constituent member may be required by the ASA to accept any advertising which such member has ruled to be in conflict with its own code or to be unacceptable for any reason. However, the ASA may require advertising which is acceptable to a constituent member to be withdrawn if the ASA rules that such advertising is contrary to the Code of Advertising Practice.

When an advertisement's conformity to the terms of the Code is assessed, the primary test is that of the probable impact of the advertisement as a whole upon those who are likely to see or hear it. Due regard will be paid to each part of its contents, visual and aural, and to the nature of the medium through which it is conveyed. Where the overall impression of the advertisement is in doubt

the ASA may, with the concurrence and at the cost of the party or parties concerned, call for a consumer reaction test by independent research.

The primary object of this Code is the regulation of commercial advertising. It applies, therefore (except as expressly provided), to all advertisements for the supply of goods or services or the provision of facilities by way of trade, and also to advertisements other than those for specific products which are placed in the course of trade by or on behalf of any trader. It does not cover political advertisements, the acceptability of which must be determined by each individual medium.

The Code also applies, as far as is appropriate, to advertisements by Government departments and agencies and to those by other non-commercial organisations and individuals.

The following are some of the main provisions of the Code:

Decency

Advertisements should not contain statements or visual presentations offensive to the standards of decency prevailing among those who are likely to be exposed to them. The presentation of the human body in particular must be treated with full consideration of its effects on all types of readers and viewers.

Honesty

Advertisements should not be so framed as to abuse the trust of the consumer or exploit his lack of experience or knowledge or his credulity.

Fear, superstition, violence, illegality

Advertisements should not, without justifiable reason, play on fear and should not exploit the superstitious. Advertisements for lucky charms, mascots, astrology, fortune telling and palm reading are not acceptable.

Furthermore, advertisements should not contain anything which might lead or lend support to acts of violence, nor should they appear to condone such acts and should not contain anything which might lead or lend support to criminal or illegal activities, nor should they appear to condone such activities.

An important provision under this heading is that advertisements should not contain anything which offends the religious or other susceptibilities of consumers.

Truthful presentation

All descriptions, claims and comparisons which relate to matters of objectively ascertainable fact should be capable of substantiation, and advertisers and advertising agencies are required to hold such substantiation readily available to the ASA Copy Committee.

Advertisements should not contain any statement or visual presentation which, directly or by implication, omission, ambiguity, or exaggerated claim, is likely to mislead the consumer about the product advertised, the advertiser, or about any other product or advertiser.

Value judgements are, by their very nature, incapable of objective substantiation. For this reason many general assertions made by advertisers, particularly about the quality of their products, fail to command universal acceptance. This does not constitute a reason, within the terms of the Code, for objecting to such claims being made, provided there is no likelihood, as a result, that the consumer will be misled about any aspect of a product that is capable of being assessed objectively in the light of generally accepted standards of judgement.

Obvious untruths or exaggerations, intended to catch the eye or to amuse, are permissible provided that it is clear that they are to be seen as humorous or hyperbolic and that it is not likely that they will be understood as making literal claims for the advertised product.

Denigration and disparagement

The following provisions under this heading are there for the protection of one advertiser against another:

☐ Advertisements should not attack or discredit other products, advertisers or advertisements directly or by implication and shall not disparage the products and/or services of other advertisers, either directly or by innuendo. In particular, advertisements should not single out a specific product or service for unfavourable comparisons.

☐ Substantiated competitive claims inviting comparison with a group of products or with other products in the same field, shall not necessarily be regarded as disparaging.

☐ When considering complaints in terms of the Code, the Copy Committee shall take cognisance of what it considers to be the intention of the advertiser.

Exploitation of name or goodwill

Once again for the protection of an advertiser, the Code provides that advertisements should not make unjustifiable use of the name or initials of any firm, company or institution and should not take advantage of the goodwill attached to the trade name or symbol of another firm or its products or to the goodwill acquired by its advertising campaign, locally or foreign, unless this is done with the permission of the other firm.

There is also a provision in the Code in terms of which advertisements should not be so similar in general layout, copy, slogans, visual presentation, music or sound effects to other advertisements as to be likely to mislead or confuse. Particular care should be taken in the packaging and labelling of goods to avoid causing confusion with competing products.

Guarantees and money-back undertakings

The Code prescribes under what circumstances the words *guarantee* and *warranty* may be used and the obligations which the use of these words place on the advertiser.

Children and young people

There is a special annexure to the Code setting out the provisions governing advertising addressed to children or young people, or likely to be seen by them. Briefly, this provides that such advertisements should not contain anything, whether in illustration or otherwise, that might result in physical, mental or moral harm to them or that exploits their credulity, their lack of experience or knowledge, or their natural sense of loyalty.

Specific categories of advertisements

There are extensive provisions covering specific categories of advertisements from antiperspirants and deodorants to toothpastes and similar products.

Medicinal and related products and advertisements containing health claims

There is a special section of the Code devoted to advertisements for medicinal and related products and to advertisements containing health claims. The advertising of medicines is regulated primarily by the provisions of the Medicines Control Act and the regulations promulgated thereunder. These are supplemented by the provisions in the ASA Code. Appreciating that a person who is ill or in pain will grasp at every possible straw held out to him, the ASA believes that it has a special obligation to ensure that medicinal advertisements comply with the highest standards of control.

Appendices

There are further, extensive provisions in appendices to the Code regulating advertising for:

☐ mail order firms
☐ slimming
☐ breast milk substitutes
☐ cigarette products

The Code also contains an extensive list of diseases to which no reference, or only limited reference, may be made in advertisements.

☐ Conclusion

Advertisements communicate effectively because advertisers are sensitive to the behaviour and attitudes of consumers. Advertisers listen to what people say and then decide what to say to consumers to convey what they consider to be important. Advertisements are prepared in a way that is meaningful to the people for whom the product, message or service is intended. Advertisers should not dictate attitudes or morality. The Code places obligations on the advertising industry to ensure that advertising, as a service, communicates effectively and reliably with the consumer, who should be informed honestly and truthfully and then allowed to choose.

☐ Appendix: Code of Advertising Practice

Preface

The Advertising Control System

The Advertising Standards Authority of South Africa is an independent body set up and paid for by the advertising industry to ensure that its system of self-regulation works in the public interest. It has an independent Chairman.

The following organisations, which are members of the Advertising Standards Authority, support and are obliged to adhere to the provisions of the Code –

The Association of Advertising Agencies (Pty) Limited
South African Direct Marketing Association
SA Printing & Allied Industries Federation
Cinemark (Pty) Limited
Newspaper Press Union of South Africa
South African Society of Marketers
South African Broadcasting Corporation (Radio)
South African Broadcasting Corporation (Television)
The Grocery Manufacturers' Association of South Africa
Pharmaceutical & Chemical Manufacturers' Association of South Africa
Specialist Press Association
The Proprietary Association of SA
SWA Broadcasting Corporation
Institute of Sales Promotion
Outdoor Advertising Association of SA
Furniture Traders' Association
Agricultural & Veterinary Chemicals Association
SA National Co-ordinating Consumer Council
ASSOCOM
Motor Industries Federation

The Code is administered by a committee drawn from the constituent member bodies. Powers are vested in the ASA Copy Committee who deal with all complaints received from the public, media and advertisers.

This Code is supplemented by individual codes which are enforced by the various member organisations. All such codes conform to the general principles laid down by the Advertising Standards Authority Code and differ only in detail where the individual needs of the medium are to be met.

No constituent member may be required by the ASA to accept any advertising which such member has ruled to be in conflict with its own Code or to be unacceptable for any reason. However, the ASA may require advertising which is acceptable to a constituent member to be withdrawn if the ASA rules that such advertising is contrary to the General Advertising Code of the ASA.

Responsibility for observing the Code rests primarily with the advertiser. But it also applies to any advertising practitioner or medium involved in publication of the advertiser's message to the public.

While the interpretation of the Code is vested in the ASA Copy Committee, its performance of this task is supervised by the Executive Committee of the Advertising Standards Authority. The decisions of the Copy Committee may be taken on appeal to an ASA Appeal Committee appointed by the Executive Committee. The Authority maintains close contact with government departments, consumer organisations and trade associations, and deals with complaints received through them or direct from the public.

Sanctions

The sanctions which exist are principally the withholding of advertising space or time from advertisers, and the withdrawal of trading privileges from advertising practitioners. These sanctions are applied by the ASA through its media members. To these sanctions has been added the sanction of adverse publicity. This is wielded by the Advertising Standards Authority which has the right to publish details of the outcome of investigations it has undertaken naming those who have offended against the Code.

Complaints

Complaints from members of the public – or those representing them – that the Code has been breached should be addressed to the Advertising Standards Authority. All that is necessary is a letter indicating the basis of the complaint. It is helpful if complainants can, wherever possible, provide examples or copies of any advertisements to which they take exception. Advice is willingly given by telephone to prospective complainants and others as to the scope of the Authority's activities and its likely reaction to any complaint, but investigations will not be undertaken without written confirmation from the complainant.

Complaints should be addressed to –
The Advertising Standards Authority of SA
PO Box 10537
JOHANNESBURG
2000

All complaints will be dealt with as expeditiously as possible. Delays may, however, occur where it is necessary to obtain technical or expert advice.

The Purpose of the Code

Advertising is a service to the public and, as such, should be informative, factual, honest, decent and its content should not violate any of the laws of the Country.

All members who subscribe to the Code shall neither prepare nor accept any advertising which conflicts with the Code and shall withdraw any advertising which has subsequently been deemed to be unacceptable by the ASA Copy Committee.

The Code is based upon the British Code of Advertising Practice and on the International Code of Advertising Practice, prepared by the International Chamber of Commerce. This is internationally accepted as the basis for domestic systems of self-regulation. It forms the foundation of this Code in which the basic principles laid down in the International Code are related to the particular circumstances of advertising in South Africa.

The main purpose of the Code is twofold. For those in advertising it lays down criteria for professional conduct. And for the public it gives a clear indication of the self-imposed limitations accepted by those using or working in advertising. Its rules form the basis for arbitration where there is a conflict of interest within the business, or between advertisers and the general public.

The provisions of the Code are mostly in general, but special rules covered by Appendices hereto apply to particular audiences such as children and young people, and to certain categories of products and services.

One may ask: with legislation protecting the consumer from dishonest and fraudulent trading practices, is there any need for a Code of Practice? The answer is an emphatic yes — for three reasons.

First, legal controls are not adapted to distinguishing between advertisements which live up to the best professional standards and those which do not. This is the concern of advertising people themselves. And this is why they have voluntarily adopted a code of conduct to maintain the standards of fair dealing and honest trading in advertising that the community is entitled to expect. They believe that professional regulations, voluntarily applied, can ensure the elimination of dubious practices more speedily and less costly than government legislation; and are also more easily adaptable to changing economic and social conditions.

The second reason for a self-regulatory Code is that all concerned agree to observe it in the broad spirit as well as in the letter, and not to circumvent it by dubious ingenuity. All accept a straightforward obligation to the public and to one another. This obligation involves advertisers in making promises that are honest and intelligible; offering performance that matches promises, and in using fair methods of selling. Advertisers also recognise that continued observance of the Code does much to advance the standing of advertising as an essential element in the marketing of goods

and services and thus promote goodwill and understanding between them and the Consumers.

Thirdly, a Code of Practice can maintain standards in an area of communication which defies legal definition — that of good manners and taste. Advertisers are expected at all times to be scrupulous in their respect for individual privacy and personal susceptibilities.

This new edition of the Code embodies several changes from the previous version. The Code now becomes a major source of guidance. Some existing provisions have been rephrased for the sake of clarity.

Definition of Advertising
For the purposes of this Code, "Advertisement" shall mean any visual or aural communication, other than editorial material, which is intended to promote the sale or use of goods and/or services or which appeals for the support of any cause and notifications of any kind and includes any displayed material. (Please refer to Clause 2 of Chapter 1).

Amendments to the Code
a. This Code of Practice and the Appendices hereto may only be amended by a majority of votes of those present and entitled to vote at a general meeting of the Authority provided that written notice of the proposed amendments shall have been given to all members of the Authority not less than one month before the date fixed for the meeting.
b. Notwithstanding the provisions of paragraph a. above the Code and its Appendices may be amended without notice at a properly constituted meeting of the Executive Committee by a two-thirds majority vote.

1. Introduction

1. Preamble
1.1 All advertisements should be legal, decent, honest and truthful.
1.2 All advertisements should be prepared with a sense of responsibility to the consumer.
1.3 All advertisements should conform to the principles of fair competition in business.
1.4 No advertisement should bring advertising into disrepute or reduce confidence in advertising as a service to industry and to the public.

2. Scope
12.1 The primary object of this Code is the regulation of commercial advertising. It applies therefore (except as expressly provided further on) to all advertisements for the supply of goods or services or the provision of facilities by way of trade, and also to advertisements other than those for specific products which are placed in the course of trade by or on behalf of any trader.

2.2 In addition the Code applies, so far as is appropriate, to advertisements by Government departments and agencies and to those by other non-commercial organisations and individuals.

2.3 The provision of paragraphs 2.1 and 2.2 above shall not be interpreted to bring political advertisements into the sphere of the ASA's functions. As in the case of any advertisement the individual medium shall determine whether any political advertisement presented to it is acceptable.

3. Interpretation

3.1 This Code is to be applied in the spirit as well as in the letter.

3.2 In assessing an advertisement's conformity to the terms of this Code, the primary test applied will be that of the probable impact of the advertisement as a whole upon those who are likely to see or hear it. Due regard will be paid to each part of its contents, visual and aural, and to the nature of the medium through which it is conveyed.

3.3 Where the overall impression of the advertisement as a whole is in doubt, the ASA may, with the concurrence and at the cost of the party or parties concerned, call for a consumer reaction test by independent research.

3.4 For the purposes of this Code –

3.4.1 the word advertisement applies to advertising wherever it may appear. It does not apply to editorial or programming publicity.

3.4.2 the word product includes goods, services and facilities.

3.4.3 the word consumer refers to any person who is likely to be reached by an advertisement whether as an end consumer or user or as a trade customer.

3.5 This Code binds advertiser, advertising practitioner and media owner, but the principal responsibility for observing its terms lies with the advertising practitioner. (Please see Sections 9 and 18 of the Trade Practices Act No 76 of 1976.)

3.6 In the event of any discrepancy between the English and Afrikaans versions of this Code the English version shall be definitive.

II. General Principles

1. Decency

1.1 Advertisements should not contain statements or visual presentation offensive to the standards of decency prevailing among those who are most likely to be exposed to them. The presentation of the human body in particular must be treated with full consideration of its effect on all types of readers and viewers.

2. Honesty

2.1 Advertisements should not be so framed as to abuse the trust of the consumer or exploit his lack of experience or knowledge or his credulity.

3. Fear, Superstition, Violence, Illegality

3.1 Advertisements should not without justifiable reason play on fear.

3.2 Advertisements should not exploit the superstitious. Advertisements for lucky charms, mascots, astrology, fortune telling and palm reading are not acceptable.

3.3 Advertisements should not contain anything which might lead or lend support to acts of violence, nor should they appear to condone such acts.

3.4 Advertisements should not contain anything which might lead or lend support to criminal or illegal activities, nor should they appear to condone such activities.

3.5 Advertisements should not contain anything which offends the religious or other susceptibilities of consumers.

4. Truthful Presentation

4.1 Substantiation

4.1.1 All descriptions, claims and comparisons which relate to matters of objectively ascertainable fact should be capable of substantiation, and advertisers and advertising agencies are required to hold such substantiation readily available to the ASA Copy Committee.

4.1.2 Should the substantiation be of such a nature that the assistance of an independent expert is required to assess it, a fee will be negotiated where necessary and recovered from the parties concerned.

The party or parties concerned will be required to deposit the fee beforehand and the Committee considering the complaint shall, at its discretion, allocate costs.

4.2 Claims

4.2.1 Advertisements should not contain any statement or visual presentation which, directly or by implication, omission, ambiguity, or exaggerated claim, is likely to mislead the consumer about the product advertised, the advertiser, or about any other product or advertiser, in particular with regard to –

1. characteristics such as nature, composition, method and date of manufacture, fitness for purpose, range of use, quantity, commercial or geographical origin.

2. value or total price actually to be paid.

3. other terms of purchase, such as hire purchase and credit sale.

4. conditions of delivery, exchange, return, repair and maintenance.

5. the terms of any guarantee.

6. copyright and industrial property rights, such as patents, trade marks, designs and models, and trade names.

7. official or other recognition or approval, awards or medals, prizes or diplomas whether in South Africa or any other country.

4.2.2 Value judgments are, by their nature, incapable of objective substantiation. For this reason, many general assertions made by advertisers, particularly about the quality of their products, fail to command universal acceptance. This does not constitute a reason, within the terms of the Code, for objecting to such claims being made provided there is no likelihood, as a result, that the consumer will be misled about any aspect of a product which is capable of being objectively assessed in the light of generally accepted standards of judgment.

4.2.3 Obvious untruths or exaggerations, intended to catch the eye or to amuse, are permissible provided that they are clearly to be seen as humorous or hyperbolic and are not likely to be understood as making literal claims for the advertised product.

4.2.4 Where informed opinion is claimed in support of a product, such opinion must be substantiated by independent evidence.

4.2.5 Advertisements should not misuse research results or quotations from technical and scientific literature. Statistics should not be so presented as to imply that they have a greater validity than is the case. Scientific terms should not be misused, and scientific jargon and irrelevancies should not be used to make claims appear to have a scientific basis they do not possess.

4.3 The Value of Goods

4.3.1 So far as is relevant, the following provisions apply to claims as to the value of services or facilities offered by way of advertisements as well as to the value of goods.

4.3.2 Consumers should not be led to overestimate the value of goods whether by exaggeration or through unrealistic comparisons with other goods or other prices.

4.3.3 The advertiser should be ready to substantiate any claim he makes as to the value in cash terms of goods offered by him at a lower price or free; and any saving to the consumer claimed to result from the offer of goods at a price lower than their actual value.

4.4 Use of the word "Free"

4.4.1 Products should not be described as "free" where there is any cost to the consumer, other than the actual cost of any delivery, freight or postage. Where such costs are payable by the consumer, a clear statement that this is the case should be made in the advertisement.

4.4.2 Where a claim is made that, if one product is purchased, another product will be provided "free", the advertiser should be able to show that he will not

be able immediately and directly to recover the cost of supplying the "free" product whether in whole or in part.

4.4.3 In particular, advertisers should in these circumstances make no attempt to recover the cost to them of the product by such methods as the imposition of packaging and handling charges, the inflation of the true cost of delivery, freight or postage, an increase in the usual price of the product with which the "free" product is offered, a reduction in its quality, or otherwise.

4.4.4 A trial may be described as "free", although the consumer is expected to pay the cost of returning the goods, provided that the advertisement has made clear his obligation to do so.

4.4.5 Advertisements offering "free" goods shall indicate that such goods are received free with every purchase.

4.5 "Up to . . ." and "from . . ." claims

4.5.1 Claims, whether as to prices or performance, which use formulas such as "up to 10 kilometres per litre" or "prices from as low as R5" are not acceptable where there is a likelihood of the consumer being misled as to the availability of the benefits offered. Such claims should not be used:

1. where the price or other advantage claimed bears no relation to the prevailing level of prices or benefits, and in particular where it does not apply to the goods or services actually advertised or to more than an insignificant proportion of them.

2. where they apply only to spoiled or imperfect goods, or to goods or services which are in some respects less complete or subject to greater limitations than the bulk of those on offer.

4.6 Direct Supply

4.6.1 Except in the case of a manufacturer who distributes to the public direct, claims that goods are available "direct from the manufacturer" and the like are not acceptable where the advertiser cannot substantiate the implication that the consumer will benefit, in terms of cash or otherwise, from the elimination of one stage or more in the normal process of distribution.

4.7 Wholesale

4.7.1 No advertisement should state or imply that goods offered for retail sale are being offered at wholesale prices unless the advertiser can prove that the prices in question are not higher than those at which goods are currently sold to retailers or other classes of trade buyers.

4.8 Fresh

4.8.1 The word "Fresh" must not be used in advertising in such a manner as to mislead or confuse the consumer.

5. Price Comparisons

5.1 By Manufacturers

Manufacturers may compare recommended retail prices without restriction, ie they may advertise

Previous recommended price: RX

New/Present recommended price: RY

or wording to this effect. The comparison must refer to "recommended" retail prices as Government Notice No 372 of 1969 04 28 issued in terms of the Regulation of Monopolistic Conditions Act of 1955 prohibits resale price maintenance.

5.2 Where a manufacturer inserts the name of a retailer the advertisement will be deemed to be a "retail" advertisement and not that of a manufacturer. It will therefore have to comply with the conditions below governing retail advertisements.

5.3 By Retailers

Retailers will be permitted to quote price comparisons and/or specific discounts in advertising provided that the following conditions are complied with –

5.3.1 Pre-publication approval is obtained from the media concerned.

5.3.2 Satisfactory documentary evidence of the price reduction must be provided to the media concerned.

5.3.3 A single price reduction or discount may be advertised for a maximum period of three months.

5.3.4 Only substantiated comparisons between an advertiser's new price and his own previous price for the product concerned will be allowed.

5.3.5 No comparison may be made between an advertiser's price and prices prevailing elsewhere or charged by other advertisers or recommended by manufacturers, or appearing on manufacturers' price lists.

5.3.6 No claims such as "5% or R10 discount on all products" will be allowed. Discounts and comparisons must be on specific products advertised.

5.4 Sale Advertising

Special sale prices may be advertised on the understanding that:

5.4.1 Sale advertising with price comparisons will be restricted to a maximum of one period of three weeks per calendar quarter, and with a minimum of two months between any two sale campaigns for the same advertiser.

5.4.2 Pre-publication approval is obtained from the media concerned.

5.4.3 Satisfactory documentary evidence of the price reduction must be provided to the media concerned.

5.5 Unacceptable Advertising

Notwithstanding the above the media concerned shall have the right, without further reference, to order the immediate withdrawal of any advertising falling within the above classifications which they consider to be misleading, inaccurate or undesirable.

5.6 Corporate Slogans

The provisions of Clauses 5.1 to 5.5 will not apply to corporate slogans, themes, statements, etc. relating to pricing. Pre-publication approval of such corporate slogans, themes, statements, etc. must be obtained from the ASA. In this regard attention is particularly drawn to Clause 4.2.2 of this Chapter.

6. Denigration and Disparagement

6.1 Advertisements should not attack or discredit other products, advertisers or advertisements directly or by implication.

6.2 Advertisers shall not disparage the products and/or services of other advertisers, either directly or by innuendo. In particular, advertisements should not single out a specific product or service for unfavourable comparison.

6.3 Substantiated competitive claims inviting comparison with a group of products or with other products in the same field, shall not necessarily be regarded as disparaging.

6.4 When considering complaints in terms of the Code, the Advertising Standards Authority's Copy Committee shall take cognisance of what it considers to be the intention of the advertiser.

7. Exploitation of Name or Goodwill

7.1 Advertisements should not make unjustifiable use of the name or initials of any firm, company or institution.

7.2 Advertisements should not take advantage of the goodwill attached to the trade name or symbol of another firm or its product or the goodwill acquired by its advertising campaign, locally or foreign, unless this is done with the permission of the other firm.

8. Imitation

8.1 Advertisements should not be so similar in general layout, copy, slogans, visual presentation, music or sound effects to other advertisements as to be likely to mislead or confuse.

8.2 Particular care should be taken in the packaging and labelling of goods to avoid causing confusion with competing products.

9. Testimonials

9.1 To be Genuine

Advertisements should not contain or refer to any testimonial or endorsement unless it is genuine and related to the personal experience over a reasonable period of the person giving it. Testimonials or endorsements which are obsolete or otherwise no longer applicable (eg. where there has been a significant change in formulation of the product concerned) should not be used.

9.2 Conformance to Code

Testimonials themselves should not contain any statement or implication contravening the provisions of this Code and should not be used in a manner likely to mislead.

9.3 Efficacy Claims

Testimonials should not contain any claim to efficacy which cannot justifiably be attributed to the use of the product, and any specific or measurable results claimed should be fairly presented. Where "before" and "after" claims are made, they should be expressed and illlustrated in such a way as to permit a fair comparison to be made.

9.4 Amendment

Where any testimonial contains an expression which conflicts with this Code, the advertiser may, with the written approval of the person giving the testimonial, amend it so as to remove the source of conflict.

9.5 Foreign Residents

Testimonials from persons resident outside the Republic of South Africa are not acceptable unless their addresses and/or country of residence are given the medium involved.

9.6 Fictitious Characters

Particular care should be taken to ensure that advertisements based upon fictitious characters are not so framed as to give the impression that real people are involved; in particular they should not contain "testimonials" or "endorsements" which may give such an impression.

9.7 Copies for Inspection

Advertisers and their agencies should hold ready for inspection by the Copy Committee, copies of any testimonials used in advertising. Such copies should be signed and dated by the persons providing the testimonials and should confirm what is said in any advertisement.

10. Protection of Privacy and Exploitation of the Individual

10.1 Advertisements should not, except in the circumstances noted in 10.2, portray or refer to by whatever means, any living persons, unless their express prior permission has been obtained. Advertisers should also take care not to offend the religious or other susceptibilities of those connected in any way with deceased persons depicted or referred to in any advertisement.

10.2 This ruling does not apply:

10.2.1 to the use of crowd or background shots in which individuals are recognisable, provided that neither the portrayal, nor the context in which it appears, is defamatory, offensive or humiliating. However, an advertiser should withdraw any such advertisement if a reasonable objection is received from a person depicted.

10.2.2 to advertisements for books, films, radio or television programmes. Press features and the like, in which there appear portrayals of, or references to, individuals who form part of their subject matter.

10.2.3 to police or other official notices.

10.2.4 to occasions when in the Copy Committee's opinion the reference or portrayal in question is not inconsistent with the subject's right to a reasonable degree of privacy and does not constitute an unjustifiable commercial exploitation of his fame or reputation. In all such cases, the propriety of any proposed advertisement should be cleared with the ASA before publication.

10.3 Particular attention is drawn to the Merchandise Marks Act 17 of 1941 and in particular to the provisions governing the use of photographs of dignitaries and reproductions of the national flag.

11. Identification of Advertisements

11.1 Advertisements should be clearly distinguishable as such whatever their form and whatever the medium used. When an advertisement appears in a medium which contains news, editorial or programme matter it should be so designed, produced and presented that it will be readily recognised as an advertisement.

11.2 In print media, wherever there is any possibility of confusion the material in question should be headed conspicuously with the words ADVERTISEMENT or ADVERTISEMENT SUPPLEMENT, and should be boxed in or otherwise distinguished from surrounding or accompanying editorial matter. For further guidance see **Appendix A.**

12. Safety

12.1 Advertisements should not, without justifiable reason, show or refer to dangerous practices or manifest a disregard for safety. Special care should be taken in advertisements directed towards or depicting children or young people.

13. Children and Young People

13.1 Advertisements addressed to children or young people, or likely to be seen by them, should not contain anything, whether in illustration or otherwise, which might result in harming them physically, mentally or morally, or which exploits their credulity, their lack of experience or knowledge or their natural sense of loyalty. For further guidance see **Appendix B.**

14. Guarantees

14.1 "Guarantee" and "warranty" are used by advertisers in two distinct senses: to describe a formal written undertaking, often with legal force, to reimburse a purchaser for the cost of the product itself, or the cost of having it put right in the event of defects becoming apparent; and more generally, as an alternative to "promise" and without any formal (particularly legal) obligation being intended to be understood. Because the possibilities of confusion are considerable the advertiser is under an obligation to be as clear as possible as to the sense in which he uses these words.

14.2 Advertisements should not contain any reference to "guarantees" or "warranties" which take away or diminish any rights which would otherwise be enjoyed by consumers; purport so to do; or may be understood by the consumer as so doing.

14.3 Where an advertisement expressly offers, in whatever form, a guarantee or warranty as to the quality, life, composition, origin, duration, etc. of any product, the full terms of that guarantee should be available in printed form for the consumer to inspect – and, normally, to retain – before he is committed to purchase.

14.4 The duration of any such formal guarantee should be stated in the advertisement and, if the availability of the guarantee is subject to a substantial limitation, an indication of its nature (eg. parts only) should also be given.

14.5 Where a phrase such as "money back guarantee" is used, it will be assumed that a full refund of the purchase price of the product will be given to dissatisfied consumers, either throughout the reasonably anticipated life of the product or within such period as is clearly stated in the advertisement, provided that the consumer is, where appropriate, willing to return the unsatisfactory product to the advertiser. On mail order advertisements see further **Appendix D.**

14.6 There is no objection to the use of "guarantee" etc. in a colloquial sense provided there is no likelihood of a consumer supposing that the advertiser in using the word in expressing a willingness to shoulder more than his purely legal obligations.

15. Money-back Undertakings

15.1 Neither "guarantee" or "warranty", nor any word derived from either, should be used in an advertisement to describe or refer to an undertaking, the substance of which is merely to refund the price of a product within a brief trial period to dissatisfied purchasers. Where such an undertaking is given in an advertisement the time within which claims must be made by consumers should be clearly stated and should make due allowance for the time taken for delivery and return of the product.

15.2 Time Limit on Offers

Where an advertiser, in an advertisement, makes an offer to refund part of the purchase price of a product under certain conditions, the period for which the offer is valid shall be stipulated in the advertisement.

16. Use of the word "new" in advertising

16.1 The word "new" may be used in all media, packaging, posters, bill boards etc. for any entirely new product or service marketed or sold during a given 12 month period.

16.2 It may also be used to advertise any change or improvement to a product, service or package, provided that the change or improvement is material and can be substantiated and defined.

16.3 The maximum use of the word "new" in the above prescribed contexts to be confined to a 12 month period calculated from date of proven first usage in an advertisement. In exceptional circumstances the Copy Committee may agree to an extension of the 12 month period.

16.4 The provisions of Clauses 16.1, 16.2 and 16.3 above shall apply *mutatis mutandis*, to advertisements and packaging announcing any change or improvement in a product, service or package without the word NEW.

III. Specific Categories of Advertisement

1. Anti-perspirants and Deodorants

1.1 Advertisements should make no claim for products taken by mouth which claim body deodorant effect.

1.2 Advertisements for anti-perspirants should not make exaggerated claims to keep skin dry either absolutely, or for a specific period.

2. Antiseptics, Germicides and Disinfectants

2.1 No advertisement for any product in these categories should claim or imply –

2.1.1 that it offers complete protection against disease, or the danger of infection unless the claims or implications can be specifically substantiated.

2.1.2 that it is a substitute for cleanliness.

2.2 Advertisements should not exaggerate the dangers of the presence of germs in the normal domestic situation.

3. Artificial Sweeteners

3.1 In advertisements for artificial sweeteners, claims making comparisons with sugar are unacceptable if they go beyond reference to sweetening power and the reduction of kilojoule intake. Examples of unacceptable claims are –

XYZ does anything sugar can do

Has all the goodness of sugar

See also **Appendix E** on "Slimming".

4. Betting Tipsters

Advertisements for betting tipsters will be accepted under the following conditions –

4.1 Betting tipster advertisers will be required to disclose to publishers their real name and permanent address. Where the business is conducted in any other name, that name is also required.

4.2 Betting tipsters may not advertise success stories or offer guarantees. No money may be requested in such advertising.

5. Charitable Causes

5.1 Advertisements claiming that the purchase of a product will support some charitable or good cause are not acceptable. (This will not preclude an advertiser from giving a donation to a charitable organisation or good cause and then advertising this fact.)

6. Cigarette Advertising

6.1 Advertisements for cigarette products must conform to the provisions set out in **Appendix H.**

7. Commemorative and other items produced in limited editions

7.1 The number of articles to be produced in any limited edition should be stated in all advertising and promotional material containing any claim that the edition is limited. Where an edition is limited by the number of persons applying within a given period, it should be described as an edition limited by time, and the advertiser should offer to inform all purchasers of the number of articles eventually produced.

7.2 Advertisements for articles made of precious metal should state the amount and the fineness of the metal involved in the pieces on offer.

7.3 Advertisements which make claims about the investment potential of the articles on sale should also make it clear that there can be no guarantee of any future increase in value.

8. Cosmetics

8.1 Claims that a product contains ingredients with special properties should be supported by acceptable medical or scientific evidence that the ingredient is indeed beneficial for the purpose referred to.

8.2 Advertisements should not contain any claim or implication that any preparation will promote rejuvenation of the skin or muscles or that hormones or vitamins remove wrinkles.

9. Employment and Instruction Courses

9.1 Advertisements for situations vacant should not mislead or exaggerate as to the nature of work, the level of remuneration likely to be obtained or the working or living conditions to be expected.

9.2 Advertisements offering instructional courses should not contain misleading promises of employment nor exaggerate the opportunities of employment or remuneration claimed to be open to those taking such courses.

9.3 Unrecognised degrees or qualifications should not be offered nor should the value of recognised degrees be misrepresented.

9.4 The Correspondence Colleges Act No 59 of 1965 and the Regulations promulgated thereunder must be consulted with the preparation of advertisements for correspondence colleges.

10. Financial Advertising

10.1 Advertisements addressed to the general public for capital or financial products or services or financial information should in addition to scrupulously observing the other provisions of this Code, so far as they are relevant, take special care to ensure that the public are fully aware of the nature of any commitment into which they may enter as a result of responding to the advertisement.

In this connection the advertiser should remember that the complexities of finance may well be beyond many of those to whom the opportunities they offer appeal, and that therefore the advertiser bears a particular responsibility to ensure that his advertisement in no sense takes advantage, wittingly or not, of the lack of experience or knowledge or the credulity of those to whose attention it is likely to come. Advertisements inviting a direct response (eg. by coupon) through the sending of money or otherwise should take particular steps to ensure thorough comprehension.

10.2 Conformity with the Law

Advertisers should take particular care to ensure compliance with any statutory legal or other requirements currently in force.

11. Franchise Schemes

11.1 Franchise scheme means a scheme where a company, firm or individual, known as a "franchisor", gives to a person, known as a "franchisee", the right, often exclusive, to sell specified products or other specified services in return for an initial payment, a percentage of the profits (or a royalty), or any other consideration.

11.2 Advertisements by franchisors seeking franchisees are not acceptable unless the franchisor has provided all the information required by media in advance of publication. Such advertisements should not mislead, directly or by implication, as to the support available or the likely reward for the investment and work required. The full name and permanent address of the franchisor should be stated in all such advertisements.

12. Hair and Scalp Products

12.1 Advertisements for any product or treatment offered for the alleviation of hair or scalp conditions, or for the improvement of the user's appearance, should conform to the detailed guidance in **Appendix C.**

13. Height Increase Courses

13.1 Advertisements for products or courses of treatment purporting to increase the height are not acceptable.

13.2 This ruling does not apply to advertisements for "elevator" shoes and similar products.

13.3 General courses of physical development, one consequence of which may be to increase the apparent height through improvement of posture, may not be advertised in such a way as to place predominant emphasis upon increasing the height.

14. Homework Schemes

14.1 Homework scheme means a scheme in which a person is invited to make articles or perform services at home for a remuneration.

14.2 Advertisements for homework schemes are not acceptable unless, when offered to media, they are accompanied by full details of the work involved and of the conditions imposed upon the homeworker. The medium concerned shall decide to what extent such details must appear in the advertisements.

14.3 Advertisements for homework schemes should contain an adequate description of the scheme and the reward to be expected. Where it is proposed to charge for machines or raw materials or components, or where the advertiser offers to buy back the goods produced by the homeworker, relevant information should be included in the advertisement. The full name and address of the advertiser should be plainly stated.

15. Imported Products

15.1 No advertisement shall give the impression that a product is imported when it is in fact manufactured in South Africa or South West Africa.

16. Inclusive Tours

16.1 Advertisements for inclusive tours should be so framed as to avoid disappointment to the consumer. In the interests of such protection the medium concerned may determine and require publication of information covering –

16.1.1 the firm or organisation responsible for the tour

16.1.2 the means of transport, whether charter or scheduled (including whenever possible name of carrier, type and class of aircraft or other means of transport)

16.1.3 destination and itinerary

16.1.4 exact duration of the tour and of the stay at each locality

16.1.5 the type and standard of accommodation and meal facilities offered

16.1.6 any special arrangements offered (entertainments, sightseeing etc.)

16.1.7 the total price of the tour as advertised (at least minimum and maximum prices) and those items which are included therein (airport taxes and other fiscal charges, incidental transportation, porterage, tips, etc.)

16.1.8 cancellation conditions.

17. Liquor Advertising

17.1 Advertisements which contain the following features will not be accepted –

17.2 Characteristics and Properties of Liquor.

17.2.1 Advertisements which suggest in an improper manner that the particular product is possessed of an abnormal potency or causes quick reaction. Nothing under this heading is intended to prohibit any factual statement of the actual strength of the product. (Examples of advertisements which would not be accepted under this heading are those stating that the product has a "kick", is "the equivalent of two tots of brandy for only 10c", is "dynamite".)

17.2.2. Advertisements which contain expressions which tend to degrade liquor as a beverage by giving it colloquial names such as "dop", "booze", "regmaker", "grog".

17.3 Consumers of Liquor

17.3.1 Advertisements suggesting consumption of liquor by members of a class who are opposed to the consumption of liquor (eg. teetotallers, prohibitionists), or are generally regarded as immature or otherwise unfit (eg. persons under the age of 18 years, destitutes, criminals).

17.4 Attitudes toward Liquor Consumption

17.4.1 Advertisements suggesting an irresponsible attitude toward the consumption of liquor.

17.5 Place of Consumption of Liquor

17.5.1 Advertisements which suggest consumption of liquor, for other than religious purposes, in proximity to churches, burial places and places held to be sacred.

17.5.2 Advertisements suggesting consumption of liquor at any place specifically prohibited by the Liquor Act.

17.5.3 Advertisements showing consumption of liquor in squalid, poverty stricken or disgusting surroundings.

17.6 Circumstances of Consumption of Liquor

17.6.1 Advertisements suggesting consumption of liquor under circumstances which are generally regarded as inadvisable, improper or illegal (eg. circumstances preceding or during any operation requiring sobriety, skill, or precision. Examples of such operations are motor vehicle driving, aeronautics, railway operations and other forms of transport, factory work, operation of machinery, caretakers, warders, office work).

17.7 Circumstances associated with Sexual Inclinations

17.7.1 Advertisements suggestive of sexual indulgence, stimuli, or submissiveness; nudity or near nudity improperly portrayed; portrayal of the female form in any compromising or suggestive situation.

17.8 Circumstances associated with Children

17.8.1 Advertisements using children except in natural

family situations, in which case they are not to appear or to be heard to be handling or consuming liquor.

17.8.2 Advertisements specifically directed to children.

17.9 Effects of Consumption of Liquor

17.9.1 Advertisements suggesting or commending or making fun of over-indulgence or its after-effects.

17.9.2 Advertisements suggesting disregard of safety or disregard of law and order.

17.9.3 Advertisements encouraging aggressiveness or physical violence.

17.9.4 Advertisements suggesting that noticeable after-effects of liquor consumption such as flushed complexion, unsteady gait, slurred speech and blood-shot eyes are not present if a particular product is consumed; or can be simply cured, concealed or removed by remedial treatment after consumption.

17.9.5 Advertisements claiming or suggesting curative properties which cannot be substantiated.

18. Mail Order Advertising

18.1 Mail order advertising should conform to the provisions of this Code, and to the requirements of **Appendix D.**

19. Marketing Act

19.1 Where the Marketing Act or any Regulations made thereunder require that the grade or description of a product must be indicated on the product pack, the advertiser shall ensure that such grade or description shall also be indicated in any advertisement for such product if the price of the product is mentioned in the advertisement.

19.2 The Regulations under the Marketing Act which govern the packaging of citrus juices and drinks shall apply, *mutatis mutandis*, to advertising for such juices and drinks.

20. Property Advertising

20.1 Information Furnished

Advertisements for real property, whether for sale or for rent, should not mislead or exaggerate or omit on such matters as –

20.1.1 the land itself and any buildings erected or to be erected thereon

20.1.2 the size of the land, availability of services, fixtures and amenities in the buildings and the suburb or location

20.1.3 the legal title and formalities

20.1.4 rights and servitudes of any kind

20.1.5 local authority and town planning requirements

20.1.6 taxes, rates and other imposts

20.1.7 the price, terms of payment and loan facilities

20.1.8 claiming extraordinary conditions of sale like "deceased estate", "owner transferred", "owner going overseas", "owner already bought elsewhere"

20.1.9 making references to Municipal valuation, Building Society valuation, cost price or replacement value

20.1.10 mentioning the name of a specific architect, builder or designer.

20.2 Property Abroad

Particular care is called for in the case of advertisements for real property located abroad. Advertising material containing detailed description of such property should include comprehensive and accurate information as stated above.

20.3 Restrictions on Transfer

When immediate transfer of the property into the name of the purchaser is not possible, this should be clearly mentioned in the advertisement in specific terms ie., "Transfer available on proclamation" or "Transfer available on opening of a Sectional Titles Register".

20.3.1 On no account should the advertiser estimate the time required for such transfer to become available.

20.4 Estate Agents

No estate agent shall –

20.4.1 by means of an advertisement, canvass clients or offer property for sale or to let unless he, in that advertisement, publishes his name and the fact that he is an estate agent, and if applicable, the name of his employer or the estate agent he represents;

20.4.2 without restriction of the generality of the aforegoing, in advertising property for sale or for letting, wilfully mislead or misrepresent in regard to any matter pertaining to such property.

20.5 Interest Rates in Property Advertising

All property advertising which refers to interest rates, other than building society rates, shall indicate –

20.5.1 Whether the rates are subsidised

20.5.2 The extent to which the rates are subsidised

20.5.3 The period of the subsidy.

21. Protein Claims

21.1 Protein claims in food advertising should conform to the Food, Cosmetics and Disinfectants Act.

21.2 References to proteins in other advertisements should avoid giving any impression that their inclusion in non-food products; eg. cosmetics, offers any nutritive benefit unless these claims can be substantiated.

22. "Sales" Advertisements

22.1 Advertisements of "sales" should conform to the provisions of this Code and to the requirements of Clause 5.4 Section II.

23. Self-Defence Courses

23.1 Advertisements for correspondence courses and the like for judo, jujitsu, karate, kung-fu and other similar methods of self-defence are not acceptable.

23.2 This does not prevent advertisements by properly

conducted clubs in which practical guidance is given by experts in such methods.

24. Slimming

24.1 Advertisements for any product or treatment offered as a means of, or aid to, slimming whether in the sense of mass loss or figure control, should conform to the detailed guidance in **Appendix E.**

25. Smoking Deterrents

25.1 No advertisement will be accepted for any smoking deterrent unless the advertiser makes clear that his product offers only assistance and not a cure, and that its success will be dependent upon the will-power of the user.

26. Solar Water Heaters

26.1 References to the National Building Research Institute, either specifically or in its capacity as a part of the Council for Scientific and Industrial Research, should not be accepted unless the material has been approved in writing by the NBRI.

26.2 It shall be the duty of the advertiser and/or his practitioner to submit the copy to the Director of the Institute, PO Box 395, Pretoria 0001, and to satisfy the medium concerned that the approval of the Institute has been obtained before any advertisement is accepted.

27. South African Bureau of Standards and the Council for Scientific and Industrial Research

27.1 No copy referring to the Council of the South African Bureau of Standards, the Bureau of Standards itself or standardisation marks of the Council shall be accepted unless it has been previously approved in writing by the Bureau. It shall be the duty of the advertiser and/or his practitioner to submit the copy to THE SA BUREAU OF STANDARDS, PRIVATE BAG 191, PRETORIA, and to satisfy the medium concerned that the approval of the Bureau has been duly obtained.

27.2 No copy referring to the Council for Scientific and Industrial Research shall be accepted unless it has been previously approved in writing by the Council. It shall be the duty of the advertiser and/or his practitioner to submit the copy to THE COUNCIL FOR SCIENTIFIC AND INDUSTRIAL RESEARCH, PO BOX 395, PRETORIA, 0001 and to satisfy the medium concerned that the approval of the Council has been duly obtained.

28. Toothpastes and other similar products

28.1 Prevention of decay

28.1.1 Fluoride toothpastes

Certain formulations containing fluoride have been shown by independent medical research to reduce the incidence of tooth decay in children. Claims made for such products should not exaggerate the results or applicability of such research. Claims as to the effec-

tiveness of such products should also be related to the need to brush the teeth regularly.

28.1.2 Other toothpastes

Claims may indicate that regular brushing with the toothpaste will help fight tooth decay.

28.2 Hygiene

28.2.1 Bad breath

It should not be claimed that a toothpaste or other product will completely destroy bacteria causing mouth odour or that it will provide long-lasting freedom from mouth odour unless such claims can be substantiated.

28.2.2 Food particles

No advertisement for a toothpaste, chewing gum or tablets intended to clean the teeth should suggest that the product will remove all food particles from the teeth or gums. It should not be claimed that chewing gum or tablets can take the place of brushing after meals.

29. TV and Radio Sets and other Domestic Appliances on Rental

29.1 Unless they fall into one of the categories dealt with in 29.3 below, all advertisements for such appliances which refer to any specific term or condition on which they may be rented should clearly state –

29.1.1 the name and main features of each appliance for which terms are quoted in the advertisement, eg. the size of the screen of a TV set

29.1.2 the minimum period for which each appliance may be rented

29.1.3 the amount of any initial payment

29.1.4 the amounts of any additional obligatory payments (eg. for aerial installation service, maintenance, accessories, or cancellation)

29.1.5 the amount of subsequent payments, when they begin, and at what intervals they become payable.

29.2 Where there is no provision for subsequent payments to be made by the week, the cost of renting may not be expressed in weekly terms unless first it is made clear, by the use of some phrase such as "equivalent to", that the weekly rate is quoted only for the purposes of comparison; and secondly, the quoted weekly payment is calculated on a basis which takes into account the amount of any initial payment and the minimum period of hire. Thus a R52,00 deposit and a minimum of 12 monthly payments of R2,60 must be expressed as "equivalent to R1,60 per week" and not as "equivalent to 60c per week".

29.3 Short classified linage, TV, radio, cinema or poster advertisements which refer to any specific financial terms or condition need not contain all the information required in 29.1 above, but they should include a statement of the total amount which must be paid to have the appliance installed and if a weekly payment is quoted, should observe the provisions of 29.2 above.

30. Water diviners

30.1 Advertisements for water diviners shall be restricted to the following details –
Name and academic qualifications, if any;
Address
Telephone Number
Field of Activity ie, indicating borehole sites for water.
30.2 Advertisements referred to above shall not offer to indicate the presence of minerals.

IV. Unacceptable Practices

1. Direct Sale and Switch Selling

1.1 Direct sale advertising is that placed by the advertiser with the intention that the products or services advertised, or some other products or service, shall be sold or provided at the home of any person responding to the advertisement.

1.2 Direct sale advertisements are not acceptable without adequate assurances from the advertiser or his advertising practitioner that the products advertised will be supplied at the price stated in the advertisement within a reasonable time from stocks sufficient to meet potential demand; and that sales representatives when calling upon persons responding to the advertisement will demonstrate and make available for sale the products advertised.

1.3 It will be taken as prima facie evidence of misleading and unacceptable bait advertising for the purpose of switch selling if an advertiser's salesmen disparage or belittle the cheaper article advertised or indicate unreasonable delays in obtaining delivery or otherwise put difficulties in the way of its purchase.

2. Unsolicited Home Visits

2.1 Where it is the intention of an advertiser to send a representative to call on respondents to his advertisement such fact must be apparent from the advertisement or from any particulars subsequently supplied; and the respondent must be given an adequate opportunity of refusing any such call.

3. Inertia Selling

3.1 Advertisements will not be accepted from those who supply goods without express authority.

4. Non-availability of Advertised Products

4.1 Advertisements should not be submitted for publication unless the advertiser has reasonable grounds for believing that he can supply any demand likely to be created by his advertising.

4.2 In particular, no attempt should be made to use the advertising of unavailable or non-existent products as a means of assessing likely public demand.

V. Medicinal and related products and advertisements containing health claims

1. Preamble

1.1 This section is supplementary to the general provisions of the Code. Special care should be taken by advertisers to ensure that the spirit as well as the letter of those provisions is scrupulously observed.

1.2 Advertisements shall not make claims concerning the safety of a product or exaggerated claims in regard to the speed with which a product can relieve pain.

1.3 No advertisement shall be so worded that, while in its literal meaning it may not contravene any of the provisions of this section of the Code, in the effect of its likely inference to the class of people to whom it is addressed, it amounts to a contravention of the Code.

2. Interpretation

2.1 The word "product" in this section is to be taken as referring also to treatments and courses of treatments and to appliances, except where the context does not permit, or as expressly provided otherwise.

3. Scope

3.1 This section of the Code applies to the following categories of advertisement –

3.1.1 those for medicines, medical and surgical treatments and appliances

3.1.2 those for toilet and other products which claim or imply therapeutic or prophylactic qualities

3.1.3 those for any product which is advertised, whether wholly or in part, upon the basis that it may improve, restore or maintain the user's health or his physical or mental condition.

3.2 Individual advertisements published by or under the authority of a Government Department and advertisements addressed directly to registered medical or dental practitioners, pharmacists, registered medical auxiliaries or nurses, may at the discretion of the Copy Committee of the ASA be excluded from the application of such of the restrictions within this section of the Code as are from time to time considered inappropriate, bearing in mind the source of the advertisement or the professional qualifications of those to whom it is addressed; provided always that such advertisements conform in every respect to the provisions of Sections I and II of this Code and in the latter case are either sent direct or are published in their respective professional journals.

4. Conformity with Legislation

4.1 All advertisements for products subject to licensing under the Medicines Control Act 1965 should comply with the requirements of the Act and any conditions contained in the product registration. In appropriate cases, the advertiser may be required to produce evidence of compliance with any condition attached to the registration by the Medicines Control Council following its assessment of the safety, quality and efficacy of the product concerned.

4.2 All advertisements for food in respect of which general, energy, kilojoule, protein, vitamin, mineral, slimming, diabetic, tonic, restorative or medicinal claims are made, should comply with the requirements of the Food, Cosmetics and Disinfectants Act.

5. Impressions of Professional Advice or Support

5.1 Claims for medical or other professional support for a product whether in copy or illustration, or otherwise, should be substantiated and the extent of such support should not be exaggerated in any way.

5.2 Detailed evidence should be held ready for supply to the Copy Committee of the Advertising Standards Authority in support of any reference to tests, whether carried out by the advertiser or otherwise.

5.3 References to tests, trials, research, doctors' preferences or prescribing habits or the use of the product or treatment in hospitals, clinics and the like may only be used if they are fully substantiated. References to tests or trials conducted in a named hospital or by a named professional or official organisation are permissible only if authorised and approved by the Medical Committee or other equivalent authority of the hospital or other organisation concerned.

5.4 Where reference is made in an advertisement to a test or other research which has been carried out other than by an independent organisation or without independent medical supervision, this fact should be clearly indicated.

5.5 Professional journals should not be named or quoted without permission, and references to such journals should not give any unjustified impression of professional support.

5.6 References to doctors, dentists, nurses and the like contained in any advertisement should refer only to those registered in the country in which they practise.

5.7 Advertisements should not refer to any "College", "Hospital", "Clinic", "Institute", "Laboratory" or similar establishment unless there exists a bona fide establishment corresponding to the description used, which is under the regular and effective supervision of a registered medical practitioner or other person holding an appropriate recognised qualification.

5.8 No address, title or description which may imply that a product emanates from any hospital or official source, or is other than a proprietary product, is acceptable for advertising unless substantiation is available from the advertiser.

5.9 Nothing herein contained shall prevent the continued use in an advertisement of the word "Doctor", or any abbreviation thereof, as part of the name of a branded product established prior to 1947 07 01.

5.10 Where in any advertisement a reference to literature is required such literature shall also be subject to these rules.

5.11 No advertisement shall contain any statements which either expressly or by implication disparage either the medical profession or the value of professional medical attention and treatment.

5.12 No advertisement shall be accepted if the advertiser fails to disclose the name of the product or the nature of the treatment advertised.

5.13 Labels of medicines for self-medication shall contain a warning that if the symptoms persist a doctor should be consulted.

6. Safety and Protection of Children and Inexperienced Persons

6.1 Particular care is required by advertisers of products within the scope of this section to avoid encouraging through their advertisements the adoption of any unsafe practices by inexperienced persons, especially by children.

7. Unacceptable claims: General

7.1 Cure

7.1.1 No advertisement should employ any words, phrases or illustration which claim or imply the cure of any ailment, illness or disease, as distinct from the relief of its symptoms, unless so registered by the Medicines Control Council.

7.2 Diagnosis, Prescription or Treatment by Correspondence

7.2.1 No advertisement should contain any offer to diagnose, advise, prescribe or treat by correspondence.

7.3 Appeals to Fear and Exploitation of Credulity

7.3.1 No advertisement should cause those who see it unwarranted anxiety lest they are suffering (or may, without responding to the advertiser's offer, suffer) from any disease or condition of ill health; or falsely suggest that any product is necessary for the maintenance of health or the retention of physical or mental capacities, whether by people in general or by particular groups.

7.4 Conditions requiring Medical Attention

7.4.1 No advertisement should offer any product for a condition which needs the attention of a registered medical or other qualified practitioner. See the list of diseases in **Appendix F** to which no or only limited reference may be made.

7.5 Encouragement of Excess

7.5.1 No advertisement should encourage, directly or indirectly, indiscriminate, unnecessary, excessive or prolonged use of products within the scope of this section of the Code.

7.6 Exaggeration

7.6.1 No advertisement should make exaggerated claims, in particular through the selection of testimonials or other evidence unrepresentative of a product's effectiveness, or by claiming that it possesses some special property or quality which is incapable of being established.

7.7 Refund of money

7.7.1 No advertisement should contain any offer to refund money to dissatisfied users of any product within the scope of this section other than appliances or therapeutic clothing.

7.8 Testimonials

7.8.1 No advertisement should contain any testimonial which conflicts with the provisions of Section II 9. Testimonials given by doctors or other qualified practitioners who are not registered in South Africa are unacceptable unless the advertisement makes clear their place of registration.

7.9 "Non-content" Claims

7.9.1 No advertisement should be based on claims that a product does not contain a given ingredient which is in actual or implied common use in competitive products in any way which may give the impression that the ingredient is generally unsafe or harmful.

7.9.2 No advertisement shall contain any reference which is calculated to lead the public to assume that the article, product, medicine or treatment advertised has some special property or quality which is in fact unknown to or unrecognised by the Medicines Control Council.

8. Unacceptable Claims: Particular Products, Treatments, Symptoms and Conditions

8.1 Diseases and conditions to which reference may not be made

8.1.1 Particular attention is drawn to the diseases and conditions listed in **Appendix F** and the provisions contained therein.

8.2 Abortifacients

8.2.1 Advertisements should not claim or imply that any products, medicines or treatments offered therein will induce miscarriage.

8.3 Acupuncture

8.3.1 Advertisements by acupuncturists or acupuncture clinics are not acceptable.

8.4 Analgesics

8.4.1 Advertisements for analgesics may not claim to induce sleep or relieve tension or calm nerves unless such a claim is associated with the relief of pain.

8.5 Bust Developers

8.5.1 Advertisements for preparations and devices purporting to promote enlargement of the breasts are not acceptable.

8.5.2 Exercises and courses, including exercises which may have an incidental effect on the bustline,

may not be advertised in such a way as to place predominant emphasis on any effect of improving, increasing or enlarging the bustline.

8.6 Contraceptives, Birth Control

8.6.1 There is no objection under the Code to the advertising of contraceptive methods, either in general or particular, provided a reference is made in appropriate cases to the fact that certain methods are available only on prescription and subject to such advertising being approved in advance by the medium concerned.

8.6.2 The effectiveness or safety of particular methods should not be exaggerated.

8.7 Corns

8.7.1 Products for the removal of corns may be advertised subject to medical approval of the product for this purpose.

8.8 Depilatories

8.8.1 Advertisements for "electric pencils" and similar products, offered for lay use, are unacceptable, as are claims for products the effectiveness of which is claimed to be based upon their "radioactive" properties.

8.9 Gargles

8.9.1 Antiseptic gargles should not be presented as cough treatments.

8.10 Hay Fever and Other Allergic Conditions

8.10.1 Advertisements referring to hay fever or other allergic conditions causing coughs, sneezing or catarrh may not suggest that the product will clear up the condition itself unless it contains appropriate antigens or be universally effective against the condition or allergy. Claims for products which do not contain antigens should be limited to the temporary relief of symptoms.

8.11 Headaches

8.11.1 Advertisements should not claim or imply that the product advertised is suitable for the treatment of frequent or regular attacks. No product may be advertised as a course of treatment for headaches.

8.12 Hearing Aids

8.12.1 Advertisements for deaf aids shall only be accepted if they offer such appliances as aids to hearing and shall not be accepted if they offer them as a treatment for deafness.

8.13 Hormones and Cell Extracts

8.13.1 Advertisements addressed to the general public should not contain any exaggerated claim to efficacy based merely upon the fact that a product includes hormones or animal cell extracts.

8.14 Hypnosis and Hypnotherapy, Psychological Treatment

8.14.1 Advertisements addressed to the general public should not contain any offer to diagnose or treat any defect, disability or condition of physical or mental ill-health by hypnosis, hypnotherapy, psychology, psycho-analysis, psychiatry.

8.15 Indigestion Remedies

8.15.1 References to lack of appetite or aversion from food, which may well be symptoms of more serious conditions, are unacceptable in connection with claims for indigestion remedies.

8.16 Laxatives

8.16.1 Laxatives should not be advertised for habitual or indiscriminate use, for the relief of abdominal pain or backache, for any benefit to complexion or appearance, or for the relief of indigestion, other than abdominal distension owing to flatulence except as permitted by the Medicines Control Council.

8.16.2. Advertising for laxatives must not contain pictures, artwork and/or copy which could mislead by creating expectations of effects other than laxation, eg. better health, body building, improved vitality, etc.

8.16.3 Laxative advertising must not encourage, directly or indirectly, the excessive use of laxatives.

8.17 Piles (haemorrhoids)

8.17.1 Advertisements should not contain any offer of products for the treatment of haemorrhoids unless the directions for the use on the container itself or its labels include advice to the effect that persons who suffer from haemorrhoids should consult a doctor.

8.18 Polyunsaturated Fats

8.18.1 Advertisements addressed to the general public for food products (or food supplements) containing polyunsaturated fats or polyunsaturated fatty acids may claim that the inclusion of such fats in the diet in substitution for other fats of different chemical constitution may retard the generation of cholesterol and help to reduce the cholesterol level.

8.18.2 Hypercholesterolemia is only one of a number of risk factors in degenerative heart disease. Care should therefore be exercised that the impression is not given that by lowering cholesterol levels the risk of heart disease is eliminated.

8.19 Pregnancy Testing

8.19.1 Advertisements for pregnancy test kits for home use may be accepted subject to their efficacy and the adequacy of the instructions supplied with them having been demonstrated to the satisfaction of a medical authority determined by the Copy Committee.

8.20 Premature Ageing

8.20.1 No advertisement should contain any claim for slowing down the process of ageing based upon a product's content unless so registered by the Medicines Control Council.

8.21 Rheumatic and Allied Pains

8.21.1 Advertisements may not refer to any medicine, product, appliance or device in terms calculated to lead to its use for the treatment of any form of arthritis, or chronic or persistent rheumatism.

8.21.2 There is no generally accepted evidence that copper bangles (or other copper objects to be worn or carried) can alleviate rheumatic or muscular pains, and such claims for them are not acceptable.

8.21.3 Bath additives may be offered to encourage the taking of hot baths for their soothing effect on muscular pain or stiffness, but no claims should be made, such as references to spa water, which suggest that the additives themselves provide any medical benefit unless so registered by the Medicines Control Council.

8.22 Sexual Weakness, Loss of Virility

8.22.1 No advertisement shall claim that the product, medicine, or treatment advertised will promote sexual virility or be effective in treating sexual weakness, or habits associated with sexual excess or indulgence, or any ailment, illness or disease associated with those habits.

8.23 Vitamins and Minerals

8.23.1 No advertisements for a product containing vitamins or minerals should make any claim –

1. that there is evidence of general or widespread vitamin or mineral deficiency

2. that a full, varied and properly prepared diet needs to be supplemented by vitamin or mineral products

3. that good looks and good health are better maintained or that irritability, "nerviness" and lack of energy can be avoided merely through consumption of additional vitamins or minerals

4. that the application of vitamins to the skin is in any way beneficial to a normal healthy skin unless substantiation can be provided

5. that the inclusion of vitamins in suntan lotions has any effect either in promoting suntan or preventing sunburn unless substantiation can be provided

8.23.2 No advertisement addressed to the general public is acceptable for a preparation which contains follic acid in quantities which may cause it to have the effect of masking the symptoms of pernicious anaemia.

8.23.3 Advertisements for products containing vitamins must comply with the provisions of the Medicines and Related Substances Control Act, 1965 (Act 101 of 1965) and any Regulations promulgated thereunder.

9. Sample Distribution

9.1 The direct distribution of samples of medicines to the lay public is prohibited.

10. Registration

10.1 In respect of products registered with the Medicines Control Council only those claims approved by the said Council may be advertised.

10.2 In respect of medicines called up for registration but not yet registered, claims in advertisements shall be limited to those submitted to the Medicines Control

Council in the application for registration provided that such claims comply with the other provisions of the ASA Code.

11. Ethical Medicines

11.1 The following provisions shall apply specifically to advertisements for ethical medicines –

11.1.1 Advertisements should be in good taste and not of a nature to offend.

11.1.2 Reproductions or illustrations of the anatomy may be used if pertinent to the ailment or treatment advertised.

11.1.3 In respect of products registered with the Medicines Control Council only those claims approved by the Medicines Control Council may be advertised.

11.1.4 In respect of medicines called up for registration but not yet registered, claims in advertisements shall be limited to those submitted to the Medicines Control Council in the application for registration.

11.1.5 In respect of medicines not yet called up for registration no claims shall appear in advertisements unless the company concerned has adequate scientific documentation on which the claims are based.

11.1.6 In advertisements in professional journals attention should be drawn to any side effects and contra indications.

12. Breast Milk Substitutes

12.1 Advertisements for breast milk substitutes must conform to the provisions set out in **Appendix G**.

13. Promotion of Medicines Through Competitions

13.1 The provisions of this paragraph shall apply to advertising for all medicines as defined by the Medicines and Related Substances Control Act, 1965.

13.2 Definitions

13.2.1 "Competition" shall mean any scheme in which persons are invited to compete with each other for a prize or prizes.

13.2.2 "Incentive schemes" shall mean any scheme whereby final sellers or persons employed by them receive financial or other incentives based on their sales of medicines.

13.2.3 "Final seller" shall mean any medical practitioner, dentist, pharmacist or any other person who sells goods by retail to members of the public.

13.3 Save as in paragraph 13.5, no advertising for any incentive scheme is permissible and no advertisement for a competition may require usage, purchase, sale or prescription of any medicine.

13.4 No advertisement may offer medicine as a prize in a competition.

13.5 The provisions of this section shall apply to advertisements directed at the final consumer and at final sellers of medicines but not to advertisements directed at the wholesale and retail trade.

14. Promotion of medicines with coupons

14.1 No medicine shall be promoted to the public through the use of coupons in advertising if the use of such coupons –

14.1.1 Could lead to the misuse of the medicine, and/or

14.1.2 Would be detrimental to the health of the consumer.

14.2 No advertisement for a medicine which is promoted to the lay public through the use of coupons shall be accepted unless such advertisement has been approved by the ASA.

Appendix A: Identification of Editorial Style Print Advertisements

1. There is an obligation on all concerned with the preparation and/or publication of an advertisement to ensure that anyone who looks at the advertisement is able to see, without reading it closely, that it is an advertisement and not editorial matter.

2. In the case of a single advertisement occupying a whole page or part of a page, the following guidelines are laid down:

2.1 The word ADVERTISEMENT should stand alone at the head of the advertisement in such size and weight of type as to be easily seen.

2.2 If the advertisement occupies less than half a page, it should be boxed in completely; or if half-page or more, separated from any adjacent matter by a distinct border.

2.3 Particular care should be taken wherever the size and style of type in the advertisement is the same as or closely resembles that of the editorial matter.

3. Where paid-for space is in the style of editorial, whether paid for by the same or different advertisers, particular care is needed to ensure that no part can be mistaken for editorial matter.

4. As a general rule, where an advertisement or series of advertisements paid for by the same organisation or by organisations under the same control extends over more than one page, the word ADVERTISEMENT should be printed at the head of each page in such a way that a reader cannot fail to see it. Similarly, where a supplement is paid for wholly by an advertiser or advertisers, it should normally be headed in bold letters with the words ADVERTISING SUPPLEMENT, and carry the word(s) ADVERTISEMENT or ADVERTISING SUPPLEMENT at the head of each page.

5. No guidance can cover every case. It may not be enough merely to follow to the letter what is said above. It may also be necessary to look again at each advertisement to see whether it is clearly distinguishable from the editorial content of the publication in which it appears and if not to take steps to ensure that it is.

Appendix B: Children and Young People

1. General

1.1 No advertisement is allowed which encourages children to enter strange places or to converse with strangers in an effort to collect coupons, wrappers, labels or the like. The details of any collecting scheme must be submitted to the medium concerned for investigation to ensure that the scheme contains no element of danger to children.

1.2 No advertisement for a commercial product or service is allowed if it contains any appeal to children which suggests in any way that unless the children themselves buy or encourage other people to buy the product or services they will be failing in some duty or lacking in loyalty towards some person or organisation, whether that person or organisation is the one making the appeal or not.

1.3 No advertisement is allowed which leads children to believe that if they do not own the product advertised they will be inferior in some way to other children or that they are liable to be held in contempt or ridicule for not owning it.

1.4 No advertisement dealing with the activities of a club is allowed without the submission of satisfactory evidence that the club is carefully supervised in the matter of the behaviour of the children and the company they keep and that there is no suggestion of the club being a secret society.

1.5 While it is recognised that children are not the direct purchasers of many products over which they are naturally allowed to exercise preference, care should be taken that they are not encouraged to make themselves a nuisance to other people in the interests of any particular product or service. In an advertisement offering a free gift, a premium or a competition for children, the main emphasis of the advertisement must be on the product with which the offer is associated.

1.6 If there is to be a reference to a competition for children in an advertisement, the published rules must be submitted for approval before the advertisement can be accepted. The value of prizes and the chances of winning one must not be exaggerated.

1.7 To help in the fair portrayal of free gifts for children, television advertisements should, where necessary, make it easy to see the true size of a gift by showing it in relation to some common object against which its scale can be judged.

2. Safety

2.1 Any situations in which children are to be seen or heard in advertisements should be carefully considered from the point of view of safety. Except in the case of advertising promoting safety or safe practices.

2.2 Children should not appear to be unattended in street scenes unless they are obviously old enough to be responsible for their own safety; should not be shown playing in the road, unless it is clearly shown to be a play area or other safe area; should not be shown stepping carelessly off the pavement or crossing the road without due care; in busy street scenes should be seen to use the pedestrian crossings when crossing the road; and should be otherwise seen in general, as pedestrians or cyclists, to behave in accordance with the Highway Code.

2.3 Children should not be seen leaning dangerously out of windows or over bridges, or climbing dangerous cliffs.

2.4 Small children should not be shown climbing up to high shelves or reaching up to take things from a table above their heads.

2.5 Medicines, disinfectants, antiseptics and caustic substances must not be shown within reach of children without close parental supervision, nor should unsupervised children be shown using these products in any way.

2.6 Children must not be shown using matches or any gas, paraffin, petrol, mechanical or mains-powered appliance which could lead to their suffering burns, electrical shock or other injury.

2.7 Children must not be shown driving or riding on agricultural machines (including tractor-drawn carts or implements).

2.8 An open fire in a domestic scene in an advertisement must always have a fireguard clearly visible if a child is included in the scene.

Appendix C: Hair and Scalp Products

1. Claims relating to baldness, hair loss, hair growth, etc.

1.1 Unless acceptable substantiation can be provided, no advertisement should contain any claim or implication that –

1. baldness can be prevented or its progress retarded

2. hair loss or thinning of the hair can be arrested or reversed

3. hair growth can be stimulated or improved

4. hair roots can be fed or nourished

5. the hair itself can be strengthened or its health, as distinct from its appearance, improved.

2. Dandruff, greasy hair and other scalp or hair conditions

2.1 Advertisements for a product or treatment offered for the control of dandruff or greasy hair should not contain any claim or implication that either condition can be permanently prevented, and should plainly state that effective control is dependent upon regular use. Nor should such advertisements contain any exaggerated claim or implication as to effectiveness.

2.2 No advertisement should contain any offer of a product or treatment for any condition of the hair or scalp which may be a symptom of systemic disease or malfunction.

2.3 No advertisement should contain any offer of a medicated product or treatment for any condition of the hair or scalp (other than those covered by 2.1 above) unless it is stated either in the advertisement itself, or in the directions for use supplied with the product, that any person suffering from the condition which the product or treatment is intended to alleviate, should consult a doctor.

2.4 In consumer advertising, care should be taken not to use unfamiliar words for common conditions such that consumers may be in any way confused or worried. Thus, by way of example, seborrhoea, pityriasis and alopecia should not be used instead of excess grease, dandruff and baldness.

3. Wigs, Hairpieces, etc.

3.1 Advertisements for wigs, hairpieces and other ways of adding hair to the consumer's own should be so drafted as to make quite clear the nature of the product or process being offered and in particular should avoid any copy or illustration that might suggest the regrowth of hair or the arrest or retarding of the balding or thinning process. Claims that such products and processes are undetectable, permanent or absolutely secure are unacceptable, unless such claims can be substantiated.

4. Individual Treatment

4.1 No advertiser should offer individual diagnosis, prescription or treatment by post for any condition of the hair or scalp.

4.2 Advertisers offering individual treatment at their premises are required to restrict their advertisements, except as provided in 4.4 below, to visiting card particulars, ie. name, address and telephone number and hours of business with a brief general indication of their business, eg. hair treatment, trichologist, etc. No illustrations are permissible. A logotype may be permitted but its acceptability should be cleared with the ASA before it is offered for publication.

4.3 No mention may be made in any advertisement covered by 4.2 above of –
1. any condition for which treatment is offered.
2. the methods of treatment employed.
3. the effects claimed for any such treatment.

4.4 The restrictions in 4.2 and 4.3 above apply to all advertisements in newspapers, magazines or the cinema, to posters, signs and unsolicited material sent or delivered directly to the consumer. Advertising material which has been requested may go beyond these restrictions, provided that in all other respects it conforms to the requirements of the remaining section of this part of the Code.

5. Hair Thickeners

5.1 Hair thickeners; that is to say products which temporarily coat the individual strands of hair with a substance which thereby lends bulk, may be advertised provided that it is made abundantly clear that the thickening which takes place is artificial and in no way conduces to any permanent improvement in the health or thickness of the hair or its rate of growth. Particular care must be taken to avoid offending the provisions of 1.1 above.

6. Cosmetics

6.1 Provided that advertisements for hair creams, brilliantines, shampoos, hair fixatives, hair lotions, hair dye and similar products do not contravene any of the advice in any section of the Code, they are not subject to any additional restrictions. It should be noted that the restriction on diagnosis and advice by post does not apply to the giving of advice on the suitability of hair colorants or other cosmetics.

6.2 Products offered for the mending of split ends of hair should contain no claim which suggests that their action is other than purely mechanical, and of transient effect.

7. Proteins and Vitamins

7.1 No advertisement for a product which is stated to contain any protein or vitamin should claim or suggest that the topical application of such substances has any effect on the health of the hair or scalp unless acceptable substantiation is provided.

8. Advertisers offering products or treatments in more than one of the above categories

8.1 Where an advertiser offers a range of products and treatments for various conditions of the hair and scalp, he should take particular care to ensure that they are clearly differentiated in any advertisement. In particular, it is not permissible for any advertiser to circumvent the intentions of the paragraph dealing with individual treatments by linking the availability of such treatments to an offer of other products or treatments or cosmetic devices, advertising for which is permitted in less restricted terms.

Appendix D: Mail Order Advertising

1. Definition of Mail Order advertisement

1.1 For the purpose of this part of the Code, the phrase mail order advertisement is to be taken as referring to all advertisements, except as expressly provided below, in which an offer is made, whether directly or by implication, to despatch goods, or have them delivered to the purchaser, upon receipt of a written order, accompanied by payment in whole or in part, without the necessity for the consumer to visit any retail establishment or to examine the goods prior to purchase. The rules in the ensuing paragraphs apply to all mail order advertisements including those by any advertiser who also conducts a normal retail business.

2. Conformity to the Main Code

2.1 Mail order advertisements should conform to all applicable sections of the ASA Code of Advertising Practice and also to the requirements of 3. to 5. below.

3. Obligations of Mail Order Advertisers

3.1 The name of the advertiser and a street address at which he can be contacted must appear in full in the body of the advertisement. Where a coupon is included in the advertisement the name and full street address of the advertiser may also appear in the coupon. Accommodation addresses may not be used. If a newspaper, magazine or post office box number is used the full street address of the advertiser must still appear in the body of the advertisement.

3.2 The name of the advertiser should be prominently displayed at the street address given in the advertisement.

3.3 Adequate arrangements should exist at that street address for enquiries to be handled by a responsible person available on the premises at normal business hours.

3.4 Samples of the goods advertised should be made available there for public inspection, except as provided below in 3.4.1.

3.4.1 Where bespoke or made-to-measure goods are concerned, or where it is the advertiser's proposal (in which case it must be clearly expressed in his advertisement) that manufacture should not be commenced by him unless sufficient public interest is manifested in the articles on offer, then models or examples of similar work should be made available in lieu of samples of the articles to be supplied.

3.5 The advertiser should refund all money paid for the goods and their despatch in the following circumstances.

3.5.1 Where goods are returned to the advertiser, undamaged, within fourteen days of receipt. If items are returned, the date of posting or the date of handing over to the carrier will be taken as the date on which the goods are returned to the advertiser. The advertiser should make it clear to consumers whether or not they may try out the goods, subject to these remaining undamaged. If no indication is given, it will be taken that trial by the consumer is permitted.

3.5.2 Where a consumer expresses a wish to be reimbursed in consequence of a delay in fulfilment of the order as provided for in paragraph 3.7 below.

3.5.3 In either case refunds should be made immediately upon receipt of the returned goods or request

for reimbursement. Credit notes or vouchers should not be supplied in lieu of cash refunds unless particularly requested.

3.5.4 Except where the publisher requires otherwise the advertiser is not expected to pay the cost of return postage (or carriage) from the consumer to himself, unless the goods supplied by him do not conform to description or are damaged on receipt, or he otherwise fails to satisfy his contractual obligations.

3.5.5 Advertisements for goods offered by mail order must contain an offer by the advertiser to refund the purchase price paid if the purchaser should be dissatisfied with the goods ordered. The advertisement must indicate a period within which the goods must be returned and such period must be not less than 14 days depending on the nature of the goods concerned. The said period of 14 days shall be determined by the dates of dispatch.

3.6 The advertiser should be prepared to fulfil all orders placed as the result of a mail order advertisement either immediately upon receipt, or within such period as is either prominently stated in the advertisement or is required to be stated by the publishers. In no case, except those detailed below, should such period exceed 28 days.

3.6.1 Where security for the purchaser's money is provided, whether through stakeholder or other schemes, longer periods than 28 days may be permitted (at the discretion of publishers) to elapse before despatch of the goods, provided that the advertiser's proposal thus to delay despatch is prominently and clearly expressed in the advertisement.

3.6.2 Where an advertisement makes it clear that a series of items are to be despatched in sequence and states the intervals between consignments, then, when advance payment for the whole series is involved, only the first delivery need be made within the 28-day period. Where a substantial sum is required in one advance payment, advertisers are required to provide security by means of stakeholder or similar schemes for that part of the purchaser's money which remains unsatisfied by the provision of goods, the outstanding money to be released to the seller at intervals as he fulfils his contract with the buyer.

3.6.3 Provided that all advertisements for the supply by mail order prominently and clearly state the latest date on which (or period within which) despatch will be effected, the following categories of goods may, at the discretion of publishers, be exempted from the requirements of despatch within 28 days.

1. Plants

2. Bespoke and made-to-measure goods

3. (Notwithstanding the provisions of chapter IV 4.2) Goods, the manufacture of which may not be commenced unless sufficient response is forthcoming (in

which case the advertiser's statement of his intention should be clearly expressed in his advertisement)

3.7 When, for whatever cause, an order cannot be fulfilled immediately and no date for despatch is quoted in the advertisement, an acknowledgement of the order, quoting a reference for correspondence, should be sent by return of post. This acknowledgement should state the anticipated date at which the order will be fulfilled. If, when that date arrives, the advertiser is still unable to despatch the goods, and in any event not later than 28 days from receipt of the original order, the advertiser should send a further communication to the consumer enclosing a reply paid postcard, and offering a refund of his money. A similar procedure should be followed where orders cannot be fulfilled within the period stated in the advertisement. If the consumer nonetheless elects to await the delivery of the goods, the progress of his order should be reported to him at intervals of not more than 14 days.

4. Conformity of Goods to Description and Sample, and to Relevant Standards

4.1 All goods despatched in response to orders received as a result of a mail order advertisement should conform both to the description of them given in that advertisement, and to any sample which may have been supplied to the publisher of the advertisement. Substitutes may only be supplied with the express consent of the person who ordered the goods for which they are replacements.

5. Goods Unacceptable for Offer in Mail Order Advertisements

5.1 "Lucky" charms, mascots or other goods which seek to exploit superstition.

5.2 Medical products except as provided in Chapter V of the Code.

Appendix E: Advertising for "Slimming"

1. Introduction: What is Slimming?

1.1 There is a good deal of confusion about slimming, about what given products can do, about whether some products work at all; and about the claims which are made for those products that can be shown to work effectively.

1.2 All advertisers, agencies and media are reminded that advertisements must conform not only to this Appendix but also to the letter and spirit of all other relevant sections of the Code.

1.3 All advertising offered for publication on either a mass loss or a figure control platform has to be checked by publishers with the appropriate media body before it can be accepted for publication. To facilitate this pre-publication checking, no new "slimming"

copy should be submitted unless at least 7 days are available for checking by media.

1.4 When a new product or new formulation is introduced or when new claims are made for an existing product, the advertiser or agency should submit full substantiation for all new claims at the same time as the copy or illustrations for the proposed advertisement, otherwise delays may be expected. Independent testimony will be required from medical practitioners registered in South Africa as to any physiological effects claimed. Testimonials from users of a product do not constitute substantiation.

1.5 Much confusion arises from the fact that wholly different kinds of product and service are sold under the general description of "slimming". The primary task of the advertiser is to ensure that his audience is entirely clear which of the possible ways of achieving "slimness" is provided or helped by his product. The word "slim" is used, so far as the human form is concerned, to cover quite different basic situations: losing mass and controlling the figure so as to achieve an impression of slimness, either by strengthening of muscles or by the wearing of garments.

2. Mass Loss

2.1 General Principles

2.1.1 Mass limitation or control by preventing the re-accumulation of excess fat, are also common objectives. References to mass loss in what follows are to be taken as referring also to mass limitation and control.

2.1.2 The only way for a person to lose mass, other than temporarily, is by burning up the excess fat his body has stored. A diet is the only practicable self-treatment for achieving a reduction in this excess fat.

2.1.3 Diet plans, and aids to dieting of the kinds dealt with below, are therefore the only products which may be offered in advertisements capable of effecting any loss in mass. Claims, whether direct or indirect, that mass loss can be achieved by any other means are not acceptable in advertisements addressed to the general public.

2.1.4 Temporary mass loss can be achieved by the expulsion of water from the body. This may not be represented in advertisements as a method of slimming.

2.1.5 Overmass in young people is sometimes associated with a defective action of the glands and it is therefore desirable that they should be advised to consult their doctors before embarking upon a slimming diet.

2.1.6 Obesity is a condition requiring medical attention and treatment. No claims referring to obesity are admissible in advertisements directed to the general public (see **Appendix F**).

2.2 Diet Plans

2.2.1 Evidence will be required from the advertiser to

show that his suggested diet(s) will provide adequate amounts of proteins, vitamins and minerals, and that the diet is capable of achieving the results claimed for it, when followed by the kind of person for whom it is intended.

2.2.2 No claim, direct or indirect, should be made in any advertisement for a diet that it contains any ingredient which in itself has the property of hastening the process of mass loss. All foods have some kilojoule count and in a balanced diet it will be necessary to have foods with higher and lower kilojoule levels. There is no ground for supposing that any specific foods have particular properties which speed up the metabolic processes which cause excess fat to be "burnt-up" and thus mass to be lost.

2.2.3 Advertisements for "crash" diets are unacceptable.

2.3 Aids to Dieting – General

2.3.1 Diet aids, such as foods, food substitutes, or appetite depressants, may not be advertised except in terms which make clear that they can only be effective when taken in conjunction with or as part of a kilojoule-controlled diet. Due prominence should be given therefore in all advertisements to the part played by the diet.

2.3.2 Any diets provided in conjunction with diet aids, whether on pack, in advertisements or otherwise, will be required to conform to the advice given above on diet plans, and details of the diets proposed should therefore be enclosed, with appropriate substantiation, when clearance of advertising is being sought.

2.3.3 Advertisements for diet aids should also conform to the advice given above as to the non-acceptability of certain claims for the individual effectiveness of specific foods or other diet ingredients.

2.4 Foods

2.4.1 Advertisements for foods offered as diet aids should make clear in what way they contribute to the diet eg. whether the particular food is lower in kilojoule than its conventional equivalent on a mass for mass basis, or a slice for slice basis.

2.4.2 Particular care should be taken to ensure that advertisements for meal substitutes do not imply that these products are effective if eaten in addition to normal meals rather than instead of them.

2.5 Appetite Depressants

2.5.1 Advertisements for appetite depressants should make clear how they work and will only be regarded as acceptable when adequate evidence has been provided by advertisers that the product is safe and effective at the level of consumption suggested.

2.5.2 Claims for the effect of appetite depressants should not be expressed in terms of food equivalent eg. equal to two eggs and ham.

Appendix F: Diseases to which no reference, or only limited* reference, may be made in advertisements

Advertisements should not make any recommendations or offer products, treatments or advice for any of the following illnesses or conditions unless these recommendations accord with a full product registration by the Medicines Control Council. So as to make the list of the widest possible use, certain of the ailments are listed more than once under different names.

A.I.D.S. (Acquired Immune Deficiency Syndrome)
Alopecia (Baldness)
Amenorrhoea
*Anaemia, other than that caused by dietary deficiency
Arterio-sclerosis
Artery troubles
Arthritis
*Asthma, except for products advertised solely for the alleviation of an attack of asthma, and the advertisement should contain a recommendation that sufferers should seek medical advice
Auditory system, any structural or organic ailment
Barber's rash (sycosis)
*Backache (where the reference is to chronic or persistent)
Bleeding disease
Blood Pressure
Breasts, diseases of or development of
Bright's disease
Cancer
Carbuncles
Cardiac symptoms, heart troubles
Cataract
Convulsions (fits)
*Circulatory conditions, except minor conditions such as chilblains, restless legs
Dermatitis (see Skin disease)
Diabetes
Diseased Ankles
Disseminated (or multiple) sclerosis
Ears, any structural or organic defect of the auditory system
Enlarged glands
Epilepsy
Erysipelas
Eyes, any structural or organic defect of the optical system
Fits (convulsions)
*Fungal infections, except athlete's foot
Gallstones
Gingivitis
Glands, enlarged, or glandular conditions
Glaucoma
Goitre

Heart troubles, cardiac symptoms
Haemorrhagic diseases
Hypertension, or symptoms thereof
Impetigo
*Indigestion, where the reference is to chronic or persistent
*Insomnia, where the reference is to chronic or persistent
The Itch (see Scabies)
Kidneys, disorders or diseases of the
Lazy eye
Leg trouble
Locomotor ataxia
Lupus
*Menopausal ailments, except minor associated conditions
Migraine
Multiple (or disseminated) sclerosis
Obesity or over-mass (see **Appendix E** – Slimming)
Osteoarthritis
Paralysis
Pernicious anaemia
Phlebitis
Prolapse
*Psoriasis, except for temporary relief
Purpura
Pyorrhoea
*Rheumatism (and backache) where the reference is to chronic or persistent
Rheumatoid arthritis
Ringworm
Scabies (the Itch)
Sexual weakness and loss of libido
*Skin diseases, except those of minor nature, where the reference is to "all or most", or skin ailments in general
*Sleeplessness, where the reference is to chronic or persistent
Seborrhoea, except for the relief of
Squint
Sycosis (barber's rash)
Thrombosis
Tuberculosis
Ulcers (all except mouth ulcers)
Urinary infections
*Varicose veins (except where the reference is confined to relief by elastic stockings)
Venereal diseases
Verrucae of the feet
*Whooping cough, except for the alleviation of symptoms

Appendix G: Breast Milk Substitutes

1. Product Information
Product information relating to breast milk substitutes

must support sound infant feeding practices and must include clear information on all the following points:
1.1 That breast milk and breast feeding are the best choice *except in exceptional circumstances.*
1.2 The difficulty of reversing the decision not to breast feed.
1.3 The negative effect on breast feeding when introducing partial bottle feeding.
1.4 Where to seek professional advice when a supplement or alternative to breast feeding may be required.
1.5 Information provided by manufacturers and distributors to health professionals regarding breast milk substitutes must be restricted to scientific and factual matters, and such information must not imply or create a belief that bottle feeding is equivalent or superior to breast feeding.
1.6 The use of breast milk substitutes must be demonstrated only by health workers, or other community workers if necessary; and only to the mothers or child minders who need to use it; and the information given must include a clear explanation of the hazards of misuse, and the importance of and methods of obtaining safe clean water for the preparation of breast milk substitutes.

2. Product Labelling
Product labelling must comply with the Foodstuffs, Cosmetics and Disinfectants Act, 1972 (Act 54 of 1972) and the Regulations (R908 and R1130) promulgated thereunder.
   Foodstuffs specifically intended for infants 12 months of age or younger:
2.1 Shall bear a label indicating on the main panel, in both official languages and in letters at least 4.0 mm in height that breast feeding should be the first choice.
2.2 Neither the container nor the label should have pictures of infants, nor should they have other pictures of texts which may idealise the use of breast milk substitutes.
2.3 To ensure optimal nutrition, explicitly worded instructions must be provided on the label for hygienic and correctly measured preparation of breast milk substitutes.
2.4 Directions for the storage and keeping before and after the package has been opened, must be provided on the label.

3. Advertising
3.1 There must be no advertising or other form of promotion to the general public of breast milk substitutes.
3.2 There must be no point-of-sale advertising, giving of samples, or any other promotion device to induce sales directly to the consumer at the retail level, such as displays, discount coupons, premiums, special sales of breast milk substitutes.

Appendix H: Advertising for Cigarette Products

1. Introduction

1.1 The purpose of this Code is the regulation of advertising and advertisements addressed to the public for brands of cigarettes.

1.2 This cigarette Code of Advertising Practice is to be read in conjunction with the Advertising Standards Authority Code for product advertising in South Africa.

1.3 The members of the South African Cigarette Manufacturing Industry have voluntarily agreed to comply with this Code of Advertising Practice and that implementation will be in the hands of the Advertising Standards Authority.

1.4 Subject to the rules, however, there is no intent to hamper fair competition or to handicap advertisers in attracting the attention of consumers. It remains legitimate for them

1.4.1 to indicate that cigarettes are enjoyed by people of many different kinds;

1.4.2 to seek to persuade existing smokers to change their brand or not to do so; and

1.4.3 in pursuit of these objectives, to employ all such techniques of artistic presentation as are used by advertisers of other types of products or services and are consistent with the spirit and the letter of this Code and of the South African Advertising Standards Authority Code of Advertising Practice.

1.5 This Code shall apply to the Republic of South Africa, South West Africa, Botswana, Lesotho, Swaziland, Transkei, Bophuthatswana, Venda and all African homelands.

2. Objectives of Cigarette Advertising

2.1 Cigarette advertising must not be directed towards increasing the number of smokers or increasing the consumption rates of existing smokers. Advertising must be directed towards existing smokers and be intended to effect a change of brand or to discourage existing smokers from changing brands.

2.2 Cigarette advertising must not be created for young people, specifically those under eighteen years of age. Advertisements should not exploit those who are especially vulnerable and those who suffer from any physical, mental or social handicap.

3. Code

3.1 No persons shall be depicted in cigarette advertisements who are under 25 years of age, except in crowd or other scenes where the background is not under control of the advertisers.

3.2 Advertisements must not show family scenes of father and/or mother handling cigarettes in front of children.

3.3 No advertising will depict or use, as endorsers, celebrities in the sporting or entertainment world nor any other person who shall particularly appeal to those under the age of 18 years provided that this shall not apply until 1st January 1983 in respect of films currently on circuit or in production.

3.4 Cigarette advertising content must, as far as possible, be directed at smokers, but must not imply that all persons or all those in a particular situation are smokers. In practice, where there are more than two persons depicted in an advertisement, not all of them will be shown to be smoking.

3.5 Cigarette advertisements must not convey exaggerated satisfaction from the act of smoking. Advertisements showing people smoking should not express unrealistic enjoyment of the cigarette, nor show people reaching with extravagant eagerness for a cigarette.

No advertisement may claim health properties for any cigarette. The smoking characteristics for the products may be illustrated or described, provided no health claim is implied.

3.7 No cigarette products must be advertised on posters or bulletin boards located in the immediate vicinity of Primary or Secondary schools.

3.8 No advertising must state or imply that smoking the brand advertised promotes physical health or that smoking a particular brand is better for health than smoking any other brand of cigarettes or is essential to romance, prominence, success or personal advancement.

4. Claims indicating mildness

4.1 A cigarette shall only be classified as "MILD" if its condensate is 17 mg or less and –

4.1.1 Its name indicates mildness, or

4.1.2 It claims mildness prominently and consistently in its advertising.

4.2 A mild version of a cigarette which is not classified as mild, must meet the requirements of 4.1 above and contain at least 20% less condensate than such other cigarette.

4.3 The term "MILD" and/or "MILDNESS" shall include the terms "LIGHT", "LOW TAR", "LOW CONDENSATE" and/or any other term indicating mildness may from time to time be used.

4.4 All condensate values shall be as determined by the South African Bureau of Standards in accordance with methods recommended by the International Organisation for Standardisation (I.S.O.) and the Co-operation Centre for Scientific Research to Tobacco (CORRESTA).

3

The South African consumer

Geo-segmentation *79*

Black values, lifestyles and psychographics *85*

The status of the black consumer *91*

Appendix: Demographics *99*

Geo-segmentation
Jocelyn Kuper

Introduction	*79*
Definition	*80*
Its value	*80*
The retail data library	*80*
Key applications	*81*
Conclusion	*84*
References	*84*

☐ Introduction

'Geo-segmentation is not the contrived invention of an over-orderly mind. It is the monitoring of marketing and advertising reality'.

The above quotation is taken from a presentation by the Newspaper Marketing Bureau to the South African marketing and advertising community in September 1985 (Argus Group 1984/1985). The concept 'geo-segmentation' had begun to emerge in the thinking of media and marketing people in South Africa, sometimes in different terminology like 'demassification' and 'geo-demographics'. It arose out of a need to limit media overspill and waste as planners saw the recession biting deep and the necessity for fine-tuning the market to maximise sales opportunities.

Similar thinking occurred concurrently in the USA. An article entitled 'Different Folks, Different Strokes' in *Fortune Magazine*, September 1985, makes the point that national marketers are learning what travelling salesmen always knew – where people live is one of the best clues to what they want to buy. The article says:

> The man in the street may believe that national media and fast-food chains are homogenizing the US into one bland culture, but smart marketers are rediscovering the importance of regional differences. For products from soups to cars, the shotgun approach of a single national advertising campaign is giving way to precisely targeted regional strategies . . . By focusing on the unique characteristics of local markets, big companies with mature products have gained market share, often at the expense of local competitors.

So what is *geo-segmentation?*

☐ Definition

Geo-segmentation is the geographic segmentation of a market based on con-sumer patterns and derived from scientific research. It rests on the premise that the more that is known and understood about where a market lives and how it shops, the more effectively a communications and marketing strategy can be devised to reach it.

☐ Its value

Geo-segmentation provides a new view of the market, assists in positioning, sug-gests new opportunities and casts many doubts on the use of mass media in the case of shrinking or static budgets.

At this point, the following quotation from a book called *Up the organisation* (and subtitled *If you're not in business for fun or profit, what the hell are you doing there?* by Robert Townsend is pertinent:

> A tight budget brings out the best creative instincts in man. Give him unlimited funds and he won't come up with the best way to a result. Put him under some financial pressure. He'll scream in anguish. Then – he'll come up with a plan which, to his own amazement, is not only less expensive, but also faster and better than his original proposal (Townsend 1970:19).

The value of geo-segmentation lies in its ability to help the marketer to come up with better and faster ways of homing in on prime prospects and making the most of budgets. It augments the principle of marketing on a 'narrow and deep' rather than a 'broad and shallow' basis. Most high potential consumers in any given product category are surrounded by masses of average or lower potential consumers. As in a gold reef, concentrated pockets of high potential consumers are surrounded by lower yielding aggregates. The challenge facing marketers is how to separate the two and exploit the high yielding pockets.

Geo-segmentation is not just another fashionable buzz-word. It follows the world-wide trend of using methods like ACORN and PRISM in the UK and the States to look at very specific regionalised markets. In South Africa it arose out of an intensive analysis of the Retail Data Library (RDL), large-scale marketing and media survey.

☐ The retail data library

This study, funded by the Argus Company, sets out to provide advertisers and their agencies with a single source data base that interrelates demographic, product, shopping and media information for male household heads and female primary purchasers across the Witwatersrand, the Vaal Triangle, Pretoria, Dur-ban and Cape Town.

More specifically, information is available on:

☐ the demographics and life-styles of female primary purchasers and male household heads
☐ shopping behaviour for a wide range of product categories and services, at specific shops and shopping centres

☐ media consumption patterns.

This marketing and media information can be interrelated at a city, town or suburban level so that advertisers can home in accurately on identified targets.

The RDL is conducted annually by the Argus Company on a very large sample. Key decision makers in the household are interviewed — the male head of the household in every 150 homes and the female primary purchaser in every 100 homes. Thus, in 1984/5 the sample comprised approximately 14 000 interviews, confined to White, Coloured and Asian respondents.

☐ Key applications

Some examples of geo-segmentation, taken from the Retail Data Library (1984/5), are given here. These illustrate a strongly skewed geo-segmented market with vastly different patterns from area to area, which makes marketing and advertising complex unless the differences are understood.

Motor vehicles

Table 3.1
Incidence of
company cars

	Total	PWV	Jhb	Pta	ER	WR	VT	CT	Dbn
Base (in thousands)	1 701	863	303	194	217	77	73	546	292
	%	%	%	%	%	%	%	%	%
Ford	15,3	16,3	14,6	11,9	21,2	19,8	17,0	13,6	15,5
Toyota	12,2	13,7	14,9	13,3	13,1	14,0	11,0	9,8	12,3
Volkswagen	11,4	14,5	14,6	14,5	15,4	13,8	11,8	7,3	10,0
Mercedes	6,5	7,8	9,7	8,7	5,3	7,3	5,4	5,0	5,3
BMW	4,5	6,5	8,7	5,7	5,7	4,6	4,2	2,5	2,3

PWV : Pretoria/Witwatersrand/Vereeniging   WR : West Rand
Jhb : Johannesburg   VT   : Vaal Triangle
Pta : Pretoria   CT   : Cape Town
ER   : East Rand   Dbn : Durban

Table 3.1 illustrates Ford's strengths on the East and West Rand and its low incidence in Pretoria. The incidence of Volkswagen as a company car is not high in Cape Town, but it does do well on the East Rand. While both Mercedes and BMW have a higher incidence in Johannesburg, Mercedes is stronger than BMW in Pretoria.

Narrowcasting to 'core Johannesburg' (ie Sandton in the north to Parktown in the south, Randburg in the west to Edenvale in the east), we see that the incidence of Mercedes and BMW company cars almost doubles. This is shown in table 3.2.

Table 3.2
Company cars

	Total	Core Johannesburg
	%	%
Ford	15,3	14,3
Toyota	12,2	16,2
VW	11,4	18,3
Mercedes	6,5	19,6
BMW	4,5	16,1

Still looking at vehicles, but this time at privately owned vehicles in Durban and comparing Whites with Asians, we see differences which could well prove useful for tactical marketing programmes and advertising opportunities. (See table 3.3.)

Table 3.3
Privately owned
vehicles in Durban

	Total	White	Asian
Base (in thousands)	204	135	62
	%	%	%
Mazda	12,4	14,1	9,2
Toyota	16,8	13,9	23,4
VW	19,2	23,5	9,3
Ford	21,8	21,6	21,6
Chevrolet	13,5	13,6	12,8
Nissan	8,7	7,7	11,4
Mercedes	7,2	7,0	7,9

**Financial
Services**

Table 3.4 illustrates Durban's aversion to bank savings accounts, and Pretoria's liking of them. Yet this does not mean that people in Durban do not save – they prefer building societies. People in Pretoria, on the other hand, do not.

Table 3.4
Incidence of
savings accounts

	Jhb	ER	WR	VT	Pta	Dbn	CT
	%	%	%	%	%	%	%
Building society savings	48	50	54	44	25	46	42
Bank savings	30	32	35	44	68	30	45

Jhb : Johannesburg   Pta : Pretoria
ER : East Rand   Dbn : Durban
WR : West Rand   CT : Cape Town
VT : Vaal Triangle

Travel

Geo-segmentation of the overseas travel market is shown in table 3.5(a). It is English speaking and located very much in Durban, Johannesburg and Cape Town. Note that the incidence of travel among people residing in the West Rand and the Vaal Triangle is so low as to be hardly worth considering.

Table 3.5(a)
Incidence of
overseas travel
(Past year)

	CT	Dbn	Jhb	ER	WR	Pta	VT
	%	%	%	%	%	%	%
English	66	84	75	45	31	17	18
Afrikaans	34	16	25	55	69	83	82

Table 3.5(b)
Overseas travel
(Past year)

	Jhb	CT	Dbn	Pta	ER	WR	VT
	%	%	%	%	%	%	%
All respondents	37	23	15	10	11	2	2

Do-it-yourself

The incidence of home improvements is higher on the East Rand, as shown in table 3.6.

Table 3.6
Incidence of home
improvements and
do-it-yourself

	ER	VT	WR	Jhb
	%	%	%	%
All respondents	43	32	31	29

However, a precision probe into do-it-yourself and home improvements in Springs and Brakpan illustrates that language and income are not the only considerations. More households in Springs chose the expensive route of getting professional help, as table 3.7 shows.

Table 3.7
Home
improvements

	Brakpan	Springs
	%	%
Done personally	36,5	20,1
Had done	23,4	28,7

The average income per household in Springs is lower than that in Brakpan, contrary to the view that the lower the income, the more do-it-yourself. (See table 3.8.)

Table 3.8
Income

	Brakpan	Springs
	%	%
A/B	39	32
C/D	61	68

Further investigation reveals the reason for this (and is set out in table 3.9) – there are more artisans living in Brakpan.

Table 3.9
Occupation

	Brakpan	Springs
	%	%
Higher managerial/professional	5,0	9,1
Intermediate professional	14,8	15,7
Supervisory/clerical	23,2	27,0
Artisan	36,1	25,3
Other	27,9	31,1

Food and groceries

This section reveals the need, even for the big chains, to be sensitive to geo-segmentation. Note from table 3.10 that fewer shoppers living in Johannesburg do one bulk shop a month compared with shoppers living on the West Rand. The pattern is reversed for weekly shopping.

Table 3.10
Pattern of average
month shopping
excluding daily
purchases such as
bread and milk

	Major metro average	Jhb	ER	WR	VT	Pta	CT	Dbn
	%	%	%	%	%	%	%	%
Bulk shop	58	43	67	68	68	69	41	44
Shop weekly	31	42	27	27	27	26	41	38
Twice weekly	11	15	6	6	6	5	18	19

It is clear from table 3.11 that advertising must be sensitive to regional differences for appropriate allocation of advertising expenditure over a month to draw in the big monthly spenders.

Table 3.11
Food and grocery
shopping patterns
(base: 451 000
'bulk shoppers')

	Mid-month (Weeks 2&3)	Month-end (Weeks 1&4)	No set time
Metro average	30	65	5
	%	%	%
Cape Town	24	71	5
Durban	23	73	4
Pretoria	39	55	6
Vaal Triangle	32	61	7
East Rand	36	61	3
West Rand	30	63	7
Johannesburg core	32	62	6
Johannesburg	37	53	10

☐ Conclusion

The foregoing are but a few examples of geo-segmentation.

By identifying regional differences the marketer can also identify regional opportunities and strategies. By employing regional marketing and media tactics he can ensure precision penetration of the market.

Thus, while geo-segmentation is not a magic wand ensuring magic solutions for all products, it can certainly give the astute marketer the competitive edge in today's economic climate.

☐ References

The Argus Group. 1984/85. *The Star Retail Data Library*. Argus Group.

Townsend, R. 1970. *Up the Organisation*. 5th impression. London: Michael Joseph.

Black values, lifestyles and psychographics

Christiane von Ulmenstein

Introduction	85
Social trends	88
Value groups	89
Markinor's segmentation	89

☐ Introduction

The values and lifestyles of the upper strata of the urban Blacks have become highly westernised, with little retention of the traditional tribal customs except for great faith in traditional doctors or herbal healers. However, this does not mean that their attitudes to life and products have become similar to those of their white counterparts.

When an advertising campaign is developed, it is not enough to concentrate on the demographic profile of the target market at which the brand is aimed.

Within a standard demographic profile of 'black housewives, 25-49, B/C income' one may be addressing vastly differing types of people, all with differing lifestyles, personalities and social values.

Segmentation of target markets along psychographic and lifestyle lines is being used increasingly to differentiate brands more creatively by utilising more finely-tuned target market definitions and more carefully defined and meaningful communication. Psychographics enable an agency creative team to get closer to genuine insights into the consumer as a *human being* who has emotions, feelings, values and social needs.

Three significant psychographic segmentation studies have been conducted in the black market in recent years.

Bates Wells (1982) were the forerunners in segmenting the black market along these lines, and developed the following segments by means of qualitative research. (The actual size of each of the segments cannot, therefore, be measured, but they become smaller as they become more sophisticated, as is illustrated in figure 3.1.) At the base of the segmentation pyramid are the *Tsotsis*, frustrated and resentful, without purpose or direction. The *Belongers* are the conservative, middle class Blacks who work hard and value their jobs. The *Mapantsulas* and *Mshozas* hold low status jobs, have little personal ambition and seek recognition from their peers. The *Cats* and *Elites* are the most advanced and ambitious Blacks, who seek to improve their jobs, income and education.

Figure 3.1
Bates Wells'
segmentation of
the Black market

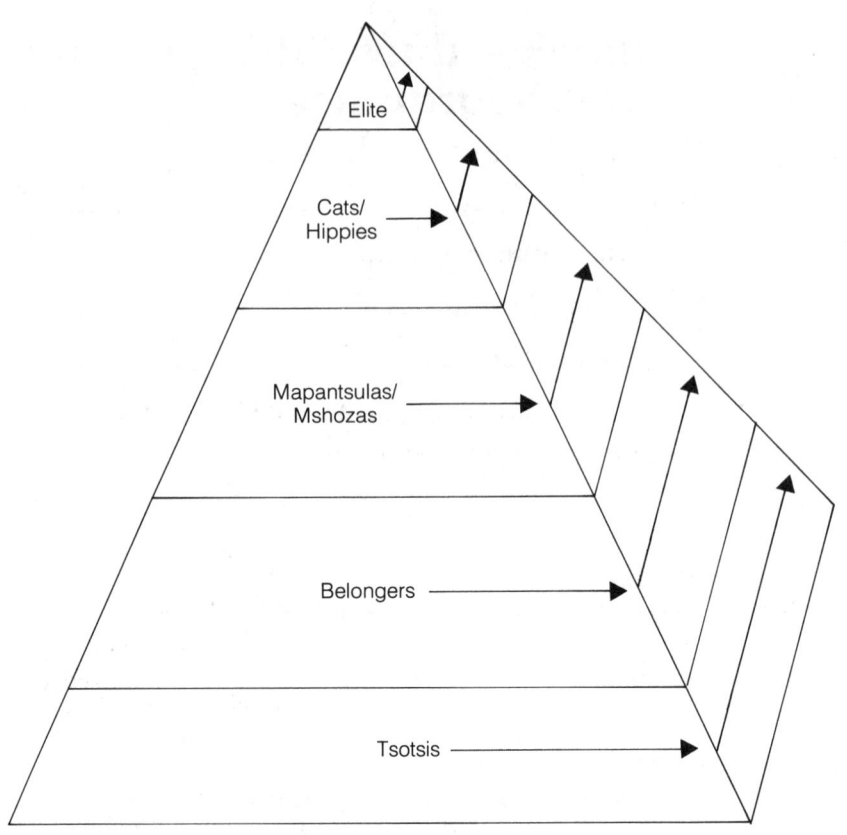

Another source of information about the values, lifestyles and psychographics of the black market can be established from a syndicated study conducted by Market Research Africa and entitled *SocioMonitor*.

SocioMonitor measures a respondent's media habits, product and brand purchasing or usage habits, financial institution usage, motor vehicle ownership, hobbies, interests, activities, demographics and social values (or psychographics). The 1985 Black SocioMonitor was conducted amongst a total sample of 1 500 adult Blacks living in cities, towns and villages (previous Black SocioMonitor studies were conducted amongst *literate* Blacks living in cities and towns), over the September/November 1985 period.

The social values are measured by means of 173 statements which are interspersed throughout the SocioMonitor questionnaire. These 173 statements are reduced to 37 social trends by means of factor analysis (see table 3.12). The 37 trends are reduced to five value groups by means of multidimensional scaling so as to produce a map of the market (see figure 3.2).

The SocioMonitor trend and value group map illustrates how each of the five value groups is made up of a number of social trends. So, for example, the *I-am-me* value group is the largest, 23% of urban Blacks falling into this group which is characterised by sensation seeking, the use of violence and aggression, the rejection of all forms of authority, and liberal attitudes toward sex.

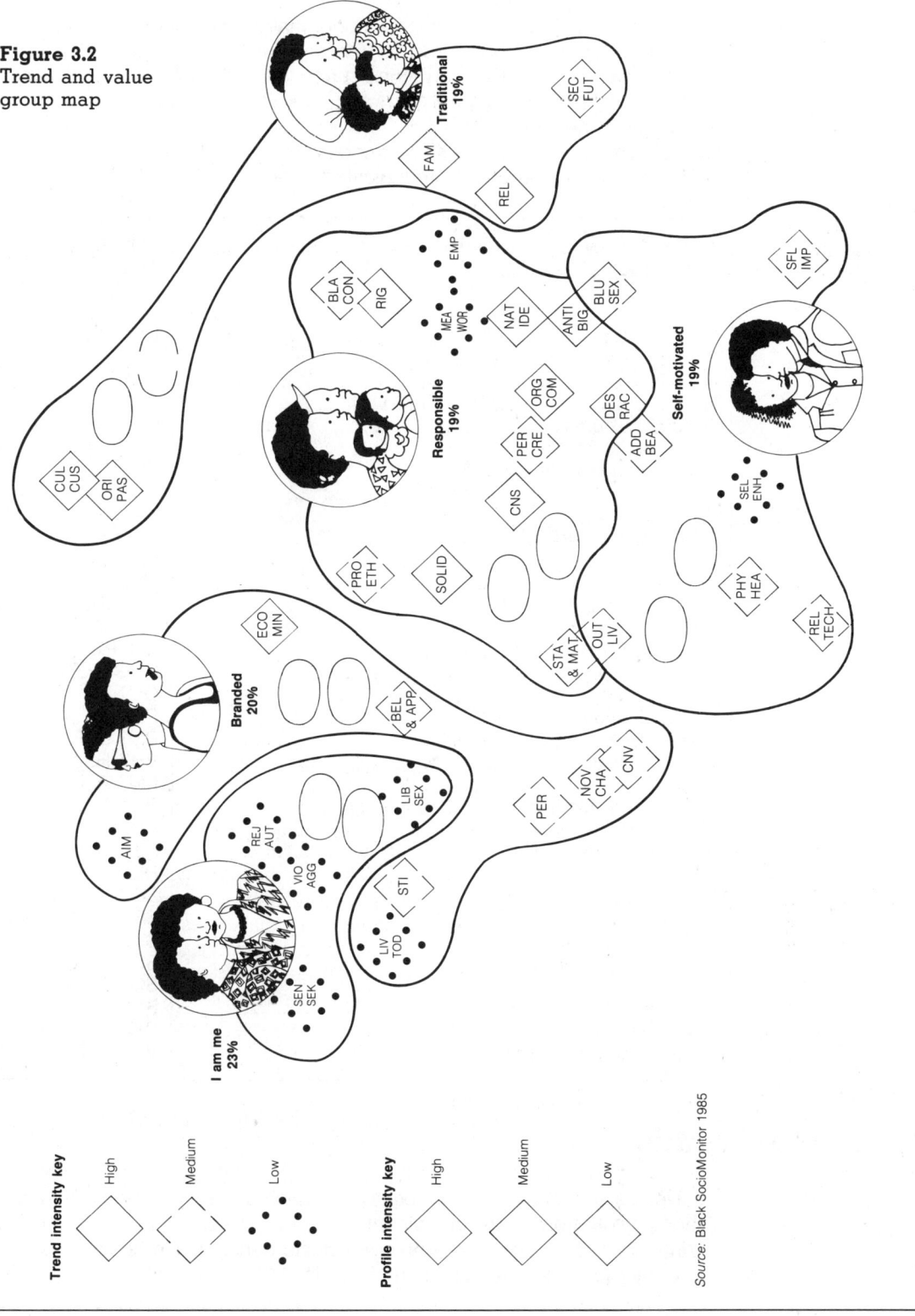

Figure 3.2
Trend and value group map

Source: Black SocioMonitor 1985

While this value group consists of younger males, the other end of the spectrum is older females, who represent 19% of all urban Blacks and fall into the *Traditional* value group. The Traditionals support cultural customs, are orientated to the past, have very strong religious and family ties, and have a strong need for security in their future.

The abbreviations for the 37 social trends which are reflected in the trend and value group map (figure 3.2) are indicated in table 3.12.

Table 3.12
SocioMonitor
social trends

Adding beauty to the surroundings	ADD BEA
Aimlessness	AIM
Anti-bigness	ANTI BIG
Belonging and approval	BEL & APP
Black consciousness	BLA CON
Blurring of the sexes	BLU SEX
Consumerism	CNS
Convenience	CNV
Cultural customs	CUL CUS
Desire for racial harmony	DES RAC
Being economically minded	ECO MIN
Empathy	EMP
Familism	FAM
Liberal sex attitudes	LIB SEX
Living for today	LIV TOD
Meaningful work	MEA WOR
National identity	NAT IDE
Novelty and change	NOV CHA
Orientation to the past	ORI PAS
Desire for an organised community	ORG COM
Outdoor living	OUT LIV
Personalisation	PER
Personal creativity	PER CRE
Physical health	PHY HEA
Protestant ethic	PRO ETH
Rejection of authority	REJ AUT
Reliance on religion	REL
Reliance on technology	REL TEC
Rigidity	RIG
Secure future	SEC FUT
Self-enhancement	SEL ENH
Self-improvement	SEL IMP
Sensation seeking	SEN SEK
Solidarity	SOLID
Status and materialism	STA & MAT
Use of stimulants	STI
Violence and aggression	VIO & AGG

☐ Social trends

The five social trends out of the total of 37 which currently characterise black attitudes most strongly are the following:
- ☐ **Anti-bigness** – a requirement for Blacks to participate in decisions affecting their jobs and the utilisation of profits

- [ ] **National identity** – a feeling of pride in South Africa, and of having a right to live and vote in South Africa
- [ ] **Familism** – family ties are of great importance and the most important non-working activity is spending time with the family. One of the ways in which family ties are enhanced is by means of religion
- [ ] **Desire for an organised community** – a feeling that community problems should be solved by members of that community, rather than waiting for the authorities to solve them
- [ ] **Rigidity** – a desire to do things in the way in which they have always been done, and to use products and brands which have always been used.

☐ Value groups

The five value groups range from the liberal radicals (I-Am-Me's) to the ultra-conservatives (Traditionals). A brief overview of each of these follows:

I-Am-Me's   These people strongly reject authority, are less family-oriented and live for today without planning for the future, having a feeling of hopelessness about their future. Their appearance is unimportant to them, they tend to be self-centered and are more likely to be loners than part of larger groups. They are likely to be younger males.

Brandeds   The people belonging to this group tend to be aimless in their ambitions, to live for today and to use brands to enhance their self-image. They seek approval of their actions from others, like trying new things, like situations with high risk and could use violence and aggression to get their way. They are more likely to be males.

Self-motivateds   These people like to own electric gadgets, are inner-directed and therefore less reliant on others for approval, are ambitious and health conscious, wish to improve themselves in respect of both their appearance and knowledge and welcome the changing role of women. They are more likely to be between the ages of 16 and 24 and in upper income households.

Responsibles   The responsibles desire harmony between the population groups of South Africa, wish to be perceived as responsible and respectable family and community members, think of others first, like to share with others, feel strongly about workers' rights to participate in corporate decision making and are patriotic and brand loyal. They are more likely to have a lower level of education and to be very involved in Church activities.

Traditionals   The people belonging to this group are conservative, very religious, value their family ties and hold their traditional customs in high esteem. They are very home oriented and are more likely to be older women with a lower level of education and in lower income households.

☐ Markinor's segmentation

Another study which attempted to segment the black market was conducted by Markinor in 1984 and identified five male and five female segments.

The major male segment was labelled '*Petrus*' and represents 40% of urban black males. 'Petrus' represents the older, more down-scale black man with traditional values, likely to be living on his own in a hostel, to support traditional customs and to have strong ties with his homeland. He has close ties with his church, does not drink regularly and is interested in soccer and boxing. The next largest segment (18%) was called 'Sydney'. 'Sydney' typifies young and smart Blacks who are concerned with their appearance and therefore buy clothes by label. They are relatively ambitious and politically aware. They enjoy going to the cinema, watching TV, listening to the radio and reading black magazines. The 'Temba' segment (12%) is fashion conscious and fairly up-scale. The quality of clothing in particular is very important to these people, whose leisure time is spent mainly in the shebeen. Boxing and soccer are their favourite sports. The 'Churchill' segment (11%) is also up-scale, but has interests which are the most westernised of the five male segments. In this segment there is the highest incidence of ownership of motor vehicles and electrical appliances, leisure time activities include going to restaurants, international hotels, cinemas and discos, and sporting interests include cricket, golf and tennis. The smallest segment (9%) is described as 'Joe' and represents the more down-scale male. This segment is not interested in its appearance and spends its leisure time in shebeens.

The segmentation among black women was more diversified, and three larger segments were identified. 'Justina' represents 36% of black urban women and tends to be a down-scale housewife whose home is important to her, who enjoys cooking, decorating, knitting and sewing, who goes to church regularly, and is not fashion conscious. 'Selina' represents one quarter (24%) of black urban women and is most likely to be employed as a domestic servant. She has close ties with her family in the rural areas, is religious, is not fashion or even quality conscious, and likes sewing, knitting and cooking. 'Berlina' represents another quarter (24%) of black urban women. She is young, up-scale, smart, slim, fashion and quality conscious, and interested in the church, politics, sport and dancing. 'Thoko' represents a very small segment (4%) which is not very fashion conscious or houseproud and whose overriding interest is going to the shebeen. 'Suzette' (3%) represents a young, very fashion conscious segment which is less interested in black customs. 'Suzette's' interests include watching soccer and boxing, reading, watching TV, going to the cinema, dancing and eating out.

☐ References

Market Research Africa. 1985. *Black SocioMonitor* 1985/1986. Users' Manual (agencies).

Markinor. 1984. *Segmenting the urban black market.* (Paper presented to SAMRA Convention 1984.)

The Bates Group of Companies. 1982. *The Future is Now.* (Own publication.)

Young & Rubicam. 1985 *Communicating with the black market.* (Own publication.)

Young & Rubicam. Results of Young & Rubicam study on black TV viewing. (Own publication.)

The status of the black consumer
Reuel J Khoza

Introduction 91

The black consumer market from a sociological
point of view 92

The black consumer market from a psychographic
point of view 94

Sociographics and psychographics: Flight from
reality or aid to marketing 96

Points to ponder when planning communications
aimed at the black sector 97

Conclusion 98

☐ Introduction

The South African market (or South African society viewed from the marketer's point of view) is a complex mosaic of sectors and segments undergoing constant and rapid change. Its multiracial, multi-ethnic nature has been investigated, written and talked about extensively by politicians, anthropoligists and scholars of multifarious description. Marketers and sociologists have thrown a great deal of light on the market's demographics, but where market psychographics, consumer motivations and the most effective mode(s) of communicating with this 'human tapestry' are concerned, as a rule a great deal more heat than light has been generated. In fact, there is a plethora of statistical information and a dearth of factual data on market lifestyle and psychographics.

The possibility of understanding the market and communicating the product, service and corporate identity to it effectively becomes particularly bleak when the black consumer is focused upon.

Some reflections on the black consumer

The black consumer is a fascinating subject for any would-be marketer for a multiplicity of reasons. A major factor in this fascination is the combination of polarities in the black segment. Depending on one's vantage point, the black segment is either complex or simple, developed or undeveloped, sophisticated or naïve, heterogeneous or homogeneous, westernised or traditionally African. Some marketers perceive it as a minefield to be explored with caution, whilst others see it as merely a satellite of the white segment. The successful few will not reveal their success strategies – and some of the latter do not even know how they made it in the first place.

What compounds the problem of understanding this segment of the South African market is that most observers and analysts approach it wearing tinted spectacles; racially prejudiced ones, anthropological ones, political ones, etc. Consequently, the black segment of the market bristles with both realities and myths.

In the bid to sort out reality from myth, concepts such as *multi-ethnic marketing*, *horizontal segmentation, the new consumer* and *the black colussus* came to the fore. These concepts highlighted and accentuated the need for fresh thinking and flexible application of universal marketing principles in a rapidly changing market.

Why sociographics and psycho-graphics?

Since the social revolution of the 1960s, marketers have increasingly accepted the idea that an understanding of changing social values is as important to successful marketing as the traditional study of demographic forecasts and economic outlook. The move to the 'marketing approach', a widespread policy shift which began in the 1950s, meant that it was not sufficient to understand consumer needs, attitudes and behaviour regarding the product category being marketed. Rather, the marketing approach demands knowledge of and sensitivity to the consumers as a total entity: who they are, how much money they can spend and, increasingly, their aspirations, concerns, beliefs, taboos, interests, values and activities, that is their psychosocial characteristics.

☐ The black consumer market from a sociological point of view

The black segment of the South African market, historically and traditionally viewed as a largely dispensable homogeneous mass of black consumers, is now thrusting its heterogeneity to the fore. It is now more like a salad with no dressing – all in the same bowl, but divided. A multiplicity of harbingers of social change account for this increasing crystallisation of segments in the black market. These include the following:

The urbanisation/ westernisation process

One of the classic indicators of social change having bearing on consumer behaviour is urbanisation. In developing countries such as South Africa, urbanisation proceeds at a high rate, eventually making possible the transformation of an agricultural state into an industrial one. Black urbanisation in South Africa is in certain ways unique. Some attributes of this uniqueness have important marketing communication implications. The politically motivated migrant labour system provides an active bridge between urban and rural Blacks. Migrant workers regularly visit kith and kin in the country, thereby bringing about *shuttle urbanisation*. In the process urban trends, fashions and fads are transmitted.

Migrants are in this sense marketing communications mediators or pollinators with a blurring effect on the urban/rural dichotomy.

Black urbanisation is also two-way in another sense. Rustic folk come to the cities, attracted by the allure of the good life and the bright lights – the prospects of a better life. At the same time industralisation is moving into rural areas, urbanising these in the process. Babelegi near Hammanskraal north of Pretoria and Isithebe in Natal are cases in point.

A stratified consumer market

Historically, the Blacks have been viewed as largely homogeneous. This casual attitude probably stemmed from the fact that whilst numerically much stronger than any other sector, the black segment was by far the weakest in terms of buying power. The black segment thus tended to be seen as a satellite of the white market. However, over the past decade or so this attitude on the part of marketers has had to undergo significant changes. Broad demographics no longer suffice.

Already, it can be seen that what used to be perceived as a pool of cheap labour and a largely dispensable consumer public is something more than that. Out of this erstwhile monolith new and pretty distinct segments are emerging, the most controversial broad classification being the emergent black middle class on one hand and the familiar working class on the other.

Closer scrutiny reveals that these groups occur in numerous forms. They occur in clusters along a continuum from minimal to ultra-sophistication. The groups are identifiable in terms of value systems, lifestyles and visible manifestations such as their manner of dress (ie self-packaging) and the material artifacts they surround themselves with. To some extent lingo is also a distinguishing feature.

Let us focus for a while on the controversial black middle class. Whilst politically nonsensical, in sociological and lifestyle terms this group raises important marketing issues. As a consumer group it evidences a broad-based thrust in elitist thinking and an increased interest in elegance — more interest in certain kinds of high-end products associated with 'high-life', more concerns with home decorating/improvement, and more concerns with appropriateness. The much talked about 99-year lease-cum-freehold schemes have also fuelled the focus on the home, helping to feed the do-it-yourself craze, as well as spurring investment in 'home technology' items such as video cassette recorders.

The advent of the working woman

Increasing industrialisation and growing demands on the family budget coupled with the intensifying wave of the Women's Liberation movement have thrust many black women into full-time occupations. This has serious implications for marketing. Because both husband and wife work, time has become a more precious commodity and items that save time are rising in value. Consider quick-to-prepare food, quick-to-use household cleaners, etc. Childbearing and rearing practices are also undergoing fundamental transformations. Black career women will no longer spend two years breast-feeding babies. In a sense it is viewed as demeaning for women to stay at home, even for the few months after their babies are born. Baby food formulae with combinations of ingredients that approximate 'mother's milk' thus come into their own.

Cost effectiveness

With the ravages of inflation and many items making excessive demands on the family budget, cost effectiveness is now emerging as a new, almost sacred, criterion to be applied, in one form or another, to almost every aspect of black national and personal life. Inflation has caused people to evolve a new economic logic. The new, overarching element in decision making among black consumers is cost effectiveness — when cost can be defined as expenditure of money, time, energy, etc. Consumers, particularly the more enlightened, are re-examining how much time, money and effort they expend on the many activities they engage in and purchases they make in the course of a given year. Marketers have to compete for consumer attention and custom against this background.

Socio-economic Darwinism and the decline of the extended family

There was a time when the extended family was the norm – the rule rather than the exception – in African life. All that is changing. Extended families are diminishing and becoming more of an exception, particularly in the urban areas. Uncles and aunts and brothers and sisters now have greater nuisance than use value.

Extended family relationships are now confined to events such as marriages, deaths and funerals, and aspects of life such as paying reverence to ancestors. Otherwise, the nuclear family is considered to stand a greater chance of a better quality of life and economic prosperity. Black families are forced by circumstances to blend their social and economic lifestyles. Herein lies a hint of a new wave of socio-economic Darwinism – less compassion for the losers and a creeping notion that society is stronger when the losers do not survive. There appears to be a growing concern with 'me and my family' (nuclear, that is) and a kind of pugilistic assertiveness that is expressed in people's personal lives and the material things they surround themselves with.

The above discourse addresses some sociological aspects of emerging consumer groupings/segments, but is by no means exhaustive. A more comprehensive exposition is to be found in MRA's SocioMonitor, which, if used with circumspection and a sound understanding of the socio-economic milieu, is indeed a potent marketing tool.

☐ The black consumer market from a psychographic point of view

This author views psychographic segmentation as the development and application of socio-psychological profiles of consumers and psychologically-based measures of lifestyles.

Lifestyle is the characteristic or distinctive mode of living of an entire society or any of its segments. Lifestyle and psychographics are important to the development of marketing strategies and the positioning of corporate identities and brands. In the South African marketing environment with its rapidly changing values (particularly where Blacks are concerned), the use of lifestyle and psychographic analyses can minimise the risks of obsolescence and reduce the amount of lag between products and consumer needs. It can lead to increases in marketing productivity and to product and service claims being more directly related to market needs, and can assist in the selection of appropriate and efficient advertising media and themes.

The following is an attempt to apply lifestyle and psychographic segmentation to the black segment of the South African market. It is largely subjective, based as it is on observations of numerous focus group discussions and analyses of the life situations of Blacks at work and during their leisure. (Clearly, a more scientific study is called for.)

This tentative typology comprises the following consumer groupings:

☐ The money-restricted consumers (survivors and sustainers)
☐ The belonger consumer group
☐ The conservative consumer groups: young/seasoned
☐ The progressive consumer groups: young/seasoned
☐ The elite consumer group

These consumer groups are described broadly below.

The money-restricted consumers

These are households and individuals whose discretionary freedom in purchasing goods and services is severely restricted by lack of money. Their buying is thus driven more by need than by choice. These are the least psychologically liberated Blacks and they are furthest from the acculturation mainstream. Their buying behaviour is dominated by survival and essential security needs. They are by and large rural, and those in the urban areas have a rural orientation; they yearn for the serenity of a rustic existence.

The belonger consumer group

Belongers tend to be strongly home oriented and prefer the traditional. Their buying behaviour is strongly influenced by an irresistible urge to become part of the group. Members of this group tend to be conforming and unexperimental. They are inclined to be formal, matriarchal, suspicious of anything new, dutiful, following, etc. Although they participate in fads, they are not the innovators – they join the fad in the third or fourth wave, that is they tend to be laggards. Their income, education and social status tend to be low. They have an aura of old-fashionness, naïveté and dependability. In their circles sameness is elevated to the status of virtue. The belonger consumer behavioural pattern accounts for the effectiveness of advertising appeals founded on popularity.

The conservative consumer group: young

Young Conservatives tend to be pre-high school drop-outs aged 15 to 30 years. They are traditionalists who indulge in ancestral worship and believe in witchcraft. In good times they are highly indulgent and tend to overspend on self-packaging and entertainment. They are very gregarious and are often known as 'Mshozas' with a clumsy approach to feminine refinement. They are avid cinema-goers, staunch soccer fans and like to organise themselves financially in saving clubs ('stokvels').

The conservative consumer group: seasoned

The Seasoned Conservatives have a limited academic background and tend to be introvert. They respect age, shop at black oriented shops, are very brand loyal, and spend excessively on clothing, travel and gimmicks. Their popular pastime is punting on horses. They enjoy old-fashioned American jazz and most of them patronise cinemas, boxing and soccer matches.

The progressive consumer group: young

The Young Progressives are the older schoolboys and girls who are psychologically liberated and better educated. They are socialites exposing a colourful lifestyle and are prominently visible and vocal. They subscribe to sexual equality, are more mobile, and probably own their own 'wheels'. Their cosmopolitan outlook is reflected in an active, extrovert social life. They discourage extended families. They prefer movies with themes of achievement, love or politics and communicate in English with a slight American slang.

The progressive consumer group: seasoned

The Seasoned Progressives are commonly known as the middle class Blacks. They are generally better educated and are teachers, business people, nurses and maybe even lawyers and doctors. Their success is reflected in the cars they drive and the bigger houses they reside in. They tend to be the trendsetters, the opinion leaders who frequently appear in media or in advertising. They prefer to speak English, have smaller families and travel extensively.

The elite consumer group

The Elites enjoy a specialised strategic role within the black community. They tend to be political activists, intellectuals, business people and professionals. They are opinion leaders, well informed, and up to date regarding local and world affairs and events. They tend to patronise white businesses and white media and frequently travel locally and abroad. They are motivated by achievement and success and the fruits thereof.

☐ Sociographics and psychographics: flight from reality or aid to marketing?

Quite a few questions have been raised about the value of psychographics and the usefulness of values or lifestyle measures. The following are some of the reasons often cited for lifestyle segmentation or psychographic research rarely working:

☐ There is a large gap between lifestyle and product and brand behaviour. The behavioural phenomenon of consumers saying one thing and doing another is said to be especially applicable to the analysis of lifestyle.

☐ Lifestyle segmentation often leads to over-segmentation. The end result, the critics maintain, is little incremental volume, increased marketing costs and, ultimately, reduced profit.

☐ Lifestyle segmentation often tells you what you already know. The question is often asked: Are we really increasing learning by slapping jargonese labels on groups of consumers that can be identified in plain English?

☐ Lifestyle segmentation has limited actionability. 'Good copy doesn't necessarily spring straight from lifestyle research', cynical copywriters assert.

This author submits that lifestyle, psychographic and sociographic research and segmentation are certainly not a rose garden, but that they can be productive – often revealing and actionable – if we follow five simple rules of use:

Keep lifestyle/psychographic analysis in perspective
As with most research techniques, lifestyle analysis is a means to an end, not an end in itself. Make sure that the dependent variable in your research is usage or behaviour. Use lifestyle analysis to improve your definition of your user groups. Do not pin everything on lifestyles and psychographics – add benefits, beliefs and demographics to your analysis.

Build an actionability up front
Review your study before you start. Talk with your brand people, your agency and especially your creative people and predict how your study might end up. If none of them know what they would do or how they could use the results, *do not do the study*.

Dig deeper than labels
A psychographic segment illustration with a label is simply not enough. What does it mean? What are the connections with your brand users and non-users? Run your lifestyle analysis through the test of face validity. Have you considered divergent as well as convergent evidence? Consider producing what your segments are not doing as well as what they are doing.

Get the communications channels wide open

Form a project team to handle follow-through actions. Get your creative and media people involved early and continuously in the research process. One of the primary benefits of lifestyle analysis is to paint visual portraits of psychographic segments for creative people to address.

Confirm your results and conclusions

A final step to confirm your communication efforts is ensuring that the right psychographic groups are on board. Set up a maintaining or tracking system to measure the effectiveness of your communication over time.

Are sociographic and psychographic measures useful?

☐ Yes – as descriptors

☐ No – as definitive targets

Experience has shown that targeting at a *product-specific* needs/wants segment results in the most successful marketing strategy and that *value clusters* should be used exclusively as a descriptive tool.

Sociographic and psychographic research can work. It can add a useful and meaningful dimension to some of our conventional methodologies. It can give you and your product/brand a competitive edge in product development, creative development and media planning. A point to remember is that there are numerous obstacles out there which can turn the promises of sociographic and psychographic research into a big disappointment.

☐ Points to ponder when planning marketing communications aimed at the black sector

It is necessary to study and understand black value systems. These are to be found in the study of culture. However, it must be remembered that black culture, like other cultures, is not static; it is dynamic. So it is as well to steer clear of pieces of advice from the pseudo-wisdom of social anthropologists who specialise in delving deep into African rustic life in a bid to understand Blacks.

The black market is not homogeneous, it is as heterogeneous as any. So when marketing to Blacks it is necessary to go through the whole exercise. The target market must be selected and defined and then segmented, that is the total market must be broken up into logical market segments/submarkets that differ in requirements, buying habits, or other critical characteristics. Once this has been done, the communication message can be tailored to meet these requirements. If this is done there is a good chance of hitting the target.

The commercial must be developed in the black mode. Blacks are motivated by the same basic needs that motivate other groups. Therefore, the copy platform must be based on the same elements. However, a white oriented commercial merely translated into vernacular languages seldom achieves equal success with a black audience. Concepts such as hunger, sickness, strength, fame, prestige, fear and even humour are surely as valid for Blacks as they are for Whites, but it is necessary to take existential experiences into account. Also, communication should be in the black idiom.

Commercials should portray people in realistic situations. This enhances credibility and improves the chances of comprehension.

Product benefits should be expressed forcefully in simple (not simplistic) and meaningful terms. In other words, the commercial should be deliberately simple as opposed to naïvely simple.

□ Conclusion

The black segment of the South African market will continue to grow in economic power and consumer sophistication and its demand to be treated with respect, understanding and finesse will increase.

The successful marketers in this segment will be those who strive sincerely to study and understand the black segment of the market through both formal and informal research. Listening and watching posts will become increasingly important.

Appendix: Demographics
Janice Dickson

Demographics of the South African population *99*

Education *102*

Projected total South African population 1980-2000 . *102*

Total population of South Africa and the black states *103*

☐ Demographics of the South African population

Table 3.13 Demographics of the South African population by area, sex, home language and education

Population (in thousands)	Total		White		Black		Coloured		Asian	
	19 128		3 467		13 576		1 575		510	
	Thousands	%	Thousands	%	Thousands	%	Thousands	%	Thousands	%
Province										
Cape	5 524	29	968	28	3 133	23	1 423	90	–	–
Natal	3 899	20	435	12	2 987	22	36	2	442	87
Transvaal	8 177	43	1 834	53	6 158	45	117	7	68	13
OFS	1 528	8	230	7	1 298	10	–	–	–	–
Sex										
Male	9 401	49	1 717	50	6 668	49	765	49	252	49
Female	9 727	51	1 750	50	6 909	51	810	51	258	51
Home language										
English or other	15 684	82	1 430	41	–	–	193	12	502	98
Afrikaans or both	3 444	18	2 037	59	–	–	1 382	88	8	2
Level of education achieved										
No school	3 187	17	2	0,1	2 929	22	224	14	32	6
Some primary school	4 881	26	15	0,4	4 358	32	431	27	77	15
Primary school completed	2 058	11	88	3	1 665	12	218	14	87	17
Some high school	5 556	29	1 086	31	3 733	28	543	34	194	38
High school completed	1 926	10	1 112	32	640	5	104	7	70	14
Some university	328	2	245	7	54	0,4	10	1	19	4
University completed	388	2	336	10	30	0,2	9	1	13	3
Other post matric	806	4	583	17	168	1	37	2	18	4

Source: AMPS May 1985-March 1986

Table 3.14 Demographics of the South African population by age, city and household income

Population (in thousands)	Total		White		Black		Coloured		Asian	
	19 128		3 467		13 576		1 575		510	
	Thousands	%	Thousands	%	Thousands	%	Thousands	%	Thousands	%
Age group										
16-24	5 923	31	776	22	4 451	33	543	35	153	30
25-34	4 617	24	796	23	3 283	24	395	25	143	28
35-49	4 576	24	905	26	3 178	23	361	23	132	26
50+	4 013	21	990	29	2 665	20	276	18	82	16
Metropolitan area										
Durban	1 003	5	253	7	431	3	36	2	284	56
Pietermaritzburg	155	1	40	1	76	1	–	–	39	8
Johannesburg and Soweto	1 363	7	405	12	854	6	69	4	36	7
Reef	1 524	8	513	15	972	7	26	2	13	3
Soweto	656	3	–	–	656	5	–	–	–	–
Pretoria	703	4	333	10	340	3	16	1	14	3
Vaal	347	2	94	3	242	2	6	0,4	4	1
Cape Town	1 067	6	380	11	179	1	508	32	–	–
W Cape	661	4	206	6	–	–	455	29	–	–
Port Elizabeth/ Uitenhage	471	3	130	4	236	2	106	7	–	–
East London	200	1	48	1	138	1	14	1	–	–
Kimberley	98	1	22	1	49	0,4	27	2	–	–
Bloemfontein	219	1	66	2	152	1	–	–	–	–
Household income										
Whites										
R3 500+	–	–	457	13	–	–	–	–	–	–
R2 000-R3 499	–	–	1 033	30	–	–	–	–	–	–
R 700-R1 999	–	–	1 605	46	–	–	–	–	–	–
R 1-R 699	–	–	372	11	–	–	–	–	–	–
Blacks										
R700	–	–	–	–	1 586	12	–	–	–	–
R400-R699	–	–	–	–	2 954	22	–	–	–	–
R 80-R399	–	–	–	–	6 926	51	–	–	–	–
R 1-R 79	–	–	–	–	2 110	16	–	–	–	–
Coloureds										
R1 200+	–	–	–	–	–	–	201	13	–	–
R 700-R1 199	–	–	–	–	–	–	421	27	–	–
R 150-R 699	–	–	–	–	–	–	717	45	–	–
R 1-R 149	–	–	–	–	–	–	237	15	–	–
Asians										
R2 000+	–	–	–	–	–	–	–	–	61	12
R1 000-R1 999	–	–	–	–	–	–	–	–	114	22
R 400-R1 099	–	–	–	–	–	–	–	–	261	51
R 1-R 399	–	–	–	–	–	–	–	–	74	15

Source: AMPS May 1985-March 1986

Table 3.15 Demographics of the South African population by household income and housewife

Population (in thousands)	Total		White		Black		Coloured		Asian	
	19 128		3 467		13 576		1 575		510	
	Thousands	%	Thousands	%	Thousands	%	Thousands	%	Thousands	%
Household income *(Continued)* Total										
A R1 600+	2 166	11	–	–	–	–	–	–	–	–
B R 600-R1 599	4 320	23	–	–	–	–	–	–	–	–
C R 80-R 599	10 468	55	–	–	–	–	–	–	–	–
D R 1-R 79	2 175	11	–	–	–	–	–	–	–	–
Housewife										
Yes	7 926	41	1 583	46	5 552	41	604	38	187	37
No	1 803	9	168	5	1 357	10	206	13	72	14
Babies										
Yes	1 550	8	180	5	1 206	9	120	8	44	9
Child										
Yes	4 541	24	659	19	3 312	24	427	27	143	28

Source: AMPS May 1985-March 1986.

Table 3.16 Demographics of the South African population by age

Age group	Whites				Blacks				Coloureds				Asians			
	1980 (Thousands)		2000 (Thousands)		1980 (Thousands)		2000 (Thousands)		1980 (Thousands)		2000 (Thousands)		1980 (Thousands)		2000 (Thousands)	
	No	%	No	%	No	%	No	%	No	%	No	%	No	%	No	%
0-14	1 247	28	1 112	20	8 902	43	13 675	39	1 022	39	1 040	30	305	37	293	27
15-24	799	18	803	15	4 153	20	7 017	20	592	23	639	18	166	20	201	18
25-34	736	16	917	17	2 799	14	5 082	15	385	15	644	18	140	17	194	18
35-49	833	18	1 233	23	2 679	13	5 245	15	351	13	722	20	130	16	224	20
50-64	557	12	900	16	1 472	7	2 612	8	179	7	338	10	60	7	137	12
65+	356	8	503	9	623	3	1 139	3	84	3	140	4	20	2	53	5
Composition of the total population																
	16%		12%		72%		78%		9%		8%		2%		3%	

Source: AMPS May 1985 – March 1986

Note: The white population is currently ageing rapidly, with reproduction below replacement levels and low mortality, so that the numbers beyond retirement age are increasing.

The Coloureds and Asians both have moderate fertility and low mortality, whilst the Blacks constitute a young population, almost 54% of the black population being under the age of 20 in 1980. Fertility is still high in comparison to the other race groups, and mortality is low.

Looking at the various age categories, amongst all races the annual rates of increase for the 0 to 14 age groups are expected to be substantially lower than the total population growth rates for the various population groups. However, in terms of absolute numbers, blacks in this age group are likely to increase from 8,9 million in 1980 to 13,7 million by the year 2000.

The increase in the 15 to 64 age group for the total South African population is expected to be approximately 10,9 million in the period 1980 to 2000. Of this increase, 8,8 million are expected to be Blacks – 4,2 million males and 4,6 females.

☐ Education

Table 3.17 Education: matriculation passes in 1980 and anticipated passes in the year 2000

	Year			
	1980		2000	
Race	No	%	No	%
White	49 239	52	43 700	31
Black	32 535	35	77 900	55
Coloured	7 226	8	11 700	8
Asian	4 819	5	7 700	6

Source: AMPS May 1985 – March 1986

Note: Latest forecasts indicate that the number of other-than-white matriculants is likely to increase more than sixfold from 1980 to the year 2000. In order to cope with this increase in pupils, at least an additional 200 000 teachers for black schools will have to be trained in the next 20 years (statistics indicate that currently only about 6 000 black teachers are being trained a year).

Figure 3.1 Projected total South African population 1980-2000*

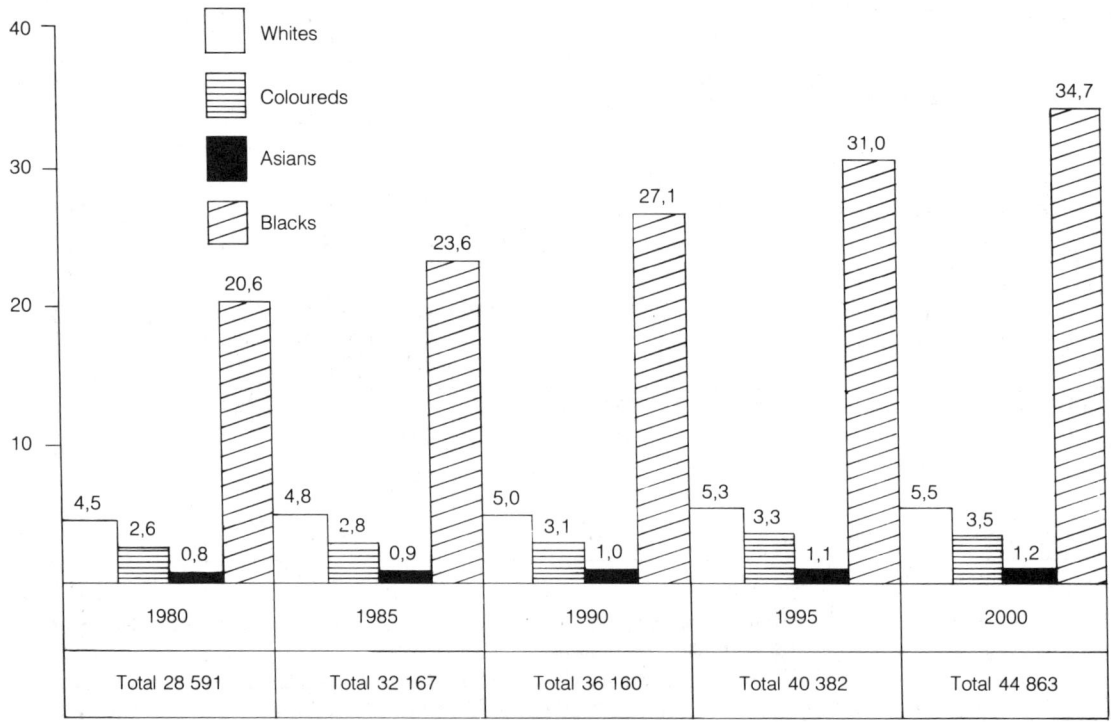

*Figures for Whites reflect annual gain of 15 000 immigrants

☐ Total population of South Africa and the black states

Table 3.18
Total population of
South Africa and
the black states

Mid-year 30 June	Total population Total (000s)	Men (000s)	Women (000s)	Whites Total (000s)	Men (000s)	Women (000s)	Coloureds Total (000s)	Men (000s)	Women (000s)	Asians Total (000s)	Men (000s)	Women (000s)	Blacks Total (000s)	Men (000s)	Women (000s)
1970	22 465	11 396	11 069	3 831	1 917	1 914	2 074	1 025	1 049	642	323	323	15 918	8 135	7 738
1971	23 022	11 656	11 366	3 916	1 959	1 957	2 124	1 049	1 075	656	326	330	16 326	8 322	8 004
1972	23 655	11 976	11 679	4 001	2 001	2 000	2 177	1 074	1 103	674	335	339	16 803	8 566	8 237
1973	24 295	12 300	11 995	4 077	2 038	2 039	2 229	1 099	1 130	691	343	348	17 298	8 820	8 478
1974	24 915	12 601	12 314	4 135	2 075	2 060	2 281	1 124	1 157	709	352	357	17 772	9 050	8 722
1975	25 466	12 834	12 632	4 233	2 115	2 118	2 333	1 149	1 184	727	361	366	18 173	9 209	8 964
1976	26 099	13 118	12 981	4 320	2 158	2 162	2 385	1 174	1 211	746	370	376	18 648	9 416	9 232
1977	26 715	13 429	13 286	4 375	2 183	2 192	2 440	1 205	1 235	765	379	386	19 135	9 662	9 473
1978	27 346	13 746	13 600	4 431	2 211	2 221	2 496	1 233	1 263	785	389	396	19 635	9 914	9 721
1979	28 092	13 760	14 332	4 476	2 229	2 247	2 555	1 254	1 301	796	397	399	20 265	9 880	10 385
1980	28 306	13 865	14 441	4 501	2 241	2 260	2 605	1 279	1 326	810	404	406	20 390	9 941	10 449
1981	28 878	14 143	14 735	4 536	2 258	2 278	2 663	1 307	1 356	827	412	415	20 852	10 166	10 686
1982	30 991	15 186	15 805	4 694	2 338	2 356	2 751	1 351	1 400	867	432	435	22 679	11 067	11 612
1983	31 415	15 394	16 021	4 768	2 374	2 394	2 797	1 373	1 424	880	438	442	22 970	11 209	11 761
1984	32 111	15 870	16 241	4 792	2 397	2 395	2 823	1 393	1 430	883	439	444	23 613	11 641	11 972
1985	33 256	16 482	16 774	4 928	2 458	2 470	2 891	1 425	1 466	899	447	452	24 538	12 152	12 386
Projections for... 1990 (No)	36 160			5 035			3 086			972			27 067		
...2000 (No)	44 863			5 467			3 523			1 102			34 771		
1990 (%)	100			14			8			3			75		
2000 (%)	100			12			8			2			78		

Note: The South African population is expected to increase from 28,6 million in 1980 to 44,9 million by the year 2000. This implies an increase of almost 16,3 million during the last two decades of this century. The expected increase for Blacks between 1980 and 2000 is about 6,6 times that for Whites, Coloureds and Asians combined, or more than 15 times the expected increase in the number of Whites alone (including a net gain of ±15 000 immigrants each year).

4

The role of the advertising agency

The role of the advertising agency   *107*

The hot agency and how to handle it   *114*

The role of the advertising agency
Len van Zyl

Origin and development of the advertising agency concept 107

The advertising agency's contribution to the client's marketing function 108

Style and structure of the advertising agency 108

The workflow procedure through the advertising agency 109

Agency remuneration 111

Closing comment 113

☐ Origin and development of the advertising agency concept

Advertising, mostly in elementary forms such as price and availability information at or near a trader's premises, is probably almost as old as the practice of buying and selling itself. (There is some evidence of this in Roman times.) However, advertising as a mass communications practice, making use of news or other entertainment media, is barely 150 years old, and not surprisingly the development of modern advertising coincides and correlates with the development of the business institution primarily responsible for the creation and production of advertising – the *advertising agency.*

During the first half of the 19th century newspaper editors in the USA used 'agents' to sell space in their newspapers for the purpose of printing advertisements. These 'space agents' received commission on the space which they sold. The various entrepreneurs who wished to communicate their wares to the readers of the newspapers were, however, tradespeople (shopkeepers, cobblers, pharmacists, tailors, etc) and were not particularly adept at writing advertisements. The 'space agents', therefore, offered to 'create' the advertisements in order to make it easier for them to sell the space to the prospective advertisers. Initially the 'agents' wrote the advertisements themselves, but later they either hired or employed writers and illustrators to perform these creative tasks – and so the development of the modern advertising agency began. Over the years the advertising agency has developed into a highly specialised and comprehensive facility for creating and producing advertisements and also, being true to its most original function, constructing and implementing media plans. Notwith-standing the fact that the modern advertising agency owes its first allegiance to its client and is no longer in the 'employ' of the media, the bulk of the agency's remuneration is still in the form of a commission earned from the media.

☐ The advertising agency's contribution to the client's marketing function

Specialisation If it were true 150 years ago that the client possessed and practised skills other than those required for writing advertisements, then it is even more so in today's highly specialised business environment. Today's client, regardless of whether he manufactures cars, food or is a financial institution, needs to invest his capital and cash resources in plants, machines and people who are capable of producing the products and services which he is offering to the market. In the same way that the lawyers who draw up a client's contracts or the architects who design his factories are not on his payroll, neither are the artists, writers and TV producers who create and produce his advertisements. These skills are bought outside from his advertising agency.

Creativity Closely aligned to the previous point of specialisation, but infinitely more impor-tant to the marketing function, is the element of creativity. No matter how rational, logical or materialistic the client's product is, the advertising almost always requires an input of emotive creativity to ensure that it commands the attention of and communicates effectively with the target audience. This creativity can be provided only by people with different talents working in an environment differ-ent from that in which the client produces his products.

Objectivity No manufacturer can be expected to be totally objective in his evaluation of the product which he offers to a defined target market. Being so closely involved with the production of his brand, the client can be forgiven for being totally prejudiced in favour of it. This is certainly not the case with the potential con-sumer, who is concerned primarily with the satisfaction of his own subjective needs, wants or desires. The consumer is not in the slightest concerned with the marketer's objectives – how much he wants to sell and what price he wants to receive for it. It is the advertising agency's task, therefore, to 'translate' the client's marketing objectives into messages which can persuade the potential consumers that their needs, wants or desires can and will be satisfied by the client's products or services. On one hand, therefore, the advertising agency represents the client to the customer, and on the other the advertising agency represents the customer to the client – hence the input of objectivity to both parties.

☐ Style and structure of the advertising agency

This ranges from the large, full-service agency employing hundreds of people, through small creative boutiques of ten or 12 strong, to a single person design studio.

Generally, the large, full-service agency works for big national or multinational corporations marketing a range of products with advertising budgets running into literally millions of rands. These large agencies seldom, if ever, work for small clients who market only one or two products or whose products are aimed more at an industrial clientele where advertising is not a very important element in the total marketing mix.

The creative boutiques usually work for medium-sized clients whose products are of a more specialised nature, for example fashion apparel, cosmetics, furniture, etc. However, this is a generalisation and one often finds that large corporate clients employ a creative boutique in addition to one or two big agencies – and giving the creative boutique one or two products which in their eyes require a particularly incisive creative approach, to handle.

The small design oriented agency usually works for industrial clients, for whom package design and demonstration pamphlets or brochures are more important than mass media advertising in national newspapers, television, radio, etc.

The full-service agency   The modern full-service agency employs a very wide variety of people specialising in a wide diversity of communicative skills and techniques. In fact, the name advertising agency could be regarded as a misnomer, since this kind of operation is truly engaged in the total marketing communications task. Such agencies have a full spectrum of departments covering market research, client service, creative, media planning and buying and production (both print and electronic) facilities, and often also offer specialist facilities such as public relations, below-the-line promotions, direct response advertising, recruitment advertising, etc. The exact size of a 'full-service' agency depends mainly on the number of its clients and the total amounts of money which these clients allocate to their advertising budgets. The number of clients and the number of products handled by the agency obviously correlate directly with the number of campaigns to be produced, and this in turn determines the number of people required in all the departments. The smallest number of staff that any agency in South Africa could employ while still calling itself 'full-service' would probably be around 20, but the top five or six agencies in this country employ between 200 and 300 people each.

☐ The workflow procedure through the advertising agency

The main ongoing contact between the client and the agency is through the client service department. Depending upon the size of the agency and of the account (and the nomenclature used by the particular agency), the client service personnel can be structured at various levels, such as client service director, account director, account manager and account executive. The client certainly can and does have personal contact with other agency executives such as the creative people, the media director or planner, the production executive, etc, but such meetings should preferably always be attended by the client service executive as well – and if this does not happen, the client service executive should at least be given a report (contact report) of such discussions. The *contact report* is the permanent written record of all discussions between and decisions made by client and agency.

At the first meeting to discuss a new campaign, the client provides the agency (client service executive) with a brief that includes a comprehensive description of the product, the target market, the competition, the client's marketing and advertising objectives and an indication of the total advertising budget. The entire agency team working on the particular account studies this brief and the agency responds with a *strategy document* (variously referred to as communications strategy, creative strategy, or advertising strategy). Ideally, the client should approve this strategy document before any actual work is commenced.

A broad indication of the creative direction as well as the media approach will be given in the strategy document and the agency will continue to work on the two parallel activities – the creative work and the media plans. If the strategy document focused on the question, 'What should the advertising achieve?', then the creative work and the media planning attempts to answer the two questions, 'How to say it?' and 'Where to say it?'. Once these two questions have been dealt with internally, the agency review board approves the work and then it is presented to the client. On client approval of the concepts presented, the decision will be taken whether to subject the campaign to pre-testing. Pre-testing is usually done by the agency's own market research department. The market research department may have done some concept testing prior to presenting the work to the client in order to give the agency conclusive evidence on a choice of two or three alternative creative approaches. Sometimes the client may insist that pre-testing is done by an outside market research organisation, but more often than not the client approves a campaign without subjecting it to any pre-testing.

After client approval has been obtained, the agency will determine the costs of production of the advertisements which must be prepared for all the different media and these production quotes will be submitted to the client before the actual mechanical production is begun. The first item on the production quote will be the finished art and photography, followed by mechanical production requirements in the case of print and film production quotes in the case of TV and/or cinema exposure. In a full-service agency the finished art will normally be done in the agency's own studio and the photography could be done by the agency's own in-house photographer, although it is more likely that the photography will be handled by an outside specialist photographer. In the case of TV, film or radio work, a full-service agency will have at least one TV/film producer and a radio producer, and they will liaise with the outside production companies, the talent agents, the musicians, etc in order to co-ordinate a total quotation. Once the client has approved the quotations for the various production elements, the production execution commences. Someone from each agency department involved in the various elements of production will be present during the production process. This includes producers and art directors on film shoots, copywriters at sound recordings and production executives at printproofing stages.

The client's presence at any stage of the production process is optional. Some clients attend TV film shoots and some attend print photographic sessions, but many clients are content to leave the entire production process to the agency, becoming involved at the stage where the agency presents proofs of the printwork or first 'cuts' (semi-finished films edited to the correct time of the commercial). The client is finally included at the stage where the material is in a highly finished state and he has to approve it for final despatch to the media which is going to expose the message. At this stage there is close liaison between the agency's media department and the production departments, as well as between the agency and the medium concerned, so as to ensure that the correct material is at the medium for placing on the correct dates.

Once the advertisements have been exposed in the media, the agency's vouchers department and accounting department comes into the act. The vouchers department assembles the proof that the advertisement has been exposed by matching the media schedules with the actual voucher copies of the publications in which the advertisement appeared, or by matching the media schedules of the media department with the flighting schedules of the broadcast authority. This administrative evidence is passed through to the accounts department, which prepares the monthly accounts which are presented to the client. Prior to the accounts being despatched to the client, the client service department becomes involved again and scrutinises each account to ensure that the vouchers match the invoices and the invoices match the media schedules. At some time during the vouching stage and this final scrutinisation stage the agency also fulfils a quality control function by checking to see whether the exposure was of a standard acceptable to the agency and its client. If a print advertisement was hopelessly under-inked or disastrously over-inked, or if a TV or radio commercial appeared in an incorrect time channel or with distorted sound, then the agency will claim either compensation or a reappearance of the advertisement from the medium concerned.

Once the campaign had been exposed in the media the client and the agency decide whether to do post-testing. A full-service agency with an effective market research department will offer this service to test whether a sufficient proportion of the target market has seen and noted the advertisements, and will probe for the target market's reaction to the advertisements. Whereas pre-testing is normally conducted at the agency's expense, post-testing, when it occurs, is usually charged to the client. However, it must be mentioned that post-testing is very rarely done. The general attitude seems to be that if a campaign is working then it is not necessary to post-test it, and if a campaign is not working then time and money should not be wasted on post-testing, but a new campaign should be begun. However, advertising is but one element in the total marketing mix and sometimes it is necessary to do a post-test to determine to what extent the advertising element is the guilty party in the overall failure of the total marketing function.

☐ Agency remuneration

The advertising agency is not an 'agent' between the client and the media or production suppliers in the strict legal sense of the word. The advertising agency acts in a principal-to-principal capacity with its client on one hand and its media and suppliers on the other. In other words, the agency is solely responsible for paying the media and the production suppliers for the service and facilities rendered by them, and likewise the agency is the client's creditor for all the money which the agency spends on advertising the client's products and services. This requires that the agency's financial accounting department is highly efficient. The agency must enjoy the most favourable terms that it can negotiate with its suppliers, but on the other hand must implement and maintain very strict debtors' control to ensure that it receives its money from its clients in sufficient time to pay its media and suppliers without the risk of having to finance the client's advertising out of its own cash resources. Of course, an advertising agency is not a capital intensive organisation as it does not possess factories, machines, raw materials, etc. Its only assets apart from its office furniture are its people; it has often been said that an agency's assets 'go down in the lift at night and come up in the lift in the morning'.

The commission system

The bulk of the agency's income is derived from commission earned on the advertisements placed in the media. This is a hold-over from the original advertising agency structure as described at the start of this contribution. Around the world the norm seems to be 15% commission to the agencies. In South Africa this figure is 16,5%, primarily due to the fact that advertising agencies in South Africa have to create advertisements in anything from two to seven different languages and for this obviously require more staff than their counterparts in other countries.

The procedure is that if the media rate card says that a full page or a TV commercial costs R10 000 then the agency bills the client R10 000, but the amount that the agency pays the medium is R10 000 less $16\frac{1}{2}\%$ = R8 350. The R1 650 is, therefore, the agency's income for the work it did creating that particular advertisement. This commission covers all the creative input as well as the administrative input and will pay for the salaries of the client service staff, the creative staff, the media staff and the accounting staff. The client is billed separately for actual, physical and mechanical production costs. Costs such as finished art, photography and mechanical production are billed to the client separately and these amounts are either subject to the same 16,5% commission or, if the figures have been quoted net by the outside suppliers, the agency grosses up the amount which it bills to the client by 19,75% so that it earns 16,5% 'commission' on the gross amount billed to the client. In a full-service agency the finished art is often prepared by the agency's own studio, in which case the agency keeps the total amount billed for the finished art.

It follows that an agency's total income under the commission system should be a minimum of 16,5% of the total of all the billings that are placed through the agency by its total number of clients. Usually the figure is slightly higher, as there are certain aspects of the work for which the agency charges and keeps 100% of the income, for example finished art, design of packages or point-of-sale material, research projects, public relations projects, etc.

The commission system of remuneration for advertising agencies has been the subject of much debate for many years. The main criticism from clients centres around the fact that the commission system does not have a direct relationship to the work input provided by the agency. A campaign consisting of one commercial and one magazine advertisement could conceivably run for two years and a million rand could be spent on its exposure. This would mean that the agency would receive R165 000 over two years for a campaign that might take six agency people only two weeks to produce. (In all fairness it must be stated that the converse could also happen, that is the agency could work for two months on a campaign which runs for a very short period only, so that it receives very little income and then has to produce another campaign.) The agency's main retort in favour of the commission system, however, is that there never is and never can be a direct correlation between creative content and the amount of time spent on a job. (The same applies in the world of art and entertainment, where a brilliant painting or an appealing piece of music can never be equated with the time which the artist spent painting or composing.) The agency world maintains that the commission system is the best incentive the agency has to ensure that it always produces the best creative work of which it is capable. It ensures that the agencies compete with each other on service and not on price, as the latter would obviously lead to price-cutting which in turn could lead to agencies cutting corners in the efforts they devote to their clients' campaigns.

One advantage which the commission system holds for both client and agency is that it makes budgeting easier. The client knows that once the advertising budget has been established that is the total which will be required because he does not have to budget separately for the agency's service. For its part, the agency knows exactly what its income is going to be as it is a standard 16,5% of the amount which the client is going to spend annually on advertising.

The fee system The alternative to the commission system is a system where the client and the agency agree on a fee for the agency's input. The initial fee is based on mutual estimates of the client's and the agency's requirements and thereafter the agency keeps timesheets and the fee is negotiated either annually or half-yearly. If the agency works for its client on a fee basis then all media commissions are credited back to the client and all other purchases made on the client's behalf are done on a net basis.

Agencies fear that when a client wants to negotiate a fee system in preference to working under the commission system, then the client's main objective is to reduce the non-media cost of his advertising. This would obviously result in a reduction in the agency's income. In South Africa the commission system is entrenched for all agencies recognised under the Joint Accreditation Committee (JAC), which is a body consisting of the agencies and the media. When an agency gains recognition from the JAC it can earn commission from the media, but that commission cannot be discounted to the client. Thus, if a fee basis is negotiated the fee must be equal to at least 16,5% of the client's total media budget.

Although the commission versus fee debate has been going on for many years in many countries, and although the systems have been interrelated in a number of countries (ie an agency may work partly on fees and partly on commission), the situation is still that between half and two thirds of all agency income is derived from commission.

☐ Closing comment

In future advertising practitioners will more than ever be expected to be highly responsible and specialised enterprises. Their task will continue to consist of the initiation, preparation, production, placing and evaluation of advertising campaigns for the product or service of the client.

The hot agency and how to handle it
Laurance Kuper

Introduction 114

Enter the creative man 115

Enter the account man 115

Enter the client 116

☐ Introduction

Whether large, small or medium-sized, the 'hot' agency is characterised by a particular attitude to advertising. Hot agencies believe that many clients can perform their own marketing and research functions, but that no client can play the role of communications consultant. Therefore the emphasis lies on the process of persuasion through communication, and at the very heart of this, hot agencies believe, is *creativity*.

Thus, while all agencies set store by creativity, the hot agency actually makes creativity a priority above all else. The better, or more mature, hot agencies will certainly have an understanding of and may even perform marketing and research functions for their clients, while younger, less experienced groups will sometimes scorn such practices in agencies.

Clients are often hard put to discriminate between the kinds of agency needs they have. Much depends on their management style and corporate culture. If the client company is highly entrepreneurial and individualistic it might be kindred spirits with a young, hot, enthusiastic agency, but if the client company's head office needs plenty of reassurance, it will probably be more comfortable with a more institutional agency. Sometimes the client company will be totally confident in its own marketing ability and will seek only the creativity of a hot agency. The client's needs should be clearly spelt out to the agency in the initial stages, as this will avoid much misunderstanding.

Creativity in advertising is a disciplined process, even if the end result may look like a spontaneous 'aha' experience. It consists of taking the client's product, analysing its strengths and weaknesses and breathing a personality into it so that it captures the imagination of the consumer public and prompts it to try the product. It is a complex area fraught with many difficulties, not the least of which is the speculative nature of trying to predict the minds of consumers who are constantly subject to a changing, challenging environment – an environment filled with competitive appeals made by other client-agency teams doing their best.

In today's era of product parity, where technology has advanced so far that most products have very marginal differences between them, the perception of the product personality has become increasingly important. In fact, it has become so important that some advertisers recognise that the image is actually as much part of the product as its physical properties (deodorants, cigarettes and fashion wear are all good examples). And it is the creative spark which often creates the difference between a successful and an unsuccessful product personality.

☐ Enter the creative man

Handling the creative man is often a difficult, but stimulating task. Inevitably, creative people see things differently. Often they see things more *objectively* than their clients, who are close to their products every day, year in and year out, and often more *subjectively*, because they have not had direct experience of the market reactions to the client's product.

The creative team usually consists of very bright people who are articulate and persuasive themselves. The good ones can usually bring valuable fresh perspectives to a client's product. Creativity has, after all, been defined by some as seeing the same thing differently from anyone else.

Unfortunately, some clients experience creative teams which become more involved with their idea than the product. They fall in love with a headline or a visual for its own sake rather than for what it will do for the product. This problem and the serious consequences of spending money with little market effect have unfortunately given creative people a bad name in some circles, and quite unfairly too, because it is usually the more junior creative people who are more concerned with building their portfolios than selling products.

Clearly, it is part of the client's role to make sure that the excitement of the idea works for the product and not for the people. The advertising should not get in the way of the product. How many times have you heard the comment: 'I remember the ad, but not the product'?

Like all other consultants, clients must manage their creative consultants carefully. They must listen hard and weigh up the innovative ideas carefully, utilise the storehouse of originality and enthusiasm and yet enjoy a good enough relationship to make sure that the rich fantasy world of the creative integrates with the demands of the business world.

It pays to remember that the prime motivation of the creative person is to 'do good work'. In his terms this means building a successful case history for the product, winning an award for the campaign, and earning the respect of his notoriously critical peers.

☐ Enter the account man

Hot agencies usually pride themselves on very close involvement and identification with the client's problems and opportunities. The account service man's role in this process is critical, as it is up to him to communicate the client's ongoing business situation to the agency in a way that is inspirational and enthusiastic. If he is good, he usually sees to it that the creative people have frequent direct contact with the client.

He must keep calling on the client to find out what is going on, perhaps with a view to an opportunity the client may not have recognised immediately. He must ensure that the client and his product remain a priority in the minds of the backroom boys who actually do the work. He must know when to stop and back off and let the creative people have their head.

It is far more difficult to be a good client service man in a creatively dominated agency than in an account service dominated agency which purports to be creative. Not many get it right. Yet those who do and their clients have the enormous satisfaction of managing 'good stuff that really works'.

☐ Enter the client

The clever client manages the relationship. He understands that the size of his budget does not necessarily matter to the people who are going to burn the midnight oil. He understands that in a peculiar way he is in competition with the agency's other clients. Much depends on the reasons for his original choice of agency, but all too frequently his original perceptions, based on a somewhat artificial presentation situation, are inaccurate and the relationship changes after the honeymoon.

Often a client inherits the agency from the marketing man who occupied the position before him. Today, more sensibly, this kind of marketing man prefers to try to make the relationship work rather than fire the old and bring in the new. His ability to manage the agency, redefine the relationship and remotivate the agency in the way he functions best is an enormous challenge.

In his attempts to be inspirational and in so doing to maintain a priority in the agency, the client should get to know and if possible like the people who do the work. Most hot agencies do good work for clients they enjoy working for. A bit of fun and enjoyment provides that extra motivation for people working on the job to ponder on and on about the product long after the working day has ended.

Most of all, hot agencies require honesty, even if it is ruthless. If a client does not like an advertisement he should say so in no uncertain terms and give his reasons for not liking it. He should listen to counter-arguments with an open mind and acknowledge where they are valid, yet have the courage to be insistent where he knows he is right.

Of course, he should be lavish in his praise if he likes the advertisement, or even certain segments of it, but he should never seek to avoid hurting feelings by being phoney. Sensitive and talented people can pick this up in a moment and the client will not get the best work.

Many clients get excellent work even though their budgets are small, their product very ordinary and their competitors far more powerful than they are. These are the clients who understand how to build up trust, mutual respect and a warm team spirit with their agencies.

When all is said and done, the management of a hot agency is not an effortless affair. It is an exciting job that requires time and effort. Good management, good communication and good relationships are the stuff that sustains any healthy client/consultant venture, and if both parties manage it, there are healthy profits to be made.

☐ Summary

The choice of an advertising agency depends mainly on successes in other campaigns and the role advertising played together with the creative ability as it is evident from previous advertisements.

Furthermore, clients will consider the agency's facilities and its experience in and knowledge of the particular industry, as well as the experience and ability of the person who will handle the account.

The extent to which the client's advertising budget can motivate the agency to perform should not be forgotten, but of prime importance is empathy between the client and his agency.

5

Management of the
advertising campaign

The importance of a good advertising brief *121*
Establishing advertising objectives *132*
The total involvement philosophy and methodology
   in planning a campaign *136*

The importance of a good advertising brief

Ludi Koekemoer

Introduction *121*

Briefing documents used by advertising agencies ... *122*

Factors advertising agencies consider to be important *126*

Conclusion *131*

References *131*

☐ Introduction

The advertising brief is a concisely written document detailing, *inter alia,* the marketing problems and opportunities, the selected target audience(s), the specific advertising objectives, an analysis of the brand/service to be advertised, the selected media mix and specific communications requirements.

Before each of these elements is discussed in greater detail, it must be pointed out that many advertising agencies criticise the use of a rigid, concise document because they argue that:

☐ creativity is an art and application of the information is where the brilliance, the magic, comes in

☐ creativity should not be forced in a direction specified in such a document. What is needed is freedom, not a forced statement of direction.

On the other hand, there are those who cannot create successfully without a briefing document because they argue that:

☐ a detailed brief, approved by both advertiser and advertising agency, eliminates possible problems and differing views as to what should be communicated to whom

☐ such a brief often provides information which may spark creative brilliance, for example information about a particular feature of the brand, frequency of use, attitudes to the brand, etc

☐ a specific detailed brief is a prerequisite for great advertising campaigns

☐ great campaigns are usually backed by extensive research. The highlights of such research are to be put into the briefing document

☐ the comprehensive research data is purposefully reduced to a statement which clearly indicates which direction to take. This provides the 'what' to say and it is now up to the creative team to create the 'how' to say it.

In my experience a briefing document is a must. It not only forces both client and advertising agency to become proactive, to conduct vital research, but it gives direction to creative thinking. Advertising is a people business, and a briefing document should not be used as a rigid tool or mould from which advertising campaigns must be produced. The briefing document cannot spell out the subtleties relating to the brand or the consumer and it is therefore necessary to provide vital information in a briefing document, but these should be discussed freely during the Plans Board (see 'The total involvement philosophy and methodology in planning a campaign'). The more discussion evoked, the better for the creative team.

☐ Briefing documents used by advertising agencies

A more detailed briefing document, used by *Mortimer Tiley* in the early 1980s, outlined the following:

☐ **The environment as it affects the advertising**
Uncontrollable variables
  − Principal competition (brands, positioning, copy platform, advertising expenditure, pricing, distribution, strengths and weaknesses)
  − Legal restraints and ASA restrictions

☐ **Consumer needs the advertising must solve**
  − The consumer need
  − Demographic profile of the target market (sex, marital status, race, age, income, community, language, education and occupation)
  − Geographic profile of target market
  − Psychographic profile of target market
  − Usage patterns of the brand/service

☐ **The major product or service benefit**
  − Primary benefit
  − Secondary benefits

☐ **Advertising objective** (eg increase awareness/comprehension/conviction; change ideas; switch brands; use the brand/service more often; try the brand/service; trade up; change a habit; add the brand/service to the acceptable list; consider our brand/service before choosing or remain satisfied)

☐ **The major advertising proposition**
  − The one fact most relevant to the advertising of the brand/service. It must be a proposition on which the advertising can act.

☐ **Advertising requirements**
  − Corporate considerations, tone, style, previous advertising strategies, etc

☐ **Media strategy**
  − Budget
  − Campaign coverage
  − Campaign timing (including seasonal details)
  − Media musts

DMB & B (D'Arcy Masius Benton & Bowles) insist on two strategy documents in their MAPS system, namely the *target consumer profile* and the *creative strategy brief.*

The target consumer profile includes the following:

☐ Target group name – Give your target group a shorthand name, something which describes who they are in a way that is relevant to your task.

☐ The 'problem' the target group seeks to solve or need it wants to satisfy – Why does the target group need your brand or category?

☐ Attitudes and experience with the category – Have they tried it? Adopted? Rejected? Positive and negative perceptions.

☐ Attitudes and experience with the brand – Awareness, trial, usage.

☐ Values and lifestyles – What do we know about the target group as people?

☐ Demographics – Age, sex, income, marital status, occupation, etc.

The creative strategy brief includes the following:

☐ Business problem/opportunity – What is the key problem or opportunity that advertising must address?

☐ Competitive set – What competitive choices is the target consumer currently considering in addition to or instead of our brand?

☐ Target consumer – In a nutshell, who is the advertising to address?

☐ Desired consumer behaviour – What action do we want the target consumer to take – try, retry, use the brand more, etc?

☐ Desired consumer beliefs – How specifically will advertising contribute to achieving the desired consumer behaviour?

☐ Consumer promise – What is the one rational or emotional benefit that will have the most influence on creating the desired beliefs?

☐ Support – What is the key idea or fact that justifies the consumer? What style or feeling will the advertising convey? What image do we wish to project?

☐ Mandatories, if appropriate – Are there any client specifics, legal requirements, etc?

Kuper Hands investigate, obtain information and reach consensus on the following aspects:

☐ the company background

☐ the product/service to advertise

☐ the internal environment (eg morale, production, distribution channels, etc)

☐ The competitors' strengths and weaknesses *vis-à-vis* ours

☐ the marketing strategy (which is defined as 'a long running time phased plan designed to achieve at a high rate of growth and return on investment a market position so advantageous that the competition can only retaliate over an extended time interval at a prohibitively high cost')

☐ the positioning strategy (where the strategic strengths must be emphasised).

Kuper Hands believe that the creative and media leap (which must be fresh and original) will then be taken by experienced advertising people who are not tied to a rigid methodology, but use research data to their best advantage. They believe that a talented, mature human mind tempered by science and not a rigid briefing document has the best ability to generate communications.

Freedman Rossi/BBDO uses a BBDO New York developed 5-point working discipline:

1 The market

2 The prime prospect

3 The prime prospect's problems
4 The positioning
5 The imagery

The *market* is analysed in great detail by means of available AMPS, Nielsen, HIPPI, past sales, etc data, as well as by analysing trends, the competition, etc.

The *prime prospect* receives particular attention because Freedman Rossi/ BBDO believes that in many cases 80% of sales come from 20% of the market. Therefore the heavy users are important, and Alan Tiley believes that the biggest single problem with defining the target audience is that it is directed at *people* rather than a *person*. An example of his description (1986) of a target audience of the *white South African heavy beer drinker* (note the picture painted about these beer drinkers) can help the creative team to almost feel at home with the person it has to communicate with:

Heavy white beer drinkers are heavily weighted towards English-speakers and the heavier the beer consumption the more it tends towards English-speakers.

Age has an influence on beer consumption − 16 to 24-year-olds are heavier drinkers. Consumption reaches a peak between the ages of 25 and 34 and starts tapering off as the drinkers get older than 35. It obviously requires the stamina of youth to drink volumes of beer, but only after one has acquired the skill.

There is not a strong relationship to income, although heavy consumption is weighted towards the B income group.

The thirst in Natal is greater than in any other province and the heat in Durban aggravates it, because heavy beer consumption is very strongly weighted to Durban, Johannesburg, Cape Town, Port Elizabeth and East London. Residents of Durban also drink more beer than the average city dweller.

The carefree, single male consumes a lot more beer than his married counterpart, but men who are divorced seem to drown their sorrows in beer − or is it to celebrate?

The work you do seems to influence the amount of beer you drink − the strongest occupational category is sales, but industrial workers and men employed in professional technical fields also drink a lot of beer.

Beer drinkers seem to enjoy drinking other alcoholic drinks too − especially cane, but you'll find gin, whisky and wine in their drinks cabinets as well. Furthermore, our research suggests that they enjoy eating potato chips and processed meat snacks with their beers.

Heavy beer consumers are heavy smokers − and the more they drink, the more they smoke (medium to heavy cigarette smokers and heavy beer drinkers).

It would seem that our heavy beer drinkers prefer to socialise instead of watching TV; research suggests that they are only moderate watchers of TV.

They are most likely to own a Ford or a Mazda, but could drive a Golf or Alfa, and the amount they spend on petrol and the rate at which they wear through tyres suggest that they drive fast. Heavy beer drinkers tend to spend more on petrol and purchase more tyres per year than the average male.

The price of beer (or is it petrol and tyres?) seems to be a factor, as there is a high incidence of overdrafts and bank loans among our prime prospects.

Our heavy beer drinker's social habits lead him to the take-away food outlet far more often than the normal male.

He is a music enthusiast, either at home or in his car, for he is more likely to spend money buying LP records or pre-recorded cassette tapes than the rest of men.

Our man is more likely to shave with a blade than with an electric razor and spends more on aftershave and aerosol deodorants to keep himself smelling fresh.

In keeping with the above image he spends more on shoes and men's clothing, but when dressing casually will probably wear jeans.

Finally, heavy beer drinkers enjoy reading *Stag* and *Scope*.

The *prime prospect's problems* are detected by a problem detection study (PDS). The following two examples prove that research which asks the consumers what they want is not good enough. The advertising agency should find out what their problems are and solve these problems with a commitment from the client, even if it means changing the action plans:

Example 5.1
Advertising
agency

What they want from an advertising agency	Order of importance	Problem detection study on advertising agencies
Good creativity	1	Agencies charge too much
Efficient client service	2	Clients do not trust them
Understand my business	3	Agencies do not know enough about their clients' products

Example 5.2
Airlines

What they want from an airline	Order of importance	Problem detection study on airlines
Reliability	1	First class tickets are too expensive
Safe	2	Not enough legroom
Friendly service	3	Wait too long for luggage

The target prospect's problem(s) should be solved and this often means that the advertiser, the marketer, has to affect certain changes before the advertising campaign can be created.

The *positioning* is done as per 'Analysis of the brand/service to be advertised' discussed later in this chapter (see p 129).

The *imagery* is considered by Freedman Rossi/BBDO to be the area in which creative work is either 'me too' or different. It has analysed many product categories' television commercials and discovered that:

☐ most underarm spray commercials show ± 5 seconds of spraying under the arm (as if people still do not know where to spray!)
☐ most car commercials show ± 10 seconds of the car driving (as if people are scared that the car will not go!)
☐ most coffee commercials show ± 5 seconds of the coffee being stirred (as if the sugar in it is important!)
☐ most airline commercials show ± 9 seconds at the end of the aircraft taking off (as if to show that it can actually get off the ground!).

These similarities result in 'me too' advertising and Freedman Rossi/BBDO believe that the advertising should break out of the imagery pool and be visually different.

A much more simple briefing document used by *McCann de Villiers* incorporates the following five points:

1 The problem or opportunity the advertising should address
2 Who are we talking to?
3 The objective
4 What the advertising should be saying
    4.1 What to say
    4.2 Evidence
5 Tone of voice

The advertising brief is an integral part of the marketing plan and I believe that it should be completed as a combined effort between advertiser and advertising agency.

☐ Factors advertising agencies consider to be important

In my discussions with the Creative Directors of some of the leading advertising agencies in South Africa, the factors given below were stated as being of prime importance in the advertising brief.

Market analysis and opportunities

An analysis of the industry, the company, the competition, market shares and share of voice (advertising expenditure by brand in the product category) should provide an indication of broad market opportunities. These will be refined once an analysis of the brand/service has been conducted.

This market analysis could include, *inter alia*, the following:

☐ The industry
  – companies involved (sales, management, strengths, weaknesses, etc)
  – growth patterns
  – specific characteristics (eg profit patterns, distribution patterns, etc)
  – technological advances and threats

☐ The company
  – history
  – management
  – policies and procedures
  – growth patterns
  – profitability
  – market share history and trends
  – sales history
  – specialisation or diversification plans
  – competence
  – size
  – reputation
  – image and standing in the industry

☐ The competition
  – who and where they are
  – their products/services advertising
  – their advertising agency and how long they have worked together
  – new launches

- market shares
- image
- growth history
- size
- strengths and weaknesses
- financial strengths
- strength of sales force/appointed dealers
- estimated budget by competitive brand/service

☐ Market shares and share of voice
- sales history and market shares in rands and in units
- market potentials
- share of advertising expenditure by brand/service
- trends over, say, the past three years.

The selected target audience(s)

The target audience consists of those people or decision-making units you want to reach with the marketing communications to motivate them to use your brand/service.

It is necessary to establish the following about the target audience(s):

☐ Who they are (demographics, psychographics, geographics)
☐ Size (eg selected individuals or masses)
☐ Purchasing and usage habits
☐ Factors influencing brand selection
☐ Knowledge of and attitudes to one brand and the competitive brands
☐ Attitudes to various prices and pricing policies
☐ Attitudes to distribution channels
☐ Attitudes to advertising campaigns of our brand and the competitive brands/services
☐ Trends relating to the above factors.

The advertiser must be able to distinguish whether the purchase decision is taken by the individual decision maker or by two or several people involved in a group decision (eg the purchase of a caravan, or a holiday flat, or a family car, etc). The target audience descriptions should outline the demographic, psychographic and geographic traits of those consumers and it is often necessary to identify a primary and secondary target audience.

Specific advertising objectives

Advertising objectives should be spelled out in detail and should be:

☐ written
☐ specific for a certain time span, for example six months, one year, etc
☐ measurable and quantifiable*
☐ decided upon with a specific target audience in mind.

Russell H Colley is of the opinion that the key to measuring advertising results is one's ability to define the advertising goals to be accomplished. Defining advertising objectives is probably one of the most difficult tasks and he suggests a

---

* I would advise students of advertising to read Russell H Colley's book *Defining Advertising Goals for Measured Advertising Results*, New York: Association of National Advertisers, 1961.

'6M' approach. (Colley 1961:23) (*Note*: These factors could form the basis of a briefing document):

Merchandise	:	What are the important benefits of the products/services to be sold?
Markets	:	Who are the people to be reached?
Motives	:	Why would these people buy/fail to buy?
Messages	:	What are the key ideas, information and attitudes to be conveyed?
Media	:	How can the prospects be reached?
Measurements	:	What method is proposed to measure accomplishment in getting the intended message across to the intended audience?

Once you have considered the six M's, you should ask yourself the following (Bovée & Arens 1982:277 & 278):

☐ To what extent does the advertising aim at closing an *immediate* sale?

☐ Does the advertising aim at *near-term* sales by moving the prospect, step by step, closer to a sale?

☐ Does the advertising aim at building a *long-range* consumer franchise?

☐ Specifically, how can the advertising contribute towards increased sales?

☐ Does the advertising aim at some specific *step* which leads to a sale?

☐ How important are 'supplementary benefits' of end use advertising (eg to help the sales people)?

☐ Is it the task of advertising to impart information needed to consummate sales and build customer satisfaction?

☐ To what extent does the advertising aim at building confidence and goodwill for the company among:
  − customers and potential customers
  − the trade
  − employees and potential employees
  − the financial community
  − the public at large?

☐ Specifically what kind of images does the company wish to build? For example:
  − product quality, dependability
  − service
  − family resemblance of diversified products
  − corporate citizenship
  − growth, progressiveness, technical leadership
  − the innovators?

The above questions are posed in a checklist provided by Bovée and Arens (1982) and each question offers a number of possible answers which could be the specific advertising objective. For example, 'How can the advertising contribute towards increased sales?'

The objective could be to:

☐ hold present customers against inroads of the competition

☐ convert competitive users to our brand

☐ motivate consumers to specify our brand

☐ convert non-users to users of our brand
☐ make regular customers out of occasional customers
☐ advertise new uses of our brand/service
☐ persuade customers to buy larger sizes
☐ remind users to buy or buy more often
☐ encourage greater frequency or quantity of use.

Analysis of the brand/service to be advertised

It is recommended that two analyses be done, namely:

☐ SWOT analysis
☐ positioning analysis.

SWOT analysis:

The SWOT analysis is an analysis of the brand/service's:

☐ Strengths
☐ Weaknesses
☐ Opportunities
☐ Threats

Extensive brand/service research is required here.

Strengths could include physical features and perceived (psychological) strengths like quality, efficacy, etc. *Weaknesses*, real and perceived, could centre around the brand's design, quality, ingredients, packaging, reputation, uses, etc. *Opportunities* are viewed *vis-à-vis* competitors' brands and could include product improvements, a new image, new uses, acceptability in new market segments, etc. *Threats* could centre around product features like differentiating qualities, availability of raw materials from overseas, threats from the distribution channels, packing problems, etc.

Once the SWOT analysis has been completed the advertiser is in a position to do a positioning analysis.

Positioning analysis:

The positioning analysis provides the basis for a strategic positioning of the brand/service which in turn can provide a guideline as to 'what' to say about the brand/service to distinguish it meaningfully from competitive brands/services.

There are many ways of positioning a brand, for example on:

☐ product features
☐ product benefits
☐ value for money (the price/quality relationship)
☐ need satisfaction
☐ exclusivity (ie what this brand has that the competitive brands do not)
☐ application (eg time of day usage, time of year, or even 'anytime')
☐ well-known and meaningful symbols (eg the *Marlboro* cowboy, *Peter Stuyvesant's* international travel symbol, etc).

An easy way to position a brand meaningfully *vis-à-vis* its competitors is to follow the following research steps (developed by Alan Tiley and Warren Harmel of Mortimer Tiley (1983)):

☐ Establish amongst the target audience for the brand the motivating factors considered before purchasing one of the competitive brands.
☐ Obtain a ranking order, that is which is the most important factor, the second most important factor, the third, etc.

☐ Obtain a rating on each motivating factor (from 0 to 100 where 0 is poor and 100 is excellent) for each brand.

☐ Plot these on a positioning chart using a different coloured disc or a different symbol for each brand, for example A, B, C, etc (see figure 5.1). Such a positioning chart can tell you at a glance whether there is a gap in the market (eg low ratings obtained on important motivating factors) and where you should improve your brand (eg your brand is rated low on the high priority motivating factors and high on the least important motivating factors).

Figure 5.1
Positioning chart

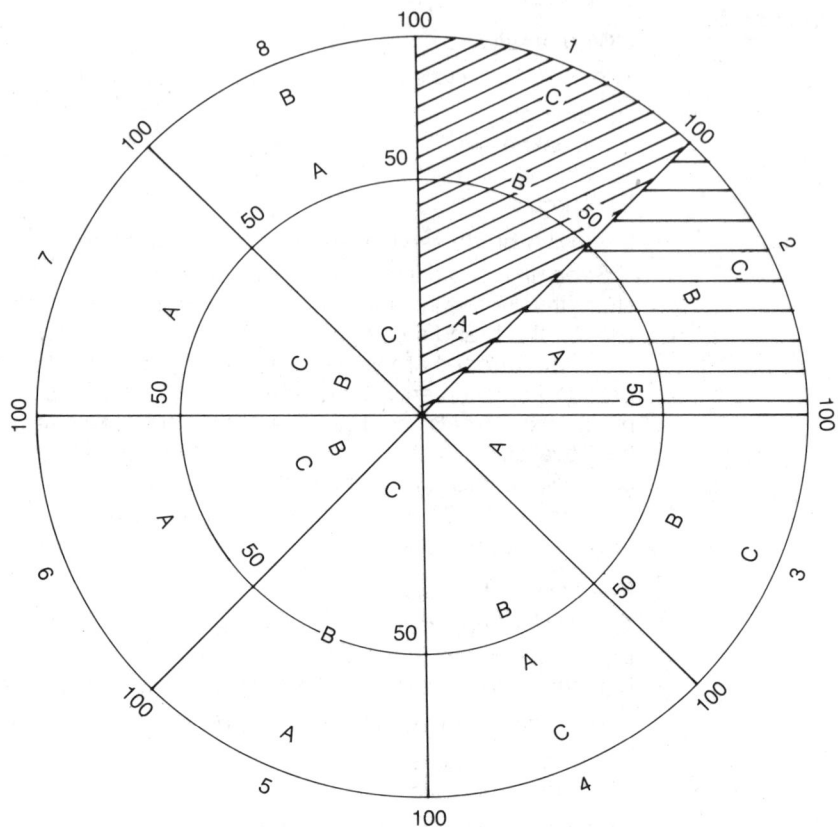

Note: Numbers 1 to 8 indicate the ranking order of the motivating factors.
0 is poor, 50 is average/reasonable and a score of 100 is excellent.

In this example none of the brands A, B or C scored high on the most important motivating factor (1), while brand C scored high on the second (2) and third (3) most important motivating factors. Brand A is perceived by the target audience to score low on the three most important motivating factors, but high on the least important factors, 5, 6, 7 and 8.

Positioning is a very important aspect in planning the advertising campaign because the consumer's perception of the brand is a deciding factor. However, the positioning should be realistic because the product should match its positioning platform or strategy.

The selected media mix

Within the confines of a given budget the media planner will select the best media mix. In the selection process discussions will take place between the media planner and the creative team because the nature and unique positioning of the brand/service can often influence the use of a particular medium. For example, if the brand is positioned as 'the most mobile lawnmower', television and/or cinema should be used to demonstrate the mobility of this lawnmower. The positioning of the brand should be such that it can be effectively translated into the ideal media mix and promotional activities to support the advertising campaign.

Specific communications requirements

Specific communications requirements include, *inter alia*, legal requirements; corporate considerations such as logos, style, type-faces, slogans, etc; and the tone of voice to be used, for example factual/rational or highly emotional, etc.

☐ Conclusion

I am convinced that a briefing document is necessary and important. The creative team does not want to be bombarded with loads of meaningless or 'nice-to-know' information. The task of the campaign planner is to obtain all the information, sift it and present the meaningful information, agreed upon by the client, to the creative team in a short, concise, to-the-point way. The creative team will have ample opportunity during the plans board stage to ask questions and the creative concept should be cracked and agreed upon within the agency before thumbnail sketches or neat layouts and copy are prepared.

☐ References

Bovée, CL & Arens, WF. 1982. *Contemporary Advertising*. Homewood, Illinois: Richard D Irwin.
Colley, RH. 1961. *Defining Advertising Goals for Measured Advertising Results*. New York: Association of National Advertisers.

Establishing advertising objectives
Grahame Tomes

Procedures for establishing objectives *132*

Determine the advertising strategy *133*

Determine the message *134*

Select appropriate appeals *134*

Conclusion *135*

☐ Procedures for establishing objectives

There are many definitions of the role of an advertisement. Whichever definition is closest to the truth, it can be said that advertising is an action tool used to help a company to achieve its marketing and sales objectives. It can be said that advertising helps to accomplish marketing and sales objectives by increasing awareness, acceptance, preference and insistence.

The combination of advertising and personal selling is the most effective, versatile, efficient and economical approach to marketing. However, care should be taken that advertising objectives are not confused with sales objectives. The objective of advertising is to communicate. The objective of the sales effort is to close a sale. It may happen that a great advertising campaign is developed, thousands of sales leads are generated, great consumer demand for a particular brand is created and the market-place is presold, but if the sales force fails to take advantage of these efforts then the advertising effort will fail.

When a company's advertising objectives are set, an objective should be written for each brand or product line and market segment. Objectives must be clearly defined (ie what action or reaction is desired in what time period in each target market), measurable, realistic and related to the market/sales objectives.

Advertising objectives may be company oriented or marketing and sales oriented. The diversity of advertising objectives within each of these types is outlined below. In practice, however, general statements must be translated into specific terms that *can be measured*. For example, a general objective such as 'increase enquiries', which would be impossible to measure objectively, should be restated in specific terms: 'Develop . . . enquiries at R . . . per enquiry from the . . . market for . . . product by . . . date'. When there is a specific objective like this the responses can be counted, the rand cost measured, the market and product identified and the exact position as at the target date specified, established. The degree to which the objectives set have been attained can then be readily determined.

The following are examples of company objectives (in general form):

☐ Identify company with product (especially if the product is well known, but the manufacturing company is not) or most successful divisions
☐ Position company in the market place *vis-à-vis* its competition
☐ Position the company as a product innovator
☐ Show that the company is 'growth oriented'
☐ If a public company, gain the attention of the financial community
☐ Create brand loyalty and identification
☐ Attract and hold high calibre personnel

Below are examples of marketing/sales objectives (in general form):

☐ Develop an awareness of and demand for your company and products
☐ Introduce a new product or application to establish buying influences
☐ Maintain market awareness of and credibility for your established successful products/brands
☐ Expand into new demographic or geographic markets
☐ Maintain goodwill and assist distributors or manufacturers' representatives
☐ Provide market with helpful information about product availability
☐ Reinforce buying decision of already sold customers
☐ Secure sales leads and qualify prospects
☐ Boost sales morale, provide recognition for and give credit to leading sales personnel
☐ Reach target markets economically – reduce selling and operating expenses
☐ Sell products in areas where it is uneconomical to use sales people

☐ Determine the advertising strategy

What is a strategy? An advertising strategy is the course of action, expressed in a plan, to accomplish a company's advertising objectives. This plan includes the policies, procedures and programmes that relate to the company, its products, markets and customers. A strategy or combination of strategies that:

☐ will best achieve the company's objectives
☐ is within the company's capabilities
☐ stays within the company's proposed budget range
☐ is based on the company's market and audience analysis

should be selected.

Strategies are not always generated exclusively by analysing a compilation of facts. The power of a 'gut feel', especially by seasoned marketing people, should never be underestimated. Their experience in working with a particular set of problems on a daily basis sometimes produces a 'sixth sense' that defies explanation yet produces the required results.

Whatever strategy is chosen, it must be elaborated and formulated into a message that will favourably impress the potential buyers of the brand/product and those who influence the buying.

□ Determine the message

The message must be meaningful – the content of the message, the specific points that must be made and the overall feeling that is to be conveyed must be decided upon. An advertising agency will create the exact wording. It should be borne in mind that most prospects are very busy living and working and in addition to their daily activities are bombarded by countless advertising messages. Thus, the single most important question to be asked is: 'Why should prospects read/listen/view this advertising communication?'. All too often the marketer who knows a great deal about his or her product becomes enamoured with some of the intricate details or specifications. Often these details are not relevant to the end user. Therefore the advertising message should address itself to one factor – the specific problems that a product will solve and how (features and benefits), or in the imagery arena how the brand or product will make the consumer feel good about that brand or product.

□ Select appropriate appeals

The following is a checklist of things that should be considered when potential appeals are selected:

The message
The message of a specific advertisement must be determined, that is what it is that must be conveyed. A good agency will be of great assistance in this area.

The agency's function
The agency provides the creative solution, that is the headline, visual elements and copy, and should not be dictated to in this regard. A company may be wrong in its approach, and if it does not like the agency solution it should merely ask for a new direction or answer. Clichés such as 'think femininity, think XYZ beauty soap' should be avoided. More specific ways in which the product can be of help to a potential consumer should be given instead.

In countries where marketers can take on their competitors directly and name names it is critical that the facts are completely accurate and that there are no skeletons in the closet which the competitor can throw back at that marketer.

Photographs of the product
Not every advertisement should feature a photograph of the product – the customer is more interested in what is going to be done for him than in what the product looks like.

Company logo
This is another sacred cow that causes problems. A logo is the name of a company presented in a special type face, or as a slogan or a symbol. A great deal can be said for following a consistent pattern in logo usage, that is slogans, type faces or symbols should not be changed constantly. Most multidivisional companies develop a manual on corporate identification usage, which is very important. However, in advertising the logo is not the most important item and need

not be given prominence. The headline, the illustration and the basic message are of prime importance. The logo should act as a signature, just as an individual name does when it is signed at the bottom of a letter.

Ask for action

When a product is advertised, some particular action should be asked for. The consumer should be told how to contact the distributor or manufacturer for additional information, the trial offer, or whatever.

☐ Conclusion

Specific advertising objectives are crucial to marketing and advertising management, because without specific objectives it is impossible to make proper decisions. These objectives help to *integrate* advertising with the marketing strategy, because this helps marketing management to make more effective *decisions* concerning *inter alia*, alternative advertising strategies and the selection of advertising media; it may serve as motivation for the advertising *budget*; and it serves as the only scientific basis for *measuring advertising's effectiveness*. The well-known DAGMAR concept (Defining Advertising Goals for Measuring Advertising Results) is certainly most applicable in formulating advertising objectives. The ultimate result of advertising must have the effect of a change of mind, attitude, behaviour or action by the target audience. It is against these changes that the effectiveness of advertising can ultimately be measured. Therefore, advertising objectives must be measurable, have a benchmark, contain a specific target market, be applicable to a specific time period and be put in writing to serve as a guide for encouraging the rest of the advertising campaign.

The total involvement philosophy and methodology in planning a campaign

Ludi Koekemoer

Introduction 136

Briefing by the advertiser 136

Planning the campaign 137

Final comment 142

☐ Introduction

Advertising is a people business. When an advertising campaign is created the advertiser and the advertising agency should not hold out on each other in any way. The role of the advertiser cannot be underestimated, while an agency, a unique factory producing unique products, should realise that the quality of the advertising produced is totally dependent on the calibre of the people involved in its creation. These people include the advertiser.

The following steps should be taken to ensure that the advertising produced will be successful in achieving the desired objectives.

☐ Briefing by the advertiser

The advertiser's brief should be in writing, but before developing it and submitting it to the advertising agency he should take the following steps.

Analyse the situation
Before planning what he wants to achieve and how to achieve it, the advertiser should analyse and review the market (eg trends, opportunities, etc), the product involved (eg strengths and weaknesses), the company (eg management, production facilities, financial resources, existing distribution channels, policies and procedures), existing advertising for the advertiser's products, the competitors (eg products, advertising employed, new launches, etc) and the economy.

Set objectives
Once the situation analysis is complete, objectives should be set for both quantifiable and qualitative aspects with regard to the products and the advertising.

Define the target market

The next step is to define the target market which will emanate from research (either secondary or primary or both). The target market should be those consumers the advertiser wants to reach and to motivate to use his product. Descriptions of the target market should outline the demographic and psychographic traits of these consumers.

> The following is an example of a description of a target market:
> ☐ Primary target market for brand X is black males
> ☐ residing in major cities in South Africa,
> ☐ aged 15-29,
> ☐ in the C and D income groups,
> ☐ Zulu, Sotho and English-speaking,
> ☐ who are economically inclined.

Complete a briefing document

It is important that the client (ie the advertiser) should complete a briefing document and that both the client and the advertising agency should sign it, indicating that they are in total agreement on all aspects. This briefing document should include:
☐ the company's history re this brand/service
☐ the brand/service to be advertised, sales and advertising history
☐ the advertising objective(s)
☐ the environment as it affects the advertising
☐ consumer needs the advertising must solve
☐ the major product or service benefit
☐ the positioning of the product *vis-à-vis* its competitors
☐ advertising requirements
☐ additional information
☐ a media strategy brief and the size of budget.

The advertiser will supply the research information necessary to give the advertising agency a clear picture from which it can design its advertising campaign. However, it is often necessary for the advertising agency to embark on further research in order to obtain more information or to distinguish between the important and less important information.

☐ Planning the campaign

Once the briefing document has been received and discussed, the following steps could be followed by the advertising agency to ensure the creation of a successful advertising campaign (see figure 5.2).

Step 1: the macro analysis The macro analysis studies the environment within which a product will be marketed and communicated and analyses environmental threats and opportunities relative to the product's advertising. Factors usually included in this analysis are the uncontrollable variables like the economic situation, the political situation and market environment and trends and opportunities; the principal competition, the company itself (ie management, resources, production capacity, strength of personnel, marketing history, etc); and, finally, the legal constraints.

Figure 5.2
The total
involvement
method

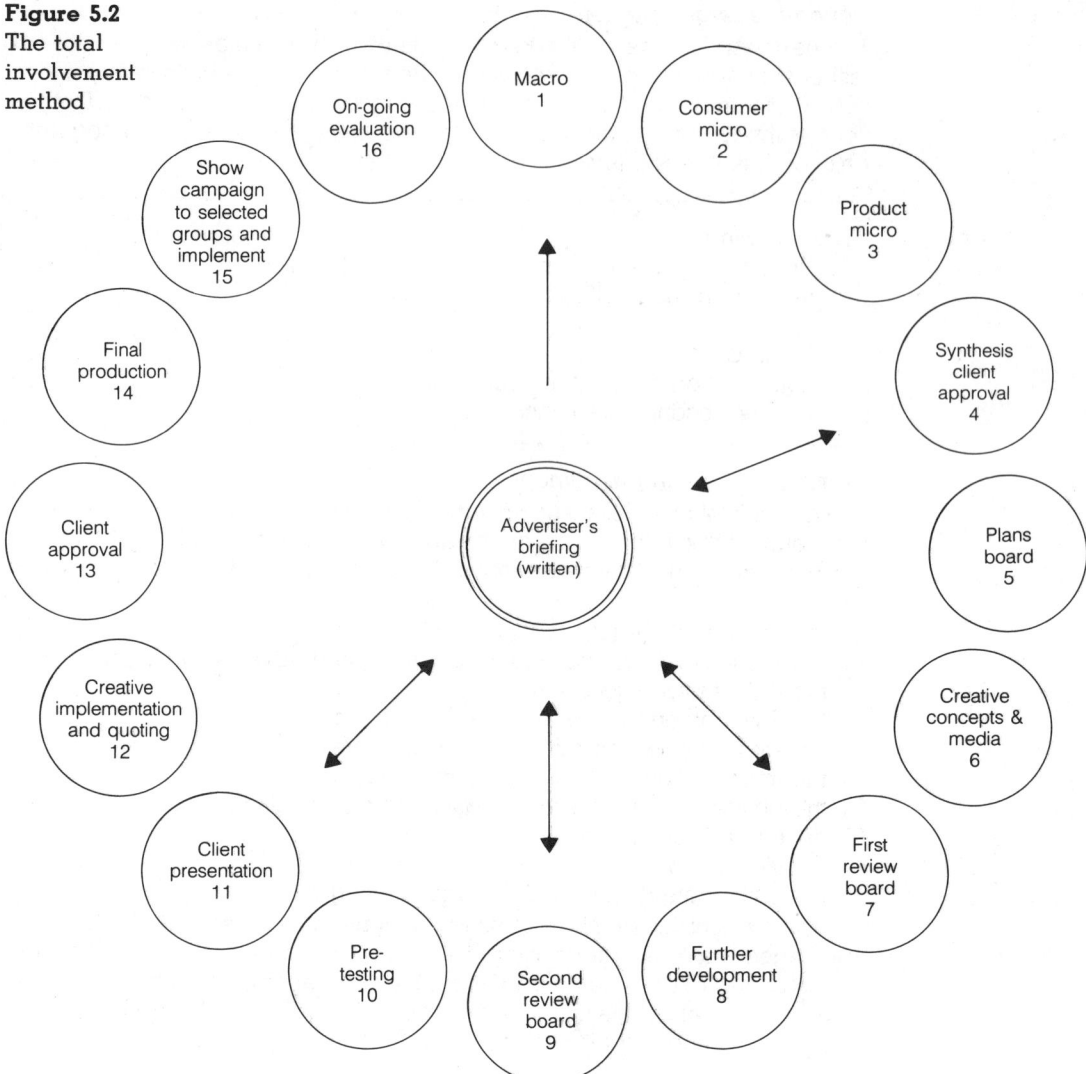

Step 2: the consumer micro analysis

Markets consist of a variety of people. Hence the geographic, demographic and psychographic factors which segment the market are studied so that the target market can be isolated and defined in terms of geographics, demographics and psychographics while its problems, wants and needs can be understood.

Step 3: the product micro analysis

Against the background provided by the macro analysis and the analysis of the needs of the target market, these needs are matched with the perceived characteristics of the product and its positioning. The product micro analysis focuses squarely on the product itself, which is the single most important ingredient in the marketing mix. It scrutinises its real and perceived attributes, benefits, strengths and weakness. Part of this analysis is to investigate existing advertising campaigns for the product and existing advertising campaigns for the major competitors.

Step 4: synthesis

The three analyses are then synthesised, that is drawn together, to evolve a succint major advertising proposition for the product. This proposition should be compared with the advertising objectives set in the briefing by the advertiser in terms of, for example, increasing awareness, increasing demand, increasing sales, increasing market share, increasing usage, creating a particular image or to improve the image, obtaining immediate reaction, a short-term campaign or a long-term campaign.

The synthesis of the macro, product micro and consumer micro analyses indicates *what* the communications need to say. It is the task of the advertising agency's creative department to determine *how* to say it after the advertiser has approved the 'what' to communicate.

Step 5: the plans board

During this stage various departments within the advertising agency get together to devise a total communications plan which includes:

☐ the creative department
☐ the media department
☐ the promotions department
☐ direct response

while attention should also be given to public relations, merchandising and product considerations.

Too often advertising is created without attention being given to media considerations, or a striking advertising campaign is designed without due attention being paid to sales representatives, merchandising, sales promotions, competitions, point-of-sale material, give-aways, etc. All of these factors should be working together to achieve the desired and stated objectives.

It is interesting to note that it may be worthwhile to leave out one of the directors at this stage in order that he might be brought in at the review board stage as devil's advocate.

Step 6: media and creative concepts

The media choice depends upon the advertising concept or theme, the target market, the size of the budget and the characteristics and benefits of the various media. It is vitally important that the money is invested in the best media and not just spent in all of the media. When the decision is taken which media to use, the following factors should be considered:

☐ Cost per thousand
☐ Reach versus frequency
☐ The quality of certain media
☐ The need for promotional support in certain media
☐ The change in media selection during certain stages of the product's life cycle

For more detailed discussions on these factors, see chapter 6 'Media Planning'.

The creative department develops a number of concepts (ie various ways of *how* to say what should be communicated) based on the advertising brief. At the same time the creative department formulates spin-offs, for example promotions, competitions, give-aways, POP material, in-store promotions, direct response ideas, etc.

Step 7: first review board

At the review board stage all initial plans and concepts are presented to members of the review board, which normally includes a campaign planner, a market researcher, the creative director, the media director and often (eg in the case of a major campaign) the managing director of the advertising agency. Each department submits its plans and has to defend its actions. It is necessary to play the 'why' game, to check plans against objectives, and to ask 'What have we not done which should also be done?'.

At this stage it is necessary to bring in the executive who has not yet been exposed to the advertising brief and present the plan to him. By playing the 'why' game and checking proposed strategies against objectives it is easier to get out of a situation where one cannot see the wood for the trees. Particular questions which could be asked by this neutral executive at this stage are: 'Do the creative ideas fit into the media selected? Will the promotional ideas work? Are these ideas practical and cost efficient? Is the television commercial simple, credible, original, relevant and something that the target audience will enjoy looking at? Is the print advertising a stopper? Is the product the hero in the advertising? Is the advertisement completely believable? Is the advertisement a likeable person? Is the theme one that will last, or does it have a very short life?'.

Step 8: further development

More often than not the various departments go back after the review board and start all over again. Some agencies even take a campaign that survives the review board, put it in a cupboard and say: 'We now have a reasonable campaign, let's see if we can do a better one'. Strategies are rethought, plans redone and it is probable that the various departments will work and improve on one of the selected advertising and promotional concepts and the media planner will prepare a semi-final media plan. It is essential that everyone involved is confident in what is selected. This time the departments will go to the second review board prepared with answers to that nagging question 'why?'.

Step 9: second review board

This is the second review. The revised plans and concepts are presented to the same team and the neutral senior executive who will act as final devil's advocate. It is often found that the most viable concept has been 'cracked' at this stage and enthusiasm for the campaign is mounting.

Step 10: pretesting

It is ideal to pre-test every campaign. The late George Gribbin, ex-president of Young and Rubicam, gave me checklists for in-house testing. The first checklist is for television scoring:

☐ Simplicity
☐ Credibility
☐ Originality
☐ Relevance
☐ Empathy

The second is for print advertising:

☐ Is the advertisement a stopper?
☐ Is the product the hero?
☐ Is the advertisement completely believeable?
☐ Is the advertisement a likeable person?
☐ Is the theme one that will last?

Sometimes it is necessary to pre-test two concepts when in doubt at the agency or when you are not absolutely sure about the interpretation of the message. I have found that it is absolutely necessary to pre-test any campaign aimed at Blacks in order to ensure that the best concept is the one that is used. Pre-testing also enables you to check whether you are communicating the right message, whether the advertising communications are credible, and whether the image of the product will be enhanced.

Unfortunately, very few agencies in South Africa pre-test campaigns and a commonly made mistake is to take a campaign designed for white consumers and modify it slightly for use in the black market. Very few such campaigns work, and often they cause more harm than good.

Step 11: client presentation

Some agencies prefer to keep the client out of steps 1 to 10 and surprise the advertiser with the advertising campaign at this stage. I believe in a policy of 'no surprises', where the client is involved constantly and the briefing document is used at the synthesis stage, the first review board stage and the second review board stage. In practice this means that the marketing director or product manager is involved, but presenting a major campaign to a client frequently involves (and should involve) the board of directors. These directors are probably going to ask the same questions which the devil's advocate and/or the client (the product manager or marketing director) asked during the second review board stage. The presentation can therefore be made with confidence to those who are responsible for making the final decision. The presenters know in advance what fears the client may have and what questions they might be asked. Approval of the campaign should be obtained at this presentation.

Step 12: creative implementation and quoting

Unfortunately, non-creative people (the advertisers) sometimes force the creative experts to change certain creative ideas, but at this stage everybody should agree on exactly what the campaign will consist of. The TV storyboards are finalised, final scripts are done for radio copy, type mark-ups are prepared for print advertising, final copy is prepared for print advertisements, model selection and voice selection (for radio and television) is done, photographers are briefed and production houses and printers are briefed in order that costs may be ascertained.

With regard to quotes, I believe that it is necessary to obtain quotes from three suppliers who have been briefed in detail. Once the quotes have been obtained they should be checked against the budget and it should be ensured that all expenses are taken into consideration. Unexpected costs at a later stage which could result in a feeling of unpleasantness between the advertising agency and the advertiser should be avoided. The agency then prepares written quotes and presents these and the final media schedules to the advertiser for final approval.

Step 13: client approval

At this stage it may be necessary to re-present the whole campaign, the final quotes and the media schedule. Written approval for the campaign and the quotes must be obtained and the media schedules must be signed.

Step 14: final production

This is the critical stage for the advertising agency when the TV commercials, radio spots, print advertising, POP items, promotional items, outdoor posters, etc are produced. From the agency's point of view it is essential to control the production and to ensure that certain standards are met. From the advertiser's point of view it is essential to be involved in the production process – to supervise what is being done, attend the shoot of a TV commercial, attend the recording sessions of the radio commercials, etc. It is often necessary to make an on-the-spot decision whilst producing a TV commercial, recording a radio spot, or producing a print advertisement. Advertisers should not expect the advertising agency to take such decisions if it means that a dispute could arise at a later stage when 'it did not work'. Sometimes additional expenses are incurred which were not budgeted for and these should be approved on the spot by the advertiser.

Step 15: expose campaign to selected staff and implement

I believe that it is necessary for the senior executives, the sales representatives, branch managers, dealers, etc to have a preview of the campaign before it breaks. It is essential to get their blessing and co-operation and to avoid surprises. Unless you have the wholehearted co-operation of the branch managers, dealers, sales representatives, etc, the campaign does not have a hope of being implemented successfully.

Step 16: ongoing evaluations

The object at this stage is to build in a measure of efficiency. This begins with the pre-campaign research and continues through pre-testing to the final post-testing (ie the efficiency versus the objectives). For example, pre and post awareness tests, image shifts pre and post, usage pre and post, etc research could be conducted on a continuous basis. A date and activity chart showing sales over time and the campaign activities should be used. All activities should be indicated on this chart so that the advertiser can see what has worked and what has not. This chart could also be used to indicate competitive reactions and activities and the effect thereof on the product sales. Nielsen data like out-of-stock situations should also be included in this chart to reflect a true picture.

☐ Final comment

The total involvement philosophy and methodology is designed to counteract the feeling that '50% of my advertising money is wasted, but I don't know which 50%'. If the advertising campaign is planned in a structured way, the necessary information is gained from the advertiser and outside sources, a total communications plan is created, the campaign is reviewed against objectives, pre-testing is carried out among the target audience and it is ensured that the production of the campaign is of a high standard and the risk of a campaign not being successful is minimised.

6

Media planning

Media planning *145*

Television in South Africa *162*

The power of radio *182*

Cinema *198*

Outdoor advertising: the neglected hero *210*

Direct advertising: media planning
  depends on identification *218*

Media planning case study: Sparkle *228*

Appendix: Media opportunities for the black market *247*

Media planning
Dick Reed

The media function in the advertising process *145*

Media attributes *149*

Media data sources *151*

Media objectives *154*

Basic media considerations *156*

Media strategy *157*

Media weighting *160*

Media plan format *161*

References *161*

☐ The media function in the advertising process

Part of the *Oxford Dictionary* definition of *medium* is 'means', and the media function in advertising is to provide the *means* or vehicle for conveying the advertisement to the target market. An alternative word in the dictionary definition is 'agency', and it is worth recalling that advertising agencies originated as media space brokers and only subsequently expanded their services to include creative, research, production and all of the rest of the range of services provided by the contemporary full-service advertising agency.

It can reasonably be argued that there are three basic decision making areas in the planning of advertising campaigns, each being of equal importance, and *media* is one of them. This is illustrated in figure 6.1, which depicts the various facets of the advertising agency's operations.

Figure 6.1
The advertising
agency's
operations

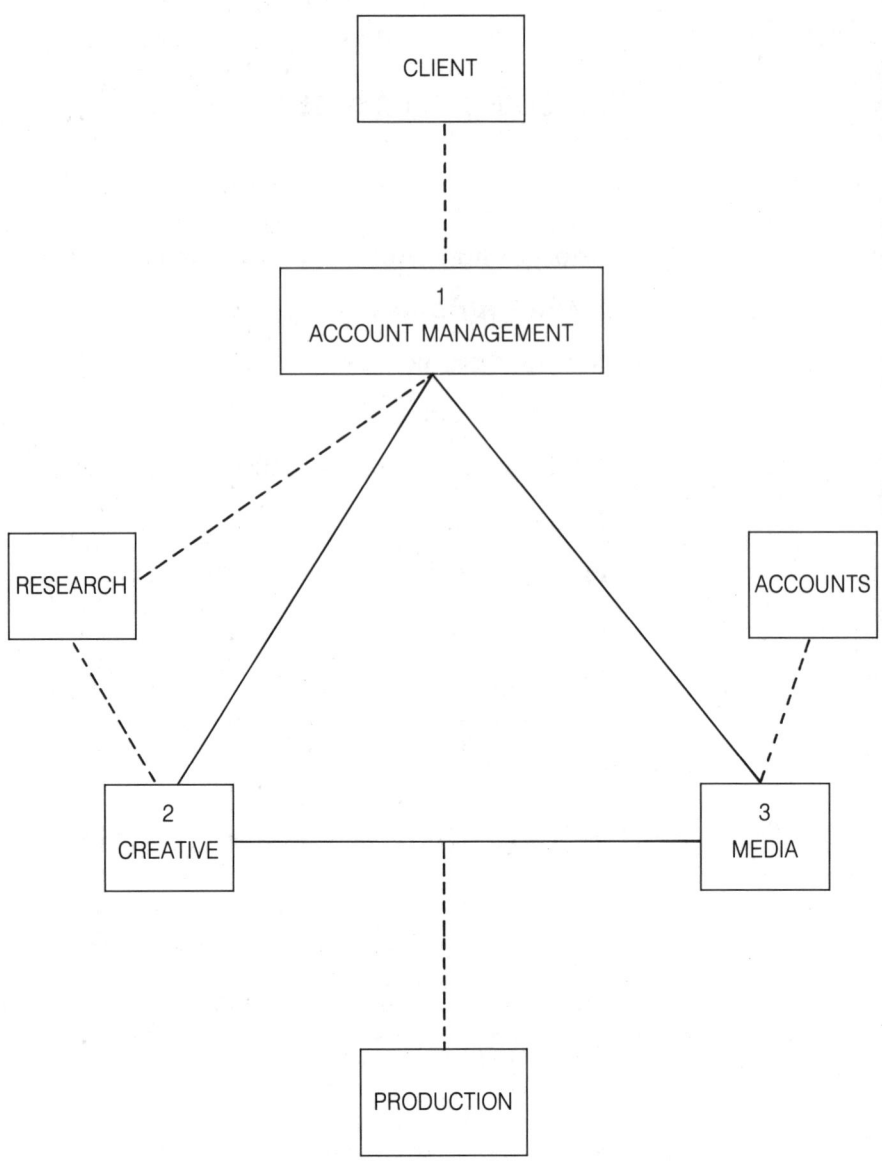

The three basic decisions are:

☐ Client/account management – What are the objectives and parameters?

☐ Creative – What do we say and how do we say it?

☐ Media – Where do we say it?

There are three participants in the media process in advertising who normally interface along the lines illustrated in figure 6.2.

Figure 6.2
Participants in the
media process

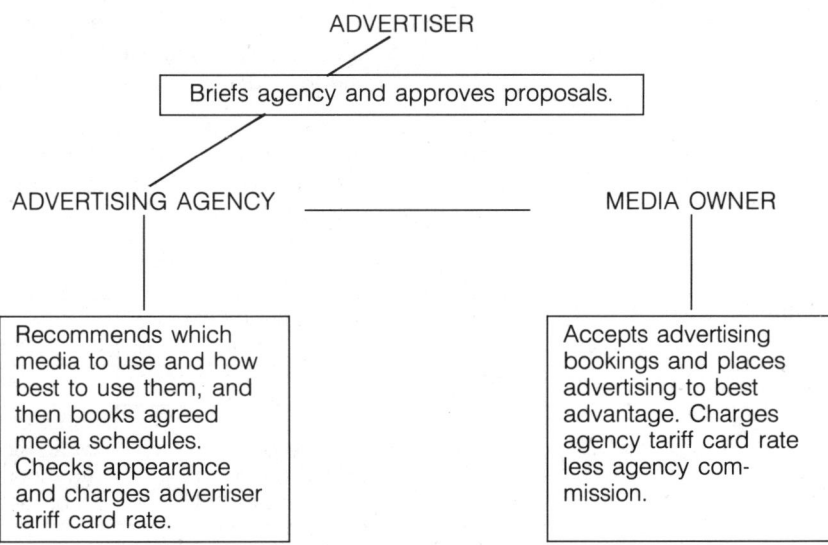

While these are the three 'professional' participants in the media process, the fuller scenario includes a fourth, the all-important target audience (see figure 6.3).

Figure 6.3
Participants in the
media process
including target
audience

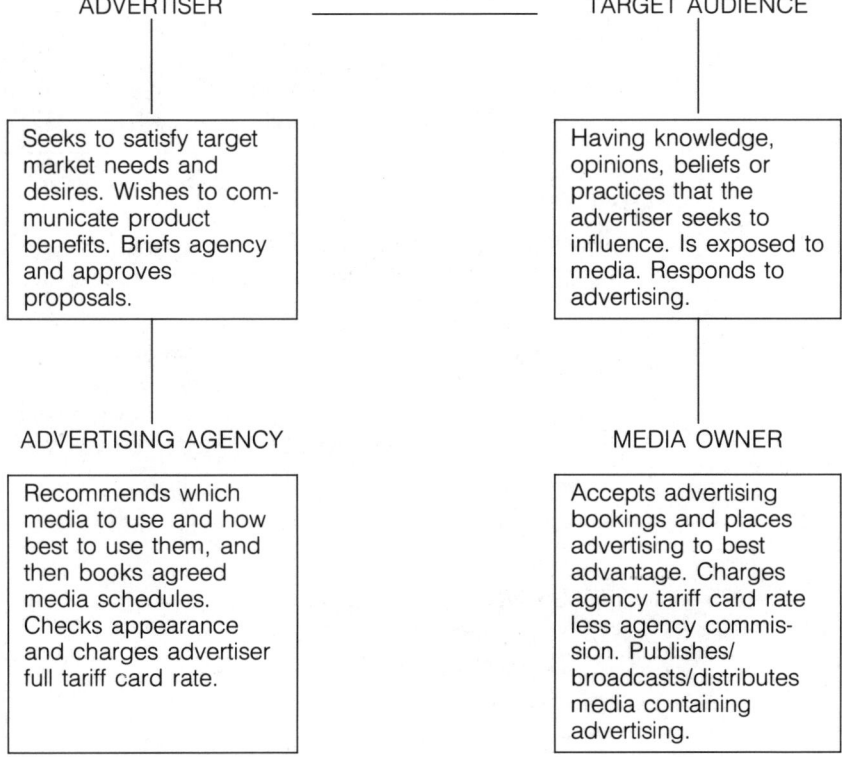

In other words, the *client* calls the shots, the *agency* figures the shots, the *medium* distributes the shots and the *target audience* absorbs the shots and if there is a response then the media process has been effective.

Media advertising in South Africa involves large sums of money, approaching 1% of our GNP. Table 6.1 compares investment in advertising as measured by Adindex for the 12 months ending December 1985 with the corresponding period for the previous year.

Table 6.1
Advertising
expenditure 1985
versus 1984

	Most recent year		Year previous		Change
	1985		1984		
	Investment in advertising (in thousands of rands)	%	Investment in advertising (in thousands of rands)	%	%
Daily newspapers	170 917	21,2	171 041	21,8	−0,1
Weekend newspapers	64 943	8,1	65 937	8,4	−1,5
Regional newspapers	48 796	6,0	44 501	5,7	+9,7
General magazines	93 036	11,5	95 305	12,1	−2,4
Business magazines	58 644	7,3	62 857	8,0	−6,7
Black newspapers	14 095	1,7	26 535	3,4	−2,4
Black magazines	11 795	1,5			
TOTAL PRINT	462 226	57,3	466 176	59,4	−0,8
Television	229 560	28,5	209 191	26,7	+9,7
Radio	75 921	9,4	72 033	9,2	+5,4
Outdoor	25 685	3,2	25 267	3,2	+1,7
Cinema	12 885	1,6	12 156	1,5	+6,0
TOTAL ALL MEDIA	806 277	100,0	784 823	100,0	+2,7

Source: Adindex

The total adspend growth of 2,7% represents a drop in advertising volumes overall of some 14% when an average media inflation factor of 16% to 17% for the year is taken into account.

These figures relate to the gross charges by the media owners for display advertising placed, but do not include GST or any production or other costs. As seen, they include only the classical 'above-the-line' media types and do not cover the broader spectrum of promotional investment that would also include:

☐ Direct mail

☐ Classified advertising

☐ Directories

☐ Shows and exhibitions

☐ Public relations

☐ Point-of-sale and window display

☐ T-shirts, novelties, etc

☐ Sports sponsorship

☐ Media attributes

Brian Allt, an internationally recognised authority on media research and Head of Market Research at the Mirror Group of Newspapers in the UK, recently wrote: 'The average Briton spends five or six hours a day with media. In a day he probably has a wider range of experience via media than he can possibly have in his "real" life' (Allt 1985: 382 & 386).

He went on to say:

When we push our advertisement through one of the media we think in terms of transferring information. This information-transfer approach tends to assume a passive recipient at the other end who will simply accept or ignore our message. We tend to forget that he will re-interpret it selectively, mix it up with current and past experience, and perhaps at best store some general emotive reaction rather than the actual message. Advertising is an intrinsic part of each medium, and part of the experience of that medium.

Allt then says:

Traditionally our media data provide us with number of readers, and so on. They tell us about the value of each reader in terms of consumption behaviour. But they tell us nothing about the value of the experience of the reader or viewer and how it varies by publication, or by programme, and in the case of a reader about its depth or duration.

Up to now media research in South Africa, as well as most of that done internationally, has given us quantitative data. This has led to media analysis and discussion often being dominated by numbers. It should be borne in mind, however, that there are three dimensions in which media attributes should be considered (see figure 6.4).

Figure 6.4
Media attributes
dimensions

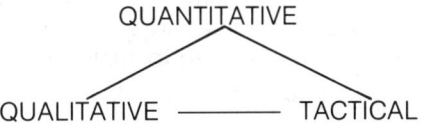

Each of the three dimensions is important, the relative importance being determined by circumstances and in relation to the plan's objectives, parameters and strategy.

Quantitative attributes

Lots of media numbers can be skilfully used to determine reach, frequency, cost efficiency and audience profile dimensions. The investment of large sums of money requires businesslike figuring of options and benefits. Computers are of great assistance in number crunching.

There are many media numbers, with varying degrees of accuracy, that are used in assessing media attributes and relative strengths. These numbers include the following:

☐ Circulation
☐ Licensed sets
☐ Readership
☐ Viewership

☐ Listenership
☐ Unit costs
☐ Cost per thousand
☐ Frequency

Qualitative attributes

There are, however, vital areas of advertising and media assessment that do not lend themselves to numeracy and which are far more judgemental. The relative impact of different media types, the size or dimension of advertisement required to achieve effective communication, the prestige or authority of one publication compared with another – one can think of many factors which rely on opinions and personal assessments in relation to the specific circumstances. Most of these cannot be quantified or, at best, are estimated on the basis of value judgements. The creative requirements of the campaign exert a strong influence in this dimension. Media work is, after all, the effective exposure of creative work.

If we were to think of media in human terms as acquaintances, we would not think of them and describe them in numeric terms. We do not evaluate or describe our friends or associates in terms of a standard set of scales. We might think of Tom as a serious sort of chap, pleasant to be with when one feels like discussing the state of the nation, and Michael as a good person to go out on the town with.

The *qualitative aspects* of media are important, but sometimes more difficult to pin down or define than quantitative dimensions. Their descriptions would be more adjectival and emotional than the quantitative scales.

Basic impact potential

Some media have more basic impact potential than others. Television, with its qualities of sight, sound, movement and colour, has more impact potential than radio, which is one-dimensional and not visual at all. This does not mean to say that television commercials are automatically more impactful than radio commercials – the creativity of usage can override the norm, but as a norm television has more impact potential than radio.

Authority or prestige

Some media have more authority or prestige. A leading financial magazine will provide a more prestigious environment for advertising an expensive motor car than a cheap photo-story magazine.

Life of exposure

Some media provide longer life of exposure – an outdoor hoarding is up and visible for a full month, whereas a 30-second commercial is visible for exactly that length of time.

Frequency of exposure

This is an essential attribute and is far more affordable and available in radio than in many other media types. By definition, frequency is more achievable in daily newspapers than weekly newspapers.

Relevance

Relevance can be a useful attribute. An advertisement for food products is likely to work better in a magazine dealing with family care and nutrition than in one dealing with TV stars.

Tactical attributes

Often, overriding factors are created by *tactical* aspects. Some media have long deadlines or contractual clauses that are binding. Other media can be negotiated at short notice and adjustments to space requirements can be made quickly and easily.

Flexibility

Flexibility is a very important tactical attribute, especially to categories like retail and automotive advertising, which can be very reactive.

Regionality

This is a vital aspect to advertisers who do not have national distribution, or who wish to upweight advertising exposure in given areas.

Competitive activity in different media

This can be assessed so that tactical decisions can be taken as to whether to meet the opposition head-on, or whether to advertise in media in which it does not have a presence.

Timing of media exposure

Timing can be very important. Appearance in a daily newspaper enables super-markets to advertise prior to peak shopping days in the week. A breakfast cereal advertiser can advertise in the morning show on radio and reach families at break-fast time.

These examples of quantitative, qualitative and tactical attributes of media are not comprehensive, but give an idea of the many different attributes that should be considered when media options are analysed.

When analysis is within one media type, for example newspapers only, com-parisons will most probably be mainly of a quantitative nature. But when inter-media comparisons are made, the qualitative and tactical dimensions can often be the more important criteria. Thus media assessment and best usage is invariably multidimensional and more complicated than it appears at face value.

The media in South Africa have more complexities than in most countries as a result of our variety of ethno-language population groupings. The *Bible* is published in 25 languages in South Africa and advertising communications are also disseminated in many languages. For example, SABC television services are broadcast in seven different languages and there are 11 primary languages used on SABC radio stations covering different areas and peoples of different languages and cultures. Standards of literacy vary considerably between differ-ent areas and peoples. All of these factors influence media exposure potentials.

☐ Media data sources

It can be debated whether advertising is an art or a science. The answer is surely that it is a combination of both – with a healthy measure of showmanship thrown in too!

Media tends more to the scientific side in its orientation towards having a lot of data on which to base perspectives of the potential and/or relative performance of different media options. This is not to say that media people cannot be artistic in their interpretation and usage of the data, and some of the most able of media people have their fair share of showmanship.

The primary data sources used in media in South Africa are dealt with below:

Audit Bureau of Circulations

The ABC, as it is commonly known, is an independent professional body with membership of publishers of publications and cinema organisations (media proprietors), advertisers and advertising agencies, that is the three sides of the advertising triangle, which makes it fully objective and representative of all interests.

The function of the ABC is to arrange the regular auditing of publication circulations and cinema attendances in a standard and correct manner so that they are comparable, and to issue the certificates to members.

ABC circulations, therefore, provide accurate and reliable circulation figures which are of great value in comparing different publications. They detail cinema attendance levels factually.

In addition to issuing ABC certificates for publications with paid circulations, the Audit Bureau also has a category of membership for newspapers with free, controlled distribution known as Verified Free Distribution (VFD). VFD certificates are issued after auditors have verified paper consumption, print orders and delivery routines.

An ABC certificate can be considered to be a data source of substantial accuracy.

Newspaper Press Union circulation breakdowns

The Newspaper Press Union (NPU) is a body which represents a large majority of publishers. The NPU has a standard set of geographical distribution areas throughout South Africa, and through the NPU the publishers release circulation breakdowns that total to their ABC circulation figure. The breakdown sheets carry a notation that, while the total is an ABC audited figure, the breakdowns by area are supplied by the publishers as unaudited detail. However, the information is accepted as being generally reliable and of real assistance to regional advertisers when they have to determine where the publications actually go.

All media and products survey

When planning the best possible advertising exposure, the planner wants to know who reads the publications, watches television, listens to the radio, goes to the cinema or travels a lot and so is potentially more exposed to outdoor and transit advertising.

This information is derived from the All Media and Products Survey (AMPS) controlled by the South African Advertising Research Foundation (SAARF), which, like the ABC, is representative of the entire industry and therefore objective and unbiased. Research of this type is complex and data is expensive to obtain and analyse, so SAARF has a funding system that requires all media owners to charge and remit to SAARF a levy of 0,5% of the cost of advertising placed by all advertisers. This is a fair system, since it ensures that all who can potentially use the data pay for it in the right proportion. Many countries in the world envy us our system, as it ensures that no vested interests can obtain control of media research.

In order to obtain this data it would be ideal if everyone in the country could be interviewed and questioned on his reading/viewing/listening patterns. However, this is not practical from a cost and logistics point of view. Scientifically developed sampling techniques make it practical for a representative sample to be interviewed, that is one out of every 100 people, and for the findings to be meaningfully projected up to the entire population dimensions. There is a known, and acceptable, margin of error.

AMPS is based on ongoing regular questioning of adults (aged 16 and older) of all races in South Africa and the self-governing states of Transkei, Ciskei, Venda and Bophuthatswana. Reports have been issued over the past 11 years so trends can be tracked and analysed.

Information in AMPS covers three dimensions (see figure 6.5).

Figure 6.5
Information dimensions covered in AMPS

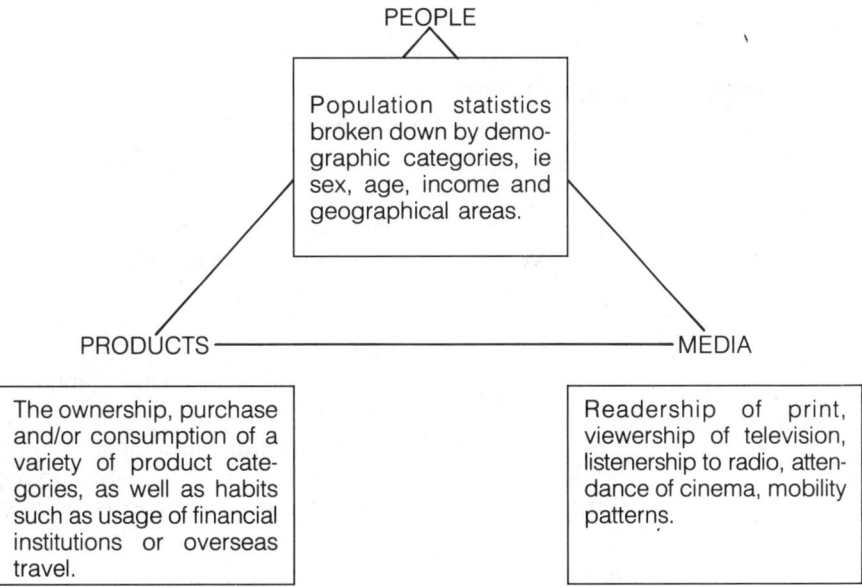

PEOPLE

Population statistics broken down by demographic categories, ie sex, age, income and geographical areas.

PRODUCTS ——————————————— MEDIA

The ownership, purchase and/or consumption of a variety of product categories, as well as habits such as usage of financial institutions or overseas travel.

Readership of print, viewership of television, listenership to radio, attendance of cinema, mobility patterns.

All this information is derived from single source integrated research so that all possible combinations and permutations of the vast data base can be calculated. This is where the use of computers becomes essential.

The accuracy of AMPS is based on a number of factors, the most critical being the accuracy and honesty of the respondents and the construction of the questionnaire, which must be such that it produces meaningful and acceptable results. This leads to areas of debate and sometimes controversy over absolute and relative levels of accuracy. This debate should never be allowed to overshadow the vast amount of data provided by AMPS. The wealth of information should be used with discretion, intelligence and flair to determine media exposure potentials. AMPS is also of great assistance to marketers who wish to obtain a perspective on their market, as AMPS product data are categorised into Heavy, Medium and Light user categories.

Individual media owner research

To supplement the 'skeleton' of industry information provided by AMPS, a number of media owners 'flesh out' the information by commissioning more detailed research into their specific areas of interest. While potentially lacking the impartiality and breadth of AMPS, this type of research can be more detailed and innovative. A prime example is the Readership Data Library (RDL), conducted and released by the Newspaper Marketing Bureau (NMB), which concerns the NMB's newspaper interests and metropolitan areas relative to them. RDL contains useful information on shopping patterns and market values related to media exposure potentials.

Tariff cards

All media issue tariff cards detailing advertising costs, deadlines, mechanical specifications and conditions of acceptance of advertising. This is essential information.

Media reference works

Catalogues of media information are compiled by two commercial organisations and are available for sale. *SARAD* is published every second month, while *PROMODATA* is an annual publication.

☐ Media objectives

The media plan is one element of the marketing programme. Planning is a process that:

☐ *begins* with the client's marketing objectives and strategy

☐ *evolves* out of decisions on advertising objectives and strategy

☐ *proceeds* to media objectives and strategy, and a specific plan for allocating funds in the manner most likely to maximise the client's return on his marketing/advertising investment

☐ *continues* through the 'stewardship' phase of monitoring the execution to be sure it conforms to the plan.

The media plan must evolve from and be fully integrated with marketing/advertising/creative objectives. From the marketing objectives and strategy the media planner should consider what aspects will impact on media selection. For example:

Source of business

Where will volume be derived?

☐ Hold current brand users (defensive)

☐ Get current users to use more (increased frequency of use)

☐ Attract customers from competitor (conquest)

☐ Expand the category

☐ Combinations/variations of the above

The advertising objectives establish the overall objectives and priorities of the communications. For example:

Role of advertising

What are we trying to accomplish?

☐ Stimulate/increase awareness and trial

☐ Maintain/sustain current position – remind/reinforce

☐ Introduce a new brand

☐ Reposition a current brand

☐ Relaunch a declining brand

☐ Prevent erosion in facing a major competitor

☐ Establish or improve image/reputation

☐ Affect attitudes

☐ Merchandise to the trade

☐ Support sales force; impress franchisees, employees

☐ Elicit a direct response – couponing, sale announcement, write-in offer, etc

Given the marketing and advertising input, the next step is to establish the media objectives. These are the guidelines for the plan which lay out precisely what is required for the media plan. They answer the questions regarding: *who* the plan must reach, *where, when, how many, how often* and for *how long,* and *what* are the required communications dynamics and environemnt.

Media objectives should take account of the following specific factors:

Target audience defined in relevant terms

Defining the target audience is important and could be as varied as:

☐ source of business/product user groups
☐ user/brand decision maker/purchaser
☐ key demographics
☐ psychographics

Geographic: Concentration/Priorities

The concentration/priorities should be stated in geographic terms, namely:

☐ National
☐ Regional
☐ Client sales areas
☐ Local markets
☐ Any 'problem' markets
☐ City/suburban/rural

Seasonality/Other Timing Factors: Concentration/Priorities

Seasonal or special time periods should be specified:

☐ Season and/or quarter (lead or coincide)
☐ Promotion periods
☐ Holiday or vacation periods/weather (if relevant)
☐ Day of week/time of day (if these factors are not critical, they should be left for the strategy or tactics section)

Reach/Frequency/Continuity: Priorities/Goals

It is essential to state (and rationalise) at least the order of priority for these three interrelated dimensions of reach, frequency and continuity.

☐ It is preferable to establish *specific goals* for each dimension, stated either as minimum levels or acceptable ranges.

☐ Priorities/goals are based on both *communications principles* and the *brand specific communication needs.* You assess the brand's needs from the marketing inputs – especially the source of business, role of advertising, awareness/attitudes, seasonal concentration, competitive considerations and any other implications from the brief.

☐ Reach/frequency/continuity objectives are, of course, also governed by the budget, so usually you must work up some rough alternatives before setting goals. You cannot set them in a vacuum – they must reflect a proper balancing of brand needs in relation to resources.

☐ *Effective* reach and frequency goals (eg at least 60% reached three or more times) are more meaningful because they recognise the need for some minimum level of message repetition to achieve effective communication for a given campaign.

☐ The *time frame* for these goals must be specified, for example average four weeks, purchase cycle, flight period, sales period, quarter or year. (*Note*: Yearly goals are usually not meaningful because of memory decay over such a long period.)

Creative requirements

Specific creative requirements must be specified:

☐ Relevant *communications characteristics* (intrusiveness, demonstrations, etc) and *environment/qualitative characteristics* (prestige, believability, etc)
☐ Specific *creative units*

Special needs or constraints

These include a variety of possible objectives. They do not necessarily apply to every plan, but in most plans one or more of the following points will be relevant:

☐ Trial-inducement – couponing, sampling
☐ Support for other consumer promotions
☐ Competition – objective of matching or exceeding competitive efforts
☐ Testing – different media, weight levels, etc
☐ Merchandisability to sales force, trade, franchisees, employees, stockholders, etc
☐ Distribution considerations – extra weight to push, or reduced weight where thin
☐ Flexibility regarding lead times and cancellation
☐ Corporate considerations – policy that could impact on any aspect of media planning or usage
☐ Priorities in case of budget increase or decrease – to allow for orderly replanning on short notice.

☐ Basic media considerations

There are four basic dimensions of media exposure, as is shown below:

IMPACT	REACH
FREQUENCY	CONTINUITY

An advertisement has to have *impact* when it is exposed, otherwise it cannot perform. Impact can be obtained through creativitiy, but it can also be obtained through taking more impactful media space units, for example:

☐ a full page instead of a half page
☐ colour instead of black and white
☐ a 60-second commercial instead of a 30-second commercial.

Impactful media space units are generally more expensive.

Media schedules providing high *reach* (that is exposure of the advertisements to a high proportion of the target audience) are generally more expensive than schedules providing low reach.

The greater the required *frequency* of exposure of the advertising, the greater the budget required.

Advertising exposure with *continuity* costs more than intermittent exposure.

Thus it is seen that the four basic dimensions of media exposure cost a substantial amount of money to achieve, and they all compete for a share of the advertising budget. Invariably, the budget is not large enough to optimise each of these four considerations. The skill of media planning is to achieve the *best balance* of the four dimensions in relation to campaign objectives.

For example, if a new model of a medium-priced car is being launched nationally, then the importance given to the *impact* and *reach* might be greater than the other two factors, as illustrated:

IMPACT	REACH
FREQUENCY	CONTINUITY

Under other circumstances, high *frequency* of exposure with *continuity* might be more essential. This could apply, for example, to an analgesic that has a selective target market.

☐ Media strategy

The media plan is the 'contact point' through which advertising strategies/executions are finally impacted against the potential consumers. Media vehicles and their mix, scheduling patterns and impact/weight levels are part of the complex strategy puzzle.

Each medium brings its own intrinsic attributes to the media plan. Each has certain attributes relative to its own communication values, its comparative values to other media, and its usefulness in various strategic situations.

Broad definition: how objectives will be accomplished

The media stratgegy spells out in broad terms *how* the objectives will be accomplished. It defines and provides the rationale for the recommended types of media (eg radio, TV, newspapers, magazines, cinema, outdoor, direct mail, etc) and for other strategic considerations (timing, scheduling, etc).

Note that the strategy is *not* the same as the tactical plan (specific vehicles and schedules, exact rands, flow chart, etc). Also, the strategy is *not* simply a reiteration of the objectives in different or expanded language.

Developing strategy requires the valuation of alternatives

Determining strategy is essentially a matter of evaluating the effectiveness of different media types and mixes in achieving the objectives within the budget.

For most brands, several different possibilities usually offer enough potential to warrant serious consideration. Therefore, determining the *best* strategy normally requires developing some alternatives to evaluate which one achieves the objectives *most effectively*. Some guidelines for working out alternatives are given below.

The goal is to come up with some *imaginative* alternatives, different from those of the current year. This is not creativity for creativity's sake, not merely irrelevant gimmickry, but innovation which contributes towards meeting the objectives more effectively.

For small budget brands it may be unnecessary to analyse alternatives if the objectives and/or budget clearly point to only one strategy, ruling out realistic alternatives.

Courtesy: RH Griffin

Little evaluation of alternative strategies may be required where historically successful approaches or client dictates make this academic (but always remember that circumstances can change). This historical success *should be indicated* as part of the rationale for the recommended strategy.

When alternative strategies are devised and evaluated, the key aim is to:

☐ consider all reasonable options (let your imagination roam at this stage – be creative and do not block out interesting possibilities prematurely)

☐ progressively eliminate, through reasoning and analysis, those with deficiencies in meeting the objectives

☐ focus on the one strategy which appears to achieve the objectives in the best manner.

Examination of alternatives does not end here. In the tactical stage there will probably have to be some alternative variations within that strategy in order to settle on the best specific plan.

Generally, the strategy statements and rationale should include the following points:

☐ Total mix and allocation by medium
  – A description of the total media mix, including a brief summary explanation of the reasons why each type is recommended and how each contributes to achieving the objectives
  – A summary explanation of the approximate allocation (or emphasis) by medium normally with a reference to this allocation meeting the objectives more effectively than the alternatives examined

☐ Television and/or radio
  – Commercial length(s)
  – Daypart mix – in some cases this may require so much detailed analysis that it becomes a tactical issue. Usually, however, it can be determined at the strategy level, at least, which dayparts will be used and probably also the primary/secondary emphasis in each
  – Other relevant considerations such as programme types, sponsorships, etc

☐ Magazines
  – Indicate whether national, regional, or local (and general description of regional/local market list)
  – Space unit(s)
  – Types of magazine (eg dual audience/women's/men's, monthly/weekly) – as with broadcast dayparts this is sometimes a tactical question, but usually it can be established strategically, at least the broad types and some indication of emphasis
  – Other considerations, such as specific types of editorial content (eg news, women's service, financial, sports, etc), editorial environment/mood, lifestyle, orientation, etc

☐ Newspapers and all other media types
  – General description of market list
  – Space unit(s)
  – Any other relevant strategic considerations along the lines of the previous examples for TV, radio and magazines

☐ Geographic allocation strategy
  – This may be included as part of the individual media elements above. Otherwise it is essential to include a section with a rationale for the mix of national versus local media. This usually requires the analysis of media weight delivery in relation to sales potential

☐ Seasonal scheduling strategies
  – Extent of concentration by season quarter or other relevant selling period
  – Any unique time of day, day of week, or other timing factors that are important strategically
  – Scheduling in terms of flighting or pulsing (burst) versus continuous advertising (drip). Since this also relates to reach/frequency/continuity objectives, it is necessary to rationalise the scheduling in terms of how it meets these objectives

☐ Other
  – Any other considerations that should be specified because they are strategies (as opposed to tactics) for accomplishing the media objectives

☐ Media weighting

When a media plan is constructed there are often elements that require comparative analysis yet represent major differentials in communication power due to their inherent strengths and weaknesses ('apples vs oranges'). In order to evaluate these media elements/options properly it often becomes necessary to apply weights to determine relative values more accurately. A number of the more common weighting techniques/concepts are dealt with below:

Creative impact weights GRPs (gross rating points)/impressions delivered by one medium may not be considered equivalent to another due to the individual communication properties of the vehicle (eg the intrusiveness/demonstrability of TV, the imaginative, creative values of radio, the longer time involvement with a magazine advertisement, etc). However, for a complete evaluation it is necessary to weigh the creative values of a GRP in medium 'A' versus 'B' or 'C'.

There are no magic numbers for what these communication relationships should be. The process is one of *judgement*, judgement representing cumulative client-account-media-creative group involvement and input regarding the specific creative objectives, specific executional requirements and specific media properties required to achieve those objectives optimally.

The following is an example. Assuming that you have a *demonstration* commercial where *visualisation* is critical, the impact values could be established with television as the optimal creative execution (1,00 weight). It is then judged that *two* print exposures would be required to be equivalent to a single TV exposure – thus print is 'impact valued' at 0,50 weight. Because of its lack of visualisation for the demonstration, it could be judged that three exposures would be equivalent to one TV exposure – a 0,33 weight. Again, these are *judgemental* weights for the *specific* creative execution for the specific *brand* – *not* industry or researched based averages

Creative impact value (example)
Television 1,00
Magazines 0,50
Radio 0,33

Once the creative impact value is assigned then the numerical process can be implemented to provide equivalent bases of information for the analysis ('apples versus apples').

'Eyes-on' adjustments

These measurements are designed to reflect *commercial/advertisement* audience delivery as opposed to *media vehicle* audience delivery more closely.

☐ Television 'eyes-on' – viewers with their eyes on the set when the commercial is running
☐ Print 'eyes-on' – readers with their eyes on the page which is carrying the advertisement

This type of weighting is currently not practical in South Africa due to the absence of information which *is* available in the USA, for example where Burke Market Research establishes the percentage of women exposed to an average commercial in relation to the audience viewing the programme (examples are 60% during daytime and 68% during prime time). For print, research studies in the USA indicate an average 85% 'pages turned' factor.

Television daypart effectiveness adjustment factors

These factors recognise the effect of variables such as programme environment, viewing environment and commercial clutter upon the target audience. While studies of attention level or commercial recall (only *indirect* measures of effectiveness) have not yielded uniform results, they do indicate a variance in scores by daypart.

☐ Media plan format

The style and presentation of a media plan can vary enormously, depending on the tastes, techniques and preferences of both originator and recipient.

A comprehensive media plan would normally include the following:

☐ A review of objectives and parameters
☐ An analysis of competitive advertising activity
☐ A consideration of media types in relation to the first two items
☐ Media strategy
☐ A recommended media plan
☐ Detailed media schedules with sizes, costs and timing
☐ Cost summaries
☐ Plan performance – details of audience delivery by medium and for all media combined (media mix).

☐ References

Allt, B. 1985 *Admap*, July/August: 382, 386.

Television in South Africa

Coen Gous, Retha Vermeulen
and Marinda van Niekerk

Introduction 162

Reasons for the use of television as an
advertising medium 165

Choice of medium 171

How to use television 172

The future 181

Conclusion 181

☐ Introduction

Can there be another medium! Clearly and undisputedly, television is the key communication development of our era and the most influential and powerful advertising medium in the world.

As a means of communication, television has it all – sight, movement, sound, and colour – conveying a total impression simultaneously to millions of people. The potential of such an audio-visual medium is almost limitless. Information, entertainment and education all have a place in television, a medium which is still expanding through new services and technology; new ways of advertising and of informing the viewer of new developments, products and services; and advanced means of broadcasting, of reaching the consumer, entertaining and educating him about local and global issues in the friendly and intimate atmosphere of his own home. All this makes up a package that is unchallenged by any other advertising medium, and in today's world it is hard to do without.

To think that commercial television was introduced to South Africa as recently as 1978! Yet only eight years later it accounts for no less than 29% of all advertising expenditure. And it is still a growing medium!

Television ownership, illustrated in figures 6.6 and 6.7, reflects its mass market penetration most accurately.

Figure 6.6
Television
ownership of
Whites and
Coloureds

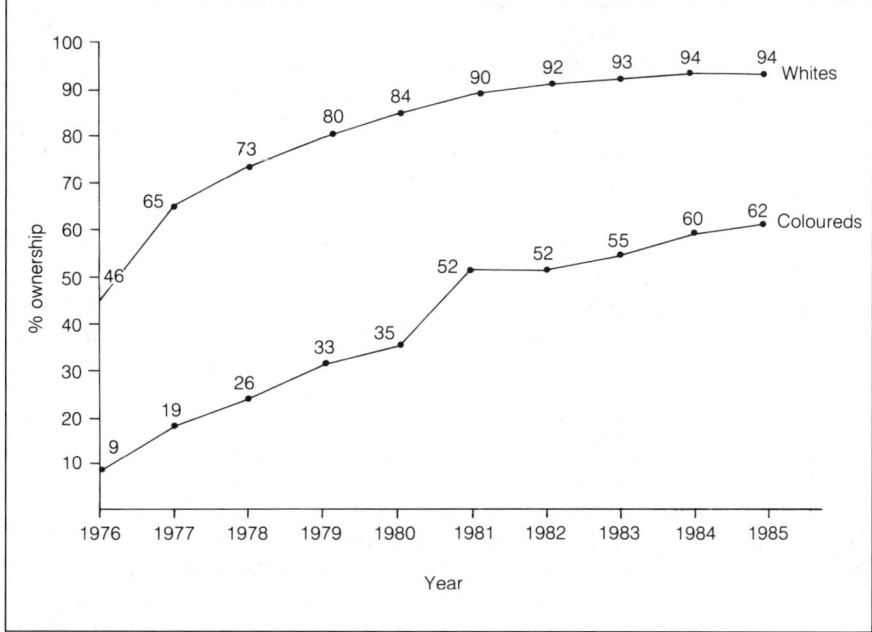

Source: AMPS (1976-1985)

Figure 6.7
Television
ownership of
Asians and Blacks

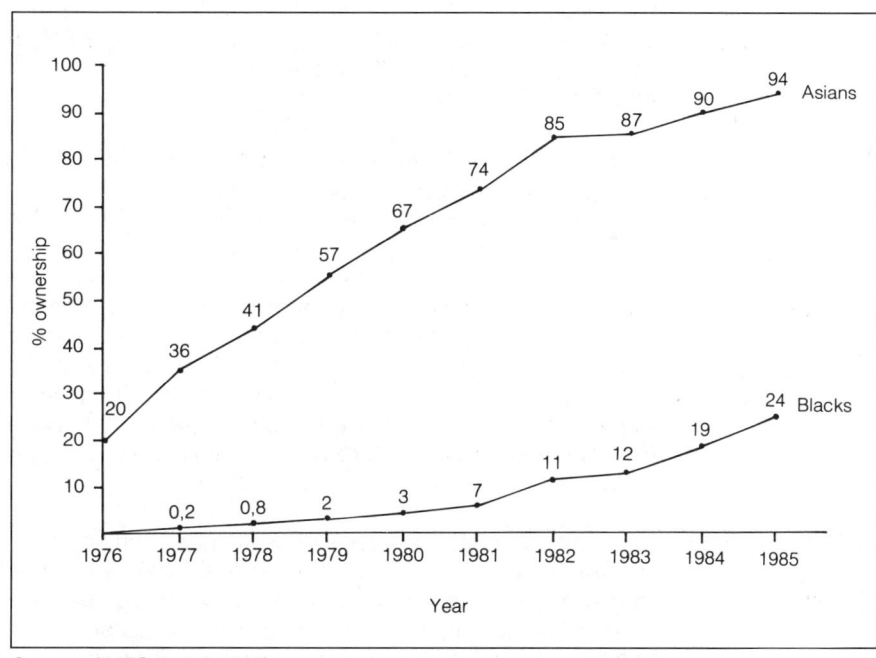

Source: AMPS (1976-1985)

Since South Africans first experienced the pleasure of watching television back in 1976 with the introduction of TV1, several other television services have been introduced. These include TV2 and TV3 (1982), aimed at the Black population, Bop TV, an independent service, and TV4 (March 1985). The first 'Pay TV' or subscription television service, M-NET, recently commenced transmission. Within ten years South Africa has been enriched by no less than six television stations, no doubt mainly because it has proved to be so successful as an advertising medium.

A brief description of the television stations in South Africa follows:

TV1

TV1 is the oldest, and still the biggest, television station. Broadcasting in English and Afrikaans, this station attracts a daily audience of 4,9 million viewers of all races, although it caters mainly for Whites, Coloureds and Asians. At the moment it is also the major television service for advertising, with expenditure higher than that of all the other stations combined. Programmes range from mass entertainment to educational, cultural, magazine and programmes catering for minority interest.

Breakfast television

The SABC introduced 'Breakfast television' on the channel of TV1 on 1 October 1986. Breakfast television is broadcast between 06h00-08h00 on Mondays to Fridays, and between 07h00 and 09h00 on Saturdays. There is a wide range of programmes on this station, including regular news bulletins, programmes aimed specifically at children, programmes for farmers, programmes for women, and even programmes for the fitness conscious.

TV2 and TV3

Like TV1, TV2 and TV3 have a full range of programmes appealing to a wide black audience in South Africa and broadcast in five major black languages. The two services are, however, transmitted to parts of South Africa only – mainly cities and major towns. TV2 is aimed at Zulu and Xhosa viewers and TV3 at Sotho and Tswana viewers.

TV4

Like TV1, TV2 and TV3, TV4 belongs to the SABC and provides mass appeal entertainment and sport programmes for South Africans of all races. In contrast to other SABC television stations, on TV4 advertising is flighted during natural programme breaks.

Bop TV

This station was the first independent television station in South Africa, broadcasting from Mmabatho in Bophuthatswana. Although targeted primarily at citizens of Bophuthatswana, it covers all Blacks living in Soweto, Dobsonville and Kagiso as well, whilst Whites living in the immediate vicinity of the SABC transmitters in Auckland Park, Johannesburg can also pick up the signal. Programmes on Bop TV are predominantly entertaining in character, and the station has a format very similar to that of TV4.

M-Net

This subscriber television service commenced transmitting in October 1986 using the SABC transmitters in Johannesburg to broadcast to viewers in the PWV area. Initially, the service will be available free of charge between 17h00 and 19h00, after which viewers will need a decoder to unscramble the signal. A subscription fee will be payable on a monthly basis. The emphasis of this service is on entertainment, and programmes are of a similar nature to programmes on TV4 and Bop TV.

☐ Reasons for the use of television as an advertising medium

Advertising time on television is being purchased for a multitude of reasons ranging from the very extreme of getting pure coverage of people to the opposite where an advertiser selects the medium for its emotional appeal. By and large, however, the majority of advertisers look at the qualitative aspects inherent in television and at the 'number' advantages of the medium, that is the quantitative aspects.

Qualitative aspects

On the commercial front the power of television has been put to use in many different ways. Television is more than a salesman.

Television educates

Television is a perfect demonstration medium. The advertiser has the opportunity to demonstrate the attributes of his product due to television's own attributes of sight, sound, movement and colour. Television is also the ideal medium to launch a new product or service, to introduce the consumer to it and to 'teach' the viewer about its benefits and uses.

Television informs

Television can make the viewer aware of the products and services available on the market and how these can contribute to his own pleasures, conveniences, tastes and actions.

Personal appeal

Due to television's unique characteristics of addressing the senses of sight and sound, the advertiser is able not only to *show* his product, but also to *talk about it* in his own creative way.

Television evokes emotion

The advertiser can make his audience laugh or cry, both of which can contribute to a product's success.

Television creates desires

By appealing to the senses of sight and sound, the advertiser can use the audiovisual characteristics of television to their full advantage. Such an appeal creates that ultimate desire for a product (like a sports car or a hi-fi set).

Television evokes hunger and thirst

No other medium can make food or soft drinks more appealing than an audiovisual medium like television.

Television makes products interesting

Uninteresting products such as insurance policies, washing powder and toilet paper can be made interesting by television advertising.

Television is believable

Research has shown that more people believe what they hear and see on television than is the case for any other medium because television is a non-static medium.

COPY

SASWITCH TV COMMERCIAL 28-04-1987

CLIENT : SASWITCH (PTY) LTD
ITEM   : 30 SEC COMMERCIAL
MEDIA : TV1, TV4, Breakfast TV

PRODUCT : UNITED/VOLKSKAS LAUNCH
KEY NO   : SWE/30/005/E/T

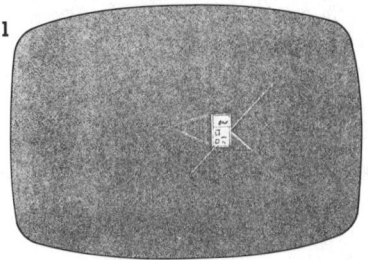

1

Volkskas ATM zooms
from infinity and
settles on right
side of frame

2

Volkskas logo pans
from outside of picture
to settle at top
of frame

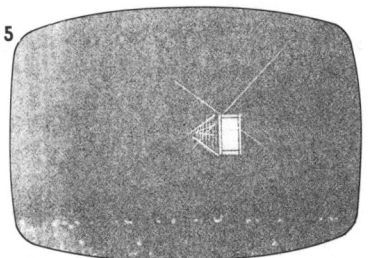

5

United ATM zooms
from infinity and
settles on right
side of frame

6

United logo pans
from outside of picture
to settle at top
of frame

9

Participating ATM cards
"Clock" wipe onto screen

MV: Throughout South
    Africa, you can now

10

Volkskas & United cards
fly in to take their
place in the circle
withdraw cash and check
your balance – at 2000
ATM's displaying the
SASWITCH Symbol

MV: Look for this symbol
    on your nearest ATM

Courtesy: SASWITCH. Launching the linking up of Volkskas and United with SASWITCH. Concept by Ludi Koekemoer

3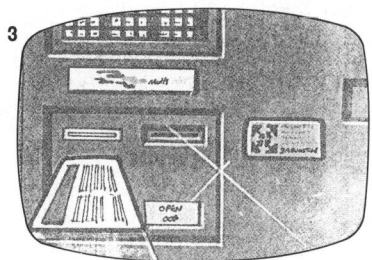

ATM card flys in upside-
down and hovers in front
of slot

4

Screen blacks out and words
appear one at a time:
"290 Volkskas ATM's join SASWITCH"

7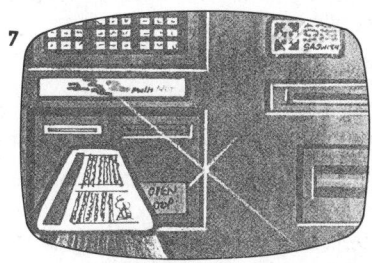

SASWITCH logo pans from
outside of TV area to
settle in its position
on the ATM

ATM card flys in upside-
down and hovers in front
of slot

8

Screen blacks out and words
appear one at a time:
"380 United ATM's join SASWITCH"

11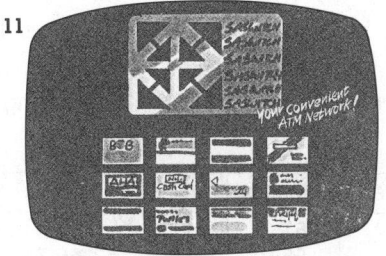

The copy fades, the slogan
"Your Convenient ATM Network"
and ALL cards reappear

MV: SASWITCH – Your
convenient ATM
network

12

Cards fade into black, logo
moves higher up and words appear

"SASWITCH HOURS" 24 hours per day
7 days per week

MV: The sun never sets
on SASWITCH

Interpersonal relationship with the viewer

Because of the intensity of interest when someone is watching television, the advertiser has the viewer's undivided attention, which improves the likelihood of getting his message across.

Television can create immediacy

People can react to the message seconds after seeing the commercial.

Viewers are in a relaxed frame of mind

Advertising tends to have a higher impact when the consumer is in a relaxed frame of mind, like when he is watching television in the friendly and intimate atmosphere of his home.

Television has a captive audience

The viewer sits in front of the TV set and wants to be entertained. Therefore, he is more receptive to an advertisement.

Embarrassing products can be made more acceptable

Products such as deodorants, underwear, toilet paper, etc, which are difficult to promote in print media or radio advertising, can be made more acceptable or even appealing through the use of humour or other creative methods.

The above are but a few of the qualitative factors which make television a successful advertising medium. Generally speaking, due to television's unique qualities all of the above create the one element essential to any advertising campaign – IMPACT!

Quantitative aspects

No advertising medium, whatever its impact, will be successful or used by the advertiser unless it reaches the right number of the right people the right number of times and is affordable and economical.

Television provides coverage

Based on AMPS reach studies, television is watched by 6 646 000 adults (16 years of age and older) of all races daily. This figure can be broken down as shown in table 6.2.

Table 6.2
Daily coverage of television by race

Race	% of race group
Whites	81,4
Coloureds	57,3
Asians	77,0
Blacks	18,6

Source: AMPS 1985

These figures, especially for Whites, compare favourably with other advertising media (see table 6.3).

Table 6.3
% penetration of different media amongst adults

	Whites	Coloureds	Asians	Blacks
TV (daily)	81,4	57,3	77,0	18,6
Radio (daily)	83,6	58,9	76,0	62,7
Daily newspapers	54,3	34,5	59,1	13,9
Weekend newspapers	76,0	54,0	73,7	29,5
All consumer magazines	93,6	54,6	69,0	38,2
Cinema (last 7 days)	9,9	3,6	3,9	3,6

Source: AMPS 1985

The average daily penetration of television has increased substantially since television was first introduced in 1976 (see figure 6.8).

Figure 6.8 Average daily viewership — all TV

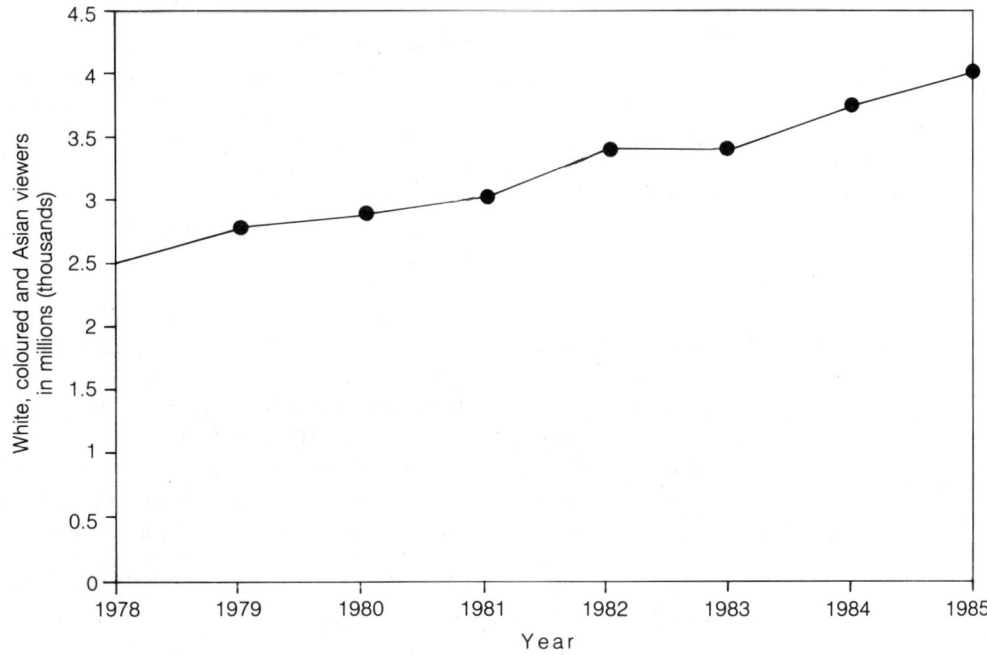

Source: AMPS 1978-1985

The high viewership of television is one of the most important reasons for television time being in such high demand with advertisers today.

Television can provide frequency

Due to the relatively high cost of advertising spots on television, it is often suggested that television cannot provide an important consideration in the selection of media, namely the frequency of advertising exposure. This is a very debatable point, but a high enough frequency will depend ultimately on various other factors, for example the size of the advertising budget, the length of the commercial, the television stations selected, the time of day used (advertising spot cost varies depending on time of day), the duration of the advertising campaign, the time of the year (spots bought on SABC stations for two months prior to Christmas are more expensive), the target market, etc.

Any limitations that television holds for the advertiser as far as frequency is concerned, however, might be outweighed by the impact that the medium provides. A frequency of, say, four (ie the average viewer will see the advertisement four times) might be considered suitable on television simply due to its impact, whilst the same frequency on radio or in newspapers might be considered to be too low.

Ultimately, the choice is the advertiser's. He will have to decide whether a frequency of four, as in our example, will be enough to reach the objectives of his campaign. However, it is significant that the majority of advertisers in South Africa regard a relatively low frequency on television to be of better value than a much higher frequency on most other media.

Television is cost efficient

Most advertisers perceive television to be on the expensive side. However, as is the case with the frequency issue, the question whether television is costly is a highly subjective one which depends on other factors like station to advertise on, time of day, length of commercial, etc. On average it costs the advertiser approximately 0,5 cents per viewer on TV1, 0,3 cents on TV2 and TV3, and 0,6 cents on TV4. Thus, it costs around R3 to reach 1 000 people, which compares favourably with magazine and newspaper advertising considering the tremendous impact of television.

Target marketing with television

Many advertisers claim that under the existing system of buying television spots it is difficult to be selective in target segmentation. This is because television is a mass medium. However, researchers and students studying viewership patterns and profiles on different stations, different days and different time periods would agree that target selectivity is possible, although it can not be as specific as it is on radio or in magazines. Nevertheless, the strategic use of television can enable the advertiser to use the medium effectively to pinpoint certain broad target segments, for example children in the afternoon on TV1, males on the sport channels, younger adults on TV4, etc. It is believed that the ultimate in target selectivity – that is programme sponsorship or selection where the advertiser has the opportunity to purchase time on a specific programme – might not be too far off. In fact, this flexibility in the system might be introduced by the SABC as early as 1987.

Current demographic viewership profiles for each race group and station can be seen in table 6.4

Table 6.4
Profiles of TV1
and TV4 viewers

	Whites			Coloureds		
	Population profile	TV1 profile	TV4 profile	Population profile	TV1 profile	TV4 profile
Male	49,6	48,2	47,9	48,6	45,3	45,2
Female	50,4	51,8	52,1	51,4	54,7	54,8
Housewife	45,8	47,1	47,3	37,3	37,3	36,5
English	41,5	39,2	50,0	12,6	84,1	75,0
Afrikaans	58,5	60,8	50,0	87,4	15,9	25,0
16-24	21,8	18,9	26,9	34,5	36,9	37,7
25-34	23,1	22,9	23,7	25,1	25,0	24,5
35-49	26,2	26,8	26,5	22,9	22,1	22,4
50 + ...	28,9	31,4	22,9	17,5	16,0	15,4
Income A/B ...	40,8	41,0	39,6	49,1	62,2	75,1
Income C	50,6	51,7	54,1	41,4	34,3	23,3
Income D	8,6	7,3	6,3	9,5	3,5	1,6

Source: AMPS 1985

Table 6.4:
Profiles of TV1
and TV4 viewers
(continued)

	Asians			Blacks		
	Population profile	TV1 profile	TV4 profile	Population profile	TV2/3 profile	Bop TV profile
Male	49,4	49,6	46,9	58,7	59,9	61,4
Female	50,6	50,4	53,1	41,3	40,1	38,6
Housewife	32,8	32,2	33,8	33,0	33,0	31,7
16-24	30,0	27,7	32,8	30,1	30,0	28,4
25-34	28,0	27,1	26,8	28,8	29,2	32,8
35-49	25,9	26,2	25,2	25,5	27,6	20,7
50+	16,1	19,0	15,2	15,6	13,2	18,1
Income A/B ...	34,3	34,3	33,3	21,2	29,5	34,1
Income C	53,1	52,9	53,9	34,7	37,6	38,7
Income D	12,6	12,8	12,8	44,2	32,9	27,2

Source: AMPS 1985

☐ Choice of medium

When an advertiser wishes to advertise his product he is faced with a choice of media, of which television is one. Medium choice is determined primarily by:

☐ The type of product – The product can affect the decision to advertise in certain media. Consumer goods of an intimate nature may not be suitable for mass advertising, and certain products are not allowed to be advertised on TV, for example cigarettes.

☐ The potential market – The potential market for certain products may not warrant specific advertising, for example cattle feed in a children's time channel on television.

☐ The extent and type of distribution system – There is no point in advertising a product which cannot be acquired by the receiver of the advertised message. For instance, if you sell a product that is available only in Bloemfontein, it might not be economical to use TV1, a national station.

☐ The objective of the campaign – This determines the type and extent of use of media, for example consumer goods for mass consumption are effectively placed in media with access to masses, of which television is a good example.

☐ The type of message – Where the product is sold on the strength of a certain appeal, like the colour and texture of food products, television may be more suitable than other media.

☐ The budget available – The budget may preclude the possibility of using certain media even if these would be best. Television is a relatively expensive medium to use and small companies do not always have the financial means to use the medium to its full value.

☐ Competitive advertising – The extent and type of advertising of competitors can influence the choice of medium. If a competitor uses television, it is likely that you would also consider it.

☐ The characteristics of the medium – These are area coverage (television could be national TV1 or regional Bop TV), audience reached (only those who own or have access to a TV set will be reached), and cost efficiency (cost per person).

☐ How to use television

The successful commercial

To convince consumers to buy your product, the commercial should be effective. Even more so with television, as you throw away a lot of money if it fails. A successful commercial should contain:

☐ a persuasive idea, which can be logical or emotional. The commercial should be an honest approach to a problem, and involve the viewer's mind and emotions;

☐ interest, which makes the commercial memorable and draws attention to the TV set. There must be something, either visual or audio, that draws the viewer's attention and makes him want to see what the commercial is all about;

☐ a simple message. If the message becomes too long and complicated the product is forgotten by the viewer, or he simply switches off.

☐ a message associated with the product. People often remember a commercial, but do not know what product it advertised.

The production of commercials

There are a number of production houses which specialise in producing good commercials. The SABC has rules on television advertising, which include the operational and technical requirements for commercials. Headings which appear are:

Film guages

These are standards for the international exchange of monochrome and colour television programmes on film.

☐ 16 to 35 mm (Com-opt)
☐ 16 to 35 mm (Com-mag)
☐ 16 to 35 mm (Sep-mag)

Guidelines for video tape

Inasmuch as a producer is inevitably viewing his work on a television monitor, such impairments as there may be due to system defects should be apparent and therefore correctable. The remarks about 'Safe Areas' apply and the producer should guard against excessive multi-generation work.

It should be borne in mind that the SABC will lay off a tape commercial onto 50,80 mm (2 inch) cassette. It is important, therefore, that the picture and sound quality of the commercial submitted should not be close to the limit of acceptability due to excessive dubbing.

Furthermore, large areas of saturated colour in the scene (particularly red) should be avoided to minimise the prevalence of head-banding.

Frame rate

All film will be transmitted at 25 frames per second. It is strongly recommended that all film produced for television be made at 25 frames per second.

Film leader and tail

All filmed commercials should be supplied with a minimum of 50 frames of black mask spacing joined to the start, preferably preceded by the SABC standard leader. (This is obtainable at all major film laboratories, but in case of difficulty details may be obtained from the SABC.) All filmed commercials should carry a sufficient tail at the end to protect the film.

Freeze frames

In order to facilitiate satisfactory transfer and packaging, a minimum of five seconds 'frozen action' is required after the full duration of the commercial.

Automatic volume compression

Automatic volume compression should, where used, be restricted to 6 dB of compression, and the onset of compression should be not less than 8 dB below what would be the overload point of the recording system if compression was not used.

The use of compression purely in order to obtain a louder sound track is decreased and will in any event result either in the level being reduced on transmission, with consequent degradation of quality, or even, in extreme cases, in rejection of the commercial.

Advertising standards

Believability is the most important element of television advertising. Unless TV advertising is entirely believable, its power to persuade and to sell will soon evaporate. Believability stems from the elimination of anything capable of being misleading or even actively confusing, unintentional though this may be. If only a few commercials do not deserve belief, doubt will be cast on all the other advertisements. Believability is in the interests of the advertiser, the medium and the public.

How can commercials be imaginative, memorable, dramatic, hard-hitting, competitive, daring and persuasive – in 60 seconds or less – and still be believable? Good basic rules are necessary. The acceptance standard in South Africa is high and probably a little more conservative than in most other countries, but as a public Corporation with a social conscience, the SABC reflects the status quo.

The preamble to the SABC's Advertising Code reads as follows (see chapter 2):

☐ All advertisements should be legal, honest, truthful and decent.
☐ All advertisements should be prepared with a sense of responsibility to the consumer.
☐ All advertisements should conform to the principles of fair competition in business.
☐ No advertisement should bring advertising into disrepute or reduce confidence in advertising as a service to industry and to the public.

The Acceptance Departments of the SABC assist advertisers with copy clearance and provide approval of commercials without delay. The acceptance procedures and standards applied by the TV1, TV2, TV3 and TV4 Acceptance Departments are identical, with the exception of certain language usage and communication requirements peculiar to TV2 and TV3.

An advisory service unit is designed to assist advertisers and agencies during the early stages of planning commercials to be flighted on TV2 and TV3. Expert advice is available on matters of custom and correct language usage. Advertisers who have to translate English or Afrikaans copy into the vernacular can do so with the help of TV2 and TV3 staff.

Bop TV applies procedures identical to those used by the SABC for accepting commercials.

1 Let me tell you about the fuel-injected Volksie Bus,

2 and how it helped me climb the Tierkloof Pas.

5 So there and then I took my braces,

6 and hitched them to this powerful new Bus and said you can tow me up the Tierkloof Pas.

9 As I sat eating Sannie's melktert, in burst the traffic cop, his name Oom Gert.
He said Sannie I've just seen a bike and a bus going a hundred miles an hour up the Tierkloof Pas.

10 And the madman on the bike make no mistake nogal ringing his bell to overtake.

3 I was on my way to Sannie van der Spuy, the melktert queen in this town Volstruis.

4 I'd been pushing my bike up the pass for hours. I was hot and sweaty and my mood was sour.
When a fuel-injected Bus pulls up to give me a ride, so I said this time I'm not getting inside.
I saw disappointment on the kids little faces.

7 Well he put his foot down and we soon reached the top and I rang my bell for the Bus to stop.

8 Then we waved goodbye and I was on my way freewheeling down to Sannie van der Spuy.

11 VO: The new fuel-injected Volksie Bus. It sings up mountain passes.

Ogilvy & Mather

Rightford Searle-Tripp & Makin

Courtesy: Volkswagen and Ogilvy Mather RST & M. An example of an enjoyable and successful commercial

**Purchase of
TV time**

Time channels

The format changes in force since September 1986 have assisted in the creation of shorter channels, effective from January 1987.

☐ Advertising channels: TV1
  14h00-18h00 (Saturday only)
  15h30-16h30 (Friday only)
  16h00-16h30 (Monday to Thursday)
  16h30-18h00 (Monday to Friday)
  18h00-19h00 (Monday to Saturday)
  19h00-20h00 (Monday to Saturday)
  20h00-20h30 (Saturday only)
  20h00-21h00 (Monday to Friday)
  20h30-21h30 (Saturday only)
  21h00-22h00 (Monday to Friday)
  21h30-close (Saturday only)
  22h00-close (Monday to Friday)

☐ Advertising channels: TV2/TV3
  15h00-18h00 (Sunday only)
  19h00-21h00 (Monday to Sunday)
  16h00-17h00 (Saturday only)
  17h00-17h30 (Friday only)
  17h30-18h00 (Monday to Friday)

☐ Advertising channels: TV4
  17h00-19h00 (Saturday only)
  18h00-19h00 (Monday to Friday and Sunday)
  21h00-close (Monday to Sunday)

Placement of advertisements

Since 1986 advertising breaks in programmes have been allowed. There are four breaks per hour, with advertising limited to two minutes per break.

Buying spots in specific programmes is also a reality. Preferred spots bought in this way will rotate in a particular programme only.

1987 rate structure

The *grid rate structure* (see table 6.5) has been designed to cover TV1, TV2/TV3 and TV4 rates and should cover every advertising eventuality in 1987. The grid is segmented into a green and red period with the following information:

☐ Green period (roughly first two weeks of a month)
  – choice of day
  – specified programme

☐ Red period (roughly last two weeks of a month)
  – choice of day
  – specified programme.

The *buying calendar* (see table 6.6) indicates the exact green and red periods and is to be used in conjunction with the grid rate structure.

Rates are no longer locked into daily channels. *The audience size determines the rate of the individual channel or programme* (see table 6.7).

Four advertising periods per year

The year is to be divided into four quarters, with the quarterly breakdown as follows:

☐ January – March
☐ April   – June
☐ July   – September
☐ October – December

Rates are announced three months in advance of the start of each quarter.

Early booking bonus

An early booking bonus has been introduced from 1987 and will work as follows:

To be in the *running* for the bonus, applications must be with the SABC on the eighth of the month. Signed contracts in the SABC's possession eight weeks *before* the commencement of the allocated month will qualify for a 10% free advertising bonus. Advertising space can be offset against the accrued bonusses at any time.

Rates

A total of seven rate cards will be issued annually as follows:

☐ First quarter
- Period 1987-01-01 – 1987-02-15
- Period 1987-02-16 – 1987-03-31
☐ Second quarter
- Period 1987-04-01 – 1987-06-30
☐ Third quarter
- Period 1987-07-01 – 1987-09-30
☐ Fourth quarter
- Period 1987-10-01 – 1987-10-17
- Period 1987-10-18 – 1987-12-19
- Period 1987-12-20 – 1987-12-31

The 1987 rate cards have been developed along projected supply and demand lines, but taking audience sizes into consideration.

The amount of advertising time available on TV1, TV2/TV3 and TV4 is 8% of normal transmission hours. Commercial content flighted during special transmission (ie tennis, rugby, etc) will be deemed to be over and above this limitation.

Commercials in multiples of five seconds, from five up to 60 seconds will normally be acceptable, with requests for spots of longer duration being dependent on availability.

For 1987, advertising rates will *remain* pro rata.

Advertising rates for the independent station M-Net in its 'open time' of 17h00-19h00 for the period 1st October 1986 to 31st March 1987 are as follows (based on a 30-second spot):

☐ 17h00-18h00   R1 260
☐ 18h00-19h00   R2 490

Table 6.5
Grid rate structure
(1987)

Tariff no	Green weeks		Red weeks	
	Specified day	Specified programme	Specified day	Specified programme
	R	R	R	R
T 1	570	630	600	660
T 2	1 140	1 260	1 200	1 320
T 3	1 710	1 890	1 800	1 980
T 4	2 280	2 520	2 400	2 640
T 5	2 850	3 150	3 000	3 300
T 6	3 420	3 780	3 600	3 960
T 7	3 990	4 410	4 200	4 620
T 8	4 560	5 040	4 800	5 280
T 9	5 130	5 670	5 400	5 940
T10	5 700	6 300	6 000	6 600
T11	6 270	6 930	6 600	7 260
T12	6 840	7 560	7 200	7 920
T13	7 410	8 190	7 800	8 580
T14	7 980	8 820	8 400	9 240
T15	8 550	9 450	9 000	9 900
T16	9 690	10 710	10 200	11 220
T17	10 830	11 970	11 400	12 540
T18	11 970	13 230	12 600	13 860
T19	13 680	15 120	14 400	15 840
T20	15 390	17 010	16 200	17 820
T21	17 100	18 900	18 000	19 800
T22	18 810	20 790	19 800	21 780
T23	20 520	22 680	21 600	23 760
T24	22 230	24 570	23 400	25 740
T25	24 510	27 090	25 800	28 380

NB:
(a) Above rates based on 30 second spot length – other durations pro-rata.
(b) Refer to Rate Chart & Buying Calendar to establish specific rates for specific days, or programmes. Green weeks and red weeks are colour-coded on the Buying Calendar.

☐ Green weeks
☐ Red weeks

Table 6.6
TV buying
calendar (1987)

January

M	T	W	T	F	S	S
		1	2	3	4	
5	6	7	8	9	10	11
12	13	14	15	16	17	18
19	20	21	22	23	24	25
26	27	28	29	30	31	

February

M	T	W	T	F	S	S
						1
2	3	4	5	6	7	8
9	10	11	12	13	14	15
16	17	18	19	20	21	22
23	24	25	26	27	28	

March

M	T	W	T	F	S	S
						1
2	3	4	5	6	7	8
9	10	11	12	13	14	15
16	17	18	19	20	21	22
23	24	25	26	27	28	29
30	31					

April

M	T	W	T	F	S	S
		1	2	3	4	5
6	7	8	9	10	11	12
13	14	15	16	17	18	19
20	21	22	23	24	25	26
27	28	29	30			

May

M	T	W	T	F	S	S
				1	2	3
4	5	6	7	8	9	10
11	12	13	14	15	16	17
18	19	20	21	22	23	24
25	26	27	28	29	30	31

June

M	T	W	T	F	S	S
1	2	3	4	5	6	7
8	9	10	11	12	13	14
15	16	17	18	19	20	21
22	23	24	25	26	27	28
29	30					

July

M	T	W	T	F	S	S
		1	2	3	4	5
6	7	8	9	10	11	12
13	14	15	16	17	18	19
20	21	22	23	24	25	26
27	28	29	30	31		

August

M	T	W	T	F	S	S
					1	2
3	4	5	6	7	8	9
10	11	12	13	14	15	16
17	18	19	20	21	22	23
24	25	26	27	28	29	30
31						

September

M	T	W	T	F	S	S
	1	2	3	4	5	6
7	8	9	10	11	12	13
14	15	16	17	18	19	20
21	22	23	24	25	26	27
28	29	30				

October

M	T	W	T	F	S	S
			1	2	3	4
5	6	7	8	9	10	11
12	13	14	15	16	17	18
19	20	21	22	23	24	25
26	27	28	29	30	31	

November

M	T	W	T	F	S	S
						1
2	3	4	5	6	7	8
9	10	11	12	13	14	15
16	17	18	19	20	21	22
23	24	25	26	27	28	29
30						

December

M	T	W	T	F	S	S
	1	2	3	4	5	6
7	8	9	10	11	12	13
14	15	16	17	18	19	20
21	22	23	24	25	26	27
28	29	30	31			

☐ Green weeks
☐ Red weeks

Table 6.7 is an example of a TV rate chart. These rates applied to the period 16/2/1987 to 31/3/1987. The SABC reviews its rates every month, depending on supply and demand factors.

Table 6.7
TV rate chart (rates effective from 16/2/87 to 31/3/87)

	TV1					
	Mon	Tues	Wed	Thurs	Fri	Sat
14h00-18h00						T11 (E/A)
15h30-16h30					T4(E)	
16h00-16h30	T3(E)	T3(A)	T3(E)	T3(A)		
16h30-18h00	T7(E)	T7(A)	T7(E)	T7(A)	T7(E)	
18h00-19h00	T8(E)	T8(A)	T9(E)	T9(A)	T8(E)	T5(A)
19h00-20h00	T22(E)	T20(A)	T22(E)	T20(A)	T22(E)	T19(A)
20h00-20h30						T22(E)
20h00-21h00	T21(A)	T22(E)	T21(A)	T22(E)	T21(A)	
20h30-21h30						T12(E)
21h00-22h00	T5(A)	T15(E)	T5(A)	T11(E)	T6(A)	
21h30-Close						T5(E)
22h00-Close	T1(A)	T2(E)	T2(A)	T3(E)	T3(A)	

TV1 Commercials to be submitted in the language of the channel, as indicated in brackets above:
E = English, A = Afrikaans, E/A = English or Afrikaans.

	TV2 & TV3						
	Mon	Tues	Wed	Thurs	Fri	Sat	Sun
15h00-18h00							T3
16h00-17h00						T5	
17h00-17h30					T2		
17h30-18h00	T2	T2	T2	T2	T2		
19h00-21h00	T7	T8	T7	T7	T8	T7	T7

	TV4						
	Mon	Tues	Wed	Thurs	Fri	Sat	Sun
17h00-19h00						T12	
18h00-19h00	T11	T11	T10	T11	T11		T13
21h00-Close	T12	T9	T12	T11	T13	T13	T11

Conditions:
1. All contracts are subject to the Broadcasting Act, 1976 (as amended), the Advertising Code and Regulations of the Advertising Services of the SABC.
2. The rates quoted include advertising agency commission on net time costs. Agency commission is not payable on rebated time costs.

3. No additional levy will be payable in respect of the South African Advertising Research Foundation Ltd. The SABC will, from its gross income, contribute the ruling percentage to SAARF.
4. These rates are exclusive of General Sales Tax under Act 103 of 1978 (as amended). GST will be added and collected by practitioners (for their clients) and by the SABC (for direct advertisers).
5. This rate card is issued for the information of advertisers and agencies and does not constitute an offer by the SABC.

☐ The future

Television can transport millions of viewers to all the corners of the earth within seconds. It is not difficult to use a television set − you just push a button − yet it is a powerful medium to which people devote a great deal of their lives.

Developments in television are being made continually in both the services offered and the television sets themselves. Large-screen sets, split-screen sets, portable sets, sets equipped with stereo speakers, remote control and wrist-watch sets all exist either in prototype or in commercially available form, making it easier for people to watch TV wherever and whenever they want.

With the introduction of cable television and satellite television, the audience has a wider variety and greater choice of programmes from all around the world. This explains why television is definitely the most powerful medium of mass communication.

Teledata, another new broadcasting service, came on stream officially on 1 November 1985. Based on the 'Ceefax' system from the BBC in the UK, this broadcast medium has already taken root in the US, Europe, the Far East and Australia. Electronic 'pages' are transmitted onto the screen and are controlled by a key-pad which enables the viewer to choose from a vast amount of information; from financial information, up-to-the-minute news and weather, sports and travel to more entertaining issues such as what's on at the movies, TV and radio, recipes and puzzles, and later expanding into educational facilities such as learning a language.

As a new and different source of advertising, Teledata offers a service which traditional media cannot provide − 'instant advertising'. It is a very flexible and fast medium. Commercials can be conceived and transmitted in a minute, removed or changed in a minute. Already, Teletext has found a special niche in other countries in that it serves as a medium which complements other media rather than competing with them.

☐ Conclusion

It is widely accepted that television advertising is one of the more successful means of advertising for a wide spectrum of products and for a diverse audience. Due to the large capital expenditure for the execution of a successful campaign, the inherent characteristics of the medium, the complexity of creating commercials, the combination of sight and sound with motion, and the massive audience it can reach, television is generally regarded as the *most powerful* advertising medium.

The power of radio
Coen Gous, Retha Vermeulen
and Marinda van Niekerk

Introduction	183
The advantages of radio over other media	184
Regional radio	187
Principles of copywriting for radio	189
How to use radio	191
Success stories	193
Radio — the future	193
References	194
Appendices	195

☐ Introduction

Fifteen years ago David Ogilvy went to one of his clients and said: 'I have discovered a new medium. Lo and behold, it is radio. The Cinderella medium' (*Viewpoint* 1981:4).

Radio's unique strengths are all too often overlooked and it has become something of a 'forgotten' medium. But radio is alive and well, especially to those who know how to capture and capitalise on its true spirit.

During 1985 more than 70 million rands were spent on radio advertising in South Africa and close on 1,9 million radio advertisements were broadcast on SABC radio alone. Radio's invisible presence is as much a part of our lives as breathing. In South Africa nearly every household owns one or more radio sets, as the following figures show (AMPS 1985:4):

	% of households owning one or more radio sets
Whites	97%
Coloureds	81%
Asians	93%
Blacks	81%

On a daily basis, radio reaches 84% of the white population, 59% of the coloured population, 76% of the Asian population and 63% of the Black population.

Radio is an extremely potent commercial medium. Not only does it provide blanket coverage of any market in terms of reach, but it also enables the advertiser to reach his market frequently because it is such an economical medium.

The introduction of commercial TV in 1978 and the expansion of the medium to provide entertainment for all race groups has perhaps drawn the spotlight away from radio and how rapidly it has developed. When TV was introduced in the USA in 1950 there were 700 radio stations. Now there are 9 000.

In the same way that people form relationships with other people, they form relationships with the media. Television can be looked upon as the 'date' for the day – viewing is carefully planned for the leisure hours after the day's tasks have been completed. From print media we get daily information which enables us to know in what context we are operating – thus we have a 'working relationship' with the print media. Outdoor advertising is the 'passing relationship' in our lives, and we all anticipate the 'one night stand' opportunity we have in cinema. But with radio we have a marriage! Radio is with us when we wake up, it travels with us from place to place, it is intimate, responds to our moods and is all too often taken for granted.

Sound creates emotions and no picture is as powerful as the human imagination. The preconception that the eye is more powerful than the ear has been proven incorrect repeatedly. The time has come to revise visual chauvinism – the fact is that the ear is an appreciably more powerful memory imprinter than the eye. Not only do you hear faster than you see, but your hearing lasts longer than your seeing. A picture fades in one second unless you strain your mind to file the essence of the idea. Hearing, on the other hand, lasts four or five times as long. This explains why it is so easy to lose your train of thought when you read printed words. Because sounds last longer in the mind, the spoken word is easier to follow.

The two factors that contribute to the effectiveness of the spoken word are that the mind holds the spoken word in mental storage much longer and that the tone of the human voice gives words emotional impact that no picture can achieve. This puts the age-old saying 'A picture is worth a thousand words' in jeopardy. How many times have you seen pictures trying to represent concepts? Think of all the pictures that one word, for example 'God' or 'love', conjures up.

There is a great deal of evidence that thinking is a process of manipulating sounds, not images. Even when pictures and sounds are involved together you see what you hear – what the sound has led you to expect to see and not what the eye tells you it has seen. The implications for the advertising industry are staggering. A transition from a visual point of view to a verbal point of view is inevitable. Of course, this does not mean that the visual does not play an important role – on the contrary, the point is that the verbal should be the driver and the pictures should reinforce the words.

Did you know that there is at least one radio service to suit each pair of ears in this country? (see Appendix 1.) Like any advertising medium, radio lacks certain virtues, shares certain advantages with other media and offers certain benefits that *no* other medium can.

☐ The advantages of radio over other media

The attributes of radio can be divided into qualitative and quantitative advantages.

Qualitative advantages

Radio relies on the 'theatre of the mind'

Radio stimulates the listener's imagination. It enables him to form his own mental image of the product and its attributes to match his lifestyle. If someone describes a beautiful, long-legged blonde he saw at the beach, you conjure up a picture in your mind's eye and will probably end up wanting to see her too – however, if he showed you a picture of her she might not be your type of woman at all!

Many advertisers use television or print media because they believe that they 'need a picture'. However, radio's direct link to the imagination may make it the most pictorial medium. The artistic use of sound in building the mind-picture is limitless. Creative radio copy can turn radio into a visual experience.

Radio is one-to-one selling

Radio allows one individual to address another in the most intimate way. It enters the home – every type of home and every type of room – and becomes a friend! Close relationships develop between listeners and radio personalities and when the editorial is interrupted by a commercial, the 'voice' becomes a friend recommending the product.

Radio relies on the spoken word

The spoken word is an extremely powerful method of communication. The human voice can be the most sincere, friendly, persuasive, natural and personal means of communication. Individual voices have high recallability owing to distinctive accents or intonations. The spoken word has also wiped out the boundaries that existed between urban and rural areas. It is readily understood by both the literate and illiterate sections of a community. Today non-readers can be as well-informed as most members of the reading public. Due to the spoken word, well-informed is no longer synonymous with 'well-read'.

Radio is mobile and highly accessible

Radio reaches the target audience while it is doing other things. You will find radio everywhere – on the beach, on sports fields, freeways and factories. Radio goes wherever people go – it is easy to listen to radio. Roller skaters and pedestrians with walkmans are living in sound – the mobility of sound can detach them from their environment so that they participate only in the reality of a radio world. Radio is as active a medium as your lifestyle!

Radio is habit-forming

People tend to plan their lifestyles around radio schedules. Radio offers warm human contact, intimate entertainment, fun and up-to-date information. In the fast-paced society we live in radio keeps thousands of lonely people company. Radio stations build up loyal audiences because people listen to 'their' programmes every day, and thus in their turn enable advertised products and services to build up brand loyalty.

Radio delivers each word of copy

With radio there is no small print. No matter whether you like or hate the message, you are involved! In other media you can select information, but every piece of radio copy enjoys the listener's attention, each word is a headline. There is no competition from any surrounding material.

Radio is an effortless medium

Listening comes naturally to people. Once you have switched on your radio you automatically participate with the reflex action of listening.

Radio offers immediacy and timeliness

Immediate reaction to radio commercials is possible – purchasing can take place within hours of hearing the advertisement. Radio's timeliness offers the opportunity of 'spur of the moment' marketing activities.

Quantitive advantages

Reach advantage

Radio reaches more people on a daily basis than any other medium. Table 6.8 shows the coverage of radio in the white, coloured and Asian market in comparison with other media.

Table 6.8
Coverage of radio *vis-à-vis* other media

Medium	Coverage
Radio daily	75,9%
TV daily	74,2%
Newspapers daily	49,1%
Any magazine	79,9%
Cinema weekly	7,5%

Source: AMPS 1985

On an average day (Mon-Fri) the penetration of the white, coloured and Asian population by radio station is as outlined in table 6.9.

Table 6.9
Penetration of various radio stations

Station	Percentage	No of listeners (in thousands)
Radio Suid-Afrika	21,2	1 179
Radio Good Hope	13,1	730
Radio South Africa	10,0	557
Radio 5	9,5	527
Radio Highveld	8,0	446
702 Music Radio	6,8	376
Radio Jacaranda	4,8	267
Radio Port Natal	4,7	261
Radio Oranje	3,9	219
Radio Algoa	3,1	172
Capital Radio	2,5	140

Source: AMPS diary January-March 1986

The coverage of radio is even more impressive in the black market. The following comparison shows the difference in media coverage of black housewives.

Medium	Total	Urban
Radio daily	60,9%	66,3%
TV daily	14,1%	39,7%
Newspaper daily	9,1%	27,3%

Source: AMPS main body May 1985-March 1986

The power of radio in the black market is dynamic. The nine black regional stations of the SABC, when used in combination, reach 7,3 million blacks nationwide on an average day (Mon-Sat). Individually, the black regional stations perform as outlined in table 6.10.

Table 6.10
Reach of SABC's black regional radio stations: cumulative yesterday (Mon-Sat)

Station	No of listeners (in thousands)	% of population
Zulu service	2 958	21,8
Xhosa service	1 057	7,8
N Sotho service	1 219	9,0
S Sotho service	1 291	9,5
Tswana service	998	7,4
Tsonga service	300	2,2
Venda service	180	1,3
Swazi service	155	1,1
Ndebele service	66	0,5
Total Nguni/Sotho services	7 318	53,9

Source: AMPS Broadcast media May 1985-March 1986

Frequency

Radio is famous for the high frequency it offers advertisers. With the outlay of a reasonable amount of money the target market can be reached numerous times. The advertiser must remember that frequency is the key to learning and remembering. It is also possible to buy as many spots as desired on one day to achieve a high frequency over a short period of time.

Radio is economical

Radio can be looked upon as a weapon against advertising inflation. The environment of the 80s is inflation. Advertisers are concerned about escalating media costs and radio provides cover and frequency at a low unit cost. Since radio is the most selective and inexpensive medium, it can be the best weapon against inflation. The SABC radio rates are presently based on a cost of between R0,40 and R1,70 to reach 1 000 listeners, depending on the station and time channel used by the advertiser. Radio compares very favourably with other media on a cost per thousand base (see table 6.11).

Table 6.11
Cost per thousand comparison of various media

Medium	Approximate cost
Radio (30-second spot)	R0,90
TV1 (30-second spot)	R4,00 +
Magazines (full page, full colour)	R4,00 +
Newspapers (quarter page, full colour)	R4,00 +

Comparison of white, coloured and Asian adult audiences

A radio commercial is economical to produce. Radio commercials can be produced for as little as R200.

Target segmentation

Although radio can be looked upon as the shotgun medium reaching each and everyone, the opposite is also true. Because of the one-to-one selling characteristic of radio the advertiser can actually target in on a specific market by using specific channels on specific radio stations (see Appendix 1 for an index of the radio stations available). The SABC radio stations are segmented into different time channels to coincide with the various lifestyles and the availability of specific target markets.

The basic SABC time channels are as follows:

☐ 06h00-08h30 – Breakfast
☐ 08h30-12h00 – Morning
☐ 12h00-14h00 – Lunch
☐ 14h00-16h00 – Afternoon
☐ 16h00-18h30 – Afternoon drive-time
☐ 18h30-21h30 – Early evening

The analysis in table 6.12 shows how station profiles can differ on basic demographics in the same time channel on different stations.

Table 6.12
White, coloured
and Asian station
profiles Mon-Fri
average quarter
hour: time channel
08h30-12h00

	Radio 5	Radio South Africa
Total	67 000	82 000
Male	54%	26%
Female	46%	74%
Age		
16-24	33%	6%
25-34	46%	12%
35-49	13%	11%
50 + ...	8%	71%

Table 6.12 clearly shows that during the 08h30-12h00 channel Radio 5 has a male bias of 54%, whereas Radio South Africa has a strong female bias of 74%; The age profile shows that 46% of Radio 5 listeners in this time channel belong to the 25-34 group, whereas 71% of the Radio South Africa listeners are 50 or older. This type of channel and station analysis enables the advertiser to pinpoint his specific target market.

☐ Regional radio

In the United States there are more than 8 000 regional services, each with a growing audience. Regional radio is radio of the future. The main characteristic of regional radio is its local involvement. The programme content of regional services is adapted to the needs of the local listeners. Regional services go for the direct link of communication between the station and the listener. The listener becomes so involved with the station that it enacts the role of a personal friend. This strong rapport between the regional station and its listener holds endless possibilities for the advertiser, especially the retailer (see the Barney's Paint Centre radio copy). He now has the chance to speak to his own community about his product. Regional services can be used successfully as an alternative to local newspapers.

Mortimer Tiley Kenyon

COPY/KOPIE

BPC'30 '13''ES

BARNEYS DISCOUNT PAINT CENTRES

JINGLE   :   COME ALONG TO BARNEY'S WHEN IT'S TIME TO PAINT ....

FV   :   What can I do about this house? It really needs painting badly. But I don't want my husband to go through the roof when he sees the bill.

PHILEMON   :   No problem madam. Just go to Barney's paint discounters. They'll tell us exactly what to do and help madam to buy the right paint and the right colour.

FV   :   You're so clever Philemon.

PHILEMON   :   Is not me madam (chuckle in his voice) ... is Barney's.

JINGLE   :   SO COME ALONG TO BARNEY'S WHEN IT'S TIME TO PAINT.

MV   :   Barney's Discount Paint Centres.

PRODUCT:	Barney's Discount Paint Centres
MEDIA:	30" Radio - Radio Highveld
COPYWRITER:	P.R.
DATE:	1/6/83
JOB NO:	7369

The following regional services are available to the advertiser in South Africa:

☐ Radio Highveld
☐ Radio Jacaranda
☐ Radio Good Hope
☐ Radio Oranje
☐ Radio Port Natal
☐ Radio Algoa
☐ 702 Music Radio
☐ Capital Radio
☐ Radio Zulu

☐ Radio Xhosa
☐ Radio Lebowa
☐ Radio Sesotho
☐ Radio Tswana
☐ Radio Venda
☐ Radio Tsonga
☐ Radio Swazi
☐ Radio Ndebele
☐ Radio Metro
☐ Radio Lotus
☐ Radio Bophuthatswsana
☐ Radio SR
☐ Radio Thoho-ya-ndou
☐ Radio Transkei
☐ Radio Ciskei
☐ Radio Paralelo

☐ Principles of copywriting for radio

Sound is a world of reality and infinite possibility. In order to utilise the power of sound to its full potential, certain principles should be followed when copy is written for radio. These are dealt with below:

Keep the copy simple

Do not talk over your listeners' heads, do not talk down to them and do not shout at them. Radio is a personal friend – remember, therefore, to talk like a friend, understand like a friend and believe like a friend. Your commercial should invite attention naturally.

Produce clear commercials

In so many commercials, words which are difficult to understand are used. The people who create the commercial know it almost off by heart by the time they complete it – but how clear is it going to be to the people it is intended for? It is important to test your commercial for clarity before releasing it – by doing this you avoid wasting money and baffling your audience.

A commercial must be well written

It is very difficult to produce a good radio commercial. The most important asset of radio as an advertising medium is the fact that it relies on the listener's imagination. With well-written copy you can make the listener 'see' what the advertiser wants him to see. Light, touch, even taste and smell can be evoked by the infinite energy of sound – take the example of the Cadbury's *Chomp* advertisement, in which the size of the chocolate is illustrated by the following question: 'How wide can you open your mouth?' Sound is a medium that can demonstrate; put some drama and energy into those commercials. It has been said that 'when you write a radio commercial for the eye instead of the ear you can expect to achieve enormous recall values'. As one eight-year-old boy said: 'I love to look at radio . . . I see the pictures better'.

Sounds can create emotions

The human voice can project love, warmth, humour, hate repulsion. A well-trained voice can project any emotion you want to portray. Cash in on radio's emotional selling value — if you succeed in touching the listener's heart you can be sure of effective advertising.

Never cram radio copy

A good rule is to allow yourself no more than 35 words for a quarter-minute spot and 65 words for a half-minute spot. So when you are busy squeezing those extra words into your script, remember that it could cost you when you hold up a recording session whilst they are taken out!

Allow yourself more air time!

It takes time to set a scene and establish a promise. It is often impossible to establish your sound effects in 30 seconds and still relate them to the product benefits. Fight for 60-second commercials — a 30-second commercial that nobody remembers has no impact!

Content

Ask yourself the following questions about the content of your commercial: Does the commercial:

- ☐ identify your brand early?
- ☐ repeat your name often?
- ☐ promise a benefit early?
- ☐ repeat the promise more than once?

The commercial will do a better job of increasing awarenes if your answers to the above are 'yes'. Remember the classic commercial for Chevrolet: 'Braai-vleis, rugby, sunny skies and Chevrolet'

The phrase is repeated over and over again, and it need not be dull — not if you have a good idea and a good writer.

Sound effects

In radio advertising sound effects can contribute to the message when used according to the following rules:

- ☐ Identify your sound effects or you may confuse your listener. The sound of rain falling in the forest is the same as that of bacon sizzling in a pan or a running shower. Remember that a sound effect is effective only when the listener knows what it means.
- ☐ Do not be afraid to use music as a sound effect. Music can be anything you want it to be. Remember Prokofiev's 'Peter and the Wolf' suite? Prokofiev tells us that the duck sounds like the melody played on the oboe. Whenever you hear the sound of an oboe you automatically think 'duck'! As long as you inform your listener about the meaning of the musical sounds, the commercial will work!
- ☐ When you have used your clearly identified sound effects build your commercial around them. Concentrate on the relationship between your product and the sound effect — like exactly how authentically German your pumpernickel bread is, just like the oompah band in a German neighbourhood, or on the reactions people have while the food is sizzling in your margarine, etc.

Radio is a local medium

Remember that you can write your commercial to suit the tastes and habits of people in specific regions. If you are advertising for Capetonians, for example, you can make use of the accent true to the region and refer to familiar faces and places, thus making it even more personal and effective.

Comedy

Comedy should be avoided unless you have someone who knows how to do it. Do not use jokes with punchlines – once you have heard the greatest joke in the world, you do not want to hear it over and over again! The best comic commercials begin with a totally ridiculous premise from which all subsequent developments follow logically. A famous example of a ridiculous premise is: 'Lake Michigan will be drained of water and refilled with whipped cream.'

Demonstration tapes

Never try to sell a radio script without a demonstration tape – It is difficult for the client to visualise what a commercial will be like from a script. With a tape you will find selling much easier and you will definitely impress your client. It also gives you the opportunity to hear whether what you have done works!

☐ How to use radio

How radio works

The interaction between client or agency and the SABC is illustrated in Appendix 2. The functions of the SABC departments are as follows:

Acceptance

South African society is multi national, with wide-spread differences in langauge, culture and religion. Therefore it is essential that advertising should conform to the standards of honesty, decency and good taste of every individual in our community. To ensure the widest possible acceptance it is necessary that all commercial copy for broadcasting on any of the commercial stations of the SABC is vetted by the Acceptance Department before transmission.

Marketing department

The Marketing Department works in conjunction with other depatments of the SABC to foster a closer and more target-oriented working relationship with advertising agencies and clients. It can assist you with your electronic media planning, as well as with any problems encountered with radio and TV research.

Administration department

This section is the hub of all administrative work which affects the advertising services of the SABC.

In the main, as far as advertising agencies are concerned, the Department of Advertising Administration handles the following:

- ☐ Air time sales administration
- ☐ Availabilities
- ☐ Contracts
- ☐ Accounts and account queries
- ☐ Budgets and financial results
- ☐ Administration of agency accreditation

Sales department

The Sales Department of the SABC's commercial services is your prime contact with all departments. There is a sales representative assigned to each advertising agency and client. He is able not only to look after your requirements with regards to planning and buying time on the stations, but also to assist you with any problems or queries you may have in connection with other departments of the advertising services.

Schedules department

The purpose of the Schedules Department is to ensure that all commercials submitted for broadcasting are transmitted at the right times on the correct dates by the predetermined stations. Therefore, it is vital that every different commercial or version thereof carries a separate code number and that agencies' scheduling instructions are explicit.

Procedures for buying radio time on SABC radio

Time

Radio time can be bought in single spots or pre-structured campaigns. Campaigns consist of an amount of spots in a number of channels across the day. Once the stations where advertising will be placed have been determined, the following aspects should be considered:

☐ The best time of the day or week to reach prime prospects
☐ The duration of the spots that will be aired — 15, 20 . . . 60 (in multiples of five seconds
☐ Budget allowances for the planned campaigns on radio

Rates

The cost of individual spots varies, depending on duration and the station and channel in which they appear. The average 30 second spot on SABC radio can cost anything between R10,00 and R1 070,00. Listenership figures are researched regularly by an independent market research organisation on behalf of the South African Advertising Research Foundation (SAARF). Rates are based on these listenership estimates, as well as on supply and demand.

The Sales Department should be contacted to make bookings and determine the availability of time in the channels on the dates that have been selected. Time cannot be held in reserve. It is booked on a strictly 'first come, first served' basis. Once booked, time cannot be cancelled within 28 days of the first flighting date for spots or campaigns.

Payment

Once the booking of a campaign has been completed the SABC forwards the account and a contract to the client/agency. This contract (two copies) should be signed and witnessed and returned to the SABC.

SABC commercial production services

The SABC has its own commercial production facility in each of the main centres of the Republic. Production staff are experts in their field with vast experience of producing radio programmes and commercials and can boast a wide depth of expertise in all the South African black languages.

SABC representatives are able to give advice on the creation of the right kind of commercial to appeal directly to a specific target market. This could be a simple 'voice-over' spot read by the duty announcer (a station service which is free of charge); a pre-recorded cameo involving one or more voices, music and sound effects; or a full-scale jingle with orchestral backing.

The representatives are also able to advise on production costs and tailor plans to suit budgets.

☐ Success stories

The testimonials below illustrate some recent feedback on the success achieved with advertising on radio.

☐ *Mr Martin Weldman of Fairway Motors, Durban:*

'After advertising my 24-hour petrol service for just one week on Radio Port Natal, business after 6 pm increased by 42%'.

☐ *Mr CW Eksteen of Blake Road Motors:*

'We would like to place on record our appreciation of the service offered by Radio Port Natal to advertisers. We have had an excellent response to our advertising and will continue to use this proven medium'.

☐ *Mr Tony Amarald, Coimbra Restaurant, Johannesburg:*

'Some years ago the Coimbra Restaurant decided to try a new form of advertising: Radio. I am presently advertising on Radio Highveld with tremendous response from the listeners.

Radio advertising, I thought, was for big business only – I was proved wrong. Radio worked for me and I know it will stay that way.'

☐ *Mr James Stock, Director of Waste Centre Warehouse, Durban:*

'The results have been quite spectacular. Our increased sales clearly reflected the benefit of radio advertising, and our image has been greatly enhanced. An added bonus which we did not anticipate is the respect with which our buyers are now treated. Our name is now well known, our buyers don't walk in cold and, although it is irrational, credit is more readily given.'

☐ *Mr Don Craye of Williams Hunt, Cape Town:*

'We moved all the stock we intended to, received enormous consumer awareness *and* people are still talking about our radio campaign.'

Need we say more?

☐ Radio – the future

Radio is not without its own technologies for the future. Satellites will change the medium by regionalising campaigns. The 'sound' of radio will change as a result of more stereo broadcasts and high fidelity. As in Britain and the USA, radio will become a 'narrow cast' medium as community radio develops locally. Small stations will cater for specific markets in any local environment. An example of community radio is student radio – currently a medium at some 12 universities and colleges and playing music, news and advertisements in canteens and residences.

However, technology will not hold listeners or advertisers. It was programming that saved radio when television came.

The society we live in is undergoing sweeping changes. Demographers are predicting smaller households, an older population, more people living alone, growth in the suburbs and minority groups and a polarisation between the haves and the have-nots. As these changes take place there will be greater diversity of interests, tastes and needs. Radio has proved that it can adapt to new tastes and new segments. Radio survived television because it adapted – it will adapt again.

Radio is a survivor – and it is inevitable that more advertisers will recognise the value of radio in the inflationary and impersonal world we are living in.

☐ References

AMPS Main Body, May 1985 – March 1986.
Viewpoint, III 1981:4 (in-house Ogilvy-Mather publication).

☐ Appendix 1: Radio stations in the RSA

Station	Broadcast area	Station characteristic
SABC radio: Radio RSA	Middle East, Africa, South America, Canada	Objective information about South Africa
SABC English and SABC Afrikaans	National	Cultural services aimed at Afrikaans and English-speaking citizens
Radio 5	National	Pop music station aimed at young adults
Radio Highveld Radio Good Hope Radio Port Natal Radio Oranje Radio Jacaranda Radio Algoa	PWV area Western Cape Natal Orange Free State Transvaal Eastern Cape	Regional stations broadcast in English and Afrikaans Middle-of-the-road Community oriented services – predominantly music stations
Radio Orion	National	All night light music service broadcasts
Radio Allegro	National	21h30-05h30 classical music daily
Radio Lotus	Natal & Witwatersrand	Asian service – broadcast in English. Asian music – community oriented
Radio Zulu Radio Xhosa Radio Lebowa Radio Sesotho Radio Setswana Radio Venda Radio Tsonga Radio Swazi Radio Ndebele	Natal, E Tvl, PWV Area & Free State E & NE Cape, Ciskei and Cape Town area N & SW Tvl – Central Tvl incl JHB Witwatersrand, OFS part of NE Cape W Tvl, parts of OFS and Witwatersrand N & NE Tvl N & NE Tvl North-eastern Transvaal Nylstroom, Groblersdal, Middelburg	Black Regional Services broadcast in vernacular as specified – music stations and general interest
Radio Metro	PWV area – broadcasts nationally between 00h00-05h00	Music station for urban Blacks broadcasting in English

Radio Stations in the RSA (*continued*)

Station	Broadcast area	Station characteristic
Independent radio: 702 Music Radio	PWV area	Pop music station aimed at young adults
Capital Radio	E Cape, Transkei, parts of Natal & Transvaal	Broadcasts in English – music and general interest programmes
Radio Bophuthatswana	Bophuthatswana & PWV area and NE Tvl	Broadcasts in English and Tswana – music station
Radio SR	Parts of Transvaal and Natal	Urban Black service – Broadcast in English – music station
Radio Thoho-ya-ndou	N Tvl, Botphuthatswana, Central Tvl and Venda	Broadcasts in Venda – music and general interest station
Radio Transkei	Transkei, SE Cape and South Natal	Broadcasts in Xhosa – music and general interest station
Radio Ciskei	Ciskei & parts of W Cape & S Transkei	Broadcasts in English and Xhosa – music and general interest
Radio Paralelo	Johannesburg	Broadcasts in Portuguese – music and general interest for Portuguese community

☐ Appendix 2: Agency/client interaction with the SABC

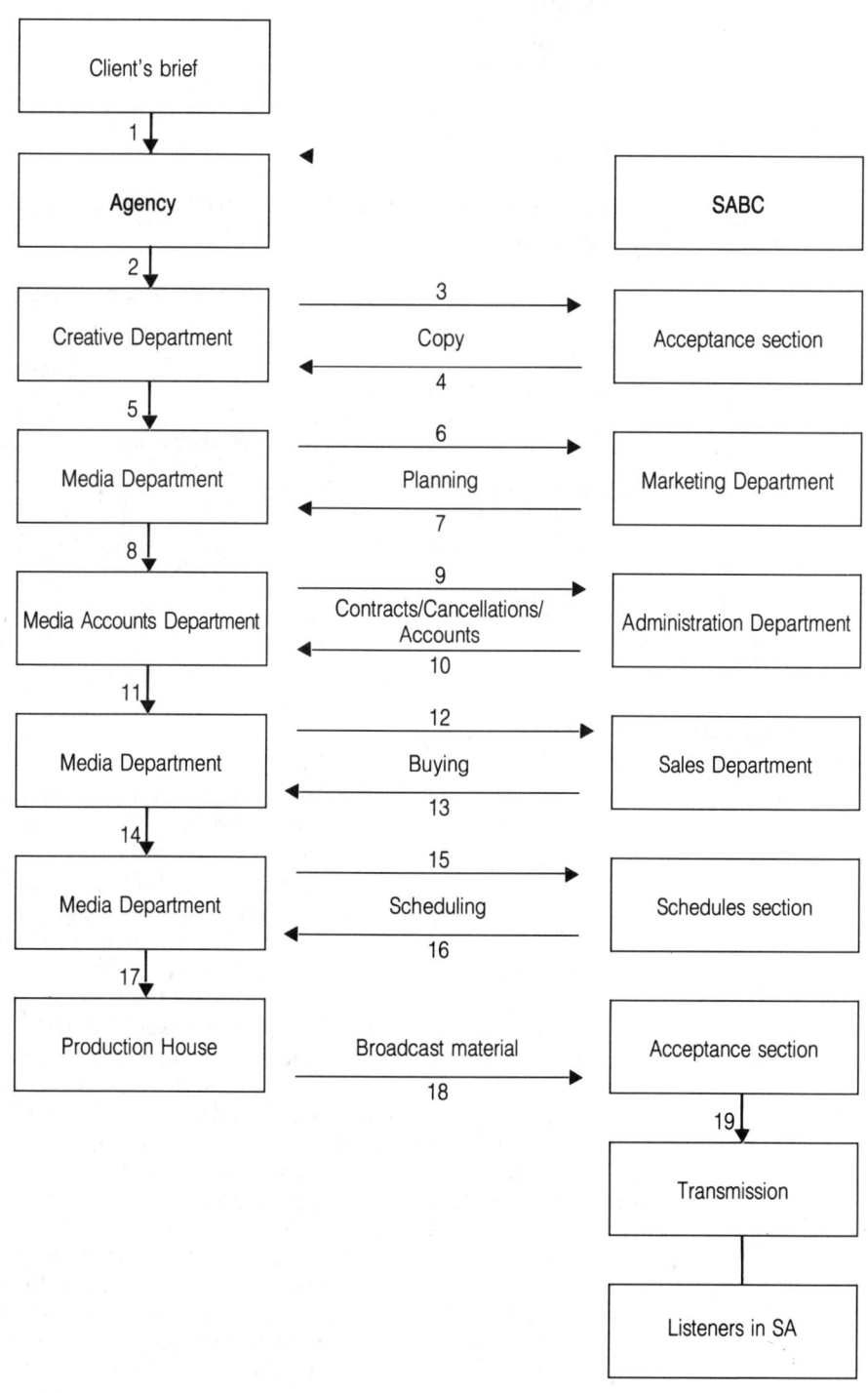

Cinema
Ludi Koekemoer

Introduction 198

Inter-media comparisons: print versus
cinema 199

Specific attributes, strengths and weaknesses
of cinema 200

Why use cinema? 201

How to get an advertiser on screen 203

Cinema's target audience 205

Closing comments 208

References 209

☐ Introduction

A truly scientific approach to media planning would imply severe conditions of experimentation such as are rarely − if ever − found in the daily routine of advertising agencies. Such an approach would require:

☐ first, that we know what we are talking about or, to put it more politely, that we define exactly what we are measuring or planning

☐ second, that measurements should be taken repeatedly under identical conditions so as to find out whether results are identical

☐ third, that one and the same experiment may be − and should be − carried out by other media planners in order to confirm the findings.

As far as the first point is concerned, *do* we know what we are talking about? Can we really define the yardstick of media planning and what is to be measured? The second and third points are mainly a matter of money and are also dependent upon the advertiser's desire to measure results.

The difficulty of defining a yardstick for media planning is best illustrated by inter-media comparisons. Are there any means of defining what is similar and different between a 30-second radio spot and the image of a poster, or can it be said that the same image on a full colour magazine page and on a poster of any size is actually the same? What are we going to compare − the first, immediate impact? Recall? Understanding? Buying intentions?

As could be expected, most media planners do not worry about the message in relation to the medium itself, and even less about details such as recall or image. The truly important thing is coverage and sales achieved, and no advertiser, not even a researcher, could blame any of them for this. Advertising is indeed for *selling*, even if this is not defined or wished for as its first result.

Our knowledge of media planning will not improve much if we continue to concentrate solely on such issues, and in the long run this will not serve the advertisers. Advertising, without doubt, is *for* selling, but it is not *about* selling. Is it not, perhaps, necessary to list all the facts and factors that influence sales before advertising starts, while it goes on, and when it stops? In today's recessionary climate marketing strategies are never the same, for salespeople or for consumers.

In summary, it is futile to compare the sales results of a magazine campaign with those of a television campaign led in two areas, however correctly they may have been matched in media planning, and to declare that so much is due to the efficiency of one medium and so much to the other. The market was not the same, the message was not the same, the salesmen were not the same and the consumers were not the same. Therefore, inter-media planning comparisons must be based on other data, on such facts as allow them to be studied on their own and in cases which allow us to check and to account for what is due to the message or image and what is due to the medium.

☐ Inter-media comparisons: print versus cinema

This analysis provides major points of difference between print media and cinema and reveals many of the strengths of each.

☐ Print is static. Film moves. You look at one and watch the other.

☐ Print is silent. Film has sound, music and effects.

☐ Print can be read. Film is heard, but can also be read via superimposition.

☐ Print imposes no time limit on the reading. Film imposes a limit which is based on its running time.

☐ Print can adjust the size of type to incorporate a long copy story which may be read by the really interested. Film can usually afford no more than 65 words within 30 seconds. Rush in the audio is film's equivalent of reducing type size, and it very rarely works.

☐ Print cannot make the reader read. Film has a far greater chance of making the viewer view.

☐ Print allows the reader to cut out a coupon and send it away. Film can simply give an address or a telephone number.

☐ Print is not read simultaneously by all members of its total audience. Film is seen by many people at the same time and can also be seen by the family as a unit (at a drive-in).

☐ Print can illustrate the product and by using several illustrations can basically simulate movement. Film has real movement. It shows the product in action and can demonstrate advantages.

☐ Print can underline, use bold type, and print a variety of typefaces and type sizes to vary emphasis. Film can employ degrees of vocal emphasis, different voices and musical underlining.

My thanks to Pax Moren, Rick Hoeksma and Vasso Theodasiou of Cinemark for their views, cooperation and information.

☐ Print can indicate pronunciation. Film can pronounce.

☐ Print has no control over the order in which an advertisement is looked at. Film controls the order and thus can tell a story the way it wants it to be told.

☐ Print is relatively quick to produce. Film is slower, but preplanning can help to reduce production time.

☐ Print is relatively cheap to produce. Film is more expensive.

☐ Print allows you flexibility within the generic medium. You can choose which print medium your advertisement is to appear in. Film is more flexible. You can pick the suburb you want to be in.

☐ Print offers several size opportunities. Film offers several time segments, but since there is no other material butting up against it every commercial is, in a sense, a full page. (Although it is appreciated that there is no real analysis possible with the audio-visual medium, it is often costed out internationally as a 30-second commercial against a full page advertisement.)

☐ Print advertisements do not intrude – people need not read them. Film commercials intrude in an entertainment medium – people must see them.

☐ Print advertisements are spaced irregularly throughout the paper. Film commercials are shown in a block.

☐ Print advertising is mainly in black and white. It concentrates on facts and news rather than on entertainment. Film may be in black and white or in colour and concentrates on entertainment rather than news.

☐ Specific attributes, strengths and weaknesses of cinema

For many years since the early 1970s, Cinemark has advocated the CRACK concept to explain the unique attributes of this audio-visual medium (Cinemark 1972):

☐ Captivity
- The members of the audience are captive, they are facing the screen. There is nothing else to distract them, their whole attention is riveted to the screen. Every day there is a fresh audience for a given feature film.

☐ Receptivity
- Normally a woman is receptive to an advertising message about dish-washers when she is washing dishes, but unreceptive to the same message when relaxing at the end of the day. However, with screen advertising the entire audience is receptive to any kind of message because it expects the screen to 'tell them something'.

☐ Audio-visual
- The screen is South Africa's big audio-visual medium. It is a medium in which two out of the five senses, namely sight and hearing, are involved simultaneously. Newspaper, magazine and radio messages are transmitted to one sense only, namely sight or hearing. It is believed that a message sent to two senses simultaneously is remembered about 65% more.

☐ Competition
  - Most advertisements compete with editorial for attention. Readers can see both editorial and advertisement at the same time. With screen advertising no such distraction exists. The screen advertisement being exhibited is the sole occupier of the viewer's time, thought and attention.

☐ Kinship
  - Cinema screen advertising can be viewed by the whole family simultaneously. In drive-ins a particular cine-ad is often the subject of immediately family discussion.

The specific strengths and weaknesses of cinema could be summarised as follows (see also Van Rooyen 1980:486):

☐ Strengths
  - Cinema involves most senses.
  - The viewer is transfixed and cannot ignore the message coming to him in near-darkness.
  - Cinema is excellent in the case of demonstrations.
  - Cinema is geographically very selective.
  - The viewer receives the message in a relaxed atmosphere.
  - Cinema offers high quality reproduction.
  - The big screen is very impactful.

☐ Weaknesses
  - Cinema reaches a general audience. The advertiser cannot select the movie that will be shown well in advance.
  - Cinema is a relatively expensive medium, especially with regard to production costs. Flighting costs per cinema per week are, however, very reasonable.
  - The time factor results in a limited message (20, 30, etc seconds).
  - Relatively lengthy preparation is necessary.

☐ Why use cinema?

South Africa boasts a dynamic and ever-expanding cinema business. Approximately 709 496 tickets are sold every week at the country's 309 four waller and 81 drive-in cinemas. In the main centres, cinema tickets are sold through a sophisticated electronic booking service, namely Computicket.

South Africa has some of the finest cinemas in the world. They are modern and luxurious and internationally recognised for their excellence. In recent years the trend has been to build cinema complexes which contain as many as eight theatres, many of them equipped with the very latest projection and dolby and stereo sound equipment.

When the announcement was made that the Republic of South Africa was going to get a TV service, the cinema industry had to reorganise itself. Large cinemas were replaced by smaller, more intimate and luxurious cinemas with an average seating capacity of 200 people. An advantage of the smaller cinemas is the fact that they can be built in suburbs and shopping centres as well as hotel complexes and are easily accessible.

But why should the advertiser use cinema? According to Cinemark, the reasons given below should be considered seriously by advertisers and media planners.

Youth medium

Internationally, cinema is established as the youth medium and South Africa's own All Media and Products Survey clearly shows that cinema is the medium for affluent 16 to 34-year-olds of all race groups. These young people are on the threshhold of their adult lives; they are still establishing their own identities and their purchasing habits, and it is during these formative years that brand loyalty is just beginning to become determined.

Captive and receptive audience

Cinema provides a truly captive audience and is probably the only medium which can claim to do so. This audience is a voluntary one. The members of the audience have paid to be present and to be entertained, and are thus in a receptive frame of mind. They see the commercials in full colour, on a large screen in a darkened auditorium, which means that distractive factors are eliminated and interest is enhanced. Because of these factors recall, that is the remembrance factor, is much higher for cinema.

Strong product identification in advertisers' own catchment area

Cinema offers the advertiser the opportunity to tailor his exposure requirements and budget to his specific 'catchment area', which, in the case of a retail business, does away with an 'overkill' situation. Furthermore, the advertiser's product can be clearly shown and demonstrated, if necessary, to highlight its features and advantages.

Remembrance factor

The impact any advertisement enjoys is of extreme importance in the communication process. Comparative evaluations have revealed the following remembrance factor percentages (information obtained by Cinemark from these companies):

	Radio	Press	TV	Cinema
Mediavision (France)	6,5%	11%	17,5%	75%
McNair (New Zealand)			45,5%	89%
Cinema Publiciteit (Belgium) .	5%	10%	15%	70%
Burke & Trendex (USA)			23%	87%
Pearl & Dean (UK)				78%
Biografstatastik (Sweden)		19%	23%	79%

Flexibility

Large advertisers can select cinemas in any combination or in any area. The very small advertiser, for example, a local hardware shop in a suburb, may find that his catchment area provides a cinema or drive-in, or both, and that he can screen his advertising exactly where it is going to be most effective.

Cost efficiency

Related to the first reason mentioned above (that is the fact that cinema is a youth medium), adding cinema to the media schedule where the target market is Whites aged 16 to 24 can lead to a reduction in cost per thousand and increase the percentage reach as well as the frequency.

Cinemark did a TELMAR computer run on AMPS 1985 figures using prime time for television and a target market of all Whites aged 16 to 24. The first run is based on a budget of R500 000 TV1 alone:

Percentage reach	93,3%
Frequency	11,2%
CPT OTS	R60,66
CPT reach	R680,50

Note: CPT cost per thousand
OTS opportunities to see

A second TELMAR run using R115 592 for cinema and the rest of the R500 000 for TV1 show the following results:

Percentage reach	96,5%
Frequency	12,8%
CPT OTS	R52,09
CPT reach	R436,30

Thus it would appear to be to the advertiser's advantage in every respect (namely % reach, frequency and CPT) to use TV and cinema combined if his target audience is 16 to 24-year-old Whites in South Africa.

☐ How to get an advertiser on screen

First of all, the advertising agency requires from Cinemark a screening proposal to present to its client. In order to be able to put one together, Cinemark must be briefed by the agency with the following information:

☐ Brand and product name

☐ Budget

☐ Campaign dates

☐ Type of commercial (see Miniad example)

☐ Type of cinema required – 4-waller, drive-in, or both

☐ Screening position, if required

☐ Whether new prints are being supplied or existing prints used in a previous campaign are to be used

☐ Language preference

☐ Length and type of film – Cinead or Cinemascope

☐ Areas required – national, metropolitan or provincial.

Once a proposed screening schedule has been worked out against the agency's briefing, a proposal, together with a print count and print cost guide, is presented to the agency and client.

When a film booking is received it is data processed for the computer, which produces a final screening schedule and invoice, complete with monthly screening costs. This takes between one and two weeks to complete, due to possible overbookings.

In addition, two weeks before screening, the computer turns out the weekly Certificate of Exhibition, which details exactly what advertisements are on each reel. This is sent out to the cinema manager in duplicate with the cans of film. At the end of each completed screening week the cinema manager signs the Certificate, certifying that the advertisements were screened as per instructions, and returns it to Cinemark with the films, which are then broken down for re-issue.

The advertisements are shown in a uniform sequence and not purely at the discretion of the projectionist. There are four formats of programme presentation, namely those of Ster Kinekor owned theatres, the Metro group of theatres, independently owned cinemas and drive-ins.

MINIAD

A Miniad is a sounded film of 20 seconds runtime comprising approximately 7 seconds of an animated introduction sequence followed by approximately 13 seconds during which time the visual message such as logo, if desired, plus name and address is progressively added. A spoken commentary is standard. A music and/or effects sound track can be provided if required.

Visual	Audio
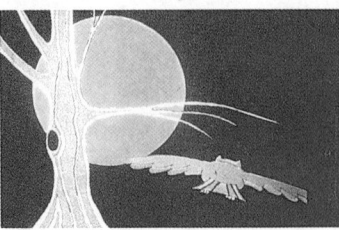	EFFECTS: Sound of owl hooting. MUSIC: Soft in background. VOICE: Feeling lonely? Why not join the late night owls in a cosy atmosphere? Bring in . . .
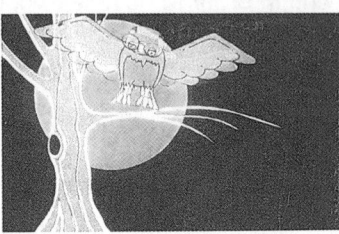	. . . your own moonshine and join us for super food and entertainment until the early hours.
	Moonshine Restaurant . . . your late night eating place. Wesbou Centre, 48 West Street, Kempton Park. EFFECTS: Sound of owl hooting. MUSIC: Up and out.

Courtesy: Cinemark

Formats of cinema programme presentation

The Ster Kinekor Group of Theatres' format is as follows:
1 Forthcoming attraction
2 *Conventional Cinead reel*
3 Forthcoming attraction
4 *Position 1*
5 Forthcoming attraction
6 *Position 2*
7 Next attraction
8 Main feature

The format for the Metro Group of Theatres is:
1 Forthcoming attraction

2	*Conventional Cinead reel*	6	Interval
3	Forthcoming attraction	7	Next attraction
4	*Position 1*	8	*Position 2*
5	*Interval advertisement*	9	Main feature

Independently owned cinemas use the format below:

1	Forthcoming attraction	6	*Interval advertisement*
2	*Cinead reel of ads number 1*	7	Interval
3	Forthcoming attraction	8	*Position 2*
4	*Position 1*	9	Next attraction
5	Forthcoming attraction	10	Main feature

The format below is used by drive-ins:

1	Forthcoming attraction	6	*Interval advertisement*
2	*Cinead reel of ads number 1*	7	Interval
3	Forthcoming attraction	8	*Position 2*
4	*Position 1*	9	Next attraction
5	Forthcoming attraction	10	Main feature

☐ Cinema's target audience

Demographics

In all four race groups (Whites, Coloureds, Asians and Blacks) cinema audiences are mainly young:

Cinema age profile percentages (4-wallers and drive-ins)

	Whites	Blacks	Coloureds	Asians
16-34 years	81%	96%	88%	90%
35-49 years	11%	3%	9%	5%
50 years plus	8%	1%	3%	5%

Source: AMPS 1985

Looking at the profile of cinema audiences (based on those who visited a cinema in the past seven days), it appears that they are in the middle to upper income groups (AMPS 1985/86):

Income	Whites	Blacks	Coloureds	Asians
	%	%	%	%
A	18	17	18	25
B	28	33	35	30
C	42	47	44	40
D	12	3	3	5

and they have a male bias, particularly in the case of Blacks and Coloureds (AMPS 1985/86):

Sex	Whites	Blacks	Coloureds	Asians
	%	%	%	%
Male	55	88	79	65
Female	45	12	21	35

Focusing particularly on the white segment of the market, AMPS 1985/86 indicates an English bias (AMPS 1985/86):

	Population	Cinema
	%	%
Afrikaans	59	48
English	41	52

and cinema's stronghold in the major metropolitan areas (AMPS 1985/86):

Metropolitan	64%
Large towns	18%
Towns/Villages	11%
Rural	7%

Psycho-graphics

In terms of values and lifestyles, *SocioMonitor* identifies four value groups. SocioMonitor 1986 provides the following details on white regular cinema-goers:

The self-motivateds (26% of regular cinema-goers)

A secure and comfortable middle and upper-middle-class feeling pervades this group of people. They are well educated and above average earners, and as such can afford to be inner-directed.

Self-motivateds are very confident people. Their self-confidence is evident in the demands they make upon themselves; they are prepared to make the most of themselves.

They seek meaningful jobs – jobs that offer them a challenge, personal satisfaction and stimulation. Psychological growth is important to them.

They are self-indulgent in that they are willing to spend a lot of time, money and effort on improving themselves – academically, creatively and appearance-wise. This effort extends to keeping fit and healthy – to taking regular exercise and eating the right foods. They have a 'back to nature' orientation which manifests itself in the purchasing of wholewheat bread, yoghurt, muesli and 'health packs'. The outdoors plays an important part in their lives and they tend to link health, natural products and the outdoors to feeling and looking good.

Self-motivateds are creative people who derive considerable satisfaction out of making things for themselves, and they tend to involve themselves in various arts, crafts and cultural interests.

The self-confidence and tolerance characteristic of this group of people allow them to accept the changing roles of women and of other race groups in society. Neither of these groups poses any real threat to them, job-wise or socially.

Self-motivateds tend to be between 25 and 44 years of age and 80% have matric or higher education. They live in A/B income households where the average monthly income is around R2 075 and they tend to be housewives or to work in clerical jobs or in a professional/managerial capacity. They tend to live in their own houses.

These people enjoy a homely life style. Although they do not enjoy eating out they enjoy having a few friends and acquaintances to dinner. They prefer to entertain people in their own homes.

Self-motivateds have a strong interest in the cultural and artistic world. They also have a marked outdoor orientation – they enjoy walking, hiking, mountain climbing, canoeing, yachting and sailing.

The self-motivated group tends to be a comfortable, settled group whose leisure activities and interests indicate their well-developed inner-directedness.

The responsibles (18% of regular cinema-goers)

Characteristic of responsibles is their need for security and stability. They are very strongly entrenched in tradition, are proud to be South African and proud of South Africa's traditions and achievements. Responsibles believe in buying local rather than imported products, because they feel that the former are as good as imported products and, an important factor to this group, they are cheaper. The unity of the family is important to this group of people, and activities involving the whole family have considerable appeal for them. Their very fierce consumerism is linked to the family and derives from their feelings of insecurity – they want the best for their families but expect 'fair play' from the products they buy. They will be very loyal to a brand, but will turn against it strongly should it let them down.

Essentially they are looking for approval at all levels – the reassurance of a big safe brand name means that they will be seen to be doing the best for their families. They tend to look to the past for guidance, finding the future both bewildering and threatening in its complexity. They tend to be rigid people, with a low tolerance for the multiple options offered by the world of the 80s and beyond. Responsibles are very resistant to change – once they have found something that meets their needs they are very hard to convert.

Hard work before leisure is the attitude characteristic of these people, who are not interested in having meaningful and stimulating jobs.

Responsibles also uphold traditional attitudes regarding the role of 'non-whites' and are not interested in increased racial contact in the interests of racial harmony.

Responsibles tend to be aged 50 or over, to be Afrikaans-speaking, to have some high school education, to live in C/D income households and to be retired.

The concept of the family is very important to responsibles, who enjoy quiet evenings at home with their families watching TV. They also enjoy going to church, having braais and watching sport. Their favourite sports are rugby, boxing and wrestling.

These people enjoy camping or caravanning. Their pleasures tend to be simple and inexpensive, for example going on a picnic, visiting the zoo, or just going for a drive.

The brandeds (29% of regular cinema-goers)

This group is characterised by its need for esteem and belonging and by its outer-directedness.

Brandeds badly want to be looked up to and to be seen as having achieved a better social and material position than their parents. Within the limitations of their education they try to achieve that status and respect via their possessions and the branded products they use. They are unlikely to fulfil their status aspirations in their work environment, and tend to work for material rewards rather than satisfaction.

Their image is very important to them – they are concerned about the impression they are creating. It is very important to them that they are accepted by the members of their group and therefore they make a conscious effort to please people they consider to be important – they are likely to change their views to please others or to use products which are used by other group members.

Brandeds continue to show very little desire for racial harmony. They continue to be aggressive, but this is now combined with a growing rejection of authority.

Brandeds tend to be male, young (aged between 16 and 34), Afrikaans-speaking (84%), and with some high school education. They tend to live in C income households and to be town or village dwellers.

These people are pleasure seekers who like being out and doing exciting things as much as possible. They are to be found at cinemas, pop concerts and night-clubs. They enjoy watching videos and playing TV games, and are not interested in participating in sport or doing exercise or gym.

Their strong interest in 'making money' is probably a function of their need to finance their high living and pay their HP instalments.

The innovatives (27% of regular cinema-goers)

The innovatives' values reflect their fundamental dissatisfaction with traditional attitudes and beliefs and with the social structure prevalent in South Africa.

In a society which is very pro-authority at all levels, members of the innovative group are strongly and increasingly against it. Their personal life styles incorporate informality, flexibility and openness to change – they do things without any rigid routine and tolerate considerable 'chaos'. They are aggressive people who are likely to take the risk of challenging authority – this could take the form of dangerous socio-political protests and calls for reform, or the more sensation-seeking 'living for today' type of protest (drug taking, speeding, etc), or specu-lation or business-related risks.

Innovatives tend to live for the present and have low expectations of a secure future in South Africa.

They are impulsive and willing to experiment with innovative products or ideas, but are also likely to become bored easily. They will be the early adopters or triers of anything new, but could drop it just as quickly.

Innovatives believe that women and other race groups should be given the opportunity to fulfil their own potential and that no artificial or socially contrived barriers should be raised.

They are predominantly English-speaking (76%), city dwellers, and have post-matric education. They tend to be between 16 and 34 years of age, to be employed in managerial/professional/executive positions (members of this group are most likely to be tomorrow's business leaders), to be students, to live in Johan-nesburg or Cape Town in flats or townhouses and in A/B income households.

Innovatives prefer a casual, informal and relaxed environment. They tend to eat out quite frequently and enjoy trying new restaurants. They go to the cinema, theatre, ballet and exhibitions. Their other interests include photography, ceramics, chess and overseas travel.

They play tennis, squash, athletics and soccer. Yoga is important, and they enjoy skin diving, surfing, yachting and hang-gliding.

The innovative group is a very comfortable, confident and psychologically as well as financially secure group.

☐ Closing comments

It has long been known by media planners that combinations of media usually work better than a single medium on its own. Within the confines of the media budget the media planner endeavours to achieve high impact, high frequency, wide reach and cost effectiveness. Cinema used in combination with television offers the media planner a solution to his problems:

☐ Cinema's big screen is impactful.
☐ Cinema is flexible and can provide high frequency.
☐ Cinema can offer reach.
☐ Cinema is cost effective, especially when used in combination with television.

Cinema is *the* medium for the younger consumers.

☐ References

Advertising Research Foundation. 1985. *All Media and Products Survey*. Johannesburg: ARF.

Cinemark. 1972. *A Guide to Cinema Screen Advertising in South Africa*. Johannesburg: Cinemark.

Lucas, GHG *et al*. (Eds). 1980. *The Task of Marketing Management*. Pretoria: JL van Schaik. (see the contribution entitled 'The Management of the Advertising Campaign'.)

Market Research Africa. 1986. *SocioMonitor*. Johannesburg: MRA.

Outdoor advertising: the neglected hero

Simon Copland

The essence of outdoor advertising 210

Outdoor is flexible 211

Outdoor costs 215

Creativity in outdoor 216

Outdoor audience 217

Summary 217

☐ The essence of outdoor advertising

Outdoor advertising can be defined as an advertising message displayed on a structure or surface prepared or erected specifically for that purpose. This definition, imperfect as it is, serves to distinguish commercial advertising activities, which will be described in this section, from the myriad visual messages such as traffic signs, shop names in neon, bumper stickers and point-of-sale placards which assail the senses.

Outdoor advertising messages are essentially ephemeral, even though some advertisers are unwise enough to leave their creative statement unchanged for years. While outdoor advertising proper sometimes employs the most modern technology (like lasers and electronics, for example), the essence of outdoor is a paper printed poster fixed with paste to a suitable backing.

Outdoor advertising has one characteristic which differentiates it from all other mainstream advertising media. *The outdoor advertising message is the medium.* There is no extraneous editorial matter to distract the viewer – outdoor is simply present in an urban environment, repeating its message over and over again.

Outdoor is considered to be one of the most cost effective of all media. In its first month, a properly planned outdoor campaign can reach as many as four out of five adults in its catchment area up to 80 times each on average.

Pure numbers, however, are not the only criterion for an effective medium and the creative content of an outdoor advertisement must be such that it can convey its message in the very short time that it is seen for. No one argues the proposition that the nature of an opportunity to see an outdoor advertisement is different from that of an opportunity to see or hear a TV advertisement or a radio spot. However, that the former is of less value than either of the latter examples is frequently stated but has yet to be proven scientifically.

The outdoor medium makes a major contribution to the totality of an advertising schedule in that it provides continuous repetition of the basic brand or service benefits at an economic cost – maintaining awareness levels between bursts of other media exposure – and thus enhances the cost efficiency of the campaign as a whole.

Rarely is outdoor used on its own (although *Marlboro* cigarettes were launched in South Africa on this medium alone by Mortimer Tiley in the early 80s). It is at its best when properly employed, that is emphasising the essentials of the campaign by repetition.

Courtesy: Mortimer Tiley and Rent-A-Sign Outdoor

Clearly, outdoor is a mass medium, but it can also be highly geographically specific. Billboards can be placed at or near locations important to an advertiser, and many a time has a board been placed on the Chairman's known route home! Because of the artificial segregation of residential areas in South Africa, the medium has been used extensively to reach non-white communities, particularly Blacks, in both urban and rural environments. Indeed, recently the emphasis has been so much on outdoor's abilities in black areas that it has almost been forgotten that Whites are just as amenable to good outdoor as anyone else.

□ Outdoor is flexible

Up to this point we have referred to the generic term 'Outdoor', but of course there is a multitude of different shapes and sizes, ranging from 26 m x 4 m to 1,5 m x 1,05 m. The standard sizes, however, are relatively few and are logically related to each other. The basic unit of size is the 'Four Sheet', which, as its name implies, is made up of four double-crown sheets, each 20″ x 30″. While the imperial sheetage sizes have long fallen into disuse, the four sheet remains, at 60″ x 40″ (or 1,56 m x 1,05 m), the unit basis for its own size and that of all bigger billboards.

One of the most popular billboard sizes, 10 ft x 20 ft, or more properly 3 m x 6 m – the '48-sheeter' – is made up of 12 four sheet pieces, each printed separately and fixed by a billposter in sequence. The '96-sheeter' is precisely twice as wide – 10 ft x 40 ft – and is made up of 24 four sheet pieces. (See figures for the arrangement of these billboards.)

Figure 6.9(α)
48-sheeter
poster

Poster size: 3 m x 6 m. Printing size: 2 900 mm x 5 800 mm. If screened neg supplied 290 mm x 580 mm at 150 #. If projections supplied must be 15 #. Bleed board print size 2 900 mm x 5 800 mm.

LAY-OUT FOR 48-sheeter

(1 015 mm)

(940 mm)	(990 mm)				(900 mm)
SHEET 1	SHEET 2	SHEET 3	SHEET 4	SHEET 5	SHEET 6
(25 mm) Underlaps SHEET 7 (50 mm) Border	SHEET 8	SHEET 9	SHEET 10	SHEET 11	SHEET 12

Courtesy: Rent-A-Sign Outdoor

Figure 6.9(b)
96-sheeter
poster

Poster size: 3 m x 12 m. Printing size: 2 900 mm x 11 600 mm. If screened negs supplied 290 mm x 1 160 mm at 150 #. If projections supplied must be 15 #. Bleed board printing size 2 900 mm x 11 600 mm.

LAY-OUT FOR 96-sheeter

(1 015 mm)											
(940 mm) SHEET 1	(990 mm) SHEET 2	SHEET 3	SHEET 4	SHEET 5	SHEET 6	SHEET 7	SHEET 8	SHEET 9	SHEET 10	SHEET 11	(760 mm) SHEET 12
(25 mm) Underlaps SHEET 13 (50 mm) Border	SHEET 14	SHEET 15	SHEET 16	SHEET 17	SHEET 18	SHEET 19	SHEET 20	SHEET 21	SHEET 22	SHEET 23	SHEET 24

According to their location, size and nomenclature vary – the four sheet (60" x 40") in a purpose-built shopping centre in a metropolitan area will be called a 'Shop ad', while the same size on a structure outside a black supermarket in the rural areas will be called a 'Point-of-Purchase (POP) Stand'. The same format is used in and around railway stations – as a 'Super-4' – and on specially designed litter bins for use in cities and towns – as the 'CBD Unit'.

Figure 6.10

(a)

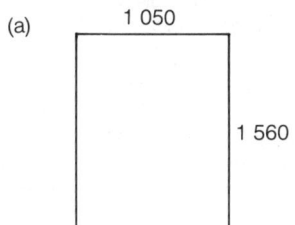

1 050

1 560

Metal size: 1 560 mm x 1 050 mm
Printing area: 1 500 mm x 980 mm
If screened negs supplied: 150 mm x 98 mm at 200 #
If projections supplied: 20 #

(b) Randfontein type B/S

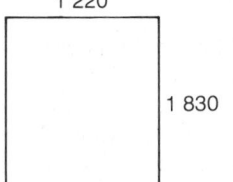

1 220

1 830

Metal size: 1 830 mm x 1 220 mm
Printing area: 1 730 mm x 1 120 mm
If screened negs supplied: 173 mm x 112 mm at 200 #
If projections supplied: 1 730 mm x 1 120 mm at 20 #

(c) PE bus shelters
   Side plate

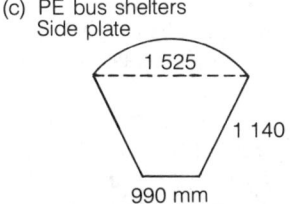

1 525

1 140

990 mm

Metal size: 1 140 mm x 1 525 mm x 990 mm
Printing area: 1 040 mm x 1 425 mm x 890 mm
If screened negs supplied: 104 mm x 142.5 mm x 89 mm at 200 #
If projections supplied: 1 040 mm x 1 425 mm x 890 mm at 20 #

(d) Backs PE

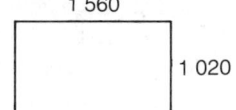

1 560

1 020

Metal size: 1 020 mm x 1 560 mm
Printing area: 980 mm x 1 500 mm
If screened negs supplied: 98 mm x 150 mm at 200 #
If projections supplied: 980 mm x 1 500 mm at 20 #

Figure 6.10
(*continued*)

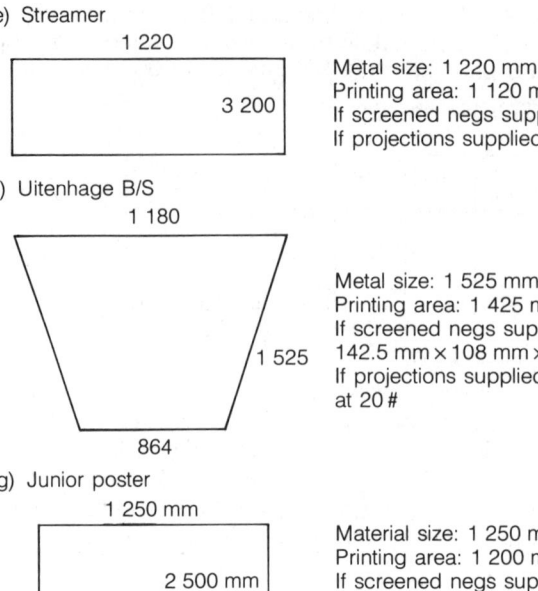

(e) Streamer

1 220

3 200

Metal size: 1 220 mm × 3 200 mm
Printing area: 1 120 mm × 3 100 mm
If screened negs supplied: 112 mm × 310 mm at 200 #
If projections supplied: 1 120 mm × 3 100 mm at 20 #

(f) Uitenhage B/S

1 180

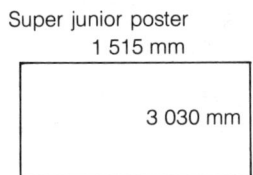

1 525

864

Metal size: 1 525 mm × 1 180 mm × 864 mm
Printing area: 1 425 mm × 1 080 mm × 764 mm
If screened negs supplied:
142.5 mm × 108 mm × 76.4 mm at 200 #
If projections supplied: 1 425 mm × 1 080 mm × 764 mm
at 20 #

(g) Junior poster

1 250 mm

2 500 mm

Material size: 1 250 mm × 2 500 mm
Printing area: 1 200 mm × 2 450 mm
If screened negs supplied: 120 mm × 245 mm at 200 #
If projections supplied: 1 200 mm × 2 450 mm at 20 #

(h) Super junior poster

1 515 mm

3 030 mm

Material size: 1 515 mm × 3 030 mm
Printing area: 1 465 mm × 2 980 mm
If screened negs supplied: 115 mm × 230 mm at 200 #

The major difference apparant between the standard 48-sheet and 96-sheet billboards is the presence and type of illumination. Obviously, the value of a billboard to a client is greatly increased if it is visible during both day and night. Often there is sufficient ambient light to make this possible – especially in the main metropolitan areas – but usually the billboard is independently lit. It can be illuminated either externally, by floodlights, or internally. The internally illuminated structure, variously termed 'Firefly' or 'Met lite', is usually placed in locations where the extra expense is well justified by heavy traffic for long periods of the 24 hours. The face of the panel is painted or silk-screened onto a translucent vinyl material stretched across the structure (in effect an enormous light box), illumination being provided by vertically placed fluorescent tubes. These structures have become very popular in the relatively short time that they have been available in South Africa.

As well as these standard sizes, there are some less well-known ones usually made to fit a particular space or type of location. The 'Junior Poster' is a case in point. In two sizes, 1,23 m x 2,46 m (4' x 8') and 1,50 m x 3,00m (5' x 10'), this double-sided monopole structure was specially designed to provide coverage of urban black townships and some major rural centres. It is placed on the road reserve and thus provides impact on both vehicular and pedestrian traffic. Another specially developed size is the 'Station Streamer', which at 1,22 m x 3,020 m (4' x 10'6'') is ideal for placement over the bridges and walkways in railway stations.

Finally, as far as specially developed structures are concerned, there are 'Bus Shelters' (see figure 6.10). These can carry either a standard four-sheet poster (single or double), or up to five specially shaped steel plate panels which have to be printed individually. Their major claim to inclusion on advertisers' schedules is their unique ability to be placed in the residential areas of cities and towns, where other types of outdoor are not permitted.

The outdoor advertising structural types described thus far are, without exception, static. Maister Outdoor Marketing (Pty) Ltd, the largest of the five or six outdoor advertising contractors (all of whom are members of the Outdoor Advertising Association of South Africa), concentrates mainly on these types of structures. Transportation advertising on and in buses, trains and other means of mass transport is, however, a major area, and ought not to be overlooked by any student of the medium.

The exteriors of buses are probably the best known of these kinds of outdoor. The opportunities range from an all-over painted double decker – the 'Supergraphic' – and the all-over painted single decker – the 'Minigraphic' – to panels and parts of panels in specific places on the bus. All the spaces are normally signwritten, that is to say hand-painted, but occasionally provision can be made for the fixture of self-adhesive vinyl decals. The fleets, which include nearly 8 000 vehicles, are handled by the six members of the Bus Advertising Association of Southern Africa.

Wherever and whenever there are crowds of people some form of outdoor advertising will be made available, regulations and rules permitting. There are superb spaces in and on the approaches to the airports of the country, spaces at the major sporting venues such as Ellis Park and the Wanderers in Johannesburg, and smaller panels available on parking meters and supermarket trolleys throughout the country.

☐ Outdoor costs

Naturally, all of these spaces have their price – prices which vary enormously according not only to the standard laws of supply and demand, but also to the number of spaces bought by a client and the length of the contract period. As a guide, however, in December 1986 space rentals were of the following approximate magnitudes (all are monthly and are inclusive of agency commission but exclusive of GST):

96-sheet billboard	R520
48-sheet billboard	R260
Shop ad 4-sheet	R 72
POP stand	R 40
Supergraphic bus (eg Johannesburg)	R650
Minigraphic bus (eg Pinetown)	R250

A 96-sheet internally illuminated Firefly might cost, according to location, as much as R3 000 per month.

One aspect of outdoor media costing which, as with every other medium, must not be overlooked, is the production and printing of the material to be displayed.

Normally, with the silk-screen process, there are three cost areas to be considered:

☐ Origination – the process up until chromalin proofs
☐ Projection – the manufacture of the full-size screens – one for each 'sheet' and for each colour
☐ Printing – the printing, collating and packing of the finished poster.

Even in general terms costs are difficult to indicate, because they vary with size, design and number of posters produced. However, as a guide one of the largest poster printers in the country gives the following estimates (net of agency commission and GST) for a 48-sheet poster with medium ink distribution:

Origination with 3 separations	±R 1 660
Projection	R 3 140
Printing of 50 posters @ R140 each	R 7 000
300 posters @ R56,45 each	R16 935

☐ Creativity in outdoor

Beauty, as well as creative excellence, lies in the eye of the beholder or art director, and so it is extremely difficult to lay down any more than the most general of guidelines for the creative use of outdoor advertising spaces. They are, first and foremost, very large spaces in relation to human scale and therefore the temptation to crowd the space with a large number of visual statements is very great, but must be strictly rejected. A bold, simple statement, the essence of the proposition about the product or service, is the best way to make outdoor work well.

It has often been said that the advertiser and his agency should start by designing and executing the outdoor component of an all-media campaign and then move on to develop this initial statement to render it suitable for other media. Often the creative treatment for outdoor is a minimally adapted press advertisement or the last frame of a TV commercial – a very false economy. Outdoor is an advertising medium in its own right and, providing certain basic rules are followed, it will prove to be most effective. In a promotional brochure sent out some years ago, Foster and Kleiser, amongst the largest US outdoor plant owners, gave the following guidelines for effective poster design:

☐ Readability
  – Is the lettering and illustration easy to define at a minimum distance of 300 feet (100 m)?
☐ Lettering
  – Is the style of type easy to read?
  – Is the lettering large enough to read with ease?
  – Have you letterspaced and wordspaced the copy carefully to aid legibility?
  – Are there too many type faces in one design?
☐ Colour
  – Has the designer taken full advantage of colour to generate viewer excitement?
☐ Clarity
  – Will the message communicate instantly?

    ☐ Economics
      − Check with your supplier on sheet arrangement for production economies.

☐ Outdoor audience

Having dealt, however superficially, with creativity on outdoor, we can now turn our attention to a consideration of the size and nature of the outdoor audience. The medium has, as we observed earlier, a fundamental characteristic which sets it apart from all other advertising media − that is to say that the message is the medium. Audiences of press and electronic media can be estimated satisfactorily by measuring the exposure of the vehicle carrying the advertisement to members of their respective audiences. Outdoor is not amenable to this kind of treatment, because there simply is no vehicle. Means must therefore be found to make generalisable predictions about the numbers of passages past a poster location or locations. This complex problem has received considerable attention in South Africa over the last ten years, but has been of abiding interest in the UK for much longer. This short overview is not the appropriate place to review the state of research into the medium − we can do no better than to recommend to the serious inquirer the following source references:

☐ Copland, BD. 1952. *The Size and Nature of the Poster Audience − Study 2.* Coventry, UK: Mills & Rockleys.
☐ Copland, BD. 1964. *Poster Audience Surveys.* London: IPA.
☐ Joint Industry Committee on Outdoor Research. 1975. *Outdoor Advertising Audiences in South Africa.* Johannesburg.
☐ SA Advertising Research Foundation. 1982 *et seq. Outdoor in AMPS.* Sandton.

☐ Summary

The outdoor medium is a complex and fascinating medium which amply repays all efforts to understand and exploit its characteristics and attributes. As the country and its populations become more numerous and mobile, so the efficiency and value for money of the medium increases. It is the one medium that requires no purchase or payment to reach its mass audiences and by its nature can only retain a neutral social and political stance. It is the *now* medium.

Direct advertising : media planning depends on identification

Jock L Falkson

Introduction 218

Identity of interest between the advertiser
and the prospective buyer 218

Correct identification of the market 223

Availability of a mailing list 225

Market segmentation 226

Turning people on 226

Creativity is the key 227

Summary 227

☐ Introduction

Media planning is based on three postulates, namely:

☐ A sale is really the natural outcome of an identity of interest between the advertiser and the buyer.

☐ The advertiser must correctly identify his market in terms of the characteristics of the people who already buy his product (or a similar product).

☐ When a list of prospective buyers can be provided (ie the names and addresses of those having the correctly identified characteristics), direct advertising is the medium of choice.

Each of these will be dealt with in more detail.

☐ Identity of interest between the advertiser and the prospective buyer

I consider the key word in advertising to be *identification*. In my view, anyone who understands this key can also understand not only *why* advertising works in the way that it does, but even to some extent *how* it works.

Complex individuals

As a person grows up in his environment he absorbs a multitude of emotional attitudes resulting from his life at home, his interaction with his family, his life at school, his life outside school, his vacations, his sporting activities, his reading, the radio programmes he listens to (whether consciously or subconsciously), the films and TV programmes he sees, his attendance at church, and all the humdrum or exciting activities going on all around him, whether he is a spectator or a participant.

By the time he is grown up and enters the adult world he will have experienced happiness, disappointment, achievement, failure, romance, love, ideals and prejudices. By then he will be the sum total of his likes and dislikes, his emotional prejudices, opinions and impressions. In fact, he will be the result of all his experiences – whether vicarious or personal.

He will be so complex by the time he is 18 that it will defy the efforts of behavioural scientists to describe him or to catalogue him. And, as he grows older, falls in and out of love, marries, divorces, raises children, works to retain – or fights to improve – his position in society and in his work situation, he will compound the complexity of his personality so much that any complete analysis of the ordinary man or woman in the street is, to all intents and purposes, impractical.

Yet this is the person with whom advertising must communicate successfully, and not only with him, but also with the others – the hundreds, the thousands, the hundreds of thousands, even the million or more – who may be regarded as making up the many segments which constitute the market.

Triggers

Every person has his triggers. Indeed, every person has a great many triggers. If advertising practitioners only knew what these triggers were they could anticipate and exploit the known reactions of people simply by pressing the right buttons. In fact, this is what they are trying to do, and the measure of their success in doing so is the measure of their profit in successfully carrying out this delicate process.

Theoretically, they want each one of their advertising messages to be 100% successful. For example, when *Time* mails 1 000 letters to sell subscriptions to its magazine, it is reaching out for the optimum result of enrolling 1 000 new subscribers. When *Mercedes Benz* takes a full page in colour in the *Financial Mail* to announce its latest 450 SE it wants every reader of *Financial Mail* to buy the car, when *Mainstay* communicates with the cinema audience and proposes that it breaks away to *Mainstay* it wants them all to do so, and so on. A hundred percent is the optimum response to any ad.

Then why does *Time* magazine get maybe a 3% response to its mail solicitation? And *Mercedes Benz* and *Mainstay* perhaps not more? (Of course the real response to any *general advertisement* which is not specifically designed to elicit a measurable response is seldom known.)

Is *Time*'s response really 3%? Or is it in fact closer to that mythical 100% on the grounds that there were only 30 people on the mailing list of 1 000 who constituted *Time*'s true prospects at that particular time? Is this conclusion tenable? Hardly. For the fact is, and this has been proved many a time, that if *Time* mailed out the very same piece to the same list say three or four weeks later, the chances are very good that another 20 or so individuals would subscribe.

Courtesy: Time Magazine. Example of a very successful mailer aimed at a specific market segment

Moreover, and this is also known from direct mail experience, if *Time* sent out an entirely different appeal for new subscribers say three months later, to the balance of that same list, it could quite conceivably gain another 20 to 30 subscribers!

What, then, is the explanation for this strange pattern? In my view, an acceptable explanation is that the first mailing contained one or more triggers which successfully found their mark on the first occasion. The second mailing picked up 20 or so new subscribers for no other reason than that *Time* made the same appeal again − thus proving something in favour of repetition. Finally, the third mailing, based on a different theme, triggered off another 30 people who had been preconditioned by earlier communications due to what psychologists call a *learned response*.

You can stay as you are for the rest of your life or you can change to Mainstay. The pure cane spirit.
Courtesy: SFW and JWT (Cape)

Theoretically, then, if all the people on the original list of 1 000 matched the existing profile of *Time* subscribers, they should all be *Time* prospects and should all eventually become *Time* subscribers. *Time* could keep trying new triggers until it succeeded in enrolling all of the 1 000 original prospects. This is an intriguing thought and it may even be true, but the reason why it is only a hypothesis and not a fact is the law of diminishing returns. This means that at some stage it will become unprofitable for *Time* to continue mailing, because the cost of getting *new* subscribers will be too high.

Inertia

Incidentally, it must be recognised that inertia is one of the greatest stumbling blocks in the way of achieving that mythical 100% response to advertising. It seems to be inertia that prevents so many people from responding to an advertising message – even one with which they identify fully. Inertia is certainly well-known to mail advertisers, hence the numerous action devices built into many mailing packages to overcome it, to get some kind of committed activity on the part of respondents. These include sweepstakes, limited time offers, gifts, premiums, yes/no competitions, mystery discount promotions, and so on. And while on this aspect, according to all expert opinion the basic success of inbound telemarketing is due to the fact that it is so simple, so convenient to indulge one's impulses. Inertia is overcome so easily – simply by reaching for the telephone and dialling a number.

Markets are seldom homogeneous; a market is not a single universal mass. On the contrary, as a rule a market is made up of several or many segments, and each segment has a specific customer profile which differs in some important respects, or nuances, from the others. Thus, it is essential for the advertiser to *identify* his market segments and his customer profiles. His success in doing so will be of primary importance to his marketing efforts.

The successful advertising message is the kind that triggers off a sense of identification on the part of the prospect. When *that* happens, the chances are good that a sale will be made or, better still, a customer gained.

To change or not to change the advertisement

I will make no attempt in this contribution to deal with media other than direct mail except to say that I seriously question the proposition which says that you never change a good advertisement, you keep running it. If my understanding of identification is right, then what you are doing after a time is merely reinforcing your message to your existing customers – preaching to the converted. Of course, this is essential and indeed required in every advertising programme, for it is your existing customers who really keep you in business and on no account must you neglect them.

However, it is just as essential to discover new customers, and for this other triggers, and hence new advertising approaches, are necessary. At any rate, even if I am not entirely correct insofar as general media are concerned (not my field of expertise), I believe that I am right when I make this proposition insofar as the direct response medium is concerned.

Thus, a mail order advertisement will run as long as it pulls profitable results. What does the mail order merchandiser do thereafter – go out of business? Not at all. He must try other approaches and other advertisements to sell the same product. In fact, he should carry on a process of continuous testing by developing new advertisements and testing them.

In direct mail, too, the proven and successful mailing package (control) is used until the results so diminish as to turn profit into loss. That is when to stop, or rather even before this happens – when the downward curve on the graph indicates that the next mailing is likely to produce a loss. But we also seek new ways to influence our market segments, for in a continuous programme of advertising we are always looking for new prospects, new customers, and to find them we also have to find new triggers.

Changing markets

Of course the market never stands still; it changes continuously, because people change. Therefore, advertising must keep pace with change. (That is why it is never really possible to stop research into your market place). The following are some obvious examples of change:

☐ A newly married couple might well be in the market for a house. Until they married they did not have this need.

☐ A new mother is in the market for dozens of items for her baby as well as for herself. Until she conceived, she had no baby or new mother's needs whatsoever.

☐ A young man who has finally saved up R10 000 is to that extent quite a different prospect to some advertisers compared with another young man who has not started saving.

☐ A travel agent who wants to promote a skiing holiday would do well to limit his offer to younger people – not to the over 50s.

☐ The outfitter who writes you a letter telling you he has just received a new shipment of shirts in your size, is likely to evoke a response in you. He has identified your size. If he offered you other sizes you would show no interest, no matter how persuasive his copy or design.

☐ A university student might well be an obvious prospect for a speed-reading course. After graduation he may never again be a prospect.

Psycho-graphics

The more we can identify people by their interests, lifestyle, hobbies, ideals, prejudices, age, wealth, education, religion, culture, physical size, politics, etc, the closer we will be to correctly identifying our market segments and customer profiles.

But while wealth is certainly an indicator for many marketers, wealth alone is *not*, psychographically speaking, a common factor. By way of example, to a yacht builder the fact that a man can afford one does not automatically make him a prospect. A boat builder must look for people who love boating and sailing, for it is among these people that he will find his prospective buyers.

Needs and wants

Of course it is necessary to bear in mind that needs and wants are basic to the marketing process, but it should be remembered that a need is not the same as a want. A need is absolutely basic. People need food – they must have it, but people do not *need* alcohol – they *can* live without it. However, many *want* and love their liquor and depending on the degree of their *want* will take steps to fulfil their desires.

The job of the direct advertiser and marketer is to identify such consumer wants and to persuade consumers to buy his product because it satisfies their needs. If he is aware of this he has a greater potential for success.

When the prospect identifies with your product or service and the things it can do for him he is in effect saying: 'Yeah! That's me. And that's for me'. That is the real meaning of identification. When this happens the person in question telephones you, or comes into your store, or fills in a reply card and exposes himself to your sales pitch. Your advertising will have done its job and, if all else is equal, you should now make the sale or, better still, you should make a new customer.

Reverse selling

I would go so far as to say that when there is an identity of interests and a sale or the acquisition of a customer is *not* the result, then the advertiser must accept that he has somehow *unsold* that customer. People sometimes refer to this process as 'reverse selling'.

And reverse selling does happen, unfortunately all too often. You can unsell someone personally or through your salesmen, and you can unsell by mail or telephone just as easily. Generally, then, the person on whom you have spent so much time and money to get him to buy from you will go elsewhere to seek satisfaction from the *sales process* itself. Customers want satisfaction not only from the product or service being offered, but also from all the people who are personally involved in negotiating the sales transaction.

☐ Correct identification of the market

A missionary will not waste his time and energy preaching to the converted – he will leave that to the parish priest. The job of the missionary, by definition, is to find new converts. In advertising terminology this means new prospects, new customers.

Of course, advertising must perform both jobs. It must seek out new prospects and also preach to the converted. Successful advertising does that, but how does the process work?

Preaching to the converted

In the advertising profession there is a school of thought which believes that it is the language and design of advertising which persuades people, for logical and emotional reasons, to buy a certain product. That advertising works in this way is surely true, but there is another school of thought that is also surely true. This school believes that most successful advertising actually preaches to the converted, that is to say it is the converted who are really being persuaded and reinforced in their views, both logical and emotional, with emphasis on the latter.

This school of thought says that it is the short man who seeks out advertisements which tell him that high heels or stretching exercises will solve his height problem. It is as well to recognise that this message will have no value for the man who is not complexed about his height: the message *Be taller!* has no relevance to such a person. If he is not complexed about being called *Shorty*, it cannot persuade him. The same holds for *Baldy*. If a man feels secure about the way he looks, he will not be in the market for a head of hair.

The lady with an underdeveloped bust will be in the market for a bust developing course. Surely it is obvious that she will seek out the advertisement which promises her the benefit she desires? When it catches her eye, therefore, that advertisement will be preaching to the converted.

Can the process be any different for cosmetics, clothes, cars, furniture, homes, travel, or whatever?

Women have an inbuilt desire to look beautiful. It is a motivation so deep and true that it is part of their psyche. Surely this is the reason why they read advertisements about cosmetics and try one and then switch to another one? The cosmetic advertisements preach to the converted.

We all buy clothes that fit our self-image. We identify and we buy. Not that we do not sometimes make mistakes — of course we do. And when someone tells a woman she does not look good in something she has only just bought, what happens? When she ceases to identify nothing on earth will make her wear that thing again.

What happens when boys and girls identify with a new look? The simple fact is that fashion changes — not because James Dean, the Beatles or the Gatsby film set out to sell the cinema audience on a change in fashion, but because the audience identified and wanted to change, and so created a new fashion.

Of course, preaching or advertising to the converted does not mean that the advertiser cannot succeed in developing innovations, new styles, new habits, or new designs. On the contrary, the advertiser is often blessed with financial success when he does so. However, is this because he has rammed a contrary thing down the throats of his prospects, or because he has anticipated the wants and desires of his market — whether by research or just plain honest-to-goodness intuition? When the market identifies, he wins. When it does not, he loses.

Therefore, the advertiser must be conscious of what constitutes the advertising process. He advertises most profitably when he preaches to the converted. But, as with parish priests, there are many sermons and many sermonisers. Not all succeed in getting their audience to identify.

Identification is the name of the direct advertising game.

The market is never wrong because the great majority will buy only when their sense of identification coincides with their decision to part with money. No marketer can stay in business on the mistakes or the contrariness of a minority of buyers. There are not enough people making enough mistakes to keep such marketers in business.

People read the books they like, go to the films they like, tune in to the radio and TV programmes they like and read the newspapers and the articles they like. They even read, look and listen to the advertising they like.

☐ Availability of a mailing list

From a direct marketing point of view, of course, the key to the identification of a market is to be found in the mailing list. The more accurately the mailing list can be tailored to the profile which has been identified as the market, the greater the chance of influencing these people to buy the product or service.

In order that the importance of mailing list identification may be understood, a fairly new concept must be introduced.

The medium is the market

You will have heard it said that the medium is the *message*, but did you know that the medium is also the *market*? This idea may seem strange, but the concept is important to all advertisers, not least direct mail advertisers. A good example to consider in the light of this idea, is the *Reader's Digest*.

The *Reader's Digest* is a medium for advertisers, this much is obvious. The *Reader's Digest* is also a market for advertisers. If this is not obvious, it will now be explained.

Although it is not possible to name them off hand, there may well be some advertisers who advertise *solely* in the *Reader's Digest*. For such advertisers the market consists only of people who read the *Reader's Digest*. However, even for those advertisers who do use other media the *Reader's Digest* is still a market or, to be more precise, a market segment. *Scope* may be another market, *Rapport* another, the *Financial Mail* another, and so on, for each medium is a market.

Let us take a mythical magazine and look closely at its readership as determined by research. Suppose the readership is 350 000. Let us assume that we find a magazine readership profile as in table 6.13

Table 6.13
Magazine readership profile
(350 000 readers)

Total	Men	Women
	224 000	126 000
Age:		
16-24	29%	27%
25-34	31%	28%
35-44	27%	22%
45-54	9%	15%
55 +	4%	8%
City/Town	89%	91%
Vill/Rural	11%	9%
Car	90%	60%
Second car	40%	20%
Travelled abroad	60%	30%
Home owner	40%	20%

	Households
Refrigerator	93%
Stereo hi-fi	66%
Television: colour	60%
black and white	22%
Dishwasher	14%
Deep-freeze	58%

Now let us consider the advertising objectives of a manufacturer of a product that would appeal to women only, say during their menopause. And let us agree that this is a ten-year span from 45 to 55.

When we turn to our research we see that only 15% of the readership of our mythical magazine audience constitutes women in this age group. The market for our manufacturer in this magazine would therefore be 18 900 individuals.

When the manufacturer turns to direct marketing he may be pleasantly surprised to learn, however, that he can find a list of 186 400 women in this age group. And since the medium is the market, these 186 400 individuals are as much a market as the readership of any magazine.

You will appreciate that the comparative examples offered are quite startling. Yet with the availability of the list of TV licensees and Voters Rolls – both on computer tape – many new and very specific markets have become available to advertisers. In many instances, therefore, direct mail may well be the advertiser's medium of choice.

☐ Market segmentation

There are products and services of specific interest to all age groups, to specific sexes, to young marrieds, to the middle aged, to the elderly, to the wealthy, to the not so wealthy, to the city or rural dweller, to the Afrikaans or English speaker, to the house or flat dweller, and so on. Each one of these parameters, singly or in combination, represents a market profile or a market segment.

It should be axiomatic, therefore, that when you can identify a market so closely you simply must use the medium that enables you to communicate effectively with that specific market.

And surely, in the light of this background, the method of looking at cost per thousand circulation or number of readers as one of the main factors in allocating advertising expenditure does not hold water?

Surely it has become essential for advertisers to look more closely at the direct mail medium: to study it, to research it and to understand it, to equate not only the cost per reader, but more logically, which media provide the advertiser with additionally profitable markets with the opportunity therefore to maximise sales and profits; to consider not only the cost per thousand, but far more importantly the cost per result; and not only the cost per result, but the cost of winning a new customer; and not only that, but the annualised sales value of the purchases of each new customer won? After all, the purpose of advertising is surely not to cause a ripple in a pond, but rather to catch fish?

☐ Turning people on

Only when you have correctly identified and profiled your market can you put your copywriters and designers to work to discover and test the triggers that will turn turned-on people on. When you discover these you will find that all-important identity of interest which should make a sale the most natural result and a customer the most likely consequence of an effectively planned and created programme of direct communication.

I hope I have provided sufficient support to prove my three postulates, namely:

☐ A sale is really the natural outcome of an identity of interest between the advertiser and the buyer.

☐ The advertiser must correctly identify his market in terms of the characteristics of the people who already buy his product (or a similar product).

☐ When a list of prospective buyers can be provided (ie those having the correctly identified characteristics) direct advertising is the medium of choice.

☐ Creativity is the key

I should end right here, but there is a fourth postulate that I would like to mention very briefly, namely:

☐ After the first three postulates have been satisfied, the professional hand of an experienced direct marketing copywriter is required to create the marketing communication.

All the philosophy discussed above is meaningless unless you have a direct mail copywriter who can put together a creative direct mail package which will cause the prospect to identify with the offer so that a sale (or a new customer) should be its natural outcome.

This relies heavily on the art of the copywriter. It relies on his knowledge of people, their lifestyles and what makes them tick. It needs the experience of a man or woman who has lived and loved and requires a knowledge of the kind of direct mail techniques which can involve people and of those which do not. It needs a deep understanding of the process of continuity and requires an understanding of the law of reciprocal interest. It requires the mature hand of someone who has enjoyed success and failure in hundreds of direct mail campaigns and needs professionalism in the art of readable writing and the art of instant comprehension. All these attributes, and many more, of course, are yours when you use a professional direct mail copywriter.

Nevertheless, the professional copywriter knows that he is not omniscient. He knows that in spite of all the richness of his experience, he cannot ever know *exactly* what is going to happen when his masterpiece is delivered by the postman. He does not know in advance which of his triggers are going to work, or just how well.

The professional copywriter will therefore explain his need for testing (not research!), because in my opinion research tells you what a person says he intends to do, whereas testing tells you what he has actually done as the only way to find out how a given group of people may react to a specific offer or mailing package. He will explain the need for testing other triggers or approaches too, and for persistence and continuity in direct mail campaigning.

Incidentally, if copy is stressed more than design there is a reason for it. The intention is not to denigrate design, for good design is essential to support good copy and good graphics are essential to convey an image of quality. The fact of the matter is that as far as direct mail is concerned, it is copy that does the actual selling. You can send out a piece containing copy only and you can sell from it; this is done all the time. But you cannot do this using design only.

☐ Summary

The success of direct advertising is dependent upon careful planning of the campaign, correct identification of the prospective buyers and knowing their needs and wants, using the best mailing list and turning people on by using the right triggers and excellent creativity.

Media planning case study: Sparkle
Courtesy of the South African Advertising Research Foundation

The media brief	228
Media objectives	230
Media strategy	231
Media specifics	241
Budget redistribution	244
Schedule performance	244
Budget summary	246
Date plan	246

☐ The media brief

Before a media plan can be put together, a foundation of sorts must be laid – the *media brief*. To simplify matters, and because it is easier to explain theory by example, we shall follow the development of a media plan for an imaginary product called *Sparkle*. *Sparkle* is a soft drink with a unique self-flavouring property. All you have to do is think of a flavour and *Sparkle* will taste of it.

Before a media brief can be put together, some basic information must be obtained on the product and the forthcoming campaign.

The advertiser's marketing objectives and strategy

An advertiser's *marketing objectives* could be the sales volume that he plans to achieve, the type of people from whom the sales are to come, and the position that he wishes his product to occupy in its market.

The shares of the total market which are held by our brand and its competitors are important. Market shares are measured through the research surveys provided, for example, by the AC Nielsen Company or the Household Consumer Audit (HCA). AMPS can supply data on the products that people use, but does not provide information at the level of individual brands.

The planner should also know how the sales of his client's product are going compared with those of competitors, how competitive brands are advertised and promoted, and what the advertiser intends to do with the product in the coming year.

As far as our imaginary soft drink is concerned, there are 12 products on the market. By now *Sparkle* has reached third place with a 10% market share. Brand 'A' leads with a 40% share, followed by Brand 'B' with a 30% share. Nine 'Other Brands' share the remaining 20% of the market. It has taken *Sparkle* five years to reach this 10% share, but it is the only brand that has shown any real growth. Most of *Sparkle's* increase has been achieved by taking market share from the smaller brands rather than from the market leaders.

The advertiser's *marketing objective* is to increase the market share of *Sparkle* from the current 10% to 15%.

The advertiser's *marketing strategy* comprises the broad means by which he intends to achieve this objective. He has told the planner that he intends to run an aggressive campaign with advertising playing a large role in supporting his sales force. The high point of the campaign will be a major promotion in November and December. This is in the second quarter of the advertiser's financial year which, since soft drinks sales peak in the summer months, runs from July to June.

Such information gives the media planner a feel for what is to happen, ultimately affecting the types of media chosen and used. It also provides guidance to the advertising agency should the advertiser require help in deciding how much money should be spent on advertising, in other words on the budget required to achieve his marketing objectives or sales targets.

Creative considerations

Creative considerations are extremely important to the media planner as it is difficult to take media decisions if you do not know *what* is to be said in the advertising and *how* it is to be presented to the consumer.

The media and creative departments within an agency, therefore, should work closely together. For example, what ideas does the creative department have? Are these ideas suitable to the requirements of the marketing operation? Are they affordable? The planner's choice of media, for example, might be affected by the requirement that colour should have top priority in the advertising campaign.

In the case of *Sparkle*, we are fortunate to have some available material; illustrations and an overseas TV commercial 20 seconds in length. The sound-track could be extended to make a 30-second radio commercial at a comparatively low cost.

Specific timing requirements

Advertising exposure can be wasted if it does not match up with the efforts of the advertiser's sales team. In the case of *Sparkle*, the client wishes to generate consumer interest in the product for a longer period than is usual for soft drinks. He aims to achieve distribution of *Sparkle* in the shops as early as July and August, and he needs advertising support of this. The dates for the major promotion are from 14 November to 30 December. The client also expects advertising to continue after the promotion up until the end of May.

The budget

Usually the advertiser states what monies are available, although sometimes the advertising agency might be approached for guidance. In *Sparkle's* case, the budget has been given as R585 000, including GST.

The media planner needs to know what the advertiser expects his budget to cover. He must enquire whether it is all to be spent on buying advertising space or time, or if reserves are to be held back to cover other costs. These might comprise, for example, the costs of actually producing the advertisements, of advertising to retailers, of direct mail advertising, or the costs of promotional materials. The planner must also inquire whether there is additional money available to cover media inflation or other contingencies. In our example 20% will be required to cover production costs and media inflation.

The amount of money available for media exposure, therefore, is 80% of the budget, less GST, which amounts to R439 000. We are fortunate in having the overseas commercial, because if an original had to be produced a much higher production cost would be incurred.

There are several ways of attempting to set budget levels. Two methods are described here:

Task budgetting method

A target is set in terms of advertising exposure. For example, an advertiser might state that he wishes his advertising to be seen by 80% of the population and for each person to have the opportunity to see at least 30 advertisements. The media planner will then work out how much it will cost to achieve this target.

Ratio method

Advertising expenditure is considered to be an integral part of the marketing budget for a specific product and a certain amount is set aside for advertising as a cost for doing business. An advertiser might work on an *advertising to sales ratio*, deciding, for example, to spend perhaps 5% of his gross sales revenue on advertising. Or he might base the amount to be spent on each case of the product actually sold.

The target market

It is essential to know who the advertising is aimed at. The planner will be concerned with their demographic characteristics (such as their race, language and sex), their social circumstances, and whether the campaign aims to reach users, non-users, or both. Regarding this last point, much will depend on whether people who do not use the product at all at present may be persuaded to do so, and on whether people who use competitive brands may be persuaded to change. The greater the media planner's knowledge of the target market the better his media plan should be.

In relation to our product *Sparkle*, AMPS can supply an overall view of soft drinks users. Whilst soft drinks are generally bought by a wide variety of people of all race groups, *Sparkle* has special appeal to women with children aged 3-15, who live in urban areas. The product is seen as being popular with mothers because of its special self-flavouring device: 'Think of a flavour and *Sparkle* will taste of it.'

☐ Media objectives

The planner is often provided with media objectives. A statement of objectives as bland as 'maximum coverage and frequency' should be rejected, for although it sounds good it means very little, lacking specific direction. A failure to supply adequate statements of objectives often means that the planner will end up by setting his own, having studied the brief and weighed up, with the help of AMPS data, what is necessary to achieve the marketing objectives.

In the case of *Sparkle*, we know that the advertiser wants to gain 5% in market share. We know the timing of his sales efforts and who our main target is, and we have demographic data which describes the target group.

Therefore, a realistic objective would be to convert more of the target market to using our brand, as well as sustaining the interest of present users. We want to try and reach as many as possible of the target market, with a good degree of repeat exposure to sustain awareness from July to May, with emphasis on the promotional period from 14 November until 30 December.

> Simplifying, we might set our objectives as follows:
> ☐ A minimum coverage of 80% of the target market
> ☐ during each month of advertising
> ☐ with people having the opportunity to see or hear an advertisement at least four times each month.

The performance of a media plan against such objectives is measurable, and how it may be measured will be described in the next section.

☐ Media strategy

Media strategies are the solutions planners propose in order to achieve their media objectives. Strategy statements reflect specifically the course of media actions to be taken, and therefore the next step in media planning.

Having set his media objectives, the planner weighs up the pros and cons of each medium against the requirements of the brief. He must also have an understanding of the media market place – the availability and the cost structure of each medium at a given time. The budget will have to be apportioned to each medium type chosen.

One of the planner's problems, however, is how to adjust the forces of impact, coverage, frequency and timing to achieve a balanced advertising schedule.

	A
Cover	Frequency
Impact	Time

	B
Cover	Frequency
Impact	Time

The above two diagrams illustrate the amount of media exposure that can be bought with a given amount of money. Square A represents a schedule where all components are equal. However, if we want to increase our campaign frequency (see B), it will be at the expense of attaining a lower coverage level. In the same way, the length of the campaign will have to be cut down in order to achieve a higher impact (a larger space size, for example).

A short review of the salient points from the media brief is necessary before we start following through the media strategy for *Sparkle*:

☐ to gain five market share points, an increase of 50% in share
☐ to achieve this through aggressive marketing, by extending the product's season, and by reaching a peak with a major promotion

☐ the prime target market comprises women with children aged 3-15, living in urban areas

☐ a 20-second television commercial is available

The next step in the media strategy procedure is to check the target market and its exposure to the various media.

Defining the target market

AMPS identifies a group of people who are users of the product category 'bottled, or tinned cold drinks', that is fizzy or bubbly soft drinks. The question actually asked of people in the Survey is: 'How many glasses do you personally drink per week?'

At this stage it might be useful to point out why women with children aged 3-15 years were chosen as the target group: It is assumed that if the mother is a regular consumer of cold drinks she will permit her children to drink them as well. So, although the target group definition has an emphasis on women, we shall in fact also aim advertising at children, who might influence their mothers to buy *Sparkle*.

A first special computer analysis is run to show the frequency of product usage in terms of glasses consumed per week. Table 6.14 shows the consumption claimed by the target population broken down by race.

Table 6.14
Cold drinks consumption: urban women with children 3-15 by race

	Users		Glasses per week	
Unweighted sample	2 090			
	'000	%	'000	%
Total users	1 131	100,0	9 722	100,0
White	315	27,9	2 304	23,7
Coloured	184	16,3	1 164	12,0
Asian	64	5,6	339	3,5
Black	568	50,2	5 915	60,8

In terms of numbers, Blacks represent almost half of all the people in the target group – 568 000 out of a total of 1 131 000. But in terms of consumption, they represent over 60% of the market. As can be seen from the table, blacks consume an estimated 5 915 000 glasses a week out of a total of 9 722 000 glasses for all people in the target group.

If the percentage that a certain race represents of the total population in the target group is divided by the percentage of the target group consumption that is accounted for by the same race, an index which is shown in the third column of figures in table 6.15 is obtained.

Table 6.15
Indices of cold drinks consumption: urban women with children 3-15 by race

	(A) Users (%)	(B) Glasses per week (%)	(B ÷ A) Penetration index	Relative index
Total users	100,0	100,0		
White	27,9	23,7	85	70
Coloured	16,3	12,0	74	61
Asian	5,6	3,5	63	52
Black	50,2	60,8	121	100

For example, Whites account for 27,9% of the population of the target group, but the number of glasses drunk by Whites is 23,7% of the total target group consumption. Dividing 27,9% into 23,7% gives an index of 85. These index numbers provide a quick guide to the relative importance of each race group as a consumer of cold drinks or to its propensity to consume the product. The index numbers will also help us to distribute total advertising effort between the race groups.

Comparisons between these index numbers are made even simpler if we divide each one of them by the largest figure. The results of this calculation are shown in the last column of Table 6.15. Thus we see that the black market could be the most valuable sector for *Sparkle*. However, this does not mean that we can or should neglect the 40% of total consumption that is represented by the remainder of the total target market.

In table 6.16 the consumers within each race group are broken down into three subgroups so that each subgroup acounts for approximately one third of the total consumption of that race group.

Table 6.16
Weight of usership of cold drinks: urban women with children 3-15 by race

	White	Coloured	Asian	Black
Total users:				
Glasses (%)	100,0	100,0	100,0	100,0
Users (%)	(100,0)	(100,0)	(100,0)	(100,0)
Light users:				
Glasses per week	1-7	1-7	1-5	1-12
Average glasses per				
person per week	3,5	3,7	2,5	5,0
Glasses (%)	34,5	32,5	31,9	34,1
Users (%)	(73,0)	(78,3)	(37,2)	(70,4)
Medium users:				
Glasses per week	8-20	8-20	5-12	13-24
Average glasses per				
person per week	13,0	13,5	7,9	17,8
Glasses (%)	33,2	32,0	30,4	33,3
Users (%)	(19,1)	(15,2)	(20,3)	(19,6)
Heavy users:				
Glasses per week	21 or more	21 or more	13 or more	25 or more
Average glasses per				
person per week	29,0	27,5	16,0	33,8
Glasses (%)	31,6	28,4	37,8	32,6
Users (%)	(7,9)	(5,5)	(12,5)	(10,0)

For example, looking down the column of figures headed 'Whites', we see that the first subgroup, 'light users', accounts for 34,5% of total glasses drunk per week by white consumers within the target group, whilst the second subgroup, 'medium users', accounts for 33,2% and the third and last subgroup, 'heavy users', accounts for 31,6% of total white consumption.

The next stage is to analyse the target group by demographics to see whether any subgroup is of particular importance when consumers are broken down, for example by area, income or age. So as not to become completely bogged down with numbers, we shall again index the results.

Table 6.17 shows data for white consumers within the target group and separately for urban Blacks:

Table 6.17
Cold drinks consumption: urban women with children 3-15, by area, income and age, within race

	White			Black		
	(A) Total	(B) Users	(B ÷ A) Pene- tration index	(A) Total	(B) Users	(B ÷ A) Pene- tration index
Unweighted sample	1 372	754		782	649	
	%	%		%	%	
Total	100,00	100,0		100,0	100,0	
Area (NPU zone)						
A	43,2	44,6	103	40,1	41,7	104
B	12,8	14,3	112	12,8	12,7	99
C	79,0	8,6	109	13,3	14,8	112
D	12,1	11,1	92	15,1	13,9	92
E	8,3	6,7	87	15,3	13,8	90
F	2,0	1,3	65	0,4	0,5	125
G	13,7	13,4	98	1,6	1,2	75
H	–	–	–	1,5	1,4	93
Household income						
A	15,1	14,6	97	37,7	34,7	100
B	32,2	32,4	100	42,0	43,7	104
C	49,2	49,5	101	4,6	20,2	94
D	3,4	3,5	103	1,7	1,4	82
Age						
16-24	9,2	11,1	121	13,9	15,2	109
25-34	41,1	43,8	107	39,9	42,8	107
35-49	44,5	41,3	93	36,4	34,2	94
50 + ...	5,2	3,8	73	9,8	7,8	80

The second of these two subgroups will serve as an example of the way the calculation has been carried out.

Looking at the first line of information, we see that 40,1% of all urban Blacks within the target group live in NPU Zone A. The same line of figures also shows that 41,7% of urban black users of soft drinks live in the same zone. Dividing the second of these two figures, 41,7 by the first, 40,1 provides an index of 104. The fact that this figure is greater than 100 simply indicates that for urban Blacks in the target group, NPU Zone A is of above average importance. Putting the same finding another way, a disproportionately large number of urban black users of cold drinks are to be found in this zone compared with the target group as a whole.

Considering all the index figures for urban Blacks in the same manner, we see that two zones are particularly above average in the concentration of cold drink users which they offer. These are Zones C and F. On the other side of the coin, Zone G is considerably below the average for all urban Blacks in the target group, with an index of only 75. Turning to household income, Group D offers below average prospects with an index of only 82, and the same is true of urban Blacks in the target group who are 50 years of age or more. Their index is only 80.

Table 6.17 shows information for Whites and urban Blacks within the target group only, simply to avoid overloading with too many data. But, from the full computer print-out similar conclusions could be drawn regarding the importance of demographic subgroups amongst coloured and Asian users of cold drinks.

Regarding the household income groups that were referred to in table 6.17 the following points should be noted:

☐ The figures which are used to define each of the groups are changed each year to take account of the effects of inflation.

☐ The figures represent monthly household incomes, so if more than one member of the family is earning their incomes are added together to arrive at the household level shown.

The figures that were used to define the income groups are in table 6.18.

Table 6.18
AMPS income
groups, by race:
Rand

	A	B	C	D
White	3 000 or more	1 600-2 999	600-1 599	599 or less
Coloured	1 100 or more	600-1 099	150- 599	149 or less
Asian	1 600 or more	900-1 599	300- 899	299 or less
Black	500 or more	200- 499	50- 199	49 or less

Having appraised the importance of racial and demographic subgroups within the total target market, the media planner can now take a general look at media coverage in order to pinpoint those media with above average penetration within the target group as a whole, or within the subsections of it.

Table 6.19 turns to this question by relating to the target market of urban women with children between 3 and 15 years of age, broken down by race into four subgroups.

Table 6.19 Media exposure: urban women with children 3-15, by cold drinks use within race

	White			Coloured			Asian			Black		
	(A) Total	(B) Users	(B÷A) Penetration index	(A) Total	(B) Users	(B÷A) Penetration index	(A) Total	(B) Users	(B÷A) Penetration index	(A) Total	(B) Users	(B÷A) Penetration index
Unweighted sample	1 372	754		679	447		383	240		782	649	
Total ('000) = %	555	315		281	184		99	64		681	568	
	%	%		%	%		%	%		%	%	
Viewed TV1 'yesterday'	85,9	87,6	102	56,6	56,5	100	77,8	79,7	102	9,1	9,3	102
Viewed TV2/3 'yesterday'	*	*		76,2	77,7	102	13,1	14,1	108	11,2	11,3	101
Viewed any TV 'yesterday'	85,9	87,6	102	57,7	57,6	100	77,8	79,7	102	14,4	14,8	103
Heavy TV viewers (3 hours per day or more)	44,0	47,6	108	30,6	33,2	108	22,2	25,0	113	9,8	10,0	102
Listened to radio 'yesterday'												
Springbok	32,6	32,7	100	33,1	32,6	98	38,4	39,1	102	*	*	
Highveld	28,3	28,9	102	*	*	*	*	*		*	*	
Good Hope	8,3	1,3	88	32,4	31,5	96	*	*		*	*	
Port Natal	6,5	6,0	92	*	*		16,2	18,8	116	*	*	
Radio 5	9,2	11,1	121	8,5	8,7	102	15,2	17,2	113	*	*	
Channel 702	6,1	7,3	120	*	*		*	*		*	*	
Radio Bantu	*	*		*	*		*	*		55,7	56,9	102
Bophuthatswana	*	*		*	*		*	*		6,6	7,2	109
Truro	*	*		*	*		42,4	48,4	114	*	*	

Table 6.19 Media exposure: urban women with children 3-15, by cold drinks use within race (continued)

	White			Coloured			Asian			Black		
	(A) Total	(B) Users	(B÷A) Penetration index	(A) Total	(B) Users	(B÷A) Penetration index	(A) Total	(B) Users	(B÷A) Penetration index	(A) Total	(B) Users	(B÷A) Penetration index
Unweighted sample	1 372	754		679	447		383	240		782	649	
Total ('000) = %	555	315		281	184		99	64		681	568	
	%	%		%	%		%	%		%	%	
Visited the cinema												
Within the last 7 days	10,1	9,8	97	5,3	6,5	123	*	*		*	*	
Within the last 14 days	15,7	16,2	103	8,9	11,4	128	9,6	10,9	120	*	*	
Read:												
Any English morning newspaper	20,7	21,0	101	23,1	23,4	101	21,2	23,4	110	15,0	15,3	102
Any English weekly newspaper	44,9	47,0	105	40,6	39,1	96	65,7	73,4	112	22,9	23,6	103
Any Afrikaans weekly newspaper........................	45,8	44,1	96	43,4	47,3	109	*	*		*	*	
Any non-white weekly newspaper	*	*		26,7	23,4	88	44,4	48,4	109	28,6	28,3	99
Any white magazine	94,2	94,9	101	43,8	41,8	95	57,6	60,9	106	20,0	20,6	103
Any Afrikaans magazine	62,2	62,9	101	52,7	57,6	109	*	*		*	*	
Any non-white magazine	5,6	6,7	120	11,3	11,4	100	13,1	15,6	119	37,6	39,6	105

*Less than 5,0%

Each of these race groups shows three columns of figures. The first represents the *coverage of different media* amongst *the race group as a whole,* expressed as percentages. The next column represents the coverage of the same media, but now amongst people in *that race group* who are *also cold drink users.* The last column of figures in each set contains *index numbers* obtained by dividing the first column into the second.

In order to understand the data a little better, look at the first line of the table opposite the heading TV1 'yesterday' as an example. The first figure on this line tells us that on average 85,9% of Whites in the target group watched TV1 on the day before a survey interview took place. Similarly, the second figure tells us that the coverage of the same medium was 87,6% amongst Whites within the target group who were also users of cold drinks. Finally, the third figure, 102, is an index obtained by dividing 87,6% by 85,9%. It tells us that the penetration of TV1 for Whites in the target group was slightly higher among cold drink users than for this subgroup as a whole, but only by a small margin.

The various percentages in the table can be turned back into actual numbers of people, because at the head of each column of figures the table shows the size of the subgroup in thousands to which that column relates. Thus, for example, the viewership of TV1 'yesterday' amongst Whites in the target group is 85,9% of 555 000 people.

By studying the pattern of the index numbers on the table, we can see which media are biased in their coverage favourably towards cold drink users within subsections of the target market. And the media planner can thus pinpoint those which are best suited to his needs. At the same time, the absolute level of coverage as shown in the first column of each set of figures is also important.

Against the white subgroup of the target market we can see that high coverage is provided by both television and magazines. Radio 5 or Channel 702, however, would not be suitable choices of media to reach Whites. The index numbers are high, 121 and 120 respectively, indicating that the coverage of these two media is biased quite considerably towards the group we are trying to reach. But in absolute terms, the proportions of Whites within the target group which they cover, 6,1% for example, indicate that 702 are too low for them to be considered as major media.

Coverage of the coloured subgroups within the target market by individual media is lower than the case of Whites. Top coverage is provided by television, by certain radio stations, by newspapers and by magazines. Media selectivity amongst Coloureds is marginal. That is to say, the index numbers are little different from 100, except in some cases where coverage is low.

Data for the Asians within the target group follows the pattern for the Whites. High coverage is provided by television, 77,8%, English weekly newspapers, 65,7%, and magazines, 57,6%. Radio, however, is not too far behind, with Truro at 42,4% and Springbok at 38,4%.

For the black subgroup within the target market, highest coverage comes from Radio Bantu, followed by black magazines, but the latter offer only a fairly low coverage, just under 40%, compared with the reach of white magazines amongst the white subsection of the target group.

Other media which do not offer high enough coverage to warrant their primary choice, for example Radio 5 which we mentioned previously, might nevertheless be used additionally if they can be afforded to build up frequency of exposure once the main media objectives have been met.

In the case of cinema, the medium must be excluded from consideration for the *Sparkle* campaign, because the production cost of converting the overseas television commercial to high quality film for cinema use would be more than could be afforded in this year's budget.

(Cinemark has advised that the cost of converting a TV commercial into a high quality film for use in cinemas will cost only about R700 if processed in the USA, and that the overall cinema production costs should not exceed R3 000.

Under these circumstances, cinema could also be considered in this exercise.)

Media factors Subsequent to defining the target market, the planner has to assess all the media options, including those provided by media for which audience data is not available, as was the case for outdoor media prior to AMPS '84. The pros and cons of each media type are evaluated with reference to the media brief and their relevance to the proposed campaign. Some indication of the cost of using each medium may be included.

The factors against which each media option should be assessed and a brief explanation thereof are discussed below. (Unfortunately, this presentation does not afford sufficient time to assess each medium against each option in relation to *Sparkle*. In any case, such evaluations are of necessity subjective to a degree and may well vary from advertising agency to agency):

Not necessarily in order of importance, we might list first the *physical characteristics* a medium offers: Does it have sound? Can it portray movement? Can it provide colour? Linked to this last point is the potential *quality of reproduction* of the visual parts of our advertisements. As with all the criteria we are noting here, the importance of the factors just mentioned will vary widely from case to case, depending on the particular product and campaign we are considering.

Naturally, the cost of any medium is important, in particular its *unit cost* – the price of a single insertion in it, or size or length relevant to our campaign's needs. The other side of the coin is whether a medium is *economical* or not – how expensive it is to buy, on one hand, adequate coverage of our target group and, on the other, adequate frequency. Production costs must also be considered – the cost of actually producing the commercial or advertisement.

Irrespective of cost, *availability* is critical; it is no good being able to afford a medium if we cannot buy the space or time we want because it is in short supply.

Another aspect of economy is the *selectivity* of different media – whether we can use them so as to reach the target group we are interested in only, or whether, unavoidably, we have to buy a wider audience with some consequent wastage of our advertising spend. Closely related is the question of *regional flexibility*: Can a medium only be used for national coverage, or can it be aimed at specific areas, at will? Regional flexibility is important in relation to a medium's potential for *test marketing* use and to provide localised *retailer support.*

A different form of media flexibility concerns timing; there are a number of related points. What is the *lead time* in using a medium – how long in advance must bookings be made; how long does it take to prepare the necessary advertising material: If we have topical advertising in mind, lead times must be relatively short. Again, what is the *length of contract* we must enter into with a media owner and how much notice of cancellation is required should our plans change or unexpected circumstances arise?

Thinking now more of the content of our campaign, how about the *message suitability* of the various media? (Here we bear in mind that some may be more suited to complex, reasoned explanation of a product's benefits, some to a single, simple advertising claim.) Then there is a *copy control*: Does a medium allow us to say more or less what we like about our product – or does the media owner exercise strict control over the permissible content of our advertising message?

Of course, there may be interaction between a medium and the advertising it carries, so we should list *'rub-off'* among our criteria – the transference, in the mind of the audience, of a medium's authority to the advertising it contains.

Then there are aspects of the conditions under which our advertisement is exposed: Will it have a chance of solus attention, or will it be closely surrounded by the *'clutter'* of many other ads; and what about the *circumstances of ad contact* – for example, will it be seen or heard at home, or elsewhere?

Finally, and without doubt most importantly, there are our feelings on the relative strengths of *impact* which the various media bestow on our advertising message.

The inter-media decision

Given that the target comprises people of all race groups, we must decide how much of the total advertising budget should be spent against each group. In this exercise we shall assume that the coloured and Asian users will be adequately covered by the white media.

Because of the premium price of *Sparkle* we hypothesise that people in the non-black section of the total target group are more likely to be able to afford to buy the product on a regular basis. Consequently, we recommend that the weight of advertising should be distributed as follows:

☐ Whites, Coloureds and Asians together – 50%
☐ Blacks – 50%

The breakdown of our actual campaign should try to match these proportions. That is to say, half of the total advertising exposures should be aimed at the white, coloured and Asian sections of the target market and half at the black section. However, when we come to look at the budget split, we shall have to allocate it in different proportions, because the cost of reaching the white, coloured and Asian audience is greater per exposure than the cost of reaching a black consumer in the target market.

It will do no harm to recap priorities at this point:

☐ We need an advertising burst in July and August.
☐ The main effort should be put into the promotion between 14 November and 30 December.
☐ Advertising should then run on from January to May.

High awareness of the advertising is required by March and therefore high coverage of the target group is also a necessity, together with a good level of report exposure.

Referring to table 6.19, the media which must be used because of their coverage of the black target group are Radio Bantu and black magazines. Although TV2 and TV3 were in their infancy when the research on which the data in table 6.19 are based was carried out in 1982, the potential coverage of the market by these television channels is also probably high. We recommend the use of this medium because of its impact on the urban black viewer and because of its fairly low unit cost. Incidentally, you will notice that not all media decisions are based solely on numbers – qualitative judgement (including gut feel) also plays a major role in media selection.

With regular exposure to advertising required, and with both name reminder and pack recognition being of vital importance in achieving high consumer recall in a modestly educated market, it is considered that outdoor advertising should also be used with 48-sheet hoardings being taken at key points in major urban areas. If these are sited in the right places, coverage of all race groups should be achieved. This medium will provide support for the more explicit message used on television and in print.

In the non-black markets TV1 must be used. SABC radio offers good support and magazines are recommended if they can be afforded.

A detailed media schedule is not included at the media strategy stage. Quite often strategies are produced a long time in advance of the advertising campaign period. Media costs change at least once a year, sometimes twice. With the allocation system currently applied on television, exact costs cannot be gauged much earlier than the September of the year preceding transmission. Consequently, to detail a schedule is frankly rather a waste of effort. Once an agreement has been reached on the media principles the detailed plan can be put together with a good chance of remaining unchanged.

Budget distribution

Here is the outline split of the budget by media type we suggest:

Radio Bantu	R49 000
TV2/3	50 000
48-sheet posters	120 000
Black magazines	40 000
TV1	140 000
'White' radio	40 920
Media total	R439 920

Note that we cannot afford to use white magazines.

Now let us recap the main reasons for selecting these media types.

☐ Radio Bantu – high coverage of all black markets
☐ TV2 and TV3 – visual impact on urban black markets with growing coverage
☐ 48-sheet posters – high visibility at key points for name reminder and pack recognition
☐ Black magazines – high coverage of the well-educated black market, which tends to be more selective in its television viewing – the magazines are complementary to TV2 and TV3
☐ TV1 – mass coverage of white and Asian markets with great impact – the medium's coverage of Coloureds is not so high, but they do view regularly
☐ 'White' radio – low-cost-unit reminder advertising, especially to mothers with children – moderate coverage but good repetition.

In the agency view, the sum of money allocated to the media campaign is sufficient only to buy the required impact over three bursts of advertising. The budget has weakened by the loss of the R35 100 which will be taken by GST. It is recommended that the three bursts are flighted in July/August, November/December and February/March.

Media strategy review

The proposed media mix will achieve the objective of high coverage during the months of exposure. But is the media list too long to provide the necessary frequency of exposure? To answer this question we should note that many of the media which are covered in AMPS duplicate one another heavily. That is to say, there is considerable overlap between the audience of some other one. Consequently, the agency's opinion is that the desired frequency pattern should indeed be reached.

From a schedule evaluation point of view, the investment in 48-sheet posters is 'wasted' because as yet there are not definite research findings in AMPS on this medium. However, experience from campaigns for other clients has shown that outdoor can certainly provide a positive input, especially when an input has been used effectively in creative terms.

The agency would have liked to include January and April in the months covered by advertising, but cannot recommend this within the constraints of the given budget. The estimated cost of providing adequate exposure in these two months and also for May, in which the client did wish to advertise, would be in the region of R85 000.

Timing plan   A detailed timing plan is not provided at this stage, simply a chart showing where the advertising effort will be placed:

	Jul	Aug	Sep	Oct	Nov	Dec	Jan	Feb	Mar	Apr	May	Jun
Television					(.............)		(.............)					
Black radio	(.............)				(.............)		(.............)					
White radio	(.............)				(.............)		(.............)					
Black press	xxxxxxxxx				xxxxxxxxx		xxxxxxxxx					
Outdoor	(.............)				(.............)		(.............)					
Promotion (competition)					(.............)							

☐ Media specifics

Television   TV1 − 20-second commercials

Time channel	Language	Cost per spot	No of spots
17h30-18h00	English	R2 300	2
	Afrikaans	R2 700	2
18h00-20h00	English	R4 200	6
	Afrikaans	R4 000	6
20h00-21h30	English	R6 900	6
	Afrikaans	R5 500	6
21h30-23h00	English	R3 900	1
	Afrikaans	R2 500	1
	30 spots =	R140 000	
	GST* =	R 8 400	
	Total TV1 =	R148 400	

(The distribution of spots by time channel reflects the probable allocation by the SABC. There is a heavy demand for the 'Kiddies Channel' (17h30-18h00) and it is not likely that a higher number of spots can be acquired.)

TV2/3 − 20-second commercials
(One spot on each service costs R1 800)

28 spots	= R50 400
GST*	= R 1 512
Total TV2/3	= R51 912

*6%, as was applicable in 1982.

Radio   Air time on the SABC service is sold in packages made up of four or five spots per day. These packages can cover day time or early morning and evening time. Air time is allocated on a monthly basis, three months ahead of flighting, unless permanent holdings are acquired. A permanent holding comprises a number of spots bought by an advertiser on a regular basis and which he must use every week of the year.

For the *Sparkle* campaign we shall buy air time as required and, in relation to this product, day time packages are more suited to reach the white, coloured and Asian target groups, but both day time and early morning/evening packages should be used to reach the black market.

Table 6.20 shows separately the proportions of the white and black consumers within the target group for *Sparkle* who listen 'sometimes' to different radio stations at various times of the day.

Table 6.20
Target group listenership to radio, by race, time channel and station

Urban women with children 3-15							
White						Black	
	Station						Station
Time channel	Spring-bok %	High-veld %	Good Hope %	Port Natal %	Radio 5 %	Time channel	Radio Bantu %
06h00-08h30	16,2	11,1	3,1	2,9	4,3	05h00-06h00	5,3
08h30-12h00	14,2	19,2	5,8	3,3	4,0	06h00-08h30	15,6
12h00-14h00	9,5	15,0	4,8	3,0	3,4	08h30-12h00	16,7
14h00-16h00	15,6	10,2	3,7	2,1	3,6	12h00-14h00	13,1
16h00-18h30	13,4	9,6	3,5	2,5	4,6	14h00-16h00	14,0
18h30-21h30	3,1	1,8	0,9	0,9	1,7	16h00-18h30	17,3
21h30-24h00	2,1	1,7	0,5	0,2	1,0	18h30-21h30	34,8
						21h30-24h00	6,3

In this example we shall assume that the agency has a radio buyer who will negotiate the purchase of the required air time, so we shall simply allocate budgets for each month of the campaign and indicate on the date plan the exact weeks in which we require spots to be flighted.

With the additional funds included, the total expenditure on the recommended stations is as follows:

Radio Bantu	R89 000 + GST R5 340 = R94 340
Springbok Radio	R35 000 + GST R2 100 = R37 100
Radio Highveld	R23 000 + GST R1 380 = R24 380
Radio Good Hope	R16 500 + GST R 990 = R17 490
Radio Port Natal	R 5 920 + GST R 355 = R 6 275
	Radio media total = R179 585

The expenditure shown here will buy approximately 200 spots on each of the white stations, and about 300 spots on Radio Bantu or 40 and 60 day packages respectively.

The budgets for each station, month by month, are:

	Bantu	Springbok	Highveld	Good Hope	Port Natal
	R	R	R	R	R
July	8 125	44 375	2 875	2 062	740
August	7 125	2 917	1 917	1 375	493
September	–	–	–	–	–
October	–	–	–	–	–
November	8 125	4 375	2 875	2 063	740
December	8 125	4 375	2 875	2 063	740
January	14 125	4 416	3 045	2 110	740
February	8 125	3 375	2 075	1 562	578
March	7 125	2 917	1 917	1 375	493
April	14 125	4 375	2 875	2 063	740
May	14 000	3 875	2 546	1 827	656
June	–	–	–	–	–
Total	89 000	35 000	23 000	16 500	5 920

Because these figures represent targets for the buyer, GST is not included.

Black magazines

The size of space to be used in black magazines has been decided by the client, and will be a full colour page. To see which publications show up best in terms of their coverage of the target market, a cost and coverage table is drawn up.

Table 6.21
Black magazines: Costs and target group coverage

		Urban women with children 3-15					
		Total			Cool drink users		
Unweighted sample		782			649		
		'000	%	CPT	'000	%	CPT
Total		681	100,0		568	100,0	
Cost full page, full colour							
Bona	R4 140	184	27,0	R 22,50	162	28,5	R 25,56
Drum	R3 200	102	15,0	R 31,37	91	16,0	R 35,16
New Dawn	R1 400	11	1,6	R127,27	10	1,8	R140,00
Pace	R3 200	113	16,1	R 28,32	98	17,3	R 32,65
True Love	R2 500	79	11,6	R 31,65	68	12,0	R 36,76
Hit	R1 200	21	3,1	R 57,14	18	3,2	R 66,67

A single insertion of a full colour page in *Bona* will cost R4 140. Amongst Blacks in our target group who are mothers with children aged 3 to 15 years, *Bona* has a readership of 184 000 or 27% of all the people in this subgroup. If we divide the space cost for *Bona*, R4 140, by the size of its audience in thousands, 184, we arrive at the cost per thousand of R22,50. Cost per thousand is abbreviated 'CPT' in this table, and the lower this figure the more efficient we may say a magazine is in reaching our particular target group.

The figures to the right of table 6.21 are the result of carrying out similar calculations, but this time in relation to black mothers with young children who are also users, according to AMPS, of cold drinks.

The audience figures in the table and cost per thousand reveal that *Bona* not only has the highest coverage of the target group, but is also the most cost effective in reaching them. That is to say, its cost per thousand figures are the next lowest in the table, in spite of the fact that we happen to know (although it is not reflected in these particular figures) that *Bona* has quite a high circulation outside the urban areas, at which we are aiming.

Remembering that the expenditure allowance for black magazines is only R40 000, we recommend only one other magazine in support of *Bona* and propose that *Pace* should be used, as it seems to have an editorial policy more in keeping with the likely interests of the person we want to reach than is the case with *Drum, True Love* or *Hit*. Consequently, the following schedule is recommended:

Bona – full page, full colour R4 140 x 6	
Pace – full page, full colour R3 200 x 5	R40 840
GST	R 2 450
Black magazines media total	= R43 290

Outdoor

In addition, 48-sheet hoardings will be used in strategic areas. For one month's flighting the cost of each will be about R180,00, but the actual price will vary in the course of booking negotiations according to the number of sites taken with each contractor and the locations of the sites. Within the budget allocated to outdoor, we should be able to buy a minimum of 110 sites for six months each, and may be able to negotiate a further 10 or 20.

The budget for outdoor is:

> Outdoor media total = R124 109
> (including GST)

☐ Budget redistribution

In the event that the television spots for which we have made provision are not actually allocated to us by the SABC, in which media should we recommend additional expenditure? In this example we would propose firstly an increase in print, and secondly in radio. In both of these cases bookings may be cancelled within one or two month's notice should additional TV air time be made available to us during the course of the advertising year.

☐ Schedule performance

In this section we set out in detail the coverage of the various sections of the target group which we forecast will be achieved by the schedules we have planned in the cases of those media for which research data are available.

For the *Sparkle* campaign we must look not only at the overall picture, but also at whether the schedule meets the monthly coverage and frequency objectives that were set out in the media strategy section.

At this stage we shall not go into any great detail in explaining how these schedule performance figures are arrived at. However, based on the information on people's reading, viewing and listening habits that is collected by AMPS, it is possible for the computer to calculate how many people within a target group will have an opportunity of seeing or hearing at least one advertisement in a particular medium, how many people will have opportunities of contact with different numbers of advertisements, and what the average frequency of exposure within the target group will be.

Before we look at the actual results of our schedule performance calculations, remember that our objective was, within each month in which we advertised, to achieve a coverage of 80% of each sector of the target market with an exposure frequency of each person having an opportunity to see or hear four advertisements on average.

Table 6.22 shows the combined performance of our schedules on television and in magazines separately for white, coloured, Asian and urban black consumers within our overall target group of mothers with children aged between 3 and 15:

Table 6.22
Estimated target group coverage, television, radio and magazines combined, and estimated average OTS/OTH, by month within race

	Urban women with children 3-15							
	White		Coloured		Asian		Black	
	Coverage %	Average frequency	Coverage %	Average frequency	Coverage %	Average frequency	Coverage %	Average frequency
July	50	4,8	65	7,9	50	6,4	70	4,9
August	45	4,0	60	5,7	45	4,7	70	4,9
September	–	–	–	–	–	–	–	–
October	–	–	–	–	–	–	–	–
November	94	8,8	75	12,1	89	7,9	82	7,8
December	83	4,1	70	6,3	80	4,0	80	5,3
January	50	4,8	65	7,9	50	6,4	70	4,2
February	94	8,8	75	12,1	89	7,9	82	7,8
March	83	4,1	70	6,3	80	4,0	75	4,0
April	50	4,8	65	7,9	50	6,4	70	4,2
May	50	4,8	65	7,9	50	6,4	70	4,2
June	–	–	–	–	–	–	–	–

In each pair of columns the first shows the coverage, month by month, within the subgroup concerned, while the second column deals with the average frequency of contact with our *Sparkle* advertising for the same months. Thus, for example, in July we estimate that our campaign will reach 50% of all Whites within our target group and that on average these people will have 4,8 opportunities to see or hear the advertising.

Reviewing the data in this table against our objective, it can be seen that our monthly target for coverage is, generally speaking, exceeded when television is used, but that the same coverage target is not achieved in most subsections of the target group in other months.

It should be borne in mind that the figures we are looking at make no allowance for the contribution of outdoor advertising to our campaign results, simply because we did not have research data on which to base an assessment in the case of this medium.

Looking in more detail at the schedule performance estimate, the important months for building up brand awareness prior to the promotion are November and December, together with February and March. The 48-sheet poster campaign will increase the average frequency of exposure in July/August, November/December and February/March. It may also increase coverage, although this could not be estimated from the research data available.

One very important point must be made absolutely clear, namely that in relation to these figures both the coverage and the frequency results rest on the assumption that we can add together opportunities to see a magazine advertisement, to hear a radio commercial or to view a TV spot without making any allowance at all for the very different characteristics of these various media or attempting to place different values on the impacts provided by exposure to them.

☐ Budget summary

Here, expenditure will be summarised medium by medium, together with other cost headings such as production, GST and the SAARF Levy. The client may also require a monthly or quarterly expenditure breakdown.

For *Sparkle*, the summary of our proposed expenditure is:

TV1	R148 400
TV2/3	R 51 912
Radio Bantu	R 94 340
Springbok Radio	R 37 100
Radio Highveld	R 24 380
Radio Good Hope	R 17 490
Radio Port Natal	R 6 275
Black press	R 43 290
Outdoor	R124 109
Media total	R547 296
Production	R117 000
Grand total	R664 296

☐ Date plan

Finally, here is the detailed date plan which shows precisely when the *Sparkle* advertising will appear:

	Jul	Aug	Sep	Oct	Nov	Dec	Jan	Feb	Mar	Apr	May	Jun
TV1												
Spots per week					43332			43332				
TV2/3												
Spots per week					43332			43332				
Radio Bantu	xxx	xxx			xxx	xxx	xxx	xxx	xx	xxx	xxx	
Springbok Radio	xxx	xx			xxx	xx	xxx	xxx	xx	xxx	xxx	
Radio Highveld	xxx	xx			xxx	xx	xxx	xxx	xx	xxx	xxx	
Radio Good Hope	xxx	xx			xxx	xx	xxx	xxx	xx	xxx	xxx	
Radio Port Natal	xxx	xx			xxx	xx	xxx	xxx	xx	xxx	xxx	
Press *Bona*	(..........)				(..........)			(..........)				
Pace	(..........)				(..........)			(..........)				
Outdoor	◄——►				◄——►			◄——►				
Promotion					◄——►							

Appendix: Media opportunities for the black market

Elana de Swardt

The urban black population 247

Television 249

Magazines 251

Newspapers 253

Radio 255

Outdoor 257

Cinema 257

Summary of all media types 258

☐ The urban black population

Table 6.23 reflects the growth of the adult urban black population from 1981 to 1985, table 6.24 reflects the population profile of adult urban Blacks in terms of sex, age and monthly household income, and table 6.25 outlines all the media types available to black viewers, listeners and readers in South Africa

Table 6.23 Urban black population (adults) in thousands

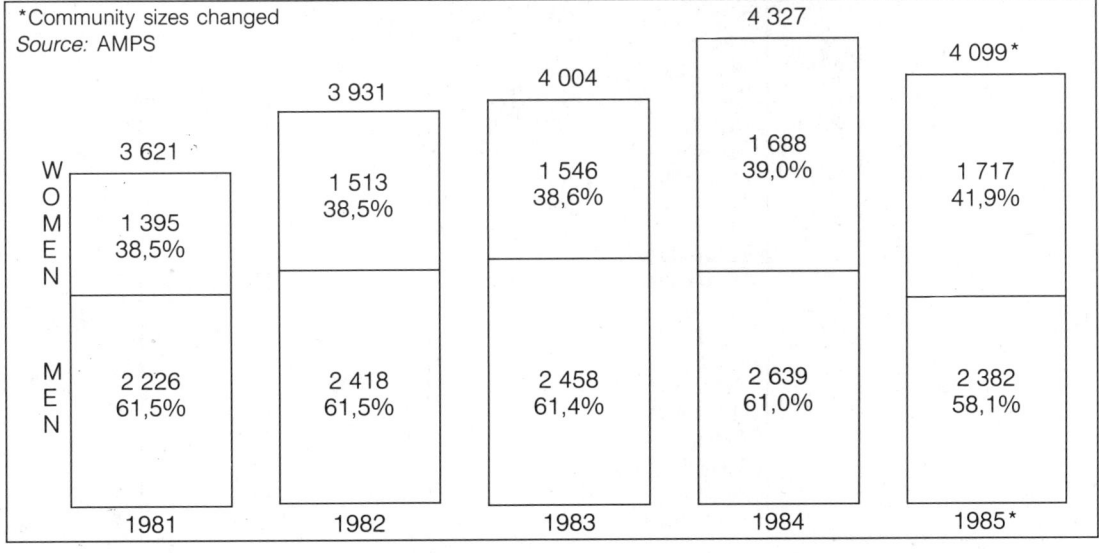

*Community sizes changed
Source: AMPS

	1981	1982	1983	1984	1985*
Total	3 621	3 931	4 004	4 327	4 099*
WOMEN	1 395 / 38,5%	1 513 / 38,5%	1 546 / 38,6%	1 688 / 39,0%	1 717 / 41,9%
MEN	2 226 / 61,5%	2 418 / 61,5%	2 458 / 61,4%	2 639 / 61,0%	2 382 / 58,1%

Table 6.24 Urban black population profile (total urban black population = 4 099 000)

% (Sex)	% (Age group)	% (Income group)	
Female 42	50+ 15,6	D 4,4	D = Less than R80
	35-49 26,1	C 40,9	C = R80 – R399
Male 58	25-34 28,9	B 34,3	B = R400 – R699
	16-24 29,4	A 20,5	A = R700+
Sex	Age group	Income group (Monthly household income)	

Source: Superbump computer run based on AMPS 85F

Table 6.25 Media types available to black viewers, readers and listeners in South Africa

TV	Magazines	Newspapers	Radio	Outdoor	Cinema	Other
TV2	Bona	Sowetan	Radio Zulu	Billboards	4 Wallers	Commuter
TV3	Pace	New Nation	Radio Seswati	Junior posters	Soweto	radio
Bop TV	Drum	City Press	Radio Ndebele	Soccer stadia	Family	Peoples
	True Love	Ilanga	Radio Xhosa	60/40 posters	circuit	club
	New Dawn	Indaba	Radio Sesotho	Bus shelters	Mine	promotions
	Hit	Imvo	Radio Tswana	Buses	circuit	Couponing
	Thandi	Echo	Radio Lebowa			(Bus
	Probe	Ink Anyesi	Radio Venda			tickets)
	SA Soccer	Phambili	Radio Tsonga			
	Sharpshoot	Lentswe	Radio Bop			
	Soccer	Highveld Voice	Radio Transkei			
	Tribute	Kangwane	Radio Ciskei			
		News	Radio			
		Lebowa	Thohoyandou			
		Gazankulu &				
		Venda Times				
		Seipone				
		Springs				
		African				
		Reporter				
		Gazanbowa				
		Times				
		Intsimbi				
		Imibono				
		Yabomdabu				

☐ **Television**

Coverage areas

TV2 is the Nguni service of the SABC covering the urban areas of Natal, the Eastern Cape and Cape Town. Languages used are Xhosa and Zulu.

TV3 is the Sotho service (SABC) and covers the central areas of Transvaal, plus Kroonstad, Theunissen, Bloemfontein and Kimberley.

Both TV2 and TV3 are transmitted in the PWV area. A map illustrating the areas of coverage is attached (see figure 6.9).

Bop TV broadcasts from Mmabatho and covers Soweto, Kagiso, some parts of the Reef and the central parts of Bophuthatswana.

Figure 6.11
Coverage areas of TV2 and TV3 transmitters within the Republic of South Africa

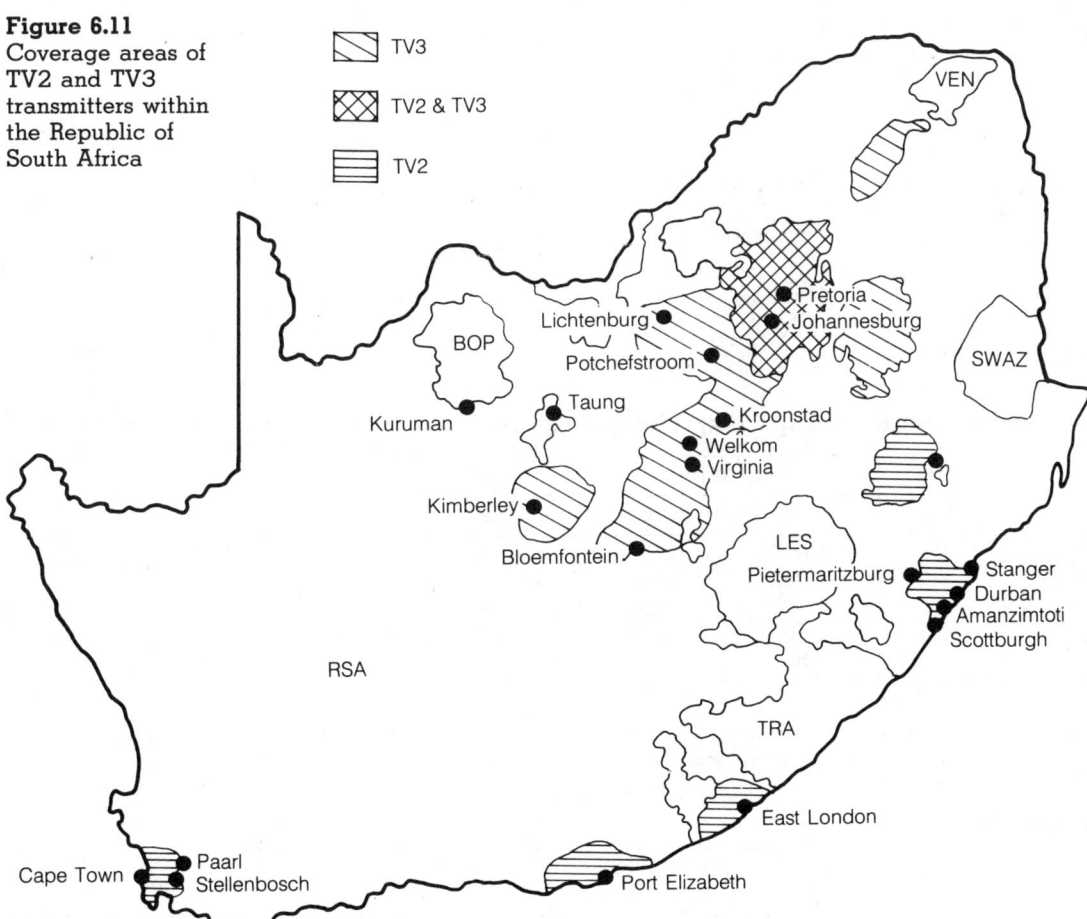

Figure 6.12
Bophuthatswana
TV

Viewership data: average day viewership urban blacks (population = 4 831 000)

	Monday to Friday		Saturday		Sunday	
	In thousands	%	In thousands	%	In thousands	%
TV2	1 015	21,0	1 116	23,1	951	19,7
TV3	1 252	25,9	1 152	23,8	970	20,1
TV2 & TV3	2 095	43,4	2 074	42,9	1 740	36,0
Bop TV*	185	3,8	192	4,0	182	3,8
TV1	861	17,8	965	20,0	656	13,6

Source: Broadcast AMPS January-March 1986

*Note that the viewership of Bop TV will be much lower due to the fact that it is measured against the total urban black population and not 'Transvaal' urban blacks.

Rates: 1986

	TV2 & TV3 individually	TV2 & TV3 combined	Bop TV
	30 seconds		
17h00-18h30	–	–	R396,00
18h00-21h30*	R2 164,00	R3 606,00	588,00
21h00-Close	–	–	600,00
15h00-18h00 Saturday	893,00	1 488,00	–

*Time channel for Bop TV is 18h00-21h00.
Availability on all stations is good.

Note: No GST is applicable on Bop TV advertising.

Viewership profiles (based on 'average day' viewership of urban Blacks)

	TV2	TV3	TV2 & TV3	Bop TV	Urban black population
Total (in thousands)	1 019	1 198	2 039	184	4 831
Men	54,6	63,0	59,9	61,4	58,7
Women	45,4	37,0	40,1	38,6	41,3
Nguni	81,5	20,6	47,5	27,8	53,8
Sotho	18,5	79,4	52,5	72,2	46,2
16-24	31,8	29,0	30,0	28,4	30,0
25-34	27,0	29,4	29,2	32,8	28,8
35-49	29,2	26,9	27,6	20,7	25,5
50 + ...	12,0	14,7	13,2	18,1	15,7
Income A	28,5	29,8	29,5	34,1	21,0
B	37,0	40,6	37,6	38,7	34,7
C/D	34,5	29,6	32,9	27,2	44,3

Source: Broadcast AMPS January-March 1986

Household monthly income
A = R700+
B = R400 – R699
C/D = Up to R399

Note:
Compared to the total urban black population, a better balance in male/female viewership is achieved by TV2, whilst Bop TV and TV3 are biased towards men.
As can be expected, Bop TV and TV3 are strongly skewed towards Sotho-speaking urban Blacks.
In line with all other black media types, the TV profile with regard to age and income is biased towards 16-34 years and A income.

☐ Magazines

Readership penetration: urban Blacks

	Total		Men		Women	
	In thousands	%	In thousands	%	In thousands	%
Population	4 098	100,0	2 382	100,0	1 717	100,0
Pace	952	23,2	587	24,6	365	21,3
Bona	1 234	30,1	743	31,2	491	28,6
New Dawn	135	3,3	68	2,9	67	3,9
Drum	860	21,0	557	23,4	303	17,6
Hit	277	6,8	182	7,6	95	5,6
True Love	613	15,0	351	14,7	261	15,3
SA Soccer	587	14,3	530	22,3	57	3,3
Sharpshoot Soccer	309	7,5	292	12,3	18	1,1

Source: AMPS 85F

Bona is still the magazine with the highest readership and has the potential of reaching a third of all urban blacks.

Note: *Thandi* and *Probe* were not included in the AMPS 1985 survey.

Rates and circulation

Rates (in rands)		Publication	Circulations*
FPFC	FPBW		
R3 600	R2 340	*Pace*	124 762
5 700	3 420	*Bona*	243 895
1 950	1 390	*New Dawn*	40 000 print order
4 430	2 576	*Drum*	112 749
1 800	1 160	*Hit*	60 396
3 392	2 024	*True Love*	92 738
1 650	1 200	*SA Soccer*	64 765
1 600	1 300	*Sharpshoot Soccer*	32 479
3 000	1 800	*Thandi*	53 596°
850	490	*Probe*	15 000 print order

Note:
All magazines are distributed nationally except PROBE which is a free magazine to black homes in Uitenhage, Port Elizabeth, East London, the urban areas of Transkei and Ciskei.
Rates as at July 1986.
*ABC July-December 1985 Domestic
°ABC August-December 1985.

Readership profiles

	Urban black population	Pace	Bona	New Dawn*	Drum	Hit	True Love	SA Soccer	Sharpshoot Soccer
	%	%	%	%	%	%	%	%	%
Male	58,1	61,6	60,2	50,1	64,8	65,6	57,2	90,3	94,2
Female	41,9	38,4	39,8	49,9	35,2	34,4	42,8	9,7	5,8
16-24	29,4	40,0	37,9	44,7	35,8	46,0	44,4	40,0	37,4
25-34	28,9	38,7	35,6	40,4	41,0	33,6	39,3	40,0	47,2
35-49	26,1	18,9	20,7	13,1	18,6	17,4	14,6	18,2	13,8
50 + ...	15,6	2,4	5,8	1,7	4,5	3,0	1,7	1,8	1,6
A	20,5	31,4	22,8	35,6	25,6	35,5	29,5	24,7	29,0
B	34,3	36,6	36,3	38,6	40,5	34,8	33,8	37,2	38,1
C	40,9	29,2	37,4	22,7	31,6	27,5	33,1	35,0	28,5
D	4,4	2,8	3,6	3,2	2,3	2,1	3,6	3,1	4,4
Readership in thousands (based on urban Blacks)	953	1 235	135	860	278	614	587	309

Source: AMPS 85F

This table clearly illustrates that most black magazine readers are in the A/B income groups, men and relatively young.
*Respondent base below 200 (137).

Non-consumer publications

Publication	Circulation	Distribution	(Cost in rands)	
			FPFC	FPBW
African Business & Chamber of Commerce Review	10 000 claimed	To all trade & other members of NAFCOC nationally	1 445	1 145
Black Farmer	3 000 claimed	Free to all farmers (NAFCOC members) mainly in the Transvaal and Bophuthatswana	1 225	895
Black Manufacturer	3 000 claimed	Also in the NAFCOC stable, it is sent to the top black manufacturers	1 225	895
e'SPOTINI	8 000 claimed	Circulated to Shebeen owners, predominantly Soweto	2 167	1 393
Taxi	6 000 claimed	Free copy to all Soweto taxi owners	1 806	1 161
Drive-on Taxi	40 000 print order	All members of the SA Black Taxi Association nationally	1 950	1 300
Inyanda News	8 000 claimed	Free to members of the Natal and KwaZulu African Chamber of Commerce	758	500

Rates as at July 1986
FPFC: full page full colour
FPBW: full page black and white

☐ Newspapers

Readership penetration: urban Blacks

	Total		Men		Women	
	In thousands	%	In thousands	%	In thousands	%
Population	4 099	100,0	2 382	100,0	1 717	100,0
Sowetan	856	20,9	603	25,3	253	14,7
City Press	776	18,9	582	24,4	194	11,3
Ilanga Weekend (Natal)	386	9,4	245	10,3	141	8,2
Ilanga Weekday (Natal)	373	9,1	249	10,4	124	7,2
Imvo (East Cape)	206	5,0	108	4,5	98	5,7
Indaba (East Cape)	197	4,8	91	3,8	106	6,2

Source: AMPS 85F

Note: Only the abovementioned newspapers are included in the AMPS survey.

Rates and circulation

Rates (R) (based on a 30x5 A4 size ad)		Publication	Circulation	Circulation area
Full colour	Black and white			
2 100	1 275	*Sowetan*	114 614 ∅	PWV
2 430	1 895	*City Press*	154 413 ∅	PWV + Dbn, PE, EL, CT
1 500	930	*Ilanga Weekend*	109 079 ∅	Durban & environments
1 500	930	*Ilanga Weekday*	109 079 ∅	Durban & environments
1 238	638	*Imvo*	52 728 claimed	Transkei, PE
1 140	675	*Indaba*	68 560	Ciskei, EL, PE, Uitenhage
1 275	713	*New Nation*	62 500 claimed	PWV, Dbn, PE/EL, CT
1 500	338	*Echo*	44 000 claimed	Pietermaritzburg
415	195	*Ink Anjesi*	10 000 free	Ladysmith
415	195	*Pambhili*	7 000 free	Newcastle
413	233	*Lentswe*	12 000 free	Klerksdorp
615	285	*Highveld Voice*	9 000 free	Middelburg
525	255	*KaNgwane News*	8 500	Nelspruit
570	300	*Lebowa/Gazankulu/Venda Times*	7 300	Lebowa
540	300	*Seipane*	5 000	Potchefstroom
420	210	*Springs Afr. Reporter*	8 500	Springs
555	285	*Gazanbowa Times*	10 000 free	Tzaneen
No colour	375	*Intsimbi*	26 000 sold	Transkei

PABC July-Dec 1985
Rates as at July 1986

Readership profiles

	Urban black population	*Sowetan*	*City Press*	*Ilanga Weekend*	*Ilanga Weekday*	*Imvo*	*Indaba*
	%	%	%	%	%	%	%
Male	58,1	70,5	75,1	63,4	66,6	52,6	46,3
Female	41,9	29,5	24,9	36,6	33,4	47,4	53,7
Income A	20,5	31,6	29,7	25,9	24,5	14,7	21,0
B	34,3	38,5	37,4	38,6	37,3	31,6	35,0
C	40,9	26,9	30,1	32,4	34,3	48,1	39,2
D	4,4	2,9	2,8	3,1	3,9	5,6	4,8
Age group							
16-24	29,4	32,9	37,3	32,1	30,6	29,9	36,4
25-34	28,9	32,3	34,7	33,8	34,8	26,7	30,4
35-49	26,1	26,9	23,3	25,9	26,3	28.9	24,0
50+	15,6	7,9	4,7	8,1	8,3	14,5	9,2
Readership in thousands (based on urban Blacks)	856,0	775,0	386,0	373,0	206,0	197,0

Source: AMPS 85F

☐ Radio

'Yesterday' listenership potential reach : total Blacks

NPU area	A	B	C	D	E	F	G	H
	PWV	Rest of Tvl excl homelands	OFS & Central Cape	Natal	Eastern Cape & Ciskei	North & West Cape	Cape Peninsula	Transkei Lesotho Swaziland & other homelands
Population in thousands	2 409	3 668	1 465	2 987	1 028	265	179	1 494
	%	%	%	%	%	%	%	%
Radio Bantu	51,8	60,2	53,5	63,8	51,9	*	63,1	35,8
Radio Botphutha-tswana	18,1	4,5	3,6	1,8	1,1	*	*	0,4
Radio Transkei	–	–	–	1,2	6,1	*	–	46,5
Radio Ciskei	–	–	–	–	17,9	*	–	1,8
Radio Thohoyandou .	0,9	5,6	0,3	0,1	0,3	*	–	–

Source: AMPS 85F

*Informant base too small

Rates: 1986

Cost per 30 seconds per day (Mon-Fri rates) in rands

	5h00-6h00	6h00 8h30	8h30-12h00	12h00-14h00	14h00-16h00	16h00-18h30	18h30-21h30
Radio Zulu	132	294	312	279	246	246	468
Radio Seswati	*	15	*	*	*	*	36
Radio Ndebele	*	6	*	*	*	*	15
Radio Xhosa	36	51	30	30	24	30	108
Radio Sesotho	18	66	63	84	78	72	144
Radio Tswana	12	45	42	42	57	60	126
Radio Lebowa	30	45	57	54	45	84	150
Radio Venda	*	6	*	*	*	*	9
Radio Tsonga	*	15	*	*	*	*	30
Radio Bophuthatswana ..	81	144	84	69	81	159	126
Radio Transkei ∅	54	———84———		63	69	126	117
Radio Ciskei ∅................	24	———24———		24	24	36	36
Radio Thohoyandou ∅	33	27	21	27	21	27	42

* Radio Zulu coverage

∅ Time channels duration different to the SABC channel structure

Rates as at July 1986

Coverage areas

Radio Zulu	Southern Transvaal, Northern Cape, Orange Free State, Natal
Radio Seswati	Swaziland and surrounding areas, including the Eastern Lowveld
Radio Ndebele	Potgietersrus, Middelburg and the Eastern Highveld, eg Standerton area
Radio Xhosa	Transkei, Ciskei, Eastern Cape
Radio Sesotho	Central OFS plus PWV area, Lesotho and part of the Eastern Cape
Radio Tswana	Western Transvaal, Kimberley, Bloemfontein plus parts of the Northern Cape
Radio Lebowa	Northern Transvaal, plus parts of the far Eastern Transvaal and Pretoria/Johannesburg
Radio Venda ⎱ Radio Tsonga ⎰	Louis Trichardt and surrouding areas down to the Eastern Lowveld
Radio Bophuthatswana	FM coverage: Bophuthatswana (from GaRankuwa across to Mafikeng to Kuruman and ThabaNchu. MW coverage: PWV and surrounding areas, ie Warmbaths, Ermelo, Bethlehem and Potchefstroom radius
Radio Transkei	Area around Transkei down to Stutterheim, Mdantsani, East London
Radio Ciskei	From Colchester outside PE in the South up to Queenstown in the north to Kei Mouth/Morgans Bay east
Radio Thohoyandou	Messina, Louis Trichardt, Pietersburg, Nylstroom, Warmbaths, Tzaneen

Listenership profiles : total Blacks

	Total black population	Radio Bantu	Radio Bophuthatswana	Radio Transkei	Radio Ciskei	Radio Thohoyandou
In thousands	13 576	7 318	832	794	213	238
	%	%	%	%	%	%
Male	49,1	51,0	64,0	43,5	61,0	60,9
Female	50,9	49,0	36,0	56,5	39,0	39,1
Age group						
16-24	32,8	37,2	46,8	*	*	*
25-34	24,2	26,4	29,4			
35-49	23,4	21,3	18,0			
50 +	19,6	15,1	5,8			
Income						
A	11,6	12,8	21,8	*	*	*
B	21,7	24,8	36,8			
C	51,0	50,9	35,7			
D	15,7	11,5	5,7			
Urban	30,2	30,9	62,6	6,9	18,3	8,8
Rural	61,8	61,1	37,4	93,1	81,7	91,2

Source: AMPS 85F
*Sample base too small

□ Outdoor

As was mentioned earlier, various outdoor types are available and can be selected on a regional and/or national basis. Rates are as follows:

	Cost per month per unit
96 sheets	R450,00
48 sheets	210,00
60/40 posters	46,00
Junior posters	84,00
Bus shelters	115,00
Minigraphic buses (Putco)	290,00
SATS rural buses	210,00
Station streamers	58,00

(All rates are negotiable)

□ Cinema

Penetration data: urban Blacks

As can be seen from the table below, cinema is a male oriented medium – 81% of all urban Blacks who attended a cinema during the last six weeks were men.

	Total		Male		Female	
	In thousands	%	In thousands	%	In thousands	%
Population .... 'Four wallers' attended last six weeks	4 099 609	100,0 14,9	2 382 493	100,0 20,7	1 717 115	100,0 6,7

Rates

According to the Cinemark rate card, there are 57 'Blacks only' cinemas in South African and 42 other cinemas which are 'non-white'. The Soweto Family Circuit is included in the 57.

The average cost per week, based on a 30-second commercial is ± R35,00. The cost per week for Soweto Family Circuit is R230,00 per week.

From September 1985, Blacks, Coloureds and Asians were allowed to attend 'white' cinemas.

Profile

Due to the relatively low female cinema attendance, the attendance profile of black men only was compiled.

	Cinema attended last 6 weeks		Population	Index Pop = 100
	In thousands	%	%	
Total	853	100,0		
Age group				
16-24	502	58,8	32,9	179
25-34	280	32,8	25,1	131
35-49	66	7,7	23,6	33
50 + ...	4	0,5	18,4	3
Income				
A	151	17,7	12,6	140
B	275	32,2	24,9	129
C	376	44,0	48,0	92
D	52	6,1	14,5	42

Source: AMPS 85F

Very similar to the profile of their white counterparts, black male cinemagoers are relatively young (16-34 years) and in the A/B income groups.

□ Summary of all media types

Penetration: urban Blacks (population = 4 099 000)

Medium	%
TV2/3	43,4
Bop TV	3,8
Radio Bantu	55,2
Radio Bop	12,7
Bona	30,1
Pace	23,2
Drum	21,0
Sowetan	20,9
City Press	18,9
Ilanga Weekend	9,4
Indaba	4,8
Imvo	5,0
Cinema − last six weeks	14,9

Source: AMPS 85F

7

Creating the advertising

Creative approaches and styles *261*
Creating effective advertising *269*

Creative approaches and styles
Ludi Koekemoer

Overseas approaches and styles 261

South African approaches and styles 264

References 268

☐ Overseas approaches and styles

Before discussing the views of a selected number of South African Creative Directors, I believe it is important to note what some of the world's most well-known advertising personalities have advocated.

Bill Bernbach: 'Execution'

Bill Bernbach established DDB (Doyle, Dane, Bernbach), an agency that has been extremely successful, in 1949. Traditionally it was accepted that a successful advertisement communicated a persuasive message. David Ogilvy's first rule for copywriters was 'what you say is more important than how you say it'. Bill Bernbach, however, believes that execution is vital and that it can be just as important as what you say. Therefore, in the Bernbach style the *execution* dominates (Aakar & Myers 1982:349).

Bernbach's philosophy that the consumer is clever enough to understand honest copy leads to an avoidance of puffery, clichés and heavy repetition. His creative approach is direct – he has pointed out that 'you must be as simple, swift and as penetrating as possible' (Higgens 1965:117 & 118). The advertisement should be visually different and should stand out from others. Bernbach asks the question 'What is the use of saying all the right things in the world if nobody is going to read them? Nobody is going to read them if they are not said with freshness, originality and imagination . . . if they are not, if you will, different' (Mayer 1958:66). A good example of DDB's philosophy is the Avis campaign. The 'We're No 2/We Try Harder' campaign admitted that Avis was No 2 to Hertz, but turned this fact into a big advantage for Avis by indicating that Avis would try harder because they were No 2. A further advantage was that all Avis departments, employees and services now had an objective, something to strive for: *We Try Harder.*

My thanks to Aubrey Malden (Ogilvy Mather Rightford, Searle-Tripp & Makin), Stoffel Matthis and Leon Strydom (D'Arcy Masius Benton & Bowles), Carl Preller (McCann de Villiers), Grahame Tomes (Freedman Rossi/BBDO), Laurance Kuper (Kuper Hands) and Derek Logan (Grey Phillips Bunton Mundel & Blake) for compiling their agencies' creative approaches and styles.

We rent the *new* Golf II and other superb cars.

AVIS

We try harder

Whatever the weather.

Courtesy: Avis. One of the most successful slogans ever used

David Ogilvy: 'The brand image'

David Ogilvy of Ogilvy Mather tends to concentrate on developing and maintaining a clear-cut brand image, mostly a prestige image. He argues that in most product categories there is no significant difference between the competing brands and the personality of the brand becomes the significant reason for selecting brand A rather than brand B.

Ogilvy is famous for his use of testimonials and distinctive prestigious individuals to convey the desired brand image.

In order that a particular brand image may be decided upon research is required and Ogilvy is very research oriented. The following 11 commandments for creating advertising campaigns are used in all Ogilvy Mather agencies around the world (Ogilvy 1964:93-103).

1 What you say is more important than how you say it.
2 Unless your campaign is built around a great idea, it will flop.
3 Give the facts. The consumer is not a moron; she's your wife.
4 You cannot bore people into buying.
5 Be well-mannered, but don't clown.
6 Make your advertising contemporary.
7 Committees can criticise advertisements, but they cannot write them.
8 If you're lucky enough to write a good advertisement, repeat it until it stops pulling.
9 Never write an advertisement which you wouldn't want your own family to read.
10 It is the total personality of a brand rather than any trivial product difference which decides its ultimate position in the market.
11 Don't be a copy cat. Nobody has ever built a brand by imitating somebody else's advertising.

Rosser Reeves: 'The USP'

Rosser Reeves of the Ted Bates agency believes one should write not for aesthetic appeal, but to create sales. He challenges the arty-crafty crowd by observing: 'I'm not saying that charming, witty and warm copy won't sell – I'm just saying that I have seen thousands of charming, witty campaigns that didn't sell' (Aaker & Myers 1982:352).

Reeves is very critical of creative approaches in which the copy is so clever that it distracts from the real message. He believes that each product must develop its own USP (Unique Selling Proposition). His guidelines for developing such a USP are (Aaker & Myers 1982:355):

☐ The proposition needs to involve a specific product benefit.
☐ It must be unique, one that competing firms are not using.
☐ It must sell. It must be important enough to influence the consumer in the buying process.

Reeves also relies heavily on product research to support specific claims. He believes that once the USP has been found it should be retained for as long as possible. Repetition of such a powerful proposition leads to habit formation and for this reason the Reeves USP approach has been very successful.

Leo Burnett: 'The common touch'

The Leo Burnett agency, located in Chicago rather than in New York, believes in using plain, ordinary people in advertising, for example the *Schlitz* neighbourhood bartender, the *Marlboro* cowboy, etc. In this respect Leo Burnett contrasts from David Ogilvy, who uses well-known personalities. Leo Burnett observed that great advertising is always deceptively simple.

He states:
It has the *common touch* without being or sounding patronising. If it takes a rationale to explain an ad or commercial, then it's too complicated for that 'dumb public' to understand. I believe the public is unable to sort out messages, not just because of the sheer flood of messages assaulting it every

day but because of sheer boredom. We try to be straightforward. We try to be warm without being mawkish. The key words are warm and believable (Aaker & Myers 1982:356).

To provide the common touch Burnett looks for the *inherent drama* of a product – the characteristic that made the manufacturer make it and makes the people buy it. The preferable approach is to dig out the inherent drama and present it in a warm, realistic manner. He believes that the inherent drama is often difficult to find, but that it is always there. Once found, it is the most interesting and believable of all advertising appeals (Mayer 1958:70).

☐ South African approaches and styles

Ogilvy Mather Rightford, Searle-Tripp & Makin: 'No rules'

Having a set of concrete rules would put us in a creative strait-jacket. It would lead to mediocrity. Mediocrity does not sell – excellence does, and excellence means sometimes breaking the rules, producing the unexpected.

We believe that all good advertising is born from a tightly defined brief and strategy. Market research and market background, facts, consumer attitudes and beliefs are used to feed, nourish and inspire our creative product – to give it direction. There is no substitute for good, hard homework. The more you know your product and the consumers' attitude towards it, the more likely you are to come up with a big idea for selling it to the consumer.

Creative advertising is the only legal way left for a company to take unfair advantage of the competition. There are people who ask whether advertising should be judged on creative excellence or the ability to sell a product. We believe that you cannot have one without the other.

With so many parity products around today, advertising can no longer be used merely to convey the basic product attributes. You need as much added value as you can get. You need an unfair advantage – creativity. Creativity can add value to the client's brand – set it apart from the competition with wit, style, flair, care, a big idea and understanding of the consumer and taste. If your advertising always looks as if it has been made with care, so will your client's product. If the big idea is memorable, the brand will be memorable too. Today, an outstanding creative product is the most effective selling tool a client can have.

David Ogilvy says:

I am sometimes attacked for imposing 'rules'. Nothing could be further from the truth. I hate rules. All I do is report on how consumers react to different stimuli. I may say to a copywriter, 'Research shows that commercials with celebrities are below average in persuading people to buy products. Are you sure you want to use a celebrity?'

At Ogilvy & Mather many successful campaigns have used celebrities, for example the *American Express* 'Do you know me?' campaign. In South Africa, the *Volksie* bus campaign with David Kramer and the *GTi* commercial with Jacky Ickx were successful. There are no rules.

The 'how' of advertising depends on people and the environment in which they work. We give our people freedom to grow, freedom to exploit their talents, and as our people get better our agency gets better. We encourage a spirit of creativity and adventurousness among all our people, regardless of their job functions, because we believe that the ability to produce exciting ideas stems from

1 The commercial revolves around a race between Jackie Ickx and Andre Arnold the World ski champion. One in a GTi the other on ski's through snowbound Switzerland. They leave the top of the ski slope together Arnold on the slopes, Ickx on the road.

3 Skier bursts into picture through white snow-bank.

4 Intercut with car moving at speeds through winding road.

5 Skier jumping over car.

6 Skier landing.

7 Ickx jumps out of car and says: "OK now I race you back up again" in French Title: ". . . now let's race back up!" in English.
Title: Europe's most popular performance car. Isn't that what you'd expect from Volkswagen?

Courtesy: Volkswagen and Ogilvy Mather RST & M

an inborn talent rather than from tutored experience. This is why, when it comes to the actual creation of advertising, we quote the following extract about the bumble-bee:

> According to the theory of aerodynamics, and as may be readily demonstrated by means of a wind tunnel, the bumble-bee is unable to fly.
>
> This is because the size, weight and shape of its body in relation to the total wing span make flight impossible.
>
> But the bumble-bee, being ignorant of these scientific facts and possessing considerable determination, does fly . . . and makes a little honey, too.

It is for this reason that we have adopted the bumble-bee as our company mascot, as it were, because we also subscribe to his aversion for rules, his rejection of scientific formulae for producing a creative product and his refusal to accept at face value the commmon criticism of self-appointed experts: 'it'll never fly'. In our experience, whenever we meet a client who shares with us the philosophy of the bumble-bee, the result is a unique combination, one which, more often than not, produces uniquely effective advertising.

You can do all your homework for as long as you like, but you will never win sales if you cannot express it with a big idea. Big ideas come from the subconscious. This is true in any creative arena – art, science and advertising. You must unlock the subconscious, nourish your mind with all the homework you like, and then fly. But flying requires talent and risk, an inbred quality to think of the unusual. It leads to the common thing done uncommonly well, and the uncommon done with commercial relevance.

D'Arcy Masius Benton & Bowles: 'OK is not OK'

D'Arcy Masius Benton & Bowles believes that every advertisement

☐ must be highly credible and above reproach in its claims
☐ should sum up the selling idea in one succinct and memorable theme line
☐ should firmly link the message to the featured product or service
☐ must capture and sustain the attention of the reader or viewer
☐ should communicate in an imaginative and unexpected way
☐ should be built around one major selling idea
☐ must emanate from a carefully conceived marketing and advertising strategy.

This agency believes that, when followed as guidelines, the preceding beliefs can help create advertising that cuts through clutter, penetrates the mind and persuades the prospect.

McCann de Villiers: 'Single-mindedness'

McCann de Villiers believes that a single-minded creative concept is more important than the execution.

Carl Preller says:

We expect the execution to be of a high standard but you cannot for example make an inferior concept work on the day of the television shoot. A single-minded, well thought-out creative concept must be exciting, fresh, new. If you try to say it all you end up saying nothing. That's why we look for simplicity and drama.

Freedman Rossi/BBDO: 'The relevant surprise'

Creativity is giving consumers what they want in a way they did not expect!

This agency believes that before talking to its prime prospects, it should *listen*. What are their likes about the brand and its competitors? What are their dislikes? It believes that because buying decisions are both rational and emotional, it should probe performance and imagery. After having listened to and understood the consumer's mind, it will know what must be said.

People do not like buying from bores or from show-offs, and they do not like being shouted at or cajoled. People like entertainment, drama, and news. So, the people must be given what they like, and the advertising message must be a relevant part of this. Most of all, the duty of a creative person is to make the message stand out in the crowd. The consumer must be surprised into noticing it. Consumers block out 99% of advertising messages, so it is imperative to get under the guard. Creativity is the relevant surprise.

Kuper Hands: 'The intuitive leap'

Laurance Kuper believes in fewer better creative people and fewer better clients. The people involved should be talented, responsible and experienced. He believes that the human mind tempered by science has the best ability to generate good, fresh original advertising – to take the intuitive leap that is far more creative than anything any methodology can offer.

Grey Phillips Bunton Mundel and Blake: 'Being visible'

Derek Logan proudly points out that Grey Phillips' success is attributable to the fact that it was the first advertising agency in South Africa to break out and be visibly different. In the early 1970s it was the one to create visible, inventive advertising, and it still does.

Logan feels that there are too many creative people and clients in South Africa who chicken out, who shy away from visible, bold advertising. He believes that good advertising emanates from a thorough brief and understanding the client and the target consumer. There is no clear-cut formula, because it is experienced gut feel that creates great advertising that will do something for the consumer.

Great advertising requires bold and brave creative people and bold and brave clients. That is probably why more than 50% of Grey Phillips' clients have been with the agency for more than 10 years.

Logan points out that the Plans Board (which is held every afternoon at 16h30), is a critical brainstorming session at which hats are removed and anybody can say what he wants to say. For example, a media person may ask: 'Shouldn't we use a celebrity to endorse the brand?', a creative person may recommend that outdoor should be used rather than another medium, etc. The Plans Board is a melting pot situation during which information is asked for and given for the purpose of identifying a single-minded idea (the 'believe something') that should be communicated. This idea is presented to the client and approved before creative work commences. Once it has been approved by the client the creative team will create the campaign and probably work its way through good ideas and better ideas until it finds something magic which will be on strategy but with lots of creative flair.

At the Review Board the campaign is presented to the account director, media planner, etc. This meeting is *not* used to pull apart the creative work. Each creative person is responsible for presenting his own work to the client, unlike many agencies where the account director or account executive presents the campaign to the client. Logan believes that the creative person has thought about it, wrestled with it and created it without considering that the client may not accept it and that he is proud to present his magic, his best to the client. He is nervous before a presentation, but nervous that the creative work may be too bold, never that it is not good enough. Great ideas are never watered down or modified.

If the client is too scared to go with the campaign then a new campaign is prepared. Again it is one that is visibly different. To be visible does not always mean the biggest sizes or the longest commercials – it means to create something that will stand out and be noticed, even in smaller sizes, even the day after.

☐ References

Aaker, DA & Myers, JG. 1982. *Advertising Management*. 2nd ed. Englewood Cliffs, NJ: Prentice-Hall
Higgens, D (Ed). 1965. *The Art of Writing Advertising*. Chicago: Crain Books.
Mayer, M. 1958. *Madison Avenue USA*. New York: Pocket Books.
Ogilvy, D. 1964. *Confessions of an Advertising Man*. New York: Atheneum.

Creating effective advertising
Ludi Koekemoer

The creative team's checklist 269

Creating effective television commercials 271

Creating effective radio commercials 280

Creating effective print advertising 281

Creating effective outdoor advertising 290

Closing comments 291

References 291

☐ The creative team's checklist

In 'Creative approaches and styles' I dealt with the importance of a good advertising brief and what such a brief should contain. From the creative team's point of view the following comprehensive checklist (completed for every brand/service to be advertised) could help in providing the necessary information:

Checklist for the creative team
☐ *History of the brand/service*

When created?	Sales history
Why created?	Image history
First name	Target market trends
Other names	Standing *vis-à-vis* competition
Significant product changes	over time

☐ *Manufacturing details*

How is it made?	Packaging benefits
Where is it made?	Can sufficient quantities be
Significant features eg special	produced?
treatments/processes, etc	Any threats?
Raw materials used	

This contribution is based mainly on the views of well-known international and South African advertising experts and my own experience. I have endeavoured to provide checklists where possible. A special word of thanks to Aubrey Malden of Ogilvy Mather Rightford Searle-Tripp & Makin for the pre-production and outdoor details, Sharon Moore of The Producers for the things to watch out for on the day of the shoot and the late George Gribbon, who enriched our lives at Mortimer Tiley for a month.

☐ *Research and market position*

Product research:
- physical
- performance
- image

Market share
Advertising research
Advertising share
Lifespan/usage research

☐ *Packaging*

Sizes available
Shape

Pack design (eg styling, colour,
   materials, etc)

☐ *Brand/service image*

Consumer attitudes (ie image,
   likes and dislikes)
Brand/service positioning
   (eg classy/luxury/effective/
   necessary/economical, etc)

Is the brand/service a necessity
   or aspirational?
Is it an impulse product?
Why is the brand/service bought?

☐ *Brand/service identity*

Trademark
Brand/service name
Symbol used
Patent information

Logo
Typestyle
Corporate requirements
Labelling

☐ *Brand/service performance*

How does it work?
What does it do?
Other possible uses?
Physical benefits (eg texture, smell,
   taste, appearance, etc)
Brand/service use

Special ingredients?
What can it do that its competition
   can't?
What can it not do?
Frequency of use?

☐ *Target market details*

Geographics
Demographics
Psychographics

Details of:
- heavy users
- medium users
- light users

☐ **Distribution details**

Is the brand/service distributed:
- exclusively?
- selectively?
- intensively?
How is it distributed, for example:
- directly to the consumer?
- via retailers?
- via wholesalers and retailers?
- via appointed agents?

Does the distribution channel need
   support?
   If so, what?
Seasonality of the brand/service?
Distribution threats/weaknesses?

☐ *Pricing details*

Price trends since launch?
Price versus competitors?
Special deals/discounts

Price mark-up policy?
Pricing threats?

☐ *Competitive details*

Who are the competition?
Where are they?
What are their strengths and
weaknesses:
– company?
– management?
– brands/services?
– other?
Performance of our brand/service
vis-à-vis their brands

Positioning details of each
competitive brand
Competitor's pricing details
Competitor's advertising and
promotional support details
Marketing communications budget
and media choice for every
brand/service

☐ Creating effective television commercials

Many creative people believe that a TV commercial should be well-written, simple, interesting, credible and entertaining. It must be stressed that a single-minded idea should be communicated in the space of 15, 20, 30 or even 60 seconds.

Producing a television commercial involves three stages, namely:
☐ the pre-production stage
☐ the production stage
☐ the post-production stage.

The pre-production stage

During the pre-production stage the advertising agency is briefed, the creative team completes its checklist, the concept(s) is created, the pre-testing is done and the storyboard is finalised. This storyboard is presented to the client and sent to the SABC/Bop TV/M-Net for approval. The production house is selected, quotes are obtained and the casting is done.

The following checklist for writing effective TV commercials could be useful during the pre-production stage (see Bovée & Arens 1982:399):

Checklist for writing effective TV commercials
☐ The opening should be pertinent, relevant, and not forced. It should permit a smooth transition to the balance of the commercial.
☐ The situation should lend itself naturally to the sales story – without the use of extraneous, distractive gimmicks.
☐ Do not jump too far ahead in the audio by describing one feature while showing another. Synchronise audio and video.
☐ Keep the audio copy concise, without wasted words. Fewer words are needed for TV than for radio. Less than two words per second is effective for demonstrations.
☐ The situation should be high in human interest.
☐ The viewer should be able to identify with the situation.
☐ Generally hold the number of elements to a minimum.

- ☐ Present a simple sequence of ideas.
- ☐ The words used should be short, realistic and conversational, not 'ad talk'. Sentences should be short.
- ☐ Words should not be wasted in describing what is being seen.
- ☐ The words should interpret the picture and prepare the viewer for the next scene.
- ☐ Remember that 60-second commercials consisting of 101 to 110 words are the most effective. Those with more than 170 words are the least effective.
- ☐ Allow five or six seconds for the average scene, with none less than three seconds.
- ☐ Provide enough movement to avoid static scenes.
- ☐ Scenes should offer variety without 'jumping'.
- ☐ The commercial should look fresh and new.
- ☐ Any presenters should be properly handled – identified, compatible, authoritative, pleasing and non-distracting.
- ☐ The general video treatment should be interesting.

Once the storyboard has been created it should be evaluated. Freedman Rossi/BBDO asks the following two questions:

- ☐ *Is it relevant?* Is the commercial making a promise or proposition that has meaning to the prime prospect? What proof do you have of this relevance? How valid is the proof?
- ☐ *Is it a surprise?* Is the promise delivered in an unexpected way? Will it give the prime prospect an affinity for the brand? Is it single-minded? Can you remember it the next day?

Aubrey Malden of Ogilvy Mather Rightford Searle-Tripp & Makin suggests that the following questions should be asked when creative work is being reviewed:

- ☐ Did you gasp when you saw it?
- ☐ Do you wish you had thought of it?
- ☐ Is it unique?
- ☐ Does it fit the strategy to perfection?
- ☐ Could it be used for 30 years? (Is it campaignable?)

Malden suggests a mnemonic for remembering what should pass through your mind when evaluating a campaign, namely 'Do I smell a rose?' Is the campaign:

- ☐ Relevant (does it answer the problem as set out in the brief and does it talk to your target audience)?
- ☐ On strategy (does it answer the creative strategy)?
- ☐ Simple (is it understood, simply? All big ideas are simple).
- ☐ Excellent (is it a big idea – stunning, unusual, unique, etc)?

He says one should look for a strong, clear consumer promise, emotional and/or rational, which is presented in a way that makes that promise unique to the brand in this day of parity products. Its execution should demand attention. Advertising is not a message delivered by someone who has something to say to someone who wants to listen. It has to compete with editorial, TV programmes and radio talk shows. Nobody reads a magazine or switches on the TV or listens to the radio especially to see or hear the ads. Advertising must 'compel' and 'interest' the audience in such a way that they want to read, listen, look at it.

The following checklist for evaluating the TV storyboard could be useful (given to me by the late George Gribbon, ex-president of Young & Rubicam Inc):

Checklist for evaluating the TV storyboard (score)
☐ Simplicity of the message
☐ Credibility of the message, the models, the situations
☐ Originality of the commercial, the idea/concept
☐ Relevance to the brand and the target audience
☐ Empathy (ie is it a likeable, entertaining commercial?)

The storyboard is finalised, presented and approved by both client and media and a decision is taken on the production house and the director.

At first discussions are informal while the agency creative team and the director agree on a common route for the treatment of the commercial, for although the storyboard is always used as a guideline, obviously it is impossible to draw each individual frame of the commercial accurately (approximately 750 frames would be needed for a 30-second commercial unless hi-speed or slow motion scenes were required). Additional shots or intercuts are agreed on and noted on the shot list.

Once the overall 'treatment' has been agreed on, the team moves on to aspects of detail. Although the film to be made lasts for only about 30 seconds, as much attention is paid to each detail as if it were a feature film running for an hour and a half. The following aspects of detail must be given attention:

Casting
A casting director is briefed on the kind of person/people required for the commercial, for example it might be a young, attractive girl of about 18 years of age, with fair hair, a good figure and good hands and possibly an acting/dancing background. A casting session is set up and a number of girls who meet the brief are sent along to be filmed on video tape. After that the agency and director sit down to select and shortlist the girls.

They judge the cast on appearance, ability to perform before the camera, personality, etc. Often the girl who seemed most suitable in person is no good on tape – you can 'put on' up to three kilograms on film. Sometimes the casting director has to cast up to 300 people, for example a stadium of extras. Each brief depends on the job.

Set/location
A commercial can be shot in two places, in a studio or on actual location.

In a studio a set is built by a set builder employed and briefed by the production house to simulate the room, house or even outdoor area required. An entire skyline can be painted on the wall or 'cyc' of the studio, and a foreground can be built from wooden or polystyrene flats recreating buildings or walls. Sometimes the floor is covered with soil which is compressed tightly to simulate ground that has been trampled by cows for decades. This may save a lot of money if the commercial is to be shot outside during the rainy season!

An actual location which meets the requirements of the commercial can be sought for example a building with Doric columns, a park with a stream and ducks, or any number of places. The obvious advantage of a location is the naturalness of everything, and the disadvantages are the time restrictions imposed by natural light, the elements and sometimes difficulty in dressing the set to exact specification.

Together the agency and production house decide whether a set or a location (or both) is suitable for the production in hand. Once a suitable design for the set has been agreed upon, the details for *propping and styling* the set/location are agreed upon. At this stage an art director and a stylist become involved. They are briefed on the feel and ambience, the colour and style of the commercial and go away to look for the items that will be used in the set. These can range from large items, such as the bed or bar needed in a room, right down to small details such as a pair of pink fluffy slippers that will peak out from under the bed, or a brass tot measure to be used for dispensing drinks in a bar scene. Sometimes the props are unavailable as the shops do not stock them, or they exist only in the mind of the art director! These can be made to specification by a special effects man, a carpenter, a glass blower, or puppetier . . . whoever is an expert in making what is required.

Wardrobe

By this time the cast, which may range from one to more than 300 people, has been approved. Now it has to be dressed. The size and dimensions of each member of the cast are recorded and a wardrobe mistress is employed to buy, hire or make suitable clothes as determined by the agency and director.

The costume could be period, or funky, depending on the storyboard, and sometimes more than one costume is needed. Again a lot of attention is paid to detail. Specific colours and designs are agreed upon and once the agency is happy with the clothes selected a wardrobe call is organised and each member of the cast tries on his clothing and is pinned for a perfect fit.

At this stage hair-styling and make-up are discussed and agreed upon. If the commercial is for a hair care product or requires specialised hair-styling, a hairdresser is employed to be on set during shooting and a make-up artist is there to powder faces, which tend to glow under the lights.

Special effects and models

Special effects and models (not the talking kind) are also discussed during the pre-production stage. Sometimes these are unnecessary, but if, for example, the storyboard shows an iron literally belching steam to indicate the effectiveness of the steam button, a modification may be needed to make the iron do just that. If the production requires 'star wars' effects, pre-production in this area is absolutely essential!

By this time most of the production details have been finalised. A pilot soundtrack may be recorded at a music studio to help with the mood at the shoot and, if acceptable to all concerned, it can be of great help to the editor at cutting stage. The agency and director discuss the voices to be used at the final stages of the commercial and depending on how many languages the commercial is to be produced in, a guide-track of the voices can also be pre-recorded to complete the pre-production process.

The pre-production meeting

Held about a week before the shoot and attended by the agency, the client, the producer and the director, the purpose of the pre-production meeting is to enable all concerned to reach agreement on the finer details pertaining to the client's commercial as discussed with the director and agency. If agreement is reached, the cast is confirmed and the wardrobe and props have been purchased, then it is on with the shoot and over to the director.

At this stage a final shot list is presented with lighting and mood boards (pictures are cut from magazines as references to help indicate the kind of feel that will be achieved). It is important that by the time the actual shoot takes place the final storyboard is buttoned down to save time (and money) once the film is rolling.

A pre-production checklist is very useful to ensure that nothing is left to chance. The following pre-production checklist and critical path was introduced by Dennis Hoines of Mortimer Tiley in the early 1980s:

Television pre-production checklist

☐ Is the commercial to be shot on film or tape?
  - any possible problems arising from this (eg complicated opticals in the case of 16 mm, location shooting in the case of VTR, deadlines, etc)?
  - is the commercial intended for cinemas as well?
☐ Locations
  - what is there to check on location (eg power, lighting, acoustics, transportation, distance, possible weather problems, alternative locations, necessary permission)?
☐ Props
  - details of interiors and sets (furniture, time of day, general atmosphere)?
  - provision for continuity?
☐ Casting
  - choice of people (age, height, colour, weight and voice)?
  - any auditions required?
  - how will the cast be auditioned?
  - any stand-ins required?
  - voice-overs?
  - model releases?
  - permission from Child Welfare when children are being used in commercial?
  - check on previous exposure of proposed models?
  - ensure availability of models?
  - English and Afrikaans aspect?
☐ Animation (where applicable)
  - artwork examples?
  - style generally?
☐ Styling
  - clothing of models, hair-styles, make-up, jewellery, etc?
☐ Shot-by-shot analysis
  - shot-by-shot analysis of time allocated in relation to the action required, and the total time available?
  - overall feel and pace of film?
  - any need to show production company similar films?
☐ Evaluation of proposed visual techniques
  - for example, zooms, fades, mix dissolves, cuts, etc?
  - discussion of opticals?
☐ Sound-track
  - sync sound, voice-overs, music (library or original), post sync, sound effects, voice dubbing into second language?
  - any pre-recording required?
  - will sync lines be memorised?
  - idiot boards required?

Figure 7.1
Critical path for film commercial

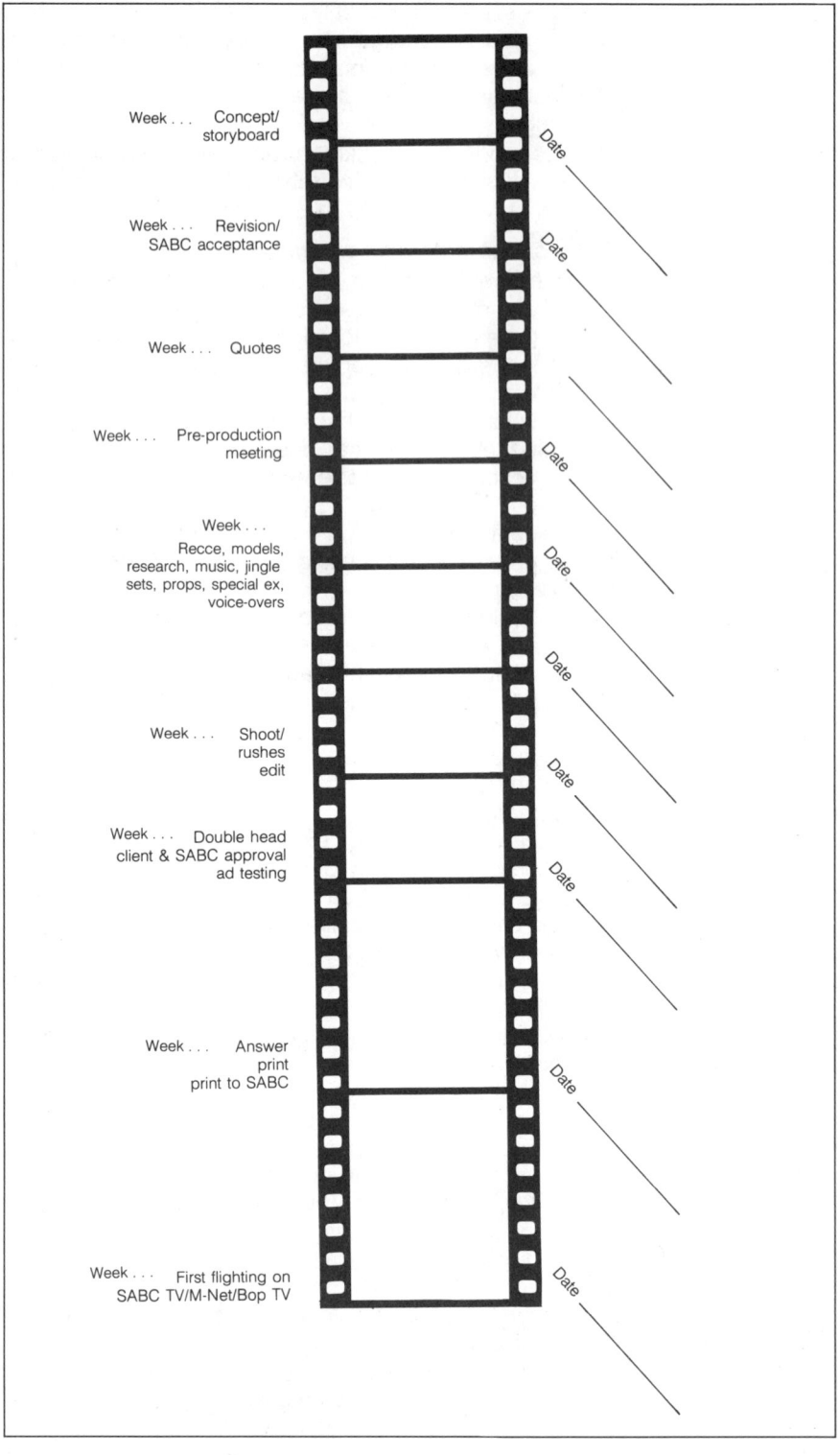

Week . . . Concept/ storyboard — Date

Week . . . Revision/ SABC acceptance — Date

Week . . . Quotes

Week . . . Pre-production meeting — Date

Week . . . Recce, models, research, music, jingle sets, props, special ex, voice-overs — Date

Date

Week . . . Shoot/ rushes edit — Date

Week . . . Double head client & SABC approval ad testing — Date

Week . . . Answer print print to SABC — Date

Week . . . First flighting on SABC TV/M-Net/Bop TV — Date

- [ ] Pack shots
  - – will pack work on TV in colour and B/W?
  - – any special requirements?
  - – provision of perfect pack specimens by client?
  - – any product demonstrations and necessary supervision?
  - – any additional props, artwork and background colours?
  - – does special product have to be made up?
- [ ] The shooting dates
  - – the shooting dates and, if possible, timetable of shoot.
  - – any stills required?
  - – who will be responsible?
- [ ] Check on responsibility allocated in respect of all the above
  - – ensure clear understanding?
  - – provision for breaks, refreshments, etc?
  - – any PR required (eg notes of thanks, flowers for helpful people, etc)?
- [ ] People to be present at shoot
  - – people to be present at shoot? who from client?
  - – who is to direct?
- [ ] Critical path
  - – when and where do we review rushes?
  - – when do we see rough cut, double head or play back?
  - – date of finally edited commercial?
  - – answer print?
  - – screening to client for approval?
  - – submission to SABC (consider early submission if advisable)?
- [ ] Number of prints or cassettes required?
- [ ] Final review and agreement of possible additional costs to be incurred?

The production stage

This is also known as the shoot day and is the responsibility of the director. Depending on the size of the production he has to control and motivate from about 15 up to 400 people (there could be a cast of thousands). Although he has an experienced and specialised crew at his disposal, it is his responsibility to ensure that each shot is right in terms of feel/lighting, etc, and that the model/actor is giving the correct performance and his best. The shoot can go on for more than a day, sometimes taking up to a week, and tempers (those of the film crew, cast, agency and client) can become very frayed. It is the director's task to keep things running smoothly.

Obviously, over the day (or more) of the shoot more than 30 seconds of film is shot. For a 30-second commercial it is perfectly acceptable to shoot two to three hours of footage, with each shot having up to 20 takes. The best of these will be chosen by the editor and cut down to make a coherent and creative 30-second commercial.

Many days, weeks and even months of preparation and planning, budgeting and payment go into the making of a successful and smooth-running shoot day(s). In order to ensure that a successful shoot will take place, certain things must be attended to:

- [ ] *Locations* must be recce'd and chosen (if not on hand, personnel are hired for this).
- [ ] *Sets* must be planned and built – there are a few companies that do this.

Courtesy: Ogilvy Mather RST & M

☐ *Props* must be briefed and hired or bought. Art directors and a stylist must be hired.

☐ A considerable amount of time will be spent *casting* good people, and the chosen people must be rehearsed, wardrobed and, where necessary, transported to the shoot.

☐ When children under the age of 14 years are to be used in a shoot *permission* has to be obtained from Child Welfare and a chaperone(s) (depending on how many children) arranged. It takes three weeks to obtain Child Welfare permission.

☐ *Wardrobe and make-up* must be styled, often in conjunction with the product and/or set, lighting, etc.

☐ The *lighting* must be discussed thoroughly. The necessary equipment must be hired and the day before the shoot the director, lighting cameraman, producer, production assistant, focus puller, camera operator, grip, gaffer, sparks, etc must attend a prelight session to perfect the mood and angles to be shot on the shoot day. On the same day the set must be assembled and propped, in which case the stylist, props person, art director and runner will be working – obviously there is an opportunity for any minor last minute changes.

☐ Any necessary *transport* must be arranged.

☐ *Props* must be collected and returned.

☐ *Camera equipment* must be delivered and returned.

☐ *The light van* must deliver and return all lighting equipment and personnel.

☐ *A construction van* may be necessary.

☐ *A catering van* would be the responsibility of the caterer or the production house or agency if necessary.

☐ *A cast bus/car* must be available to pick up and take home the cast – it must be on hand (with a driver) during the period of the shoot as well as on rehearsal days and post-production days such as post-sync sessions, etc.

☐ If *animals* are a requirement in the commercial their transport must be arranged.

☐ Flights must be booked and transport to and from airports and hotels must be arranged.

☐ Personnel and transport must be on hand at given times to handle any *freighting* required.

☐ *Equipment* must be booked.

☐ *Cameras* – sync or wild. Camera supporting gear – ie dolly, heads, crane/jib, legs, tracks, batteries, fitters, film magazines, motor, generator, lenses, sound equipment and stock, loud communication equipment and various stills and Polaroid Instant viewing of shots and sound, that is video link/record.

☐ *Stock and processing*. Stock is either 35 mm/16 mm or video stock and is arranged dependent on the complexity of the commercial and bought, stored and transported to shoot. Material that has been shot is then packaged. Sound and visual are sent off to the relevant processing laboratories (Irene for film) and the sound man packages and delivers his material to the editor involved in the commercial.

If the commercial has an extremely tight schedule, as the incoming shoot comes off the film is dashed to the labs at noon for processing and again at 16h30 for night or early morning processing. Processed negs will come off at noon so that time is saved. A day can be crucial to a tight schedule.

The post-production stage

If the commercial is shot on film the post-production stage consists of:
☐ editing
☐ producing additional elements
☐ sound mix
☐ interlock
☐ optical print
☐ answer print
☐ approval by client and medium (eg SABC)
☐ producing release print and video transfer.

If the commercial is done on video tape the post-production stage consists of:
☐ editing
☐ adding ancillary elements
☐ sound mix
☐ final tape/master copy
☐ approval by client and medium (eg SABC)
☐ duplicating final tape.

Editing the footage is a critical stage. First *the editor* edits to a rough cut, guided by the storyboard, the music, the sound-track and the magic captured on the day of the shoot. The rough cut is very rough; it is jumpy, the colour has not been equalised and corrected and it is full of editing marks. The agency is called in to view the rough cut on the editing table and suggestions are made and decisions taken about improving the commercial. Further editing is done while the final sound-track is recorded. Meanwhile, *additional elements* such as logos, slogans, etc are produced and shot and the editor incorporates these for the double head stage. The film is still reasonably rough – colour equalisation has not been done – but the picture sequence is matched with the sound-track. At this stage the client is called in and the edited version is approved.

Then the *sound mix* is done to ensure that the voices, the music and the special effects are synchronised and interlocked. The next stage is to produce an *optical print* incorporating fades, dissolves, etc. The *answer print* is produced and sent to the medium for final approval. Once this has been obtained colour correction and grading is done and the final *release print* is produced for cinema or a *video transfer* is done for SABC TV/M-Net/Bop TV.

If the commercial is done entirely on video tape the various stages could all happen in one day. Video editing is computerised and the editor can experiment on the spot with various intercuts, fades and dramatic effects, while colour correction is done right there. Doing a commercial on video has the advantages of speed, versatility, strict control, etc, but it is restrictive to some extent because it is confined to what can be captured in a studio and it cannot be used for cinema in video format.

☐ Creating effective radio commercials

Radio commercials normally run for 30 seconds, although shorter and longer time segments can be booked. A radio commercial can consists of voice(s) only, music and voice(s) or music, voice(s) and sound effects. The more elements it contains the fewer words can be used to describe the brand/service, its benefits, etc. The maximum word count for radio commercials in English or Afrikaans should be:

Length of commercial	English or Afrikaans	English copy to be translated into other languages
10 seconds	25 words	20 words
20 seconds	45 words	35 words
30 seconds	65 words	50 words
60 seconds	125 words	100 words

The following checklist for writing radio commercials may be useful to copywriters:

Checklist for writing radio commercials

☐ Is my copy simple? (Remember that difficult verbal messages are hard to hear and grasp).

☐ Did I use fewer, but better words? (Remember that you should not exceed 65 words for a 30-second commercial).

☐ Did I use a dramatic device/stopper early in the commercial? (Remember that if interest is not created in the first six to eight seconds, the message will probably be lost).

☐ Did I use the right tone of voice/emotional approach? (Remember that touching the listeners' hearts ensures success).

☐ Did I speak to my target audience in their own language? (Remember that the brand/service is the star of the commercial).

□ Was I specific? (Remember that generalities should be avoided as they are meaningless).

□ Did I repeat the promise more than once? (Remember that if a promise is meaningful it should be repeated or said in different ways. If it is not meaningful, leave it out).

□ Did I help the target audience to identify the brand/service? (Remember that radio is a reminder medium and the target audience needs help in visualising the brand/service).

□ Does the commercial flow smoothly? (Remember to read the commercial aloud to check on possible tongue-twisters, smooth flow and proper length).

Bovée and Arens (1982:424) outline 17 creative ways for selling on radio:

1 *Product demo* — telling how a product is used or the purposes it serves
2 *Voice power* — where the power of the commercial is in the casting of a unique voice
3 *Electronic sound* — synthetic sound-making machines create a memorable product-sound association
4 *Customer interview* — a product spokesman and customer discuss the product advantages — often spontaneously
5 *Humorous fake interview* — variation of the customer interview in a lighter vein
6 *Hyperbole or exaggerated statement* — overstatement arouses interest in legitimate product claims that might otherwise pass unnoticed; often a spoof
7 *Sixth dimension* — compression of time and events into a brief spot involving the listener in future projections
8 *Hot property* — commercial adapts a current sensation — a hit show, performer, or song
9 *Comedian power* — established comedians do commercials in their own unique style, implying celebrity endorsement
10 *Historical fantasy* — situation with historical characters revived to convey product message
11 *Sound picture* — recognisable sounds used to involve listener by stimulating his or her imagination
12 *Demographics* — music or references appeal to a particular segment of the population, as an age or interest group
13 *Imagery transfer* — musical logo or other sound reinforces the effects of a television campaign
14 *Celebrity interview* — famous person endorses product in an informal manner
15 *Product song* — music and words combine to create musical logo selling product in the style of popular music
16 *Editing genius* — many different situations, voices, types of music and sound are combined in a series of quick cuts
17 *Improvisation* — assigned a situation, performers work out the dialogue extemporaneously; may be post-edited.

□ Creating effective print advertising

The four requirements of a newspaper or magazine advertisement are that it must attract attention and create initial interest, communicate relevant product information and maintain interest, induce adoption of the relevant information into the target audience's systems of beliefs and attitudes to the product and persuade the reader to purchase the product, purchase it more often, or to be favourably inclined to the advertised brand/service. A print advertisement consists of three important elements which must be decided upon by the creative team, namely the verbal elements, the visual elements and the design elements.

In this section I will provide checklists on the four requirements and on the three elements.

Attracting attention

The following is a checklist for attracting attention:

Checklist for attracting attention

- ☐ Does the advertisement reflect the brand/service favourably without directing undue attention to itself?
- ☐ Is the brand/service and main message presented powerfully and distinctively so that the reader can grasp it at a glance?
- ☐ Does the device that attracts attention also tell the product story?
- ☐ Does the advertisement contain a visual/illustration that performs the task of selecting the audience for the advertisement?
- ☐ Do the objects and/or people in the advertisement appear lifeless or dull? (Remember that moving objects can bring life, interest and excitement to the advertising message).
- ☐ Is the illustration relevant to the basic message of the advertisement?
- ☐ Does the headline capture the reader's attention?
- ☐ Is the headline specific, relevant and understandable?
- ☐ If the appearance of the brand is vitally important in the ultimate purchase is the brand emphasised in the illustration?
- ☐ Is the visual emotional enough?
- ☐ Is the advertisement not too cluttered?
- ☐ Do the people and objects face into the advertisement?
- ☐ Does the colour treatment of the advertisement give eye-appeal?
- ☐ Does the advertisement have a focal centre that dominates and attracts?

Communicating relevant information

A checklist for communicating relevant information is given below:

Checklist for communicating relevant information

- ☐ Does this advertisement tell the target reader to use this brand/service to get this specific benefit?
- ☐ Does the selected benefit have the greatest interest for the greatest number of target prospects?
- ☐ Is the satisfaction offered concrete, direct and immediate?
- ☐ Is the language used meaningful, natural and understandable to the target readers?
- ☐ Did I use positive rather than negative words?
- ☐ Is the copy readable?
- ☐ Is the illustration relevant to the brand/service, the benefit or main message of the advertisement?
- ☐ Does the advertisement communicate a favourable brand image which distinguishes it clearly from competitive brands?
- ☐ Do the symbols used conform to the brand/service and the audience?
- ☐ Are the people and objects real?
- ☐ Is the brand/service the star of the advertisement?

☐ Does the first paragraph contain the most newsworthy item?
☐ Is the copy cluttered with uninteresting or less important claims?
☐ Is the advertisement addressing the target reader personally?
☐ Does the advertisement tell/show the target reader what the brand/service will do for him?

Adoption of the information

A checklist of questions to ask about the adoption of the information is given below:

Checklist for the adoption of the information

☐ Are the right emotional appeals used?
☐ If sex appeal is used, is it overdone or irrelevant?
☐ If humour is used, is it a quiet, sensible use of amazing copy/illustration?
☐ Does the advertisement impart pleasant information?
☐ Can the reader identify with the model in the illustration?
☐ Is the advertising message believable in all respects?
☐ Are there too many superlatives or exaggerated claims in the body copy?
☐ Should the advertisement perhaps have contained some information about what the brand/service cannot do?
☐ If a testimonial approach is used, are the testimonial claims written in language the testifier would actually have used or the reader would expect him to use?
☐ Is the illustration normal, natural and unposed?
☐ Will the advertisement build the desired brand image for the brand/service?

Persuading the reader

The following is a checklist about persuading the reader:

Checklist for persuading the reader

☐ Is the advertisement persuasively different?
☐ Is the advertisement a stopper?
☐ Does the advertisement have vitality?
☐ Does the advertisement communicate the relevant product information quickly and easily?
☐ Does the advertisement offer a reward for reading it?
☐ Does the advertisement reinforce positive attitudes to the brand/service?
☐ Is the depicted brand image relevant to the target reader's desires and sufficiently meaningful to motivate him to buy the brand/service?

The verbal elements of a print advertisement

The verbal elements consist of headlines, body copy, slogans and payoff lines. Some copywriters prefer to work with what they call the *copy platform*. The copy platform involves:

☐ the product promise and support evidence
☐ the USP
☐ effective selling arguments
☐ the target audience to be reached
☐ the emotional tone or mood
☐ the objective of the advertisement.

The copy platform is a tool that guides copywriters in creating a meaningful promise before they write their headline and the body copy.

Headlines

The following is a checklist for effective headlines:

Checklist for effective headlines

☐ Is the headline an attention-getter?

☐ Will the headline draw the target readers into the body copy?

☐ Is the headline meaningful or too general?

☐ Did I avoid cliches?

☐ Does the headline contain words that will help select the target readers?

☐ Is the headline brief without sacrificing saying something meaningful?

☐ Did I use the right words? (Remember that short words are mostly concrete while long words are often abstract).

☐ Is the headline positive? (Remember to avoid negative headlines).

☐ Does the headline promise a benefit or reward to the target reader? (Remember that consumers buy need-satisfying benefits and a headline specifying the major benefit will be effective in most cases).

☐ Is the headline not too cute or too clever?

☐ Is the headline co-ordinated with the other elements of the advertisement?

Body copy

The major purposes of body copy are to inform the target reader, to satisfy his curiosity, to answer any questions he may have about the brand/service, to support the headline and illustration and to persuade him to purchase the brand/service or to be favourably inclined towards it. A checklist for writing body copy is given below:

Checklist for writing body copy

☐ Is the first paragraph short and interesting?

☐ Did I leave out relevant information purely for the sake of avoiding long copy?

☐ Does the headline and illustration make some or most of copy unnecessary?

☐ Does the ad need copy at all (ie perhaps the headline and visual say it all)?

☐ Does the copy spell out in adequate detail and in attractive terms the satisfaction to be derived from using this brand/service?

☐ If the product is expensive or the story complex, is the body copy giving enough detail?

☐ If the copy is long, is it easy to read and separated by logical captions?

☐ Does every word in the body copy work for me? (Remember to make the point directly and specifically).

☐ Does the body copy tell the reader to buy this brand/service to get these specific benefits?

☐ Is the body copy truthful and honest?

☐ Did I copy other advertisements? Key phrases?

Slogans

The third verbal element is slogans. Much of what applies to headlines also applies to slogans. Slogans are often words or phrases which express an advertising idea in condensed form. Sometimes the brand/service positioning translates into a slogan, sometimes a particularly good headline ends up as the slogan.

Over the years many verbal devices such as puns, metaphors, rhyme or alliteration have been used to spell out the advertising idea in the form of a slogan.

The following is a checklist for writing slogans:

Checklist for writing slogans
☐ Is the slogan connected with the brand/service's major benefit/reward?
☐ Will the slogan arouse curiosity on the part of the target reader?
☐ Is the slogan a focusing point of the advertisement?
☐ Is the advertised brand/service a low price item? (Remember that slogans are best suited to corporations, convenience goods and impulse items).

The visual elements of a print advertisement

The visual elements are usually the *illustration(s)* and the *logo*. In most advertisements the illustration is the most important feature of the advertisement. It can and should enhance the overall effect by specifically attracting attention, communicating relevant product benefits, strengthening the headline and body copy and visually expressing ideas or images that are difficult to express in words. A checklist for choosing illustrations is given below:

Checklist for choosing illustrations
☐ Does the illustration visualise the key idea or benefit of the brand/service?
☐ Will the illustration successfully attract the reader's attention?
☐ Is the illustration simple and compelling?
☐ Does the illustration reinforce the headline rather than compete with it?
☐ Does the illustration have a single, meaningful focal point?
☐ Is there good eye movement in the illustration or does it cause eyeball gymnastics?
☐ Should the illustration be in black and white with one or two additional colours or in full colour?
☐ Should the product be shown in use?
☐ Should the illustration show how to use the product?
☐ Does the illustration show the pack? (Remember it helps Mrs Housewife to identify the brand on the grocery shelf).
☐ Can the reader identify the user benefit in the illustration?
☐ Does the humour in the illustration create a positive and lasting impression?
☐ Should the illustration be a photograph or a drawing?
☐ Should the illustration show 'before' and 'after' photographs?
☐ Is the illustration credible?
☐ Does the illustration create the desired brand, user and situation images?
☐ Will the illustration motivate the target reader to use the product or to be favourably inclined towards it?
☐ Is the logo too dominating, or too small?

The design elements of a print advertisement

The question is often asked: Which kind of layout works best? This is not an easy question to answer, because it depends on the objective of the advertisement, the budget constraints (eg a lack of funds may influence the art director to use an unusual shape in order to attract more attention), what should be depicted, etc. However, readership surveys (Bovée & Arens 1982:342, 343) in the USA indicate that the highest scoring advertisements usually use the standard layout with a single dominating illustration that occupies between 60 and 70% of the total advertising space. Next in line are advertisements consisting of one large and two smaller pictures. These pictures should stop the reader and be interesting. Readership drops considerably if the body copy of an advertisement is more than 50 words long, while the headline should fill only 10 to 15% of the advertisement.

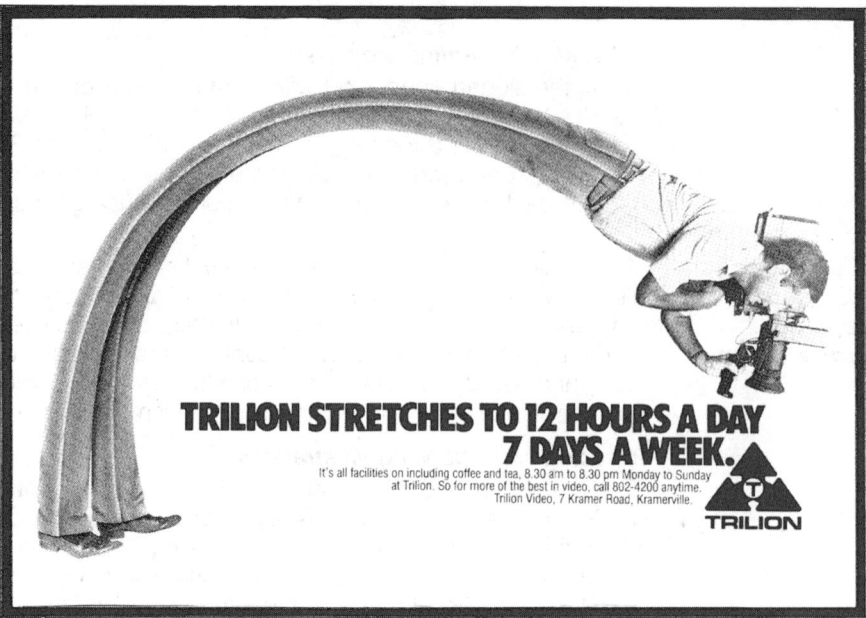

Courtesy: Trillion. Unusual visual and excellent eye movement

Design deals with such important aspects as *balance*, *movement*, *proportion*, *contrast*, *continuity*, *unity*, *clarity/simplicity* and the effective use of *white space*. There are no ready-made formulas to ensure that effective layouts are created, but if the abovementioned factors are taken into consideration, a thumbnail sketch is prepared, the rough layout is better than the thumbnail in its design and the comprehensive layout is checked on these aspects, a good design can be achieved.

Below is a checklist of design principles (Bovée & Arens, 1982:341 & 342).

Checklist for design principles

☐ *Balance*   The reference point that determines the balance of a layout is the optical centre. The optical centre is about one-eighth above the physical centre, or five-eighths from the bottom of the page. Balance is the arrangement of the elements as they are positioned on the page – the left side of the optical centre versus the right, and above the optical centre versus below. There are two kinds of balance, formal and informal.

  – *Formal balance*   Perfect symmetry is the key to formal balance: *matched elements* on either side of line dissecting the ad have equal optical weight. This is used to strike a dignified, stable, conservative image.

  – *Informal balance*   By placing elements of *different* size, shape, intensity of colour, or darkness at different distances from the optical centre, a visually balanced presentation can be achieved. Just like a teeter-totter, an object of greater optical weight near the centre can be balanced by an object of less weight placed further from the centre. Most advertisements use informal balance because it makes the ad more interesting, imaginative and exciting.

1 Thumbnail sketch
2 Layout
3 Final advertisement

Courtesy: SASWITCH. Three stages from thumbnail sketch to layout to final advertisement

☐ *Movement*   The principle of design that causes the reader of an advertisement to read the material in the sequence desired is called movement. This can be achieved through a variety of techniques.

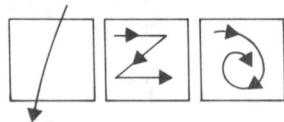

- Through the use of *gaze motion*, the placement of people or animals in the advertisement so that their eyes direct our eyes to the next important element to be read.
- By the use of mechanical devices such as pointing fingers, rectangles, lines or arrows to direct attention from element to element or, in television, by moving the actors or the camera or by changing scenes.
- Through the use of comic-strip sequence and pictures with captions that force the reader to start at the beginning and follow the sequence in order to grasp the message.
- By using white space and colour to emphasize a body or type or an illustration. Eyes will go from a dark element to a light, from colour to non-colour.
- By taking advantage of the natural tendency of readers to start at the top left corner of the page and proceed on a diagonal Z motion to the lower right corner.
- By using size itself, which attracts attention because readers are drawn to the biggest and most dominant element on the page and then to the smaller elements.

☐ *Proportion*   Elements in an advertisement should be accorded space based on their importance to the complete advertisement. For best appearance, elements frequently use varying amounts of space in some proportion, such as three or two, to avoid the monotony of equal amounts of space for each element.

☐ *Contrast*   An effective way of drawing attention to a particular element is with the use of contrast in colour, size or style. For example, reverse (white letters on a dark background), or a black and white ad with a red border, or an ad with an unusual type style creates contrast and draws attention.

☐ *Continuity*   Continuity refers to the relationship of one ad to the rest of the campaign. This is achieved by using the same design format, style and tone for all advertisements, by using the same spokesperson in commercials, by incorporating an unusual and unique graphic element in all ads, or by the consistent use of other techniques such as a logo, a cartoon character or a catchy slogan.

☐ *Unity*   Unity is the ad's bonding agent. It means that, although the ad is made up of many different parts, these elements relate to one another in such a way that the ad gives an harmonious impression. Balance, movement, proportion, contrast and colour may all contribute to unity of design. In addition, many other techniques can be used:
- type styles from the same family
- borders around ads to hold elements together

- overlapping one picture or element over another
- judicious use of white space
- graphic tools such as boxes, arrows or tints.

☐ *Clarity and simplicity*   Any elements that can be eliminated without damaging the effect the advertiser is trying to achieve should be eliminated. Too many different type styles; type that is too small; too many reverses, illustrations or boxed items; and unnecessary copy make layout complex and too busy. It makes the advertisement hard to read and hurts the overall effect desired.

☐ *White space (isolation)*   Visit a local shopping centre and notice the stores that stock lower-priced shoes. They normally display as many styles in the window as possible using virtually every foot of space available. Then go to a store carrying high-fashion, expensive shoes, and note how they selectively display a few shoes in their windows. Simply by looking at the window displays you get a certain image of the price of the merchandise carried by the store. The same image is conveyed by advertisements in their use of white space.

White space is the part of the advertisement that is not occupied by other elements (even though the colour of the background may be black or some colour other than white). White space can be used to focus attention on an isolated element. Put a vast amount of white space around a block of copy and it almost appears as if it's in a spotlight. White space has a great deal to do with the image the artist desires to create.

Judging the creative print work

Before submitting a layout and copy to a client the creative team should evaluate the print advertisement.

Schultz and Martin (1979:75) suggest the following questions:
☐ Is the advertisement on or off the written strategy?
☐ Is the advertisement honest and in good taste?
☐ Is the advertisement clear?
☐ Is the advertisement an unconventional solution to the problem?
☐ Is the advertisement arresting to a consumer of the medium?

George Gribbon suggests the following pertaining to print advertising:
☐ Is the advertisement of yours a stopper?
☐ Is the product the hero?
☐ Is your advertisement completely believable?
☐ Is your advertisement a likeable person?
☐ Is the theme one that will last?

Derek Logan of Grey Phillips Bunton Mundel and Blake uses the Grey measure:
☐ Someone (the identified target audience).
☐ Something (what the brand/service does for the consumer, eg you are selling sleep, not *Horlicks*).
☐ Somewhere (the right media choice).
☐ Somehow (creative considerations like style, tone of voice, etc)
☐ Believe something (the single-minded promise).
☐ Reason(s) why (the reason why the brand/service can deliver the single-minded promise).

The most important factor is the 'believe something', the single-minded promise that must be communicated with creative flair.

☐ Creating effective outdoor advertising

Aubrey Malden of *Ogilvy Mather Rightford Searle-Tripp & Makin* states that outdoor is the fastest communicator of all media.

It is a medium where ideas should communicate fastest. The message should be telegraphic and immediate. The audience is usually moving – in cars, in buses, (or on foot) – and does not have time to be intrigued. You cannot take a poster home to read as you can an intriguing print advertisement. The message should be simple and uncluttered. Some say it should communicate within three seconds, others two seconds. Boil down your brief on outdoor until it is very simple.

Print can include many copy points, posters cannot. Posters are usually used as a 'reminder' or an 'awareness' medium. The secret is not to try to communicate too much – 'less is more'. Use less words, and one simple visual – a logo might even work better than a packshot.

For many years creative people thought that 'outdoor' meant 'posters' – pieces of printed paper. Do not limit your thinking. Recently Araldite Glue in the UK stuck a car, using *Araldite*, on a billboard with the line 'Also sticks handles to teapots'. In South Africa, for SPL, a billboard was wrapped in a huge chain and padlock with the line 'Liberate your Main Frame'.

Courtesy: SPL and Ogilvy Mather RST & M. Example of an unusual creative approach

You do not always need words, but if you do you should consider using no more than ten. In an advertisement for *Nike* in the States the billboard used a huge cutout of a football player to great effect. The *Nike* logo was the only word on the poster.

Derek Logan of *Grey Phillips Bunton Mundel & Blake* says that outdoor is a static medium and that it calls for a swift message. There are no rules like a 'one word headline' or a 'large packshot'. The creative concept is king and will dictate what it takes to make it work — maybe ten words in the headline or a multitude of packs. Willards Crinkle Cut chips, for example, may best be communicated on a corrugated surface for the hoarding. Here the Crinkle Cut aspect is highlighted by using the physical aspects of the hoarding in conjunction with the message. Logan therefore stresses that the message should be communicated in a creative, relevant way.

Laurance Kuper of *Kuper Hands* is of the opinion that when planning a campaign the creative team should think outdoor first. It should be possible to posterise good press advertisements or to use them on outdoor media. When creating outdoor advertising it is necessary to be succinct and single-minded. Outdoor is a flexible medium and it is possible to use the background and the location and go beyond the confined space. Outdoor is visual and big, and because the same people drive past it and see it again and again the relationship between the medium and the viewer must be created.

Freedman Rossi/BBDO has three rules for creating effective outdoor advertising:
- Use six words or less.
- Create a 'visual scandal'.
- Think outside the box.

Carl Preller of *McCann de Villiers* uses three words: 'simplicity and drama'.

Finally, *Aubrey Malden* of *Ogilvy Mather Rightford Searle-Tripp & Makin* recommends that when judging outdoor, look at it quickly and ask:
- Is it simple?
- Is the communication immediate?
- Will it stand out?
- Is it on strategy?
- Will it make me gasp if I drive or walk by?
- Can it be even simpler?

☐ Closing comments

Whether the task is to create effective television or radio commercials, print advertisements or outdoor advertising, the key is a good brief and creative freedom where ingenuity and flair can be expressed in a unique way to grab (capture) the target audience's attention, to communicate meaningful product/service information and to motivate the target viewer, listener or reader to act in the intended manner as spelt out in the advertising objective(s).

☐ References

Bovée, CL & Arens, WF. 1982. *Contemporary advertising*. Homewood, Illinois: Richard D Irwin Inc.

8

Advertising research

Will the consumer be able to decode your advertising
   message correctly? *295*

The pre-testing of advertisements *310*

Measuring advertising effectiveness *320*

Multivariate analyses: understanding data *328*

Advertising research: the media *334*

Marketing research into industrial advertising
   and media *344*

Will the consumer be able to decode your advertising message correctly?

Annemarie van der Walt

Introduction 295

The frame of reference acts as a filter 296

Perception 298

Perceptual defence 301

Message content strategies 304

Summary 309

References 309

☐ Introduction

The question in the title is one which frequently confronts advertising practitioners. It is, unfortunately, a question for which there is no ready answer, since correct decoding of marketing information hinges on the consumer's perception of the communication content. The advertiser uses symbols such as words, pictures, sounds and shapes to encode a message with a certain meaning. These symbols are transmitted to the consumer as sensory stimuli. Only when the consumer perceives the stimuli in the way intended by the advertiser will he be able to decode the message correctly. The main objective of the advertising message is to *persuade* the consumer. The consumer must be persuaded to purchase the product, to change his attitudes or behaviour, or to regard the marketer and his product in a positive way. The marketer cannot hope to attain this objective if his message fails to reach his target market or if the target audience misunderstands the meaning of the symbols contained in the message.

The process of decoding depends to a large extent on the flow of information through the consumer's frame of reference, which acts as a filter. In this process some symbols may be disregarded, get lost, or may be changed beyond recognition. A person's frame of reference consists of all his previous experiences, beliefs, likes, dislikes, habits, prejudices, feelings and other psychological reactions of unknown origin. A person's frame of reference is unique to that person, which implies that many different meanings can be ascribed to the symbols used in executing a message – thus changing the message in an indefinable way.

Before the information can begin to flow through the filter the consumer must be exposed to it. He must be able to see, hear, feel, taste or smell it. Merely seeing or hearing, however, cannot be referred to as perception. *Perception is seeing or hearing in terms of the person's frame of reference.* Unfortunately, the word 'perception' is often used in an incorrect or confusing way in texts. A person cannot refuse to *see* something placed before him. However, he can protect himself by not *perceiving* it correctly.

This contribution deals with the extremely complicated topic of consumer perception and the perceptual defence barriers which a consumer erects to protect himself against undesirable information. Finally, the merits of a few message content strategies such as the use of humorous appeals, card stacking and repetition are discussed. It is clear that an advertiser should do everything in his power to facilitate correct decoding of the message he has designed, for consumer perception is the key to correct decoding of advertising messages.

☐ The frame of reference acts as a filter

In this section a factual description of the filter is given. Exactly how this filter works remains a mystery which may never be solved. In short, it entails the evaluation of every stimulus (bit of information) to which a person is exposed in the light of previously held beliefs, emotions and behavioural intentions. All these evaluations are summed in an overall orientation or attitude towards a certain object. If the advertising message for a certain brand of instant coffee, for example, is the object, all the symbols used to execute the advertisement (verbal as well as pictorial) will be transmitted into sensory stimuli and evaluated one by one to form the overall orientation, impression or attitude toward this brand of instant coffee. The message is perceived in the light of the foregoing evaluation, after which the person will be able to make a decision – to buy or not to buy the instant coffee. This very complicated process happens without the person being aware of what has really happened.

The frame of reference consists of three main components through which all information must flow, namely the cognitive, affective and behavioural components. The information flow and the three components are illustrated in figure 8.1.

☐ The *cognitive component* consists of the total configuration of beliefs and knowledge about a certain object, as well as actual experience gained previously. Any information in conflict with the cognitions (things that one 'knows' to be true) causes an imbalance, referred to as *cognitive dissonance*. Because this imbalance makes a person uncomfortable, he may try to alleviate it by deliberately distorting the message.

☐ The *affective component* involves feelings, emotions and prejudices. Prejudices are the result of previous faulty interpretations and cannot be changed easily. People actually sometimes believe their prejudices to be universal truths, in which case a mere advertisement cannot persuade them to change their minds.

☐ The *behavioural component* has to do with reactions, intentions and habits. Information contrary to what one usually does, one's habits and intentions (previously formed) will not be accepted easily. Sometimes not even a demonstration of the merits of accepting the information will change well-established habits.

Figure 8.1
The flow of
information

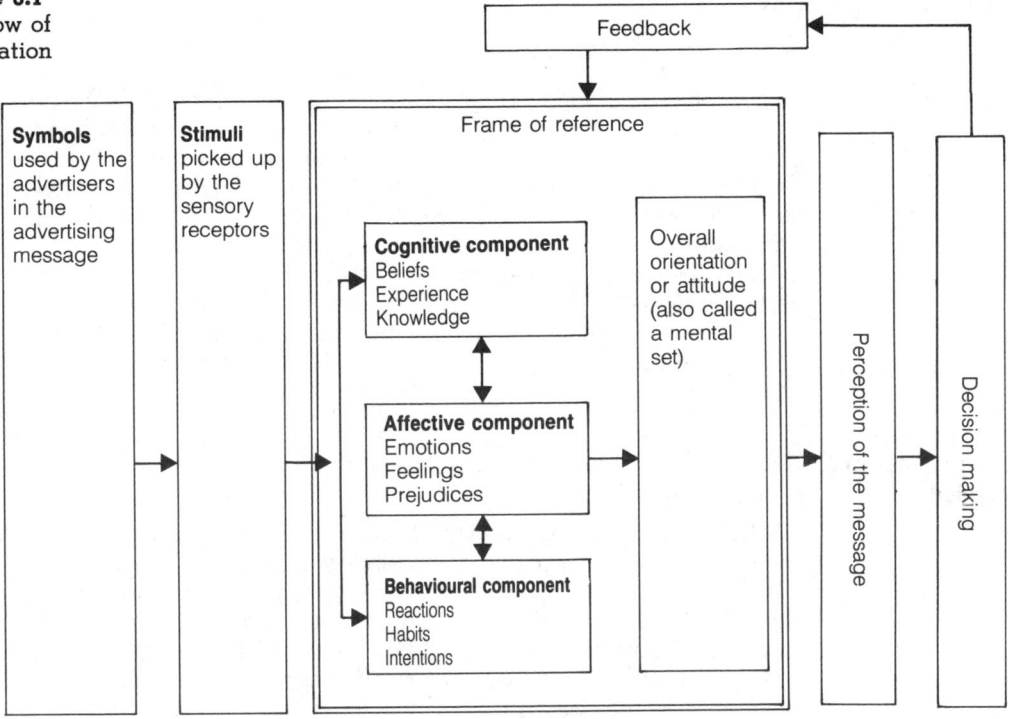

When one says that a certain message has been perceived, this means that the stimuli have passed through all three components of the individual's frame of reference in such a way that the person is ultimately able to come to a decision. It does not mean, however, that that person has perceived the message in the correct, approved or desired way, or that the decision will be positive. Feedback from decision making, whatever it entails, is incorporated into the structure of the frame of reference. A decision, for example, that a specific product is of poor quality and not worth the price will, therefore, become part of the frame of reference and continues to influence all further information regarding the product.

As can be seen in figure 8.1, the three components influence each other. A bad experience with a product (cognitive) will make one feel frustrated (affective), and result in the intention to warn one's friends against it (behavioural). The intention then becomes part of the cognitive component as well as the affective component. When it is seen in this way it is surprising indeed that any information ever succeeds in passing the filter unaltered. Two individuals may receive the same message under the same conditions, but each may assign a different meaning to it because a person's frame of reference is unique to a particular person.

It was stated in the introduction that mere seeing, hearing or feeling cannot rightly be called perception, although the word is often misused in this way. Some texts distinguish between *perception* (seeing) and *apperception* (seeing in the mind's eye), but otherwise the word perception is used interchangeably to denote both concepts. The meaning of perception as it is used in this contribution is discussed in the next section.

☐ Perception

Perception defined

Perception occurs when the sensory receptors receive stimuli via the brain, code and categorise them *and assign certain meanings* to them, depending on the individual's frame of reference. There are at least ten sensory receptors, but usually only five of these are appealed to by marketing messages. These senses are *sight, hearing, taste, touch* and *smell*. In print and audio-visual advertising sight and sound stimuli are used, while potential consumers are also allowed to touch, taste or smell mechandise in retail stores. Advertisers sometimes suggest the experience of other sensory stimuli such as warmth, cold and kinesthesis (movement) in an attempt to make the message more realistic and to facilitate corrrect decoding. All symbols must contribute something to the consumer's understanding of the meaning of the message.

The perceptual process

There are four distinct activities involved in the perceptual process, namely exposure, attention, interpretation and recall.

Initially, perception begins with *exposure* to stimuli and occurs when the stimuli come within the range of one or the other of one's senses. Obviously, if a consumer is not exposed to a message nothing further can happen. Personal selling has an advantage over advertising in that the sales representative can make sure that the potential consumer is exposed to the sales message – the disadvantage being the limited reach of a single sales representative whilst many potential consumers may be exposed simultaneously to a single advertisement in the mass media (that is to say those potential consumers who wish to notice the advertisement!). Usually the individual is exposed to a great deal more stimuli than he is able to process.

When the consumer is exposed to a certain message he must make a special effort to pay *attention* to the details of the message. Attention is a function of a person's subjective needs and interests, as well as of the characteristics of the stimulus. Bright colours, loud noises and movement may contribute towards capturing attention.

Exposure and attention do not invariably lead to *interpretation*. Interpretation is uniquely individual, since it is based on a person's understanding of the meaning of the message. When interpretation occurs the stimuli are placed in categories of meaning based on the individual's previously gained knowledge and experience. If there is no background knowledge the message can easily be misinterpreted. The advertiser can aid consumers in the task of correctly categorising stimuli by providing them with appropriate cues. 'Like Grandmother used to make' is a headline which attempts to position the message in a familiar environment of which the consumer is supposed to have adequate background knowledge. Consumers may find it difficult to interpret information about a uniquely new product of which they have had no previous experience. This is the reason why it took so long for microwave ovens to be totally accepted.

Even if the information is received, attended to and correctly interpreted, this will serve no purpose if the person is unable to *recall* it when he is required to act. The advertising message has failed if the consumer cannot remember the name of the product and the product benefits at the point of purchase. In-store promotions are used to aid failing memories and to facilitate recall.

Characteristics of perception

The characteristics of consumer perception are generalisations which have important implications for the design of advertisements which will have a good chance of being decoded correctly. They are dealt with below:

Consumer perception is limited by thresholds

All the senses have some limit on their responsiveness to marketing messages. There are three thresholds, namely the *lower threshold*, beyond which a stimulus cannot be received; the *upper threshold*, beyond which increased stimulation produces no increase in response; and a *difference threshold*, which is the smallest increment of stimulation that can be perceived by the consumer. The stimuli contained in the advertising message must exceed the lower threshold in order to expose the consumer to the full impact of the message. Stimuli should also exceed the difference threshold (the so-called jnd – just noticeable difference threshold) in order to make consumers aware of fine differences between stimuli which are almost identical. The existence of the jnd threshold seriously influences the ability of consumers to distinguish between similar advertising themes. The me-too types of advertisements, where marketers tend to copy each other's theme and/or messages, may result in confusing the consumer because the jnd threshold is not exceeded.

Consumer perception depends on the source of the marketing stimulus

Messages from a respected or credible source are more readily perceived than information transmitted by other, less respected sources. This is the reason why word-of-mouth advertising is so effective. Testimonial advertising, where a well-known personality or an expert recommends a certain course of action, is often persuasive due to the credibility of the source of the message.

Consumer perception depends on symbols

Symbols are cues which aid perception. Many different symbols are used in advertising illustrations – a baby may symbolise mother love, a white dress innocence, long blonde hair sex appeal, trees and green grass freshness, a combination of bright colours (flowers or balloons) youth or happiness, etc. This means that pictorial cues in advertising illustrations must be considered carefully. Cues which create the required mood or emotion should be used to reinforce the verbal message. Pictures are not the only form of cues. Words, sounds and unusual noises can be used as cues to trigger undesirable reactions. Using the word 'strong' in connection with a detergent may trigger the idea that it may harm delicate fabrics.

Consumer perception is of short duration

Most of the things a consumer perceives are temporal. Thus information has difficulty in holding the consumer's attention for long periods. The temporal nature of perception is the reason why repetition of the message and reminder advertising are so important. Even a popular product can fail if advertising is discontinued.

Consumer perception is holistic

This means that perception tends to be summational. Consumers take many different sensations almost simultaneously and sum these sensations into a complete and unified whole. Every bit of information passes through the filter and is combined in an overall orientation to whatever he is engaged in decoding.

Do you know the meaning of these symbols?

From the description of the characteristics of perception above it is clear that influencing consumer perception is no easy task. To complicate matters even further, the individual can purposely or subconsciously erect defence barriers every step of the way, by not *exposing* himself to information, by not paying *attention* to it, by *interpreting* the meaning of the information wrongly or by 'conveniently' *forgetting* the message when action is required. It is not only advertisers who are subjected to this treatment. Teachers, preachers, parents and politicians are also confronted with these barriers when they want to persuade their target audience to a particular point of view. This defensive action against information is called *perceptual defence*.

☐ Perceptual defence

Two reasons can be advanced for the fact that people apparently feel a need to defend themselves against information. These reasons are:

☐ perceived risk
☐ perceptual overload.

Perceived risk   One answer to the question why consumers find it necessary to protect themselves against unwelcome or undesirable stimuli can be found in the perceived risk of consumer decision making. Consumers must constantly make decisions regarding which product and services will best satisfy their needs. Because the consequences of such decisions are often uncertain, the consumer faces some degree of risk when making purchasing decisions. It should be stressed that the consumer is influenced only by the risk he perceives, regardless of whether or not such risk actually exists. If no risk is perceived there will be no reaction, even in very dangerous situations. Perceived risk is the basis of fear appeals, where the consumer's attention is drawn to the grave consequences of not changing his behaviour or attitude or not reacting in the prescribed way.

There are several kinds of risk associated with purchasing decisions. Some people are more vulnerable to some kinds of risks than others, and some are vulnerable to all kinds and experience great difficulty making up their minds. The uncertainties associated with different kinds of risks are shown in table 8.1.

Table 8.1
Risks and
uncertainties

Risk	Uncertainty
Functional	Will it work? Will it last?
Physical	Is is safe to use?
Financial	Am I wasting money?
Social	Will my family and friends approve my choice? Will they admire me?
Psychological	Will it make me feel (look) good? Will it impress others?

All these risks are involved to a greater or lesser extent with the consumer's ego or self-esteem. High risk perceivers are sensitive to risk, lack self-confidence and have egos which can be easily bruised by making a 'wrong decision such as wasting a lot of money on a product which in any case may not work properly and may also make them look ridiculous. Consumers constantly look for information which may reflect negatively on their self-esteem. The defence barriers are therefore attempts at ego protection.

Perceptual overload

Another reason why consumers find it necessary to erect defence barriers is that they have limited capacities to process all the information directed at them. Perceptual overload occurs because the mind of the individual fails to comprehend all the sensations, often of conflicting nature, which bombard his senses at any given moment. Marketing stimuli include an enormous number of variables, all of which compete for the consumer's attention. Different colours, sizes and shapes and many conflicting messages are but a few examples of the variables. Even one advertisement consisting of a headline, an illustration and copy material contains literally hundreds of separate stimuli. So much information confuses the individual and renders decision making virtually impossible.

Perceptual defence occurs throughout the perception process, that is during exposure, attention, interpretation and recall. Man's ability to be selective when dealing with information helps him to adjust and to make consumer decisions without undue difficulty. It is understandable that these decisions will not always be completely logical or rational.

Perceptual defence barriers

The four defence mechanisms or barriers are:
☐ selective exposure
☐ selective attention
☐ selective interpretation
☐ selective recall.

Each one of these mechanisms and its implications for advertising decisions will be considered individually.

Selective exposure

The readership and listenership figures for print media, radio and television give some indication of the degree of exposure which an advertisement in these media may enjoy. However, exposure depends not only on what the consumer selects to read (to listen to or to watch), but also on the tendency that people have to deliberately seek out messages which are pleasant and to actively avoid painful or threatening ones. When my son was small he had a favourite storybook and insisted on 'reading' the story every day. The story was about naughty little Timmy playing in the garden snipping off flowerheads with garden shears. Timmy's parents told him repeatedly not to play with the shears lest he cut his hand. A little bird hopping along the fence also uttered warnings. My son knew the story by heart and 'read' the text while looking at the pictures. The second to last picture showed Timmy crying, his cut finger dripping with blood, but just before he came to that page and that picture my son would close the book firmly, absolutely refusing to turn the page and saying 'Naan', his word for 'finished'. This story illustrates perfectly what is meant by selective exposure.

Exposure to a message means only that it has been seen. There is no guarantee that the individual will choose to pay attention to it.

Selective attention

A person will pay attention only to messages which fit in with his frame of reference. Consumers have a heightened awareness of stimuli which meet their needs and a depressed awareness of stimuli irrelevant to their needs. Thus they are likely to pay attention to advertisements for products which may provide need-satisfaction. A consumer with unfulfilled needs or who has a particular problem will scan the environment for relevant information and pay attention to this information to the exclusion of other non-applicable material. Bright colours, unusually loud noises, music, or other attention-getting devices are used to capture attention amidst the 'noise' of many other competing messages. In order to understand an advertising message the consumer must pay attention to the total message, but even if he does pay attention to all the details in a message this does not mean that he will interpret it as intended by the marketer.

Selective interpretation

The information which has succeeded in passing the barriers erected against exposure and attention 'flows' through the filter which enables the consumer to discard some bits of information, to change the meaning of others, or to place undue emphasis on certain sections. The result may be quite different from what the communicator originally intended. Faulty decoding due to selective interpretation may be the result of misindexing the message or distorting its meaning.

Misindexing refers to the way people tend to classify or categorise the meaning of the message and can often be ascribed to poor message construction. Misindexing occurs:

☐ when the advertisement is so novel or amusing that the situation itself becomes the message while the most important part, namely the brand of the product and the promised benefits, are overlooked

☐ when the attention-getting device is inappropriate and the device itself becomes the message, with the result that the advertisement is likely to steer thoughts away from the real meaning of the message

☐ when me-tooism confuses the consumer.

Distortion refers to the way the meaning of a message is changed by the consumer, purposely or more often subconsciously. Stimuli in conflict with a person's previously held beliefs, likes, dislikes and habits create an imbalance in the cognitive structure of the consumer, making him feel uncomfortable. In order to rectify this imbalance the consumer must either bring about changes in his cognitive structure or change the meaning of the message. The latter is a much easier course of action. The typical reactions of a consumer suffering from this kind of imbalance are to rationalise (by giving socially acceptable reasons for not accepting the message), to deny the importance of the message, or to look for loopholes to escape the implications of the message. A social drinker distorts the message in the 'Drink or Drive' advertisement by saying: 'I need to drink to be able to relax' (rationalisation), 'I won't get drunk on a few beers' (denial) and 'The food that I have eaten will reduce the alcohol level in my blood' (loophole).

The meaning of the message can be distorted by *levelling*, which means that an important bit of information in the message is overlooked (when it is the name of the product being advertised that is overlooked the consumer may end up buying the competing product!). The meaning of the message can also be distorted by *sharpening*, where the consumer reads additional information into a message – information which does not actually appear in the message. Reminder advertising relies on the consumer's ability to sharpen the message and to add information gained from previous advertising campaigns.

If the nature of the message does not fit into the person's frame of reference it may be *discarded* entirely. People may reject messages about which they have no background knowledge, which they are prejudiced against, or which are contrary to established habits.

Selective recall

Even if the message is interpreted correctly and deemed acceptable, the consumer may be unable to recall it when he is required to act, for example in the store. Selective recall may sometimes work to the advantage of the advertiser, for example the *positive sleeper effect* which causes the consumer who has not been convinced by the advertisement to react in the desired way (by purchasing the product) anyway. The only possible reason for the positive sleeper effect is that recall was not complete; and consumer forgot the nature or theme of the message and remembered only the recommendation that the product should be bought. The positive sleeper effect can also be advanced as a reason why negative publicity sometimes causes an increase instead of a decrease in the demand for the product. The *boomerang effect* in recall causes the consumer to reverse his 'at-home' conviction and intention to purchase the product and to take the directly opposite course of action by purchasing a competing product. One reason which can be advanced for the boomerang effect is that the consumer could not recall the differential product benefits mentioned in the original advertisement. This means that the message has not crossed the jnd threshold.

Total recall may also be difficult due to the noise of many other competing stimuli. Therefore the advertising message should be simple and straightforward, distinctly different from that of competitors in order to avoid further confusion. The KISS (Keep It Simple Stupid!) principle should be the rule for designing advertising messages in a competitive market. Effective point-of-purchase reminder advertising can assist recall and reinforce tentative acceptance of advertising messages.

It is very difficult to transmit a marketing message in an advertisement in such a way that it is noticed, understood and remembered (therefore correctly decoded) as intended by the advertiser. The merits of different message content strategies will be discussed in the next section. This discussion addresses the problem of how to create messages which will make decoding easy. As has been repeatedly emphasised, correct decoding of the advertising message is a prerequisite for persuasion and positive (purchasing) action.

☐ Message content strategies

Card stacking   Card stacking is a message content strategy aiming at giving as much information as possible in a single advertising message. All the attributes possessed by a brand are mentioned to allow consumers to select those attributes they deem to be important for brand evaluation. The cost and temporary nature of television advertising often precludes this strategy. Gilson & Berkman (1980), however, quote an example of a television commercial which has been made 'stupefyingly busy' with flashing data, continued comment and changing scenes. This was done deliberately to keep the audience interested through many repetitions – every time they see it a further bit of information is added until at last they know all the details of the message.

In print advertising card stacking can be used in the copy. A mix of facts, figures, technical details, rational and emotional appeals, benefits and uses are brought to the attention of the consumer, who can take his time to process every bit of information in the message. On one hand this shotgun approach may provide enough information to satisfy divergent consumer needs, but on the other it may result in confusion and the message being discredited by its audience.

Card stacking may retard message wear-out because consumers are occupied with information processing. This effect may be enhanced by variety in the theme or a slow unfolding of brand attributes throughout the campaign.

The problem with card stacking is that although it may be attention-grabbing at first, the consumer is inclined to level it by focusing on only a few attributes and can therefore distort the meaning of the message. The consumer may also be so confused by the mass of information that he is unable to recall crucial aspects – such as the name of the product!

Fear appeals   A threatening advertisement arouses a fear response. Physical or social threats are often used in persuasion because it is an accepted fact that unpleasant things may sometimes be learnt as readily as pleasant things. It has been found, however, that increasing the threat reduces persuasion. Initially a threat may attract attention, but as the threatening content increases consumers distort the message, looking for loopholes or means of denial. A moderate amount of fear is maximally persuasive, as can be seen in figure 8.2.

Figure 8.2 Fear appeals and the degree of persuasion

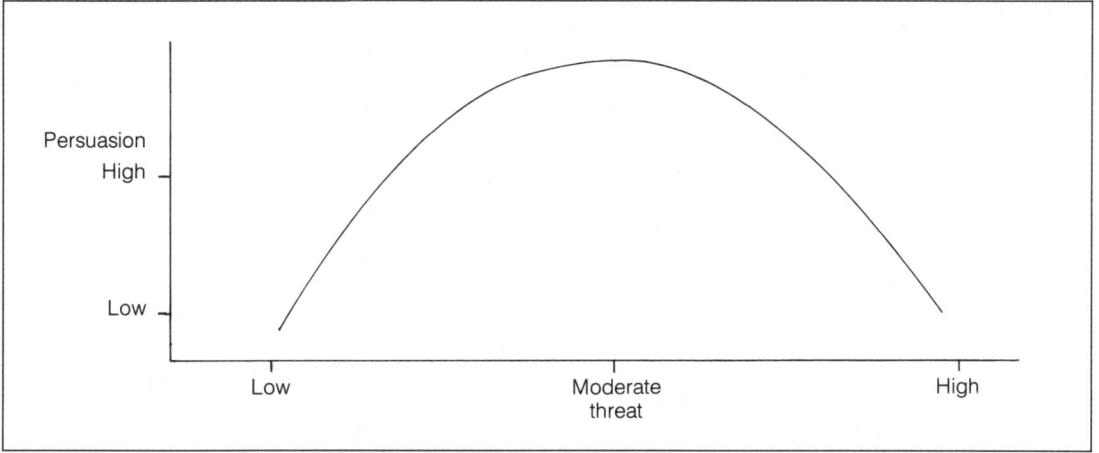

Figure 8.2 shows an inverted U relationship between the degree of threat contained in the message and the level of persuasion effected. A moderate threat appears to have the best effect.

A fear-producing message results in an emotional response in the consumer, who must adapt in order to deal with the threat. The advertiser, however, is not really interested in emotional reactions. His purpose is to obtain action in terms of his product. This means that the adaptive action must be spelled out in the advertisement. The message must provide a means of coping with the danger and dire consequences which it is suggested will be the result of non-compliance. If this crucial aspect is neglected the consumer may devise unacceptable means of coping with the danger, for example by ignoring or distorting the threatening message which he will be tempted to do in any case.

The search for loopholes or a means of denial can be overcome by using a highly credible source to deliver the message. In testimonial advertising a well-known personality can recommend methods of dealing with the implied threat. If a low-credibility source is used the audience is given the opportunity to think of counter-arguments and other means of dealing with the threatening appeal. The problem, of course, is to find a spokesperson who will be regarded as highly credible by the whole audience. Today people tend to be hypercritical. Even the opinions of people of exceptionally high standing (for example Nobel Prize Winners) are bound to be discredited by some. If the spokesperson is discredited the entire message will be rejected.

Where the required behaviour is negative in nature, for example to stop smoking (or else be vulnerable to cancer), to drink less (or else become an alcoholic), to eat less (or else become obese), persuasion becomes even more difficult. It seems to be easier to persuade people if positive action is advised, for example to use W-brand toothpaste (or else face the dentist), to drink X-brand analgesic (or face the consequences of failing to do your job properly due to a headache), to take Y-brand food supplement (or face the danger of becoming fat), to use Z-brand wrinkle cream (or face the unpleasant consequences of ageing prematurely). Virtually all medicine and drug advertisements contain threatening appeals of one kind or another.

The threat of social disapproval is commonly used in consumer advertising. These appeals can be effective because they focus the consumer's attention on the expectations of others. Most people actively look for ways of obtaining the acceptance and approval of others. Overtly positive appeals can also imply a vague social threat, for example if the mother-in-law is highly complimentary about the cleanliness of the bathroom the implication of her disapproval is clear. The threat of disapproval can, of course, be overcome by using a certain germ-killing household detergent. In the same vein, if the girl with fresh breath is courted and kissed the implication is that girls who do not use a mouthwash will be ignored by boys. Many people lack self-confidence and are therefore especially vulnerable to threats involving social ostracism. This means that what the advertiser regards as a low degree fear appeal may seem excessively threatening to a timid consumer, who will then fail to decode the message correctly.

Humorous messages

Humorous messages are designed to be amusing and entertaining, to provoke smiles or laughter. Examples of humour are word-play, jokes, satire, irony or under- or over-emphasis of a specific situation. The perception of humour differs from person to person – like beauty it 'is in the eye of the beholder'. What one person may find funny another may regard as childish nonsense, what makes one person smile may irritate or confuse another. Nothing makes a poorer impression than an advertisement that tries to be funny, but fails. Humorous appeals are very popular because they are considered to be attention-grabbing. Humour can also create goodwill for the sponsor due to its entertainment value. However, the humorous appeal may be so distracting that the real message is misindexed – then the amusing situation or joke itself and not the product benefits or the recommendation that the product must be bought becomes the message.

Some advertisers condone joking about the product or its inherent qualities, but it can be highly 'dangerous' to poke fun at one's brand. Persuading the target market to accept the benefits of a branded product in a competitive market is a serious business and therefore it would be a mistake to make the product offering seem silly or inconsequential. Poking fun at the consumer, for example by making him look stupid, is even more dangerous. It may lead to denial and message rejection.

There is evidence that humorous appeals are generally no more persuasive than straightforward messages. Therefore, it may, if the attendant dangers of misindexing, distortion and rejection are taken into account, not be worthwhile to waste time developing and executing a humorous theme.

Message repetition

Repetition of a persuasive message increases the likelihood of the consumer remembering the message. Increased repetition is closely linked to complete message recall. A *concentrated schedule*, where many repetitions of the same advertisement are concentrated in a brief timespan during the schedule, has proved to be effective during the schedule, but if the advertisement is discontinued the message is soon forgotten. A better strategy may be *flighting*, where a concentrated schedule is repeated at more or less regular intervals. In the period inbetween, reminder advertising can be used to continually focus attention on the brand name and product benefits. A well thought-out theme is an advantage in a situation where advertisements must be repeated so often that there is a possibility of boring the consumer into not paying attention. A slogan or jingle designed to emphasise the brand and main benefit and which will remind consumers of the product and the nature of a foregoing concentrated schedule is invaluable in this regard.

However, boring or irritating the consumer may not be such a bad idea. 'It matters not whether they think well of you or ill of you so long as they remember your name.'

Irritating appeals

There is evidence that a highly irritating message can often be effective, causing sales to increase. The portrayal of unattractive people with bad manners and unpleasant habits in advertisements does not deter consumers from buying the product. The only reasons which can be advanced for this phenomenon are the attention value of anything that irritates a person and the fact of selective recall – the irritating details fade, leaving only the name of the product and its benefits in the mind of the consumer. Few advertisers, however, are brave enough to use a really irritating theme in case it backfires, creating ill-will and casting a negative reflection on the company and product image.

Labelling

Labelling involves name giving. People who are labelled tend to attempt to live up to expectations by complying with and following the approval or recommended behaviour pattern. This content strategy is apparently based on the dictum 'Give a dog a bad name'. Reference to the audience in flattering terms such as 'responsible citizens', 'discerning buyers', 'dog lovers', 'valued contributors', 'neat housewives' and 'high-powered executives' by a credible communicator have persuasive impact.

Rational appeals

Rational appeals are those which emphasise logical or socially acceptable reasons for buying the product, for example quality, durability, economy, functionality, and exclude emotional elements. A completely rational advertisement consists mainly of copy material, and the illustration – if there is one – shows the product in use. Dissonant consumers tend to use the rational appeals mentioned to rationalise their purchasing decisions, thereby alleviating the unpleasant feeling caused by cognitive dissonance (the car is bought because of its low fuel consumption and not because it is a status symbol). Consumers like to create the impression that they are rational buyers, always getting the best deal.

Courtesy: RH Griffin

It makes them feel uncomfortable if they know in their heart of hearts that they have reacted in an emotional manner.

Emotional appeals

Emotional appeals are directed at the social and ego motives such as friendship, love, security, prestige, status and self-esteem. Advertising illustrations are ideal vehicles for these appeals which imply satisfaction of social and ego motives. Most illustrations in which models (families, social groups, male and female couples) are portrayed in a variety of activities make emotional appeals of one kind or another.

A mix of rational and emotional appeals has been found to have greater persuasive impact than either one or the other alone. Such advertisements usually comprise rational appeals in the copy and implied emotional appeals in the illustrations.

Today there is a tendency toward a greater degree of rationality, with less emphasis on promises of emotional need-satisfaction. Unrealistic promises which cannot be kept (for example that a certain perfume will make a girl irresistible to men) have fallen into disfavour.

□ Summary

The different kinds of message content strategies – humorous messages, continuous repetition and a mix of rational and emotional appeals – all have one thing in common: they are all designed with an eye on facilitating correct decoding of the message. The consumer must perceive the advertising message as intended by the marketer – if not, the consumer will not fully understand the meaning thereof. It is unlikely that such a message will persuade the consumer to buy the product being advertised.

The consumer's acquisition of information proves to be problematical. Every bit of information to which the consumer is willling to expose himself is evaluated against the cognitive, affective and behavioural components of the individual's frame of reference. Information which does not fit into this frame is rejected, while aspects of the message which are contrary to what the person knows, believes or likes can be misunderstood or distorted either deliberately or subconsciously. The consumer erects barriers against perception and eventual persuasion. These barriers are selective exposure, selective attention, selective interpretation and selective recall. It is no easy task to overcome all of these barriers in a single advertisement. Nevertheless, it is the task of the advertiser to design a message which will stand a good chance of crossing the barriers and, therefore, of being decoded correctly. The general principles to be adhered to have been sketched and the pitfalls to be avoided have been highlighted. The principles do not succeed, however, in providing a simple solution to the problem, because there is no easy solution.

□ References

Assael, H. 1984. *Consumer Behaviour and Marketing Action*. Boston, Massachusetts: Keny Publishing Co.

Cohen, D. 1981. *Consumer behaviour*. New York: Random House.

Gilson, C & Berkman, HW. 1980. *Advertising Concepts and Strategies*. New York: Random House.

Hawkins, DJ, Best, RJ & Coney, KA. 1983. *Consumer Behaviour Implications for Marketing Strategy*. Plano, Texas: Business Publications.

Shiffman, LG & Kanik, LL. 1978. *Consumer Behaviour*. Englewood Cliffs, New Jersey: Prentice-Hall.

Williams, TG. 1982. *Consumer Behaviour Fundamentals and Strategies*. St Paul: West Publishing Co.

The pre-testing of advertisements
Gordon Hooper

Introduction	310
What is copy research?	310
The PACT agencies	311
The PACT perspective	311
The PACT principles	312
Summary	318
References	319

☐ Introduction

Copy research is a field characterised by debate, controversy and dissatisfaction amongst users and practitioners. It is a field which embraces a broad diversity of schools of thought and has a history spanning a hundred years.

Copy research is one of the major arms of the broader field of advertising research. Copy research itself is divisible into several sub-elements, of which pre-testing is one. This contribution has the objective of leaving the reader equipped with a sound understanding of the broad nature of pre-testing and a set of principles to ensure successful, conflict-free pre-testing projects.

☐ What is copy research?

Dubois (in Ferber 1974:3) presents a useful classification scheme for copy research. Copy research can be classified along two major dimensions. In one dimension methods can be classified according to the stages of advertising development, as follows:

☐ Testing basic themes, ideas or appeals
☐ Testing elements of advertisements such as headlines, pictures, jingles, story sequences
☐ Pre-testing whole adverts in a rough or finished form
☐ Pre-testing the effect of repetition to simulate a campaign
☐ Post-testing single advertisements in their normal media
☐ Post-testing whole campaigns in their normal media.

At each of these six stages of testing there is another dimension which reflects what we are trying to find out or measure. This dimension includes the following classification categories:

☐ Assessing the advertisement for impact, attention value or interest
☐ Testing advertisements to assess the message communication
☐ Testing to measure the perceptual impact ability of the advertisement on consumer attitudes
☐ Testing to estabish the effect on consumer purchase behaviour
☐ Testing to establish what executional variables are causing the change in attitude or behaviour
☐ Testing to establish the likely effect the advertisement will have on the (re-)positioning of the product.

This classification system yields a 6 × 6 matrix of 36 cells, in many of which we can choose among a large number of testing methods. This contribution is concerned with the third classification stage: pre-testing whole advertisements, in rough or finished form.

☐ The PACT agencies

Early in 1980 21 of the world's leading advertising agencies formed a committee to seek resolution to the confusion and concerns about copy research. They named the committee PACT, for Positioning Advertising Copy Testing. Two years later the PACT committee issued its 'consensus credo' consisting of a perspective and nine principles. This contribution outlines and discusses the perspectives and principles of the PACT credo.

The PACT agencies recognise the legitimate needs of advertisers for conducting copy research and the concerns of creative people about it. Also, they recognise the divergent views and perspectives embracing copy research and the profusion of methodologies which have resulted. The aims of PACT and its outlook are well summarised by this extract from the prologue to the credo (1982:13):

We believe we have an obligation − based on our unique position − to speak out about issues of vital concern to us all and to minimise meaningless and unnecessary conflict. PACT is an expression of our consensus. Through PACT, we bring our collective experience and the convergence of our professional opinion to share with:
  − client and agency management
  − agency creative people
  − our own research colleagues

PACT represents a platform for "positioning advertising copy testing". It is not intended as a primer on how to test copy − though it has clear implications for test methodology.

☐ The PACT perspective

The PACT perspective represents the shared view of the PACT agencies on the role of copy research. It includes the following five areas:

☐ The role of copy testing begins only after the groundwork has been laid by fundamental strategic research. Advertising executions should not begin until agreement has been reached about the advertising strategy. Unless agreement has been reached on what the advertising is supposed to do (its objectives), agreement can never be reached about what to test or how to test it.

☐ Advertising is an execution of an underlying strategy and as such is an expression of that strategy. Copy testing cannot separate out the effects of strategy versus execution. It can only evaluate their combined effects. If two or more executions are tested to select the best option, it is important to judge the executions from the same strategic platform.

☐ Since both advertiser and agency are concerned with the market-place effectiveness of an advertisement and should be concerned with understanding the advertising process, both share a common goal of running effective advertising and learning how effective advertising works. It is surprisingly common to find an advertiser pre-testing an advertisement 'behind the agency's back'. This malignment of copy testing goals is the fuel of copy research conflict.

☐ Truly rigorous research costs large sums of money and it is often not necessary to undertake painstaking studies. Often the minimum of research is all that is required to help the subjective decision-making process. However, in cases where these decisions involve high risk, cost control compromises should be kept to a minimum.

☐ The users of copy research must be judicious in their interpretation of the results. It is usually easy to present several rather different interpretations of a set of results. All copy research methods have limitations, and it is a professional prerequisite that the research limitations are fully communicated and understood by all parties.

☐ The PACT principles

The PACT agencies drew up a set of nine fundamental principles underlying a good copy testing system. The rest of this contribution takes each of these principles in turn, discusses its relevance and implications, and looks at ways of incorporating it in copy testing practice and methodology design.

Principle I   *A good copy testing system provides measurements which are relevant to the objectives of the advertising.*

Advertising, like the other elements of the marketing mix, contributes towards the attainment of marketing objectives. In order to achieve marketing objectives, advertisements or campaigns must achieve certain advertising objectives.

Advertising objectives come in many varied forms, and their nature depends on the advertising philosophy adopted and the particular strategy decided upon. For example, advertising objectives may set out to increase brand or brand benefit awareness, or alter negative perceptions, or induce product trial, and so forth. Unless advertising objectives and strategy are agreed upon, there is nothing to pre-test. A relevant pre-test system cannot be designed unless agreement is reached as to what the advertisement is supposed to do, and to whom.

Principle II   *A good copy testing system is one which requires agreement about how the results will be used in advance of each specific test.*

This is a key principle if conflict is to be avoided. Sound management practice has always embodied the concept of nurturing commitment to and a sense of ownership of a project amongst the participating parties. The PACT agencies recommend that the involved parties develop an agreed set of action standards before the research is conducted. These action standards might include specifying the percentage attention level, minimum percentage negative response, or percentage increase in brand association with certain key attributes.

The practice of specifying how the results will be used ensures a mutual understanding of the goals of the research. It also minimises the conflict over interpretation once the test results are in. But, most important of all, prior discussions of this nature are key to the proper positioning and design of the pre-test system.

Principle III

A good copy testing system provides multiple measurements – because single measurements are generally inadequate to assess the performance of an advertisement.

It is commonly believed that the ultimate measurement by which advertising should be judged is its contribution to sales (except in the case of corporate image advertising). It is also accepted amongst advertising researchers that there is no universally accepted measurement which acts as a surrogate for sales. When an advertisement is pre-tested its likely sales effect is what is under scrutiny, and the interested parties use non-sales related measurements to aid their subjective judgement as to the possible sales effect of the advertisement.

Modern thinking recognises that there cannot be a single best measure of advertising effectiveness and proposes that careful interpretation of multiple measures gives the best aid to sales effect judgement.

Principle IV

A good copy testing system is based on a model of human response to communications – the reception of a stimulus, the comprehension and the response to the stimulus.

Very much related to the principle of multiple measurements, this principle views advertising as performing on several levels. It must be received, it must be understood, and it must make an impression. The PACT agencies recommend that measurements be taken on reception, comprehension and response. In addition, they recommend measurements for executional diagnostics. They recognise that a host of different methodologies exist for gathering these measurements. The researcher needs to have a good command of all the available techniques to be able to select procedures best suited to the particular advertisement under evaluation.

The remainder of this section on Principle IV is devoted to discussion of the major approaches available for gathering measurements in each of the four categories.

Measuring reception

Reception is concerned with questions like 'Did the advertising get through?', 'Did it attract consumer attention?', and 'Was it remembered?'.

Methods of measuring reception fall into two major categories – direct reception measures and indirect reception measures. Possibly the most popular direct approach is that of '*recall*'. The underlying philosophy is that if an advertisement cannot be remembered, it has not been received. Many research vendors offer a syndicated day-after-recall service. The day after a TV advertisement is flighted a random sample is drawn and telephonically interviewed to establish the percentage recall score for the advertisement. This score is compared with 'norms' which are developed by product category. There are two main criticisms of day-after-recall approaches. In the first place, several studies (Ross 1982:14; MacLachlan 1983:9) have shown that recall scores are not related to persuasion or buyer behaviour measurements. Second, norms are averages made up of good and bad advertisements and comparing recall measurements to norms can only lead to 'average' advertising!

Another favourite way of measuring recall is the '*clutter*' approach. Print advertisements under test are mixed with other advertisements and editorial material in a folder. Respondents are given a certain time to browse through the folder and are then asked to recall the advertisements they saw. A similar approach involving television programme content and advertisements is applicable to TV copy. The relative recall scores of all the advertisements in the clutter environment indicate the relative reception potential of each advertisement. The clutter approach has the same problems of relevancy and comparison to norms as the day-after-recall method. It has one other problem as well. All the 'competitive' advertisements in the clutter should, like the new test advertisement, be unseen by the respondents to guard against the biasing effects of previous exposure. This is usually very difficult to achieve.

Mechanical methods for measuring reception directly are in use in America, and include techniques like the eye camera method, the HRB Singer test, tachistoscopy, galvanic skin response and the binocular rivalry method. These techniques all try to get around the problem of asking respondents to articulate their reaction to the advertisement.

Indirect methods of measuring or judging consumer reception to an advertisement involve interpreting responses to open-ended questions like 'What thoughts or feelings did you have while watching this ad?' or evaluating the ratings given to the advertisement on a set of attributes like 'shows a situation I can identify with', 'was meaningful to me', 'is the kind of advertising I like', and so forth. Indirect methods like these require more interpretation than direct methods, which tend to be of a more go/no-go nature.

Measuring comprehension

Comprehension is concerned with questions like 'Was the message understood, identified with the brand, believable, and was there anything confusing or unclear?', the underlying philosophy being that it is all very well to gain attention, but the message must be understood and believed before attitudes and behaviour can be affected.

Comprehension measures are relatively easy to acquire, and the *standard communication check* must be the most popular pre-test method aside from focus group discussions. In essence, comprehension methodologies involve asking respondents to play back the main message and ancillary messages. These questions can be asked after a brief exposure to the advertisement, or after a detailed exposure, or both.

To establish believability and clarity, direct or indirect methods can be used. Respondents can be asked directly whether they believe the advertisement and whether they found anything hard to understand. Indirect methods overcome 'eagerness to please the inverviewer' bias and involve analysing the ratings given to the advertisement on attributes like 'believable', 'honest', 'confusing' and 'easy to understand'.

Some advertisements do not communicate a rational message, but are more concerned with communicating an image message. Standard communication check procedures do not work in these cases because respondents cannot articulate the message. Keon (1983:7; 1984:8) proposes a method for evaluating the image communication of advertisements. This method involves showing respondents a portfolio of advertisements with all brand identification removed or hidden. Respondents are asked to say which brand each advertisement is for. A misclassification matrix is developed and mapped using multi-dimensional scaling. The method uses the existing images of the brands in the market-place to establish a relative image communication measure for the test advertisement. This method, called Trinodal Mapping, has enjoyed only limited application due to the problem of evaluating a new, unseen test advertisement amongst exposed advertisements, and due to the fact that the technique precludes the development of a new, unique image.

Measuring response

Measuring response, or persuasion as many writers label it, is the most difficult area to achieve in copy research. The difficulty stems from the usual problems of unproven validity and from the broad nature of possible 'response'. The advertising model or philosophy employed, together with the advertising objectives set, will determine the nature of response sought. The measurements taken will pertain to the defined response sought. Response measurements are concerned with questions like 'Did the consumer accept the proposition?', 'Did the advertisement affect perceptions or attitudes, and if so, which ones and how strongly were they affected?', and 'Did the advertisement induce product trial?'.

The most common method for evaluating response is the simple propensity to purchase question. Respondents are asked to rate their likelihood of purchasing each of the brands in the category before and after seeing the advertisement. Almost any measure of likelihood-to-buy can be used: score out of 10, ranking of the brands, constant sum allocations, and so forth. Any change in propensity to purchase or liking for the test brand is deemed to be as a result of seeing the advertisement, and this change is used as a measure of response or persuasion.

Another major school of thought in the area of measuring response is that of before and after attitude shifts. This form of measuring response is particularly pertinent to the belief models of advertising, which relate behaviour to beliefs and have the objective of affecting behaviour by affecting beliefs.

In essence, a respondent's beliefs about and attitudes towards the brands in the category are measured before and after seeing the test advertisement. Any one of many techniques available for measuring brand image can be used. Any shift in attitude is deemed to be as a result of being exposed to the advertisement. Obviously, an advertisement performs differently in a pre-test environment from in an armchair environment. Or, more accurately put, respondents behave differently towards advertising in a pre-test environment. It is important to realise that attitude shift methods do not reflect the exact change in perception to be expected, but rather which beliefs are likely to be affected by the advertisement and the relative degree of that effect.

Other methods set out to measure actual purchase response. The coupon redemption system exposes respondents to the advertisement in a shopping mall interview and issues them with a 'cent off' coupon. By analysing the coupon redemption behaviour researchers make inferences about the response to the advertising.

Consumer panels, coupled with split-cable television, are being used in America to evaluate response to test advertisements. Half of the panel members are exposed to the test (TV) commercial in a normal viewing environment and their purchase behaviour is compared with that of the other half of the panel members who were not exposed to the advertising.

Developing executional diagnostic information

Knowing the reception, comprehension and response characteristics of a test advertisement is one side of the story. Knowing why the advertisement performs as it does is the other side. Diagnostic information about how the creative elements and execution relate to impact, communication and persuasion are extremely useful for improving or fine tuning the advertisement. Executional diagnostics are the key to understanding how the advertising works. To quote the PACT agencies (1982:13):

> Questioning about consumer reactions to the advertising execution (eg perceived differentiation from other advertising, reactions to music, to key phrases, to presenters or characters, to story elements, etc) can provide insight about the strengths and weaknesses of the advertising, and why it performed as it did.

As elegant as it might sound, obtaining executional diagnostic information is not easy. The simplest, most used and most dangerous method is direct questioning. Respondents are asked to say what elements they like and what elements they dislike about the test advertisement. At face value this method seems reasonable, but the writer's experience has shown that the natural consumer cynicism towards advertising often causes meaningless answers to these direct questions. This problem applies particularly to the dislikes. If one specifically asks for criticism, one gets criticism, even though this criticism may not be relevant.

Indirect methods for getting executional diagnostic information are preferable. The best-known method is that of Mary Jane Schlinger (1978:16). The 'Schlinger Scales', as they are known, consist of a set of 36 statements which could be used to describe the test advertisement. The advertisement is rated on a seven-point scale for each statement and the scores are factor analysed to arrive at a score for the advertisement on each of six underlying dimensions – relevant news, brand reinforcement, stimulation, empathy, familiarity and confusion. The statements remain constant between successive copy tests and a set of data upon which to base comparisons is collected.

Other writers, notably Moldovan (1985:11), Green and Schaffer (1983:4) and Mehrotra, Van Auken, and Lonial (1981:10) have extended the Schlinger approach to correlate the statement ratings, or the resulting orthogonal factors, with measures of persuasion. These approaches establish not only how the advertisement rates on the various executional descriptors, but also which executional elements are associated with the response (persuasion). Stewart and Furst (1985:17) and Hornik (1980:6) propose similar approaches, but using rating scales which include more intrinsic characteristics of the advertisement such as the visual, the style, the use of colour, the quality of photography, information content, setting, tone, and so forth.

As with all the measures described thus far, the question of exactly what to measure should be answered by analysing the objectives, strategy and creative approach to the strategy.

Principle V   *A good copy testing system allows for consideration of whether the advertising stimulus should be exposed more than once.*

It is well known from communications theory that learning from test material is higher after multiple exposure than after one exposure, and that the marginal contribution to learning diminishes with successive exposures. The PACT agencies recommend that there are situations, given the objectives of the advertisement and the test methodology employed, where multiple exposure methods must be considered. This is particularly true for situations of high risk, or for subtle or complex communications, or for questioning about executional diagnostics.

Research into the question of multiple exposure in the pre-test situation is scarce, and methodologies for achieving multiple exposure evaluations are cumbersome, expensive and time-consuming. Donius (1983:2) conducted a study in conjunction with the American Association of Advertising Agencies to establish the effects of multiple exposure on measures of reception and response. He concluded that reception or recall measures improve with multiple exposure, and likewise for benefit perception. He also concluded that measures of overall persuasion were relatively unaffected by multiple exposure. These results indicate that the decision to use single or multiple exposure testing methods is dependent on the decision about what measures are relevant. From Principle I, this in turn relates to the advertising objectives.

Principle VI   *A good copy testing system recognises that the more finished a piece of copy is, the more soundly it can be evaluated and requires, as a minimum, that alternative executions be tested in the same degree of finish.*

Pre-testing advertisements in a rough form has a number of attractions. Diagnostic or evaluative guidance can be obtained before money is spent on production, and more strategies and/or executions can be evaluated. Also, creative people tend to be more flexible and open to changing a commercial which is in rough form.

The question arises as to what extent production values, what is 'added' to the commercial by production, affect the copy test results. Appel and Jackson (1975:1) showed that pre-post constant sum persuasion scores give the same ranking of advertisements, whether in rough (filmed animatic) or finished form. Kanter (1978) conducted a large survey into the question of degree of finish. He tested advertisements at various stages of finish, from simple line drawings with a rough voice-over to live action visuals. He compared the performance over a range of measurements and concluded that the better the state of finish, the more representative of the final commercial the results are. He also concluded that line drawings or simple art renderings are not representative enough to be pre-tested.

Schlinger and Green (1980:15) conducted a large-scale study into the comparative performance of storyboards versus finished commercials on the Schlinger Scales. They found that the production values added to an advertisement are substantial. In particular, advertising becomes more attractive and stimulating and less irritating. Perceived clarity of the communication is increased, as is the ability to communicate mood or image. Schlinger and Green also concluded that production does not directly affect persuasion scores.

Principle VII   *A good copy testing system provides controls to avoid the biasing effects of the exposure context.*

The PACT agencies recognise that different results for the same commercial will emerge, depending on the conttext of the test exposure. Commercials can be tested on-air or off-air, in a clutter of other commercials or programme content, and so forth.

Ideally, advertisements should be tested in the environment in which they will finally be exposed, but this is usually impossible to do. Researchers must be aware of the differences between test and real world environments, and should try to estimate the likely effects on the test results. If two of more executions are to be evaluated, they should all be tested in exactly the same environment to preclude differences resulting from exposure context.

Principle VIII   *A good copy testing system is one that takes into account basic considerations of sample definition.*

Obviously, the sample must be big enough for the test results to be interpreted with a good degree of confidence. But, more importantly, the sample should be representative of the defined target market at which the advertising is aimed.

Isn't it funny how all hi-fit ads are boring . . . until you're in the market for a hi-fi!

Respondents in a copy research experiment must be screened so as to make sure that they are members of the target audience as defined in psychographic terms. Target audience respondents tend to be much more involved in the advertising, find it more believable, and are less cynical about it.

Principle IX   *A good copy testing system is one which can demonstrate reliability and validity.*

If a system is to be reliable, it must produce the same results each time the advertisement is tested. If a system is to be valid, the results should be relevant to and predictive of market-place performance. The PACT agencies recognise that proving reliability and validity is expensive, and in many cases impossible. They urge researchers to be aware of the questions of reliability and validity when constructing a pre-test system. They also urge the industry to conduct research to improve knowledge about the reliability and validity of the commonly used measurements.

Ostlund, Clancy and Sapra (1980:12) researched the degree to which advertisers and agencies consider the reliability, sensitivity and validity of the methodologies they use to conduct copy research. They showed that the majority of American advertisers and agencies (80 to 90%) conduct copy research with no formal standards for reliability, sensitivity or validity.

☐ Summary

Given the diversity of opinion and the conflict which characterises copy research, the PACT agencies present nine principles for a good copy testing system and a perspective on the role of copy research.

The aim of the perspective and principles is not to dictate methodology, but rather to be used as a tool for focusing on the copy test task at hand and putting together the most meaningful test design possible.

The principles and perspectives also have implications for the management of, and key actor relationships within, a copy research project. Adopting the PACT recommendations should lead to fewer 'bad' advertising decisions and less conflict in copy research.

☐ References

Appel, V & Jackson, B. 1975. 'Copy Testing in a Competitive Environment'. *Journal of Marketing*, January.

Donius, JF. 1983. 'Campaign Simulation via Multiple Exposure On-Air Copy Testing'. *Journal of Advertising Research*, 23, (2).

Ferber, R. (Ed). 1974. *Handbook of Marketing Research*. New York. McGraw-Hill.

Green, PE & Schaffer, CM. 1983. 'Ad Copy Testing'. *Journal of Advertising Research*, 23, (5).

Hooper, GA. 1986. 'The Pre-testing of Advertisements', Unpublished Thesis, University of Witwatersrand.

Hornik, JH. 1980. 'Quantitative Analysis of Visual Perception of Printed Advertisements'. *Journal of Advertising Research*, 20, (6).

Keon, JW. 1983. 'Product Positioning: TRINODAL Mapping of Brand Images, Ad Images, and Consumer Preference'. *Journal of Marketing Research*, XX.

Keon, JW. 1984. 'Copy Testing Ads for Imagery Products'. *Journal of Advertising Research*, 23, (6).

MacLachlan, J & Myers, G. 1983. 'Using Response Latency To Identify Commercials That Motivate'. *Journal of Advertising Research*, 23, (5).

Mehrotra, S, Van Auken, S & Lonial, SC. 1981. 'Adjective Profiles in Television Copy Testing'. *Journal of Advertising Research*, 21, (4).

Maldovan, SE. 1985. 'Copy Factors Related to Persuasion Scores'. *Journal of Advertising Research*, 24, (6).

Ostlund, LE, Clancy, KJ & Sapra, R. 1980. 'Inertia in Copy Research'. *Journal of Advertising Research*, 20, (1).

PACT agencies. 1982. 'Positioning Advertising Copy Testing'. Unpublished Credo of 21 US Advertising Agencies, September.

Ross, HL. 1982. 'Recall versus Persuasion: An Answer'. *Journal of Advertising Research*, 22, (1).

Schlinger, MJR. 1978. 'Attitudinal Reactions to Advertisements'. Working Paper, Unpublished.

Schlinger, MJR & Green, L. 1980. 'Art-Work Storyboards versus Finished Commercials'. *Journal of Advertising Research*, 20, (6).

Stewart, DW & Furst, DH. 1985. 'Analysis of the Impact of Executional Factors on Advertising Performance'. *Journal of Advertising Research*, 24, (6).

Measuring advertising effectiveness
Clive K Corder

Introduction	320
Planning advertising research	320
What to measure	321
When to measure	321
Techniques of measurement	322
Conclusion	327

☐ Introduction

The steady increase in advertising budgets has highlighted the need to measure the effectiveness of this expenditure and resulted in the rapid development of research techniques. Unfortunately, it has also led to a great deal of confusion regarding definitions, methodologies and levels of validity.

Arguments over the rationale for testing advertising effectiveness continue. There are few internationally accepted procedures for pre-testing and post-testing, and advertisers may easily be confused by the numerous alternative methods available.

Nevertheless, the effectiveness of advertising can and should be measured and a guide to the use of research in this field follows.

☐ Planning advertising research

A sound programme of advertising research cannot be set up if there is no clear indication as to who the target market is and what the advertising is trying to do. The most valuable elements in advertising effectiveness measurement are the ability to measure against predetermined standards and to study trends over time.

Advertising research presupposes that the objectives of the advertising have been defined and agreed upon by all concerned. These should be set out in writing and might include, for example:

☐ a definition of the target group in terms of demographics and type of user
☐ the levels of product and brand awareness to be achieved

☐ the desired product, user, situation and image aspects to be conveyed
☐ the type of buying predisposition or response required.

☐ What to measure

For many years the development of advertising effectiveness research was inhibited by the argument that the objective of advertising is to increase sales and that the effectiveness of advertising can only be measured in terms of increased sales. However, sales and advertising can rarely be directly related, since advertising is only one aspect of the marketing mix. The rationale behind measuring advertising effectiveness is not to correlate advertising expenditure with sales, but to isolate and define the objectives of advertising and to measure performance against these criteria.

Advertising effectiveness research works on the presupposition that if advertising is going to improve sales, it must be successful in achieving:

☐ Exposure – it must be seen and/or heard by the target audience.
☐ Awareness – awareness of the brand, product or service, must be developed
☐ Understanding – it must be understood
☐ Credibility – it must be convincing
☐ Image – the right image of the product or service must be created
☐ Propensity – the likelihood of buying must be improved and trial must be generated
☐ Reinforcement – the positive relationship with the regular brand must be reinforced.

All of these factors can be measured, not once, but on a regular basis. Targets against which performance can be evaluated can be set. Follow-up diagnostic research can investigate why performance in any particular area is not being achieved.

It is from these basic assumptions that advertising effectiveness research has developed.

☐ When to measure

The field of advertising effectiveness research can be conveniently divided into 'before' and 'after', that is *pre-testing* and *post-testing*. Both phases are important and should not be regarded as alternatives in any comprehensive advertising testing schedule.

Advertising development (pre-tests)

This covers tests conducted at all stages before the actual flighting of an advertisement in any medium, from concept stage to final video or pull. The objective of pre-testing is to see whether and how far an advertisement is likely to achieve its objectives in terms of impact, registration and response.

Pre-testing can be carried out using either qualitative or quantitative research techniques, depending upon the degree of completion of the test material and the type of information sought. In all cases care should be taken to select respondents who match the defined target market for the campaign as closely as possible. In pre-testing, advertisements should be shown in as realistic a setting as possible, with sufficient impact so that it is possible to measure effects.

Post-tests

Post-testing can be divided into two classes:

Initial reaction

This type of research supplies fast feedback on the impact of and reaction to individual advertisements after initial or early exposure.

Extended campaign testing

This is perhaps the most important and most valuable element in advertising effectiveness research. It is the measurement of the cumulative effect of a series of advertisements or a whole campaign in terms of meeting defined targets. It can also provide answers to tactical and strategic questions such as:

- [ ] Is the media right?
- [ ] Should the campaign be changed or re-run?
- [ ] Is the budget adequate?
- [ ] What are my competitors achieving, and how does the effectiveness of my campaign compare with theirs?

☐ Techniques of measurement

In this section a few of the available methods of pre-testing and post-testing advertising will be dealt with in more detail.

Pre-tests: concept development and testing

A key step in the development of a campaign is establishing the basic concept or concepts. Previous research, brainstorming sessions, creative ideas and existing campaigns, both local and overseas, may all suggest a wide range of possibilities. These can be narrowed down by judgement to the few which hold most promise.

Specific concepts can be tested by means of group discussions or quantitative interviews with semi-structured questionnaires. The material for testing can be in the form of verbal descriptions of each alternative concept and need not include visuals, which tend to be rather ambiguous, especially when roughs are used.

Pre-tests: communication check

This method is used once an advertisement has been developed, even if only to a rough stage. It measures how successful an advertisement is likely to be in achieving product and brand registration and in getting across the desired message or brand image.

In the case of print, a representative sample of the people in the target group is exposed to the advertisement for a short time, two to ten seconds. The people in the sample are then asked what was advertised and what they can recall. The advertisement is then left exposed and further questions on reactions, feelings, interests and perceptions are asked. When a TV or cinema commercial is being tested, the initial exposure is usually with other advertisements inbetween an interest film. The test commercial is usually shown again prior to more detailed probing.

Post-tests: initial reaction

Despite intensive pre-testing, advertisers often want a very fast feedback on consumers' immediate reactions to advertisements when exposed to them in market conditions.

Two methods which are widely accepted for measuring the initial impact of and reactions to advertising are day-after-recall testing (DART) for television commercials (the method is also suitable for radio spots) and Starch for press advertisements.

Day-after-recall testing (DART or DAR)

Day-after-recall testing is used to measure the impact, communication feedback, product registration and reaction to an initial or early showing of a television commercial. The research method generally used is in-home or telephone interviews. Small samples of approximately 100 people in the target group who were viewing during the commercial break are taken.

In the South African context DART tests are complicated by the use of different languages. Generally it is necessary to wait until the commercial has been shown at least once in the languages being tested. Then a new dimension is added to the results, namely the impact of the advertisement in the home language and in other languages.

Starch

The main aim of a Starch test (named after Daniel Starch, who pioneered the service), is to measure the impact of advertisements in newspapers and magazines. Interviewers carry a copy of the specific issue of a publication in which the advertisement to be tested appeared. Interviewees are asked if they read that particular issue. Then they are asked to page through the publication and say which pages they looked at, whether they saw the advertisement, and how much of it they read.

Three standard measurements are used:
☐ Noted
☐ Seen/Associated
☐ Read most.

'Noted' is a measure of an advertisement's power to secure the attention of readers. It is the percentage of readers of the current issue who remembered, when interviewed, that they had seen the advertisement in the particular publication.

'Seen/Associated' is a measure of an advertisement's power to make brand or sponsor impressions. It is the percentage of readers who have seen or read any part of the advertisement which clearly indicates the product (or service) advertised.

'Read most' is a measure of an advertisement's power to arouse and hold reader interest. It is the percentage of readers who read 50% or more of the written portion of the advertisement.

These scores can be based on all respondents in the target group, all readers of the publication, or all page readers.

In practice, several different advertisements in the same publication are measured or, where a survey is being done for only one advertisement, the interview is often extended to cover the impact of particular aspects of the advertisement, for example copy points, visuals, trademarks, etc. Usually contact samples large enough to produce 100 to 150 readers of the publication are used.

Results of Starch tests differ considerably according to the page on which the test advertisement appears. They also vary by product class and often quite different results are obtained for males and females. Nevertheless, the simplicity and reproduceability of the Starch technique allows norms to be built up and trends to be monitored, from which very useful information can emerge, for example on the effects of page position, advertisement size, colour, layout, editorial content, etc on advertisement noting.

Post-tests: Extended campaign testing

Although it is important and useful to pre-test and post-test individual advertisements in specific media, it is even more important to be able to monitor the cumulative effect of a series of multi-media advertisements or a whole campaign. A campaign should be measured in terms of its efficiency in carrying out its objectives, in giving maximum value for money spent, and in out-performing current competitive advertising in both these aspects.

It is in the field of extended or campaign advertising post-testing that research methodology has developed most rapidly during the past few years. Post-testing techniques are numerous and vary in complexity from fairly simple measures of awareness, usage, image, etc to the increasing complexities of multivariate analysis and disaggregative model building.

Most extended post-testing procedures are based on fairly large (300 or more) representative samples and use a wide range of questions designed to measure not only advertising performance, but also a wide spectrum of data relating to a brand's positioning and performance in the market.

If the effects of advertising are to be measured, then some method which can identify who has been exposed to an advertisement or a campaign and the degree of that exposure, is necessary. This problem has taxed the ingenuity of researchers for decades. Numerous solutions have been put forward, ranging from simply asking respondents to recall if they have seen or heard any advertising, to split-runs for magazines and newspapers, controlled exposure via cable television, and complex probability models based on media consumption and media exposure schedules at the individual respondent level. One approach which is yielding outstanding results and has gained acceptability with clients and agencies alike is *Adexpose*.

Adexpose

In an Adexpose survey, informants are shown actual miniatures of press advertisements and posters and a series of key stills from TV and cinema commercials that were used by leading brands during a selected time period prior to fieldwork. Exposure levels for informants are obtained by a simple recognition procedure involving card-sorting and categorising each advertisement under on of three headings:

☐ I have seen this ad many times
☐ I have seen this ad once or twice
☐ I have not seen this ad before

Whilst this may seem simplistic, both in South Africa and overseas visual recognition tests of this nature have proved to be a very accurate guide to actual advertising exposure. The procedure can be extended to include radio, using either recognition or recall.

Using each informant's levels of claimed advertising recognition as a basis, an exposure score can be calculated for each respondent. A weight can be given to the exposure scores for each brand in each medium on the basis of the amount of money spent by that brand in each medium. Respondents can now be allocated, in terms of the exposure to the advertising for each brand, into a series of groups ranging from nil, low, medium to high exposure. It is possible to answer a number of key questions about the effectiveness of the advertising for each brand under test:

☐ Has the campaign reached the intended target group, and who has been exposed at this point?

☐ What is the duplication between the reach of different media, and what portion of the market has been heavily exposed?

☐ What is the relationship between advertising exposure and standard measurements of marketing achievement such as:
  − spontaneous and prompted brand awareness
  − brand usage and second choice brand
  − credibility of advertising claims
  − slogan recognition
  − brand image on specific attributes
  − propensity to buy
  − trial and usage?

Results are in the form of a series of response functions such as 'recognition of the brand', 'spontaneous awareness of the brand', and 'associations between the brand and certain attributes' (see figures 8.3 to 8.6).

Figure 8.3
Recognition of brand A's advertising campaign

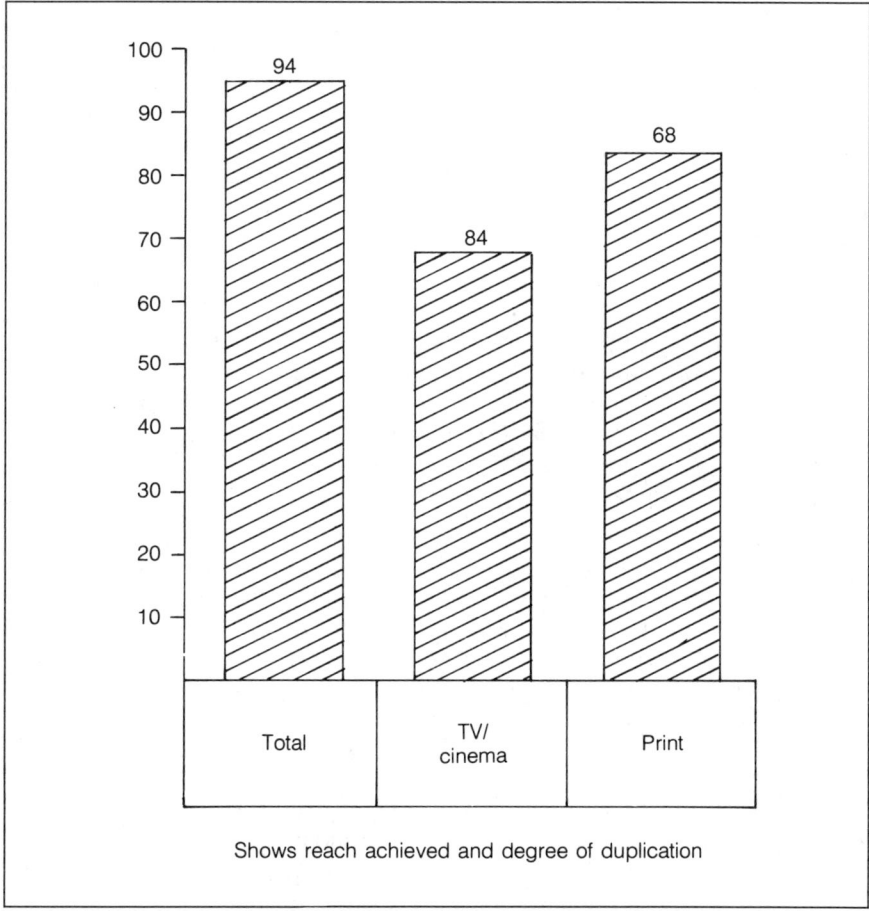

Shows reach achieved and degree of duplication

Figure 8.4
Spontaneous awareness of brand A within exposure groups

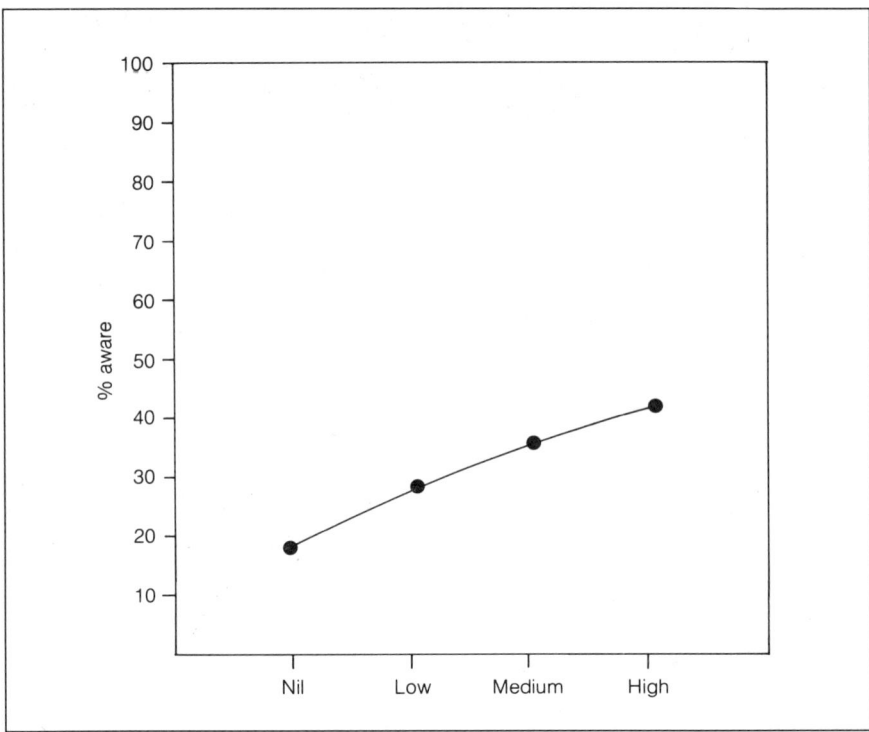

Figure 8.5
Brand A on attribute A

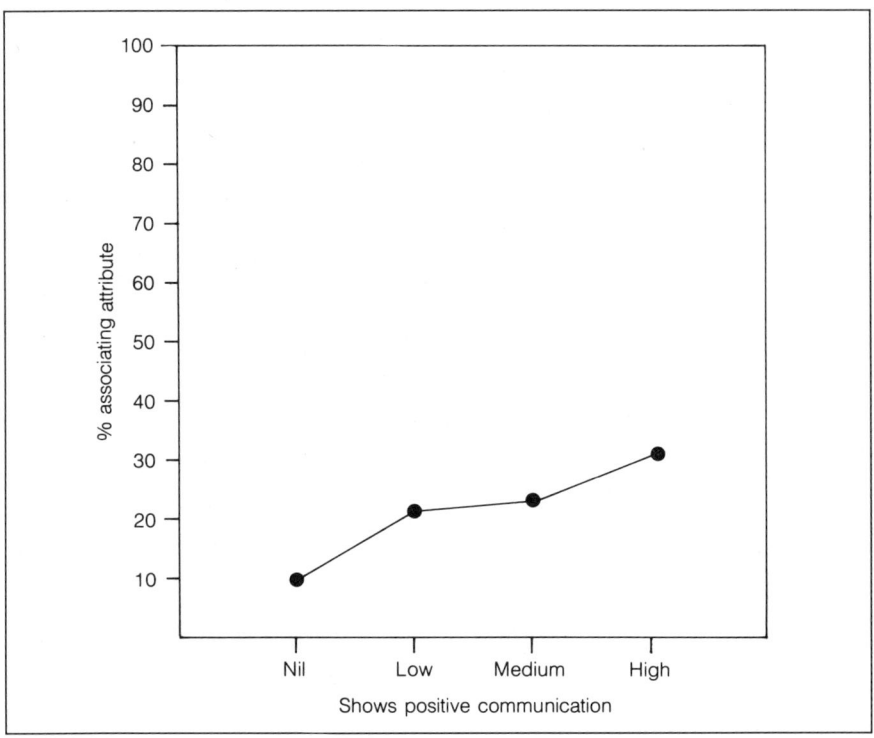

Figure 8.6
Brand B on
attribute C

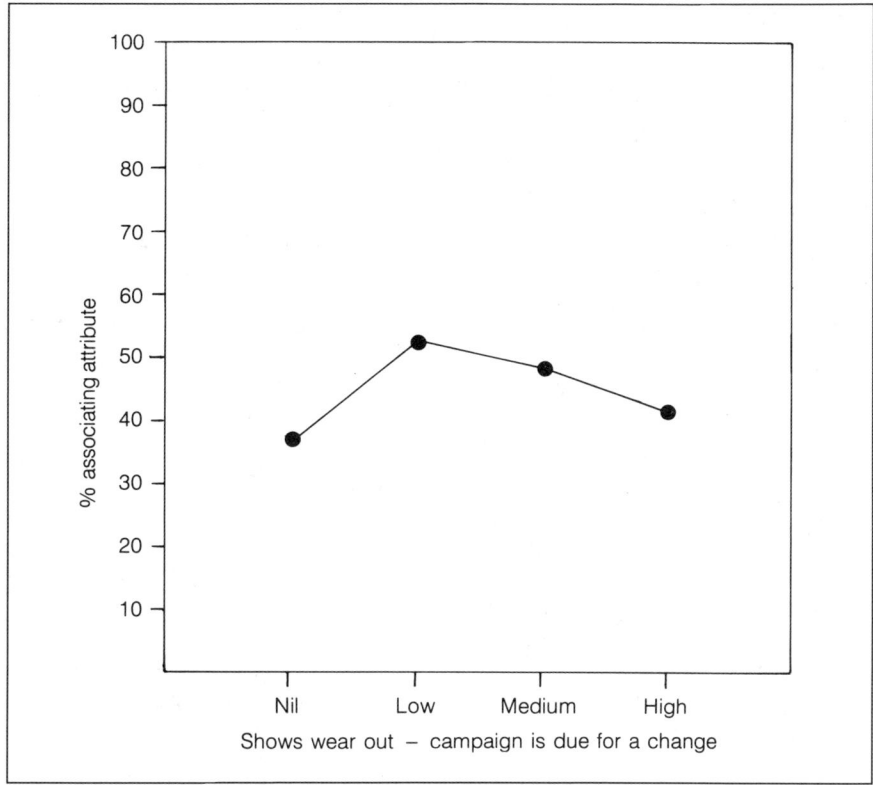

□ Conclusion

Only a handful of the dozens of methods used for pre-testing and post-testing advertising have been described. The complexity of the communication process, increasing knowledge of how the brain works and changing technology all ensure that the measurement of advertising effectiveness will continue to be a dynamic area of research development.

The Adexpose recognition technique is an exciting breakthrough in the development of methods to post-test advertising effectiveness.

Multivariate analyses: understanding data

Erik du Plessis

What is multivariate analysis?	328
Why multivariate analysis in an advertising course?	328
Predictive and descriptive techniques	329
Perceptual mapping	330
Summary	333

☐ What is multivariate analysis?

Although measurements are usually taken on single dimensions, in the real world they are mostly interdependent.

If the height, weight and colour of the eyes of a sample of people is measured, it will be found that there is a high correlation between the height and weight measurements and no correlation between the eye colour and the other two variables.

When the results from such a study are analysed, the following conclusions may be drawn:

☐ 'Height' and 'weight' are measurements of the same thing (say 'size').
☐ Height is predictive of weight, that is if we measure height we can predict weight.
☐ Because they are similar, we need measure only one of them.
☐ Eye colour is not related to the concept size (ie height or weight).

In the above example the interrelationship between a few univariate measures have been studied and as a result some fairly strong conclusions have been drawn. The purpose of multivariate analysis is to study the interrelationship between variables and arrive at certain conclusions (as the example shows).

☐ Why multivariate analysis in an advertising course?

There are numerous multivariate analysis techniques available – any analysis which is concerned with inspecting the interrelationship between measurements is a multivariate analysis – and these techniques often 'appear' the same to the novice. The major difference between the techniques is the aim of the analysis. This determines the interpretations that can be made and also those that cannot be made from the analysis.

Since the early 1970s multivariate techniques have increased in popularity, and since the advent of the micro computer there is an increasing number of researchers and consultants conducting these analyses commercially. Unfortunately, this 'have technique – will travel' attitude means that quite often the research problem is redefined to suit the technique rather than the correct technique being used for the analysis.

Although the practising advertiser need not be an expert in statistics, it is becoming increasingly important that he has a working knowledge of the objectives of multivariate techniques so that he can take advantage of their strengths while ensuring that the appropriate technique is used.

☐ Predictive and descriptive techniques

Multivariate techniques can be divided into those that have prediction as an objective and those that have description as an objective.

Predictive techniques

The predictive techniques are:
☐ Multiple regression
☐ Multiple discriminant analysis (MDA)
☐ Conjoint measurement

Multiple regression

This technique seeks to develop a model of the relationship between a dependent variable and independent variables. For example, you may want to explain the sales volume (dependent variable) of a brand by relating this to economic factors, levels of distribution, advertising budgets, price, etc.

Multiple discriminant analysis (MDA)

In this case the objective is to use a set of independent variables to 'predict' the classification of dependent variables. For example, you have a set of measurements on a number of individuals, including the brand they use. This can be subjected to MDA to determine what differentiates the users of one brand from those of another.

Conjoint measurement

Conjoint measurement seeks to determine the relative importance of each product attribute in creating on overall desirability for the product. It is different from multiple regression in the way the data is collected and analysed. For example, respondents are handed a number of descriptions of product formulation and asked to indicate their preference. The attributes are set at different levels (eg some descriptors show a low price and others a high price). This information can then be used to devise product strategies.

Descriptive techniques

The descriptive techniques are:
☐ Factor analysis
☐ Cluster analysis
☐ Non-metric multidimensional scaling
☐ Correspondence analysis

Factor analysis

This is a set of techniques that try to reduce a large number of variables to a lesser number of underlying factors. In a typical application of factor analysis a large number of potential measurements (eg attitudes or needs) are identified in a preliminary study. Then factor analysis is used to identify underlying factors – which are then used as measurements in the main study.

Cluster analysis

This is also a set of techniques, the aim of which is to form meaningful groupings of people or products in terms of their similarity. One application would be to find groupings of products that are similar and therefore competitive.

Non-metric multidimensional scaling

By inspecting a data set of brand preferences this technique sets out to identify brand groupings that are competitive.

Correspondence analysis

By inspecting a data matrix this technique sets out to determine the rows and columns that are similar in terms of their distribution. For instance, the input matrix may be a table of brand/attribute association data. The result of the analysis will show which brands are perceived as 'similar' relative to the attributes, and which are seen as different (ie brand cluster analysis). This will also show which attributes differentiate between the brands (ie discriminant analysis).

☐ Perceptual mapping

Strictly speaking, perceptual mapping relates to any graphic presentation (mapping) of brand/attribute data (perceptions). Technically, this means that any simplistic presentation of perceptual data qualifies under this heading.

Perceptual maps can be drawn using any of the abovementioned multivariate statistical techniques. However, since the analysis objectives of the techniques differ, it is obvious that the way in which a perceptual map is interpreted will depend upon the technique on which it is based. When confronted with a perceptual map, the advertising practitioner should always ascertain which technique was used to derive the map.

South African practice

Perceptual maps are most frequently derived from either multi-dimensional scaling or correspondence analysis. The former is basically a technique developed in the USA and the latter a French technique.

In South Africa, correspondence analysis has become the more popular technique for deriving perceptual maps.

Using perceptual maps in advertising strategy

Due to the increasing popularity of perceptual maps an example is given here.

Table 8.2 is an (hypothetical) example of a brand attribute matrix. Correspondence analysis of the data results in map 8.1.

Table 8.2
Brand positioning

	BR1	BR2	BR3	BR4	BR5
Cheap	20	30	40	**50**	20
Quality	60	30	20	20	20
Taste	10	20	15	10	20
Smell	30	20	10	20	15
Pack	20	30	10	**50**	40
Male	30	20	**50**	10	15
Female	**60**	50	30	10	40
Fragrance	**40**	**40**	10	10	20
Useful	20	10	40	30	15

From this map it can be 'read' that Brand 3 is positioned as a male brand and Brand 4 is positioned as being cheap and as having a nice pack. Brands 1, 2 and 5 are positioned as being 'fragrant', with Brand 1 being feminine and Brand 5 having a pleasant smell.

Map 8.1
Brand positions

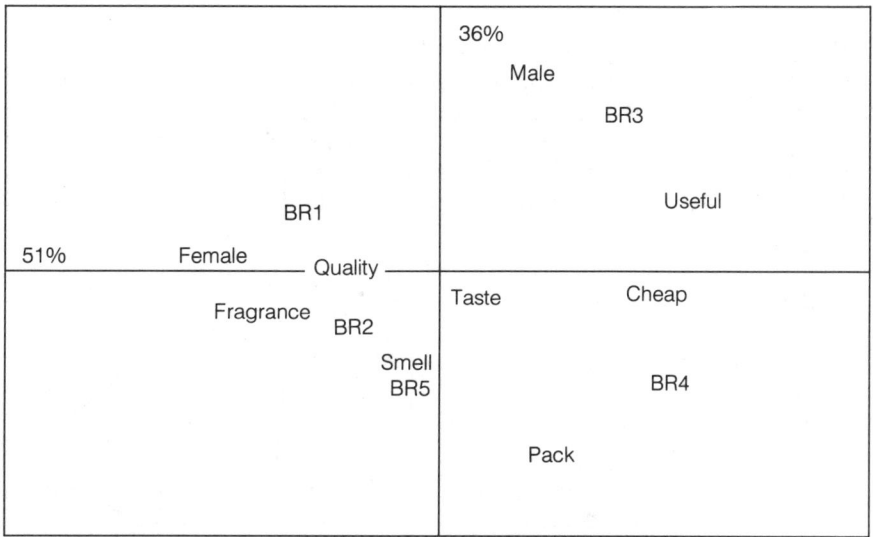

On the basis of this 'map' of the brand positions, the strategist can decide whether the position of his brand is desirable or whether it should be moved.

Having decided that the brand's 'positioning' should be moved, the strategist can conduct tests on a number of advertising concepts against the attributes and determine the positioning effect that the proposed advertising will have on the brand position.

Suppose that the strategist believes that his brand (BR5) should be positioned more towards 'packaging'. Map 8.2 shows the strategic positioning effect that concepts A, B, C, D and E will have.

Map 8.2
Concept positions

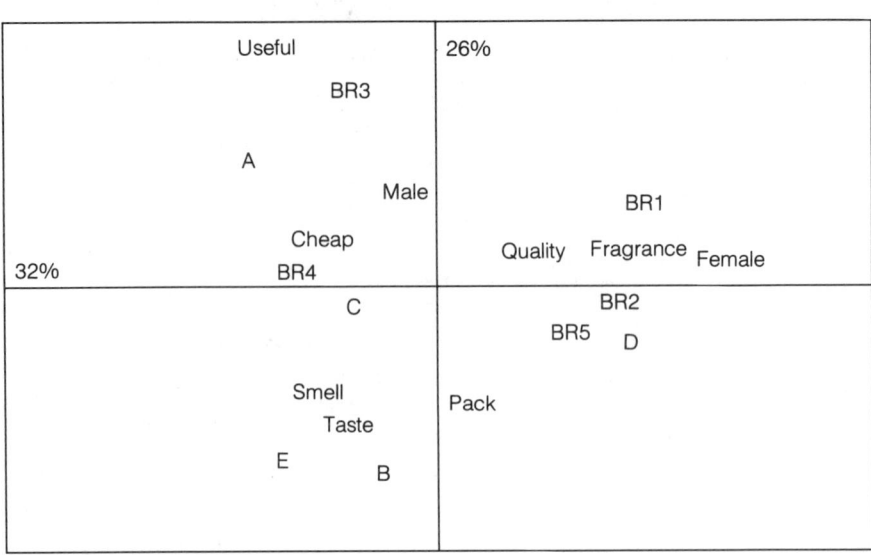

Now suppose that the advertiser opted for concept 'B' (see table 8.3). After the campaign has been flighted for a specific period the brand position can be re-tested so that it can be seen to what extent the position has in fact changed. Map 8.3 shows the (hypothetical) result of such an exercise, with BR5-A the position of Brand 5 among the audience exposed to the advertising.

Table 8.3
Concept
positioning

	Brand					Concept				
	BR1	BR2	BR3	BR4	BR5	A	B	C	D	E
Cheap	20	30	40	50	20	40	10	40	20	40
Quality	60	30	20	20	30	15	15	50	5	10
Taste	10	20	15	10	20	20	20	15	15	50
Smell	30	20	10	20	15	40	50	30	10	40
Pack	20	30	10	50	40	15	**40**	20	40	30
Male	30	20	50	10	15	40	20	15	30	20
Female	60	50	30	10	40	10	15	10	50	15
Fragrance	40	40	10	10	20	20	10	5	20	10
Useful	20	10	40	30	15	50	5	10	5	5

Table 8.4
BR5
advertising
effect

	BR1	BR2	BR3	BR4	BR5	BR5-A
Cheap	20	30	40	50	20	20
Quality	60	30	20	20	30	15
Taste	10	20	15	10	20	20
Smell	30	30	10	20	15	50
Pack	20	30	10	50	40	15
Male	30	20	50	10	15	15
Female	60	50	30	10	40	10
Fragrance	40	40	10	10	20	5
Useful	20	10	40	30	15	

These analyses allow for the evaluation of the strategic effect of a campaign. They are also useful in that they aid decisions as to whether a campaign is approaching the end of its life – that is whether it is no longer achieving any incremental positioning improvements.

Map 8.3
BR5 advertising
effect

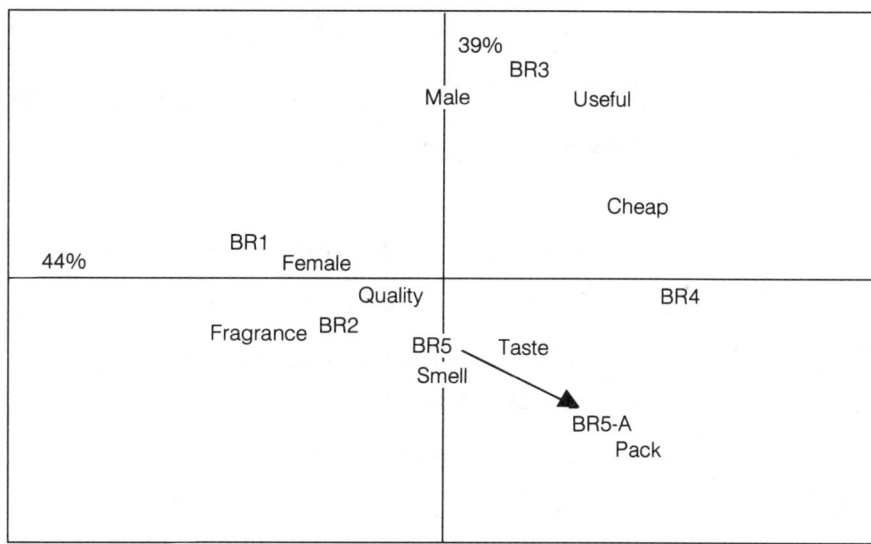

**The techniques
do not add**

As a concluding note it must be stressed that these techniques do not add to the data or the sample. They are only analysis tools. In other words, the techniques do not compensate for poor sampling or poor research design – they can only analyse relative to the sample and relative to the measures that were used. This is especially important when decisions regarding the product attributes on which brands are measured are made.

These techniques have been usefully applied in studies where measures of the products are taken on performance related criteria, on personality criteria and even photographs. However, if the measures that are used are performance related, the technique should not be expected to yield useful lifestyle or personality information (or vice versa). Therefore, the advertiser should ensure that the research design is such that the results will be relevant to the advertising process.

□ Summary

Multivariate analyses enable the advertising researcher to analyse the interdependence and correlation between more than one dimension or variable. It is a *quantitative* rather than a qualitative technique which can be expressed visually in the form of perceptual maps.

Advertising research: the media
Marius Leibold

The nature of advertising media research	*334*
Print media research techniques	*335*
Television, cinema and radio media research techniques	*339*
Outdoor advertising media	*341*
References	*342*

☐ The nature of advertising media research

Media selection research is concerned with testing the effectiveness of the particular vehicles of transmission of advertisements. The five main media are:

☐ Print
☐ Radio
☐ Cinema
☐ Outdoor advertising.

Each of these media consists of different types of transmission vehicles (for example magazines, newspapers, brochures, etc in the case of print advertising) and the aim of media research is to establish the size, composition and reaction of audiences to the different advertising vehicles.

Media research has two distinct but associated functions to perform, namely:

☐ to provide audience measurements, that is accurate estimates of the number and kind of persons who are given the 'opportunity to see' (ots) advertisements carried by a given medium

☐ to indicate the effectiveness of these opportunities, that is allow reasonable predictions to be made as to the influence of the advertisements on persons who are given such opportunities to see.

The difference between advertising media research and advertising content research is one of focus of attention in that *media* research is concerned mainly with establishing the size and kind of audience (the number of ots's), whereas advertising *content* research is concerned mainly with how the audience responds to particular advertisements (the effect of the various ots's).

Seeing that media research involves questions concerning how many people are exposed to given advertising messages, how many times each person is exposed to each medium, and how effective each exposure was, it is not surprising that media research studies tend to be expensive. Since the results are of interest to advertisers, potential advertisers and companies involved in the media, such research is typically conducted by outside research agencies rather than individual advertisers or companies in the media.

Different types of techniques have been developed to assess the size, composition and responses of audiences of the various vehicles of transmission. However, certain techniques are common to more than one vehicle, and for the sake of brevity they are discussed according to the main categories of media.

☐ Print media research techniques

The techniques most frequently employed in print media research differ somewhat, depending on whether the researcher attempts to measure issue readership, reading frequency, page audience, or advertisement audience. Therefore, before listing the main techniques of print media research it is necessary to establish each of these concepts clearly.

Being an issue reader is said to provide an 'opportunity to see' (ots) an advertisement carried by the issue. However, seeing that some readers do not avail themselves of this opportunity, issue audience is often not equivalent to page audience, which is defined as the number of people exposed to a given page (or spread) in a given issue. Being a member of the page audience increases the likelihood of seeing an advertisement on that page, but does not necessarily guarantee it (except when the advertisement is a full page spread). Consequently, it is useful to distinguish page audience from advertisement audience, which comprises those persons who have contact with the advertisement itself.

These distinctions reflect the necessity for careful print media research which avoids taking readership surveys at face value. Such surveys often fall short in that they qualify respondents as readers irrespective of the proportion of an issue they have actually read, or of whether they have actually purchased the issue or not, which could give misleading estimates of the effectiveness of the particular newspaper or magazine.

Measurement of issue readership

The two major techniques for measuring issue readership, which is the number of persons who have read a particular issue of a newspaper or magazine, are:
☐ recall tests
☐ recognition tests.

Recall tests

These tests require the respondent to remember whether he has seen a particular issue of a newspaper or magazine. It may be conducted in an aided or unaided form. In aided recall the respondent is assisted by 'scaled-down' versions of the issue containing just enough information, for example cover pictures and main editorial features, to stimulate the respondent to remember sufficiently.

Recognition tests

The respondent is supplied with copies of different issues and asked which he has bought or read. Such tests typically involve showing the respondents issues of a publication and asking them to glance through them. Respondents are declared readers of particular issues only when they affirm having had prior exposure to such issues (Simmons 1961:470).

An estimate of the total readership for a particular publication is made on the basis of the size of the readership of one or more typical issues of the publication, as compiled through extensive interviewing of respondents. This is usually done, in its simplest form, by multiplying the size of the readership for an average issue with the number of issues involved, which provides an estimate of the total number of persons reached by the given publication.

Measurement of reading frequency

A problem which arises with the measurement of issue readership is which particular issues to use in the tests. Because of the costs involved only a few issues are studied in a given year, despite the fact that readership of individual issues may vary widely. The question of reading frequency arises from the fact that for a particular newspaper or magazine there are many persons who are irregular readers, that is they do not read every issue or are only occasionally exposed to one or more issues. Thus, it is an invalid assumption that a given individual either is a member (reader) or is not (non-reader) of the audience – the reading frequency should be taken into account.

The probability that an individual has contact with the average issue of a publication is known as his reading frequency for that issue. Issue readership must be combined with reading frequency measures to provide a guide to the total number of persons who are likely to be exposed to an insertion in a particular publication. The three main techniques for assessing reading frequency are:

☐ consumer panels
☐ recognition tests
☐ subjective estimates (Orpen 1979:120).

Consumer panels

A group of individuals or households are chosen randomly and either keep a complete diary or retain all publications purchased during a stipulated period.

Recognition tests

Respondents are shown various issues of a particular publication and asked which they have bought or read.

Subjective estimates

This involves a group of individuals who are asked to indicate, on either a numerical or a verbal scale, how often they read or buy issues of a particular publication. On a numerical scale they indicate which of a number of illustrative percentages best describes their usual or typical behaviour, for example, 100%, 75%, 25%, etc of all issues. On a verbal scale they indicate which of several phrases is the most accurate description, for example, 'always', 'never', 'occasionally', etc.

Measurement of page audience

It is a fact that people differ widely in what and how much they read in a given issue of a publication. The measurement of page audience scales the audience down to those individuals who at some state in their readership of the issue have contact with a particular page. This provides an estimate of those persons who were in a position to see an advertisement featured on that particular page. The four main techniques of assessing page audience are:

☐ glue spots
☐ eye cameras

☐ self-reports
☐ scale estimates (Orpen 1979:120).

Glue spots

This technique involves the placement of a small, hopefully imperceptible seal of glue at the corners of given pages of a publication. A person, who could be a member of a pre-selected group of respondents, is counted as being within the audience for a pair of pages if the glue seal between them is found to have been broken.

Eye cameras

This involves filming a respondent in a reading situation by means of a hidden video camera. In this way it can be determined not only which pages were opened and for how long, but also the general direction of looking on the page.

Self-reports

These involve the use of recall (aided and unaided) and recognition measures in order to define the page traffic as the proportion of the issue audience claiming to have read a particular page.

In unaided recall a respondent is included as page traffic if he states that he looked at particular items on a particular page. In aided recall the respondent is given a list of some of the items on a particular page and is asked whether he remembers seeing that particular page when he read the issue of the publication.

In recognition tests the reader is usually taken through the issue page by page and asked to indicate whether he remembers reading each page in turn.

Scale estimates

This technique involves presenting respondents with some form of scale and requesting them to choose the scale position that best describes their own behaviour regarding the degree of thorough or less thorough reading within the particular issue of a publication. The scale can be either numerical (eg number of pages looked at on average) or verbal (eg read 'some', 'most' or 'all' of an issue).

Measurement of advertisement audience

As was explained earlier, page audience is not necessarily advertisement audience, unless it concerns a full page advertisement. Advertisement audience research could perhaps be regarded as being on the borderline of advertising message/content research, but it is customary to include measures of the number of readers who have contact with specific advertisements under the heading 'media research'.

The two main techniques for assessing advertisement audience in print media are:

☐ recall tests
☐ recognition tests

Recall tests

In unaided recall tests the respondent is simply asked questions about the advertisement, especially concerning the product or service featured. Typically, the name of the advertised product or service and/or identifying features of the advertisement are presented verbally and the respondent is asked if he can remember seeing the advertisement in a particular issue of a particular publication.

In aided recall the respondent is assisted in remembering by 'prompts' of various kinds. These 'prompts' commonly include the front covers of the relevant issue(s) of the publication, abbreviated forms of the advertisement, or a set of brand or company names associated with the advertised product or service. In aided recall it is usual to restrict the respondents to those who claim to have read the particular issue of the publication in which the advertisement appeared, and to ask them to 'play back from memory' what they can remember about particular advertisements. Aided recall tests of this kind are often known as 'impact' tests, which were first popularised by the Gallup-Robinson research group in the USA (Orpen 1979:122).

Major advantages of the recall method are the following:

☐ A large number of standardised questions can be asked within one survey.
☐ Recall measures are usually fairly stable over the length of the test period, although some information is forgotten.
☐ Recall of advertisements is independent of the position of the advertisement in the publication.
☐ Specific advertisements are not presented, which helps to avoid the confusion often inherent in recognition tests.

The major disadvantages of the recall method are the following:

☐ The skill of the interviewer contributes to the value of the information, which is consequently subject to bias.
☐ It is likely that the respondent's responses originate from his previous knowledge of the advertising of the product or service, and not from the actual advertisements themselves.
☐ There is a tendency among respondents to underclaim seeing particular advertisements, particularly in the case of unaided recall.

Recognition tests

Recognition tests involve actually showing the relevant advertisement to each respondent who claims to have seen a particular issue and asking questions about it. The questions centre around three aspects:

☐ Whether the respondent remembers seeing the advertisement
☐ Whether the respondent noticed the name of the product, service or advertiser
☐ Whether the respondent has read a certain percentage of the written material.

Three different Starch readership scores (named after Daniel Starch, who pioneered the service) are prepared for each advertisement: 'noted', that is the percentage of readers who say they saw the advertisement in the publication; 'seen/associated', that is the percentage who correctly identify the product and advertisers with the advertisement; and 'read most', the percentage who say they read more than half of the written material in the advertisement (Kotler 1984:655). A 1981 study examined the accuracy of Starch score predictors and concluded, *inter alia*, that for low-involvement consumer decisions brand recognition ('associated') may be sufficient, whereas actual readership ('read most') is probably necessary in high-involvement cases (Rossiter 1981:63-68).

The major advantages of the recognition method are as follows:

☐ There is less reliance on the memory of the respondent, as in the case with recall tests, with consequently more reliability of results.
☐ It is possible to ask questions which are more comprehensive and probing than those in recall studies.
☐ Corrections can be made for possible overclaiming by respondents.

The major disadvantages of this method are the following:

☐ A state of confusion is often induced in the respondent by the presentation of many different advertisements, and he tends to claim to have seen more advertisements than is actually the case.

☐ There is a tendency for advertisements presented early on in the interview to yield higher readership scores than those presented later in the interview.

☐ Some respondents deliberately falsify responses in order to impress the interviewer. In order to 'control' the falsification factor, some advertisements that have not yet appeared may be interspersed with regular advertisements.

In South Africa, the majority of print media research is conducted under the auspices of the South African Advertising Research Foundation (SAARF), which is made available to the advertising industry in the periodic All Media and Products Survey (AMPS) reports. The SAARF and AMPS reports have been subjected to a fair amount of criticism over the years, especially with regard to their readership questionnaire. The SAARF managing director, Mr Gert Yssel, aptly states that 'Readership research is an extraordinarily difficult problem . . . it is not just South Africa that is grappling with its complexities'. (SAARF 1985:1).

Following a recommendation by the committee, the SAARF board decided to take the unusual step of publishing an additional volume to the interim report for 1985. It reviews a number of factors affecting readership research and explains the problems involved, especially with regard to the methods used in AMPS. The extra volume also includes a discussion of the Direct Link Method (DLM), which was developed by Dr Wally Langschmidt (founder and past chairman of Market Research Africa), as well as reservations about the technique and some of its assumptions. Basically, the DLM involves an adjustment of copy-purchase claims of respondents back to audited circulations of the particular media involved, which provides a key to controlling respondents' inflated readership claims.

☐ Television, cinema and radio media research techniques

Television, cinema and radio are very different from print media when it comes to the measurement of the size of their audiences, as such media leave no visible trace that they have been 'received'. The programme and the advertising message are often mixed and it is difficult to divorce them. However, the attention of research efforts is on the programmes themselves rather than on the effectiveness of the advertisements per se.

There are six main techniques that can be employed to assess the size of the audiences of different programmes and hence indirectly the effectiveness of different television and radio channels or stations. These are:

☐ telephone interviewing
☐ personal interviewing
☐ meter recording
☐ diaries
☐ cameras
☐ hidden offers (see Orpen 1979:124-126 and Boyd et al 1985: 758-760).

In the case of cinema, only personal interviewing, diaries and hidden offers apply.

Telephone interviewing

Two approaches can be used with this technique, viz *coincidental* or *non-coincidental* approaches. Coincidental interviews involve telephoning people and simply asking them what television or radio programmes they are watching or listening to at the time of the telephone call. Non-coincidental interviews involve telephoning people and asking them what programmes they listened to or watched during some particular time. This system has the advantage of speed and economy, but has significant limitations:

☐ The results may not be valid, since only homes with telephones are included.

☐ Such procedures do not produce any continuous information about the audience. Neither the number of homes reached over a period of several programmes, that is the cumulative audience, nor the total audience for a given programme at any one time can be established, since no measure of tuning in or out is obtained.

☐ Calls must be limited to certain hours of the day and night, such as before 22h30 at night, in order to avoid unco-operative responses. There may also be the tendency on the part of some respondents to report that they are viewing a more socially acceptable programme than they are.

Personal interviewing

With personal interviewing, too, coincidental or non-coincidental interviews can be used. In the former instance people are visited, usually at home, and asked whether they are listening to the radio or watching television at the time of the interview. In the case of non-coincidental personal interviews, people are visited, usually at their homes, and interviewed personally about the particular programmes they listened to or watched during a specific period, or about which cinemas they frequented.

Obviously this technique is more expensive and time-consuming than telephone interviewing, but it has the advantage that the results are generally more valid. It has the disadvantages that one cannot easily establish the cumulative audience and that interviewing has to be limited to acceptable hours of the day and night.

Meter recording

This technique involves fixing to radio and television sets devices which indicate precisely to which channels they are tuned and when they are switched on or off. One such device is called an *audimeter* and is used by the AC Nielsen Company in the USA to report the following facts:

☐ Total audience – number and percentage of television homes tuned to each network programme for a minimum of six minutes

☐ Average audience – equivalent to the number of television homes tuned to the full programme (the average number of homes minute by minute)

☐ Share of audience =

Number of homes watching a specific programme
Number of homes watching any programme at that time

Seeing that the audimeter sample remains essentially the same from month to month, a measure of the cumulative audience can be obtained. Data can be broken down by household characteristics such as region, city/town, size, age of male head, total family income, and presence of children. In South Africa the use of this technique is likely to become operational only later when, amongst others, the introduction of subscription television will facilitate its use.

While this technique provides more accurate and objective data than any of the other methods of measurement for the audio-visual media, it has the major drawbacks that there is no guarantee that the viewers or listeners are actually listening to or watching the programmes involved and that it does not indicate who is viewing (Bearden et al 1981:187-191).

Diaries

Diaries are basically self-reports. Respondents have to record in a specially designed diary their radio listening or television/cinema viewing, or both. The assumptions are that panel members will co-operate by recording their listening or viewing at the time it occurs, and that they will do it accurately. A continuous panel operation can provide useful duplication data, not only between radio, television and cinema, but also between programmes and other media to which the individual was exposed. Meters are often used in conjunction with diaries, thus providing a monitoring function on the diary technique. If the assumptions are valid the diary method has the advantage of obtaining data on individual viewing programmes. However, it cannot provide a precise minute-by-minute audience flow, which the audimeter does.

Cameras

Cameras can be used to monitor the behaviour of people during periods when particular radio and television programmes are broadcast. The advantages of this technique are that it can indicate the presence or absence of individuals unambiguously and reveal valuable information about how people listen to or watch programmes. However, it has the major disadvantage that respondent behaviour may be affected by the presence of the camera. It also does not indicate anything about the effect of the programmes on the listener or viewer, and it is therefore customary to combine this technique with in-depth interviews and questionnaires.

Hidden offers

This technique involves offering some reward, such as discounts, samples, etc to listeners or viewers during the course of a programme, usually at a relatively inconspicuous point (hence the term 'hidden'). It is important that the reward is 'hidden' in the programme in order to justify the assumption that most or all of the programme has been listened to, or watched, and also that the reward is substantially desirable to elicit an actual response. Furthermore, it is assumed that the larger the number of offers that are applied for the larger the audience of the programme.

☐ Outdoor advertising media

Outdoor advertising is considered to be the oldest form of advertising and one of the most ancient forms of communication.It presents media research with a number of major difficulties which are not found in the study of other media, and it is therefore not surprising that there is a lack of in-depth audience research. The difficulties are basically twofold:

☐ There is no easily identifiable unit of measurement such as a publication or programme. Outdoor advertising is characterised by posters, bulletins and spectaculars displayed at specific sites or on specific vehicles for particular periods of time.

☐ In outdoor advertising the qualification for inclusion in the media audience has to be indirect, typically on the basis of a passage past a display site or an encounter between an individual and a public transport vehicle.

The main objective of outdoor media research has been to provide an estimate of the number of passages made by a random sample of the population past a random sample of sites (whether they 'move' past the site, as with posters, or the site 'moves' past them, as with public transport vehicles (see Orpen 1979:127). The four main techniques used to provide such estimates are:

☐ journey records
☐ key point recording
☐ location cards
☐ driving simulation.

Journey records

This technique requires individuals to indicate, through interviews, questionnaires or travel diaries, their exact movements during a certain period, typically the seven days prior to questioning. These journeys are then compared with the location or routes of the relevant outdoor advertising media. The main advantage of the journey record technique is that it allows the collection of information about all sites in a certain area, but it has the disadvantages that it relies upon the respondents' memories and is a time-consuming and expensive process.

Key point recording

This technique involves selecting a random sample of sites or routes, listing them in a formal questionnaire, and asking respondents to indicate if, during a certain period (typically seven days prior to questioning), they passed these sites or used these routes. The posters or billboards which appeared on these routes or sites are not mentioned at all, that is questioning pertains to routes or sites only.

The advantages of this technique are its speed and simplicity, but it has the disadvantage that false claims are often made in attempts to please the researcher.

Location cards

Photographs or sketches of each site or vehicle and its advertisements are produced and presented to respondents in the form of a number of location cards. The respondents have to indicate which of these they saw during a specific period. Although this technique has the advantage that the respondents indicate not only that they passed, but also that they noticed the outdoor advertisement, there is the disadvantage that false recognitions may be given.

Driving simulation

Telecom Research in the USA simulates an actual driving situation, in which a respondent sees a moving scene while his eye movements are measured by an eye-movement recorder (Kleppner 1983:237).The system measures impact, viewer involvement and brand-name awareness. This technique is useful for analysing general driving observations and the location of specific advertisements, but has the major disadvantage of directly affecting the acuteness of the respondent's observation, thus invalidating the predictive power of the technique.

☐ References

Bearden, WO et al. 1981. 'Attentive Audience Delivery of TV Advertising Schedules'. *Journal of Marketing Research*, May:187-191.

Boyd, Westfall, & Stasch. 1985. *Marketing Research: Text and Cases*. 6th ed. Homewood, Illinois: Richard D Irwin.

Kleppner, O. 1983. *Advertising Procedure*. 8th ed. Englewood Cliffs, New Jersey: Prentice-Hall.

Kotler, P. 1984. *Marketing Management: Analysis, Planning and Control*. 5th ed. Englewood Cliffs, New Jersey: Prentice-Hall.

Orpen, C. 1979. *Advertising; Buying; Selling: A Behavioural Science Approach*. Johannesburg: McGraw-Hill.

Rossiter, J. 1981. 'Predicting Starch Scores'. *Journal of Advertising Research*, October: 63-68.

Simmons, WR. 1961. 'Controlled Recognition in the Measurement of Advertising Perception'. *Public Opinion Quarterly*, 25:470.

South African Advertising Research Foundation. 1985. 'No Room for Complacency'. *Outlook*, December:1.

Marketing research into industrial advertising and media

George Klein

Corporate versus product advertising	*344*
Advertising and the industrial decision maker	*345*
Trade press advertising expenditure	*346*
The size of industrial advertising budgets	*347*
The trade journal press	*348*
Industrial journals that look and sound alike	*348*
The need to measure industrial readership	*349*
The objectives of industrial readership research	*350*
References	*352*

☐ Corporate vs product advertising

Industrial advertising divides itself clearly into *product type* and *corporate type* advertising. Large companies often indulge in corporate advertising where exciting, colourful, highly conceptualised artwork intertwines and blends with clever words. Smaller companies cannot afford the luxury of corporate advertising and therefore confine their media exposure to product advertisements which are generally regarded as boring by the agency's creative team. Boring or not, the advertiser and his agency must take a critical look at how the target market wants to be communicated with.

Industrial buyers and specifiers are pragmatic individuals. Consequently, they look for product facts, specifications, appplications and quality assurance supported by recognisable local or international standards. They also look for price indications and contact names within the supplier company. In traditional advertising terms this does not make for exciting campaigns devised by the 'creative team' because there is little creativity expected by industrial buyers.

Many creative campaigns that have won first prize in advertising competitions have failed dismally at the industrial buyer level simply because they do nothing to support the sales marketing teams except to vaguely amuse and often to mystify the potential customers.

The greatest motivation for a decision maker to buy or specify a particular product is fear of buying the wrong product. The implication is that the industrial buyer will not easily switch to another source of supply unless he is assured that the alternative product will not let him down and make a fool of him. This fact should be taken into account when industrial advertising campaigns are conceptualised.

Thus, the industrial buyer is rarely impressed or amused by symbolism, humour and abstruse promises that he cannot feel, smell, touch or appreciate in terms of cost savings.

How well are advertisers meeting these demands?

Trade readership surveys conducted by this author into different industries indicate that generally advertisers and their agencies are communicating well with their audiences: around 80% of the readers find the advertising either 'very' or 'fairly' informative to them in their decision making. The greatest demand, however, is for more technical information and, where possible, price indications.

The following typical comments highlight this requirement:

- ☐ give test results in the advertisement
- ☐ more attention to product and less to photography
- ☐ copy is too long – give basic facts only
- ☐ give contact person names and phone numbers
- ☐ mention product applications
- ☐ compare old with new product
- ☐ fewer girls draped over products
- ☐ more about spares
- ☐ more up-to-date information
- ☐ too many repeat advertisements
- ☐ ads too interested in own company prestige – not sufficiently customer oriented
- ☐ more colour
- ☐ ads should relate to the particular industry only
- ☐ too many old products are advertised – not enough new ones
- ☐ ads should tear out for filing
- ☐ fewer catch phrases that have no bearing on the product or service
- ☐ advertisements should appear less frequently, but be of better quality.

☐ Advertising and the industrial decision maker

If advertising is to work it must be noticed by the industrial decision maker, and a more elusive character in terms of definition has yet to be found. The area of decision making has been the subject of various papers and books over the years because there is no simple answer to what motivates an industrial decision maker and who, in fact, he is.

It is generally accepted that whereas in a home the decision making unit (DMU) usually comprises the husband and wife team, but may also be either one or the other (in other words up to two people are generally involved), in the industrial market the DMU can include up to seven or more individuals who are continually changing their identities and job functions as they change jobs. Consequently, the DMU within any one target company may change its shape between the appearances of advertising insertions.

For advertising to be optimised, the advertisement must be noticed by as many of the DMU within the buyer organisation as possible. In practical terms, it must have as high a 'pass-on readership' as can be achieved within as short a period as possible. Pass-on readership is, therefore, an important measure of an advertisement's possible effect. This measure of readership is dealt with in more detail later on.

Unlike the consumer sector, the industrial sector has two distinct types of decision maker. One is the *specifier*, who neither buys nor uses the product but is vital to the seller because he advises the buyer about what to buy. The specifier is typically a professional person such as an architect, a consulting engineer or a Government official. His opinion matters a great deal and therefore advertising must take note of his presence in the decision making chain of people and events. The other type of decision maker is in the more recognisable form of the in-company buyer, engineer, manager, director, etc.

An analysis of job titles in past readership surveys defies all description. There is no standardisation of what people should be called. A 'Human Resources Manager' who also carried out important technical buying functions for his company has been found and there are 'Procurement Directors' who are so senior that they do no procurement. But seniority also varies widely from truck drivers and typists through to managing directors and group chairmen. It all depends on the company ethos and the personalities of the people involved.

No wonder, therefore, the serious concern of advertisers who have really given this problem some thought (many advertisers have never really considered the DMU as a problem) about trying to identify who has, in fact, noticed their advertising.

Readership research has also established that in some sectors of the economy the target market hardly reads at all, yet large budgets are being poured into advertising. The only audience that such advertising is reaching is the advertiser's competitors and his own staff. For example, readership research has shown that the journals aimed at the food and catering industry are read mainly by the advertisers themselves, who scan the journal to see what their competitors are advertising. The people who should be reading the journals are catering managers, hotel managers, food and beverage managers, restauranteurs and dietitians, but very few of these people have the inclination to read.

☐ Trade press advertising expenditure

Market Research Africa (Pty) Ltd's service known as *Adindex* measures expenditure on advertising. The author's analysis of the expenditure on the trade press since 1972 shows a compound growth in value terms of 21% per annum – from R4,9m in 1972 to R58,4m in 1985. Growth in advertising expenditure hit a high of 41% in 1981 and a low of −15,9% in 1985 (Adindex). In fact, 1980 was a boom year in South Africa, when GDP reached 7,4%.

The 1985 recession hit all the major sectors of the advertising industry and the industrial sector was no exception. During the year of recession industrial advertising accounted for 12,6% of total adspend on print media. However, during 1983, which was a relatively good year for industrial advertising, it accounted for 12,3% of total adspend. Consequently, the industrial sector is moving in tandem with the total advertising industry.

The expenditure indicated by Adindex is an estimated 20% below actual expenditure because some of the less important journals are not included. Nevertheless, Adindex is the best measure of industrial advertising activity available in South Africa.

Of all the major types of media available, print accounts for 89%, television 8%, outdoor and radio 1% each, and cinema less than 1%. Clearly, therefore, the trade press is the main vehicle for industrial advertising.

☐ The size of industrial advertising budgets

From the information available it is difficult to identify the size of business-to-business (ie non-consumer) industrial advertising budgets per advertiser company because, apart from the engineering sector of Adindex, the other sectors may also have some non-consumer element included in the adspend figures. However, taking the engineering sector as an indicator, the highest recorded budget in 1985 was R997 000 spent by a quasi-Government enterprise, and the smallest, unrecorded, in the words of the advertiser, 'R1,50' – which is quite a wide range.

During 1985 the distribution of advertising expenditure in the engineering sector as outlined in table 8.5 clearly shows the range of budgets. Approximately 600 industrial companies advertised during the year.

Table 8.5
Advertising
expenditure

Rands	%
up to 20 000	56
21 to 40 000	22
41 to 80 000	14
81 to 100 000	2
101 to 120 000	1
121 to 140 000	1
141 to 150 000	1
151 to 200 000	1
201 to 400 000	1
401 to 800 000	1
801 to 1 200 000	*
over 1 200 000	*

Source: Author's analysis of MRA's Adindex Report, 1985

*Less than 1%

Table 8.6
Number of trade
and financial
journals as at
January 1984

Industry	Number of journals
Advertising and Publishing	6
Agriculture	40
Automotive	5
Building and Civil Engineering	22
Chemistry and Chemicals	3
Clothing	4
Commerce	7
Computers	8
Electrical	12
Engineering	12
Exports	3
Food and Beverages	3
Hotels and Liquor	6
Industrial and Industry	10
Medical and Paramedical	24
Mining	14
Municipal	8
Paper, Printing and Packaging	7

Table 8.6
Number of trade
and financial
journals as at
January 1984
(continued)

Industry	Number of journals
Plastic	3
Shipping	3
Textiles	3
Transport	13
Other	216
TOTAL	350

Source: Author's analysis of *SARAD*, January 1986

☐ The trade journal press

SARAD Publishing Co (Pty) Ltd lists most of the journals and newspapers that are published in South Africa. This directory lists approximately 350 names of financial and trade journals that carry business-to-business advertising. About 250 of these are the more pertinent publications that can be regarded as media for advertising to commerce and industry.

The number of journals in the main sectors are given in table 8.6 however, these numbers may change significantly, depending on the health of the economy. Since the figures were obtained several publications have closed. There is no doubt that the South African industrial press is over-traded and a shakeout of publications will only serve to bring better order and raise the quality of the remaining journals.

The number of journals and expenditure on advertising in a particular industrial sector has nothing to do with the importance of that specific industry to the total economy. The extent of duplication of journals can be seen in table 8.6: Industries such as Mining has 14 journals, Transport has 13, Building and Civil Engineering have 22, and Medical has 24. Obviously an advertiser and its agency must experience severe problems choosing which journal will best serve its purposes.

☐ Industrial journals that look and sound alike

The large number of journals offered to South African readers has resulted in considerable confusion among readers as to what, in fact, they are reading. Some publishers, competing with each other in a limited market, follow others by using similar titles, similar layouts and similar articles. Others may opt to purposely initiate changes to make their journals look different. They may change the format or the type of paper, use more colour, staple the pages or allow the sheets to fold loosely into the journal, or make other attempts at differentiation. However, it is the similarity of titles that confuses readers most. The confusion may go so far as to cause an advertiser to use a journal different from the one he thinks he is using and makes readership research in the industrial journal area extremely difficult.

Industrial readership research cannot be carried out by telephone without the reader being shown pictures of the journal front page or even the journal itself. These pictures may be forwarded by post prior to the telephone interview to overcome this difficulty.

Even when titles or journals are shown to readers they may still identify the journal incorrectly. Past readership research has included several dummy titles of journals that do not exist and has picked up a significant number of 'readers' of the non-existent journal. Therefore, the researcher must do everything possible to reduce the 'total error' in his survey. In most research there is an element of 'total error' that has a lot to do with research methodology and little to do with sampling, respondent selection, the questionnaire and other variables. The trained researcher must be able to anticipate sources of error and must reduce if not entirely eliminate them.

☐ The need to measure industrial readership

Industrial budgets allocated to above-the-line advertising in South Africa are fairly limited and when the economy turns down they are the first to be cut in the company's overall cost structure. Added to this, the cost of advertising rises steadily each year, with the increases usually well ahead of the inflation rate. Consequently, many industrial companies consider advertising to be a luxury.

There are many sceptics in industrial companies who cannot see the need for advertising. They would far rather spend additional funds on placing another company representative on the road because they can measure his cost against sales – a measure which industrial advertising defies in most instances.

However, once a company decides to embark on advertising it is faced with the daunting task of choosing media which will optimise its adspend. If the advertiser is handling his own placement of advertising then he opens his door to the many advertising salespersons who will show irrefutable evidence that their journal is the best in terms of exposure to the advertiser's target market. With all this evidence, the majority of which is supported by only the vaguest of proof, the advertiser often opts for journals he personally likes and reads, as he does not have much else to go on.

If the advertiser has placed media selection in the hands of an agency, he has a somewhat better chance of having a more objective selection of journals made for him. But this depends largely on the experience of the agency in industrial markets – unfortunately many agencies have only a passing interest in these markets and can offer little, if any, advice.

Whoever chooses the media is faced with a choice of several journals – 22 if he is in the building and construction industry, and not many less if he is in other sectors of the economy. Added to this number are the many other journals that impinge laterally on these industry specific journals – journals that cover all sectors of the economy, such as the financial and the general engineering press. The choice may extend to 40 journals that a specific reader may 'read, glance at or page through'.

In order to diminish the real threat of wasting advertising budget on the wrong media, readership information is necessary to give guidance to whoever has the task of selecting the media.

If readership research is used, it must address itself to whatever parameters are useful to media selection. Certain of these have been well established in consumer media research, namely:

☐ Journal penetration – which journals are being read?
☐ How frequently are they being read?
☐ How recently have they been read?

These are the major parameters for readership research. However, the industrial advertiser normally needs to know considerably more to assist him in his selection.

The following are further measures that are useful in media selection. Some are borrowed from consumer readership research, while others are specific to industrial markets:

☐ How thoroughly are the journals read?
☐ How journals arrive on the reader's desk, that is whether subscribed to personally or via the company or by means of unsolicited mailing, etc
☐ Extent of pass-on readership – the number of readers per copy
☐ Number of copies obtained by the establishment
☐ Reader's place on the circulation list, that is he obtains journals first, second, etc
☐ Reader lag time – how long it takes for the journal to reach the pass-on reader
☐ What happens to journals after they have been read?
☐ Multiple readership – how many readers of a specific journal also read other journals
☐ The readers' main areas of responsibility
☐ Level of usefulness of journals in helping people to reach purchasing decisions
☐ For what type of equipment or materials is the reader a decision maker in buying?
☐ How informative industrial advertising is perceived to be and how advertising could be improved.

The above list of objectives for industrial readership research is the result of what publishers, advertising agencies and advertisers have asked for in past readership surveys. Each of these is dealt with in more detail in the next section.

☐ The objectives of industrial readership research

It is not the intention to discuss readership research methodology beyond giving a brief description of the objectives for industrial readership research which have been found to be useful by a mix of industrial advertisers, their advertising agencies and trade journal publishers. Of all the objectives, however, the advertiser's main interest is in which journals are being read by his target market and the identification of the decision making unit (DMU) as it relates to the advertiser's product range. Several of the other objectives merely provide more detail about the main objectives and allow the agency to assist clients in media selection. The publisher's interest is clearly to be able to show the advertiser the benefits of advertising in his pages. In spite of the scientific approach being adopted toward media research, the industrial advertiser's gut feel and the fact that, over many years, he has grown to like specific journals is still an important influencing factor in media selection. In some instances gut feel is better than all the research carried out simply because of the advertiser's very narrow and specific product range.

The following are notes on industrial readership objectives that have been found to be useful:

Journal penetration

This is a ranking of journals that have passed the 12-month filter of claimed reading, in other words the percentage of the sample that claim to have read a specific journal in the past 12 months, arranged in decreasing order of mention. The definition of what constitutes a 'reader' needs to be examined carefully.

Reading frequency – how many issues of the journal are being read?

When is a reader a reader? A respondent who reads all six issues of the last six published is possibly more important than one who reads only one out of six issues. Consequently, readers are weighted so that a reader of only one issue is counted as 1/6 or 0,167 of a reader, a reader who claims to have read three out of six issues is counted as 1/2 or 0,5 of a reader, and one who has read all six issues is counted as one reader.

The result of this analysis is that a more conservative and possibly a more practical measure of journal readership is obtained.

Reading recency – when last was the journal read?

This is a measure of readership to indicate the time lag before a specific journal is read. Do respondents read a specific journal any sooner than other journals? Are weekly journals, as a group, read sooner than, say, fortnightly or monthly journals? The implications are that if an advertiser wishes to be noticed soon after the publication date of his advertisement, an early journal readership is preferable to a later one. However, several other measures of readership must also be considered.

Thoroughness of reading

Another measure of readership is in terms of how thoroughly journals are read. Four levels of thoroughness ranging from 'read thoroughly' to 'hardly look at it' may be used. Are some journals read more thoroughly than others?

How journals are obtained

How do journals arrive on the reader's desk – through personal subscriptions, company subscriptions or unsolicited mailing? Even the fact that the respondent may not know could affect his interest in the journal.

Number of readers per copy – pass-on readership

A measure of the number of readers per copy, also called 'pass-on readership', is a useful means of establishing how many readers are likely to see a specific issue and, therefore, how many are likely to be exposed to the advertisement.

Number of copies obtained by the establishment

How many copies of each journal are obtained by each establishment? Some free issue trade newspapers and journals are circulated to several persons in the same company. In some cases the same individual may receive more than one copy.

Reader's place on the circulation list

This is a measure of how long it may take a reader to receive a specific copy. This information, cross-tabulated with the reader's buying authority, is a useful measure of how fast and how effective the exposure could be.

Reader's lag time – how long it takes journal to reach the pass-on reader

This is another measure of the delay in journals reaching a reader.

What happens to each journal after circulation throughout company?

What is the final destination of a journal? How soon is it thrown away, or is its usefulness extended by placing it in a reception area, taking it home, or placing it in a library? The longer it remains in circulation, the greater the number of readers that may see a product's advertisement.

Multiple readership

This is a measure of the percentage of readers of a specific journal that also read other journals and indicates the overlap that an advertiser would be exposed to by advertising simultaneously in two journals that are read by the same reader. The campaign's objective may be to obtain audience saturation and, therefore, to seek a high level of overlap in the media schedule. However, the objective may also be to spread exposure as widely as possible with little reader overlap.

Respondent's major decision area

This is a measure of the area of responsibility in terms of buying decisions that the respondent is active in.

Usefulness of journals read

Journals usually have various broad areas of coverage. The following break-downs have proved useful:

☐ company and industry news   ☐ product news section
☐ overseas news   ☐ special surveys
☐ product advertising   ☐ feature articles on specific subjects

How useful is each of these sections to readers on a scale ranging from 'very useful' to 'completely useless'?

Reader's purchasing responsibility and value level of his authority

This is a measure of the respondent's seniority according to the level of his daily buying authority. A relatively low percentage of respondents has no buying authority as such because of the tender procedure adopted by their establishments. Nevertheless they are decision makers in the buying process but do not consider themselves to have the necessary buying authority.

Type of equipment or materials that reader is responsible for

This is one of the most crucial questions for the identification of the target reader.

How informative is industrial advertising?

On a scale ranging from 'very informative' to 'very uninformative', how informative is industrial advertising generally to decision makers for the buying of goods and services for their establishments?

☐ References

Klein, G et al. 1984. Reports on trade readership. Johannesburg Market Research Africa. Adindex. Johannesburg. SARAD. Johannesburg: Sarad Publishing Co Ltd.

9

Industrial advertising

Advertising industrial goods, specifically
   capital equipment *355*
Communicating effectively with industrial buyers *369*

Advertising industrial goods, specifically capital equipment

Chris F van Veijeren

Introduction	355
Distinctive features of industrial marketing and advertising	356
Classifications of industrial goods	357
Identifying and reaching buying influences	358
Buying motives	359
The actual distribution of industrial marketing costs	363
The industrial advertising plan	366
Final conclusions and general guidelines regarding industrial advertising	367
References	368

☐ Introduction

For both the academic and the practitioner in the marketing field, the paucity of literature on the marketing of industrial goods remains a problem. Therefore, it is the intention in this contribution to pay particular attention to the role of industrial advertising in the marketing of capital equipment. For a number of reasons it can confidently be expected that the marketing of capital equipment will remain important on the local scene. The structure of South African industrial life is such that it will require continued importing of industrial goods of many kinds. The need for international competitiveness will probably make imports, particularly of sophisticated capital equipment, mandatory. Despite the national objective of employment creation in South Africa, automation will probably increase – for instance, it occurs more and more in the automotive industry. There are a number of reasons for this, including the requirement for cost containment, higher quality standards, and imported designs that are contingent upon automated manufacturing processes.

It is a feature of a developing economy that the percentage that is represented by industrial goods continues to increase *vis-à-vis* consumer goods. Thus it is estimated that the market for industrial goods in the USA is between 65 and 70%

of the total market for industrial and consumer goods. The marketing costs for industrial goods are not as high as is the case for consumer goods, but have nevertheless been rising, particularly in the case of direct selling. Thus, effective industrial advertising can play an important role in lowering the total costs of marketing industrial goods and it can be predicted with safety that industrial advertising will play an ever-increasing and more important role in industrial marketing.

☐ Distinctive features of industrial marketing and advertising

There are a number of specific and distinctive features of industrial marketing that have a definite influence on industrial advertising. Those having most relevance to industrial advertising are discussed below.

The number of industrial customers is usually limited

Typically, market segments are more distinct than is the case with consumer markets. Therefore, especially where specialised segments are concerned, industrial advertising makes use of specific trade journals.

The assumption that buying is on a rational, objective and economic basis

There are counter-indications, however, that the buying of industrial goods does not always occur on this basis, since buying decisions are not made by organisations, but by people. Obviously, the industrial advertiser will have to find a suitable balance between the objective and the subjective in his advertising appeal.

Most industrial buying decisions are made by a group of people

This group is normally referred to as the decision making unit (DMU) and the industrial advertiser should identify and recognise the role of a number of persons who usually influence the buying decision.

Information is essential

Because the industrial buyer is a professional buyer, information on industrial products is essential. For the industrial advertiser the dilemma is to present substantial technical information without allowing the copy to become dull.

The buying process often extends over a long period

One American study showed that for the average industrial purchase 1,4 years elapsed between the realisation of needs and the final decision as to the make to be purchased (Buckner 1967:4). Under these circumstances the industrial advertiser would be aiming his message at his potential customer for a considerable period of time.

Many industrial buyers are conservative and resistant to change

This has to be taken into account when industrial advertising copy is prepared.

Word of mouth advertising

There is evidence of the importance of 'word of mouth' advertising based on the general credibility of the marketer.

Specialised service is extremely important

Owing to the technical complexity of many industrial products, specialised service is extremely important. Advertising such a specialised service may give an industrial marketer a way to differentiate an otherwise undifferentiated product.

The buyer buys his perception of the capability of the supplier

Particularly with regard to capital equipment, the buyer may be buying something that is completely unspecified – indeed, he is buying a vague promise of something that is to be delivered at some future, uncertain date. In effect, the buyer is buying his perception of the capability of the supplier and obviously advertising can play an important role in the creation of this perception.

The geographical concentration of industrial markets

One striking feature of industrial markets is their geographical concentration. In fact, in South Africa it has been calculated that some 70% of the total industrial production is concentrated in less than 1,5% of the geographical area. In the light of this, for industrial advertising one would want to find media (if available) with a concentrated geographic focus.

To summarise, it is clear that many of the distinguishing characteristics of industrial goods have an important bearing on industrial advertising and consequently the marketing practitioner would be wise to bear these in mind.

☐ Classification of industrial goods

A number of classifications of industrial goods are presented in table 9.1. The last column of the table is particularly interesting as it links the classification with the role that advertising can play.

Table 9.1
Types of industrial goods and advertising strategies pursued

Type of industrial goods	Typical marketing situation	Typical advertising strategies pursued
Capital goods	Capital goods are usually differentiated and distinctive goods. Industrial advertising should stress the generalised reputation of the supplier, since the goods will often be judged in terms of the image of the supplier. Products may be complex and require personal selling.	Stress the image of the supplier (eg his R & D capabilities). Credibility is important. Stress distinctive features and benefits of the product, emphasising its 'unique selling propositions'. Personal selling may be important.
Industrial raw materials and spare parts	Products tend to be undifferentiated. Marketing problem is how to achieve at least some differentiation. Advertising strategy may seek to differentiate by stressing service factors.	Stress the total system within which, for example, spare parts operate. Pay more, but you get regular supply 'of consistent quality'. Underplay product characteristics since products are equal to competitive offerings.

Table 9.1
Types of industrial goods and advertising strategies pursued (continued)

Type of industrial goods	Typical marketing situation	Typical advertising strategies pursued
Industrial supplies (consumables)	Competition keen, with many suppliers who can offer essentially the same product. Peripheral services may become even more important to achieve distinction. Differentiation as far as products are concerned is difficult to achieve.	Create an image of 'one-stop' shopping, of a supplier that can offer the whole range of supplies. Advertising should cast the net wide, since many potential new buyers may require these products.
Industrial services	Some services may be offered as part of the abovementioned products. Certain services (eg marketing consulting) are very dependent on the calibre of the individuals involved and the image of the organisation.	Advertising should contribute particularly to the general image of the organisation. Credibility is important.

Table 9.1 outlines the situation in which the marketer of a specific type of industrial goods (or service) typically finds himself. The last column in the table outlines the advertising strategies usually pursued and some useful generalisations can be drawn from these. Using table 9.1 as its basis, table 9.2 provides guidelines for advertising. In table 9.2 the type of industrial goods and advertising strategies are linked.

Table 9.2
Some advertising guidelines linking the type of industrial goods and advertising strategies

☐ The more differentiated the industrial goods, the more likely that product features and benefits may be stressed. *Comment:* Since capital goods are more likely to be differentiated than industrial supplies, more opportunities for creating unique selling propositions (USPs) are presented by capital goods.
☐ Since capital equipment usually represents large (single) expenditures in absolute terms, the generalised reputation of the supplier will remain important.
☐ The less differentiated the product: – the less important product features and benefits will be – the more important price will be – the more important supplier-related aspects (such as service aspects, eg delivery service, reliability of supply, credit, etc) will be – the more important industrial advertising to find new clients who can buy the same products will be.

☐ Identifying and reaching buying influences

An important distinctive feature of industrial marketing is that the buying decision is usually taken by many persons in the buying organisation, all of whom influence the final decision to some extent. Understandably, they are known as *buying influences*.

A buying influence can be defined as follows: 'A buying influence is any person who becomes involved in or contributes to the problem solving or decision making activities in the buying process'. Thus industrial marketing differs from the marketing of consumer goods, where the final consumer is usually able to decide for himself what he wants to buy and has to consider relatively few (if any) other persons in his decisions.

Two reasons in particular explain why anyone finds himself in the position of a buying influence. First, a person's organisational position may provide him with the authority of responsibility to influence certain buying decisions, and second, a person may have certain expert knowledge necessary for a particular buying decision.

In addition to being able to identify the buying influences, it is especially important that the industrial advertiser is able to recognise whether any person(s) among the buying influences dominates or represents a specific decision. Just as some markets distinguish a 'centre of gravity' in the different buying phases, so we can speak of a centre of gravity in buying influences. What this amounts to is that very often one or more persons may have an especially important influence on some particular buying transaction, and the identification of such a person or persons may facilitate the industrial advertiser's task.

A typical example of persons representing such a 'centre of gravity' is to be found in the South African building industry, where influential people in the design phase determine the materials to be used and the equipment to be installed in a building during the building stage. They are known as *specifiers*. The industrial advertiser should understand the flow of influence in the entire buying chain and should direct his advertising at these specifiers early on in the buying process.

Number of buying influences

The persons who make a particular buying decision are referred to in the literature as the decision making unit (DMU). Notice that in practice the constitution of the DMU is subject to periodic, and in extreme cases even rapid, change, especially in industries that undergo rapid technological development or expand owing to take-overs or mergers.

The DMU consists of a number of persons. For example, a *Business Week* study concluded that on average 3,5 persons are involved in a typical non-repetitive purchase, while 4,4 are involved in a repetitive purchase. *Factory* magazine, on the other hand, determined that 11,9 persons – exclusive of the purchasing department – are involved in an average purchase (Thorelli 1966:16). The findings show that on average six persons are concerned with an industrial purchase (Industrial Advertising Research Institute 1967:93).

This author calculated that in the South African metal industry, 5,4 people influence a buying decision in companies with more than 1 000 employees, 4,5 persons influence a buying decision in companies with between 501 and 1 000 workers, 3,7 persons influence a buying decision in companies with between 201 and 500 employees, and 2,4 persons influence buying decisions in companies with between 21 and 200 workers.

☐ Buying motives

For many years one of the classic distinctive features of industrial advertising has been the assumption that the industrial buyer approaches his task rationally and objectively with a view to deriving the maximum economic benefit for his company. It can be argued that since goods are bought for business purposes, it can be expected that reason and judgement rather than emotional reactions will be the dominant factors influencing purchases. However, much in the literature indicates that this assumption of objectivity cannot be taken for granted and that emotional factors do play a part in the industrial buying process.

Emotional determinants of the buyer's activities

One of the most detailed studies of the emotional factors concerned in the industrial buying process was undertaken by Robert Shoaf and was based on the techniques of motivational research. The following principal findings of the study undoubtedly have important implications for the industrial marketer (Shoaf 1959:9):

1 The industrial buyer is more human in his buying habits than industrial marketers realise.
2 While administrative, production, engineering, and purchasing managers differ functionally, they all have common management interests.
3 Needs exist everywhere in industry, but industrial marketing is not doing a sufficiently creative job in changing them to wants.
4 To the extent that products and services become more objectively alike, the buyers' final decisions are based more and more on subjective emotional factors.
5 Your customers are your best prospects.

In his commentary on Shoaf's study, Lazo (in Hancock 1960:265) points out that 'fear is one of the major influences in industrial buying. Fear of displeasing the boss. Fear of making a wrong decision. Fear of committing the company to substantial outlays. Fear of making a mistake. Fear of losing face with the boss or with one's associates. Fear of losing status. Fear, indeed, in extreme cases, of losing one's job.' Robertson (in Hancock 1960:273) says the following: 'These particular respondents (buying influences) showed, in effect, some degree of fear of having superiors disagree with their actions or opinions . . . This suggests that many buyers are apt to stick to what they think management want rather than to recommend what, in their judgment, is best.'

According to Lazo (in Hancock 1960:265), one of the main implications of the above is the image of the conformist and 'organization man' as the buyer who ' . . . needs personal reassurance. He needs confidence. He needs to be able to have faith in people. But let's not overlook the basic truth that purchasing executives are *purchasing people*, and that as long as people are people, they are going to continue to behave like people, to be influenced like people, and to buy like people'. This may appear to over-emphasise the emotional factors in the industrial buying process, but Lazo points out elsewhere that 'the buyer is both rational and emotional', which is certainly a more balanced view. The whole question is perhaps best summarised by Fullerton (in Shoaf 1959:55) as follows: 'They (industrial customers) have economic buying motives — but they're still human beings'.

Another study of buying motives brought to light further interesting data, among them the fact that product quality is decisive in the various buying influences. 'The report indicates that no reason for buying is a major appeal to more than a third of its buyers' (Industrial Advertising Research Institute 1959:93). The importance of approval for the actions of the buying influence is described as follows: 'The findings indicate that the final decision-maker in a purchase is influenced by his superiors and his associates. He "wants" to be reassured that he has made the right decision' – a conclusion that agrees with Lazo's finding (in Hitchcock 1960:265). The report is also important because it applies to the industrial situation the motivational research which so far has been applied mainly in the field of the marketing of consumer goods, and 'the indirect techniques are a source of added information on buying motives, ideas and basic attitudes which can go undiscovered if market researchers depend on direct-type questioning entirely' (Industrial Advertising Research Institute 1959:17).

Behavioural buying model

Kernan and Sommers' *behavioural matrix model* provides insight into the approach the industrial marketer can use to analyse the buyer's probable buying motives in different situations so that he can adapt his selling strategy to them. Two basic series of variables are distinguished:

☐ the role and nature of the organisation concerned ('institutional role commitment'), which may be innovative, adaptive or lethargic

☐ the occupational role type of the buyer, which may be novel, established or obsolete (Kernan and Sommers 1966:59).

An example of the use of this model is when the marketer stresses to the hyperconservative (obsolete) buyer employed by an antipathic (lethargic) undertaking the 'safety' of the purchase of a particular product for his undertaking. In fact, in this case the advertising should emphasise the general credibility of the marketer to engender a feeling of security in the buyer.

Buying reasons influencing choice of capital equipment: a South African survey

Obviously, the industrial advertiser is interested in why the buyers of capital equipment buy one make of capital equipment in preference to another. The results of a research survey undertaken in the South African metal industry by this author are shown in table 9.3.

Table 9.3
Choosing capital equipment: results of a South African survey (710 replies)

Reasons for choosing between alternative brands of capital equipment	%
Possible savings resulting from the use of the equipment (eg savings in operating or maintenance costs)	18,9
Reliability of the equipment	16,5
Quality of the products produced	14,3
Price	13,6
Other sought-after characteristics (eg desired capacity, longevity)	10,2
New equipment identical to current equipment leading to standardisation	9,7
Technical service aspects (eg technical service readily available)	4,6
Delivery	3,2
Financing available (eg supplier offers credit, leasing, etc)	3,0
Other reasons	6,0
	100,0

Source: Van Veijeren, CF. DBA study in the SA Metal Industry, p 109

It is interesting to note that economic reasons seem to be more important than others such as technical reasons. Possible savings were mentioned as the most important reason, reliability as the second, quality of the products produced as the third and price, possibly surprisingly, as the fourth most important reason. It is interesting to note the position of price, which is certainly consistent with modern marketing philosophy to try and get the 'heat off' price and stress other non-price competitive factors. There is no doubt, however, that the difference in preference among the various reasons is relatively small, and that in practice these various factors are considered simultaneously. One buyer said: 'We cannot answer this question as it entirely depends on our particular circumstances at a given time and the kind of equipment under discussion'. Another buyer said: 'All aspects are taken into account'.

The industrial advertiser is faced with a dilemma – ideally he should stress a particular USP (or only a limited number of features or benefits) from the point of view of good communication, but a number of factors all seem to play a role. On top of this, the motives of each of the members of the DMU (decision making unit) at the various levels and functions of the organisation may differ.

Importance of the image of a company

Increasing attention is being paid to the image that a company projects in the market-place, and nowadays it is recognised that the 'beliefs' of clients are based more often on perceptions than on reality. Furthermore, the way in which service is provided forms part of the total package of the product. A client's combined impression of the product and the services offered is often also based on his impression of the general reputation of the marketer. Clearly, the industrial marketer's advertising has much to contribute to the creation of such an image.

An American study provides a striking illustration of the importance of a good image of the undertaking to the industrial marketer. In a survey undertaken in the chemical industry in the USA, industrial salesmen had to indicate which factors – placed in order of importance – they considered to be most important in industrial marketing (Messner 1963:45). The results are shown in table 9.4.

Table 9.4
Factors, in order of importance, influencing the sale of machinery and tools

Factor	% of salesmen who mentioned the factor
Product quality and performance	98
Salesman's integrity and reputation	85
Technical service and handling	67
Punctuality in delivery	59
Reliability of delivery	50
Prices and discount	45
Completeness of the product line	43

Source: Messner 1963:45

As expected, product quality and performance headed the list, but the salesman's integrity and reputation came second, thus showing that the subjective appraisal of the seller's undertaking is important in industrial sales. Factors such as technical service and handling, punctuality in delivery and reliability of delivery are sometimes judged subjectively as well. In other words perceptions play an important role and these may well be favourably influenced by advertising.

The general reputation and reliability of a marketer is often referred to as his 'high-credibility' undertaking (Levitt 1965:49). Usually, the higher the credibility of a company the easier it becomes for its salesmen to 'get in' and get a good hearing. Due to the complexity of the capital goods sales situation, the closer one moves to the final sale the more important the role of the salesman tends to become. In fact, in the final sales situation Levitt, in his classic study, found the following:

'However, to get favourable action in final decision-making situations (adoption), a good presentation by an anonymous company is much better than a poor one by a well-known company. Hence, face to face presentation is more important in the final analysis than advertising or public relations' (Levitt 1965:88).

Healy (1969:19) distinguished four situations in which the image of an undertaking is important for marketing purposes, namely

□ where the undertaking and the product have the same name – for obvious reasons

□ where the product has a subsidiary role and the accent falls mainly on the service

□ where the product (or service) has not been standardised and the credibility of the undertaking is highly important

□ where the product or services of rival undertakings do not differ much from those offered by the undertaking.

□ The actual distribution of industrial marketing costs

In practice, industrial companies use both personal selling and advertising. Thus it is interesting to note the results of an actual study of these components for 745 US firms (see table 9.5).

Table 9.5
Marketing costs of
745 companies

Cost item	%
Advertising	1,6
Direct selling	6,3
Warehouse and delivery	2,1
Other marketing costs	2,9
Total of sales	12,9

Source: LAP report No 8015.4

From these generalised results for industrial marketers it would appear that they spend about four times as much on personal selling as on advertising. Another interesting trend is that the smaller the sales of a company, the higher its spending on marketing and advertising tends to be. This is shown in table 9.6

Table 9.6
Marketing costs by
amount of sales
(%)

Sales volume	No of advertising firms		Direct selling	Warehouse & delivery	Other marketing costs	Total % of sales
Under $1 million	38	2,8	7,8	2,2	3,8	16,7
$1-25 million	419	1,8	7,1	2,2	3,2	14,3
25-50 million	95	1,3	5,3	2,1	2,6	11,3
50-100 million	92	1,4	4,9	2,0	2,3	10,5
100-250 million	43	0,8	4,3	1,9	1,6	8,6
250-500 million	24	0,8	4,9	2,4	1,5	9,6
Over 500 million	28	1,2	5,8	2,3	2,3	11,6
Average	745	1,6	6,3	2,1	2,9	12,9

Source: LAP Report No 8015.4

Cost of industrial sales calls

One of the crucial arguments in favour of industrial advertising hinges on the costs of an industrial sales call in relation to the cost per publication contact. Soaring personal selling costs have become particularly important in the South African context, where we have the world's third most expensive motor cars, relatively expensive petrol and large distances. The McGraw-Hill Laboratory of Advertising Performance has monitored these costs over many years and found that the average cost of an industrial sales call was $205,40 in 1983 in the USA, a figure that was 15,4% higher than in 1981. 'The average cost of getting a person to see an advertisement in a business publication is just 18c (US), 5,9% higher than in 1981' (LAP Report No 7020.6). It should be borne in mind that this study refers to industrial goods in general and not to capital equipment specifically. One could reasonably expect that the cost of an industrial salesman's call would be considerably higher due to the more complicated nature of the product that he sells. In one instance known to the author, the costs of one sales call made by salesmen from a specialised industrial rubber goods company in South Africa amounted to R875. Amounts of R70 to R200 are probably more common in South Africa.

Table 9.7
Changes in the cost of a sales call (US) since 1942

1942		$ 9,02
1977		$ 96,79
	10 salesmen	$128,69
	50 salesmen	$ 70,06
1980		$170,00
1981		$200,00
1983	10 salesmen	$290,00
	Average	$205,40

Source: LAP Reports. 1983 figure from LAP Report No 8013.7

It is interesting to note why the cost of personal selling is so high: The average salesperson works longer than 9½ hours a day, but can devote only three hours and 42 minutes to face-to-face selling. Travelling, waiting, attending sales meetings, making reports and doing other paperwork use up more than half of his time (LAP Report No 7023.1). The average salesperson spends a working day on the following activities:

- ☐ Face-to-face selling 39%
- ☐ Travelling and waiting for interviews 32%
- ☐ Reports, paperwork, sales meetings 24%
- ☐ Service calls 5%

Sales calls required to close a sale

Of course in practice there is one further problem, and that is that it takes a number of sales calls to successfully close an industrial sale, a matter which has also been researched by the Laboratory of Advertising Performance (see table 9.8).

Table 9.8
Number of sales calls required to close a sale

6% of sales were closed after 1 call
9% of sales were closed after 2 calls
34% of sales were closed after 3 calls
18% of sales were closed after 4 calls
13% of sales were closed after 5 calls
7% of sales were closed after 6 calls

Source: LAP

In a later research study the number of sales calls required to close a sale were found to be 5,5 and the total cost for one was found to amount to $1 129,70 (LAP Report No. 8051.2).

Calculation of the average cost of getting a person to see an ad

In a US study the circulation figures for 29 business publications were taken individually and multiplied by 80%, which is the actual average issue readership (LAP Report No. 7020.6:3) This study also found that the average seen score is 55%, which was then multiplied by the previously obtained score. An example of this calculation is shown in table 9.9.

Table 9.9
Example of 'seen advertising costs'

46 000 circulation
x 80% average current issue readership
————
36 800
x 55% average seen score
————
20 240
$3 600 (cost for 1 page at the 2 colour, 6 time rate): 24 240 = 14,8c

Source: LAP Report No 7020.6:3

The major point that emerges from this calculation is the small cost of a 'contact' through the print medium. Since this cost relationship is so favourable compared with the cost of personal selling, the question is why the capital goods marketer cannot simply use the print media only. This choice will now be discussed.

Comments on the cost and choice of personal sales and advertising

From the previous section it is quite clear that the industrial marketer is faced with a dilemma: On one hand the costs of industrial salesmen's sales visits have risen steadily over the years and have now reached very high levels. On the other, the effectiveness of selling in the face-to-face situation must obviously be higher than is possible with industrial advertising. But industrial advertising has at least three important contributions to make to assisting the industrial sale, namely:

☐ finding new prospects for the product, usually at a very attractive rate from the cost effectiveness point of view

☐ contributing to the general image of the marketer

☐ contributing some specific product characteristics, ideally unique to the marketer's offering and not offered by anybody else.

The main factors in favour of personal selling over industrial advertising and vice versa are presented in figure 9.1. In practice the choice is never an either/or choice (one or the other), but rather one of the logical mix of personal selling assisted by industrial advertising.

Figure 9.1
Factors
influencing the
choice between
personal sales and
industrial
advertising

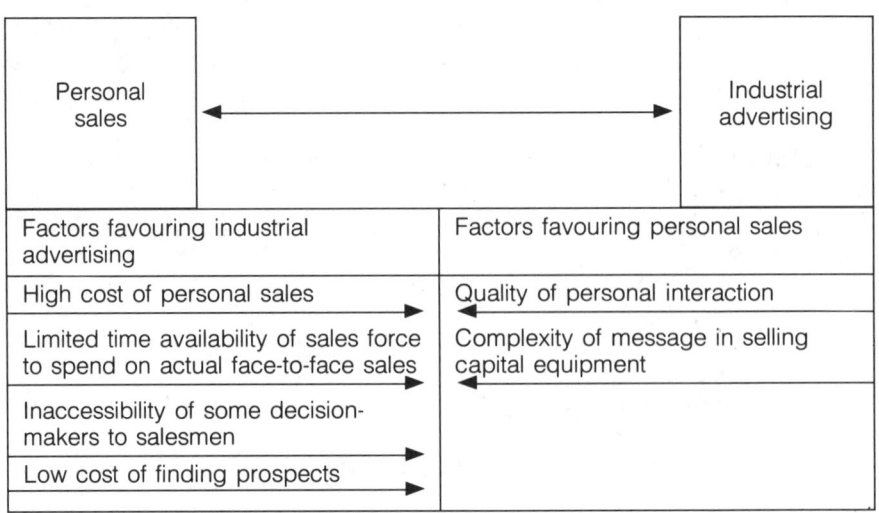

☐ The industrial advertising plan

It is important to formalise the results in a formal written document. In fact, research conducted by Thune and House (1970) has clearly demonstrated the value of formal written planning. In their study they contrasted the performance of formal (ie written) planners with informal (mainly verbal) planners, and found that the formal planners clearly outperformed the informal planners (Thune & House 1970:81-87).

The advertising plan is part of the promotional plan, which in turn is part of the marketing plan, which again is one of the functional plans forming part of the overall corporate strategy. In fact, various plans can be thought of as being part of a hierarchy of plans. The interrelationship between them is set out schematically in figure 9.2

Figure 9.2
Interrelationship of
the advertising
plan with the
marketing and
corporate plans

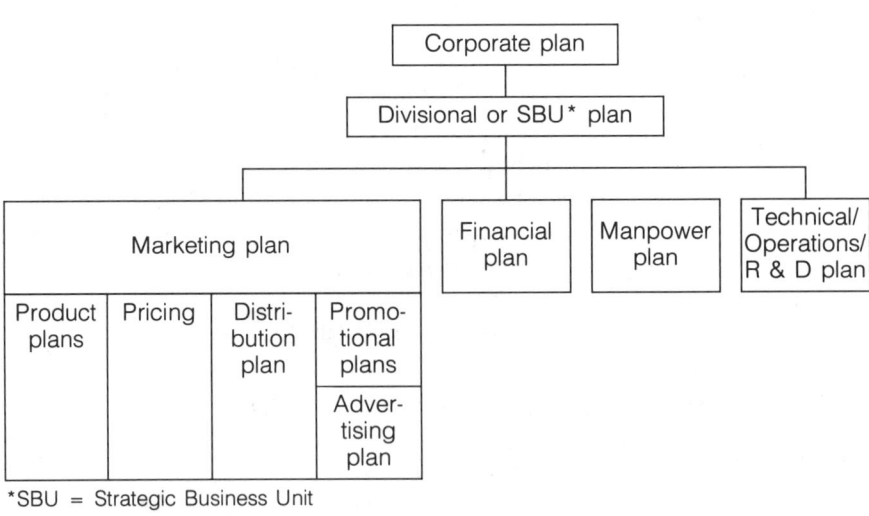

One important principle that should be taken into account when the interrelationships between these plans are considered, is the planning principle of internal consistency. Clearly, the advertising appeals that form part of the corporate plan should also be reflected and executed in the advertising plan. On the other hand, if it becomes clear at the advertising plan level that a certain advertising appeal as directed by the corporate plan is unrealistic (eg the company cannot really live up to the claims), it is important that feedback of this nature should be sent up in the planning hierarchy. A close interrelationship of this nature is obviously particularly important.

The process outlined above is often referred to as a hierarchy of planning, the major objective being to ensure consistency of objectives between the various levels of planning. These various levels are shown in figure 9.2 and are typically the corporate, the divisional (or the Strategic Business Unit or SBU level) and the functional level. One of these functional level plans will be the marketing plan.

The format of an industrial advertising plan

What should be included in the industrial advertising plan? The list can probably never be complete, but it could be expected that at least the elements outlined in table 9.10 should be included.

Table 9.10
Format of the advertising plan

Objectives	State concisely the current situation that advertising should address. Ideally, objectives should be quantified.
Major advertising strategies	Strategies should state how the objectives should be achieved. Major appeals, themes and tone of advertising should be stated.
Budgets	Budgets should state how much money is available, which in turn should be based on the advertising objectives to be achieved. Budgets should reflect how much is to be spent on the major types of advertising media.
Media schedules	Media schedules should reflect the implementation of the advertising plan, since what is being done, when it is being done and how much it will cost will be reflected in the schedule.
Control of expenditures	Feedback on the actual expenditures makes comparison with the envisaged expenditures possible and can act as a control phase.
Advertising evaluation	At least some attempt should be made to determine whether the whole advertising action was effective. This may imply that money should be set aside for advertising research.

☐ Final conclusions and general guidelines regarding industrial advertising

The costs of personal selling (particularly the travel component) appear set to rise continuously. It seems reasonable to suggest that other forms of communication, particularly industrial advertising, will become increasingly important.

The perception of a marketer's image rather than reality seems to be whát counts in practice. Industrial advertising can contribute considerably to the establishment of a marketer's general image or credibility.

Many members of buying organisation's DMUs are inaccessible to personal selling; industrial advertising offers an important approach to reach them effectively.

As far as buying motives in industrial marketing are concerned, subjective factors at the personal level cannot be discounted.

☐ References

Buckner, H. 1967. *How British industry buys.* London: Hutchinson.

Hancock, RS.(Ed). 1960. *Dynamic marketing for a changing world.* Chicago: AMA.

Healy, IAM. 1969. 'PR men told to study their markets'. *Industrial advertising and marketing,* March: 1969.

Industrial Advertising Research Institute. 1959. *Motives in industrial buying.* Princeton, NJ: NIAA Industrial Advertising Research Institute.

Kernan, JB & Sommers, MS. 1966. 'The behavioural matrix − A closer look at the industrial buyer'. *Business Horizons*, Summer: 59.

Levitt, T. 1965. *Industrial advertising.* New York: McGraw-Hill.

Shoaf, RF. 1959. 'Emotional factors underlying industrial purchasing.' Cleveland 13, Ohio: Sponsored by *Steel.*

Thorelli, HB. 1966. 'Who makes the purchasing decision?'. *Marketing Insights,* 31 October :16.

Thune, SS & House, RM. 1970. 'Where long-range planning pays off'. *Business Horizon,* 13: 81-87.

Communicating effectively with industrial buyers

Ludi Koekemoer

Introduction *369*

Characteristics of industrial marketing *369*

Characteristics of industrial buyers *370*

Profiling *371*

Contact cycles methodology *373*

Evaluating the campaign *374*

References *375*

☐ Introduction

Industrial marketing is dynamic and challenging. It reflects the ever-changing nature of the market-place due to changes in the political arena and the economic situation and improvements in technology, and it is growing significantly in complexity and sophistication.

Marketers and advertisers who need to communicate with the industrial market should realise that their marketing communication strategies will be different from marketing communications addressed to individual consumers or households.

☐ Characteristics of industrial marketing

The critical function performed by an industrial company (by every economic organisation) is the creation of customer or client satisfaction through the provision of goods and services carefully developed in response to customer needs and wants (Webster 1979:3). Industrial marketing concentrates on the marketing of goods and services to other industrial, intermediate and institutional clients or customers. These customers use the goods purchased in their production processes. Sometimes goods like raw materials, component parts, etc become part of the final industrial or consumer product. In other cases capital equipment is used in the production process and comprises physical production facilities. Goods may also be bought to be used as supplies in operations, repairs or maintenance activities. Examples are cleaning materials, fuel, etc. Services refer to all intangible 'products' and are often part of a package when physical products are bought, for example training which goes with a machine, after-sales service, etc.

Briefly, the distinguishing characteristics of industrial marketing are the following (Marx & Dekker 1982:539 & 540):

☐ There are relatively few buyers, in some cases even only a single buyer. This is particularly significant in *profiling,* discussed later.

☐ The demand for industrial products is derived from the demand for the final consumer goods produced by the industrial company.

☐ In many cases purchasing decisions occur more on the basis of economic, rational factors than on emotional factors.

☐ In certain instances (eg expensive capital equipment) more than one person is involved in the buying decision process.

☐ Detailed information (and sometimes demonstration) is important to the industrial buyer or decision-making unit (DMU).

☐ The negotiating and purchasing process often extends over a longer period and impulse buying seldom occurs.

☐ The purchasing process is often characterised by an unwillingness to change and therefore personal selling becomes very important.

☐ Face-to-face communication plays an important role.

☐ DMU's or industrial buyers often insist on specialised services due to the complexity of certain types of industrial products.

☐ Market fragmentation occurs and profiling the DMU or industrial buyer becomes very important.

☐ The industrial market is a highly concentrated market, for example in the PWV area, Cape Peninsula area, Durban/Pinetown area and PE/Uitenhage area.

☐ The 80:20 principle often occurs, that is 80% of the business is generated by 20% of the industrial firms. In many cases this ratio could be 95:5.

☐ Characteristics of industrial buyers

Industrial buyers are rarely individually responsible for the buying decision. Each person uses different criteria based on his experience, education, background, personality, sense of responsibility, etc to evaluate a supplier or product.

Industrial buyers have access to a multitude of information sources such as:

☐ sales representatives (eg personal selling)
☐ direct mail advertising material
☐ professional and technical conferences
☐ trade journals
☐ newsletters
☐ exhibitions and trade shows
☐ press releases.

They need product knowledge and consider the technical specifications and advantages, perceived risk, time factors (eg lead times), problem-solving attributes and price factors and relate these to their expectations (ie both personal and business/company related).

Reciprocity (ie I will buy from you if you buy from me) is often considered to be good business sense.

The orientation of the industrial firm is significant in industrial marketing and more specifically in profiling (identifying the buyer or DMU by name), because if the firm is more financially oriented, financial management will be most likely to make the buying decision. If, however, the firm is production oriented, the production manager or production buyer will probably make the decision.

☐ Profiling

Profiling is a systematic process of identifying the industrial buyer or decision-making unit (DMU) in a given firm by name.

Obviously, the first step is to segment the market into firms that buy or are potential buyers of the company's products. Once these firms have been identified it is necessary to obtain a profile of the buyer(s) responsible for purchasing the company's goods and services. It is necessary to know the following about each buyer:

☐ Is the buyer an individual or a DMU?

☐ If the buyer is an individual, his name, sex, age, type of job, level in the company, years of experience in that job, education, training, hobbies, interests, etc, must be ascertained, while it may be very useful to have information regarding his wife, his children (eg school level, participation in sport, etc), his holiday preferences, his and his wife and children's dates of birth, his wedding anniversary date, his aspirations, etc. Even details about his secretary may be useful.

☐ If the buyer is a DMU, the composition of the group, information on the group leader or most influential person, and on the DMU's decision-making process is important. (For example, one member of the group could be solely responsible for gathering information, but have no decision-making powers. It would be a waste of time to convince this person to buy your product, since he could be too junior with no authority. He could, however, pretend to be responsible for making the final decision.)

Once the profiling is complete, a list of each buyer or DMU's details which will be used in the contact cycle methodology (see 'Contact cycles methodology' must be compiled and fed into the computer.

If it is decided that the target prospects will be reached via advertising media like technical publications, etc, profiling provides a clear-cut target market segmentation.

It has been my experience that many advertisements in the industrial market are never read by the industrial buyer himself, or do not persuade him to consider buying the advertised product. For this reason it is essential to assess the results of the advertising campaign and to relate costs to effect. This can be illustrated in three simple graphs. (see figure 9.3, based on the advertising output curve and the advertising elasticity of demand in Marx & Dekker 1982:293).

Figure 9.3 shows that there is a certain noise level in the market, and that if expenditure on advertising is between Ro and Rx you will have no effect. Above Rx a particular effect, which could be awareness, the establishment of a particular image, the generation of leads, etc, can be achieved. It is essential to measure the specified objective effect on a regular basis to establish whether the money invested in the advertising is working for you or even against you.

Figure 9.3 illustrates three alternatives. Figure 9.3a shows that the more you spend on advertising, the more effect you will achieve. In figure 9.3b the effect is good up to a point, but more money will not increase the effect. In figure 9.3c the advertising works up to a point and then actually turns against you. This is often the case with humorous approaches, which attract attention initially, but after a while put readers off.

Figure 9.3
The advertising effect curve

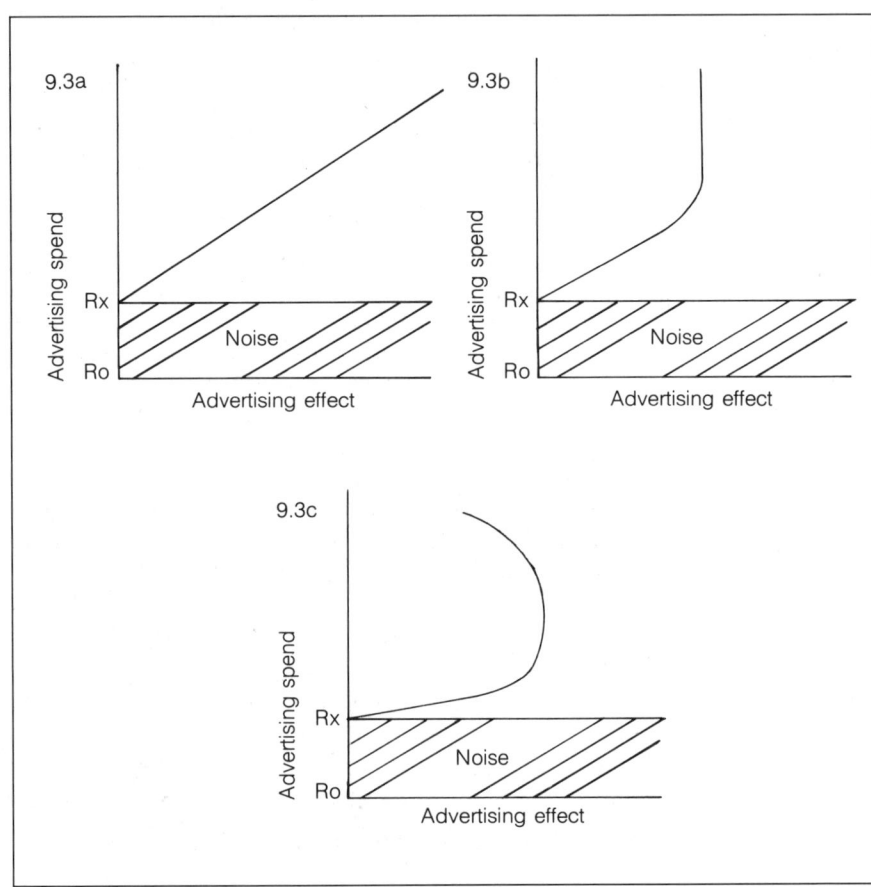

☐ Contact cycles methodology

A successful contact cycle is a preplanned cycle of profiling the prospect, then sending the buyer/DMU something visual and finally clinching the deal (see figure 9.4). The visual element could be a pull of the advertisement, a brochure, etc.

Figure 9.4
Contact cycle in industrial marketing

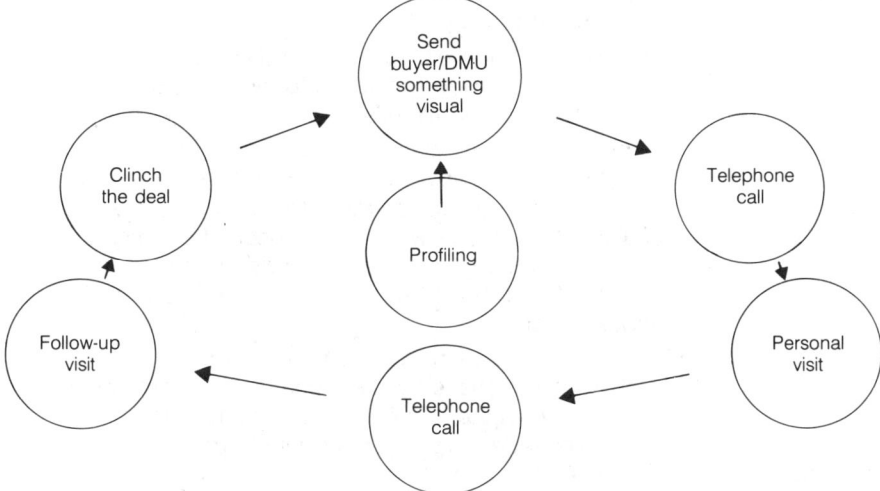

It is critical to do the profiling accurately, as this determines what visual element will be sent to the prospect. Does he want a letter, a brochure, a specification sheet, or a catalogue? On the other hand, if his secretary is known to block information, a telex or telegram may have to be sent.

The contact cycle is programmed in such a way that the advertiser/marketer knows exactly when to telephone the prospect. This call should be made one or two days after the prospect has received the mailing. The purpose of the call is to inform the prospect of who sent the mailing (to introduce yourself if he does not know you), to ensure that he has received the visual element sent and to arrange for a personal visit to discuss the matter.

Due to the fact that a careful profiling of the prospect provides accurate information, a personalised visual element or something which will capture his imagination must be prepared and sent to the prospect. This may mean that a number of different visual elements must be prepared, each with a specific prospect of DMU in mind. It is worth the money!

During the personal visit stage an effective presentation must be made to persuade the prospect to buy your product. Because industrial buyers are not readily willing to change, more information is often asked for as a stalling tactic during this stage. This gives you an opportunity to obtain the information and to telephone the buyer again to:

☐ thank him for the time he afforded you
☐ inform him that you have the additional information
☐ arrange a meeting

The follow-up visit in a critical one, as you will either clinch the deal or the buyer will give you a legitimate reason why he cannot give you the order (eg he has a long-term contract until such and such a date), or a flimsy reason, or a definite 'no'.

Prospects must then be grouped into three categories, namely:

☐ clients
☐ warm prospects
☐ long-term prospects.

A new contact cycle must be worked out for those prospects who have become clients and the policy should be to look after them, to get to know them very well, and to provide excellent service to them.

A contact cycle must also be worked out for the warm prospects. Experience has shown that the advertiser should position himself as his prospect's no 2 supplier. Regular contact, including visual material, telephone calls and personal visits should be made with the prospect. The moment the prospect is not satisfied with his current supplier or needs something in a hurry which his regular supplier cannot deliver, he must immediately call you and not start considering various suppliers.

Long-term prospects should be programmed into a lower key contact cycle which is characterised by fewer contracts per time period but with sufficient frequency to show the prospect that you have no intention of forgetting him. The idea is to change warm prospects into clients and long-term prospects into warm prospects and clients.

☐ Evaluating the campaign

The most important measure is *sales*. Often the sales figure is regarded subjectively as 'good', 'reasonable' or 'poor' without consideration being given to the investment in advertising and related costs incurred to generate the sales. The percentage return on investment is a very important measure to use and can easily be measured in four steps (see figure 9.5).

In *step 1* the media cost, advertising material cost and production cost (creativity and printing) are added to the cost of contacting the prospect to determine the total contact cycle cost.

In *step 2* the number of contacts is multiplied by the percentage of prospects who are willing to meet with you to discuss your product(s). This gives you the total number of leads and if you multiply this by the percentage conversion (ie successful sales) you get the total sales figure.

In *step 3* your net profit is calculated by deducting cost of sales from the sales figure to give gross profit. Deducting the contact cycle cost calculated in step 1 from the gross profit margin will give you net profit.

In the final step, *step 4*, the net profit is divided by the contact cycle investment (total cost) and multiplied by 100 to get the return on investment.

In this way you can quantify your communications/sales strategy. Constant measuring of different strategies will tell you which are better than others – not which strategy produced the largest sales figure regardless of cost, but in relation to cost.

Figure 9.5
Return on
advertising
investment
calculation

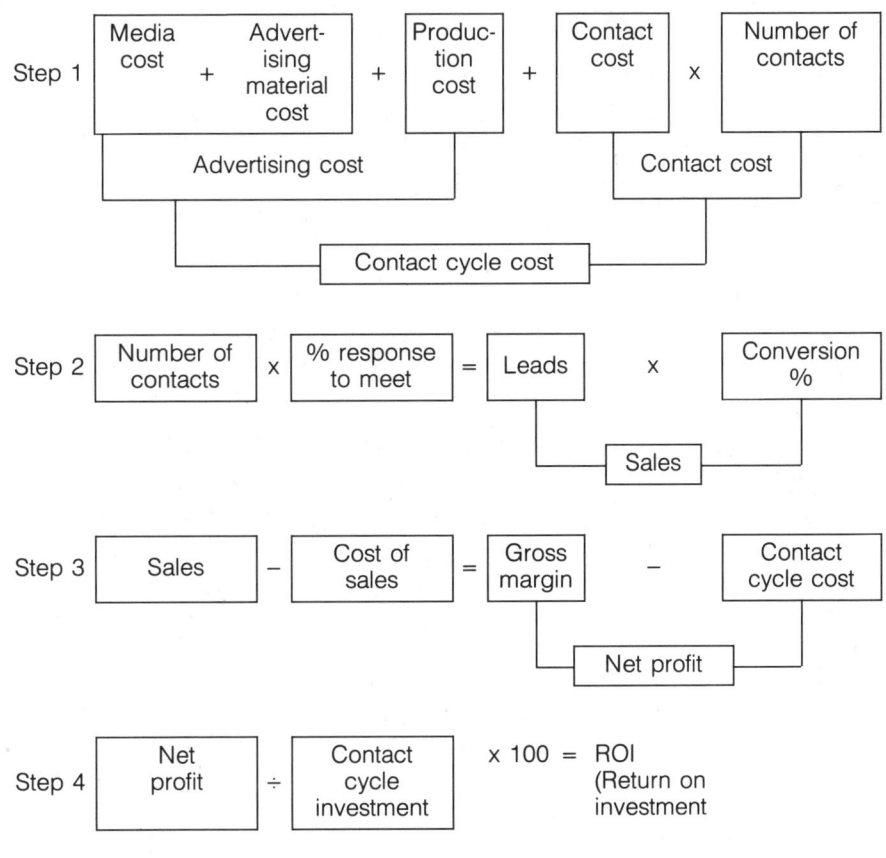

□ References

Webster, GE. 1979. *Industrial Marketing Strategy*. Ronald series on Marketing Manage-
    ment. New York: John Wiley & Sons.
Marx, S & Dekker, HJ. 1982. *Marketing Management: Principles and Decisions*. Pretoria:
    HAUM 1982.

10

Advertising to Blacks

Advertising to Blacks in print media   *379*

Communicating with the black market on television   *391*

Advertising to Blacks in print media
Ludi Koekemoer

Introduction	379
The literacy problem	380
The choice between audio, visual and print media	381
Advertising in print media	382
References	390

☐ Introduction

The question 'Why should the black market be singled out rather than regarded as part of the masses of consumers residing in South Africa?' often arises. The primary objective of advertising is to create awareness among a specific target audience of the existence, availability and usefulness of the advertised product or service and to stimulate interest in and enthusiasm for purchasing the product or service. Each target audience should be analysed and my experience in the black market suggests that it should be treated differently from other target audiences for the following reasons:

☐ Education
☐ Culture and tradition
☐ Perception
☐ Habits

With regard to the *educational* aspect, there are many Blacks in South Africa who are illiterate and cannot read or write. This phenomenon is more prevalent among older Blacks, and it is much easier to reach them by radio and television because these media reach them in their home languages. The use of printed media for advertising requires that the target audience is able to read and this automatically eliminates the illiterate from such media as newspapers, magazines, leaflets, brochures, etc.

As far as *cultural* and *traditional* issues are concerned, the role of the black man, the black woman and the black child is often different from that of their white counterparts. Furthermore, their spiritual beliefs and fears often play a significant role in their consumer behaviour. With regard to *habits*, for example eating habits, their enjoyment of food is different. The more they enjoy their food, the wider they open their mouths whilst eating, while in a white household the children are taught to eat with their mouths closed. Handing over money or an object to another person with the left hand is an insult to a black man, whilst this action is not significant among Whites.

Many such examples exist and their every day experiences lead to habits which are often different from those of their white counterparts. We also find that the way in which they dress, their use of cosmetics, wigs and jewellery, etc is often different from that of Whites. A common mistake made in advertising is to create an advertisement for the black market by a white creative team which does not understand the subtleties involved in the minds of its black audiences.

Perception is something which is closely related to education, culture, tradition, every day experiences and habits and many advertising agencies fail to understand that Blacks often interpret advertising messages literally. For example, if an advertising model is shown lying down (supposed to be resting or relaxing) he could be perceived to be lazy. A model dressed in a very expensive leather jacket could be perceived to be a Tsotsi rather than somebody who is well to do. I will never forget when I lectured to the marketing students at the University of Fort Hare on retail marketing and explained why a retail outlet such as OK Bazaars puts certain products on certain floors and uses music and colour combinations to stimulate the buying atmosphere. Towards the end of the lecture one student stopped me and mentioned that almost a third of the class had never been inside an OK Bazaars. I felt like someone trying to explain to a blind person what green looks like. I then realised that Blacks' perceptions are sometimes totally different from those of Whites, simply because they have not experienced the same things as their white counterparts, or because they may have experienced things which Whites have not experienced.

☐ The literacy problem

Soweto has often been called the pulse of the urban black market. A number of literacy studies have been conducted among Blacks in Soweto and a recent study conducted by the author indicated that the literacy rate of Sowetan Blacks over the age of 16 is 76%. This means that 24% of the adult Blacks in Soweto are still illiterate. The literacy rate will increase as more youngsters reach the age of 16 and they are far more literate than their older counterparts. However, it must be borne in mind that approximately 61% of all Blacks still reside in rural or non-urban areas. Should the language in which Blacks are communicated with be the vernacular languages, English or Afrikaans? Most black people prefer to speak English for reasons which range from historical, to status, to political. Nevertheless, the majority of black people are required to know one or both of the official languages. This language could be English if the black person works for a multinational company in Johannesburg, but could be Afrikaans if he works as a farm labourer on a farm in the Orange Free State.

Accurate statistics regarding the literacy of the black peoples in the various regions of South Africa are extremely difficult to come by, but my research suggests that the literacy rate could be as high as 78% in the urban areas and as low as 30% in the rural areas. This is important not only when a decision has to be made as to what medium to use in advertising to Blacks, but also with regard to the three-dimensional perception issue.

Three-dimensional perception is a phenomenon relating to a person's education and every day experiences. The higher his educational level, the less likely he is to experience problems with three-dimensional perception. A study conducted by the author found that Blacks aged 16 to 20 who had no schooling experienced exactly the same problems with three-dimensional perception as white children between the ages of three and six (pre-school children). People with no education cannot perceive depth, and therefore a picture of a person standing in the foreground with a house in the background will be seen out of perspective and the size relationships will appear to be wrong. Everything will be seen on the same level. This often creates problems in advertising, because Blacks who have little or no education consider advertisements of this type to be unbelievable. Their opinion is based on the fact that they cannot perceive in three dimensions.

☐ The choice between audio, visual and print media

Chapter six, 'Media planning', contains a contribution on media opportunities for the black market. Note should be taken of the coverage of TV2 and TV3, the viewership data for television, the readership penetration of magazines and newspapers, the listenership reach potential of radio and the penetration of cinema. The crucial question, however, is whether the target audience is educated.

It would be a total waste of money to advertise a product aimed at illiterate Blacks in magazines or newspapers. Furthermore, the product to be advertised could be better suited to an audio-visual medium such as television or cinema, or an audio medium such as radio. On the other hand, when the advertiser wants to communicate important information to his target audience and back it with proof in the form of an illustration, outdoor or printed media should be used.

Television is fast becoming the most popular advertising medium in the black market because it appeals to virtually all the senses, but its coverage is still somewhat limited to urban areas only. Broadcast AMPS January to March 1986 Report suggests that the average day viewership of TV2 is as follows (the TV2 languages are Zulu and Xhosa and the urban black population is 4 831 000):

☐ Mondays to Fridays 21,0%
☐ Saturdays   23,1%
☐ Sundays   19,7%

The corresponding figures for TV3 are (the TV3 languages are South Sotho, North Sotho and Tswana):

☐ Mondays to Fridays 25,9%
☐ Saturdays   23,8%
☐ Sundays   20,1%

It is noteworthy to record that Blacks are avid viewers of TV1:

☐ Mondays to Fridays 17,8%
☐ Saturdays   20,0%
☐ Sundays   13,6%

Channel switching between TV1 and TV2/3 occurs quite frequently.

When we look at radio, especially the 'yesterday' listenership potential reach, it is evident from AMPS '85 that Radio Bantu is the most popular radio station and its 'yesterday' listenership is as follows:

☐ PWV area   51,8%
☐ E Cape & Ciskei   51,9%

- ☐ OFS & Central Cape 53,8%
- ☐ Rest of Transvaal 60,2%
- ☐ Cape Peninsula 63,1%
- ☐ Natal 63,6%

According to AMPS '85, the newspaper which achieved the highest readership penetration was *Sowetan*, with a readership of 20,9% of urban Blacks. This is not, however, a nationally distributed newspaper. Magazines obtaining more than 20% readership penetration according to AMPS '85 were *Drum* (21%), *Pace* (23,2%), and *Bona* (30,1%) (urban Blacks).

It is envisaged that more and more Blacks will become regular viewers of television as their affluence and access of electricity increase. On the other hand, Radio Bantu remains a popular radio station and black readership of newspapers and magazines will increase as black literacy increases.

☐ Advertising in print media

An exhaustive list of principles relating to the various aspects of advertising in print media, for example attracting attention and creating initial interest, communicating relevant information and maintaining interest, inducing adoption of the relevant information and persuading the prospect are given in *Print Media Advertising, Some Basic Principles* (Koekemoer 1978). A select number of principles will be discussed here, in particular those which have proved to be important or to have more relevance to every day advertising attempts or campaigns.

Attracting attention and creating initial interest

☐ A successful advertisement reflects the brand or service favourably without directing undue attention to itself.

Selectivity is practised when a prospect pages through a newspaper or magazine. The prospect should be able to see immediately which brand or service is advertised and will not spend time and effort searching for the product or brand name when it is hidden. Some advertisers try to move away from the so-called stereotyped format by adopting an unusual approach which may attract the prospect's attention. Although novelty can be successful in attracting the prospect's attention, it is no guarantee that the advertising message will be communicated successfully. Experience suggests that novelty often creates confusion, and trying to be clever results in misunderstanding of the advertising message. It is not suggested that a 'clever piece of advertising' will be ineffective, but that the advertisement should not attract attention to itself – it should skilfully attract attention to the product or service advertised. Semi-nudity is often used to attract the readers' attention to an advertisement, but whilst the attention-value of the model in a bikini is high, the attention-value of the product in the advertisement could be low.

☐ No amount of advertising copy can attract the prospects' attention more effectively than an illustration.

In print advertising the presence or absence of a picture or illustration can cause marked differences to the attention-value of an advertisement. The illustration could feature people, a situation and the product. It performs the task of selecting the audience for the advertisement. An illustration can also depict rewards by featuring what the product will do for the consumer. Illustrations are especially suited to setting the mood for the prospect or creating a certain atmosphere, for example of empathy, quality, efficiency, freshness, etc. Illustrations help prospects to identify the product and create a user image and a situation image. An advertisement without an illustration is dull, uninteresting and unattractive – the old saying 'a picture is worth a thousand words' is relevant here.

☐ A picture of a person using a product is more natural and attention-grabbing than a still life of the product.

People are more interested in other people doing things in various situations than they are in a product on its own. Stationary objects and people in an advertisement often appear lifeless, posed, unnatural and dull. A good illustration of a person using the brand can attract the prospect's attention and arouse his interest so that he reads the copy to establish what the product can do for him. Moving objects bring life, excitement and interest to the advertising message. In advertising aimed at Blacks, the use of a series of pictures progressing from left to right, top to bottom, is extremely successful because it tells a story, moving logically, from problem identification to the products that should be used to the end result, which is satisfaction. Furthermore, these pictures are proof that the user has in fact obtained satisfaction from using the brand.

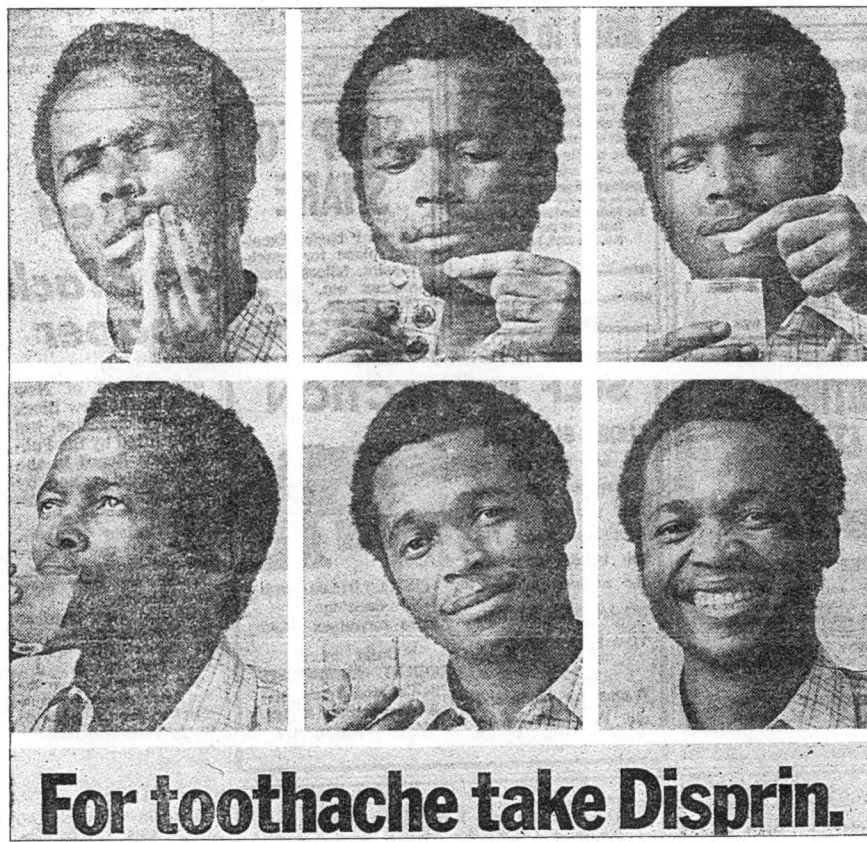

For toothache take Disprin.

Courtesy: Reckitt & Colman South Africa. The best example in South Africa of a series of pictures telling a story – no body copy is necessary

However, any illustration used must be relevant to the basic message of the advertisement. For example, an illustration of a black woman cleaning her house in her best dress and high heel shoes, or smiling happily as she does the dishes is totally out of keeping with reality. Careful attention should be paid to make-up, clothing, jewellery, the background setting, etc. Note that it has been proved that pictures rather than drawings should be used to illustrate advertising aimed at Blacks.

☐ A headline should be specific, relevant and understandable.

The headline enables a prospect to selectively screen those advertisements in a newspaper or magazine which offer him a specific reward or promise satisfaction of a particular need. Advertisers should not make the prospect guess what the advertisement is all about, and therefore advertisements often alert the prospect by means of headlines such as 'What every pregnant woman should know', or 'Men rate Gunston great'. However, the use of headlines involves a compromise – the more selective they are the fewer readers will be attracted to them, but the higher their attention-value.

Headlines should be in understandable language which can be interpreted without any confusion. It must be remembered that many Blacks have very little education and may experience difficulties comprehending the use of a second language, that is, English. Therefore, headlines should be simple, relevant and understandable. Brief headlines are necessary because of the readers' span of attention, but their content is more important than the exact number of words used.

☐ The more important it is that emotional associations are made with the brand or service, the more the visual should be emphasised.

Black readers respond more quickly to emotions portrayed in pictures than to emotions expressed in words. Emotions are close to the readers' heart and illustrations can be used effectively to attract attention and to create a certain mood or atmosphere, for example happiness, enjoyment, love, fear, empathy, distress, etc. An illustration featuring a deeply concerned mother next to the bed of her ill child will immediately evoke the prospects' emotions if she has been in a similar situation. An expression of pain is easily portrayed in an illustration, but difficult to describe in words.

An advertisement containing a headline and lengthy body copy without a supporting visual will have little attention value. However, when an advertisement is prepared, care should be taken not to feature too much. In the words of Rosenblum: 'You can feature the picture, or you can feature the headline, or you can feature the price, or you can feature the body copy. If you try to feature all, you feature none' (in McClure & Fulton 1964:224).

☐ A colour advertisement will attract attention more successfully than a black and white advertisement.

A black and white advertisement will attract less attention than a similar advertisement in colour. Brighter and richer colours, especially contrasting colours, are effective in attracting attention. Colour treatment of an advertisement also gives eye-appeal. Most products used by consumers have coloured packages and using these colours in the advertisement makes the product seem realistic. Colour treatment also helps in product identification, while an important atmosphere or image can be portrayed effectively through the use of the right colours.

When advertising to Blacks, certain connotations could be attached to the intended mood or image by using colours in a certain way. Blacks' perception and interpretation of colours are somewhat influenced by their cultural heritage and every day experiences. I am of the opinion that the use of colour should be researched because it should be dictated by the situation.

Communicating relevant information and maintaining interest

☐ A successful advertisement will tell the prospect to use a particular brand or service to obtain a specific benefit.

The target audience consists of prospects who may have specific needs and desires *or* vague needs and latent desires. In his advertisement the advertiser must stress the most important needs and desires to prove to the prospect that he needs to make use of this brand or service. He could do this effectively by stressing, elaborating or outlining a specific product benefit which offers the prospect a meaningful reward.

When advertising to Blacks it is important that the advertiser does not try to include a wide variety of different benefits in the advertising message. The less important benefits will weaken the impact of the message and in many cases even confuse the prospect. In my experience the most successful advertisements are those which are single-minded in their message and appeal and which outline only one major benefit. It is better to express the selected product benefit directly (using a direct statement or describing a reward) rather than indirectly. It is also better to prepare a series of advertisements, each concentrating on *one* benefit, than to have one advertisement dealing with a large number of benefits.

☐ Advertising copy should use language that is meaningful, natural and understandable to the prospect.

Black readers are not on the same verbal level as white copywriters. The 'skilled-with-words' copywriter is often tempted to use impressive, incomprehensible language or words which have a completely different meaning to the prospect. The problem with using high-falutin words is not only their literal meaning, but also the underlying feelings, emotional overtones and attitudes of which these words are symbols. Words have different connotations for different people. The meaning of a word is also greatly influenced by the context in which it is used. For example, the expression 'I feel great' could be perceived as an expression of good health in a vitamin advertisement, or as an expression of self-pity in an advertisement portraying a person getting out of bed with an obvious hangover.

Advertising copy should present concepts that are natural land understandable to the reader. It should be written with specific readers in mind, for example children, teenagers, housewives or fashionable ladies or men. The language used should depend upon the type of product advertised and the image of the brand. When advertising to Blacks, it is safer to use simple, short, direct statements.

In his book *The art of readable writing*, Rudolf Flesch (1974) outlined a formula for measuring the ease of reading any piece of copy:

☐ Multiply the average sentence length by 1,015
☐ Multiply the number of syllables per 100 words by 0,846
☐ Add the two products
☐ Subtract this sum from 206,835
☐ The 'Reading ease' score is . . .

As can be seen from the above, the Flesch formula takes into account the average sentence length and the number of syllables per 100 words, but does not give an answer to the question of the comprehension of the language used.

The reading ease score rates a piece of copy on a scale of 0 (practically unreadable) to 100 (easy to read for any literate person). The ease of reading score of any advertising copy is linked with the educational standard attained by the reader. Table 9.11 outlines the reading ease categories and the percentage of adult Blacks in Soweto capable of reading advertising copy falling within Flesch's reading ease categories. This table indicates that according to the educational levels attained by Blacks in Soweto, copy with a 'very easy' reading ease score would be readable by 100% of Blacks. A copy with a reading ease score of between 80 and 90 ('easy to read') would be readable by 96% of black readers, and fairly easy copy would be readable by 87% of black readers. Copy falling within Flesch's 'standard reading ease' category (for which Std 4 to 5 is required) would be readable by 73,5% of black readers, while 'fairly difficult' copy would be readable by only 42,5% of Blacks. Where Std 10 is required, that is to be able to read 'difficult' copy, only 7% of Blacks would be capable of reading such copy, and copy falling within Flesch's 'very difficult' reading ease category will be read by only 2,5% of the Blacks living in Soweto. It must be stressed that the sample consisted of Blacks already reading newspapers like *Sowetan* and magazines like *Bona*, *Pace*, etc.

Table 10.1
Percentage of adult Blacks in Soweto capable of reading copy falling within Flesch's reading ease categories (1986)

Education level	Adult black readers in Soweto: 1986	Flesch's reading ease categories	
		Score	Description
0-Std 1	100,0%	90-100	Very easy
Std 2	96,0%	80- 90	Easy
Std 3	87,0%	70- 80	Fairly easy
Std 4 and 5	73,5%	60- 70	Standard
Std 6 to 9	42,5%	50- 60	Fairly difficult
Std 10	7,0%	30- 50	Difficult
College/University	2,5%	0- 30	Very difficult

Note: The sample in Soweto consisted of 500 black men and women who regularly read a newspaper or a magazine aimed specifically at Blacks.

The ease of reading could be improved by using shorter sentences and words with fewer syllables. This is especially recommended for advertising aimed at Blacks.

☐ Symbols used to create a particular brand/image must conform to the product as well as to the audience to be effective.

Advertising communication depends heavily on symbols to convey a message or to create a brand image. Words are a familiar type of symbol used in print advertising and the choice and composition of phrases and sentences is important. Colour and contrasting colours are used extensively to portray symbolic meanings, for example green for freshness, red for strength, yellow for goodness, brown for maturity, etc. Numbers are also used to communicate symbols. 'No 1' is often used to symbolise the best or the most popular, while large numbers such as 35-million denote popularity, size, or security.

Symbols are attributable to people and to products. Advertisements classify products and the people who use them into different categories symbolically. Many advertisements use the symbol 'economy' or 'economically minded' by using words to the effect of 'save money', 'cut costs', or 'lasts longer'. In advertising aimed at Blacks the symbol of success is extremely popular while the American symbol is still useful. Blacks respect a good, hardworking, conservative personality or an opinion leader such as a doctor, nurse or church minister. Since

1976, and especially in later years, respect for elderly people and teachers has wained. Blacks interpret cars as symbols of success, and symbols of strength and acceptability appear to be strong motivating factors among black men. Young black females aspire to be beautiful, modern and popular and lightness of skin and fineness of features are still symbols of beauty. However, advertisers should be careful when depicting a sexy image. The use of sex appeal is extremely dangerous and works only if the nudity or sexiness is relevant to the product and the audience. Overdoing sex appeal will cause the brand image and user image to deteriorate.

□ The first paragraph should contain the most newsworthy item.

The illustration and headline should attract attention and create initial interest in the advertising message. The first paragraph should follow on this message logically and lure the prospect into reading the body copy. It should be concrete and specific and enable the prospect to quickly identify either the answer to his particular problem or the product reward from using the product. When advertising to Blacks the use of long copy or copy which is cluttered with uninteresting or minor claims should be avoided. In many cases an advertisement without body copy has communicated better than a similar advertisement cluttered with long copy. If it is important to use copy, subheads containing news or curiosity appeal should be used effectively to get readers to read the copy that follows.

Inducing adoption of the relevant information

□ Sex appeal in advertising should not be overdone or used irrelevantly.

The more conservative type of person may be negatively predisposed towards the use of sex appeal in advertising, while the more liberal person may not perceive it as being objectionable. It has been proved over and over again that the use of sex appeal in advertising aimed at Blacks is often detrimental to a brand image or the user image. Contrary to popular belief, Blacks are conservative when it comes to showing affection and the blatant use of sex appeal, for example a sexy illustration, is not acceptable to them.

Used cleverly, however, sex appeal can be very effective in attracting a prospect's attention. It should not attract attention to itself, but to the brand or the desired message. The use of sex appeal is best suited to products which could logically use such an approach, for example soaps, shampoos, bubble baths, underwear, deodorants, etc.

The use of sex appeal should not be overdone, because a too open flaunting of sex appeal may repel many people in the target audience and could depict a model as the type of person with whom the prospect does not want to identify.

□ It is dangerous to use humour in advertising aimed at Blacks.

Humour is normally used in an atmosphere of relaxation to attract the prospects' attention and to impart pleasant information. However, it is probably the most difficult emotional variable to introduce successfully into print advertising aimed at Blacks. The problem occurs when a white creative team decides on a humorous approach. What may be humorous to the creative team may not be perceived as humorous by the black prospects. Typical white humour is not understood by Blacks and it is essential to use their type of humour.

Some products do not lend themselves to a humorous approach; it is difficult to be humorous about illness, stress, a lack of security, etc without overstepping the boundaries of good taste.

Used skilfully, humour can interest the reader in what is to follow, but most humorous approaches have a very short lifespan.

☐ The prospect should be able to identify with the model in the illustration. It is easier to induce adoption of the user and situation images if the reader perceives a particular model to be relevant to his cognitive structure or can associate or identify with the model in that advertisement. Blacks' attitudes to white baby models and to young white models are favourable, but they respond negatively to older, more conservative white models because they see them as being representative of the South African Government and the people who deny them basic human rights.

The model's actions are also an important factor and in this regard it is very important to establish the typical role which the black man, the black woman and the black child should play.

The setting of the illustration is important because models are identified with on the basis of their overt behaviour, their clothing, their make-up, their jewellery, their facial expressions and other objects in the illustration.

Testimonial approaches are often used – either a well-known personality or a typical consumer may be quoted. Testimonial statements can be believable if properly used and if the testifier is identified in the advertisement. Many testimonial claims are presented with transparently false enthusiasm. Such claims may sound artificial and forced, as though they were written by a copywriter, because they often use the kind of language a copywriter and not a testifier would use. Therefore, the use of consumer language is extremely important and if a well-known personality is used, it must be ensured that he does in fact use the product or would logically use such a product. On many occasions Blacks have criticised advertising aimed at them because they feature well-known personalities endorsing products they would not use, for example a soccer player smoking a certain brand of cigarette, because a soccer player is not supposed to smoke.

A leading washing powder advertisement was severely criticised because the models featured in the advertisement were wearing clothing that placed them in an image category different from that expected by the readers. It must be stressed again that Blacks interpret messages literally, and therefore if you talk about a husband with coal-dust on his overall, then the advertisement should feature the husband and the coal-dust on his overall and, if his family is shown, it should be the type of family a man who worked for the South African Railways would have.

☐ A prospect will adopt the advertising message if it is believable in all respects. The advertising message communicated by the headline, the illustration, verbal claims made about the brand and irrational appeals should be believable in all respects. Many headlines claim product superiority which is not substantiated in the illustration or in the body copy, and many illustrations depict unbelievable or unrealistic situations or solutions to problems. Many copy claims claim something which the product or service cannot do, and many emotions portrayed are irrelevant or lack realism.

The brand image will be adopted if the message is believable and in line with the prospect's past experience of using that particular brand. If at all possible, claims should be backed by the results of tests conducted on the brand, awards won by the brand, or guarantees and seals of approval.

Blacks are highly critical of advertising aimed at them and believability is probably the most important element in advertising to this market segment. Belief is inherently a matter of feeling and emotion based on past experiences and cultural and tribal background, and the more the reader can identify the message as speaking to him the more he will believe in the promise or the reward.

Persuading the reader

Advertising is planned with persuasion as its major objective. Persuasion could be described as a planned attempt to influence people to behave in a certain way. It is my contention that attracting the reader's attention is a first requirement in the persuasion process, because if the reader does not see your advertisements it has no chance of communicating relevant information or inducing adoption of this information. The success of an advertisement could be measured in terms of the awareness it creates, the extent to which it communicates the intended message, the achieved brand, user and situation images, and sales.

A first requirement in any decision making process is effective advertising communications. In order to communicate effectively to Blacks it is necessary to understand their physical needs and psychological needs and make-up, their perception of the product's usefulness, their past experiences with the brand and competitive brands, their resistance to buying the product, the satisfaction they require and their interpretation of certain advertising methods or devices used to communicate to them. These devices could include headlines, illustrations, emotions, symbols, copy, etc.

Indirectly, the following principles could be used to measure the success of the persuasion process:

☐ Advertisements which attract a prospect's attention and create initial interest will be more persuasive than those which do not.

☐ A persuasive advertisement will offer a reward for reading it and this reward should be sufficiently attractive to induce the prospect to continue reading it.

☐ A persuasive advertisement will reinforce positive attitudes or beliefs about the product or service among current users and/or favourably modify attitudes or beliefs about the product among potential or non-users.

☐ The brand image must be relevant to the prospect's desires and sufficiently meaningful to persuade the reader that it will be to his advantage to buy the brand.

Direct measures of persuasion often include direct action measures where checks are made on the sales results achieved by an advertisement. This is applicable to retail type advertising or where special offers are advertised, but image creating advertising cannot be measured in this way. The advertising researcher therefore tries to measure an advertisement's persuasiveness by using 'intention to buy' measures. These measures are often crude and unqualified and can at best be a prediction of what is likely to happen in the market-place.

My recommendation is that the attention value of an advertisement and the reasons why it is successful or not successful in attracting attention should be established. Similarly, the extent to which the relevant information is communicated should be researched and practical problems eliminated. The extent to which the information is adopted into the reader's system of beliefs and attitudes should be assessed and again problems should be identified and eliminated. This means that a successful advertisement is one which successfully attracts attention to the product and main message and which communicates relevant product information to the reader. This information is successfully adopted into the reader's system of beliefs, attitudes and emotions towards and about the brand.

As a closing comment, it is necessary to stress that the black market is a volatile, rapidly changing market which is fast becoming urbanised and westernised, and therefore it is absolutely necessary to research every advertising execution to assess its viability.

☐ References

Flesch, R. 1974. *The Art of Readable Writing*. 25th ed. London: Harper & Row.

Koekemoer, CL. 1978. *Print Media Advertising, Some Basic Principles*. Johannesburg: Insight.

McClure, LW & Fulton, PC. 1964. *Advertising in the Printed Media*. New York: Macmillan.

Communicating with the black market on television

Christiane von Ulmenstein

Introduction	*391*
Model selection	*393*
Advertising techniques	*393*
Length and speed of commercials	*394*
Dubbing of commercials	*394*
Media planning	*394*
The use of music	*394*
Product and brand advertised	*395*
Conclusion	*395*
References	*395*

☐ Introduction

Prior to the inception of TV2 and TV3, the major communications medium used by advertisers to reach the black market was radio. Radio commercials were relatively inexpensive to produce, and were created mainly by white creative teams. The introduction of TV2 and TV3 on 31 December 1981 created an urgent need for information on how to communicate with the black market effectively, particularly because of the substantial investment involved in the production of television commercials. In order to enhance the effectiveness of television commercials aimed at the black market, a number of South African advertising agencies and marketing research houses conducted research studies aimed at an understanding of black TV viewers' attitudes to various aspects of television advertising.

As a result of these research studies a number of guidelines for enhancing the effectiveness of advertising aimed at the black market have been established. Guidelines regarding model selection, commercial length, dubbing, media planning and music will be given here.

☐ Model selection

One of the most important elements determining the success of a black television commercial is the choice of models.

The pool of black acting talent is still reasonably small, and black television viewers are frequently exposed to the same actors in TV2 and TV3 programmes, as well as in black commercials. Research has established that model overexposure leads to advertising credibility problems, particularly when black television viewers cannot associate well-known models with housewife roles in TV commercials. The repeated exposure of models in black television commercial is in itself disliked (Young & Rubicam 1985).

Commercials which feature white models and which are dubbed into the vernacular languages for flighting on TV2 and TV3 are disliked. First, Blacks resent the fact that their own actors are being kept out of work if they are not used in such commercials, and second, such commercials communicate that the brand advertised is aimed at Whites only.

Attitudes to multiracial commercials, that is commercials in which models from more than one population group appear, have been of particular interest to advertisers. Blacks react positively to multiracial commercials in principle because they reflect South Africa's multiracial society. However, it is crucial that integrated ads portray equality of the Whites and Blacks featured and depict realistic situations. Blacks are particularly sensitive to integrated commercials in which there is a token inclusion of Blacks, they appear last or for a short while only, or are depicted

1 When you're a long way from your next meal . . .

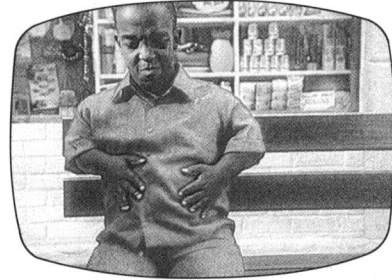

2 and you're too hungry for something small, you need something . . .

5

6

Courtesy: Cadbury's and Young & Rubicam

in subservient roles. Furthermore, the settings in which the Whites and Blacks interact in the commercial must reflect the degree of interaction of Whites and Blacks in South African society. For example, multiracial commercials which are set in sporting situations and in restaurants and hotels are far more acceptable than those set in private homes.

☐ Advertising techniques

It has been established that Blacks' and Whites' understanding of and response to the traditional advertising techniques of slice-of-life, spokesperson, celebrity endorsement, hyperbole (ie deliberate exaggeration to make a point), aspiration and product demonstration do not differ (Young & Rubicam 1982).

The advertising technique of product demonstration appears to be particularly well received in instances where the product advertised is relatively unfamiliar to Blacks. The advertising for *Tastic rice*, for example, is one of the best liked, because it demonstrates to housewives how to cook rice (Young & Rubicam 1986).

While humour can be used successfully as an advertising technique, it is important to note that the humour used must be pertinent to the black culture, and not merely be a translation of 'white' humour. The current *Lunch Bar* and *Black Cat* commercials are examples of the successful use of humour as an advertising technique (Young & Rubicam 1986).

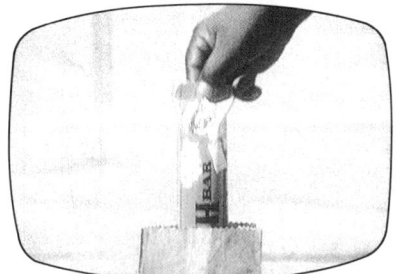

3 that's bigger than your hunger. Cadburys Lunch Bar.

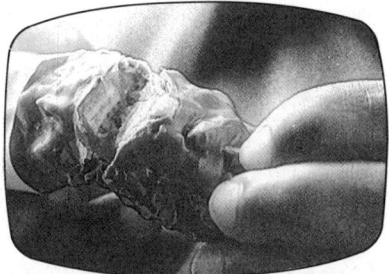

4 The snack that's packed full with wafer, roasted nuts and tasty toasted rice covered in a delicious double layer of Cadburys chocolate.

7 Hey man, you look like you could use a little nourishment yourself.

8 Cadburys Lunch Bar. It's bigger than your hunger.

☐ Length and speed of commercials

The commercials which appear on TV2 and TV3 are often perceived as being too fast, and their intended messages may not be properly understood. This is particularly likely in the case of commercials which are translated directly from English into the vernacular languages, as the latter need more words to communicate the same message (Young & Rubicam 1985). It is advisable to produce commercials of at least 30 seconds, but preferably longer.

☐ Dubbing of commercials

It has already been indicated that dubbed versions of 'white' commercials are strongly disliked, not only because they keep black actors out of work, but also for the implied discrimination in the depicted target market.

In addition, dubbed commercials are often perceived to be out of sync, which is disliked by black TV viewers. Many Blacks find it unrealistic that white models speak Zulu, Sotho, etc. More TV viewers prefer TV commercials to be in a pure vernacular language (60%) than in a mixture of vernaculars and/or English (30%). Only a small proportion of black TV viewers would prefer to see commercials in English only (7%) (Young & Rubicam 1986).

☐ Media planning

The choice of media also often creates sensitivities. Blacks have been found to be heavy channel switchers, watching an average of 2,7 TV channels per evening (Young & Rubicam 1986). Since they are therefore likely to be exposed to both white and black TV channels, they are aware that certain commercials are flighted on white channels only.

However, different advertising executions of the same concept for the same brand for white and black commercials are accceptable to black TV viewers, because they recognise the differences in white and black lifestyles and customs. However, they do reject advertisements which are clearly aimed at the lower classes or which talk down to them (Young & Rubicam 1985).

☐ The use of music

The music used in commercials should reflect Blacks' taste in music (Young & Rubicam 1985). Directly translated jingles or music taken straight from white commercials is disliked if it is not relevant to Blacks. Township jazz appears to be preferred to other types of music.

☐ Product and brand advertised

Loyalty to brands is characteristic of black consumers, and it is usually the first brand in a particular product category advertised to the black market that achieves a following in the black market. In many instances such a leading brand name has become the generic name for the product category (eg *Sta Soft*, *Colgate*). It has been estabished that attitudes towards a particular product category may strongly influence attitudes to the advertising of brands within that category (Young & Rubicam 1986). The commercials for *Surf* and *Omo*, for example, are among the list of commercials best liked by black television viewers. In the detergent market these two brands dominate the black segment thereof and therefore the strength of these brand names influences advertising attitudes, particularly because the advertising messages are credible, based on the consumer's personal experience of them.

The linking of sport with alcoholic beverage or cigarette advertising is disliked, because such commercials are perceived to encourage sportsmen to drink (and thus to cause alcoholism) or to smoke. Alcoholic beverages and cigarettes are labelled 'bad' products, and black housewives dislike the fact that these are advertised so heavily on audio-visual media (Young & Rubicam 1985).

☐ Conclusion

Black TV viewers are very positive about advertising, because they consider it to be informative and educational, as well as entertaining.

When there are commercial breaks on TV, 60% of black TV viewers tend to watch the commercials, and only 11% watch them reluctantly and without interest. Commercial breaks *within* programmes are an annoyance to some TV viewers. When there are commercial breaks on TV, black viewers tend to enjoy watching them (Young & Rubicam 1986).

One major guideline to successful communication with the black market is the aspect of *realism*. The choice of models, props, wardrobe, setting, music, interaction with white models, and interaction with the product being advertised must reflect what would be realistic in the view of black consumers. Realism in black TV commercials enhances their chances of being understood and reduces the danger of credibility problems.

While adhering to the guidelines for communicating with the black market presented above may eliminate the risk of ineffective communication, advertisers still run the risk of making mistakes in their communication with the black market. It is advisable, therefore, that *all* advertising campaigns which are developed for the black market are pre-tested so that negative attitudes to the advertising campaign can be avoided.

☐ References

Young & Rubicam. 1982. Viewer Response Profile Study.
Young & Rubicam. 1985. Window on the Black Market.
Young & Rubicam. 1986. Study on Black TV viewing, attitudes to advertising and attendance of multiracial cinemas.

11

Retail advertising

Retail advertising   *399*

Retail advertising
David Buirski

The 'essence'	399
Continuity and image	400
Editorial value	400
Going in-house	400
The retail advertising man	402
Retail advertising issues	402
Retail advertising philosophy	403
Comparison of retail and branded advertising in the four divisions	406

☐ The 'essence'

In order to do successful retail advertising it is imperative to find that indispensable quality or element – the 'essence' of a client's business.

In the case of a branded product this is relatively easy, since only a single product is dealt with. However, in the case of a supermarket chain for example, it is far more difficult because hundreds of products, each with its own individual character, are dealt with. To complicate matters further, the essence of a retailer, unlike that of a branded product, can and does change.

For example, in the beginning a leading retailer carried a large range of branded products at low prices. The essence of its business was therefore fairly easy to establish, and resulted in an advertising campaign which stated simply: 'For Branded Goods You Know, At Prices Really Low'. Later the essence of its business changed; the inclusion of housebrands meant that the original slogan was no longer strictly true.

Therefore it could be said that the more complex a store becomes, the more difficult it is to establish its essence. This is not necessarily true. A hypermarket, for example, is a store where you can buy almost anything you need under one roof at extremely low prices. Appropriate essence slogans for such a store are 'One-Stop Shopping, Non-Stop Saving', 'Everything under one roof', etc.

What should an advertising agency do when confronted with a new client who has no real essence or whose essence is confused? In this case it is advisable to extract a unique element which in advertising terms becomes the 'essence'. A good example of this is another supermarket chain whose agency perceived that its unique property – its essence – was the fact that it had far more super-markets in South Africa than any other company. The essence statement there-fore became 'Just up your street'.

When a leading clothing retailer changed its essence statement to 'Low Prices for the People', in line with the fact that it had over 500 stores throughout South Africa it was therefore, within range of virtually every South African of every race, sales increased dramatically within a short time, confirming the importance of 'essence'.

☐ Continuity of image

It is extremely important that the essence statement and image is maintained. Only one chain in South Africa has consistently maintained its image; the others have chopped and changed countless times – to their detriment.

Too many retail advertisements are treated as individual units, the emphasis being placed on product and price only. Such advertisements do not form part of a properly conceived campaign and therefore do not offer consumer con-tinuity/confidence.

☐ Editorial value

Advertising must be backed up by editorial articles that afford it credibility. The value of these editorial articles is generally underestimated.

☐ Going in-house

When the issue of who to place your advertising with arises, there are usually only two alternatives:

☐ Use an advertising agency
☐ Go in-house.

Neither of the above traditional alternatives is ideal, and there is a third alterna-tive called the 'in-house agency' option. Of the traditional alternatives the adver-tising agency route is preferable, because it attracts a better calibre of staff and therefore better advertisements.

The following factors must be taken into consideration when the decision is made to take your advertising in-house:

☐ Will there be a financial benefit?
☐ Will the advertising be as effective as with an agency?
☐ Will the service from an in-house operation be as good as the service from the advertising agency?

The risks associated with going in-house are listed below:

☐ It is difficult to attract a suitable calibre of staff
☐ Possibility of tunnel vision occurrring

☐ The boss syndrome – give the boss what he wants, not what he needs
☐ Possibility of inferior advertising
☐ Lack of staff stimulation.

There are many reasons why a suitable calibre of staff cannot be attracted. A few of these are the following: Creative staff are not happy working in-house, because the job lacks the excitement of being part of a team that handles many different accounts covering all aspects of the market – many people feel that being locked into a single account is boring and their portfolios become thin. Working in-house lacks the glamour of an advertising agency. Several years ago the issue of going in-house was being seriously considered by several large South African food chains. We thought they would find it difficult to attract qualified staff. In order to test this belief we circulated a questionnaire among our staff informing them that our client X was going in-house and asking if they would consider this move. Their answer was a resounding NO!

The benefits of going in-house are the following:

☐ Possible financial savings
☐ The advertising team dirties its hands, gets to know its own business
☐ Immediacy – closer lines of communication.

We have been aware of these factors for many years and have decided that the best way of doing really effective retail advertising is by combining the benefits of the advertising agency and the in-house operation and forming what we call the *in-house agency system*.

The in-house agency system

Our major client is a good example of how the in-house agency system benefits the client. A few aspects of this system will be examined in relation to this client.

Our agency has six separate teams in the various provinces located in close proximity to our client's hypermarkets. To service their supermarket divisions we have eight separate teams, once again located close to our client's regional offices. This adds up to 14 separate units for a single client.

Local opportunity

The question: 'Why so many individual units?' could be asked. Each region has different target markets, different newspapers, different needs and different competition.

As I see it, whether through an advertising agency or in-house, the problem is that advertisements are usually created and despatched from Head Office and therefore in many cases do not relate to the differences in the regions. Thus, Head Office advertising is often irrelevant and unable to react quickly enough to local situations or to answer opposition advertising. In fact, Head Office is often unaware of these local opportunities.

As for dirtying their hands – getting to know their client's business – because they are on the spot these individual teams soon get to know their regional client's business intimately.

Function of Head Office

Head Office has the important function of creating national campaigns and seeing to it that a client's essence, image and disciplines are adhered to in the regions.

Creative boredom

Creative people become bored working in-house – surely the same applies to people working on one supermarket region? The answer to this is 'yes', but because an advertising agency has many accounts when this occurs staff can be rotated and put onto different accounts. This is not possible in an in-house operation.

Financial savings

The total buying power of an advertising agency should be greater than that of a single in-house operation, therefore savings should be made on both media and production costs.

☐ The retail advertising man

Is the retail advertising man any different from other advertising people? I think the answer must be 'yes', for various reasons.

Retail advertising agencies have to prepare far more advertisements per month than a branded products agency with the same billing, which means that more staff are required, resulting in higher expenses. Therefore it becomes imperative that the retail artist is more productive, it must be accepted that more people will be required per million rand billing than in a branded products advertising agency. Of course, the same applies to account service and every other facet of the agency. They have to have more stamina. The retail man has to have quick reactions, for example an account executive must be able to see a client at a moment's notice, the creative department must be able to prepare advertisements at a moment's notice, and the media department has to book advertisements overnight in order to meet competition and a very tight deadline. The retail advertising man has to think quickly; often he does not have time to debate an advertisement the way that a branded product advertising man is able to.

Fortunately, over the years it has been found that there is a certain type of person who enjoys the urgency of retail advertising and has the stamina required to cope with the pressure. Called *marathon runners*, such people form the backbone of retail advertising and are in great demand.

☐ Retail advertising issues

Stricter controls

Because of the high volume of work going through the traffic system, there have to be stricter controls and disciplines.

High production costs

The retail advertiser's production costs are extremely high because of the large volume of different advertisements and the number of items featured in each advertisement. These costs can be increased substantially by client and agency error occurring due to sheer volume and lack of time for attention to detail. Research indicates that these extra costs can be as high as 30%. Clients should be educated in the basics of production. When this is put into practice costs have been reduced by as much as 40%.

The negative retail advertising image

One of the largest stumbling blocks a retail advertising agency faces is the fact that creative people generally find working in a retail advertising agency unglamorous and lacking in creative opportunities, and feel that working for a retail agency will not further their career, that specimens suitable for their portfolio are rare. Therefore it is important that the image of retail advertising is improved and promoted.

Fortunately, the world-wide swing to retail and below-the-line advertising is helping to change this image. More and more traditional agencies are casting covetous looks at retail business and opening retail divisions of their own, which means that branded creative people are being exposed to the opportunities in retail. It is becoming easier to attract 'branded' creative people to retail agencies than it was in the past.

Creative awards

One of the ways of up-grading the retail image is by creating specific awards for retail excellence.

Motivation

Advertising agency people generally work under pressure, retail people even more so. Motivation is important. It is therefore imperative that these people are stimulated constantly by participation in training seminars, creative workshops, etc.

Incentives such as university, creative and management courses must be provided, as well as incentives in the sport and recreational areas.

☐ Retail advertising philosophy

I have read many advertising philosophies related to branded products, but I have yet to come across a philosophy which is related specifically to retail advertising. This may explain why the standard of retail advertising is generally not as high as that of branded advertising and may be due to the fact that throughout the world there are very few specialist retail advertising agencies. Generally, retail units are offshoots of branded agencies, often simply to meet existing clients' retail needs or because other agencies are opening retail divisions. Just as the essence of a client's business is of paramount importance, so too is the retail philosophy which forms the basis of a retail agency's structure − without this philosophy every advertisement, every campaign is a hit-and-miss affair depending on the everchanging needs and/or whims of account executives and clients. No advertising philosophy is the same, but there are certain key elements which form the basis of any philosophy.

The following are some of the key elements of an advertising philosophy:

Essence

Establish the 'essence' of your client's business.

Individual identity

In order to stand out, every client must have an individual identity, one that is not confused with that of the opposition.

Consistency and continuity of image

Having carefully researched and established an image, stay with it, do not be side-tracked. Nothing does more damage to an advertising image than constant change. Consumer confidence will never be built this way.

Colour

Tests as to the effectiveness of colour as opposed to black and white advertisements have indicated that colour is more effective and cost efficient than black and white.

Urgency

Retail advertisements should be urgent, because people are more likely to react to a shout than to a normal voice. If you have something to say, be bold.

Action

A moving object, an object in action, draws more attention than a stationary one − a rocket in the act of blasting off has far more impact than an immobile one. Retail advertisements should take this into account.

Product understanding and involvement

Dirty your hands, become involved at floor and store level. Understand the nitty-gritty of your client's business. Spend time working within his company.

Topicality

Take advantage of whatever news is making the headlines and use it to attract the readers' attention.

Benefits

State the benefits as clearly and as simply as possible.

Simplicity

Keep your ads and your main message simple, bold and easy to understand.

Specific target markets

Avoid the temptation of using a successful retail concept for another client whose target market might be different. Generally, the handwriting of agencies should not be as obvious as it is at present.

Editorial value

This aspect should not be overlooked and is probably more important than the advertisements themselves, for the articles add credibility and believability to a campaign. Naturally, editorial must form part of your campaign and be related in every way.

Promotions

Promotions are the life-blood of any retailer. It is virtually a matter of promote or die. Promotions should be regular and co-ordinated, and to have full impact should be store-wide.

Unsuitable co-op items

Do not feature items simply because the supplier is paying for their exposure. If the item does not warrant appearing in the advertisement leave it out.

Avoid the price and product only type of advertisements

If this is the kind of advertising being used, the consumer is being conditioned to look at advertisements for bargains and that is all he will go to the store for. For the bulk of his purchases he will go to the store he perceives to be the best for overall value.

The importance of price or the perception thereof

Make prices and captions and copy relating to low price bold.

Courtesy: Young and Rubican Retail

Campaigns, not single ads

Every advertisement no matter how small, must form part of a campaign, thereby forming the link of continuity.

The importance of in-store signage and ticketing

Generally, this aspect is neglected. An example of how important this is follows: A chain controlling two clothing operations, each with a different target market and identity but serviced by the same display department, somehow switched basic price tickets, so that Store A received Store B's tickets. This mistake was not realised until there was a dramatic change in client profile. Store A's client profile changed from a 70% white and 30% coloured to a 30% white and 70% coloured profile – in only eight weeks! Imagine what this would have cost if the client had deliberately attempted to switch his profile.

☐ Comparison of retail and branded advertising in the four divisions

I believe the following comparisons to be a useful exercise as they highlight certain important retail aspects:

☐ Client service (see table 11.1)
☐ Creative (see table 11.2)
☐ Media (see table 11.3)
☐ Production (see table 11.4).

Table 11.1
Client service

Retail	Branded
Often without marketing qualifications. Rarely worked in client's organisation	Marketing qualifications. Often worked in client's organisation
An advertising all-rounder with knowledge of all facts. Often has creative background	A specialist, relying on back-up from other disciplines, eg media, production, creative
Retail market requires an individual with great resources of stamina and able to react instantly to the volatile retail market repeatedly	Advanced strategic planning means less volatile market, fewer changes
Often works from little or no marketing information and has to use own intuition and experience – 'gut-feel'	Works from exhaustive marketing and research reports which require a great deal of time
Only rarely required to produce detailed documentation	Required to produce marketing strategy documents, etc
Always working against the clock	Often has adequate time
Regular (almost daily) client meetings	Infrequent client meetings

Table 11.2
Creative

	Retail	Branded
Time	Limited time to meet deadlines. Must be fast worker	Time to prepare ads – speed not essential
Conceptualise	Tighter deadlines mean less time to think	Ample time for strategic thinking
Service/Creativity	Emphasis on service	Emphasis on creativity
Visual/Copy	Generally think in pictures and headlines	Generally think in words
Disciplines	Must adhere to disciplines	Disciplines not as important
Productivity	Must be productive to meet the large number of advertisements required	Productivity not as important
Job opportunities	Limited due to few retail agencies	Ample job opportunities
Pressure	Under constant pressure	Under occasional pressure

Table 11.3
Media

	Retail	Branded
Target market	Defined by catchment area	Defined by demographics (sex, age, income) or psychographics (lifestyle)
Media approach	'Hot media' – a quick reaction is essential	'Cold media' – quick reaction is not always essential
Price	Essential for retail price comparisons	Benefits of product/service, not price
Deadlines	Short deadline essential in the competitive retail market to facilitate late product and price changes	Not of major importance. Campaigns usually planned to cover a long period
Advertising frequency	Very high frequency of store advertisements – every advertisement is different	Less frequency of the same advertisement
Media usage	Local media eg local newspapers, free sheets and knock-and-drop related to catchment area	National media utilised for cover of target market
Size of advertisements	Large advertisements essential to dominate page and show range of merchandise in local media	Large size advertisements not essential

Table 11.3
Media
(continued)

	Retail	Branded
Colour	Because advertisements usually appear only once, use of full colour is limited to avoid high production costs. Frequent use of spot colour for impact and lower production costs. Frequent use of full colour inserts	Full colour used to create mood and to show product at its best
Positioning of advertisement	Front half positioning essential for maximum readership in newspapers	Positioning in magazines is not critical – readership is uniformly high through-out the publication

Table 11.4
Production

	Retail	Branded
Quotations	Similar	Similar
Ordering of material	Similar	Similar
Time needed for reproduction	Extremely limited, because products and prices are often changed at the last minute to meet compe-tition	Ample time, because cam-paigns are planned well in advance and feature benefit, not price
Cost	Extremely high, because advertisements appear only once and tight dead-lines and frequent price changes mean expensive overtime	Not as high, because the same advertisements are repeated and less over-time is required

12

Advertising services

Advertising the products and services of non-profit
organisations *411*

Advertising the products and services of non-profit organisations

Annemarie van der Walt

Introduction	*411*
Product offerings of non-profit organisations	*412*
Characteristics of non-profit marketing	*414*
Advertising research in non-profit marketing	*415*
Image formation	*417*
Non-profit advertising campaigns	420
Reinforcing the advertising message	425
Summary	426
References	426

☐ Introduction

Marketing by non-profit organisations has come to be known as *social marketing*, because these institutions generally market social services of various kinds. The word 'services' is purposely used to describe the products of non-profit organisations, because most provide services. However, the product offerings of non-profit organisations include not only services, but also ideas, causes, places and personalities.

There is little evidence that the social marketing function is – or should be – very different from the commercial marketing function. The products and services of non-profit organisations must be marketed in essentially the same way as consumer and industrial products – by the careful integration of the four marketing instruments. It is a fallacy, therefore, to think that advertising is the only tool that can be used for social marketing. In fact, many failures in the marketing of social services can be ascribed to attempts to equate advertising with marketing.

Before attempting to communicate with the public (the target audience) about a service, idea or cause, it is extremely important to ensure that the service, idea or cause, (the product) will be acceptable to the target audience, that this product will be readily available to the target audience (distribution) and that the sacrifice demanded of the target audience (price) reflects exactly the benefits to be received as a result of using the service or adopting the idea.

Before advertising as a communication method is focused on, the uniquely different characteristics of the products and services of different non-profit organisations will be scrutinised.

□ Product offerings of non-profit organisations

In the introduction it became apparent that there is some confusion regarding the terminology 'products' and 'services'. Therefore, it is necessary to get some idea of what is meant by the products and services of non-profit organisations. The product offerings of non-profit organisations include services, ideas, causes and personalities, which are more or less intangible (except personalities of course!) when compared with most other consumer and industrial products. Intangibility can be expressed in a continuum, as shown below:

Tangible   Intangible

Industrial products	Consumer products	Services	Causes	Ideas

All of the product offerings in this continuum consist of a collection of utilities which provide benefits to consumers. Usually, an industrial or consumer product on the left-hand side of the continuum consists of a physical product, a service component and an idea. A BMW dealer, for example, sells a physical object, services of repair and warranty and the idea of prestige and luxury. The physical reality of this product provides a powerful base upon which to build a description of what is being provided. The different components of tangible product offerings facilitate the formulation of the marketing strategy and especially the design of an advertising message.

Due to the abstract nature of the services, causes and ideas presented on the right-hand side of the continuum, it is difficult to describe what is being provided and it requires extra effort to present the benefits in advertising messages. The product offerings of non-profit organisations are on the right-hand side of the continuum – they are virtually all intangible, but usually some effort is made to afford them a modicum of tangibility in the form of symbols such as uniforms, badges and flags, as indicated in Table 12.1.

Table 12.1
The product offering of non-profit organisations

Non-profit organisation	Idea	Service	Products
Unisa	Education	Lectures	Study guide
National Road Safety Council	Road safety for drivers and pedestrians	Film shows	Booklet
SA Armed Forces	Patriotism	Training Physical fitness	Uniform Flag
International Training and Communication (ITS)	Community involvement	Speech training	Badge
DR Church	Religion	Charity to the needy	Magazine

Berry (1980:24-29) gives an eloquent description of the differences between products (goods) and services: 'A good is an object, a device, a thing; a service is a deed, a performance, an effort. When a good is purchased, something tangible is required; something that can be seen, touched, perhaps smelled or worn or placed on a mantle. When a service is purchased, there is generally nothing to show for it. Money has been spent, but there are no additional clothes to hang in the closet and nothing to place on the mantle.'

In the remainder of this discussion, when the 'products of non-profit organisations' are referred to they will include services, ideas, causes, personalities, etc. This is a short cut and will obviate listing all of the different kinds of product offering every time.

There are two main types of non-profit organisation, namely:

☐ public institutions (such as the Consumer Council), which use tax revenues and are supported by the state and often referred to as the second sector
☐ private organisations, which receive financial support in the form of grants, subscription fees, through fund-raising activities, or any combination of these sources and are referred to as the third sector.

This contribution deals with both types of non-profit organisation mentioned above, which include the following:

☐ cultural organisations (eg museums)
☐ knowledge-oriented organisations (eg schools, universities)
☐ philanthropic organisations (eg charities)
☐ social cause organisations (eg feminist groups)
☐ religious organisations (eg church associations)
☐ public institutions (eg Consumer Council)

Courtesy: RH Griffin

☐ Characteristics of non-profit marketing

There are several distinctive characteristics which directly affect the marketing activities of non-profit organisations and especially the way in which their product offerings are advertised.

Broader mission

Non-profit marketing usually has a broader mission. The objective of a business is to achieve long-term profitability while catering for the needs of consumers. In non-profit organisations societal needs are served while an attempt is made to break even. Because profit is not the bottom line the true measure of achievement in non-profit organisations is not expressed in monetary terms, but rather in levels of patronage, usage of service, or levels of participation in a programme. These measures are not easily determined, and it is difficult to prove the success of any advertising campaign. On the financial side, deficits are usually viewed as inefficiency or ineffectiveness by those who are responsible for funding. There are usually severe budgetary constraints due to limited resources, which means that non-profit organisations cannot advertise freely to attain their objectives. The social goals of non-profit organisations include persuading people to adopt an idea, disseminating useful information about beneficial practices, or changing harmful behaviour.

Inseparability of services

The inseparability of services is another distinguishing characteristic of non-profit marketing. This means that the 'consumer' is tied irrevocably to the production of the service or idea in order to derive benefit from it. Furthermore, a service or idea is very perishable – failure to attend an art exhibition, for example, is a lost opportunity which may never be repeated. Services and ideas cannot be stored.

Lack of trained personnel

Most, although not all, non-profit organisations lack personnel trained in marketing, because marketing is often regarded as being of lesser importance. The staff is usually so involved in fund-raising and creating ideas and services that it does not realise that the publics at which these ideas and services are directed will not automatically accept whatever it is offering. Marketing is usually regarded as the job of the PRO.

Many divergent publics

The product offerings of non-profit organisations are usually not targeted at distinct market segments, but rather at many divergent 'publics', each with its own interests, preferences and demands. The services of a university, for example, are aimed primarily at present students who are the users of these services. However, the product offering cannot be tailored to the demands of these consumers. Lecturers, prospective employers and even the Department of Education are involved in curriculum decisions. The requirements of all these 'publics' must be met fully, otherwise potential students hearing of deficiencies will be demotivated. The result could well be empty lecture halls! Obviously, it would be very difficult to design an advertising message with an impact on all these publics, and many different advertising campaigns, each designed for a specific audience, would be prohibitively expensive.

Complaints and criticism

These are the daily bread of non-profit organisations. Because of their broader societal mission, non-profit organisations seem to stimulate critical public scrutiny. Secondary publics, such as donors and reporters, will have a strong interest in how the non-profit organisation uses its funds. These people are not always in agreement about the correct or most efficient way of doing things. This results in conflicting criticism which is difficult to disprove because of the lack of standards of performance which can logically be expected. How many drivers, for example, can be persuaded to use safety belts by a single advertisement, however well designed? Uninformed publics often complain that advertising expenditure is a 'pure waste of money'. Conversely, others may perhaps criticise the same organisation for not allocating sufficient funds to the advertising campaign and therefore failing to create the necessary awareness, interest and acceptance for the product offering. Complaints about the poor quality of Government services and the 'misuse of funds', for example, are a national sport in South Africa. However, experts are of the opinion that severe critical attitudes can be changed by using marketing techniques and communicating (by means of advertising) with citizens.

It is clear from this brief discussion that the distinctive differences between the marketing function of a business and that of a non-profit organisation can be ascribed to the latter's greater diversity of conflicting objectives, to the fact that it is more likely to be under public scrutiny, and to the problems involved in appealing to many different publics at the same time with limited funds.

The problems facing those who are employed to create effective advertising campaigns in such a situation are daunting indeed.

☐ Advertising research in non-profit marketing

In commercial firms it is imperative to launch advertising research projects in order to determine the effectiveness or impact of the advertising message and to determine consumer needs, preferences and prejudices before attempting to create a persuasive message. It is generally known that the effectiveness of an advertising message cannot be measured easily. A sharp rise in sales figures indicates a positive reaction on the part of the target market, but it does not prove without doubt the persuasive power of the advertising message. Advertising *awareness* (the number of people who are aware of the product), advertising *recognition* (the number of people who are able to recognise the advertisement), and advertising *recall* (the number of people who remember the advertisement) are usually tested by means of research projects to give some indication of the effectiveness of the message. It is virtually impossible, however, to determine how many people have been persuaded by the message. Measuring awareness, recognition and recall have as much relevance to non-profit advertising as to profit-seeking enterprises advertising products and services.

Advertising research is also done to gather information about consumers and to serve as a basis for the creation of an advertising message. Consumers express their needs, preferences and prejudices in their responses to surveys and the advertising message is designed to promise need-satisfaction and the product benefits demanded by consumers. This brief explanation makes research sound easy, but there are many problems and pitfalls. In non-profit marketing there are even more! The usage rate of a social service or the adoption rate of an idea cannot be quantified as easily as sales figures. The patronage level and the number of subscribers or donors give some indication of the reception the service or idea enjoys, but once again these figures do not prove the persuasiveness of the advertising message.

Respondents in research projects cannot easily grasp and assess the meaning of social services and ideas. For example, the benefits to be received as a result of adopting a certain idea or the dire consequences of refusing to adopt the idea may or may not be felt at some future time. Respondents may either be *unable* to express their real feelings and reactions to advertising messages regarding social services or ideas in words which will be understood by the researcher, or they may be *unwilling* to do so. Very few people, for example, would be willing to state that they do not wish to donate money to a charitable cause because they are too stingy and uncaring to do so. When questioned they will rationalise and give socially acceptable reasons, reasons which are, however, not the real reasons for their lack of charity. This means that direct questioning will result in biased answers and meaningless research results.

The problems involved in sampling are daunting. Reference has already been made to the diversity of the publics, the target audiences for advertising messages of non-profit organisations. Drawing properly representative samples from all these target audiences may prove to be impractical and too expensive.

Focus-group interviewing is probably the only research method which can be used to pre-test non-profit advertising messages and campaigns. Focus groups can be organised to include members of all the target audiences. A focus group can also consist of a panel of experts. These knowledgeable people act as a testing board for ideas and the use of symbols which will convey the advertising message correctly. In focus-group interviewing the story board (of an intended advertisement) can be scrutinised carefully and systematically to determine whether the real message is clear and unambiguous. Advertising practitioners, whose responsibility (unenviable!) it is to create attractive and attention-grabbing advertising themes for the intangible product offerings of non-profit organisations, are often so involved with the uniqueness of the theme that they sometimes forget the human limitations of the audience which must interpret the message. The advertising practitioner 'falls in love' with his creation and often finds it impossible to accept the fact that the public remains disinterested and is often simply too ignorant or uncaring to recognise the true merit of the message which has been created with so much care.

In a focus-group discussion the practitioner comes face to face with the recipients of the message and may well be surprised by the different interpretations that evolve. Very often post-testing by means of focus groups reveals weaknesses which should have been noted and corrected even before the campaign was launched. Advertising practitioners often assume that consumers are fully able to absorb and process information, while in fact their ability to do so is limited. The failure of fear-inspiring appeals to motorists in the United States to wear safety belts and of the so-called Anti-drug Campaign, which seemed to stimulate rather than discourage the demand for drugs, clearly show that consumers do not always comprehend the gist of persuasive messages directed at them. The reasons for both these 'failures' were revealed in post-testing — in these cases proper pre-testing would probably have revealed deficiencies and misconceptions, thereby saving time, money and valuable lives. The conclusion which can be drawn here is that focus-group interviewing is an essential step in planning an advertising campaign for a non-profit organisation.

☐ Image formation

The name (brand name) chosen for a non-profit cause, service or idea is of crucial importance, as it lends some substance to a very vaguely defined product offering and, if well-chosen, will go a long way to creating the desired image. The name must be meaningful, short, easily pronounceable, ideally identical in English and Afrikaans, and easy to remember. Non-profit organisations tend to lean towards acronyms (like SANTA or AA), which are often meaningless, unpronounceable groups of letters. A strange name will require more advertising effort if it is to become familiar to the public and more advertising rands will have to be spent just on making it known. An emblem (or logo) is often used in conjunction with the name. This emblem is supposed to reflect the nature of the product offering in a symbolic way. A good example is the red cross emblem used by the Red Cross. Few, if any, people are ignorant of the meaning of this cross. The emblem is a symbol which assists the consumer to visualise the non-profit cause, service or idea and therefore assists in image formation. It is obvious that the name and emblem cannot be chosen at the whim of the founders or executives. It should be designed by advertising experts and tested rigorously. Focus-group interviews are once again probably the best research method which can be used. Participants in the focus-group discussions can be asked to rank alternatives according to preference and also to form free associations. Alternatives evoking negative associations should, of course, be excluded.

Non-profit organisations should avail themselves of every possible opportunity to emphasise their name and emblem. Absolute consistency in the spelling of the name, the lettering and the colours used is a prerequisite for image creation. The stronger the positive association between the name, the emblem and the nature of the cause, service or idea, the easier it will be to design effective advertising messages. If members of the target audience are unaware of the meaning of the name and emblem, they will have to be taught to recognise it by having their attention and interest attracted to it. Valuable advertising rands are wasted on intermittent advertising campaigns for 'unknown' product offerings. Conducting infrequent advertising campaigns with long silences inbetween will invariably lead to forgetting and the necessity for a re-education programme for every new campaign. The general public should be kept consistently aware of the name of the non-profit organisation by reminder advertising between intensive campaigns. Slogans emphasising the name can be used as a means of achieving consistency and continuity. Many non-profit organisations tend to jump from one intensive advertising campaign to another at a later stage as funds become available. The flow of information should, however, never really be discontinued lest the consumer forget the name (and the message).

Teaching the name and what it stands for is not sufficient. If information on how to obtain the service is not readily available, a negative reflection may be cast on the image of that service. Because services, causes and ideas cannot be moved, stored or displayed in convenient locations (shops?), the advertising message must provide 'evidence' of the existence of the intangible product offering. The advertisement must therefore assist with the proper 'distribution' of the product offering from the producer to the consumer. People sympathetic to causes or wishing to donate to worthwhile charities often encounter difficulty when trying to obtain relevant information. Recently, massive publicity was afforded to hungry school children on the Rand, but contact telephone numbers or exact locations where donations could be made were not given, the public was merely told to 'contact the nearest Welfare Office' (wherever that might be!). Wishing to donate something to the house being built for the use of out-of-town cancer patients, this author was not sure where to find the relevant information – in the telephone directory under National Cancer Association?, Cancer Association?, South African Cancer Association? – or is it called Toktokkie? This demonstration of one person's ignorance points to a lesson imperfectly taught, learned and implemented. Often well-intentioned impulses disappear due to similar frustrations. All advertisements or promotional material prepared for a non-profit organisation should also help with the distribution of the product by providing telephone numbers, addresses or answer coupons. The final step in successful persuasion is to obtain action or active involvement on the part of the audience. Active involvement should be made easy!

Courtesy: National Cancer Association

If the non-profit organisation is large enough to support branch offices, the image of the organisation will be enhanced and proper distribution of the product offering will be facilitated. Branch offices can conduct their own marketing programmes according to the needs of the public in their area. The National Road Safety Council, for example, has branches in most major centres. These branch offices distribute information and promotional material to schools, organisations and opinion leaders in the vicinity. However, the main office is responsible for national advertising.

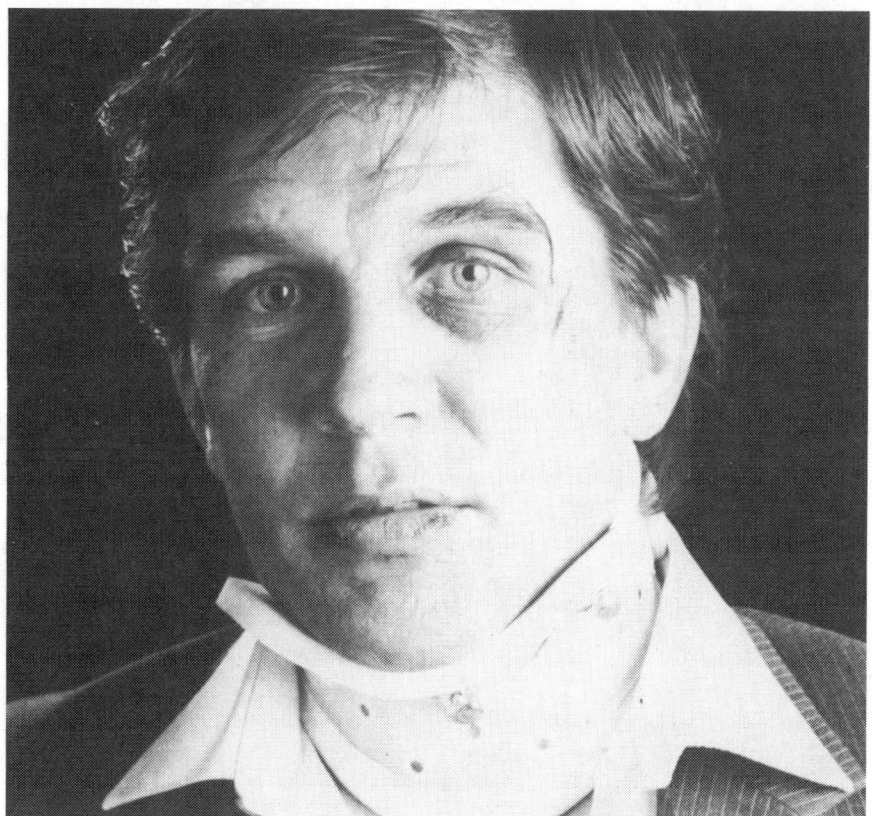

The best thing that can happen if you've never had an accident before.

If you've never had a car accident before, now is the time to start worrying! Because, admit it, you might just be getting the tiniest bit complacent about driving. It might just begin to look too easy.

And the moment you drop your guard could well be your last moment on earth. If you get off with whiplash and a few bruises, consider yourself fortunate. Because from now on you'll be a more alert driver — and you're still alive.

Take it easy, yes, but guard against dead easy.

Look. Think. And stay alive.

Courtesy: National Road Safety Council. An appeal to the South African public to be alert and to avoid accidents

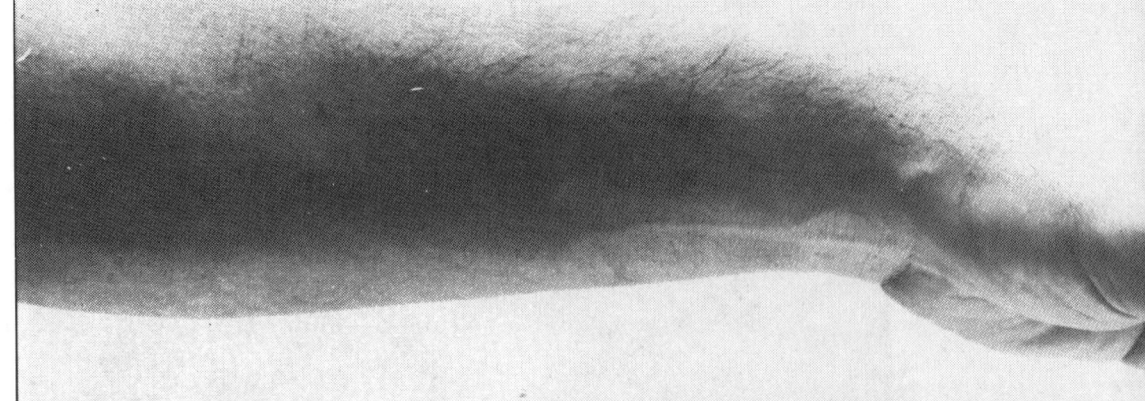

Friends don't let friends drive drunk

Courtesy: SA Breweries. A good example of an advertisement arousing emotion in the public

☐ Non-profit advertising campaigns

Different kinds of non-profit advertising campaigns will be discussed in this section.

Public service advertising

Public service advertising is presented in the conventional formats of advertising, that is typical newspaper or magazine space, radio or television time units, or outdoor posters. These advertisements urge the audience to implement or support some kind of social or economic cause deemed beneficial by consensus of opinion of the general public. Public service advertisements usually urge some kind of specific action. These advertisements are non-political and non-commercial and concentrate on 'good works' with which almost everyone agrees, such as conservation or the prevention of child abuse. Often media time will be

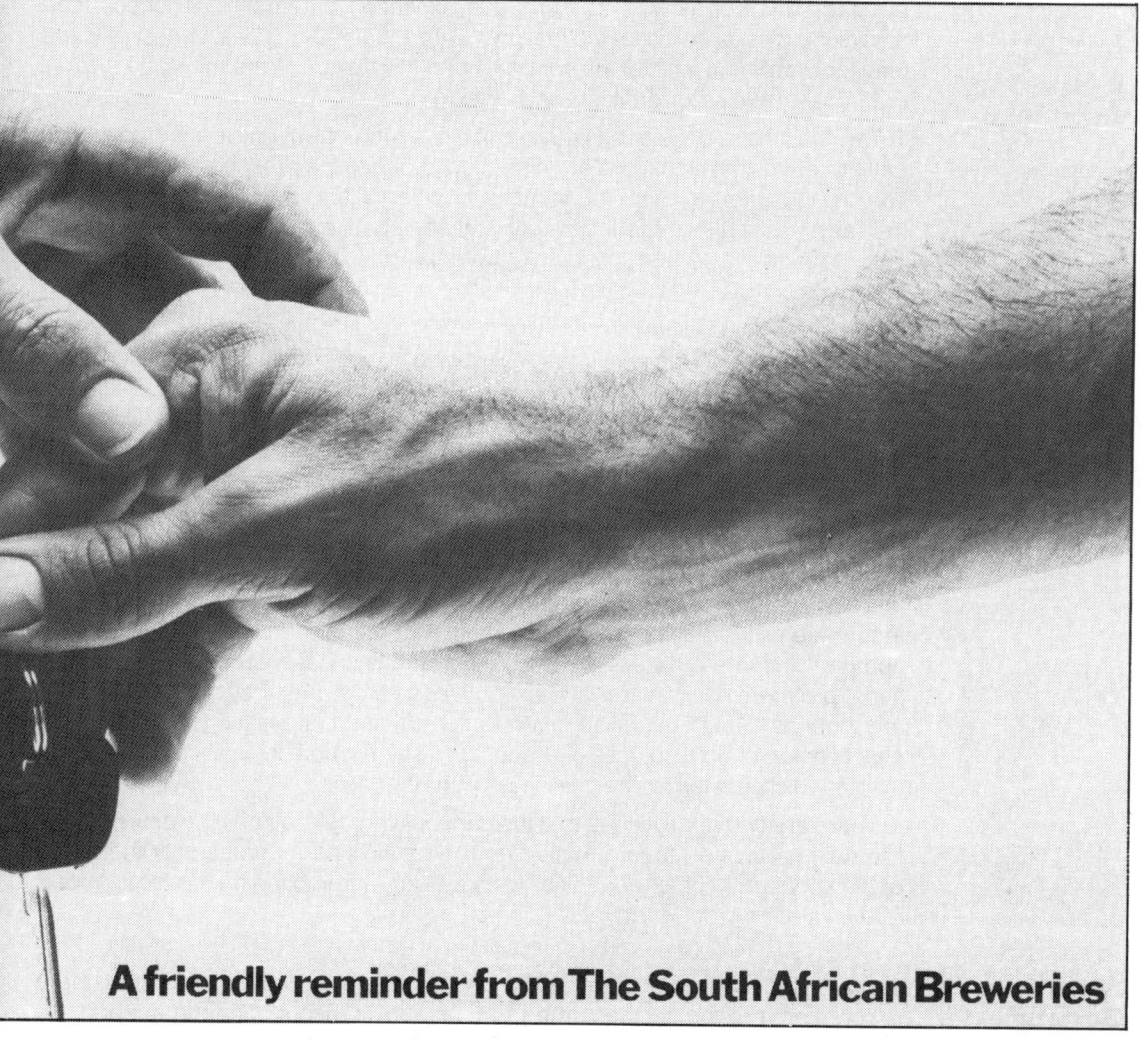

A friendly reminder from The South African Breweries

donated to institutions for the exposure of their advertisements, otherwise the institution or association responsible will have to pay for the advertising time.

The appeals in public service advertising usually have a serious emotional tone. Fear appeals are often used. A typical advertisement on the topic of road safety, for example, will show the fearful results of not paying attention to the message. Consumers tend to defend themselves against fear-producing messages by denying the importance of the information or ignoring or purposely misinterpreting the messages. Mild fear appeals are more successful in capturing attention and ensuring reaction. The 'it could have been you' type of message is used to appeal to pity and compassion, requesting donations or assistance to alleviate suffering. Good examples are the advertisements which show an illustration of the agonised face of a hungry baby or the heartbreaking efforts of a disabled child trying to walk. Humorous appeals are seldom used for public service advertising. One example which attracted much attention comes to mind. This appeal was humorous in execution but implied a serious fear-provoking message. It showed glasses full of liquor moving past very swiftly and inevitably colliding amidst the sound of breaking glass – the message implies the consequences of drinking and driving.

The most frequently used medium for this type of advertising is direct mail. Letters requesting donations are often addressed to the prospective donors personally, thus making them much more meaningful and difficult to ignore. Direct mail as an advertising medium is currently being misused by many advertisers. This leads to waste and ineffective advertising.

Cause advertising

Cause advertising differs from public service advertising in that it is sponsored by business while public service advertising is not. These advertisements are also presented in the conventional formats. They do not encourage action, but are aimed at influencing legislation, gaining a following or moulding public opinion. Cause advertising is sometimes called *advocacy* and usually presents information on controversial topics. Businesses often underwrite cause advertising campaigns in order to demonstrate their societal responsibility and in doing so may of course obtain goodwill for themselves. The chosen theme may or may not be relevant to the sponsor's product. A close relationship between the type of business and the cause being underwritten will cast a positive reflection on the image of the business. Sometimes the theme of the cause has nothing in common with the business of the sponsor and is chosen according to the personal preferences or interests of executives in order that they might profit from any publicity which might be given to the cause. It is difficult to compare the effectiveness of both courses of action, but it seems more logical to choose some theme which relates to the business of the sponsor.

There are two approaches to cause advertising. Sometimes the entire advertisement is devoted to information on the cause and it carries only the name of the sponsor. In other advertisements a slogan promoting the cause is added to the regular product advertisements.

Advertising by Government institutions

Although the services of Government institutions are not usually advertised, there is some advertising by the Armed Forces, the Transport Department and the Department of Posts and Telecommunications. While these advertisements are usually informative and extremely rational, elements of emotional appeal can be detected in some of them. The advertisement for the South African Railways shows a happy family travelling by train, and the Airways advertisement portrays a little boy welcoming his father home from a business trip.

Political advertising

Political advertising can be intended either to boost the acceptability of highly placed Government officials or candidates, or to build an image for a certain political party. This type of advertising is 'old hat' in the United States, where it has been refined to a fine art. In South Africa this type of advertising campaign, aimed at influencing public opinion, is just begining to gain momentum – and there are many rumours that marketing consultants and advertising agencies are being used to promote certain personalities and political parties. The government launched an aggressive advertising campaign – the first in South Africa – in January 1986.

The advertisement consisted of a two full page draft of a letter by the State President:

```
INFLUX CONTROL HAS BEEN ABOLISHED.
THE PASS LAWS HAVE GONE.
THE PRISONS ARE EMPTIED OF THE VICTIMS OF THIS UNHAPPY SYSTEM.
NO SOUTH AFRICAN WILL EVER SUFFER THE INDIGNITY OF ARREST FOR
A PASS OFFENCE AGAIN.
A NEW ERA OF FREEDOM HAS BEGUN.


THAT IS THE REALITY.


        When I made the promise to scrap the pass laws by July 1
    a new spirit of optimism was felt throughout the land.
        Now that promise has been fulfilled.
        And the lies and accusations of those who said it would
    never happen have been proved as empty as the cruel and selfish
    ideologies they would force upon an unwilling nation.
        We are a land of many different groups.  Each with a right
    to freedom.  Each with a right to protection.  Each with a right
    to share in the prosperity of the greatest nation in Africa.
        To those skulking criminals who sneak around at night,
    killing and maiming innocent people in the most cowardly way,
    I say beware.
        The new South Africa will be a land where all decent people
    can sleep with their doors open.  A land where we can look each
    other in the eye.  Without fear or hatred.
NB      And it will come about.  Not because I say so, but because
    my government and I have the power to make it happen.
        That is the reality.
        The time for retribution is over.
        Yes, it is the time for all South Africans to act like men.
    Not lie snivelling with their heads under their pillows.  It is
    time to stretch out our hands and look each other squarely in the
    eyes round the negotiating table.
        You have heard my commitments.
        You have seen that in my hands negotiation is the most
    powerful weapon of all.
        But I will not suffer the slaughter of innocents.  I will
    not contemplate any path towards change other than peaceful
    evolution.
        This I can promise you:  when the history of the new South
    Africa is written, it will not be in blood.
        It will be written in the one thing our enemies fear the
    most - peace and goodwill.

                                        P.W. Botha
                                        State President
```

Courtesy: Bureau for Information

There is also evidence of market research projects launched to determine voters' preferences and prejudices. In order to steer clear of the dangers of discussing local politics, American examples will be quoted to illustrate the level of refinement which has already been reached.

There is some controversy about the use of modern advertising practice in political image-building. Arguments against political advertising tend to emphasise the complexity of political issues and the impossibility of designing an advertising message that will do justice to the issues. However, it is not impossible. An advertising executive, George Lois, points out rather irreverently that the Twelve Apostles were the first advertising agency that succeeded in selling its Candidate to the masses. The strongest argument in favour of using advertising in a political campaign is that advertising is probably the only way in which to reach the masses. Not everyone is able to attend political meetings (normally less than 15% of the voters do) or even to understand what is being said at them. One could argue that voting decisions based on information (truthful information) gleaned from advertisements would probably be more logical than those based on ignorance.

Marketing a political candidate not only entails designing persuasive advertising messages and selecting the most appropriate media, but covers the formulation of an entire marketing plan including the correct positioning of the 'product' (candidate or political party), making sure that the message is conveyed to voters, and disseminating the correct information.

Ronald Reagan's political campaign is an excellent example of this approach. The campaign commenced in 1965, and was based on research to determine how the candidate should be positioned. This resulted in a television advertisement which showed Reagan standing in his book-lined study – a log fire burning in the grate. This warm, friendly, informal and cosy atmosphere allowed ordinary people to identify with the candidate. Today, 20 years later, the image which President Reagan portrays is still the same.

The example quoted above illustrates the success of the 'slice-of-life' appeal, which can be used in many different ways to convey to consumers what the product means, how it should be used, what its benefits are and at whom the advertisement is directed.

The image created in this way cannot be a facade. The candidate should not be shown to be what he is not, because he will betray himself by unconscious gestures and expressions. Voters will perceive this and disregard the message in its entirety. In this way the chances of the candidate may be decreased and the image of the political party tarnished. The editorial or non-advertising approach to message construction is usually followed. The candidate is shown in action, making a speech or giving information on political policy matters.

Media selection is perhaps even more important in political advertising than in advertising of any other kind of product or service. In South Africa, posters are used to try to reach and influence voters. Posters usually consist of a flattering photograph of the candidate, a slogan or brief indication of the policy of the political party and the distinctive logo in 'corporate' colours. In the US an integrated approach is followed and campaign buttons, posters, caps, banners, balloons, slogans and jingles are used.

Television advertising is favoured by political parties with attractive candidates – the unphotogenic candidate does not come across very well. However, Hitler proved to be extremely persuasive on film, and he had an unprepossessing appearance. Even so, many people are convinced that John F Kennedy's success was directly attributable to his boyish good looks and attractive television personality.

Print advertising can also be used to advantage. Richard Nixon's advisers decided to advertise in prestigious magazines such as *Life*, *Look* and *McCall's*. The longer copy of print advertising proved to be an advantage. The illustration of the advertisement portrayed Nixon as a family man surrounded by his attractive family. This portrayal of Nixon as a family man was supposed to capture the interest of American women.

☐ Reinforcing the advertising message

Advertising is not the only tool that can be used to communicate with the target audience. Other communication tools are personal selling, publicity and promotion techniques. All four of these tools should be used in an intergrated way in order to convey the message properly.

Personal selling is a very important tool in industrial marketing. In non-profit marketing personal contact is also sometimes used to communicate with selected members of the target audience and to persuade them to act (often to give a donation or to become a member). This is a rather expensive method of communication because of its limited reach, but a personal message has much more persuasive impact than a non-personal message in the mass media. Boys' Town, for example, employs a contact person to convey information about this worthy cause and to request assistance. The message communicated on a personal basis should be supported by a message in the mass media (advertising). Conflicting information will harm the image of the non-profit organisation.

The use of publicity increases the advertiser's credibility because the message appears in neutral media such as newspaper reports, magazine articles, or television discussions. A good PRO will attempt to obtain as much positive publicity for the product from impartial sources as possible, but free publicity will be forthcoming only if the story is newsworthy or if the general public can benefit from the product offering. Sometimes the PRO will engage in a great deal of effort to obtain a favourable mention of the product offering or the name of the non-profit organisation. Often the non-profit organisation hoping to benefit from publicity will have to advertise in the medium first. The information in the advertisement must be essentially the same as that contained in the report or article. Sometimes a publicity story will be overly enthusiastic, promising benefits which cannot be supplied. Such conflicting messages are bound to result in disappointment and negative attitudes on the part of the receiver. Advertising and publicity should support one another. Publicity is not always positive. Negative publicity can cause much harm and cast a negative reflection on the image of the non-profit organisation. It has already been mentioned that non-profit organisations are open to criticism and all kinds of complaints which are, of course, regarded as very newsworthy by the media. Negative publicity must be countered at all costs; the public must be reassured and presented with the correct information. The alleged misuse of funds is an extremely popular but negative publicity which can cause considerable harm. Needless to say, negative publicity should be avoided as far as possible.

Sales promotion and advertising are complementary promotional tools. The message relayed by one must be reinforced by the other. Sales promotion techniques are short-term incentives to encourage action and are not intended to influence attitudes or to communicate product information. They are often referred to as below-the-line advertising.

Coupons, competitions, contests, displays, demonstrations, exhibits, etc are all examples of sales promotion. If this promotional tool is used in an imaginative way it can help the non-profit organisation to obtain publicity. A display of the drawings of disabled children, for example, may attract the attention of many interested potential donors, as well as the news media, resulting in invaluable publicity. The message should then be reinforced by an advertisement in the news media requesting donations.

Non-profit organisations often use the promotional tools singly or alternately. Ideally, all four tools should be used to communicate the message.

☐ Summary

It has been shown that the advertising function is an aspect of the marketing activities of both profit and non-profit organisations. There is no reason to believe that there is a distinct difference in the way in which these two types of organisations approach commmunication with their target audiences. The product offering of non-profit organisations includes mainly intangibles such as services, causes, ideas and personalities. Because this product offering differs from that of consumer and industrial firms, executives often believe that advertising is the only tool which can be used to market services, causes, ideas or personalities. This is a fallacy. The product itself must provide need-satisfaction and benefits to target consumers, it must be distributed in such a way as to make it easily obtainable, it must be worth the price asked (donation), and all the promotional tools must be used to relay the message to the target audience. Advertising is not a panacea: It cannot stand alone; it cannot compensate for other weaknesses in the marketing strategy; and it cannot solve all marketing problems. Many non-profit organisations suffer from a 'do good' mentality which results in directing all marketing efforts to this objective. Good organisation, management efficiency and an acceptable product offering are often considered to be of secondary importance or the inevitable result of good intentions. This leads to unrealistic expectations about what advertising can accomplish for the non-profit organisation.

☐ References

Assall, H. 1985. *Marketing Management Strategy and Action*. Boston: Kent Publishing Co.

Berry, LL. 1980. 'Services marketing is different'. *Business Day*, 24-29.

Bloom, PN & Novelli, WD. 1981. 'Problems and challenges in Social marketing'. *Journal of Marketing*, Spring: 79-88.

Fine, SJ. 1981. *The marketing of ideas and social issues*. New York: Praeger.

Finegold, PC & Knapp, ML. 1977. 'Anti-drug abuse commercials'. *Journal of Communication*, Winter: 20-28.

Fox, KFA & Kotler, P. 1980. The marketing of social causes: The first ten years. *Journal of marketing*, Fall: 24-33.

Gilson, CG & Berkman, HW. 1980. *Advertising Concepts and Strategies*, New York: Random House.

Kotler, P. 1982. *Marketing for non-profit organisations*. Englewood Cliffs, New Jersey: Prentice-Hall.

Lovelock, CH & Weinberg, CB. 1984. *Marketing for public and non-profit managers*. New York: Wiley.

Murphy, PE & Enis, BM. 1985. *Marketing*. Glenview, Illinois: Scott, Foresman and Co.

Pride, WM & Ferrell, OC. 1985. *Marketing Basic Concepts and Decisions*. Boston: Houghton Mifflin.

Robertson, LS *et al*. 1974. 'A controlled study of the effect of television messages on safety belt use'. *American Journal of Public Health*, 64:1074.

Rothschild, ML.1978. 'Political advertising: A neglected policy issue in Marketing'. *Journal of Marketing Research*, February: 63-67.

Rothschild, ML. 1979. 'Marketing communications in non-business situations or why it's so hard to sell brotherhood like soap'. *Journal of Marketing*, Spring: 11-20.

Russ, FA & Kirkpatrick, CA. 1982. *Marketing*. Boston: Little Brown.

Schoell, WF. 1985. *Marketing Contemporary Concepts and Practices*. Boston: Allyn and Bacon.

13

Direct response advertising

Direct response advertising   *429*

Direct response advertising
Joost van Nispen

Introduction *429*

Benefits of direct response advertising *430*

Direct response advertising objectives *431*

Future developments *434*

Data base marketing *436*

☐ Introduction

'There's a fight brewing below the surface of the advertising business today. A fight between professionals and amateurs, discipline and anarchy, communication and exhibitionism, selling and entertainment' (David Ogilvy 1982).

In the fight referred to by David Ogilvy, the professionals in direct response advertising have always been firmly on the side of *selling* rather than entertaining. And, as Ogilvy predicted, the fight is slowly being won by those who stand for professionalism, discipline, communication and selling. Over the last four years, direct response advertising has become the fastest growing form of advertising in the world – including South Africa.

Direct response advertising is not just a new – or separate – form of advertising. On the contrary, direct response is a new way – a different way – of looking at *all* your advertising and marketing.

In its simplest form, direct response is:
☐ Any form of advertising
☐ using any medium
☐ that allows you to reach a specific market
☐ with a specific message
☐ to create an immediate action.

Action is the key word in direct response advertising. After your message has been seen, read, or listened to, what do you want the consumer to do? You want him to *act*.

Direct response does not pretend that advertising can do the entire marketing job on its own. It sets itself a far more practical goal, namely to elicit a response from selected target markets that are addressed, as far as possible, as *individuals*.

Because it is so important, it will be repeated that direct response advertising is *any* form of advertising, in *all* possible media, that allows you to reach a *specific* market with a *specific* message in order to create an *immediate* action. This definition translates into certain *immediate benefits* to the advertiser and marketer.

☐ Benefits of direct response advertising

It is measurable and fully accountable

Direct response allows you to match spending with revenue. Every response, every lead, every sale can be traced back to its original source, irrespective of whether it is a particular advertisement or insert in a magazine or a specific mailing to a specific list segment. Through coding you always know where it comes from, how much it cost, and how much revenue it generated for you. This means that you can repeat your winners and maximise the cost efficiency of your future efforts.

It is testable

Direct response allows you to measure the effectiveness of your campaign as you go along. Because of its measurability, you can test different strategies, executions, mailing lists and media to maximise your return on investment. You can 'look before you leap', so that when you leap, you leap profitably.

It is this continued testing at minimal expense and risk that enables each marketer to know exactly what works best for him. It increases sales and decreases cost per sale, and that is exactly what direct response is all about.

It is targetable

Direct response allows you to talk exclusively to your prime prospects. There is little wastage in direct response. You reach only those people who have a need for your product or service and are in a position to make use of it, and you communicate with them as *individuals*, one at a time, with specific messages relevant to their particular needs. Your message becomes a *personal* one, and exponentially more effective.

This targeting makes direct response ideal for the segmented markets we find in the 1980s, whether in consumer or business-to-business communications. Key decision makers can be reached in a professional and involving way.

Direct response uses a *scalpel* and not a *scattergun* approach. If you know your prime prospects you can communicate with them on an ongoing basis. If you do not, it allows you to find them by soliciting response to more broadbased offers and helps you to build a list of such prospects. As David Ogilvy puts it: 'If you want to sell contact lenses to prime prospects, there are only two cost-effective ways to go about it. You either buy a list of people who wear spectacles, or you *build* such a list by placing an advertisement that says "Breakthrough for people who wear spectacles. For exclusive information – without any cost or obligation – fill in the coupon below".'

It is involving

Direct response allows you to tell the whole story, uninterrupted by distracting messages. With direct response you can mention every possible benefit and advantage and answer any possible objection. There is no limit on time or space to tell your story, and no clamouring *competition*.

You can also communicate person to person and in the prospect's language – be it technical, friendly, sympathetic or professional. Direct response makes each recipient feel valued and important enough to be addressed personally.

It is multi-media

Direct response allows you to generate results without being restricted to the mail. It uses mail, magazines, newspapers, point of sale, telephone, radio and television. Through all these media it makes people act, and makes them act *now*.

Direct response is also ideally suited to the new interactive electronic media, from *Beltel* to the interactive cable network *Qube* in the United States. This remarkable vehicle allows consumers to actually place their orders through television.

Now that you have seen what direct response is and what it can do for marketers, how does it fit into the overall marketing mix?

> Direct response fits into the marketing mix whenever you want to generate *immediate, measurable results* from your advertising.

This is the general principle. Let us now be specific. Whenever you want to achieve any of the following objectives, direct response becomes an essential – and often the only – part of the marketing mix.

☐ Direct response advertising objectives

If you want to sell things directly

Direct response can sell products by *mail order*, directly off the page. Or it can market financial or insurance products – or almost any other product – *directly* without intermediaries.

If you want to generate trial

Direct response can make sampling exercises far more effective by limiting free samples to those who *request* them. It can help you to segment your market by finding out demographic and psychographic information about your prime sampling prospects.

If you want to generate traffic

Direct response can get consumers to 'vote with their feet' – to come in and test-drive your car, to come into your store to respond to a special offer, or to visit your computer dealership.

If you want to convert traffic into turnover

Traffic generation is only the first step. With direct response you can stimulate turnover as well – especially in retail.

A mystery discount with a guaranteed minimum of 20% discount and a chance to get 30%, 40% or 50% off – even to get your purchase *free* – generates significantly more traffic *and* turnover than a straightforward 25% discount, and at the same unit cost to the retailer.

The same holds for the cumulative point system as used by airlines in so-called frequent flyer programmes. For example, one point per kilometre flown, plus bonus points for business and first class, get *more* people to select your airline (generating traffic) and a greater proportion to upgrade (generating turnover).

If you want to increase turnover

There are only three ways to increase your turnover:

☐ Sell to more people
☐ Sell more to people
☐ Sell at a higher price

Courtesy: Time Magazine

How direct response helps sell to more people, *and* sell more to people – through communicating with *existing* clients – has already been discussed, but what about selling at a higher price?

Direct response is the one way to establish with certainty what price a market is prepared to pay. Frequently different prices are tested in split runs, and it is surprising how often the higher price out-pulls the lower ones. *Testing* is the name of the game in direct response. You need never hit or miss on price policy.

If you want to utilise your sales force more effectively

At a time when the cost of maintaining a sales force is sky-rocketing – it is becoming increasingly difficult to find *good* sales reps – it is foolish to have them run around making cold calls and carrying a few product brochures.

A smart marketer would not waste his sales staff's time like that. He would advertise to *generate leads* – prospects who have shown an interest in his product or service and want more information.

When this approach is used the success rate of sales calls increases dramatically. The rep is now an *invited guest*, there for the specific purpose of satisfying the prospect's curiosity about a product. *What a sales opportunity!*

However, direct response can do more to assist a sales force. The *prospects* or customers can be segmented by sales potential. While the sales force concentrates on those prospects with the highest potential, an ongoing direct mail programme allows you to keep in touch with the others – profitability – because they will eventually become *prime* prospects.

If you want to communicate with your existing customers

In direct response your existing customers are your best source of *future* business. Through ongoing communication you will turn individual customers into loyal, ongoing *clients* and, eventually, into *advocates* of your products, your service, your business.

This process is called 'moving your customer up the loyalty ladder'. No target market gives you as low a cost per sale as your existing customers. Therefore, *always treat your existing customers better than new business*. Give them advance notice before you advertise to the public at large. Give them something special. Do something *exclusive* for them. The results will surprise you.

Once your customers become *advocates* you can even encourage them to find *new* customers for you. In direct response we call this 'member-get-member'. These formalised referral programmes have added significantly to the loyal customer base of such diverse marketers as car manufacturers and dealers, credit card companies, vending machine distributors, airlines and travel agents, car rental companies, industrial marketers, retailers, fund-raisers, you name it.

If you want to generate applications of any kind

Direct response can assist you in getting new credit or retail card holders, to generate subscriptions to magazines and newspapers, and to get prospects to apply for insurance or investment products, or for club membership of children's book clubs or prestigious health spas, gyms and golf clubs.

If you want to involve your staff in your sales efforts

It has already been said that of all target markets, none gives you as low a cost per sale as your existing customers. I will now go one better than that.

Even more cost effective than existing customers are *your own staff*. They are the single most important factor that can literally make or break your campaign. When you involve them in your campaign, when you motivate them to make that extra effort and tell them what you would like them to do, your sales can *double*.

Whenever we do a campaign, our advertising to staff receives as much thought and attention as any print or broadcast advertising aimed at the consumer. For example, when we were about to advertise the Standard Bank's *Gold Fund*, investments increased dramatically as soon as the staff campaign had broken, well before any other advertising or direct mail appeared.

Now I would like to expand on the relationship between direct response advertising and traditional advertising and marketing. I believe it is in this area that we will see some exciting developments in the future; developments that will be nothing short of *revolutionary!*, that will change the nature of marketing and the face of advertising for all time. The revolution has already started – because of market changes, increasing fragmentation and greater scepticism among customers, and a more hard-nosed business approach by marketers who are now less bowled over by great visuals and want *results*.

☐ Future developments

What are the developments shaping the marketing of the future? I see four distinct ones:

☐ Marketing objectives win over media objectives
☐ Continuing recessionary mentality
☐ Mass market breaking up
☐ Reversal of cost structures

Marketing objectives win over media objectives

First, advertising decisions will be based more and more on marketing objectives and media will be ruthlessly analysed to see if they help achieve those objectives.

When you think of some of the products that appear on television that have no right to be on television, you will see what I mean. For instance, a marketer who is prepared to pay the price of reaching two million viewers when his market is a handful of farmers is not understanding his marketing objectives. And neither is his advertising agency. He is allowing his subjective media preference to dictate his advertising strategy.

I am constantly surprised how often even major marketers decide to produce a new television commercial simply because 'It's time for a change', and then use marketing considerations to rationalise this decision. Not too long ago this was the rule rather than the exception, and advertising agencies encouraged it. Or a client might want to 'try direct mail' (as he puts it), so his sales promotion manager – or even his secretary – grabs a pen and writes some 'do-it-yourself' letters. And then they proclaim to the world that 'direct mail doesn't work'.

In both these extreme cases the media choice came first and the strategic and marketing considerations second. This approach is still prevalent, but I am convinced that it will be totally eradicated over the coming years. Marketers will set objectives, identify target markets, rank them in order of priority and develop optimal communication strategies.

Continuing recessionary mentality

I am convinced that the freewheeling, high-spending days of the 70s will never return, not even when we see a dramatic economic upturn. The recession has taught marketers a lesson they are not likely to forget – ever!

'Advertising must help make the cash register ring'. Clients will not accept the hemming and hawing so often heard from advertising agencies when it comes to judging the effectiveness of advertising. They are going to insist on less self-serving, more objective means of measurement.

There is an analogy I would like to share with you. Let us assume that you have 100 salesmen who together are responsible for 100 000 rands' worth of sales. Would you be satisfied with that information? Of course not! You would want to know how each salesman was doing, because you know that at times 20% can be responsible for 80% of your sales. Unless you were a philanthropist, you would fire the losers and hire more winners. Nevertheless, what would not be tolerated in a sales force is still being routinely accepted by major advertisers all over the world.

Incredibly, the majority of marketers still know only the overall performance of their entire advertising campaign, and not that of each individual element. Whereas, as we have seen with direct response, *every element* of the campaign is regarded as a salesman. You can know how each is doing – not by how it looks or by how it sounds, but by how well it works.

In direct response you cannot really be fooled – certainly not more than once. Because of this, direct response will become an increasingly more attractive option to those marketers who insist on rigorous standards of measurement.

Mass market breaking up

Thirdly, the mass market is no longer a 'mass' market. It is naturally segmenting itself into smaller and smaller groups.

Pepsi Cola had only one product in one type of bottle. IBM had only large computers; no medium-sized systems and no PCs. McDonald's had only one hamburger; no *Big Macs* and no *Chicken McNuggets*. Now there are at least four kinds of *Pepsi*, six major IBM product lines and seven kinds of McDonald's for consumers to choose from. People either need, or just demand, choices. Successful marketers provide these choices.

Products for mass markets are becoming rarer. Instead, there are many different products for ever smaller market segments. To survive, we must re-examine whether traditional mass media – radio, television, newspapers and magazines – are the appropriate media to reach small market segments.

Can mass marketers afford to spend substantial sums on mass media, knowing that much of their circulation is wasted, or should they re-focus their thinking and direct their spending towards building loyalty among their customers and trial usage among their best prospects? Suddenly, direct communication with selected *individuals* becomes an attractive alternative, particularly in view of the recent and prospect decline in data processing costs. Direct response, as we have seen, can help you on both sides of this equation.

Reversal of cost structures

Finally, I believe that we will see an accelerating reversal of traditional cost structures. Specifically, the cost of media, salespeople and overheads will continue to rise, while the costs of data processing will continue to go down.

The cost of a sales call in 1985 was $300; a 300% increase over 1977. And there is no end in sight. During the same period, commercial rents in the US tripled in many major metropolitan areas. Conversely, the cost of storing and retrieving 1 000 bits of information tumbled from thousands of dollars to just a few cents – micro chips have become cheaper, smaller and more efficient and the computers that drive them have become simple, easy-to-use inexpensive 'toys'.

This means that:

- [ ] there will be fewer and more costly visits by salespeople to prospects and clients
- [ ] cold calls become ever more expensive
- [ ] there will be greater pressure to sell low-margin products in more innovative ways

☐ Data base marketing

Because of this reversal of traditional cost structures, *data base marketing* has become the latest buzz-word in the direct marketing community. Data base marketing is really an old idea in a new guise.

Simply by recording your customers and prospects by name, home and work addresses and important demographic and psychographic characteristics, you can now selectively:

- [ ] offer the right services and products directly – without the involvement of a salesperson
- [ ] obtain qualified leads for your sales force
- [ ] keep in regular contact with your customers and prospective buyers in a way that is relevant to them

I believe that the formation of a data base will become the corner-stone of the new advertising that I see emerging.

The advertising of the future will include *narrowcasting* as well as *broadcasting*. Measurements will be applied to determine the exact effectiveness of advertising. Response techniques will help marketers to identify prime prospects. Advertising will communicate *with* consumers more and more rather than talk *at* them. And marketers will be far more conscious of the necessity for appropriate positioning of their products and services to various target markets, and in all media.

The advertising of the future will aim to integrate the creation of a long-lasting favourable image and positioning of your product or service with the immediate generation of ongoing sales directly attributable to the advertising.

Direct response advertising will be uniquely positioned to play a key role in defining the advertising of the future. In David Ogilvy's words: 'Direct response is the wave of the eighties . . . It may well become the advertising of the nineties'.

14

Telemarketing

Telemarketing: the medium of the 80s *439*

Telemarketing:
the medium of the 80s
Mike Falkson

Introduction 439

Benefits of telemarketing 440

Co-ordinating with your field sales force 442

Your customers are your best prospects 444

Training telephone sales representatives 445

Keep it ethical 447

Hidden pitfalls of telemarketing 448

Using the telephone to build business 449

Isn't telemarketing too expensive? 450

☐ Introduction

Every decade has an identity that sets it apart. The 80s are no different, for the challenges they present are as obstinate as any faced before.

Inflation is driving up costs in business and industry and eroding the buying power of consumers. Capital for expansion and modernisation is difficult to find. High interest rates are boosting the cost of maintaining inventories and slowing down collections. Competition is getting stiffer and more difficult to meet, threatening the very existence of companies. Travel and hotel costs are escalating the expense of visiting prospects and customers. Lowered productivity in sales and servicing has resulted in escalating marketing costs.

These problems are not new – we have faced many of them before. What makes them so difficult to resolve and us so vulnerable to them is that they are all coming at us at the same time.

This situation calls for creativity, adaptability and innovation. It requires business executives to find new imaginative ways of conducting conventional business, especially in marketing and distribution. Managers need to reassess their assumptions about advertising effectiveness, sales force deployment, market share, marketing, research and other variables.

Telemarketing is an essential factor in the marketing communications mix. This has been demonstrated, field-tested and successfully implemented. It works, and it is cost effective.

Telemarketing can be applied to any and all the functions of marketing – from order taking to full account management. It can be used to respond to inquiries, supplement or replace personal selling, qualify leads, sell to marginal accounts profitably, increase orders, increase advertising effectiveness, replace traditional retail shopping and render instant and cost effective personal service to customers when they need it most.

In essence, then, telemarketing is a system with a specially staffed facility. It should have specially trained professionals supported by special management and marketing information systems. It should be programmed to execute and implement defined sales and service programmes to identified target markets.

Because telemarketing is result oriented, it is now recognised as the means for achieving such key objectives as deeper market penetration and greater market share, controlling sales and service costs, and making advertising more accountable to cost-per-result analysis.

☐ Benefits of telemarketing

Increases sales

Telemarketing is a low cost means of contacting customers and prospects over a broad geographic area quickly. Because communication is two-way, it allows sales personnel to move customers and prospects to a buying decision persuasively and efficiently. Sales volumes can be increased by the expert use of such techniques as up-selling, cross-selling and turning service calls into sales calls.

Supports the field sales force

Once a customer relationship has been established, repeat visits do not always have to be made face to face. The combination of telemarketing's personalised contact with face-to-face selling can raise sales productivity to new levels.

Also, through inbound telemarketing, leads from promotional campaigns can be skilfully qualified. If the prospect is preconditioned over the telephone, the subsequent face-to-face visit can result in a truly productive sales call. Dead-end sales visits can be almost totally eliminated.

Expands market share

Telemarketing deepens market penetration. It can expand your market without expanding your field sales force. It can conveniently match your advertising's geographic reach. You can co-ordinate promotion with extended sales territory coverage to increase sales and enlarge your market share.

Allows intensified sales activity

This is especially valid for those geographic areas and market segments that are low in sales volume. Telemarketing can also support the selling and promotional programmes of your distributors.

Cuts sales costs

The need for highly skilled, well-trained salespeople, coupled with the skyrocketing increases in travel and other sales expenses, have more than tripled the cost of sales calls in the past ten years. An equally skilled and trained but smaller telemarketing staff can cover an even larger territory, with dramatic results – and there are no travel or mileage allowances or hotel, lunch or entertainment expenses to contend with. Thus, productivity is high while the cost per sales contact drops sharply.

Enhances customer service

Your customers can receive speedy answers to product and service problems. Convenient, available service prevents customer problems from developing into deep-seated dissatisfactions. Customers can also obtain information on product usage when they need it most. As a side benefit, product and distribution difficulties are easily recognised and can be promptly rectified, cost effectively.

Increases advertising effectiveness

Advertisement response rates can be improved by inviting customers to place orders with a tele-response centre. Thus, instead of completing an order card or coupon and having to mail it, your customer merely makes a telephone call. The advantages are: prospects can make the purchase while the idea is strong; it is more convenient to telephone than to fill in and mail a coupon; a telemarketing specialist can influence the customer's decision to close a sale; and, since communication is two-way, there are additional opportunities to upgrade, cross-sell and sell alternative items. You will find, as many other businesses have, that you can actually close more sales with telemarketing.

Timely cost/benefit analysis

Prompt response helps you to test the pulling power of direct mail or general advertising. Changes can be made before you make an irreversible commitment to a direct mail promotion.

Prompt data, for example number of inquiries, number of sales, income per sale and cost per sale, can help measure effectiveness.

Targets the market

The selling effort can be targeted directly to specific markets, for example companies employing more than 100 people and having a turnover in excess of R5 million. You can determine the effectiveness of a promotional programme to select telemarketing targets quickly and inexpensively, because responses are quicker by telephone. Management systems can provide rapid analysis of programme performance.

Takes orders

Order taking usually begins with a catalogue or other mailed promotion, or a magazine or newspaper advertisement. The prospect is encouraged to place an order through the convenience of a telephone response centre. An order-taking operation offers the potential for upgrading and cross-selling. In addition, simple marketing research may be done.

Renews subscriptions

Renewals via telemarketing produce what might take several letters to accomplish. Now an integral part of many magazine circulation subscription programmes, the initiating call technique has also been used successfully to sell other products to former customers. More and more publishers are relying on telemarketing for their renewals. *Time* magazine has been using telemarketing for the last five years to achieve high response rates here in South Africa.

Customer service

Customer service is a concern, irrespective of whether you sell to business or consumer accounts. Quickly resolving a problem is a sure way of maintaining relationships with existing accounts.

Qualifies sales leads

Sales lead qualification is designed to eliminate wasted face-to-face sales visits. The better the qualification, the greater the sales potential. Thus, telemarketing supports field salespeople by targeting and preconditioning prospects, which leads to more closed sales and an improved cost/revenue ratio. Many industrial companies insist on qualifying each lead before allowing a face-to-face visit.

Sells to marginal accounts

Marginal account management by means of telemarketing allows a marketer to capitalise on the revenue potential of small accounts. Such marginal accounts, often spread over a wide geographic area, can be handled profitably because of telemarketing's low cost.

Account management

Full account management is at the very zenith of the marketing spectrum. It involves order taking, answering questions about order status, inventory availability, delivery schedules and billing, and product consultation. A full-service operation can include both selling and customer service.

Increases profits

Add them all together – more sales, lower sales costs, greater market share, deeper market penetration, improved advertising effectiveness and enhanced customer service – and what do you have? Greater efficiency, greater productivity and greater profitability.

☐ Co-ordinating with your field sales force

As the cost of the average industrial sales call continues to soar business executives continue to search for ways to make their field sales forces more efficient. More often than not telemarketing is seen as a solution to the problems of those companies caught between increasing sales costs and the need to generate an ever greater volume of sales.

First, you should be aware that when you set up a telemarketing sales force it is bound to affect your field sales force. For one thing, the telemarketing operation can enable you to reduce the size of the field sales force or, in some instances, eliminate it altogether. This can be accomplished by having your telephone sales reps take over some of the sales force's functions such as prospecting and qualifying sales leads. In some cases telephone reps may be able to take over the entire selling and account management function.

It may well be possible to use telemarketing to reduce the costs of direct selling while continuing to generate the same amount of turnover. One way of doing this would be to have telephone reps handle those activities which are just too costly to justify the attention of individual salesmen. Telephone communicators could also take over marginal accounts or those which are geographically remote.

The telemarketing department is an ideal mechanism for opening new accounts in new markets. The objective here would be to build up enough sales in new markets before assigning a field salesman to handle it. Telephone reps can be used for cold calling into geographic areas in which no previous customers exist and to prospect for orders within industries which have not previously bought from you. New product lines can be introduced by telephone.

Of course, the telephone can be used to increase sales in existing markets. This can often be accomplished simply by giving existing customers a special 'hot line' number to use for ordering products between visits by the field sales force. Outbound calls can also be made on a regular basis to encourage customers to place additional orders between sales visits or to find out if additional sales visits are desired.

A telephone sales force makes it possible to ensure that a lead prospecting programme systematically blankets a given area. Telephone reps can place calls to all businesses of a certain size and type within the target area. It will often be found that sales are generated from companies which the field sales force has previously ignored. How often have you heard a salesman say: 'I passed that place every day for years and I never thought they'd be interested!'?

Telemarketing could also be used to ensure that all sales leads are followed up by the field sales force. When field salespeople are responsible for their own prospecting there is no way for management to know if and when leads are being followed up. A centralised telemarketing operation can track the sales leads. When a prospective customer requests a sales visit not only is the appropriate salesperson notified, but an entry to this effect is entered into the data base. Regular reminders are sent to the salesperson (and to his supervisor) until a report is received from the field indicating the result of each sales lead.

Supplementation is a strategy whereby the telephone sales rep and the field sales rep work together to generate a lead and to convert the lead to a sale. In this sense the telephone rep is said to supplement the work of the field salesperson. Supplementation lends itself to at least three levels of activity:

Generating leads

In some telemarketing operations the reps may do nothing more than generate leads. This may be done by outbound prospecting or by generating inbound calls from interested prospects.

Screening and qualifying

For example, the telephone communicator must find out whether the prospect is truly a qualified potential buyer. He should determine how 'hot' the lead is by asking if the company intends to purchase the new item within, say, three or six months.

The telephone rep should ask if the prospect is currently using a particular item and, if so, which make and model. If the prospect is currently using a competitor's product, the telephone rep should ask if he is dissatisfied with that product and, if so why? He should also ascertain who will use the item, who influences the choice, and who has the final decision making power.

Initial follow-up

The telemarketing department should do some of the initial follow-up necessary to bring the prospect closer to a buying decision. This may involve answering questions, mailing sales literature, discussing price and terms, etc. It is extremely valuable to do this sort of follow-up *before* a field salesperson is asked to give an actual demonstration of the product. Having telephone reps handle initial follow-up allows the field salespeople to use their time talking to prospects who are closer to a buying decision.

Another strategy used in co-ordinating field and telephone sales forces is *substitution*. In this case the telephone reps take over the entire sales function on some or all accounts.

Ordinarily, accounts would be assigned to one sales group or another on the basis of size. It is typical in the business-to-business sales situation for 50% of the accounts to provide 80 to 90% of the turnover. The remaining half provide only 10 to 20% of the business, but often take up half of the field salesperson's time. By shifting some or all of these marginal accounts to the telephone force, a company can allow its field salespeople to concentrate their personal efforts on those accounts which yield the best results.

Some businesses have more than one product line. It may be possible to sell one group of products by telephone while another may require demonstration because it is so complex. In this case, accounts that purchase complex products would be retained by the field sales force while others would be handled by telephone.

☐ Your customers are your best prospects

Telemarketing works best where a relationship already exists between the marketer and his customers. Marketers who understand this principle will make it the first objective of their marketing strategy to cultivate existing customers – with the aim of getting them to increase the amount and frequency of their purchases.

Telemarketing can also do an extremely cost effective job of reactivating inactive customers. Most ex-customers would be immensely flattered to receive a telephone call saying: 'We miss you, please come back!'.

The other objective is to win new customers for your company. Telemarketing can do an equally cost effective job in this area.

In all three areas, it is proven telemarketing wisdom to precede the telephone campaign with a *direct mail campaign*. This will cream the mailing list to produce a high quality result at the lowest relative cost. It is then up to telemarketing to maximise the response, and this it can do extremely well. Results of up to 30% are not uncommon where a two-pronged attack is planned in the form of an integrated marketing campaign. In fact, an integrated campaign will always evoke a response two to ten times greater than that evoked by direct mail used alone. The same holds good for telemarketing used in conjunction with space advertising. Advertising can motivate a greater number of readers to respond to an offer, to request more information, or to place an order by telephone.

One of the major advantages of the telephone as a marketing medium is that you are assured of message delivery.

While print and broadcast media obviously play an important role, the telephone is the only interactive medium that gives your company the chance to reach out and speak to every person in each of your market segments, to ask questions, to obtain information, to provide information and even to overcome problems. All these aspects can be handled instantly when you use telemarketing in support of your other activities.

☐ Training telephone sales representatives

Would you be surprised to hear that it has frequently been demonstrated that a person who is an absolute whizz in a face-to-face or an eyeball-to-eyeball situation can prove to be a dismal failure when it comes to selling over the telephone? That is because effective face-to-face salesmanship relies on interpersonal relationships; reactions to a look of pleasure or surprise, a wink, a grin, a handshake, a joke, and so on. Successful telephone sales on the other hand, spring from a carefully prepared and tested script and a voice that smiles! A ten-point training plan for putting together an effective team of telephone reps is set out below.

Thorough briefing

Telephone sales reps should be thoroughly briefed before any telephone marketing programme is implemented. A checklist system for monitoring the result of each call will simplify the telephone rep's task by minimising the time spent on paperwork and maximising the time spent on the telephone.

Successful oral communication

Oral communication is an art few people take the time to master. Effective use of the telephone as a marketing instrument requires far more than merely seating your star salespeople at telephones and asking them to dial the numbers.

Here is one way to teach the telesales technique: The trainer announces that there are certain unchanging rules for successful telephone sales. He then writes the words 'Rules for Successful Telephone Sales' on the blackboard or easel. At this point he states that the people in the room probably know more about telephone marketing than they realise and asks them to list what they think would constitute good attitudes and work habits for telesales people. With a little guidance from the trainer, the trainees will come up with all of the following, which should be listed on the board:

☐ Be articulate
☐ Be enthusiastic
☐ Smile
☐ Use the scripts and prepared material
☐ Control the call
☐ Know when to say goodbye

This information should remain on the board for the remainder of the training.

Each of the attitudes and work habits should be discussed as they are mentioned. Smiling should be emphasised as the habit that can be of the greatest benefit and the one that is most frequently forgotten. It should be pointed out that smiling has a physical effect on the voice box. The effect of smiling on the voice should be demonstrated.

When the topic 'controlling the call' is dealt with, the trainees should be encouraged to sound mature, talk louder than normal and respond quickly to any questions or objections. They should also be told that using the scripts and prepared material will make them more persuasive, since they are not used to using persuasive speech. It should also be pointed out that the scripts fit the image of your company and are legally acceptable, whereas other things the reps might say may not be. Reps should be told not to let every rejection get them down.

Correct verbal speed

Facial expressions plus a natural tendency to do a little lip reading from time to time usually enable people to understand one another more easily in face-to-face sessions. However, when the telephone is employed the voice and the words are the only influences at work. Talking too quickly will often lead to distrust at the other end of the line. The listener may feel that he or she is being pressured into something.

Conversely, speaking too slowly creates impatience, loss of interest and a desire to hang up before the sales message is complete. Cultivating the proper speech rate is one of several things that must be taught to those selected to serve as telephone reps.

Role playing

Proper training and role playing with those who will sit on the telephone for four to five hours daily to represent your company must be a primary consideration in the planning of an effective telemarketing operation.

Communication is a two-way affair. A properly prepared script will include a series of questions to encourage response and meet possible objections. The latter should be answered effectively with answers usually developed from the original test programme.

Telesales reps must be trained not only to deliver their scripts in the most persuasive way possible, but also to listen carefully to what the person at the other end of the line says.

Interpersonal relations and etiquette

Another important element of a good training session is a period of instruction designed to heighten your future reps' ability to deal with customers maturely and courteously. This involves reminding them to say 'please' and 'thank you' and to let the customer hang up first. On the other hand, you will probably find that it pays to offer more extensive training in this area. One rude sales rep can cost your company a great deal of business. As with sales techniques, there are a variety of instructional materials available.

At JC Penney Life Insurance, transactional analysis (TA) concepts are drawn on to help train new telephone reps in dealing more effectively with customers. According to Arnie Sealove, assistant vice-president of JC Penney Life Insurance, 'The TA training has helped our communicators to be more objective and to deal with customers on a more mature level. It's one of the reasons for the continued growth in telephone sales here.'

Motivation

If your reps are involved in up-selling, selling add-on items, or converting service calls to sales calls, you will find that it pays to inspire them with more than just commission. Imaginative incentives are certainly in order.

Product knowledge

This is probably the most important single part of the training. Your reps must know your company's products inside out. Films or video presentations should be employed to show the products and how they are used. After each product presentation the trainer should do a little role playing in which he acts the part of a customer asking the trainees questions about the products. This section of the training may last anything from an hour to two weeks or more, depending on the number and complexity of the products.

Taking orders

When an order is actually placed or an appointment made, details such as date, name and address, quantities, prices, styles, etc should be read back to the customer immediately to eliminate (or at least minimise) the possibility of error. When a complex offer is being made it is wise to check from time to time by asking 'Do you follow me?', or 'Is that clear?'.

Repeat and confirm

A verbal 'yes' on the telephone is often quickly forgotten unless confirmation is received by the prospect within a few days. Telephone sales reps must also reinforce the prospect's affirmative response by repeating whatever the person has agreed to.

Controls

The *number of calls* is a key element in the cost of a telemarketing programme. Therefore it is important that your telesales reps are trained to get through to the decision maker on each call. He or she should not waste time talking to a secretary or an assistant. There is nothing to be gained from going through a script with someone who has no authority to buy. When a business executive is called it is to be expected that a good secretary will challenge your right to talk to him. However, training for this situation with a pre-tested script will help telesales reps to get through quickly and efficiently.

The lengths of the individual phases of training and the amount of emphasis placed on each will vary, depending on the scope and complexity of your operation.

□ Keep it ethical

Continued acceptable use of the telephone as an important marketing tool depends on the manner in which marketers employ this powerful marketing medium.

Calls must offer real benefits and should be short and truthful. They must be made at reasonable times, taking into account the occupational, cultural, ethnic and religious practices of the prospect. It is important that the scripts are created in such a manner that they enable the communicator to terminate a call promptly and courteously when the response indicates antagonism or even a lack of reasonable interest. This means that communicators must be trained to pay attention to what they hear and to what they say. Of course, scripts must furnish them with the logical responses to anticipated suggestions or objections.

The South African Telemarketing Association has adopted the following code of ethics to which all telemarketers in this country would be wise to pay heed:

Prompt disclosure

All telephone marketing contacts should promptly disclose the name of the sponsor and the primary purpose of the contact. No one should make offers or solicitations in the guise of research when the real intention is to sell products or services or to raise funds.

Honesty

All offers should be clear, honest and complete so that the recipient of the call knows the exact nature of what is being offered and the commitment involved in placing an order. Before making an offer, direct marketers should be prepared to substantiate any claims or offers made. Specific claims which are untrue, misleading, deceptive, fraudulent, or unjustly disparaging of competitors should not be used. All documents confirming the transactions should contain the means for the consumer to contact the telephone marketer.

Terms

Prior to commitments by customers, telephone marketers should disclose the cost of the merchandise or service, all terms, conditions and payment plans and the amount or existence of any extra charges such as shipping and handling.

Reasonable hours

Telephone marketers should avoid making contact during hours which are unreasonable to the recipient of the calls.

Automatic dialling equipment

No telephone marketer should solicit sales using automatic dialling equipment unless the telephone releases the line immediately when the called party disconnects.

Name removal

Telephone marketers should remove the name of any contact from their telephone lists when requested to do so.

Minors

Because minors are less experienced regarding their rights as consumers, telephone marketers should be especially sensitive to social obligations and responsibilities.

Prompt delivery

As a normal business procedure, telephone marketers are urged to ship all orders as soon as possible.

Cooling-off period

Telephone marketers should honour cancellation requests which originate within three days of sales agreements.

Unlisted numbers

Telephone marketers should avoid calling telephone subscribers who have unlisted or unpublished telephone numbers unless a prior relationship exists.

☐ Hidden pitfalls of telemarketing

The first pitfall is that it looks so terribly simple — because anyone can speak on the telephone. Of course anyone can, but very few people can market successfully by telephone. And this is the business you are in when you enter the telemarketing mode.

Speaking well on the telephone is certainly essential, but it is just one of the elements which must be correctly handled as part of an overall marketing strategy. You have the same situation in direct mail. Almost anyone can write a letter, but there are barely a handful of professional direct mail writers in South Africa who have the creative ability to produce a letter which will bring the advertiser measured success.

The telephone is like the postage stamp in direct mail — both permit delivery of the message. However, what that message is to be, who should receive it, when and how it should be communicated, with what specific purpose, what should precede the phone call, what should follow the call, what information should be elicited, what information should be recorded on a data base and when you should make the next call are just some of the things which must be carefully considered and structured into telemarketing strategy.

Once you have finally developed your marketing strategy you have to test it and improve it until you have achieved a cost effective programme.

What else is there to do after you have achieved a cost effective, profitable programme? Well, you had better watch it and guard it as carefully as you manage your sales force, because the fact that you have an effective sales force does not permit you to fire the marketing or sales managers – or the area manager.

The same holds for your in-house telemarketing unit. This requires company commitment from board level down. The telemarketing unit itself – no matter how small – requires a competent operations manager, supervisor and lead communicator. Their role is to ensure that the programme is carried out correctly. They must be alert to unexpected situations which could hurt results, able to turn adversity into profit and must ensure honesty – no matter what the temptation – and courtesy – no matter what the provocation. It is your company's name that they are using, and your company's image and reputation that are on the line.

Telemarketing results are measured and monitored by the hour. A downward trend must immediately trigger an investigation: 'What's happening? Why is the programme falling down? Is it just one communicator who is having a bad spell, or is the falling trend general among all the communicators?'. Similarly, the fact that one communicator is producing twice the average result must be investigated. 'Why!? What is he doing so right, or is he perhaps doing something not so kosher?'.

Telemarketing is *not* as simple as it looks or sounds. It is just as complex a medium as direct mail and it must be expertly managed to be effective. A short list of reasons why many in-house programmes fail follows:

☐ No dedicated telemarketing management and/or supervision
☐ Ineffective hiring practices
☐ Poor, insufficient training of communicators
☐ No constant monitoring of communicators by experienced supervisors
☐ No daily motivation of communicators
☐ Poor script writing, incompetent revision
☐ Poor testing and evaluation of scripts
☐ Communicators permitted to ad lib
☐ Unprofessional attitudes expressed over the telephone
☐ Poor telephone speaking techniques and manners
☐ Poor handling of objections
☐ No job satisfaction
☐ No stand-ins available for illness of communicators
☐ Dishonesty of communicators (white lies, high pressure tactics, etc, especially rampant when commissions are paid)
☐ Insufficient remuneration and/or fringe benefits
☐ Not cost efficient
☐ Uncongenial working environment
☐ Necessity to keep hiring (communicators regard their work as temporary and average six weeks on the job)

By eliminating these pitfalls you could be well on the way to success.

☐ Using the telephone to build business

Take your primary sales media – television, radio, newspaper and/or direct mail – integrate it with the telephone and you will have created a more powerful marketing formula, every time. The telephone is an essential tool in this multi-media era, and its success when tied to other media is well documented. In combination with direct mail, for example, telephone marketing programmes have proved to be two to ten times more effective than direct mail alone.

☐ Isn't telemarketing too expensive?

Robert Stone, chairman of the internationally-known direct marketing agency Stone & Adler, Inc, once said:

> In this day of multi-media, we are finding more and more that the telephone is becoming an integral part of the media mix. True, a telephone call is a more expensive contact than any other direct resonse medium. But what really counts is cost-per-result. And here telephone is often less expensive. In my opinion, to pass up the opportunities in telephone marketing because you are afraid of cost is to be blind to a proven marketing opportunity (personal communication).

I totally agree with him, because we find that the cost-per-result is the most important factor.

15

Below-the-line advertising

Below-the-line activities   *453*

Below-the-line activities
Christina Burlock

Sales promotion in South Africa 453

The key to successful sales promotions 455

Tried and tested motivators 456

Can a promotion be evaluated? 459

References 460

☐ Sales promotion in South Africa

World over, the use of sales promotions has escalated dramatically in recent years.

In the UK, 'below-the-line' has shown a 250% growth in five years, compared with a mere 63% growth in 'above-the-line' spending during the same period! (Peterson 1985). England's 'below-the-line' spend exceeded that of advertising as far back as 1976. In the USA, the cross-over point was reached some years earlier − in 1970.

Two thirds of the UK 'below-the-line' spend comprises trade deals, discounts and price-offs. If statistics were available, South Africa would probably plot a similar developmental pattern − a recent dramatic growth in the monies invested 'below-the-line', two thirds being spent on trade deals and price-offs.

The remaining third is made up of the more tangible and visible activities known as 'sales promotions'.

Why such rapid growth? The first and most obvious reason for the rapid growth in sales promotions is the extreme youth of the industry. In the early 70s Lever Brothers offered a R5 000 cash prize to purchasers of *Surf*. At the time, this was one of the biggest prizes ever offered in South Africa! The 'science' of sales promotion has evolved rapidly since then, with budgets of R250 000 for trade, sales or consumer incentives not uncommon today.

The second reason is a logical extension of the first. As more sales promotions were produced, the marketers and promotion houses became more expert, which in turn produced better results. Encouraged by the effectiveness of sales promotions in terms of improved sales or share gains, marketers continued to increase their 'below-the-line' spend.

Finally, there is the cost factor. Since the advent of television many advertisers have become 'disenchanted' with the 'less effective' media. Those who cannot afford to appear on the box tend to look at sales promotion as the 'next most effective' method of promoting sales and support their press, radio or outdoor advertising with comparatively heavy 'below-the-line' spends. The top marketing companies also tend to spend heavily on sales promotions, having saturated television.

Sales promotion in South Africa and overseas

The Institute of Sales Promotion in South Africa (ISP) uses the same definition of sales promotion as the ISP in England. Looking at this definition, and comparing it with those in American textbooks on promotions shows that the *principles* of sales promotion are universal, but in practice South Africa stands alone:

> All manner of marketing devices and techniques applied *tactically* or *strategically*, in such a way as to *emphasise, enhance or add to* the communication of the *basic proposition of a Brand*, Group of Brands or Service, with a view to *increasing acceptability* by *consumers* or *distributors*, excluding the techniques of media theme advertising, basic product display, the Press Relations area of Public Relations activity and Direct Mail as defined by that Association.
> (From the South African Institute of Sales Promotion Code of Practice).

This is a long, complex definition, but the essence can be gained by looking at the italicised words. (One of the most fundamental mistakes made in the area of sales promotion is to underestimate the necessity to '*emphasise, enhance or add to . . .* the *basic proposition of a Brand*'. All too often the brand is 'forgotten' in the excitement of 'trips to Disneyland', 'dream kitchens' or '5 bakkies to be won'!).

The words that should be added to the definition here in South Africa are 'within the confines of the law'. Sales promotion in South Africa is governed by two major Acts, a plethora of government regulations and a host of self-regulatory bodies. Together they create restrictions unique to South Africa. But they also offer protection to consumers, protection very necessary when the unique make-up of the South African population is considered.

Sales promotion and the law

The two major Acts that restrict sales promotion activities are the Gambling Act, 1965 (Act 51 of 1965) and the Trade Practices Act 1976 (Act 76 of 1976 as amended).

The Gambling Act prohibits any game of chance. Bingo, lotteries and forecasting the outcome of a sporting event (ie football pools), all popular sales promotion activities in other countries, are outlawed here.

South Africa's Trade Practices Act was amended on 14 February 1984. The intention was to free trade coupons from their previous restrictions, thus allowing them to be supplied in 'advertisements', or in connection with the sale of goods, or the provision of services, provided they comply with the amended section 10 of the revised Act. The end result, however, was confusion. The amendment was worded in such a way that lawyers could interpret its meaning in a multitude of ways. Just when you thought it was safe to use a trade coupon . . .!

Whilst the Gambling Act discourages creative promotions, lawful schemes may be devised where chance (as opposed to skill) determines the distribution of prizes. However, the question whether a scheme is lawful is not easily answered, and the issues are often blurred. It is always better to err on the side of caution to avoid the high legal costs which follow a prosecution, even if the defense is successful.

When assessing the legality of a promotion, be advised to seek professional advice. There are members of the legal profession who are well versed in the relevant Acts and the various cases that serve as precedents or guidelines as to how the courts might interpret the Law. In general terms a company lawyer is not the best adviser. He is not as knowledgeable about the Acts in question as a competitive, aggressive marketer needs him to be. Use the experts.

An illegal or suspect sales promotion is all too easy to stop in its tracks. A member of the public (or usually a competitor) simply has to walk into a police station and file a complaint. The Advertising Standards Authority could also take action against a company running a promotion that contravenes its Code of Practice. If warranted, the ASA has the power to prevent the offending company from advertising in almost any major media in the country!

Examples of illegal promotions abound, but the risk of being contested is high and the penalties are often expensive. Successful sales promotions do not depend on getting around the law, but on the skill of the promotions consultant in getting *to* the target market.

☐ The key to successful sales promotions

A list of all the different types of promotional activities certainly helps to illustrate the vast scope of sales promotion, but it will not make you an expert. Someone with a knowledge of coupons, consumer competitions or sales force incentives can create a successful sales promotion, provided he or she knows *how to motivate* and *who to motivate*. These two simple factors are the key to success.

The *Klim* 'win a Dairy Cow' competition is a good example of a successful promotion based on this essential 'knowledge' of the target audience. The aim of the exercise was to increase the sales and market of *Klim* in the *rural* Black market. As the manufacturer's sales force did not call on the rural trade, the first 'target market' that had to be 'motivated' was the wholesale trade.

A 'proposed' plan was put to each wholesaler together with the question: 'We need your advice . . . if we were to action this plan, how many free "kits" do you think you'd need for your customers?'. The 'motivation' here was simply the ego appeal of being asked advice . . . and everyone gave it gladly. At the same time, they unconsciously committed themselves to a performance level, an easy commitment because the plan was not 'actual' and the kits were 'free'. Both these aspects reduced the 'stress' associated with decision making.

Once the wholesalers' commitment and the quantities required had been researched, the actual 'kits' were produced. The kits were flashed 'Win a Dairy cow with *Klim*'. A letter inside the kit explained how the retailer could win his cow. He simply had to erect the point-of-sale material and hand out the entry forms provided. If one of his customers won a cow, then he would also win. A large reply-paid envelope allowed the retailer to submit all his customers' entries free of charge.

The motivating factor in the case of the retailer was, of course, the cow. To him, cows are 'labola', status symbols, symbols of wealth, givers of milk. Cows produce calves and ceremonial occasions demand the slaughter of an ox or cow – the prize had enormous appeal.

As the trader handed out entry forms to his shoppers, sales of *Klim* soared. The entry form featured a crossword puzzle (called Jackpot in the Black market) and the clues demanded a careful study of the copy on the sides of the *Klim* tin. This simultaneously educated the reader as to the merits of *Klim* as a product and brand.

A solitary cow provided the motivation to pursue the competition and become involved with the brand. The end result? Two hundred and forty thousand entries from (rural) consumers. The point-of-sale material long outlived the promotion, the big full-colour pictures of that treasured animal, the cow, ensuring the product's popularity. Flanking each picture of the cow were pictures of satisfied consumers and pack shots – a perfect sales proposition. *Klim* moved from second place to brand leader in the Transkei, and from third place to second in South Africa!

To the best of our knowledge, cows had never been offered as prizes before that competition. And that is the moral of this story! Sales promotions should not be dictated by lists of what has been done in the past, but rather by the desires, needs, aspirations and fears of their target markets.

☐ Tried and tested motivators

There are common responses that run throughout most levels of society:
- ☐ Most people like a bargain.
- ☐ Most people want something for nothing.
- ☐ Most people are, to a degree, competitive.

These traits are most commonly exploited with the three ageless appeals:
- ☐ Save!
- ☐ Free!
- ☐ Win!

Some examples of these proven motivators are dealt with below.

Price promotions

Price cuts and bargains are likely to interest about 75% of all housewives. The propensity to purchase depends on the product, the amount of the saving and the ease of availability.

Two for the price of one

These offers are used extensively to gain trial, being an 'optimum' bargain. 'Three for the price of one' would be rejected as 'too generous, must be something wrong', and anything less than 'Two for the price of one' allows room for debate: 'I don't really need it', or 'I might not like it'.

In South Africa, many marketers have had to withdraw '2 for 1' stocks when the combined 'weights' of the products do not comply with the metrology regulations governing that product category.

Get this much free

This is a good sales motivator when flashed on-pack to indicate the amount of stock free. Depending on the circumstances, this offer has certain legal sensitivities and should be cleared before actioning.

Price-off coupons

Certainly not as popular in South Africa as in the USA, coupons still have some merit in terms of inducing trial. Insensitive couponing on cosmetics, perfumes, etc, can destroy a brand's credibility or desirability. Coupons on medicinals are carefully controlled by the Medicine Control Council.

The administration involved in the redemption of coupons can be handled by the product manufacturer or ceded to a coupon clearing house.

Pre-printed price-offs

Discounts or price-off offers should be printed on-pack only after approval has been gained from the distributing outlets.

Added value offers

A way of inducing purchase without lowering the price of a product or service is to add some other form of 'value', for example 'Get a R5,00 kite for R1,00. Send R1,00 plus the label from this bottle'. Since these promotions fall within the realms of the Trade Practices Act, legal advice should be sought on the correct phrasing of the offer.

Trading stamps

Outlawed until February 1984, trading stamps are now permissible provided they comply with the stipulations of the amended Trade Practices Act.

Self-liquidating offers

In this form of promotion all the promoter's costs are repaid by monies received from the respondents. The most common use of a self-liquidator is to create interest in a pack by using a panel as the main communication media. The item offered should be either novel (such as a distinctive coffee set as used in a heavily exposed coffee TV commercial), or extremely attractively priced. Certain companies specialise in the fulfilment of such offers, handling the packing and postage, etc on behalf of the promoter.

In-pack premiums

The value of the premium cannot differ from one pack to the next, as this would contravene the Gambling Act.

Competitions   Paton Tupper's research and in-house investigations show that roughly 50% of housewives show more of an interest in bargains/price-offs than in competitions, about 25% are more interested in competitions than in price-offs, and approximately 25% do not react to either stimulus.

Of the 25% interested in competitions, a small percentage ($\pm$ 3%) are regular or 'professional' entrants – and as such are extremely fickle, switching from one brand to another for the sake of the competition presently running. A slightly larger percentage ($\pm$ 6%) enter competitions fairly frequently, but display the same useful interest in the product as they do in the competition itself. The bulk of those interested ($\pm$ 15%) enter infrequently, triggered only by prizes that appeal strongly to them.

However, the *audience* of a competition can be far wider than these figures indicate. The ability to attract readers is the first criterion that a competition should meet. Once a reader's attention has been gained, the entry form should create sufficient interest in the product to increase brand awareness, encourage trial and, ultimately, sell the product to a now-convinced consumer. The success of consumer competitions should be judged on the resultant sales, and *not* on the number of entries received.

The White South African male is, in general terms, not responsive to 'ordinary' competitions. To achieve some measure of success the promotion should be precisely targeted and expressly challenging. The 1985 *Camel* Okavango Challenge and the 1984 and 1985 *Castle Lager* Tavern Tour of Europe ('Have You Volunteered?') are good examples of specific and successful targeting.

Blacks enjoy consumer competitions provided they are simple and, preferably, entertaining. In order to encourage a higher percentage response rate among Black consumers, marketers should spend a portion of their budgets publicising the winners. Suspicion and mistrust that the marketer has not honoured his commitment will impact negatively not only on the response to his future promotions, but on his product's sales as well!

Character merchandising

The use of TV characters (most of which are available for a fee from the licensor) almost guarantees a higher than average interest level. Characters have been used to increase the appeal and impact of competitions,.as well as a vast range of merchandise such as sweets, snack lines, kiddies' clothing, etc.

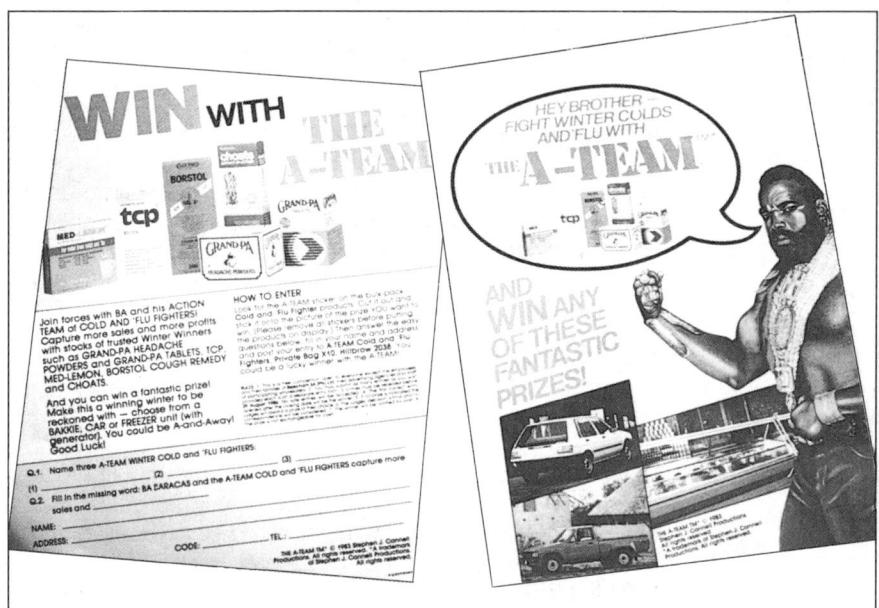

Using the popularity of the A-team to promote products to the black market

On-pack competitions

There are several dangers in this route. The competition 'closing date' can 'age' the pack and hinder sales if the pack is still on-shelf after the promotion ends. Certain trade sectors do not allow consumer competitions in their stores, and therefore do not accept stock featuring on or in-pack competitions.

Nevertheless in 1985 *Body-on-Tap* shampoo enjoyed considerable sales success through in-packing real and fake diamonds. Through the media, consumers were invited to pick out the packs containing the real diamonds (test of skill).

Personalised in-store competitions

Although the prizes are far smaller than those offered in national competitions, the prize-per-store route encourages consumer participation through the increased chance of winning: 'Win this braai in this store'. The presence of a physical prize aids the salesman in negotiating good display space and encourages the store's participation (as it is guaranteed that one of its customers will win.)

Media-linked competitions

Media support (especially TV) certainly increases the response to competitions. Certain radio stations and magazines will exchange a measure of free competition 'exposure' for the right to award your prize to one of their listeners/readers.

Incentives

Motivating the sales force

Salesmen are usually highly competitive people. More often than not they thrive on being pitted against each other (or an opposition company). In some companies sales incentives are viewed in a negative light ('they are paid a salary to sell – keeping their jobs should be incentive enough.'). A more enlightened attitude is to acknowledge that 'selling' today is not exactly 'challenging'. Incentives provide the challenge that brings the best out of a basically competitive person. The rewards do not have to be financial or material. Recognition, status and pride are the real motivating factors!

A danger in sales force motivation is to create a 'race for the top' amongst the top two or three people, the rest giving up knowing full well that they cannot compete at that level. Better overall results are achieved when *every* salesperson is motivated (eg *every* salesman to achieve target goes into the draw for a week in Mauritius). Under these circumstances, the 'challenge' should still exist for the most competitive performers (eg *plus* the two salespersons highest over target win a week in the Bahamas).

Incentive travel

Incentive travel is the term used to describe the scheme whereby if a pre-set target is reached the entire company (or the entire sales force) enjoys a five-star holiday together at some exotic destination. It sounds expensive, but it is not! The sales target is set at a level that will yield normal company profits plus sufficient additional profit to pay for the entire venture.

To investigate this route further, contact an agency specialising in incentive travel, a 'regular' travel agency will not have the necessary expertise.

Motivating the trade

'Trade marketing' is developing rapidly in South Africa. Good trade relationships have to be built up over a period of time, based on mutual respect for each other's business requirements.

☐ Can a promotion be evaluated?

Sales promotions are possibly the most measurable of all the marketing tools. The areas of evaluation are the following:
☐ Sales force reaction – are the salespeople excited and motivated to sell?
☐ Trade reaction – has the promotional activity had a positive effect on the trade's attitude to the brand?
☐ Sales in – are the sales figures above the norm for that period?
☐ Are the sales equal to those targeted for the promotional period?

☐ Displays – photographic evidence, trade visits or sales managers' report-backs are studied.

☐ Consumer response – Coupon redemptions and entry forms received are indicative of the level of awareness gained by a promotion. Unfortunately, since promotions usually differ in terms of the motivation offered and communication methods used, it is difficult to assess what levels of response should be received.

☐ Sales 'out' – with bar coding, sales figures of goods through the major trade are available almost immediately.

☐ Brand shares – short and long-term gains should be visible in audited markets.

Finally, although sales promotions are all too often viewed as 'short term' and 'tactical', *responsible* promotional activities should aid long-term 'brand building'. Promotions should *support* and *enhance* the basic brand proposition. Do yours?

☐ References

Petersen, C. 1985. Sales promotion in action. London: Associated Business Press.

16

Promoting prescription pharmaceuticals

Promoting prescription pharmaceuticals *463*

Promoting prescription pharmaceuticals

John Edmunds

Introduction *463*

Communication activities and their importance *465*

The basic elements of the promotional mix *467*

References *474*

☐ Introduction

Promoting prescription pharmaceuticals to health care professionals, the consumer's decision makers, has many aspects in common with true consumer marketing.

Successful promotion, that is brand preference or insistence, is in fact due to an educational or learning experience which results in a change in habit. In other words the prescriber or recommender (in the pharmacist's case) has to 'unlearn' old patterns of behaviour.

Regardless of the vehicle of promotion, the message transmitted to the receiver (eg prescriber) must be put across in a logical, structured fashion making maximum use of a centralised theme based upon a unique selling proposition (USP). It is this USP that positions the product in the market-place, giving it its relationship to the competitors' products and carving out for it a niche in the prescriber's armamentarium.

When engaging in ethical pharmaceutical promotion one has all the tools at one's disposal that one has for consumer promotion, with the exception of certain media such as outdoor, television, radio and the lay press. Of course, this should be taken into account when off-prescription medicines for self-medication are promoted directly.

One significantly unique feature of prescription drug promotion is the use of and often dependence upon the salesman, who is known by various titles in different countries (eg medical representative or medical detailer).

When the copy and layout of either a brochure or an advertisement is designed, or when a personal sales presentation is structured, one important axiom should be considered constantly. The higher the level of education or knowledge of the target audience the greater the need to present the promotion in a form which fosters a dialogue. Ignorant people have to be told *why* a particular product will serve their needs; knowledgeable people have to be convinced by logical argument that the product *will* serve their needs. The latter people wish to feel that they made the decision themselves and that the promotional campaign merely assisted them in arriving at their decision.

Medicine is a benefit versus risk situation, and to obviate a sense of post-prescription cognitive dissonance the prescriber must feel that all factors were known and considered by him. The most important aspect of this process, especially due to the educational standard of the target group, is that all statements must be believable.

Consumer behaviour and the communication process are aspects vital to the design of any programme, and an understanding of these should permeate all aspects of the campaign, be it print, audio-visual or personal. At this point it is imperative to understand that the theme should dominate and permeate all three elements of the promotional mix. The decision maker should be viewed as an information processing and decision making entity.

The communication process is essentially tri-elemental:

☐ source
☐ message
☐ receiver (destination)

In personal communication the receiver is an individual, and in mass communication the destination is a group (see the contribution entitled 'The nature and process of advertising' in chapter 1). The distinction is drawn here because it cannot be assumed that all of the members of the group receive. Furthermore, in mass communication an additional communicative element is required, namely the medium (of communication). The transferral of the message communicated cannot be guaranteed, because between the source and the receiver it is subject to distortion or 'noise' emanating from varying sources, internal to both the source and receiver, or external.

Three basic requirements for effective communication exist:

☐ It must be designed to gain the receiver's attention.
☐ It must be understandable by both receiver and source.
☐ It must arouse receiver need and be able to satisfy this need.

To achieve these criteria the communicator needs to have a knowledge of his audience. The marketer should be able to classify the target market's motives, and in medical marketing these go beyond the basic physiological needs, which are solely patient owned. Prescriber needs must be addressed, namely to effect a cure or disease control in the patient without causing further harm and, if the quantity of life cannot be increased, to improve the quality of life. Preferably, both quantity and quality should be enhanced.

If they were asked what the important needs are, most medical practitioners would answer in words to the above effect. Needs often ignored are the needs of the prescriber himself and satisfaction of these centres around the self-actualisation, ego-bolstering, ego-defensive and affectional needs of the prescriber. These needs should not be condemned: the prescriber is a person and as such has the same needs as the average man. In fact, he would not have achieved professional status without an above-average motivation, essentially in the achievement or self-actualisation areas.

Due to the health care professional's training, his level of perception is in a highly developed and specific state. Understanding of this factor is vital, because both perception and learning are involved in the interpretation of any stimulus (communication is a stimulus). This leads to a further behavioural element in the health care professional communication process, namely selective perception. The professional mind is highly selective regarding which stimuli will be allowed to contribute to the learning process.

This in turn leads to apperception (perception in the light of previous experience) and how it influences decisions, and selective retention (the rate of retention and forgetting different signals). Again, these aspects are more highly developed among professional people, especially when communication with them is in their areas of specialisation.

□ Communications activities and their importance

Promotion is a costly process and the elements of the mix vary in importance, with managers being bludgeoned into using the various elements at different levels of intensity. The bludgeoners are often those people who as marketers in their own right are intent on selling their particular medium.

Several surveys in the UK (see table 16.1), South Africa (see table 16.2), and the USA (see table 16.3) have been published and in fact reflect similar findings. These should be used to form a basis for promotional mix decisions.

Table 16.1
United Kingdom: sources of information about therapeutic risk for a range of self-selected adoptions of new drugs

	Therapeutic risk		
	High	Medium	Low
Representatives	25	31	39
Mailings	14	17	19
Journals	19	8	9
Colleagues	12	14	8
Consultants	18	8	4
Other sources	12	22	21
Total number of sources used	125	154	89
Average number of sources used	2,77	2,70	2,34
% Professional sources used	49%	30%	21%
Average time taken to adopt (weeks)*	74	51	49

*Time taken to adopt is the period between release onto the market and first use.

Source: Journal of Royal College of General Practitioners, 1975, vol 25.

Therapeutic risk is a function of the pharmacological activity of the medicine. The more benign the disease the less toxic the medicine and the lower the risk. For example, a cough mixture is considered to constitute short-term therapy and is a low risk product, whereas medicines for the treatment of heart rhythm disturbance are high risk products and the duration of therapy is most probably lifelong.

To maintain market share for a low risk product an intensive promotion at representative level is required, because due to its 'representative' sensitive nature the prescriber could easily switch. The opposite could be expected of a high product – other factors play a more major role in convincing the prescriber. Therefore, irrespective of the number of representative calls, the prescriber is unlikely to change under this influence alone.

Table 16.2
South Africa:
communications
activities in
descending order
of importance as
they affect the
doctor in his
practice

Communications activities	Mean score out of 15
Medical journals	11,06
Continuing medical education lectures	10,71
Medical Association organised congresses	9,65
Reference works	9,20
Company organised seminars	9,19
Medical representatives	9,19
Medical newspapers	7,99
Samples	7,71
Company organised social functions	7,22
Detailing aids	6,79
Product advertising pieces	6,68
Medical exhibition	6,56
Pharmaceutical company home journals	6,18
Product related give-aways	6,18
Direct mail	5,76

Source: Marplan Pharmaceutical Communications Study, March 1981.

Table 16.3
United States of
America: adjusted
comparison of
findings regarding
sources
influencing a
doctor to prescribe
a new drug

Source	Ferber & Wales study	Coleman study	Fond du Lac study	Gaffin study
Detailmen	21,1%	20,9%	38,2%	44,0%
Medical journal article	22,8%	18,9%	25,4%	17,0%
Direct mail	15,4%	30,1%	8,7%	22,0%
Medical journal advertisements	5,4%	2,2%	8,8%	15,0%

Source: Smith, Mickey C. 1975. *Principles of Pharmaceutical Marketing.* Lea & Fabigen.

Without a detailed analysis and correlation, an appreciation of those elements of the promotional mix that apply to medical marketing can be made by inspection. Note that the relationships between the elements are reasonably consistent in the three countries and at different times. Also, if highly specific correlations are to be made the details of the methods of research are necessary. It is also apparent that the relative importance of each element does not vary much over time.

Promotional spend

When a promotional budget is designed the major problem is the level of spend to be decided upon.

Consumer markets generally devote an advertising share of about 1,7 times that of the share of sales planned during the initial two years and thereafter maintain their share of advertising in line with their share of sales.

The pharmaceutical industry has a somewhat different ratio and is more closely related to the year of introduction and year's post introduction.

Table 16.4
The ratios of
promotional
expenditure % to
market share %

Year 1	4:1
Year 2	2 or 3:1
Year 3	1:1
Year 4	1:1

Sources: Peckham Sr, James O. 1975. *The Wheel of Marketing.* Nielsen Marketing Research. Slatter, Stuart P. 1977. *Competition and Marketing Strategies in the Pharmaceutical Industry.* London: Croom Helm.

Marketers must realise that promotional spend means total marketing spend across the mix. Too often one (or more) element(s) is reduced or withdrawn while the ratio in the other elements is maintained, and the reason for the drop in share is questioned. It is simple — the total ratio has been reduced. Reduce in one area and it is necessary for the spend in the other elements to be increased. For example, if personal promotion is stopped media expenditure must be increased to a level to compensate and to allow the total spend to remain at the required ratio, within the terms of the expectations for the product.

It is interesting to study the level of promotional expenditure as a percentage of sales in selected countries (see table 16.5).

Table 16.5
Promotional
expenditure as a
percentage of
sales in selected
countries

Country	Promotional expenditure as a % of sales
USA	22
West Germany	22
Italy	22
South Africa	22
Belgium	21
Canada	21
Sweden	18
India	18
France	17
Turkey	16
UK	15

Source: World trends in the pharmaceutical industry, 1976-80, Scrip & Stockton Institute

☐ The basic elements of the promotional mix

The detailer (medical representative)

When the advertising or promotion of pharmaceutical products is considered the role of the medical representative cannot be ignored. This individual is somewhat unique among salespeople, because he (becoming more and more 'she' as the profession attracts well-qualified women) tends to be the vehicle for the transmission of the advertising message. It is the medical representative who:

☐ carries the advertising brochure to the potential prescriber
☐ uses the brochure during the sales presentation
☐ verbalises the message

In over-simplistic terms, the medical representative is to the ethical product what television and radio are to the consumer product. The only differences are that the situation is more personal (a one-to-one situation), the message is longer and, hopefully, dialogue ensues.

Thus, no chapter on medical advertising would be complete without a discussion of the role of the medical representative as part of total promotion and the inclusion of the detailer's oath (Sutton 1960:19).

The Detailer's Oath:

I do hereby solemnly swear that I will tell the doctor the truth, the whole truth and nothing but the truth; that I will not make exaggerated claims of superiority or safety; that I will always give adequate assurance and proof that what I say about a product is true; that I will constantly remind myself that no medication is 100% effective in all patients and that even a placebo will cause distressing side effects in some patients and that the difference between the product I am detailing and the product the doctor has been using, is much smaller in his eyes than in my own, and any exaggeration of this difference will only serve to confirm his previous prescription writing habit.

This oath highlights the need for truth in advertising in this industry. Prescription pharmaceuticals are destined for compromised people to enable them, with the assistance of drugs, to resume their useful place in society. The degree of usefulness is disease related and impacted by the efficacy of available medication. Drugs are used to provide that minimum degree of comfort to ensure the bearability of life in those who are chronically or terminally ill. Unlike the majority of consumer product promotions, pharmaceuticals must be approached with the seriousness and promotional integrity that the situation in which the ultimate consumers find themselves deserves. Granted, there are certain situations that generate a level of humour or the opportunity for situational comic relief. However, it is necessary to be extremely wary of humorous campaigns, because they can all too easily backfire and the salespeople should be aware of this.

Promotion is a serious business and one that is difficult to control at the salesperson level. Detailmen and women go about their calls with a minimum of supervision; as in most selling jobs it is an isolated one. It differs from the majority of similar roles in that the salespeople take few orders: the presentation is made and the salesperson moves off and hopes for prescription of the products.

Market research is possibly the only method of obtaining an accurate assessment of the performance of a representative. Unfortunately, the format in which most market research is available from professional market research companies is too global to indicate the performance of individuals. therefore, it is necessary to break down the sales per area in-house, using this information together with sound field manager judgement to rate the representatives' effectiveness.

The sales force budget usually accounts for over 50% of the average company's promotional budget, hence the need for effective control, training, motivation, direction and confidence that the person is calling on the prescribers.

Ideally, a medical representative should have the following attributes:

☐ Education
☐ Integrity
☐ Initiative
☐ Empathy

Education

The ideal representative should have a tertiary education, preferably at degree level, although a technician's qualification in a medical area is acceptable. However, due to the shortage of graduates in medically related sciences, pharmacy or nursing, and even in the arts, people who have left school with a university entrance level pass are accepted and trained in-house by companies.

A training scheme devised by the Pharmaceutical and Chemical Manufacturers' Association in cooperation with the Department of Health has been launched through the correspondence division of the Witwatersrand Technikon. The final diploma, to be awarded by external examination, is the National Diploma in Pharmaceutical Marketing, to be passed in three parts. The first part is confined to basic medical sciences and on the attainment of part one the representative will be registered as a Certified Medical Representative. Apart from the individual's level of education, intensive and extensive training has to be performed in-house and this is product related.

Integrity

Direct supervision, or the lack thereof, was mentioned earlier. It is impossible to oversee the daily and hourly activities of a medical representative. It is easy for a representative to be dishonest, not to make calls, or to claim calls not made ('ghost calling'). Furthermore, incorrect claims can be made for the salesperson's own reasons, with the possibility of disastrous results.

Representatives carry samples of products to be handed to doctors free of charge. These are valuable and the system is wide open to abuse such as distribution to non-registered people and disposal or barter for personal gain. The integrity of the individual is paramount.

Initiative

Representatives work on their own, often in isolation from their immediate manager. They are often placed in situations requiring decisions and should be able to make these accurately; there are times when a patient's health may be at stake. Complicating this is the need for the individual to identify commercial opportunity and to recognise buying signs.

Empathy

Empathy is difficult to develop; it is largely an innate characteristic. It is the art of projecting one's personality into that of the other person, thereby developing a level of understanding or comprehension of that person's motives. The outcome is to be able to sell to that individual, within the framework of his needs and terms of reference. All too often the representative rambles on, completely by-passing the decision maker's area of interest. Interest in a product must be identified, developed and finally translated into action – the action of writing the prescription for the right indication in the right patient.

Personal selling is an art. It is something that can be developed provided the individual has sufficient intelligence to understand the scientific implications of the product and a personality capable of projecting both the salesperson *and* the product to the receiver (prescriber). Complementing the art are the powers of persuasion and communication, and for the latter a salesperson needs word power, that is articulacy, fluency, grammatical sensitivity and verbal knowledge. In countries in which more than one language is spoken this is difficult to achieve in those other than the mother tongue.

Structuring a presentation can be done only by the salesperson himself. It is usually based on the thematic guidelines and factual attributes of the product as perceived by the marketing person or the product manager. Personal selling is a form of persuasion based essentially on psychological factors employing a two-way flow of communication. The objective is either to change the decision maker's attitude in favour of the product being sold, or to reinforce the existing favourable attitude.

When selling it is best to involve as many of the decision maker's senses as possible. It is for this reason that one of the functions of the product manager, in conjunction with the advertising agency, is the development of what are commonly known as visual aids (VAs). A VA is usually a four to six page promotional piece, printed on suitable board, designed to assist the representative to lead the doctor through the sales presentation. It makes use of an attention-grabbing opening panel followed by copy including graphical representation highlighting the USPs of the product. Where possible, independent third party evidence is used.

The representative attempts to establish a dialogue, because in discussion the doctor's interests are probed, his questions are answered and his objections are or should be overcome. Backing this process are reprints on the appropriate subjects which are lifted from scientific journals and emanate from reputable medical units and practitioners world-wide. In fact, third party evidence in this reprint form is one of the most effective means of selling a product. The doctor does not consider the representative to be an authority and assumes, usually rightfully, that the company is biased. Hence the need for 'journal' evidence and the importance attached to medical journals in the three tables quoted earlier.

At the end of the presentation the representative should close firmly, achieving a commitment from the doctor to prescribe the product. It is then customary to leave starter and sample packs for the doctor to give to his patients. The medical representative performs the following functions in the product acceptance sequence:

☐ Brand awareness
☐ Brand recognition
☐ Trial (samples)

He also encourages brand preference and brand insistence, or should one say brand loyalty, be reinforcing the prescriber's decision once he has been convinced that the drug performs within the parameters of the maker's claims and that it is a cost effective form of therapy.

Media advertising

Prescription pharmaceutical advertising is somewhat traditional in its selection of media. Outdoor advertising is essentially non-existent, as are radio and television exposure. This is due to the nature of the product and the attitude of the target market, the medial practitioner. Doctors jealously guard exclusivity and object to prescribing products perceived by themselves to be consumer products. It is for this reason that marketers must decide early on in their pre-launch decision phase whether the product will become a consumer or a prescription product. For example, depending upon its ingredients and scheduling (the scheduling of a product is the Department of Health's indication as to whether a product is available on or off a doctor's prescription), a cough mixture is suitable for either.

As in all areas, there are exceptions to this rule. An example of this is a cough mixture which commenced life in the market place during the 1950s and was promoted as an ethical at a time when many doctors and pharmacists were still of the persuasion that old-style prescriptions were best for their patients and were compounded *secundum artum* in single-man dispensaries. Needless to say, over the years the product developed the prescription market, became one of the prescriber's standbys and continues to occupy a position among the brand leaders.

A decision was taken during the late 1970s to change the fashion cycle of the product in an endeavour to expand out of the prescription-only field, which due to its competitive nature and fragmentation had little scope for significant growth. The product was promoted through the lay press, radio and television, it recorded a significant sales growth and apparently did not lose many, if any, of its existing prescribers. Perhaps it is the nature of the product: doctors perceive cough mixtures as low risk products, unlike an anti-hypertensive drug, which is medium to high risk. However, it is a courageous marketer who diversifies at the risk of losing his major franchise, that of the prescriber.

This desire for exclusive product knowledge on the part of the prescriber and pharmacist confines media advertising to mailings, professional journals and tabloid newspapers. Latterly, professional tabloids are proliferating and have achieved a level of popularity among the profession as they are easy to read, 'newsy' and do not include a high level of technical detail, which makes scanning easy.

According to the Marplan study tabulated earlier, mailings are not favourably ranked and in fact are becoming passée due to the build-up of professional resistance to 'advertising'. However, over a three-year period, that is 1979, 1980 and 1981, my personal experience has been a 15% plus response to mailings containing a reply-paid card which, if returned, carried an inexpensive gift of a medical nature or a free sample for the responder. Whether the response was a result of the doctor reading the advertising or whether the receptionist merely took the card through with a 'sign here, there is something for nothing' attitude cannot be established.

A foray into audio promotion was instituted in 1969. Tape recordings were made of medical lectures on various topics and each lecture was interspersed with medical product advertising (which was relatively expensive). These tapes were distributed free of charge to the medical profession. As a concept it was excellent and was based on the premise that doctors could listen to the tapes in the comfort of their own homes or whilst driving to rooms, hospitals or house calls. Durability of product was the marketing plus to the advertiser, as the intention was for the doctors to build up a tape library. The concept lasted some ten years before it was discontinued, possibly due to a lack of support by advertisers. The exact reasons for its demise are not known to me, but I assume that the anticipated durability did not achieve expectations and the advertising did not result in the anticipated level of prescription generation. Neither of the companies that I was associated with during this period used this particular medium.

Journal and tabloid remain the stalwarts of non-in-house promotion. Advertising is advertising and the principles stand, irrespective of whether it is to the professions or to the lay public. The advertisements themselves must adhere to the principles of copy and layout and must be pitched at the level of the audience. Despite the fact that most marketers work through advertising agents, be they small or full service, it is necessary to have a working knowledge of the art to make an appreciation of the work created by the agency.

In South Africa it is customary for the product or brand manager to work together with the agency's account executive and to hold discussions with artists and copywriters regarding the formulation and execution of the advertising. In the main, the agency does not have a high degree of product knowledge or a scientific background. For this reason the product manager needs to perform an analysis of selling points and benefits, zeroing in on the product's unique selling proposition, which in its turn must be believable by the audience. Furthermore, the theme chosen should be compatible with the campaign as a whole and conducive to the furtherance of market segmentation, desired-product profiling and positioning.

The visual aid (VA)

Layout principles pertain equally to press advertisements and visual aids (brochures or leave pieces) used by the representative. I prefer to call them visual aids because they are, in essence, the visual back-up to the 'audio' presentation made by the salesmen. During the selling procedure (or 'detail', to use the jargon of the pharmaceutical industry) the representative leads the doctor through the VA which is used in place of the back-up visuals used in a platform/audience presentation. Visual aids contain diagrams, graphs and copy (the selling copy contains third party quotes which are indexed together with accepted scientifically oriented product detail in print). At the conclusion of the presentation the VA is left with the potential prescriber as an additional reminder. These sales aids usually find their way into the trash can; what is intended and hoped for is a brief reread by the doctor before it is discarded.

Mailings are often identical to VAs used by the detailman or specifically designed for the function intended. In the latter case a sequence of related mailings is designed to follow up each other. To encourage readership of the contents various ploys such as teasers on the envelope, a competition based on the series, token free gift or sample offers, etc are employed.

The one problem in pharmaceutical promotion is the evaluation of the effectiveness of individual moieties of the campaign. The promotional mix is highly interdependent, one upon the other, with the salesman being the pivot. Isolation and subsequent evaluation is extremely difficult, and even complex analysis may result in spurious findings. Advertising's old premise, namely '50% is wasted – which 50%?' – holds.

Give-aways, complete with advertising message, are worthy of mention. (Other terms for these are 'durables' or even 'executive toys'.) They range from expensive desk sets, paper weights and steel ball games to rulers, pens, statuettes or quite ridiculous little toys. Some medical practitioner have desks cluttered with these, others take them home and some merely discard them. Give-aways describe their intended function – to give a lasting product reminder to the decision maker. Their actual durability depends upon the receiver's perception of the gift. For the selection of such a gift the marketer needs a degree of understanding of his 'audience' and to be empathetic to its needs. Without this he may incur a high level of expenditure and end up merely increasing the load of the garbage collectors. On the other hand, a well considered and selected give-away can have a life span of many years.

The advertising codes of ethics of the various Pharmaceutical Manufacturers' Associations or regulatory bodies around the world tend to place limitations on the material worth of 'advertising or promotional gifts' to the medical profession. On the other hand, it has been known for companies to 'give away' carved chess sets, expensive gold pens and the like. Furthermore, some countries limit the gifts to medically or product related items – in this case stethoscopes or other diagnostic equipment are freely distributed suitably engraved with advertisements.

Professional meetings arranged by pharmaceutical companies with the target audience, be it medical practitioners, pharmacists or nurses, with or without

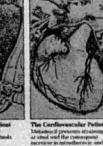
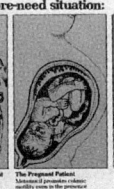

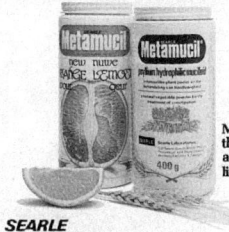

Courtesy: GD Searle

their spouses, are used by various companies regularly or from time to time. Some of them are viewed by the professional guests as a good exercise for a night out, and little notice is taken of either the product or the advertising message. Others can make a major impact on all or a selected few of the guests. In common with all parts of the advertising mix, their success depends upon the nature of the product, the method of projecting the product's image, the selection of the target audience, and even the day of the week suited to the Town or City concerned.

The concept for a promotion and the implementation thereof is a serious affair, and a costly one if it is misdirected.

Finally, promoting prescription pharmaceuticals requires more than just classical advertising. It requires sound knowledge of the product and the target audience (the doctor), and the importance of visual aids and give-aways cannot be underestimated.

☐ References

American Medical Association. 1956. Fond du Lac study.

Coleman, JS, Katz, E & Menzel, H. 1957. 'The Diffusion Innovation amongst Physicians'. Publication A 239 of the Bureau of Applied Social Research. Columbia University.

Ferber & Wales, HG. 1958. 'The Effectiveness of Pharmaceutical Promotion', Bulletin No 83. The Bureau of Economic Research, College of Commerce and Business Administration. University of Illinois.

Smith, Mickey C. 1975. *Principles of Pharmaceutical Marketing*. Lea & Febigen.

Sutton, D. 1960, 'A Plea for Detailmen to Tell the Truth'. *Medical Marketing*, 13 April: 19.

17

Glossary of
advertising terminology

Glossary of advertising terminology 477

Glossary of advertising terminology
Courtesy of D'Arcy Masius Benton & Bowles
Dick Reed and
Joost van Nispen

Media terminology *477*

Research terminology *486*

Film/video production terminology *487*

Print production terminology *490*

Direct response *495*

☐ Media terminology

ABC figure
The average circulation per issue of a member publication, audited over a six-month period by the Audit Bureau of Circulation of SA.

Above-the-line advertising
Advertising in the conventional media such as press, radio, television, cinema and outdoor.

Adspend
Advertising expenditure by an advertiser or a group of advertisers in conventional media during a given period.

Adindex
The ongoing survey of adspend conducted by Market Research Africa (Pty) Ltd. Adindex measures the amounts spent in all conventional media, on a monthly basis, for all categories of products, services and retailers. Production expenses and promotional costs are not included.

Age groups
The four standard age groupings used in the AMPS report are: 16-24, 25-34, 35-49 and 50+.
However, data is available for analyses as follows: 16-19, 20-24, 25-34, 35-44, 45-49, 50-64, 65 and over. Data on children is also available.

All media and products survey (AMPS)
The annual survey undertaken by the South African Advertising Research Foundation (SAARF) into readership, listenership and viewership of media and the usage of certain products. AMPS provides the basic data upon which most media planning in South Africa is based.

'All or most' readers
In AMPS the readership of magazines and newspapers can be further qualified by thoroughness of reading. A reader who claims to have read 'all of it' or 'most of it' is considered a very thorough or fairly thorough reader of that publication.

All races
In AMPS 'all races' means white, coloured, Asian and black adults as measured in the survey.

Audience
People who have an opportunity to see or hear an advertisement by virtue of their being exposed to the 'vehicle' which carries the advertisement.

Audience (cinema)
AMPS measures the attendance habits of people at drive-in cinemas and 'four-wallers', that is conventional cinemas. Respondents are asked about the recency

and frequency of their visits, and what type of venue they went to. To evaluate cinema as a medium, we usually measure the cumulative reach of the target market over six weeks. Thus we can compare the potential of cinema with the potential of other media types and make a strategy decision. However, AMPS gives us a measure of exposure to the medium as a whole. To evaluate a particular schedule we must look at the attendance figures of the selected cinemas.

CINEMARK attendance figures at cinemas are published every six months, some are audited by the ABC, others are estimated or supplied by the cinema. These show the average weekly audience at each venue, and include children.

Audience (TV/radio)

The number (usually expressed in thousands) of adults listening to or viewing a station.

☐ The average quarter-hour audience figure reflects the average number of people likely to be reached by one spot within that time channel.

☐ The total net audience of a station is the number of people (counted once only) who tune in to that station during the course of one day.

☐ The 'yesterday', seven-day and four-week audience figures reflect the cumulative audiences built up over one day, one week and one month respectively, and indicate the potential reach of the station or time channel over those time periods.

Audience accumulation

The increase in audience reached by a medium using successive issues or broadcasts.

Audience duplication

A measurement of the overlap of audience between different media (external), between successive issues, or broadcasts of the same medium (internal).

Average frequency

The *average number* of times an individual reached will have an opportunity to be exposed to the media. When the performance of a media schedule is measured, this is calculated simply by dividing the gross number of opportunities to see by the number of people reached at least once. Average frequency is deceptive, because not everyone is reached the same number of times. Some people will see more and some less than the average.

Example: $\dfrac{\text{Gross OTS}}{\text{Net reach}}$ = Average frequency

$\dfrac{3\,883}{355}$ = 10,9

This reads that 355 000 individuals will have a total of 3 883 000 opportunities to see an advertisement, some once only, others many times − but on average 10,9 times (see Frequency distribution).

Below-the-line advertising

Any advertising or promotional activity outside of conventional media. This may include direct mail, pamphlets, point-of-sale material, competitions, give-aways, demonstrations, sampling, coupons, etc. A separate budget is usually set aside for this.

Bias or skew

When the profile of product users is compared, for example with the population profile, any significant difference between the two would indicate a bias.

For example:

	Population	User	Index
English	42%	62%	1,45 = strong bias
Afrikaans	58%	39%	0,67
Male	49%	52%	1,06 = slight bias
Female	51%	48%	0,94

Billboards (radio)

The opening and closing announcements of a sponsored feature or programme. These are of limited duration and may contain only a product mention such as '. . . brought to you by the makers of XYZ brand'.

Black-and-white, B/W

This refers to a newspaper or magazine advertisement printed in black only. No colour is used.

B + 1 col, B + 2 col

Black plus one colour, black plus two colours. Also known as 'spot' colour.

Broadcast/narrowcast media

Broadcast media include most radio and television stations. However, one could consider Bop TV to be 'narrowcast', that is beamed to specific audiences. Second channel or closed-circuit television available in some hotels and apartments would be narrowcast, as would cable TV and shopping centre radio stations.

Broadsheet

The newspaper page size most commonly used by South African dailies and Sundays. Type area varies from 54 to 55 cm deep by 10 or 11 columns wide. American broadsheet is 52 cm by 9 columns.

Burst

A concentration of advertising exposures in a short period, for example a pre-holiday burst for camping equipment. A pattern of bursts, rather than continuous advertising, produces peaks of high brand awareness followed by periods of very low awareness. This suits some campaigns, but for others continuity over long periods is essential to sustain good levels of recall.

☐ A *launch burst* is used to cut through the competitive advertising in order to build rapid awareness for a new brand.

Campaign

All advertising and related efforts on behalf of a product or service, directed towards the attainment of a predetermined goal.

Candidate media (list)

All those media eligible to carry a particular campaign. From an evaluation of these the final schedule is selected.

Checkerboard

A size option offered by some magazines, which consists of two quarter pages positioned diagonally, in the top left and lower right quarters of a page. The rate usually applied is 80% of the full page cost.

Child AMPS

A survey recently completed by SAARF into the readership, listenership and viewership of media and the usage of certain products by children. The age groups covered were 8 to 15 years for Whites, Coloureds and Asians and 10 to 15 years for Blacks. The AMPS 83/84 Child Report follows the survey conducted in 1979 on Whites only, and in 1980 on Blacks only.

Christie diagram

A graph showing the relative cost efficiency and reach of candidate publications. The vertical axis shows the cost ranking with the most economical publications towards the top. The horizontal axis shows the reach, with the greatest being towards the right. Publications which deliver both good reach and cost efficiency will fall into the top righthand quarter.

Clutter

The effect produced by a multitude of advertisements within a medium, which necessitates the use of striking creative treatment, dominant size, or special positioning to achieve noticeability for one's advertisement. Alternatively, one might consider choosing a less cluttered medium.

Column centimetre, ccm

A newspaper space measurement that is one centimetre deep and one column wide. Rates are quoted per single column centimetre.

Thus: 20 cm × 5 cols = 100 ccm at R5,65 = R565,00.

Communication ability

Media communicate differently, and people react to media in different ways. For example, a cinema or TV commercial will have far greater impact than a radio spot or a poster. By applying a weighting we can therefore attempt to place qualitative as well as quantitative evaluations upon the candidate media types. Each medium's ability to deliver a message to a particular target market can then be assessed (see Effective rating points).

Controlled circulation

The circulation of a business, trade or technical publication, issued regularly free or mainly free to individuals engaged in a specific business, industry or profession, who are selected according to their job title, function, qualifications or other characteristics relevant to the interests of the advertisers (also called 'qualified circulation').

Cosmic

A trade name for a suite of computer programmes based on a formula derived by Metheringham and designed to give optimum media schedules based on cost and response.

Cost effectiveness

A method of comparing the value of different media for a specific campaign.

Cost per thousand (CPM, C/TH)

This refers to the relative cost of reaching 1 000 prospects in a particular target market through a given media type or individual medium.

For example: Target market – white housewives

Publication	Full page full colour cost	No of housewives reading publication	Cost per 1 000
Fair Lady ...	R4 250	614 000	R6,92

It is a valuable tool for comparisons between media provided that care is taken to base the costs on comparable sizes. It is also used to compare relative efficiencies between schedules.

Cover, coverage or reach

The unduplicated number (in thousands) or percentage of the target market *potentially* exposed to the advertisement at least once may be termed net cover or net reach. Why potentially? Because reach is really a measurement of exposure to the medium, and not necessarily to the advertisement (see also Reach and frequency).

Daytime/drivetime radio

Daytime or housewife-time refers to the time channels between 08h30 and 16h00 which have been 'packaged' by various radio stations to facilitate the buying of time for campaigns aimed at this target market. Drivetime really refers to the morning and late afternoon time slots when commuters are listening in their cars.

Demographics

The characteristics of a person or group of people expressed in terms of their age, income, social class, education, sex, race, area, size of community, etc.

Direct mail/direct response advertising

☐ *Direct mail* usually consists of a letter, pamphlet or catalogue, sometimes several items, mailed directly to prospects whose names and addresses have been taken from some selected list. It can be a very efficient way of reaching a narrowly defined target group.

☐ *Direct response advertising* can be placed in any medium (even on TV or radio) and is characterised by a requirement on the part of the prospect to send in a coupon, telephone or write to the advertiser, or respond in some way in order to obtain the product or service. This obviously encompasses straightforward mail order advertising, but can also be used to sell insurance and travel, etc.

Domination

☐ A media technique for achieving greater impact than your competitors by heavier spending in a medium or media group.

☐ A creative tactic of using size to achieve more impact than other advertisements on the page or spread.

DPS, double-page spread

Two full pages facing each other in a magazine or newspaper and forming one advertisement.

½ DPS

Two horizontal half pages facing each other and running across the bottom of two pages.

Duplication

Very few people restrict themselves to one magazine or one newspaper. Therefore, there is duplication of audience when more than one medium is used, as the same people may read one, two, three or more of the publications listed. If one adds up the percentages of target market reached by each one of five magazines, for example, it will generally be over 100%. Actual coverage, when duplication is removed, might be 80%.

Editorial environment

The medium can affect the message by its editorial compatibility or otherwise. A subjective judgement of the editorial suitability of one medium over another must sometimes be made, even when both reach the same target market.

Effective rating points (ERPs)

In assessing each medium's ability to deliver a message to a particular target market, a communication ability weighting can be applied to the GRPs – thus a truer comparison can be made with effective rating points.

For example:

On an expenditure of R100 000 one might achieve:

	GRPs	Comm ability index	ERPs
Magazines	579	0,60	347
Television	463	0,90	417
Radio	2 553	0,20	510

'Ever' users

AMPS contains data on a number of general consumer products. Users are divided into light, medium and heavy categories. 'Ever' users are the sum total of these, that is all persons who claim to use the product.

Exclusive readers

Those readers of a publication who do not read others on the schedule.

For example:

	White readers (in thousands)	Duplication	Exclusive readers
Sunday Times	1 239	(34,8%) 431	808
Rapport	1 379	(31,3%) 431	948

Frequency

(See Reach and frequency.)

Frequency distribution

When one or more schedules are evaluated, an important factor to consider is the frequency distribution, or breakdown of the target market reached at different levels of exposure.

Example:

	Schedule A	Schedule B
1 or more exposures	94,9%	89,0%
3 or more exposures	86,4%	86,5%
6 or more exposures	74,6%	79,3%

Although Schedule A has the highest overall reach, that is 94,9% of (unduplicated) target consumers exposed at least *once*, Schedule B has a better reach at the '6 or more' level and might be the preferred media schedule. The ideal number of exposures desired will vary greatly between campaigns. It must be stressed that frequency and reach measurements should be treated with caution. They reflect the potential exposure to the *medium* and tell us nothing about actual perception of our advertisement (see Noting probability).

Frequency of media exposure

The number of times an individual is exposed to a medium within a given period.

Full colour, F/C, 4-colour

Black plus cyan, yellow and magenta are used in newspapers and magazines to produce full colour.

Full page, F/P, FP

An advertisement occupying the full print area of a newspaper or magazine page.

Thus: FP/FC = a full page in full colour.

Free sheet

A local newspaper distributed free to homes, shops and offices in a given area. Usually, a fixed number are 'dropped' individually into mail boxes along set routes on a regular weekly, fortnightly or monthly schedule. The ABC issues Verified Free Distribution Certificates to free publications that have satisfied the auditors.

Gross impacts, gross OTS

The *total number* of potential exposures of the target market to the media schedule. Since many people will have more than one 'opportunity to see', the number of different people reached (net reach) will be considerably less. *Note:* Gross OTS measures the total potential exposure to the media carrying the advertisement, and not necessarily exposure to the message itself.

There are two ways to calculate gross OTS:

☐ Simply multiply the average issue audience (average quarter-hour audience for a radio or TV time channel) by the number of insertions or spots.

For example:

Publication	WCA readers (per thousand)	No of insertions	Gross OTS
Huisgenoot	1 879	× 6 =	11 274
Reader's Digest	1 596	× 6 =	9 576
		Gross OTS:	20 850

☐ Gross OTS is also a cost-related concept. By dividing total expenditure in a medium by its cost per thousand, one can arrive at gross OTS.

For example:

Publication	FPFC cost	No of insertions	Total cost
Huisgenoot	5 120	× 6 =	R30 720
Reader's Digest	5 800	× 6 =	R34 800
			R65 520

Therefore: $\dfrac{\text{Total cost}}{\text{Cost/000}}$ = Gross OTS

$\dfrac{\text{R65 520}}{\text{R3,14}}$ = 20 860

Gross rating points (GRPs)

Gross rating points are used to describe the gross weight of a given media effort against a defined target market. Quantitatively speaking, gross rating points are equal to *reach* multiplied by *frequency* (GRP = R × F). GRPs therefore describe the gross weight of advertising that is being absorbed by the target market in the campaign period.

Example: A schedule providing a net reach of 75% and average frequency of 4,6 will yield 345 GRPs:
75 × 4,6 = 345.

However, other schedules could yield the same GRPs:
69 × 5 = 345 (slightly lower reach, slightly better frequency)
15 × 23 = 345 (very low reach (15%) and high frequency)

The GRPs therefore are not in themselves 'good' or 'poor', but are a useful tool for comparing alternative schedules or evaluating the relative effectiveness of different media at a given budget level.

Gutter

In a newspaper, the unprinted margin at the centre fold is called the gutter. If an advertisement is designed to 'run across the gutter' it presupposes a position on the centre page so that it can be printed unbroken through this margin.

Heavy user

What constitutes light, medium and heavy usage levels of the various products covered in AMPS varies widely from category to category, but generally speaking 'heavy' means above average.

Examples of 'heavy' usage:

Tea	: 5 + cups per day
Instant coffee	: 4 + cups per day
Table wine	: 6 + glasses per week
Beer	: 7 + glasses per week

Household

The AMPS definition of a household is one person living alone, or a group of persons (not necessarily members of one family) who live together and whose food and household expenses are managed as one unit.

Housewife (AMPS definition)

In the AMPS survey a 'housewife' is defined as a female who is wholly or partly responsible for the day-to-day purchases for the household. She may be married, single, divorced or widowed. She may or may not work part or full time.

Image transfer

The ability of a radio commercial or print advertisement to recreate in the imagination of the audience, a television or film commercial. The secondary medium is then acting as a reminder and reinforcer of the primary audio/visual medium.

Impact

This is the impression made by the advertising message on the audience. High impact may be achieved by large sizes, the use of colour, or dramatic creative treatment. In the media trade-off between impact, reach and frequency, one may have to sacrifice the greater impact of a DPS in order to achieve the necessary frequency. Or the reverse may be true. Impact may be of prime importance, in which case frequency or reach or both would have to be reduced to meet the budget.

Impact covers four different areas:
☐ Creative impact
☐ Media impact (eg TV vs radio)
☐ Space impact (eg DPS vs full page)
☐ Environmental impact (eg editorial suitability)

Impact/impression

☐ The extent and degree of consumer reaction to an advertisement or campaign.
☐ The degree to which a medium affects its audience.
☐ OTS multiplied by the probability of recalling the advertisement.

Impact factors, IF

When schedules are analysed or the cost efficiencies of publications are compared, an impact factor can be applied to downweight a schedule or a medium. This endeavours to put a realistic value on the likelihood of the advertisement being seen.

Example:

Publica-cation	Size	Cost	Read 000	IF	WTD read	CPT
Reader's Digest	DPS/FC	R5 800	1 596	0,80	1 277	R4,54
	FP/BW	R3 645	1 596	0,40	638	R5,71
	BUYLINE	R1 215	1 596	0,25	399	R3,05

In the above table impact factors have been used to downweight different sizes of advertisements in the same publication according to their probable noticeability. This gives us a 'weighted' readership and cost per thousand which is a truer basis for comparison (see Noting scores).

Income groups

AMPS divides the *monthly total household income* of each race group into four categories:

	Whites R	Coloureds R	Asians R	Blacks R	W/C/A R	All races R
A	3 500 +	1 200 +	2 000 +	600 +	3 000 +	1 400 +
B	2 000 to 3 499	700 to 1 199	1 100 to 1 999	300 to 599	1 400 to 2 999	500 to 1 399
C	700 to 1 999	150 to 699	400 to 1 099	50 to 299	300 to 1 399	50 to 499
D	699 –	149 –	399 –	49 –	299 –	49 –

These are the *1984* AMPS definitions. The figures are updated each year in line with earnings.

Insertion

A single placement of an advertisement in a medium, usually applied to print only.

Insert

A loose leaflet, pamphlet or booklet inserted into a magazine or newspaper. These are usually preprinted by the advertiser, and the carrier publication charges a fee such as R30 per thousand to include the advertising insert.

IOC ranking

An impact-over-cost table arranges the candidate publications in order of their cost efficiency in reaching the target market.

Example:

Publication	Cost	Read %	Read 000	CPT	Index
Pace	R3 200	20,6%	339	R 9,43	100
Bona	R5 200	30,6%	504	R10,33	91,3
Hit	R1 200	6,8%	111	R10,77	87,5
Drum	R3 850	18,8%	309	R12,44	75,8

Notice that *Hit* ranks above *Drum* in cost efficiency here, but only reaches one third as many target readers. A Christie diagram usually follows an IOC ranking, and this allows one to compare both reach and cost efficiency simultaneously.

Knock-'n-drop

Door-to-door delivery of a free magazine, newspaper, advertising package or sample to all householders in the area selected.

Loading (TV, cinema)

The SABC applies a loading on television rates for the high-demand period from 14 October to 15 December. Cinemark applies a 20% peak time loading on exhibition rates from September to December each year.

Market weights

Relative values applied to various characteristics, for example demographic groups, in order to establish the worth of different segments for a particular product.

Media mix

The combination of two or more media types called for by the strategy. Each element in the media mix will contribute different strengths to the campaign. For example: The Sunday press might be used for a launch to achieve fast country-wide awareness, radio might provide regional reminders, while outdoor could be used to focus attention on local promotions. The choice of the correct media mix for each campaign is dependent on the objectives.

Minigraphic (bus)

A single-decker bus which is painted *all over* in the advertiser's colours and design (as opposed to panels only).

Multiple pick-ups

The number of occasions on which a publication is picked up by one reader before it is discarded. A magazine which contains plenty of good, interesting editorial will obviously offer the advertiser more opportunities to see than a flimsy magazine which can be read in a few minutes.

Net cover, net impact reach

The *unduplicated* number (per thousand) or percentage of the target market potentially exposed to the schedule at least once, that is each person is counted once only, regardless of the number of opportunities to see they may be exposed to (see Gross impacts).

Net unduplicated audience

The total number of different individuals reached one or more times, irrespective of the number of potential impacts on each individual provided by the schedule and of the duplicated reach of the different media.

Noting probability

Research (Starch-INRA Hooper, USA/Gallup, UK) into the noting of advertisements of different sizes in magazines and newspapers has provided us with tables of 'scores'. Depending on the percentage of the page used by the advertisement and the use of colour (if any), the probability of its being seen by readers has been calculated. This gives us a fairly realistic method of comparing the effectiveness of alternative schedules.

Noting scores

The proportion of the readers of a publication who recall having seen at least part of an advertisement. This is an aided recall technique.

Objectives

In order to plan an advertising campaign effectively, one must have set objectives in mind:
- *Marketing objectives* – the effect on market share, distribution, etc
- *Advertising campaign objectives* – the effect on the consumer, awareness, etc
- *Media objectives* – the specific reach, frequency and continuity desired

Clearly-stated objectives give positive direction to the planning and enable potential success or otherwise to be measured.

OFC, OBC, IFC, IBC

These indicate special positions on the cover of a magazine, namely outside front, outside back, inside front, inside back. A premium is paid for such guaranteed positions.

OTS, OTH

These are opportunities to see and opportunities to hear – the number of potential chances that a target consumer has to see or hear the advertising message. Gross OTS is the total number of such exposures delivered by a schedule. Average frequency is that total divided by the reach and is the average OTS of everyone reached (see Frequency distribution).

Outdoor advertising

All signs and posters are classed as 'outdoor' even though many are to be found inside shopping malls and railway stations.

The medium includes:
- hoardings, billboards (48-sheet, 96-sheet)
- illuminated signs of various kinds
- shop-ads (at shopping centres and CBDs)
- pop stands (at black trading stores)
- station streamers, target signs, postabenches (at railway stations)
- junior posters (in black townships)
- stadium hoardings (at sports stadiums)
- buses
- bus shelters

Page traffic survey

A survey designed to establish readers per page of a publication.

Paid circulation

Actual sales of a publication, either by subscription, bookshop, or street sales, as opposed to free distribution or complimentary copies.

Penetration

- In media, the same as 'coverage'.
- In marketing, incidence of usage or ownership, also the extent of distribution.

Point-of-sale advertising

Advertising matter or display structure usually prepared by the manufacturer for use by the retailer on the retailer's premises at point of sale.

Primary readers, pass-along readers

Primary readers are those who personally buy, subscribe to, or receive a publication and claim to read the publication frequently and intensely. Secondary readers, known as 'pass-along' readers, are often considered to be less committed to the publication and therefore less important to the advertiser. This may or may not be true.

Profile of readership or audience

The demographic composition of the readers, viewers or listeners reached by a particular medium. By comparing the profiles of various magazines, for instance, one can find the best match to the target market with the least wastage.

Psychographics

Lifestyle and attitudinal aspects of the target consumer, as opposed to demographics. For instance, the man who is in the market for a *Ferrari* would have very different 'psychographics' from the man who buys a *Rolls Royce*, although they may well be in the same age and income brackets.

Purchasing cycle

The pattern of habitual repeat buying of the product. A soap powder may have a weekly cycle, toothpaste and coffee a monthly cycle, cooldrinks a daily cycle, and durables a cycle lasting many years. Knowing the purchase cycle of the product helps establish the frequency desirable in an advertising campaign.

Reach and frequency

These are two very important, if somewhat misleading, concepts in media planning. Media objectives are normally formulated in terms of reach (how many people) and frequency (how often). The performance of a media schedule is therefore measured in terms of reach and frequency.

A typical example of a magazine schedule analysis is the following:
Target market: white females 16-24 (total 374 000)
Schedule results:

Gross OTS	: 3 883
Net reach/000	: 355
Net reach %	: 94,9
Average frequency	: 10,9

Net reach is the unduplicated number or percentage of the target market potentially exposed *at least once*. Average frequency is calculated simply by dividing the gross OTS by the number of people reached, and is therefore the *average* number of times individuals may be exposed. This is deceptive, because it does *not* mean that 94,9% of the target has 10,9 opportunities to see. We need to look at a frequency distribution to see what percentage of the target market will be reached at different levels of exposure (see Frequency distribution).

Readership (average issue)

AMPS measures the *average* number of people who have read an issue of a publication, be it a daily, weekly, fortnightly or monthly. By 'read' they mean 'personally read or paged through all or part of a copy'.

Readers per copy (rpc)

This figure is arrived at by dividing the total average issue readership (AMPS) by the average issue circulation (ABC). It is a highly controversial subject, because some wild figures have been thrown up, such as 12,3 rpc for a Sunday newspaper! We feel that readers per copy figures produced this way are meaningless and best ignored.

Reading thoroughness

Respondents are also asked to indicate whether they read all, most or some of a publication, or only glanced at it. Obviously, a medium with a high proportion of 'all or most' readers offers a better chance of the advertisements being read than one with a lower thoroughness of reading score.

Recency and frequency of reading

To establish recency, AMPS asks the respondent to indicate all the publications read or paged through in the past 12 months, and when last this was done. AMPS then questions the respondent on the past six issues (ie six months for monthlies, one week for dailies) to establish frequency of reading. A heavy reader of a particular publication would be a '5/6 or 6/6 reader'.

Regionality

The areas in which a campaign is to be conducted. This may follow the product distribution pattern, or be directed at weak sales areas, or be concentrated in areas of high consumption (such as coastal resorts for sun-tan preparations).

SAARF levy

By agreement, a levy of 0,5% has been placed on advertising expenditure in all media included in the AMPS survey. It is used to fund the media and products research conducted by the SA Advertising Research Foundation for the benefit of advertisers. Some media owners have incorporated this into their rates (eg SABC), others bill this as a separate amount.

Schedule

A tabulation of all advertising, usually including costs and dates, relating to an advertising campaign.

Share of voice

The product's percentage of the total competitive advertising spend. If Brand A instant coffee spent R250 000 and the total spend of all instant coffees was R2 million, Brand A's share of voice would be 12,5%. One can also calculate the brand's share of voice within a specific medium, such as TV1, to assess the strength of the campaign against the other brands using the medium.

Short-life, long-life publications

Monthly magazines such as *Your Family* and *Reader's Digest* would be described as 'long-life' publications because they probably stay in the home for several weeks. At the opposite end of the scale are daily newspapers that are generally discarded within 24 hours and so have a 'short life' in which to reach the target market (see Multiple pick-ups).

Six-out-of-six readers

Readers of a publication who claimed in the AMPS survey to have read every one of the last six issues. In the case of a monthly this would be over a period of six months, for a fortnightly over three months, and for a weekly over six weeks. A 6/6 or 5/6 reader is a 'heavy' reader of and closely identified with a particular publication.

SocioMonitor

An ongoing research programme which has been conducted at two-yearly intervals since 1976. The aim of the study is to provide a comprehensive, conceptual framework describing people's values and lifestyles in such a way that their behaviour in the market-place and in society can be explained and better understood.

SocioMonitor identifies four main value groups in SA society:

☐ *Responsible we* (conservative traditionalists motivated by essentially protestant values and a desire for security and stability)

☐ *Branded me* (conservative but materialistic, motivated by status, esteem and conspicuous consumption)

☐ *Innovative me* (hold radical views and believe in taking risks and living for now, tend to be liberal and pro-reform)

☐ *Self-motivated me* (tend to be inward-looking and concerned with self-expression and fulfilment)

The psychographic profiles of media and brands can be matched to each other using SocioMonitor, thus adding a qualitative element to the media choice, which may be of greater significance than the sheer numbers of reach and cost per thousand.

Soft data

Information about media which cannot be quantified.

Solus, semi-solus, special positions

A guaranteed position as the only advertisement on a page is known as a *solus* position. *Semi-solus* guarantees that only one other advertisement will be placed on the page. A *special* position is one that is negotiated and guaranteed, such as 'opposite leader page', or 'inside front cover' of a magazine. All such positions normally carry a loading.

Strategy, tactics

In media planning terms, the *strategy* is the broad selection of media types that will be used to attain the objectives set. The *tactics* refer to the specific usage of particular media vehicles and their deployment to achieve the agreed strategy.

Supergraphic (bus)

A double-decker bus that is painted *all over* in the advertiser's colours and design (as opposed to panels only).

Synergy

The 'rub-off' that occurs between two or more campaigns from the same advertiser if a similarity of design, logo and execution is present. A packaged-goods manufacturer may, for instance, produce a wide range of brands, all carrying the same trade mark. If his advertising reflects this 'synergy' the effectiveness of each campaign will be enhanced. In media terms, this might mean co-ordinating exposures to maximise this advantage.

Tabloid

A newspaper page size that is half that of broadsheet. It varies from 39 to 42 centimetres deep by seven columns wide. Tabloid is the size most commonly used for feature sections like the *Star* 'Tonight!' and for free sheets like the *Randburg Sun*.

Target market, T/M

The particular consumers at which the advertising effort is to be aimed. They should be defined both demographically and psychographically. The more carefully a target market is identified and described, the more accurately both creative and media strategies will be directed.

Task budget

A media budget which has been calculated to achieve specific objectives. This may be based on the share of voice demanded to meet marketing objectives. It may be calculated to buy the required weight of advertising in terms of reach and frequency (GRPs) in the selected media types.

Universe

The total population within a specified group or target market, expressed in computer analyses in thousands.

Example:

W/C/A women + children = universe: 1 168

This means that there is a total of 1 168 000 white, coloured and Asian women with children aged 3 to 15 years.

Urban/rural

In AMPS, a *city* is an urban centre with 30 000 + Whites. A *town* has between 5 000 and 29 999 Whites. A *village* has 200 to 4 999 Whites. *Rural* communities are largely farming areas.

We classify city/town as urban, and villages as rural. An anomaly occurs in this method of definition, because large black townships exist which are classified rural despite concentrated populations.

☐ Research terminology

Ad-hoc research

Research at a particular point in time; once-off research, not continuous.

Benchmark survey

This research is the first major study conducted to act as a measurement against which all future research is evaluated.

Concept test

A test to establish respondents' reaction to an idea – usually a new type of product – or to establish which of several product claims respondents regard as most valuable. No visual material is presented at this stage.

Consumer panel

A continuous sample of households (persons) from which information on buying habits, media habits, and so on is obtained.

Continuous research

Research in which data is collected on a continuous basis to measure changes that could occur in the market-place. This is usually conducted once a year/every two years, and is also called a tracking study.

Cross tabulating

Here we determine the relevance between different subcategories of the population (ie how different age/income groups and others compare with the population profile).

Demographic features

These are features of a sample such as age, sex, language, income, race, etc.

Depth interview

An interview conducted without a questionnaire and where the interviewed person is encouraged to talk freely without direction/interference from the interviewer. This interview (also called unstructured, qualitative or non-directive) aims to uncover attitudes/feelings that would not be established via direct questioning.

Desk research

Research which utilises internal records, published data and other existing material without conducting actual research in the field.

Dustbin audit/check

An observational method in which the interviewer records the tins, wrappers and packages found in the consumer's dustbin.

Filter question

A question or series of questions designed to eliminate those respondents ineligible for the particular subject.

Group discussions

An assembly of a suitably small sample of respondents who are interviewed in groups of convenient size, each discussion group being led by a suitably qualified person who controls the flow of the group's ideas in order to elicit the necessary information.

Homogeneous

Composed of similar constituent parts – as compared with heterogeneous, which means composed of dissimilar constituent parts.

Incentive

Some small reward (gift) given to respondents or panel members to encourage their co-operation.

Informant

Also 'interviewee', 'respondent', or 'subject'. A member of the sample who gives information, answers, etc.

Margin of error

Deviation from the true figure originating in a complete census. The smaller the sample the larger the margin of error.

Monadic evaluation

When an advertisement is evaluated in isolation – in contrast to paired comparison, where two ads are evaluated *vis-à-vis* each other.

Open-ended questions

Questions which are left open to be answered in any manner by the respondent. No prompting or clues are provided by the interviewer.

Perceptual mapping

A technique which identifies what gives products/services identity in the market-place. The data is plotted on a horizontal/vertical axis and further identifies the groupings of brands which consumers perceive to be similar. Perceptual maps also identify the attributes (or features) which create an identify for a brand, or alternatively those which are not relevant in creating an identity.

Playback/feedback

In advertising research this is a respondent's verbatim report of the elements recalled in a specific advertisement.

Population

Group of persons being investigated from which some are selected in a systematic fashion to form a sample (also called 'universe').

Precoded questions

In contrast to open-ended questions, precoded questions have the answers supplied on the questionnaire. The respondent's answer is merely ticked alongside the appropriate box (ie 'yes/no' answers/rating scales/association statements).

Punchcard

Card onto which code symbols are punched to represent the responses given to questions.

Qualitative research

Study of attitudes and beliefs of consumers or users and the reasons for their purchasing habits. Usually involves small sample sizes.

Quantitative research

Study of the extent of product/brand usership/usership habits/buying behaviour carried out with large samples.

Recall method

A research technique to determine the extent of respondents' ability to remember an ad and its contents – either with or without presentation of test material.

Reliability

The extent to which a result is due to systematic effects, that is will remain consistent from sample to sample.

Representative

That which reflects the characteristics in similar proportions to their ratio in the universe as a whole (ie respondents selected by age, income and other factors should represent their ratio of the population).

Sample

A selected representative part of a group of units (the population or universe) from which the behaviour of the population or universe may be inferred.

☐ Cluster – a sample in which groups or households of people are selected at each sampling point.
☐ Random – a sample in which each item in the universe has an equal chance of being selected.
☐ Stratified – a sample in which a predetermined proportion is drawn from known divisions or strata of a population.
☐ Quota – information is collected from a predetermined number of people across demographics.

Starch rating

The numerical score developed through an application of the recognition method of print advertisement research as applied by Daniel Starch and staff. Readers of the publication in question go through the publication, page by page, indicating those advertisements and sometimes editorial elements that they 'recognise' as having read. The extent of readership is also probed. Starch reports show 'noted', 'seen/associated' and 'read most' figures.

Syndicated research

A method whereby passenger questions are included on national studies conducted regularly. Each client pays only for the number of questions and not the whole survey (also called Omnibus surveys).

Tabulation

Summary of survey results in the form of statistical tables.

Tachistoscope

Equipment which permits visual presentation of objects for very short periods of time, that is respondents have time only to glance at the object.

Validity

The extent to which a result is free from bias measured by reference to independent sources. This contrasts with *consistency*, which has to do with the agreement of the data.

☐ Film/video production terminology

Animatic

A 'mobile' storyboard. Each frame of the storyboard is filmed and a voice-over added. This is used primarily as a pilot for research and business presentations.

Animation

Drawings that are photographed in sequence, one frame at a time, to give the illusion of motion.

Answer print

A print of the finished commercial in which the picture and sound-track are put together for the first time (see also Composite print).

Audio mix

The putting together of two or more sound-tracks to make a single master track. It is at the audio mix that the sound is balanced and any special sound effects are added.

Blimp

A soundproof housing around a camera. It muffles the camera noise so that it will not be picked up by the microphones.

Casting session

The audition where actors read for the parts in a commercial.

Casting tape

Videotape recording of an actor's audition.

Clapstick

A pair of hinged boards that are attached to the top of the slate. The sticks are banged together at the beginning of each sound take, making a visible mark on the film that can be matched to the sound of the clap on the sound-track to help the editor synchronise the sound-track to the film.

Composite print

A film print with both picture and sound-track on a single piece of film.

Continuity

Scenes occurring in the order required in the script. Also, consistency of props, positions of props and actors from scene to scene.

CU (close-up)

A very close shot of the subject matter. A close-up of an actor, for example, might show only his head and shoulders.

Cue sheet

Prepared by the editor in preparation for mixing the sound-track, the cue sheet shows where the special sound effects and music should come into and go out of the track.

Cut

☐ Editorial term − to edit or shorten a scene by cutting the film. Also, to go from one scene to another without opticals.

☐ Production term − director's command to stop the action in a scene and turn off the camera and sound-recording equipment.

Cutaway

An insert scene used to break away momentarily from the main action in a scene.

Dissolve (lap dissolve)

A transition from one scene to the next by overlapping the fade-out of the first scene to the fade-in of the next.

Dolly

A mobile platform on which the camera is mounted and the cameraman can sit.

Double exposure

Two separate scenes shot on the same piece of film.

Double head (DH) (sep mag)

Sound and picture on separate pieces of film shown together in synchronisation.

Dubber

A high quality sound recorder that feeds into a mixing console.

Dubbing

The process of recording several sound-tracks and mixing them into one composite track.

ECU

Extreme close-up.

Edge numbers

Numbers printed on the edge of the original negative. These correspond to numbers on the rough cut and are used to conform the negative to the approved rough cut.

Editing

The process of splicing scenes together in a proper order and mixing them to the previously recorded sound-track.

Editorial sync

The lining up of the picture and sound-track in an editing machine so that they are directly opposite each other.

Effects

An all-inclusive term for opticals, which includes fades, dissolves and more complicated opticals such as split-screen effects.

Effects track (SFX)

A track with no dialogue, only sound effects and/or music that is to be mixed into the sound-track.

Equalise

Balance the sound-track so that everything is heard at the same level.

Establishing shot

Wide shot used to orient the viewer to the environment of the scene.

Extra

A performer best described as part of the background. He has no dialogue.

F-number

F-stop on a camera; any one of the series of markings on the lens barrel that indicate the aperture setting.

Fade

An optical effect in which a scene goes from full light to blackness, or vice versa.

Film magazine

A container for the unexposed film that will be used to shoot a commercial. The film magazine is loaded in a darkroom and then attached to the camera. When all the film in a magazine has been exposed the film is transferred to cans and the magazine is reloaded with unexposed film.

Film prints

Positive pictures made from the film negative.

Filter

Any number of glass or gelatin devices placed in front of the camera lens to give various effects. Some filters darken the sky, others simulate night conditions. Still other filters are used to balance colour values under varying lighting conditions.

Final approval

The decision, after editing is complete, to accept the film without further changes.

Fine cut

The rough cut edited to time, with the scenes as they will appear in the final commercial.

Flag

Any opaque screen used to shade unwanted light off walls. It is also used to keep light from hitting directly into the camera lens (sometimes called a 'gobo', 'cutter' or 'mask').

Flat

A painted background supported by a wooden frame. Flats are often used as background for scenes.

Gaffer

Crew member; electrician who works with the cameraman to light the set.

Grading

Estimating the amount of light that must be passed through the individual scenes in the master of a film to produce the correct exposure in a print. This operation is carried out by a grader and is usually done by eye.

Grip

Crew member; does heavy moving and lifting during the shooting day. Also helps set flags and gobos.

Inter-negative

A negative that is made for the purpose of running off release prints. It is made either from a reversal master (such as 16 mm Ektachrome) or a print, preferably a special duping print. An inter-negative is also made as one stage in making opticals (mixes, fades, wipes, overlays, etc).

In the can

An expression used to indicate that a film has been exposed and put into a metal can.

Jump cut

The uneven action between two cuts. This occurs when a section of film is removed from a continuous-action scene and the film is respliced.

Leader

Blank film at the beginning and end of a commercial used for threading purposes.

Limbo

Word used to signify an absence of background, with the subject being shot in only a pool of light.

Lip sync

The simultaneous filming and dialogue recording of a scene.

Mag track

Any sound-track on magnetic tape.

Married print

Print of a sound film carrying both picture and sound-track. Normal print of sound film for projection.

MCU (medium close-up)

A shot that usually frames the actors from the waist up.

Mix

The combination of the various sound elements into a single sound-track.

Mute

A picture negative or positive print without the sound-track.

Optical negative

Negative of the commercial with all the opticals in it.

Opticals

Special video effects (dissolves, fades, mixes, wipes) added during the process of printing a film.

Outtakes

Takes of scenes that were shot but not used in the final commercial.

Package clean-up

The removal of the net weight statement and other extraneous small type that form the face of the product package. This is done in television commercials because the small type is not readable in a commercial except in a very close shot. Cleaning up the package front makes the package look uncluttered and allows the viewer to concentrate on the product's name.

Post syncing

The recording of sound effects and lip sync to edited silent footage.

Pre-production

The period between approval of the advertising concept and the shooting of the commercial. During this time a director is chosen, actors are cast, sets are built and all other preparations are made to shoot the commercial.

Pre-production meeting

A meeting that brings together all the agency, client and production company people to discuss the final details of the production of a commercial.

Release prints (TX)

The final prints of the commercial ready for distribution.

Residual (re-use fee)

A fee paid to a commercial performer for repeat showings of a commercial. The amount is based on a formula laid out in the contract with the advertising agencies.

Rough cut

The first edited version of a commercial.

Rushes

Film that has just been exposed by a film camera. In the case of a print, a print of scenes exactly as they were shot in the camera without any cutting or editing having taken place.

Scenario

The detailed script of a commercial combining all words, music, sound and visual effects.

Scratch track

A rough, temporary recording of the voice-over announcer's lines, usually spoken by the producer. It is used to help edit film that was shot silent and is replaced at the sound mix by a track recorded by a professional announcer.

Script

The written text of a commercial.

Sound effects (SFX)

All sound other than dialogue, narration and music. Sound effects are usually recorded separately and mixed with the dialogue track to create the mixed mag track.

Split screen

A frame optically divided into two or more areas with a different action taking place in each.

Storyboard

A series of pictures drawn by the art director to show the proposed flow of an advertising concept. The storyboard places the words and pictures of a concept in relation to each other for the first time.

Sync

The perfect synchronisation of picture and sound-track.

Tracking

Moving the camera dolly while the camera is filming a scene.

Trims

Pieces of film cut from scenes being edited into a rough cut.

Voice-over (VO)

Announcer lines recorded after the commercial is edited. These lines are placed in scenes shot without sound and usually describe what the viewer is seeing.

Wipe

An optical effect; one scene is brought into another by moving a line across the frame.

Work print

A print from the original footage used to edit the commercial. The rough cut is created from the work print.

☐ Print production terminology

To list all terms connected with the graphic arts would fill a book. Many would be too technical and of little value to anyone other than a skilled craftsman. In this section only the terms commonly used in advertising and printing today are defined.

Airbrush
- ☐ In artwork, a small pressure gun shaped like a pencil that sprays watercolour pigment by means of compressed air. Used to correct and obtain tone or graduated tone effects.
- ☐ In platemaking, used with an abrasive-like pumice to remove spots or other unwanted areas.

Antique finish

A term describing the surface, usually on book and cover papers, that has a natural rough finish.

Art

All illustrations and copy used in preparing a job for printing.

Ascender

The part of the letter that rises above the main body, as in 'b'.

Author's alterations

In composition, changes and additions in the copy after it has been set in type. Often called 'AAs'.

Backing up

Printing the reverse side of a sheet already printed on one side.

Black-and-white

Originals or reproductions in single colour, as distinguished from multicolour.

Bleed

If the printed image extends to the trim edge of the sheet or page, it is called bleed.

Blind embossing

A design that is stamped without metallic leaf or ink, giving a bas-relief effect.

Blowup

A photographic enlargement.

Blueprint

In offset-lithography and photo-engraving, a photoprint made from stripped-up negatives or positives, used as a proof to check position of image elements.

Break for colour

In artwork and composition, to separate the parts to be printed in different colours.

Circular screen

A circular-shaped screen which enables the camera operator to obtain proper screen angles for colour halftones by rotating the screen.

Collate

In binding, the gathering of sheets.

Colour correction

Any method, such as masking, dot etching, re-etching and scanning, used to improve colour rendition.

Colour separation

☐ In photography, the process of separating full colour originals into the primary printing colours in negative or positive form.
☐ In lithographic platemaking, the manual separation of colours by handwork performed directly on the printing surface. An artist can pre-separate by using separate overlays for each colour.

Contact screen

A photographically-made halftone screen on film having a dot structure of graded density used in vacuum contact with the photographic film.

Continuous tone

A photographic image that has not been screened and contains gradient tones from black to white.

Contrast

The tonal gradation between the highlights, middle tones and shadows in an original or reproduction.

Cyan

One of the subtractive primaries, the hue of which is used for one of the four-colour process inks. It reflects blue and green light and absorbs red light.

Density

A measure of the relative blackening of photographic images.

Descender

That part of the letter which extends below the main body, as in 'p'.

Die-cutting

The use of sharp steel rules to cut special shapes, like labels, boxes and containers, from printed sheets. Die-cutting can be done on either flat-bed or rotary presses. Rotary die-cutting is usually done in line with the printing.

Die-stamping

An intaglio process for the production of letterheads, cards, etc; printing from lettering or other designs engraved into copper or steel.

Direct screen halftone

In colour separation, a halftone negative made by direct exposure from the original on an enlarger or by contact through a halftone screen.

Doctor blade

In gravure, a knife-edge blade pressed against the engraved printing cylinder that wipes away the excess ink from the non-printing areas.

Dot

The individual element of a halftone.

Dot etching

In photography, chemically etching silver halide halftone emulsions to increase or reduce the amount of colour to be printed. Dot etching negatives increase colour; dot etching positives reduce colour.

Dot spread

In printing, a defect in which dots print larger than they should, causing darker tones or colours.

Double dot halftone

In lithography, two halftone negatives combined into one printing plate, having greater tonal range than a conventional halftone. One negative reproduces the highlights and shadows; the other reproduces middle tones. This should not be confused with duotones, or printing with two black plates.

Double-page spreads

Double-page spreads cause no particular problem when used across the centre spread. Two facing pages in other positions may not always line up precisely, owing to the difficulty obvious with running headlines. Generally there is no solution apart from designs that make any misalignment less obvious. Perfect binding needs special attention. Some of the image may be lost from the centre of the picture. This could be up to 20 mm unless precautions are taken by the printer. In any case, it is generally difficult to open a perfect bound book or magazine so that it is completely flat and it is therefore best to avoid placing vital subject matter in the centre. It is essential to consult with the printer and binder.

Drop-out

Portions of originals that do not reproduce, especially coloured lines or background areas (often on purpose).

Dummy

A preliminary layout showing the position of illustrations and text as they are to appear in the final reproduction. A set of blank pages made up in advance to show the size, shape, form and general style of a piece of printing.

Duotone

In photomechanics, a term for a two-colour halftone reproduction from a one-colour photograph.

Emulsion side

In photography, the side of the film coated with the silver halide emulsion which should face the lens during exposure.

Enamel

A term applied to a coated paper or to a coating material on a paper.

Etch

☐ In photo-engraving, to produce an image on a plate by chemical or electrolytic action.
☐ In offset-lithography, an acidified gum solution used to desensitise the non-printing areas of the plate; also, an acid solution added to the fountain water to help keep non-printing areas of the plate free from ink.

Fine etching

In platemaking, dot etching on metal to correct tone values on photo-engravings and gravure cylinders.

Fixing

Chemical action following development to remove unexposed silver halide to make the image stable and insensitive to further exposure.

Flush left (or right)

In composition, type set to line up at the left (or right).

Format

The size, style, type page, margins, printing requirements, etc of a printed piece.

Galley proof

A proof taken of type standing in a galley, before being made up into pages.

Gutter

The blank space or inner margin from printing area to binding.

Halftone

The reproduction of continuous-tone artwork, such as a photograph, through a crossline or contact screen, which converts the image into dots of various sizes.

Hard copy

In phototypesetting, typewritten copy on ordinary paper produced simultaneously with magnetic or paper tape on most keyboards.

Highlight

The lighest or whitest parts in a photograph represented in a halftone reproduction by the smallest dots or the absence of all dots.

Lamination

A plastic film bonded by heat and pressured to a printed sheet for protection or appearance.

Layout

☐ The drawing or sketch of a proposed printed piece.
☐ In platemaking, a sheet indicating the settings for the step-and-repeat machine.

Letterset (dry offset)

The printing process which uses a blanket (like conventional offset) for transferring the image from plate to paper. Unlike lithography, it uses a relief plate and requires no dampening system.

Magenta

One of the subtractive primaries, the hue of which is used for one of the colour process inks. It reflects blue and red light and absorbs green light.

Magenta screen

A dyed contact screen.

Makeready

☐ In printing presses, all work done prior to running, namely adjusting the feeder, grippers, side guide; putting ink in the fountain; etc.

☐ Also, in letterpress, the building up of the press form so that the heavy and light areas print with the correct impression.

Mask

☐ In colour separation photography, an intermediate photographic negative or positive used in colour correction.

☐ In offset-lithography, opaque material used to protect open or selected areas of a printing plate during exposure.

Middle tones

The tonal range between highlights and shadows of a photograph or reproduction.

Negative

In photography, film containing an image in which the values of the original are reversed so that the dark areas appear light, and vice versa.

Newsprint

Paper made mostly from groundwood pulp and small amounts of chemical pulp and used for printing newspapers.

Offset gravure

Printing gravure by the offset principle, and generally done on a flexographic press by converting the anilox roller to a gravure image cylinder and covering the plate cylinder with a solid rubber plate.

Origination

Types of original

Originals may be in different physical forms, although basically of two types:

☐ a transparency, viewed by transmitting light
☐ reflection copy, viewed by reflected light

Transparencies may be:

☐ original transparencies – that is the film used in the camera to photograph the original scene
☐ duplicate transparencies – that is a copy of the above
☐ print film transparencies – that is made via a colour negative
☐ conversions – that is transparencies made from reflection copy
☐ colour negatives – but consult the repro house before considering their direct use

Reflection copy may be in the form of:

☐ photographic colour prints (these must be specially made; ordinary 'en prints' will not produce decent results)

☐ dye transfers
☐ water colour paintings
☐ wash drawings or airbrush art
☐ poster colour paintings
☐ oil paintings or other similar materials

Transparencies

A transparency is suitable for all methods of reproduction. The luminosity (or brightness) range of a reproduction will usually be less than that of the transparency and some tone compression, therefore, occurs in reproduction. It is normal practice in graphic reproduction to keep most tone compression in the shadows while maintaining good highlight contrast. If required, detail in particular parts of the tone scale can be specially retained or emphasised, but with consequent loss elsewhere. Clear, written instructions over a stat should be given in such cases. Advertisements, for example, frequently call for low key pictures in an attempt to convey some 'atmosphere' and it is important to communicate this concept to the trade house or printer.

The ideal transparency for reproduction has the following properties:

☐ Colour balance is neutral when viewed under standard lighting conditions. Colour casts, either overall or local, are absent. (Local colour casts tend to reproduce in a more obvious form and are difficult to correct. Overall casts on individual transparencies can be removed more easily, but are still best avoided since visual assessment is made more difficult.)

☐ All the colours fall within the gamut of the combination of inks to be used. This can be judged from the printer's colour chart. (Colours falling outside the gamut of the four-colour process will not be accurately reproduced. If this cannot be tolerated, an extra colour must be printed. However, it should be realised that for some newspaper and magazine printing using machines with only two or four printing units this will not be economical. Therefore, only an approximation of some colours may be possible.)

☐ Freedom from dust, scratches, finger marks, stains, mottle and evidence of uneven processing.

The image is sharp and has a fine grain structure, particularly if enlargement is envisaged. This will be dependent on the artistic effect required.

☐ It has been exposed to give a highlight density within the range 0,3 to 0,55. The highlight area referred to in this context is that containing the lowest density in which image detail is to appear in the reproduction. Catchlights will have a lower density than specified above.

In order to retain detail in the reproduction of a high key subject (ie a subject in which the majority of important tones are in the highlight to midtone part of the tone scale), the transparency should have a highlight density in the range 0,5 to 0,6 (ie slightly higher than normal). Overexposed transparencies will lack colour saturation and have 'burnt out' highlights (ie containing no detail). Underexposure gives poor shadow detail.

□ The shadow density is within the range 1,8 to 2,4. This is the density of the deepest shadow in which image detail is to appear in the reproduction. Original transparencies will frequently have higher densities and these areas will reproduce as solid colour not containing detail. The maximum density at which it is required to reproduce detail should be stated, if possible.

□ It is nearly the same size as the reproduction which is required. However, size changes are a normal part of the reproduction process (see later comment regarding size limitation of input). The printer's specification should give details.

□ It is wrong reading, that is, the image is reversed left to right when looking at the emulsion side. All original transparencies will naturally meet this requirement. Duplicate transparencies may not.

Duplicate transparencies

Original transparencies may be duplicated for the following reasons:

□ To enlarge or reduce a transparency near to the size required for the reproduction, or to enlarge a small portion of a transparency to final size. Image quality and subject matter can then be assessed visually easily.

□ To bring a number of original transparencies to the same end (Dmin – Dmax) densities.

□ To remove colour casts.

□ To make several duplicates so that simultaneous publication in a number of places may occur.

□ To correct local colour casts by hand retouching and to make general alterations. This is more safely done on a duplicate than on the original.

□ To produce page ready copy. As advised earlier, same size to final reproduction is one of the ideal characteristics of reproduction transparencies. However, maximum and minimum size limitations of the separation equipment to be used must be considered before any duplicate is made.

Reflection copy

Recommendations for the production of reflection copy depend somewhat on the facilities available at the trade house or printer in question, and reference should be made to their specifications. Where there is a choice, it is recommended that reflection copy be produced 1,5 to 2,0 times final size, unless the original is for small reproductions.

Photographic colour prints

These may be used very satisfactorily if of high quality – they must be made especially for the purpose.

Generally, colour prints are produced when there is extensive retouching to be done.

Retouching

Whenever originals are retouched there is the possibility of metamerism. If metamerism does occur the retouched areas will appear correct on the original, but any subsequent reproduction will show errors. In the case of photographic originals, metamerism can be avoided by using only those dyes recommended by the manufacturer of the material concerned. In particular, colour prints and dye transfers should not be retouched with poster colours, since metameric effects are almost inevitable.

Positive

In photography, film containing an image in which the dark and light values are the same as the original. The reverse of negative.

Pre-press proofs

Proofs made by photographic techniques to eliminate the expense of making press proofs.

Process colours

In printing, the subtractive primaries – yellow, magenta and cyan, plus black in four-colour process printing.

Process printing

The printing from a series of two or more halftone plates to produce intermediate colours and shades. In four-colour process: yellow, magenta, cyan and black.

Progressive proofs (progs)

Proofs made from the separate plates in colour process work showing the sequence of printing and the result after each additional colour has been applied.

Right or wrong reading

This refers to the image orientation of an original, transparency, film or plate when the emulsion is towards the observer.

Saddle wire

In binding, to fasten a booklet by wiring it through the middle fold of the sheets.

Scanner

An electronic device used in the making of colour and tone corrected colour separations.

Screen angles

In colour reproduction, angles at which the halftone screens are placed in relation to each other to avoid undesirable moire patterns. A set of angles often used is: black 45°, magenta 75°, yellow 90°, cyan 105°.

Self cover

A cover of the same paper as inside text pages.

Show-through

In printing, the undesirable condition in which the printing on the reverse side of a sheet can be seen through the sheet under normal lighting conditions.

Spiral binding

A book bound with wires in spiral form inserted through holes punched along the binding side.

Transparent copy

In photography, illustrative copy such as a colour transparency or positive film through which light must pass in order for it to be seen or reproduced.

Trim marks

In printing, marks placed on the copy to indicate the edge of the page.

Undercolour removal (UCR)

In process colour web printing, colour separation films are reduced in colour in areas where all three colours overprint and the black film is increased an equivalent amount in these areas. This improves trapping and reduces ink costs.

Varnish

A thin, protective coating applied to a printed sheet for protection or appearance. Also, in inkmaking it can be all or part of the ink vehicle.

Vignette

An illustration in which the background fades gradually away until it blends into the unprinted paper.

Web press

A press which prints from rolls (or webs) of paper.

☐ Direct response

Direct mail

Any advertising *medium* in the same category as radio, television, newspapers, etc. It is a medium that conveys advertising messages to a *list* of *individual* prospects with the help of the *Post Office*, in the same way that radio conveys messages to a *mass* of *unknown* prospects with the help of the *SABC*.

Direct marketing

This is the broadest and least scientific term of all. Even the International Direct Marketing Association is continually refining and redefining the term. For the purpose of this book, it shall be defined as:

> The marketing of products and services in a way that involves – at some stage of the marketing process – the recording of a particular name and address, to form a data base for future marketing activities.

Direct response advertising

Direct response advertising can be regarded as:

> The advertising of products and services in all media involving either the building of a data base, or the exploitation of one.

Mail order

A form of *marketing* in the same way that *retail* is a form of marketing. In mail order, a prospect is invited to buy products by sending in his order through the *mail* rather than going to a shop and placing his order at the *retail outlet*. Note that the *invitation* to order through the mail could appear in advertisements or inserts in magazines, in a mail order commercial on television, as well as in a direct mail package. Note also that a mail order purchase is not necessarily fulfilled through the mail. Apart from being mailed, the product bought could be sent by rail, personally delivered by a salesman, or be available for collection at a retail outlet.

Telemarketing

Closely related to mail order is telemarketing, in which the telephone is the medium through which the order is placed. Often mail order and telemarketing promotions are combined, giving the prospect the choice of ordering through the mail – by sending in an order form – or over the telephone – by telephoning a number and charging the purchase to a credit card.

Index

A

Account man *115*
Adexpose survey *324*
Adindex *346*
Advertising *24*
    a communication process *18*
    and competition *38*
    and consumer prices *40*
    and economic utility *39*
    and manipulation *44*
    and monopolies *39*
    agency *9, 107*
    audience *337*
    brief *121, 126*
    by government institutions *422*
    campaign *137*
    characteristics of *19*
    Code of Practice *173*
    control *48*
    control system *54*
    defined *16*
    earliest forms of *3*
    effect curve *372*
    effectiveness research *321*
    expenditure *10, 148*
    how it works *21*
    in South Africa *6*
    on radio *193*
    periods (TV) *177*
    proposition *139*
    pull-through effect *29*
    since the invention of printing *5*
    some basic principles *382*
    strategy *133*
    techniques *393*
    terminology *477*
    to Blacks *379, 385*
Advertising objectives *127, 132, 136, 154*
    direct response *431*
Advertising research *295, 320*
    non-profit marketing *415*
Advertising Standards Authority *43, 48*
Affective component *296*
Agency remuneration *111*
Agency's function *134*
AMPS *152*
Appeals *134*
Association of Advertising Agencies *43*
Attracting attention *282*
Audit Bureau of Circulations *152*

B

Behavioural
    buying model *361*
    component *296*
Below-the-line *453*

Bill Bernbach *261*
Billboard *212*
Black
    consumer *91*
    consumer market *94*
    market *85, 391*
    radio stations *186*
    SocioMonitor *86*
    television commercial *392*
    TV viewers *395*
Board on publications *45*
Body copy *284*
Brand positions *331*
Briefing *136*
    document *122, 137*
Buying radio time *192*
Buying reasons, capital equipment *361*

C

Card stacking *304*
Cause advertising *422*
Changing markets *222*
Checklist
    for television *140*
    for TV commercials *271*
    for TV storyboard *273*
Children and young people *70*
Cigarette products *76*
Cinema *7, 198*
    profile *205*
    urban Blacks *257*
Client
    presentation *141*
    relationship *116*
    service executive *110*
Clutter approach *314*
Code of Advertising Practice *48, 50, 54*
Cognitive component *296*
Cognitive dissonance *28*
Colour advertisement *384*
Commission system *112*
Communication *445*
    process *464*
Communications plan *139*
Company objectives *133*
Competitions *457*
Comprehension, measuring *314*
Concept positions *332*
Consumer panels *336*
Contact cycles *373*
Copy
    platform *283*
    research *310*
Copywriting for radio *189*

Cost
    of personal sales *365*
    per thousand *186*
Coverage
    of radio *185*
    of television *168*
    TV2 and TV3 *249*
CRACK concept *200*
Creating
    outdoor *290*
    print advertising *281*
    radio commercials *280*
    television commercials *271*
Creative
    advertising *264*
    approaches *261*
    impact *160*
    implementation *141*
    man *115*
    requirements *156*
    strategy brief *123*
    team's checklist *269*
Creativity *227*
    outdoor *216*

D

DAGMAR concept *135*
Data base marketing *436*
David Ogilvy *262*
Day-after-recall testing *323*
Decision-making unit (DMU) *345, 359, 371*
Decode advertising message *295*
Decoding *295*
Definition of advertising *55*
Demographics of populations *99*
Descriptive techniques *329*
Design
    elements of print *285*
    principles *286*
Direct advertising *218*
Direct mail campaign *444*
Direct response advertising *429*
    benefits of *430*
    testing *433*
Distortion *303*
Distribution of industrial marketing costs *363*

E

Economic arguments against advertising *37*
Education *102*
Effective advertisement *22*
Effective communication *464*
Elements of promotional mix *467*
Emotional appeals *308*
Emotional associations *384*

Evaluate print advertisement *289*
Evaluating the campaign *374*
Executional diagnostic information *316*
Eye camera *337*

F

False and misleading advertising *43*
Fear appeals *305*
Features of industrial marketing *356*
Fee system *113*
Field sales force *442*
First 'advertising specialist' *5*
FLESCH formula *385*
Flow of information *297*
Formal balance *286*
Full-service agency *109*
Functions of SABC *191*

G

Geo-segmentation *79*
Glue spots *337*
Gross rating points *160*

H

Headlines *284, 384*
Hidden offers *341*
Hot agency *114*
Humorous messages *306*
Humour in advertising *387*

I

Image formation *417*
Image of a company *362*
Imagery *125*
Impact of advertisement *202*
In-house agency *400*
Incentives *459*
Industrial
    advertising *344, 355, 356*
    advertising budgets *347*
    advertising plan *366, 367*
    advertising strategies *357, 358*
    buyers, characteristics of *370*
    decision maker *345*
    goods, classified *357*
    journals *348*
    marketing *369*
    readership objectives *351*
    readership research *350*
Inertia *221*
Informal balance *286*
Inter-media comparisons *199*
Inter-media decision *238*
Integrating advertising with marketing strategy *30*
Irritating appeals *307*

L

Labelling *307*
Leo Burnett *263*
Listenership, total Blacks *255, 256*
Literacy problem *380*
Logo *134*

M

Macro analysis *137*
Magazine readership profile *225*
Mail order advertising *63, 71*
Mailing list *225*
Market analysis *126*
Market identification *223*
Market segmentation *226*
Marketing
    communication *23*
    communication aimed at black sector *97*
    objectives *133, 434*
Mass communication media *45*
Measure industrial readership *349*
Measuring
    advertising effectiveness *320*
    response *315*
Media
    attributes *149*
    available to Blacks *248*
    brief *228*
    choice *139*
    considerations *156*
    data sources *151*
    expenditure *13*
    exposure *236*
    factors *237*
    objectives *154*
    opportunities, black market *247*
    owner research *153*
    plan *154, 161*
    planning *145*
    planning case study *228*
    process *147*
    reference works *154*
    selection research *334*
    specifics *241*
    strategy *157*
    strategy review *240*
    weighting *160*
Medical advertising *467*
Medical representative *468*
Medicinal and related products *65*
Medium choice *171*
Merits of advertising *41, 46*
Message *134*
Meter recording *340*
Methods of pre-testing and post-testing *322*

Micro analysis *138*
Moral values *45*
Multivariate analyses *328*
Music, use of *394*

N

Nature of advertising *16*
Newspaper Press Union *43, 152*
Newspapers, urban Blacks *253*
Non-profit
    advertising campaigns *420*
    marketing *414*
    organisations *411*
    organisations, types of *413*

O

Outdoor *257*
    advertising *210*
    advertising association *215*
    audience *217*
    costs *215*
    media research *342*

P

PACT perspective *311*
PACT principles *312*
Page audience *336*
Penetration
    urban Blacks *258*
    of media *168*
    of radio *185*
Perceived risk *301*
Perception *296, 298*
Perceptual defence *301*
    barriers *302*
Perceptual mapping *330*
Perceptual overload *302*
Perceptual process *298*
Personal interviewing *340*
Personal selling *24*
Persuading *283*
Persuasion process *389*
Pharmaceuticals, promotion *463*
Pitfalls of telemarketing *448*
Point-of-purchase stand *213*
Political advertising *422*
Population of South Africa *103*
Positioning *125*
    advertising copy testing (PACT) *311*
    analysis *129*
    chart *130*
Post-production stage *279*
Post-testing *111, 142, 321*
Poster design *216*
Poster size *212*
Pre-production meeting *274*

Pre-production stage 271
Pre-testing 110, 140, 310, 321
Predictive techniques 329
Present situation 136
Price promotions 456
Prime prospect 124
Principles of advertising code 56
Print
     verbal elements 283
     visual elements 285
Print media research 335
Process of communication 18
Product
     labelling 75
     life cycle 25, 26
     offerings 412
     positioning 27
Production 141
     of commercials 172
     stage 277
Profiles of TV1 viewers 170
Promotion
     evaluated 459
     mix 23
     of pharmaceutical products 467
Promotional expenditure as percentage of sales 467
Propensity to purchase 315
Property advertising 63
Psychographic segmentation 85, 94
Psychographics 206
Public service advertising 420
Publicity 24, 425
Pull-through effect of advertising 29

R

Radio
     advantages of 184
     advertising 182
     stations 195
Rate structure (TV) 178
Rational appeals 307
Reach/Frequency/Continuity 155
Readership
     urban Blacks 251
     profiles, urban Blacks 252, 254
     research, industrial markets 350
Reading frequency 336
Recall tests 335, 337
Reception 313
Recognition tests 335, 336, 338
Regional radio 187
Reinforcing the message 425
Repetition 307
Research techniques 339
Response measurement 315

Retail advertising 399
     issues 402
     philosophy 403
Retail and branded advertising 406
Retail data library 80
Review board 139
Role of advertising
     in marketing 23
     in society 37
Rosser Reeves 263

S

SAARF 152
SABC 7, 43
Sales
     calls 364
     force 28
     promotion 24, 453
Schlinger scales 316
Screening proposal 203
Segmentation
     Markinor's 89
     of black market 86
     of target markets 85
Selective recall 304
Sex appeal in advertising 387
Six Ms 128
Slogans 284
Social trends in the black market 88
Societal factors and advertising 41
Sociographics 92, 96
SocioMonitor 86, 206
South African Bureau of Standards 64
South African consumer 87
Specific categories of advertisement 60
Standard communication check 314
Starch test 323
Strategy document 110
Subjective estimates 336
Successful sales promotions 455
SWOT analysis 129
Symbols 20

T

Target
     audience 127, 155
     consumer profile 123
     market 137
Task of advertising 24, 28
Techniques for assessing reading frequency 336
Teledata 181
Telemarketing 439
     benefits 440
     Association Code 447

Telephone
    interviewing *340*
    sales *445*
Teletext *181*
Television *7, 162*
    ownership *163*
    pre-production checklist *275*
    reasons for use *165*
    stations *164*
    use of *172*
Testimonial approaches *388*
Testing in direct response *433*
Time channels (TV) *176*
Timing plan *241*
Total South African population *102*
Trade journal press *348*
Trade Practices Act 76 of 1976 *43*
Trinodal mapping *315*
TV rate chart *180*
Types of non-profit organisations *413*

U

Unacceptable claims *67*
Unacceptable practices *65*
Unique selling proposition (USP) *39*
Urban black population *247*
Urban Blacks *85*
Urbanisation *92*
Use of television *172*

V

Value groups *89*
Verbal elements of print *283*
Viewership, all TV *169*
Viewership profiles, urban Blacks *251*
Visual aid (VA) *472*
Visual elements of print *285*

W

Workflow procedure through advertising agency *109*
Working woman *93*